HAVERING SIXTH FORM
COLLEGE LIBRARY

INTERNATIONAL BACCALAUREATE

D1381917

BIOLOGY

Minka Peeters Weem
with
Christopher Talbot and
Antony Mayrhofer

All rights reserved except under the conditions described in the Copyright Act 1968 of Australia and subsequent amendments. No part of this publication may be reproduced, stored in a retrieval system, or transmitted in any form or by any means, without the prior permission of the publishers.

While every care has been taken to trace and acknowledge copyright, the publishers tender their apologies for any accidental infringement where copyright has proved untraceable. They would be pleased to come to a suitable arrangement with the rightful owner in each case.

This material has been developed independently by the publisher and the content is in no way connected with nor endorsed by the International Baccalaureate Organization.

Copyright ©IBID Press, Victoria.

www.ibid.com.au

First published in 2007 by IBID Press, Victoria.
Corrected and reprinted January 2008.

Library Catalogue:

Peeters Weem M, Talbot C, Mayrhofer A.

1.Biology

2. International Baccalaureate. Series Title: International Baccalaureate in Detail

ISBN: 978-1-876659-02-8

All copyright statements, '© IBO 2007' refer to the Biology guide published by the International Baccalaureate Organization in 2007.

IBID Press express their thanks to the International Baccalaureate Organization for permission to reproduce its intellectual property.

Cover design by Adcore.

Published by IBID Press, 36 Quail Crescent, Melton, 3337, Australia.

Printed in China through Trojan Press Book Printers.

PREFACE

This book and CD has been prepared to help students in their studies of Biology. It has been designed around the IB syllabus and the chapters correspond to the topics in the syllabus for the Standard and Higher Level Sections.

Students taking the Biology exam at Standard Level need to study all the material in Chapters 1 to 6 and choose two Options from Chapters 12 to 18. Students taking the Biology exam at Higher Level need to study all the material in chapters 1 to 11 and choose two Options from Chapters 15 to 19. For more details, please consult the IBO Syllabus Guide.

This book is intended as a framework for studying this course. However, please be aware that, to obtain the best possible results, it is necessary to study as wide a range of resources as possible. This should include other media, such as internet sources.

In particular, your own practical work will assist you in developing an understanding as well as an appreciation of the depth and richness of Biology. Some further materials are being developed and information can be found at www.ibid.com.au

It is important to consider both TOK and Internationalism when studying any IB subject. Some TOK considerations have been included where appropriate in the text but students are encouraged to explore the concepts further. Internationalism is woven into the text and students are encouraged to share their own examples with their class mates.

The Exercises at the end of the chapters and Answers in the back of the book are provided to help check understanding and recall of basic facts. They are not provided by the IBO and are not necessarily aimed at IB level. Teachers and IB Coordinators can supply students with past IBO papers to help them develop a sense of the level required for the examinations.

The Authors

EDITOR'S NOTE

This project has involved teachers, authors, proof readers, artists and many other people on several continents. It has been done within an extremely tight timeframe and involved thousands of emails across the world and many different software applications. We are pleased, and trust that you will also be pleased, with the final product which went to Press with no known errors. However we know from experience that some typographic and other errors will have escaped our proofing process and will emerge as students and teachers start using the books and CDs.

If you wish, you can help us and yourself in the following ways:
• Send us an email at rory@ibid.com.au with details of any errors that you notice
• Please visit www.ibid.com.au for errata sheets which will be produced promptly when needed and be freely available as necessary
• Check our website and other publicity regarding our 'Student Guides to Internal Assessment' and 'Volumes of Investigations' for the Core, HL and Options in Biology, Chemistry and Physics. These materials are currently in preparation and are due for publication later this year.

THE AUTHORS

Minka Peeters Weem grew up in the Netherlands and started her involvement with the IB at the age of 16 when she was invited to join UWC of the Atlantic in the UK. After her IB Diploma, she returned to the Netherlands to study Biology at the Agricultural University of Wageningen where her studies for her Master's degree involved research in Animal Behaviour, Pharmacology and a teaching degree. Minka started to work for the International School of The Hague and has since taught in Paris, Bahrain, Hong Kong and Switzerland. She accepted the position of Head of School and commenced work at the European International School in Lagos, Nigeria in August 2007.

Minka strongly believes in international education and supports the IBO in making international programmes available to students in many countries, both in international and national schools, either private or state. To Minka, the last sentence of the IBO Mission Statement is the most important : *"These programmes encourage students across the world to become active, compassionate and lifelong learners who understand that other people, with their differences, can also be right."*

Christopher Talbot graduated with honours in Biochemistry from the School of Biological Sciences, University of Sussex in the United Kingdom. He has a Masters Degree in Life Sciences (Chemistry) from the National Technological University (NTU) in the Republic of Singapore. He also holds a Certificate in Computing for Molecular Biology from Birbeck College, University of London in the United Kingdom. He is currently teaching IB Chemistry and Theory of Knowledge in the Anglo-Chinese School (Independent), Republic of Singapore. He previously taught IB Chemistry, IB Biology, Computer Studies and Theory of Knowledge at the Overseas Family School, Republic of Singapore, where he was TOK Coordinator and subsequently Curriculum Area Leader for the Science Department.

He is the author or co-author of the *Student Guides to Internal Assessment for use with the International Baccalaureate Chemistry, Biology and Physics Programmes* and the *Chemistry Practice Examination papers (IBID Press 2007)*. He has also written books aimed at the Singapore Cambridge A-level Chemistry syllabus and acted as a freelance Editor for Oxford University Press. He has moderated IB Chemistry coursework and is a qualified IB Chemistry workshop leader.

Antony Mayrhofer graduated from the University of Sydney with a Bachelor of Degree Science majoring in Biochemistry and a post-graduate Diploma of Education. He has been teaching International Baccalaureate Diploma Programme Biology since 1990. He has been an assistant examiner of Scripts since 1996 and has been a Senior Moderator of Biology Internal Assessment since 2000. He was a member of the curriculum review committee that produced IB Biology Subject Guides including the new Biology Guide for exams from 2009 onwards. He has been a Deputy Chief Examiner of Biology since 2002 and as such is involved in the development of IB Biology curriculum and assessment material.

Antony is the IB Diploma Programme Co-ordinator at St Paul's Grammar School, Sydney, Australia, one of the largest IB schools in the Asia Pacific Region. He had previously held the position of Head of Science at the School. Antony has also had substantial involvement in the development of the NSW State Board Of Studies Biology Syllabus for senior students in that system. He is Chair of the Association of Australasian IB School's (AAIBS) standing committee.

ACKNOWLEDGEMENTS

IBID Press wish to acknowledge the advice and assistance of the following people in the development and production of these materials to support the teaching of IB Biology.

Chief author
Minka Peeters Weem

Contributing authors
Christopher Talbot
Antony Mayrhofer

Proof readers
Jessica Miller
Christopher Talbot

Layout
Julie Rogers - Desert Sun DTP

Project management
'Science Teaching And Resources'

Photographs, artwork & graphics
Manohar Hullan
Michael Badenoch
IBID Press
Science Teaching And Resources
Slapton Ley Field Centre in Devon (UK)
The authors

CONTENTS

Chapter 13   Option B: PHYSIOLOGY OF EXERCISE

Chapter 14   Option C: CELLS AND ENERGY

Chapter 15   Option D: EVOLUTION

Chapter 16   Option E: NEUROBIOLOGY AND BEHAVIOUR

Chapter 17   Option F: MICROBES AND BIOTECHNOLOGY

Chapter 18   Option G: ECOLOGY AND CONSERVATION

Chapter 19   Option H: FURTHER HUMAN PHYSIOLOGY

STATISTICAL ANALYSIS

Science is concerned with the systematic study of the natural world around us. Biology is particularly concerned with the study of living organisms and includes all levels of life from molecules to ecosystems. In the study of biology, scientists make careful observations and in many cases develop hypotheses, conduct experiments and gather data. Data may be quantitative measurements or qualitative descriptions of phenomena or the results of experiments. Once gathered, data needs to be analysed in an appropriate way to decide whether or not it supports the relevant hypothesis.

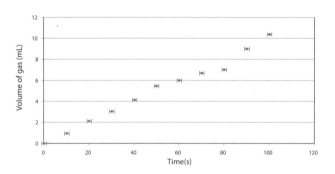

Figure 101   Total volume of gas collected against time

1.1.1	State that error bars are a graphical representation of the variability of data.

© IBO 2007

All measurements are subject to errors and it is important to recognise this in the way the data is recorded and manipulated. Error bars can be used to show either the range of the data or the standard deviation (*see Topics 1.1.2 and 1.1.4*) on several repeats of one experimental measurement.

Consider a photosynthesis investigation where a student is collecting and measuring the gas released by a plant against time. In the Excel-generated scatter graph in Figure 101, each of the time measurements was measured with an analogue stopwatch and has an error or uncertainty of ± 1 s. For example, a time of 40 s has a lower limit of 39 s and an upper limit of 41 s. X error bars were selected with a value of 1. The display was selected to show both the upper and lower limits, so the entire range of the uncertainty or error is displayed.

(Please refer to Chapter 2 - Data collection and processing of The IBID Student Guide – Biology for further examples and detailed instructions on adding error bars with Excel).

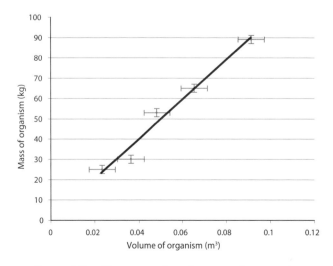

Figure 102   The mass of marine organisms against their volume

Error bars can be displayed for the values of both variables. In the Excel-generated graph in Figure 102 the mass of the marine organisms is measured using scales with a precision of ± 2 kg. The volume of the marine organisms is measured with a precision of ± 0.006 m³. Notice the error bars are small and they all fall on the trend line (*see Topic 1.1.6*), indicating that the measurements are reliable.

(Please refer to Chapter 2 - Data collection and processing of The IBID Student Guide – Biology for a detailed discussion about errors or uncertainties and precision versus accuracy).

1.1.2	Calculate the mean and standard deviation of a set of values.

©IBO 2007

When sampled biological data are recorded as a series of values representing variables, it is useful know their **mean** and **standard deviation**. The mean is the sum of all the values divided by the number of values. In everyday language, it is often called the 'average'.

MEAN

For example, consider the following data:
2; 4; 8; 11; 12; 13; 14; 14; 23; 24; 25

The mean is calculated manually as follows: $\frac{150}{11} = 14$.

However, the mean can be calculated more rapidly by means of a calculator or Excel.

Usually, the mean is easily calculated, but described below are two examples where simple means are **not** appropriate.

Example 1

If the means of samples themselves are 'meaned', an error can arise if the samples are of different sizes. For example, the mean of the means in Figure 103 is 8, but this does not take into account the different sample sizes. A more accurate mean is a weighted mean: ((7.0 x 5) + (8.0 x 8) + (9.0 x 2))/(5.0 + 8.0 + 2.0) = 7.8 A weighted mean gives weights to different numbers in proportion to their importance.

Mean	Sample size
7.0	5
8.0	8
9.0	2

Figure 103   Table of means and sample sizes

Example 2

When calculating a mean of ratios (for example, percentages) for several groups of different sizes, the ratio for the combined total of all the groups is not the mean of the proportions for the individual groups.

For example, if 40 rats from a batch of 100 are male, this implies 40% are male. If 120 rats from a batch of 240 are male, this implies 50% are male. The mean percentage of males (50 + 40)/2 = 45% is **not** the percentage of males in the two groups, because there are 40 + 120 = 160 males in a total of 340 = 47% approximately.

STANDARD DEVIATION

Means do not give a complete description about a sample of data. The **standard deviation** summarises the spread of the data around the mean (*see Topic 1.1.3*). The standard deviation measures how widely spread the values in a set of data are. If the data points are close to the mean, then the standard deviation is small. Conversely, if many data points are far from the mean, then the standard deviation is large. If all the data values are equal, then the standard deviation is zero.

Standard deviation is often abbreviated to SD, s.d., s or σ. Figure 104 shows a manually-worked example for a sample of shells where x is the length and f is the frequency,

x	f	fx
35	1	35
37	2	74
38	2	76
30	2	60
42	2	84
44	1	44
	$\Sigma f = 10$	$\Sigma fx = 373$

Figure 104   Table with shell data

The mean, $\bar{x} = \frac{373}{10} = 37.3$; $= \bar{x}^2 = 1391.3$

Standard deviation, $s = \sqrt{\frac{\Sigma(x - \bar{x})^2}{n}} = 4.49$

where x represents each value, $\bar{x}$ represents the mean of the measurements and n represents the number of measurements. The equation shows that the standard deviation is the root mean square deviation of values from their mean.

The formula above strictly applies to an infinite population. For calculating the SD of a sample change the denominator n to n-1. The difference has little effect on the SD value if the population is very large.

The IB Biology syllabus does not require you to do manual calculations or memorise the mathematical formulas, but it is helpful to observe how the statistics are generated for the simpler statistical functions.

The standard deviation and the mean can be rapidly calculated by means of a graphical or scientific calculator or using 'Excel' software.

The screen shots in Figures 105 to 109 and the instructions describe how to enter the data from Figure 104 and perform summary statistics on a TI graphical calculator (one of the recommended calculators for the IB Mathematics courses).

Press STAT

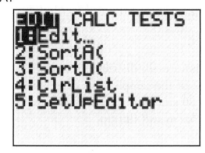

Figure 105

Press ENTER and enter the numbers (shell sizes or *x*) into L1 and then enter the respective frequencies *(f)* into L2.

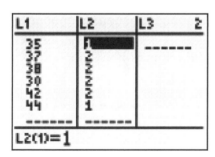

Figure 106

Press STAT and use the arrow key to select CALC.

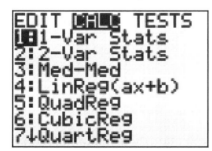

Figure 107

Press ENTER to obtain a summary of the data entered.

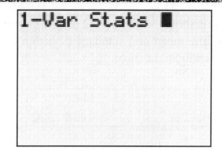

Figure 108

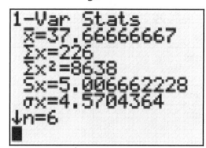

Figure 109

The top value ($\bar{x}$) is the mean. The fourth value (Sx) is the standard deviation, assuming that the data is from a sample of the population. The fifth value (σ) is the standard deviation assuming that the data represents the entire population.

Figure 111 shows some data from an Excel spreadsheet describing the length of two groups of sea shells, such as those shown in Figure 110. Use the Descriptive Statistics function from Data Analysis in the Tools Menu of the Excel program.

Figure 110   Sea shells

Seashell Number	Group 1 (Small Shell) length(mm)	Group 2 (Large Shell) length(mm)
1	10.2	16.8
2	11.6	19.7
3	9.7	18.5
4	13.3	22.5
5	8.3	20.7

Figure 111   Data table for small and large seashell length

CORE

The output is shown in Figure 112 for the Group 1 small shell data. The mean and standard deviation have been manually highlighted in bold.

Mean	**10.62**
Standard Error	0.852877482
Median	10.2
Mode	#N/A
Standard Deviation	**1.907092027**
Sample Variance	3.637
Kurtosis	-0.229700866
Skewness	0.411499631
Range	5
Minimum	8.3
Maximum	13.3
Sum	53.1
Count	5

Figure 112   Output data for shell length (generated in Excel)

1.1.3	State that the term standard deviation is used to summarize the spread of values around the mean, and that 68% of the values fall within one standard deviation of the mean.

©IBO 2007

If repeated measurement of continuous Biological variables, such as the height or weight of humans from a large population, are plotted, a close approximation to a normal distribution is obtained. The normal distribution has some very special characteristics.

Data which is normally distributed will exhibit a bell-shaped curve which is symmetrical around a centrally located mean. The curve is known as a **Gaussian curve**. Many statistical functions and tests assume that the data approximates to a **normal distribution**.

A normal distribution curve is shown in Figure 113. Note that that most values are close to the mean and only a few values will be far from the mean.

The standard deviation provides information on the range within a Biological sample (provided it is normally distributed). Consider the following data: the mean height of a human population is 180 cm and its standard deviation is ± 10 cm.

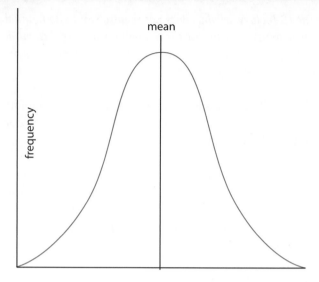

Figure 113   A normal distribution curve

If the data is normally distributed then 68% (approximately two thirds) of the sample have heights which are within 10 cm of 180 cm, that is, 68% of the sample have heights between 170 cm and 190 cm.

In addition 95% of the sample heights lie within two standard deviations of the mean. In this example, two standard deviations = 2 x 10 cm = 20 cm. In other words 95% of the sample have heights between 160 and 200 cm. Figure 114 illustrates these two values.

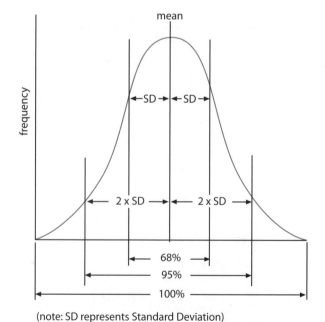

(note: SD represents Standard Deviation)

Figure 114   The normal distribution curve showing values for standard deviation

CORE

1.1.4 Explain how the standard deviation is useful for comparing the means and the spread of data between two or more samples.

©IBO 2007

A small value of standard deviation indicates that the data is clustered closely around the mean value. A large value of standard deviation indicates a wider spread around the mean. Figure 115 shows Gaussian curves for the frequency distributions of two statistical populations with differing standard deviations (spreads).

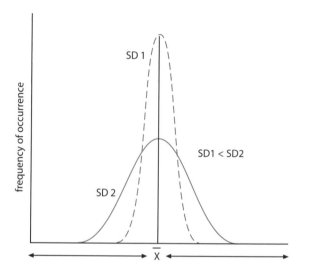

Figure 115   Normal distribution curves with large and small distribution curves

1.1.5 Deduce the significance of the difference between two sets of data using calculated values for t and the appropriate tables.

©IBO 2007

Suppose a student measured and recorded the length of leaves from two similar trees. The data is displayed in an Excel spreadsheet *(Figure 116)*.

The processed data can be displayed graphically in the form of a bar chart. Error bars can be added with the standard deviation of the two samples. They will give a visual indication of the variability of the data.

The mean for sample 1 is obviously lower than the mean for sample 2. However, is this difference statistically significant? This depends not only on the difference between the means of the two samples, but also on the difference between their standard deviations. The **Variance** is the square root of the Standard Deviation.

Sample 1	Sample 2
7.85	12.50
8.51	12.94
13.66	6.26
11.03	6.10
6.59	13.19
8.04	10.74
14.16	6.06
8.13	12.53
6.79	15.45
11.06	15.64
5.83	15.19
10.73	14.93
6.68	7.94
5.02	8.28
10.37	12.65
Standard deviation	Standard deviation
2.761473899	3.545349066
Mean	Mean
8.963333333	11.36

Figure 116   Lengths of leaves from sampling two similar trees

The **t test** compares two sets of data and indicates the probability (P) that the two sets are essentially the same. P varies from 0 (not likely) to 1 (certain). The higher the probability, the more likely it is that the two sets are the same, and that any differences are just due to random chance. The lower the probability, the more likely it is that that the two sets are significantly different, and that the differences are real. In Biology, the critical probability to show difference is usually taken as 0.05 (or 5%). A critical value is a value that a statistic must exceed in order to have a hypothesis test result in rejection of the null hypothesis. An example of a t test performed on the data from Figure 116 is shown in Figure 117.

	Variable 1	Variable 2
Mean	8.96333	11.36
Variance	7.625738	12.5695
Observations	15	15
Pooled Variance	10.09761	-
Hypothesised Mean Difference	0	-
df	28	-
t Stat	-2.065517	-
P(T<=t) one-tail	0.0241207	-
t Critical one-tail	1.7011309	-
P(T<=t) two-tail	0.0482415	-
t Critical two-tail	2.048407	- ·

Figure 117   Data table for t test

CORE

(Please refer to Chapter 2 - Data collection and processing of The IBID Student Guide – Biology for detailed instructions on performing t-tests with cell formulas and the built-in Statistical functions of Excel).

The difference is statistically significant since the two tailed probability is much lower than 0.05. This indicates that tree 1 has statistically smaller leaves than tree 2.

t tests can also be performed on a TI calculator as shown in the screen shots in Figures 118 to 122.. For example, a two-tailed t test can be performed on the following values (of bird wing spans): 2, 7, 9, 10, 13, 15, 18 and 20 cm to establish whether the population mean is 10 cm.

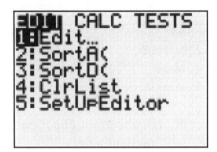

Figure 118   Screen shot A

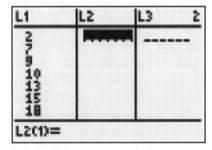

Figure 119   Screen shot B

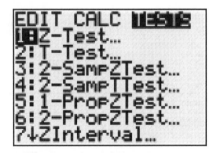

Figure 120   Screen shot C

Move the cursor over the respective sections and enter ten (for the mean) and indicate that the data is in L1.

Figure 121   Screen shot D

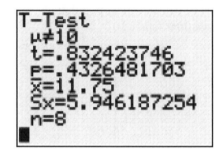

Figure 122   Screen shot E

A two tailed test is a statistical analysis in which the alternate hypothesis states that a difference exists. The null hypothesis can be rejected in either tail of the theoretical distribution.

TOK   What is an objective standard?

An objective standard is one without bias. Natural science claims that it is without bias as its findings are based on observations made objectively. The t test determines if there is a statistical difference between two sets of data in an objective way. Statistical tests reveal probable difference between events or likelihood of an event. However, it is often not well understood that the probability that something will (or will not occur) is not a guarantee that it will (or will not) occur.

1.1.6   Explain that the existence of a correlation does not establish that there is a causal relationship between two variables.

©IBO 2007

Biological data should always be plotted to show the relationship between two sets of data. A **line graph** should be plotted if the independent variable is under the control of the student performing the investigation. If both variables are dependent (that is, measured) then the values should be plotted in the form of a **scattergram**.

Regression and **correlation** are methods used when testing relationships between samples of variables. If one variable is known or assumed to be dependent on the other in a linear manner then a linear regression technique is used to determine the line of best fit.

A **correlation coefficient** can then be calculated which indicates how well the experimental data fit the line of best fit. Correlation coefficients are expressed as a number between -1 and 1. A positive coefficient indicates a positive relationship while a negative coefficient indicates a negative relationship (between the data and the line of best fit).

A positive correlation means that if the value of X increases, the value of Y will also increase. A positive correlation could be found between the amount of sugar in a jelly and the number of bacterial colonies growing on the jelly after a fixed amount of time.

A negative correlation means that if the value of X increases, the value of Y will decrease. A negative correlation could be found in the amount of salt in a jelly and the number of bacterial colonies growing on the jelly after a fixed amount of time.

The closer the value is to -1 or 1, the stronger the relationship between the variables, that is, the less scatter there would be about a line of best fit. A coefficient of 0 implies that there is no relationship between the variables.

Figure 123 shows examples of correlation with linear regression lines. In (i) and (ii) the correlation is good; for (i) the correlation is positive and the correlation coefficient is close to 1; for (ii) the correlation is negative and the correlation coefficient is close to -1; in (iii) there is weak positive correlation and the correlation coefficient would be close to zero.

Care must be taken when interpreting correlation coefficients, because if two variables are highly correlated it does not necessarily mean that one causes the other. In statistical terms, correlation does not imply causation.

There are three possible relationships between two variables, X and Y:

- Causation: Changes in X cause changes in Y.
- Common response: Both X and Y respond to changes in some unobserved variable.
- Confounding: The effect of X on Y is mixed up with the effects of other variables on Y.

An example of a correlation without a causal relationship could be found in the following: since 1950, CO_2 levels in the atmosphere have increased. During the same period, crime levels have gone up. The correlation between these data does NOT mean that increased crime levels are caused by carbon dioxide levels going up.

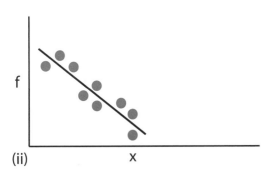

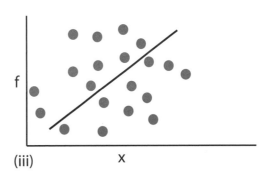

Figure 123   Correlation with linear regression lines

EXERCISES

1. The number of eggs in the nests of a sample of a species of bird is shown below. Find the mean and sample standard deviation of these numbers of eggs. Perform the calculations manually and on a graphical calculator.

   5   3   5   3   4   2   0   2   1   2

2. In a clinical trial, a population of patients was given Drug A or B. The mean times in minutes for blood clotting are shown in Figure 124.

Drug A	Drug B
61.6	39.3
64.6	26.3
55.6	32.4
45.2	21.5
50.6	60.3
70.5	24.3
67.7	36.4
57.5	47.4
66.5	33.2
42.3	57.2

   Figure 124

   (a) What is the null hypothesis?
   (b) What is the alternate hypothesis?
   (c) Perform a two tailed, unpaired test for the data and calculate the t statistic for the t test.
   (d) What is the critical value of t for P<0.05?
   (e) Is the t statistic greater or less than the critical value of t?
   (f) Can the null hypothesis be rejected?

CELLS

2.1   Cell theory

2.2   Prokaryotic cells

2.3   Eukaryotic cells

2.4   Membranes

2.5   Cell division

CORE

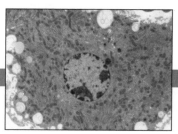

2.1 CELL THEORY

2.1.1   Outline the cell theory.

2.1.2   Discuss the evidence for the cell theory.

© IBO 2007

For a very long time, people did not know cells existed. The discovery of **cells** was linked to the developments in technology, in particular the ability to produce high quality lenses for **microscopes**. A series of steps led to the discovery of cells, most of them being related to the advances in technology. You can see that it involves a sequence of discoveries, often made by scientists in different countries.

1590-The Dutch optician *Zacharias Jansen* invents the compound microscope. A compound microscope has 2 lenses which provides greater magnification.

1665-The Englishman *Robert Hooke* studies cork with a compound microscope and names the structures 'cells'.

1675-*Antonie van Leeuwenhoek,* another Dutchman, discovers unicellular organisms.

1838-*Mathias Schleiden* from Germany suggests that all plants were made of cells.

1839-*Theodor Schwann*, also from Germany, suggests that all animals were also made of cells.

1840-The Czech *Jan Evangelista Purkinje* names the cell content 'protoplasm'.

1855-*Rudolf Virchow* from Germany suggests that 'all cells come from cells'.

TOK   What is a scientific theory?

The natural sciences use the scientific method to explain the physical world. The scientific method begins with observations. These observations are used to develop a possible explanation, or hypothesis. The hypothesis is tested through further observations or experiments. Each observation or experimental result is compared to the hypothesis to determine if the hypothesis is valid. If the hypothesis is supported repeatedly it can be confirmed.

Scientific theories or laws are the result of the thorough testing of hypotheses in a wide range of circumstances. The term theory in a scientific sense means that the hypothesis is supported by a large body of evidence and is the best explanation that scientists agree upon. The cell theory flowed from several related hypotheses that were tested over many years. It was confirmed as a theory after many observations and experiments made by a large number of scientists.

If new evidence comes to light that contradicts or does not fit the explanations made by a theory, the theory will need to be re-examined to determine if it is still valid. The theory may be modified or rejected altogether if it cannot account for the new observations.

CORE

The **cell theory** was developed and includes the following elements:

- All living organisms are composed of cells, and the products of cells (e.g. hair and scales).
- Cells are the smallest units of life.
- Cells only come from pre-existing cells.

The cell theory is widely accepted and advances in technology have allowed us to greatly increase our knowledge of cells. In particular the development of the electron microscope (EM) has allowed us to study the ultra structure of cells (*see Topic 2.3*) in more detail than Robert Hooke could ever have imagined.

2.1.3	State that unicellular organisms carry out all the functions of life.

© IBO 2007

Unicellular organisms are fully functioning individual organisms so they need to be able to carry out all functions of life. The functions of life include:

- **metabolism** which includes respiration and excretion
- **response** to stimuli which is also known as sensitivity
- **growth** includes both in cell size and number
- **reproduction**, whether sexual or asexual
- **homeostasis** which means maintaining relatively stable conditions inside the body
- **nutrition** which means the source of food

2.1.4	Compare the relative sizes of molecules, cell membrane thickness, viruses, bacteria, organelles and cells, using appropriate SI units.

© IBO 2007

Some **organelles** can be seen with the light microscope, others cannot. To study the internal structure of a cell, we need an electron microscope in all cases. Although even large cells are too small to see with the unaided eye, it is important to have an understanding of the relative sizes of cells and organelles. The following are 'typical sizes' only.

Eukaryotic cell	10 - 100 μm	$= 10 - 100 \times 10^{-6}$ m
Prokaryotic cell	1 - 5 μm	$= 1 - 5 \times 10^{-6}$ m
Nucleus	10 - 20 μm	$= 10 - 20 \times 10^{-6}$ m
Chloroplast	2 - 10 μm	$= 2 - 10 \times 10^{-6}$ m
Mitochondrion	0.5 - 5 μm	$= 0.5 - 5 \times 10^{-6}$ m
Bacteria	1 - 4 μm	$= 1 \times 10^{-6}$ m
Large virus (HIV)	100 nm	$= 100 \times 10^{-9}$ m
Ribosome	25 nm	$= 25 \times 10^{-9}$ m
Cell membrane	7.5 nm thick	$= 7.5 \times 10^{-9}$ m
DNA double helix	2 nm diameter	$= 2 \times 10^{-9}$ m
Hydrogen atom	0.1 nm	$= 0.1 \times 10^{-9}$ m

Because these objects are very small, we use special units to measure them. The micrometre (μm) is one millionth of a metre (10^{-6} m) and the nanometre (nm) is one thousand millionth of a metre (10^{-9} m) or one thousandth of a micrometre.

The largest known bacterium (*Epulopiscium*) was found in fish in the tropical waters surrounding Lizard Island, Australia. It is over 1 mm in length.

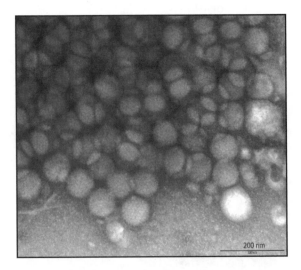

200 nm

Figure 201   An adenovirus

Some eukaryotic cells are larger than is indicated in the table above. Animal cells are often smaller than plant cells. The yolk of an egg is one cell. Each sap-filled vesicle of an orange is one cell.

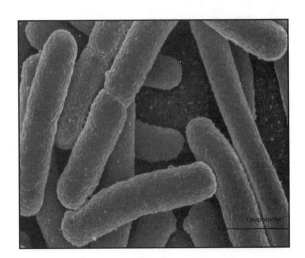

1 micrometre

Figure 202   A bacterium (E. coli)

TOK   What is the use of microscopes?

Knowledge claims made from the senses are filtered through the limitations of sense receptors and subsequent manipulation in the brain. Observations assisted by technology usually flow through other filters. Almost all cells, and everything sub-cellular, must be viewed through a microscope of some sort or another. A monocular light microscope produces a two dimensional image of a specimen whereas a binocular microscope may reveal more of the three dimension nature of a specimen. In most cases light microscope specimens are so small and thin that the detail of their contents are very difficult to see so they are treated with stains to allow observation of key cellular features.

Specimens prepared for viewing with an electron microscope must be specially treated so that the microscope examines an artefact of the original specimen. Electron micrographs are routinely colourised. Colourisation often hides the scope of the difference between images from an electron micrographs compared with images produced by a light microscope.

Some would argue that colourisation is done to reduce awareness of the numerous filters that electron microscopes bring to bear on our perception of the microscopic world.

2.1.5	Calculate linear magnification of drawings and the actual size of specimens in images of known magnification.

©IBO 2007

Diagrams and photographs can be shown larger or smaller than reality. To indicate the real size of the object, the magnification can be indicated next to the diagram or picture or a scale bar can be given.

Magnification
× 2

Figure 203 – A magnified image

Calculating magnification using the scale bar

The **scale bar** has a size indicated with it. This is the size it would really be but it would then be too small to see. So the image has been magnified to the picture you see. You can use a ruler to measure the (magnified) scale bar in the picture.

The two sizes of the scale bar are related via the formula:

magnified size = real size × magnification

so   magnification = $\dfrac{\text{magnified size (ruler)}}{\text{real size (scale bar)}}$

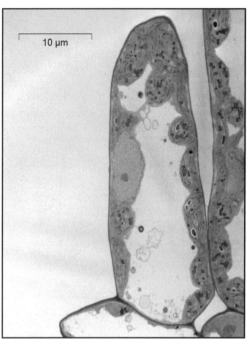

10 μm

Figure 204   Plant cells

Once you know the magnification, you can calculate the actual size of a cell organelle. You can use the same formula to calculate the real size from the measured, magnified size and the magnification.

real size = $\dfrac{\text{magnified size (with your ruler)}}{\text{magnification}}$

magnified size = real size × magnification

so   magnification = $\dfrac{\text{magnified size (ruler)}}{\text{real size (scale bar)}}$

Worked example

Figure 205 shows an electron micrograph of a liver cell.

The real size of the scale bar is given as 10 μm but you can measure the scale bar and find that it is 20 mm (approx.).

so using   real size = $\dfrac{\text{magnified size (with your ruler)}}{\text{magnification}}$

Magnification = 20000/10 = 2000×

CORE

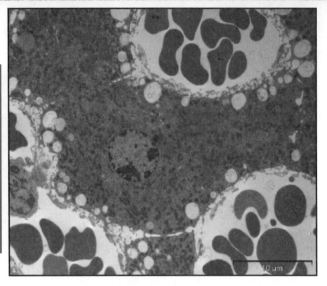

Figure 205   A liver cell

If you now want to find the size of the nucleus in Figure 205, you need to use the magnification you just calculated.

so real size   = 14 mm / 2000
                = 14000 μm / 2000
                = 7 μm

| 2.1.6 | Explain the importance of the surface area to volume ratio as a factor limiting cell size. |

© IBO 2007

The size of a cell is limited by its need to exchange materials with its environment. If a cell becomes too large, its diffusion distance becomes too long to be efficient and its surface to volume ratio becomes too small to allow the necessary exchange.

The rate with which a cell produces heat/waste and consumse resouces (food and oxygen) is directly proprtial to its volume. However, since the uptake of resources and the removal of heat/waste goes via the cell membrane, the rate of uptake/removal is proportional to its surface area.

A cube with sides of 1 cm has a surface area of 6×1 cm $\times 1$ cm $= 6$ cm^2 and a volume of 1 cm $\times 1$ cm $\times 1$ cm $= 1$ cm^3 which means a surface area: volume ratio of 6:1. This means that every 1 cm^3 of volume has 6 cm^2 of surface area.

A cube with sides of 10 cm has a surface area of 6×10 cm $\times 10$ cm $= 600$ cm^2 and a volume of 10 cm $\times 10$ cm $\times 10$ cm $= 1000$ cm^3 which gives a surface area: volume ratio of 600:1000 = 0.6/1.

1 cm cube
Surface area = 6cm^2
Volume = 1cm^3

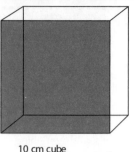

10 cm cube
Surface area = 600cm^2
Volume = 1000cm^3

Figure 206   Different size cubes

This means that every 1 cm^3 of volume has 0.6 cm^2 of surface area. This is one tenth of the surface area per cm^3 volume if you compare it with the smaller cube.

As you can see the volume increases more rapidly than the **surface area** which eventually creates a problem for the cell.

Ways of dealing with this are to increase the surface area by protruding extensions *(see Figure 207)* or by flattening the cell. Multicellular organisms face the same problem. This is why, for example, we have lungs (structures in lungs increase the surface area available for gaseous exchange) and a circulatory system (blood carries materials round

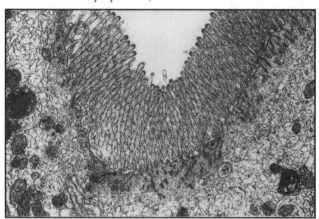

Figure 207   Epithelium in the gut

the body, reducing the diffusion distance). The nucleus is generally very much smaller than the whole cell, which helps it exchange substances with the rest of the cell.

| 2.1.7 | State that multicellular organisms show emergent properties. |

© IBO 2007

Emergent properties are those where the whole is more than the sum of their parts. A good example of emergence is a termite hill or the human brain. In the case of the brain,

CORE

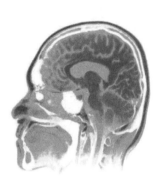

Figure 208
An anthill

Figure 209
The human brain

the individual neurons are not capable of thought but the communication and cooperation between the neurons makes it possible for the brain to think.

Multicellular organisms show **emergent properties**. This means that the organism can achieve more than the sum of what each cell could achieve individually. This is caused by the fact that cells interact, allowing them to perform

tasks together that they not achieve, even in part, if they were alone. Figures 208 and 209 show good examples of objects with emergent properties.

2.1.8	Explain that cells in multicellular organisms differentiate to carry out specialized functions by expressing some of their genes but not others.

© IBO 2007

While every cell contains all the genetic information to carry out every function, only a small portion of the genetic material is activated. A cell in your toes has the information on how to make the pigment which colours your eyes, but will not use it. So cells differentiate by expression of some of their genes and not others. The genes which are not expressed by the cell, remain present in the nucleus but are packed away so tightly that they cannot be accessed. **Euchromatin** is light grey when viewed with an

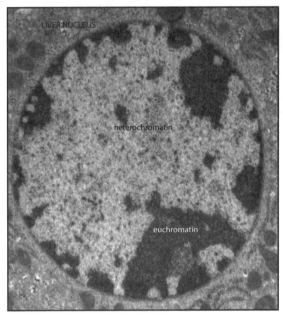

Figure 210   Chromatin

EM and heterochromatin is dark grey. Euchromatin often represents the genes that are used (transcribed), *see Topic 3.4,* while **heterochromatin** tends to contain the inactive genes.

Cells affect each other. The differentiation of any one cell is determined by the cell's position relative to others and by chemical gradients.

TOK   What are emergent properties?

From a natural science perspective, the levels of life may be considered to be emergent properties, that is, each level emerges from a level below. For example, at the simplest level, the pumping action of the heart emerges from the interaction of the physical action of the various tissues that form it with the chemicals and nerve impulses entering the tissues. Looking at life in terms of its emergent properties is helpful in developing an understanding of the complexity of life and the interaction of its various components. One of the limitations of taking this approach to life is that to look at biological processes individually means that we miss the immense level of interaction integral to all living systems.

By looking at a process, tissue or organ in isolation we will understand how it functions, but lose a sense of the organism it is part of. In fact, this can lead to a loss of understanding what life is. A heart can continue to pump outside of the body for some time given appropriate conditions. Is it still alive? Looking at life as an emergent property may be seen to imply that life is just a series of chemical and physical interactions without any sense of purpose. Whether this is the case or not is not for natural science to decide.

CORE

2.1.9	State that stem cells retain the capacity to divide and have the ability to differentiate along different pathways.

© IBO 2007

Stem cells are unspecialised cells. An embryo is a source of stem cells because the cells can become any type of cell and are 'totipotent'. After many division, the zygote has become a ball of cells or blastocyst. These cells can become almost any type of tissue and are considered 'pluripotent'.

Another source of stem cells is the umbilical cord of a new born baby. Cells from the blood of the umbilical cord are considered 'multipotent' because they can become a limited number of other particular types of cells. Adults still have some stem cells in their bone marrow which can be used to treat diseases such as leukemia.

Stem cells are different from 'normal' cells in two ways:
1. Stem cells are undifferentiated. This means that they have not yet specialised into a certain type of cell. As a result, all (or most) of their genes can still be expressed.
2. Stem cells are self-sustaining. They can divide and replicate for long periods of time.

The most interesting characteristic of stem cells is their ability to differentiate into specialised cells when given a certain chemical signal. Theoretically, you could make a stem cell replicate and then differentiate into liver cells and grow a new liver this way.

In reality, research has only been going on since about 1998 when a group led by *Dr. James Thomson* at the University of Wisconsin developed a technique to isolate and grow the cells. In some countries, stem cell research is restricted by legal measures. In Denmark, Spain, Sweden and the UK, stem cell research is allowed using cells from embryos less than 14 days old but only Denmark and the UK allow the

creation of embryos for research purposes. In the USA in 2006, President George W. Bush vetoed a bill which would have allowed Federal money to be used for research where stem cells are derived from destroyed embryos.

2.1.10	Outline one therapeutic use of stem cells.

© IBO 2007

The therapeutic use of stem cells is sometimes referred to as cell therapy. In cell therapy, cells that do not work well are replaced with healthy, functioning cells.

The most common example of **cell therapy** is a bone marrow transplant. This technique has been used for more than 40 years. Cells in the bone marrow produce blood cells. People with leukemia can receive a transplant of healthy, functioning bone marrow which may cure their disease.

Cell therapy is also used in experiments to graft new skin cells for people who have been severely burned. Another use is to grow new corneas for people whose eyesight is failing. In all of these cases, the transplanted cells need to become part of the body and need to continue to function well as part of that body for the therapy to be a success (*see Figure 212*).

TOK   How should stem cells be used?

Therapeutic cloning is a controversial issue for many people. Stems cells are very flexible, making them ideal for experimentation. Potentially their development can be channelled to replace body tissue that has been damaged or does not function as it should. Examples of possible uses include growth of replacement heart valves, treatment of diabetes mellitus and Parkinson's disease. However, to treat such conditions, significant scientific hurdles such as immune system rejection of stem cells will need to be overcome. There is also the risk that manipulated cells could follow pathways that are unexpected, such as the development of tumours. Use of human embryonic stem cells for experimentation requires the destruction of a human embryo. To many people, destruction of the embryo means the death of a human individual. This is unacceptable to most cultures and religious traditions. Where such cultures and religious traditions are influential, such experimentation is limited or not possible. Today scientists are divided in their ability to research the ability of stem cells by cultural and religious as well as legal restrictions.

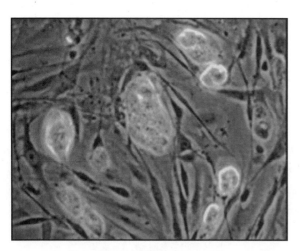

Figure 211   Mouse stem cells

The Promise of Stem Cell Research

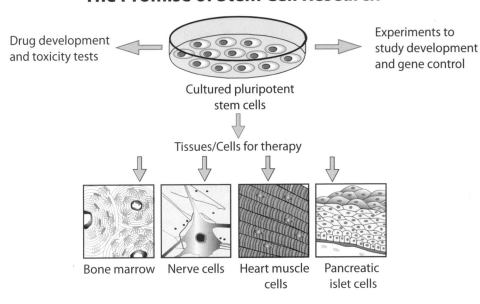

Drug development and toxicity tests

Experiments to study development and gene control

Cultured pluripotent stem cells

Tissues/Cells for therapy

Bone marrow   Nerve cells   Heart muscle cells   Pancreatic islet cells

Figure 212   The promise of stem cell research

2.2 PROKARYOTIC CELLS

2.2.1   Draw and label a diagram of the ultrastructure of *Escherichia coli (E. coli)* as an example of a prokaryote.

© IBO 2007

You have probably heard of *Escherichia coli*, commonly known as *E. coli*. They are very common bacteria, e.g. many of them live in your gut at any time. Using a scanning **electron microscope (SEM)**, you would see an image of the outside of *E. coli* like the one in Figure 213 whereas a transmission electron microscope (TEM) would produce an image like the one shown in Figure 214.

When we combine a number of transmission EM pictures, we can deduce the structure of *E. coli*. It is shown in Figure 215. You should be able to draw and label a diagram similar to this.

2.2.2   Annotate the diagram with the functions of each of the named structures.

2.2.3   Identify structures from 2.2.1 in electron micrographs of *E. coli*.

© IBO 2007

The various strucures in **prokaryotic cells** have particular functions as follows.

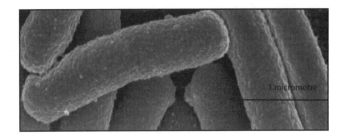

Figure 213   Escherichia coli cells (3D)

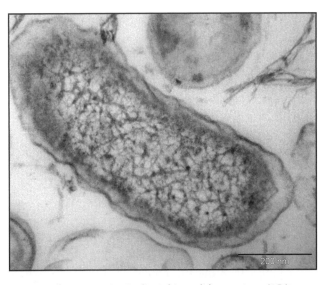

Figure 214   An Escherichia coli bacterium (2D)

15

CORE

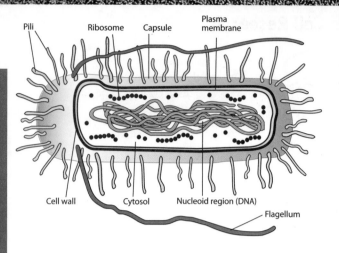

Figure 215   Diagram of a prokaryotic cell

CELL WALL

The **cell wall** is made of protein-sugars whereas plant cell walls are made of cellulose.

It gives the cell its shape, protects the bacterium from external damage and prevents bursting if the cell has taken up a lot of water (e.g. in a hypotonic medium). It also achors the pili and flagella which help some bacteria move.

PLASMA MEMBRANE

The **plasma membrane** controls which materials enter and leave the cell, either by active or passive transport. It is selectively permeable.

CYTOPLASM

Cytoplasm is a watery fluid that contains enzymes that control metabolic reactions in the cell and also contains the organelles of the cell.

PILI

Pili are thin protein tubes. They are found on the outside of the plasma membrane. Refer to Figure 216.

There are two types of pili: attachment pili (sometimes known as fimbriae) and conjugation pili (sometimes known as sex pili). Prokaryotes are likely to have many attachment pili. At the end of the pilus, there is a sticky section which allows *E. coli* to stick to a surface such as the cell membrane of another cell.

There tend to be only a few **conjugation** pili. They are much longer than the attachment pili and play a role in bacterial conjugation. They build a bridge between the

cytoplasms of two bacterial cells and allow a plasmid to be transferred from one bacterial cell to another. Figure 217 shows a photograph of bacterial conjugation.

FLAGELLA

Flagellae are long thread-like structures, made of protein. They are attached to the cell surface and they allow the bacterium to move in a fluid environment.

RIBOSOME

Ribosomes consist of RNA and proteins, they play a key role in protein synthesis. The process is called translation (*see also Topic 3.5*). Prokaryotic ribosomes are 70S. This means that they are slightly less dense than eukaryotic ribosomes which are 80S. Figure 219 shows a 3D reconstruction of a ribosome.

NUCLEOID REGION

The **nucleoid region** of the cell contains the DNA which contains the genetic material.

It is the area from which all processes in the cell are controlled.

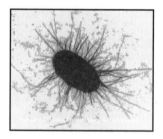

Figure 216   Bacterial pili

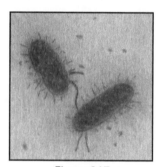

*Figure 217
Bacterial conjugation*

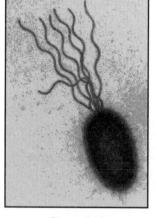

*Figure 218
Bacterial flagella*

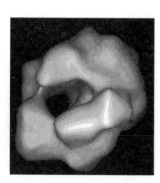

*Figure 219
3D model of a ribosome*

CORE

2.2.4   State that prokaryotic cells divide by binary fission.

©IBO 2007

Prokaryotic cells divide by **binary fission**. The process of binary fission starts with DNA replication which is followed by the separation of the two circular strands of DNA to either side of the cell. Then cytokinesis occurs, where the cell divides into two. Each new cell receives about half of the cytoplasm. Subsequent growth will restore each cell to full size. Figure 220 shows an EM of bacterial binary fission which is almost complete. Figure 221 shows this process of binary fission diagrammatically.

Figure 220   Bacterial fission - photograph

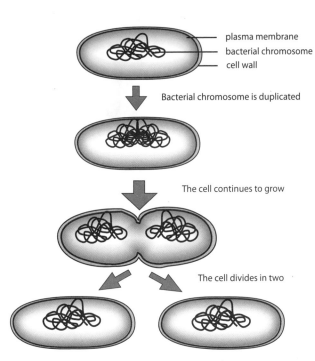

plasma membrane
bacterial chromosome
cell wall

Bacterial chromosome is duplicated

The cell continues to grow

The cell divides in two

Figure 221   Bacterial fission - diagram

2.3 EUKARYOTIC CELLS

2.3.1   Draw and label a diagram of the ultrastructure of a liver cell as an example of an animal cell.

©IBO 2007

Figure 222 has been drawn on the basis of microscopic observations of a number of **eukaryotic cells** such as liver cells.

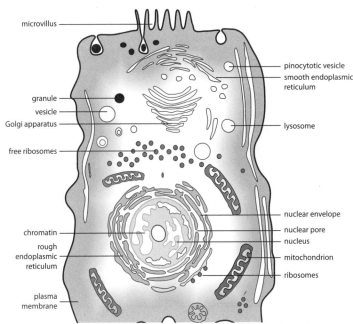

microvillus

pinocytotic vesicle
smooth endoplasmic reticulum

granule
vesicle
Golgi apparatus

lysosome

free ribosomes

nuclear envelope
chromatin
nuclear pore
rough endoplasmic reticulum
nucleus
mitochondrion
ribosomes
plasma membrane

Figure 222   The ultrastructure of a eukaryotic cell

2.3.2   Annotate the diagram with the functions of each named structure.

2.3.3   Identify the structures in 2.2.1 in electron micrographs of a liver cell.

©IBO 2007

Figure 229 shows a list of cell organelles, commonly found in eukaryotic cells, with their functions.

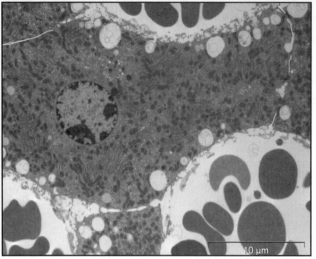

Figure 223   An electron micrograph of a liver cell

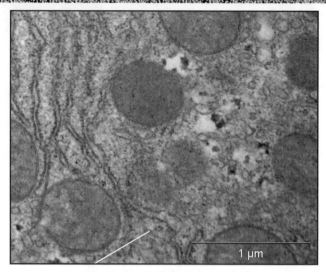

Figure 226   Golgi apparatus

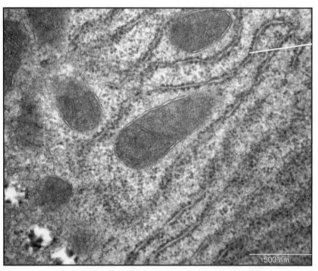

Figure 224   Ribosomes and rough ER

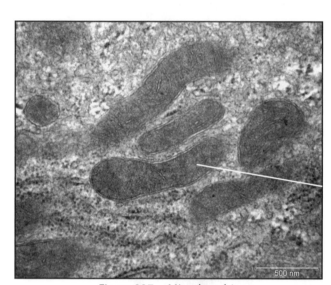

Figure 227   Mitochondria

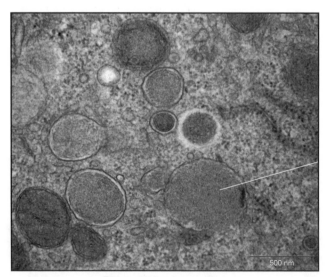

Figure 225   Lysosomes

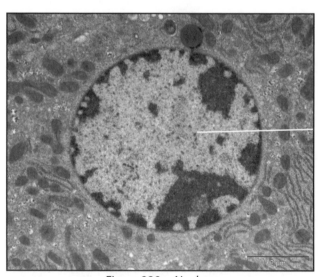

Figure 228   Nucleus

CORE

Cell organelle	Structure	Function
(free) ribosome	made of two subunits, both made of protein and RNA free ribosomes make proteins that are used in the cell	site of protein synthesis *(see Topic 3.5)*
rough endoplasmic reticulum - RER	RER is membrane with ribosomes attached. RER makes proteins that are exported via exocytosis in order to be used outside the cell	site of protein synthesis *(see Topic 3.5)*
lysosome	contains hydrolytic enzymes e.g. lysozymes which can break down substances in the cell	fuses with and digests old cell organelles and material taken in via endocytosis (intracellular digestion); it also can burst and cause autolysis of a cell
Golgi apparatus	stack of flattened, membrane-bound sacs, forming an extensive network in the cell	intracellular transport, processing and packaging of proteins
mitochondrion	the link reaction and the Krebs cycle take place in the matrix; the electron transport chain is found on the cristae of the inner membrane	involved in the release of energy from organic molecules
nucleus	largest cell organelle contains DNA	controls the activity of the cell by transcribing certain genes and not others *(see Topic 3.5)*

Figure 229 Cell organelles structures and functions table

2.3.4 Compare prokaryotic and eukaryotic cells.

©IBO 2007

Figure 230 summarises some of the similarities and differences between prokaryotic and eukaryotic cells.

2.3.5 State three differences between plant and animal cells.

©IBO 2007

Figure 231 summarises some of the main differences between plant and animal cells.

2.3.6 Outline two roles of extracellular components.

©IBO 2007

Extracellular components are found associated with both plant and animal cells. **Cellulose** is the best known example of an extracellular component in plant cells. Bone, cartilage and connective tissue are examples of tissues with a very important extracellular component in animal cells. Following are some more details about cellulose and cartilage.

The main component of plant cell walls is cellulose. The **cell wall** is a non-living secretion (an extracellular component) of the cell and it serves several purposes:

- The cell wall provides support and mechanical strength for the cell and in turn the tissues of the plant as a whole. It determines the shape of the cell.

- As the plant cell takes up water, the intra-cellular pressure increases. The cell wall will limit the amount of expansion and prevent the plant cell from bursting. The cell will continue to take in water due to osmosis but the same amount of water will be expelled due to the pressure of the cell wall. The cell is now turgid and mechanically quite stable. Many plants depend to a large extend on turgor to keep them upright.

- Cellulose is a carbohydrate and plants can use the cell wall for carbohydrate storage.

CORE

Feature	Similarities	Differences	
		prokaryotes	*eukaryotes*
genetic material	DNA	naked DNA	DNA associated with proteins (histones)
		circular DNA	linear DNA
		DNA found in cytoplasm (nucleoid area)	DNA enclosed in nuclear envelope
protein synthesis	ribosomes	70S (mass and size)	80S (mass and size)
respiration		no mitochondria but uses plasma membrane and mesosomes	mitochondria
ultrastructure	internal membranes	no internal membranes present	compartmentalise the cell into areas with different functions

Figure 230   Comparing prokaryotic and eukaryotic cells table

Feature	Plant cell	Animal cell
cell wall	cellulose cell wall and plasma membrane	only plasma membrane
chloroplast	present in photosynthetic cells	absent
vacuole	large, permanent vacuole, filled with cell sap	small, temporary vacuoles may be present
reserve food	carbohydrate stored as starch and also plant oils	carbohydrate storage as glycogen and some stored as animal fat

Figure 231   Differences between plant and animal cells

- The cell wall provides a barrier for **pathogens** (disease causing organisms). Plant cells store specific proteins in the cell wall that recognise pathogens and start a 'defense response' to them.

Plasmodesmata are narrow channels through the cell walls. They connect the cytoplasms of cells next to each other to make it easier to exchange molecules.

Hyaline **cartilage** in animals is a tissue that has cells within a lot of extra-cellular matrix (ECM). The ECM of cartilage is a gel which contains certain kinds of glycoproteins. They associate with water and collagen and are responsible for the firmness and resilience of the cartilage. Figure 232 shows a photograph of cartilage. Notice that the cells which produce the ECM are clustered in groups of 2-3 within a 'sea' of ECM.

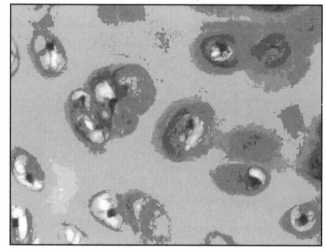

Figure 232   Hyaline cartilage

CORE

2.4 MEMBRANES

> 2.4.1 Draw and label a diagram to show the structure of membranes.
>
> 2.4.2 Explain how the hydrophobic and hydrophilic properties of phospholipids help to maintain the structure of cell membranes.
>
> ©IBO 2007

Figure 233 shows a diagram of the **fluid mosaic model** of membrane structure. Figure 234 is an electron micrograph of the membrane (see pointer) of a liver cell and the thickness of the membrane can be calculated approximately using the bar.

If you were to build a membrane, you would start with a phospholipid molecule which consists of a phosphate head which is polar and 'hydrophilic' and 2 fatty acid tails that are nonpolar and 'hydrophobic'. This arrangement is shown in Figure 235 (a).

You would then combine the phospholipids to form a bilayer. The polar phosphate heads would be on the outside of the layer because they can interact with water (hydrophilic). The non-polar fatty acid tails are hydrophobic and will be away from the water on the inside of the bilayer. This arrangement is shown in Figure 235 (b).

The phospholipid bilayer could form the outside of a sphere, similar to a thin layer of soapy water forming a bubble. If the layer of soap represents the membrane, then the air inside the bubble represents the cytoplasm. This arrangement is shown in Figure 235 (c).

This is the basic structure of a membrane. The function of the plasma membrane is to keep the cell content separate from the outside so that the cell can have a higher or lower concentration of certain molecules, e.g. glucose or enzymes. In order to achieve this function, the plasma membrane must be able to control which substances enter and leave the cell.

The phospholipid bilayer is quite effective in stopping molecules from going into or out of the cell. Since the membrane has a non-polar layer in its centre and two polar layers on either side, it is very difficult for both polar and non-polar molecules to pass through both layers.

However, every cell needs to exchange materials with its environment and molecules need to enter and leave the cell. This is one of the functions of proteins that are found in between the phospholipid molecules.

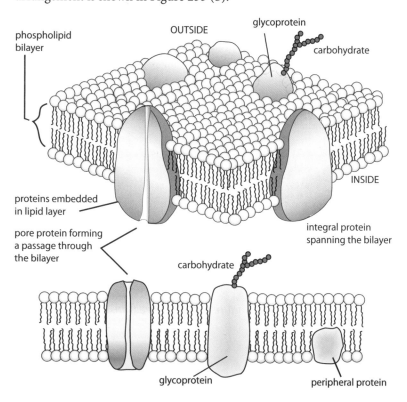

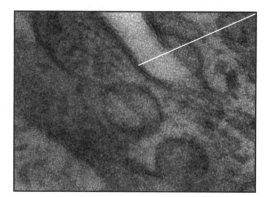

Figure 234 Electron micrograph of a plasma membrane of a liver cell

Figure 233 Diagram of a plasma membrane

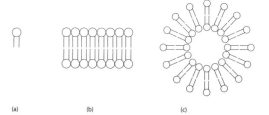

Figure 235 Molecular structure of membranes

CORE

Two kinds of membrane proteins are recognised

Integral proteins are those in which most of the protein molecule is found in between the phospholipid molecules of the membrane; they interact with the cytoplasm on one side, with external molecules outside the cell and with the hydrophilic section of the membrane in between.

Peripheral proteins are mostly found outside the phospholipid bilayer in the cytoplasm but interact with the phosphate heads; they may not be permanently associated with the membrane.

Some proteins have a carbohydrate group attached to them. They are then called glycoproteins.

Last but not least, plasma membranes contain cholesterol. Figure 236 shows that cholesterol is quite a large molecule. It is usually positioned between the fatty acid tails of the phospholipids and reduces fluidity and permeability. (*Note; The IBO syllabus does not require students to memorise the structure of cholesterol.*)

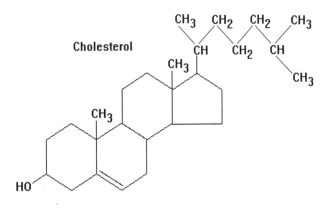

Figure 236   Structure of cholesterol

Membranes have varying amounts of cholesterol. If a membrane has a lot of cholesterol, it will be very stable and not very permeable. Membranes of intracellular organelles such as mitochondria have less cholesterol. They are more fluid and more permeable.

In summary
- the main component of membranes is a phospholipid bilayer
- membranes also contain integral and peripheral proteins
- some of these proteins are glycoproteins (proteins with a carbohydrate attached)
- membranes contain cholesterol

This arrangement is quite stable because any change in the relative positions of the phospholipid molecules decreases the interactions between polar parts of molecules and increase interactions between non-polar groups and water.

2.4.3   List the functions of membrane proteins.

©IBO 2007

Proteins in the plasma membrane can have various functions as follows.

- Hormone binding sites - **hormones** transported by the blood will only act on cells that have the appropriate protein receptor on the outside of their membrane.

- Immobilised enzymes (also called membrane-bound enzymes) - enzymes arranged into systems in order to make it easier for a sequence of reactions to occur. A good example is the electron transport chain on the cristae of the mitochondrion (*see Topic 8.1*).

- Cell adhesion - integral proteins can stick out and bind to specific protein molecules in adjacent cells or they can bind to an extracellular matrix (*see Topic 2.3.6*).

- Cell to cell communication - either via direct contact between the membrane proteins of adjacent cells or via signals such as hormones or neurotransmitters.

- Channels for **passive transport** - they are often small proteins where the outside is hydrophobic and the inside of the hollow tube is hydrophilic, allowing polar molecules to enter the cell as shown in Figure 237.

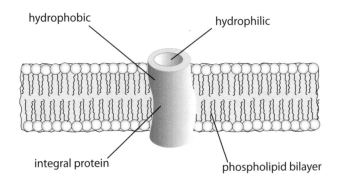

Figure 237   Passive transport

CORE

- Pumps for **active transport** - e.g. Na$^+$/K$^+$ pump in nerve cells, using ATP to transport Na ioins back outside the axon and K ions back in. This is illustrated in Figure 238.

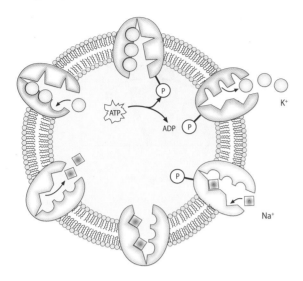

Figure 238   Active transport

Simple diffusion is possible for small, non-polar molecules. They can diffuse across the membrane without additional assistance. However, for polar molecules (ions), the membranes forms a barrier that is difficult to cross without help. There are two possibilities for facilitated diffusion, both using proteins in the membrane. They are channel proteins and transport proteins.

Channel proteins create a hydrophilic pore in the membrane through which small charged particles (ions) can diffuse into the cell *(see Topic 2.4.3)*

Transport proteins can help move substances such as glucose into the cell. The transport protein has a binding site specific for glucose. Once glucose binds, there will be a change in the structure of the protein which carries the glucose molecules across the membrane and releases it inside the cell. The transport protein goes back to its original shape and is really to move the next glucose molecule into the cell.

(see also Topics 6.1.6 and 6.1.7)

2.4.4	Define diffusion and osmosis.
	©IBO 2007

DIFFUSION

Diffusion is the movement of gas or liquid particles from a region of high concentration to a region of low concentration.

OSMOSIS

Osmosis is the passive movement, or diffusion of water molecules, across a partially permeable membrane, from a region of lower solute concentration to a region of higher solute concentration.

2.4.5	Explain passive transport across membranes in terms of simple diffusion and facilitated diffusion.
	©IBO 2007

It is important to remember that both simple diffusion and facilitated diffusion are passive transport. This means that they do not require energy but it also means that the direction of the diffusion is down the concentration gradient.

2.4.6	Explain the role of protein pumps and ATP in active transport across membranes.
	©IBO 2007

Active transport requires energy. It will not take place unless ATP is available. Active transport often moves particles against the concentration gradient, that is from low to high concentration. An example is the sodium-potassium pump. *Refer to Figure 238.*

Be aware that the proteins involved in active transport are often also referred to as transport proteins. The process is not very different from facilitated diffusion but remember that active transport requires energy (ATP) and may go against the concentration gradient.

Transport proteins are sometimes called carrier proteins or membrane pumps e.g. the sodium-potassium pump. A protein in the plasma membrane can move sodium out of the cell and potassium into it even though the concentration of sodium outside is higher than inside and vice versa for potassium. This is important in the functioning of nerve cells. The proteins involved in this process are selective. *Refer again to Figure 238.*

CORE

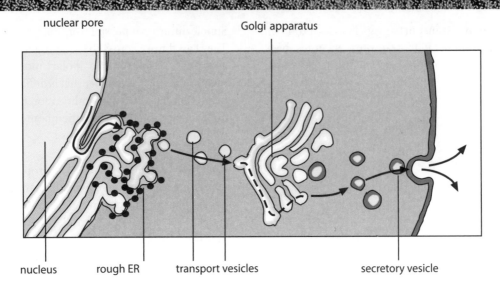

nuclear pore

Golgi apparatus

nucleus

rough ER

transport vesicles

secretory vesicle

Figure 239   Formation of vesicles for exocytosis

2.4.7	Explain how vesicles are used to transport materials within a cell between the rough endoplasmic reticulum, Golgi apparatus and plasma membrane.

©IBO 2007

As Figure 239 illustrates, intracellular transport often involves the use of vesicles.

From the fluid mosaic model, it can be seen that membranes are not static structures. The molecules making up the membrane can move in the plane of the membrane. Also this structure has some flexibility so that small amounts of membrane can be added or removed without tearing the membrane (this is called endocytosis and exocytosis), (*see also Topic 2.4.8*). Since the structure of the plasma membrane is essentially the same as that of the nuclear envelope, the endoplasmic reticulum (ER) and the Golgi apparatus, it is possible to exchange membrane sections between them.

The RER produces the proteins that are intended for export and the function of the Golgi apparatus is to prepare substances for exocytosis. This involves wrapping the substance in a section of membrane from

the Golgi apparatus. This membrane then joins the cell surface membrane in the process of exocytosis. *Refer to Figure 239.*

Many of the substances which the cell 'exports' are proteins and hence the following organelles and processes are involved:

1. The nucleus which contains chromosomes that, in turn contain genes coding for proteins. Messenger RNA (mRNA) is then made by transcription and passes from the nucleus to the cytoplasm.
2. The rough ER which contains the ribosomes which make proteins, intended for export, by translation.
3. The protein then goes into the lumen of the RER, is surrounded by membrane and moves to the Golgi apparatus for processing before it leaves through the cell surface membrane by exocytosis.

There is no continuous connection between the rough ER and Golgi apparatus. There is, however, an indirect connection made by membrane-bound secretory vesicles, which bud off from the ER and move to the Golgi apparatus, where the membranous components fuse and the contents of the vesicles are delivered for modification within the Golgi apparatus. In turn secretory vesicles from the Golgi

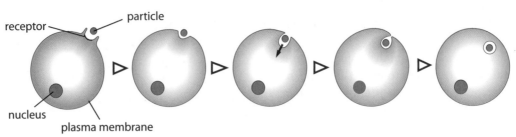

receptor

particle

nucleus

plasma membrane

Figure 240   Diagram of endocytosis

CORE

can leave the cell via exocytosis at the plasma membrane, where again fusion of membrane components occurs. *Refer again to Figure 239.*

2.4.8	Describe how the fluidity of the membrane allows it to change shape, break and reform during endocytosis and exocytosis.

©IBO 2007

ENDOCYTOSIS

Endocytosis is the process by which the cell takes up a substance by surrounding it with membrane. This process requires energy (ATP). Cells use endocytosis to take in substances that cannot enter the cell in other ways because they are highly polar and/or too large. Examples of endocytosis would be white blood cells taking up bacteria. The process of endocytosis is shown in Figure 240. *Refer also to the animation on the Student CD.*

Two different types of endocytosis are recognised, pinocytosis (when the substance is fluid), which is sometimes called "cell drinking" and phagocytosis (when the substance is solid), which is sometimes called "cell eating".

Figure 241 presents an overview of the processes by which materials can enter a cell.

	ATP required	Concentration gradient
Diffusion	no	down
Facilitated diffusion	no	down
Osmosis	no	down
Active transport with carrier proteins	yes	against is possible
Endocytosis	yes	against is possible

Figure 241   Overview of processes by which materials can enter a cell

EXOCYTOSIS

Exocytosis is the reverse of endocytosis and results in materials being removed from cells. It also requires energy in the form of ATP. *Refer also to the animation on the Student CD.*

2.5 CELL DIVISION

2.5.1	Outline the stages in the cell cycle, including interphase (G1, S, G2), mitosis and cytokinesis.

©IBO 2007

As discussed in *Topic 1*, the cell theory is considered to have three important aspects:

* all organisms are made of one or more cells.
* cells are the units of life.
* cells only arise from pre-existing cells.

The **cell cycle** of growth, duplication and division can be divided into several stages as shown in Figure 242.

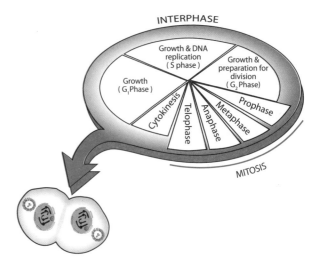

Figure 242   The cell cycle

There are some important terms that you need to understand.

Mitosis refers to the process of nuclear division.

Cytokinesis occurs after mitosis and is the actual physical division of the cell and is therefore not included in mitosis.

Stage G1 refers to the period of cell growth and increase in number of cell organelles.

Stage S indicates the synthesis of DNA otherwise known as replication.

Stage G2 is the preparation for mitosis.

CORE

2.5.2 State that tumours (cancers) are the result of uncontrolled cell division and that these can occur in any organ or tissue.

©IBO 2007

Mitosis and cell division are usually under strict control, only producing new cells needed for growth or repair. Tumour repressor genes produce proteins which inhibit cell division. Proto-oncogenes are genes that produce proteins which stimulate growth and cell division. If mutations occur in these genes, cell division can become uncontrolled, resulting in a tumour. This can occur in any organ or tissue. Figure 243 illustrates the main stages in the growth of a cancer.

Certain kinds of radiation and certain chemicals are known to be carcinogenic, mostly they increase the chances of mutation, although some seem to increase the effect of mutations already present. Viruses inserting their genetic material into the chromosomes of the host, may also contribute to the formation of tumour cells. Certain forms of electromagnetic radiation also increase the rate of mutation (mutagenic) and are therefore also carcinogenic. There is a strong correlation between the amount of ultraviolet light and the incidence of skin cancer. A series of genetic changes in a cell is needed before it becomes a tumour cell. However, the changes accumulate over the years, making cancer quite common in the aging population and a very common cause of death.

Some tumours are harmless or benign e.g. warts. Others may become malignant and spread to other tissues and other parts of the body and are then called cancer. Cancer can be treated in a number of ways:
- surgical removal
- radiation therapy
- chemotherapy

SURGICAL REMOVAL
Surgical removal of the tumour cells before they can grow further and spread

RADIATION THERAPY
Radiation therapy (**radiotherapy**) using a strong ionising or nuclear radiation beam which can be directed to a precise point and will 'burn' all cells in the area

CHEMOTHERAPY
Chemotherapy uses chemicals that destroy all rapidly dividing cells by medication. Unfortunately this also

includes cells responsible for the growth of hair, cells which form the lining of the gut and sperm -producing cells. This cause the side-effects involved with this treatment.

2.5.3 State that interphase is an active period in the life of a cell when many metabolic reactions occur, including protein synthesis, DNA replication, and an increase in the number of mitochondria and chloroplasts.

©IBO 2007

Only a small part of the cell's life cycle is in mitosis, which is the division of the nucleus. Cytokinesis is the division of the cell and follows immediately after mitosis. It can even start before the last phase of mitosis is completely finished. Most of the time in the cell cycle, the cell is in interphase.

Stages G1, S and G2 together are called **interphase**. Rather than being a 'resting phase' as once thought, Interphase is a very active period in the life of a cell, where many biochemical reactions, DNA transcription and translation and DNA replication occur.

In order for the cell to function properly, the right reactions must take place at the right time. Within a cell, chemical reactions usually only take place in the presence of the correct enzyme. Enzymes are proteins and are produced by the process of transcription and translation (*see Topic 3.5*).

As described above, replication of DNA takes place during the S phase of interphase.

The number of **mitochondria** and **chloroplasts** in the cell increases mostly during G2 phase. All through interphase, the chloroplasts and mitochondria absorb material from the cell and grow in size.

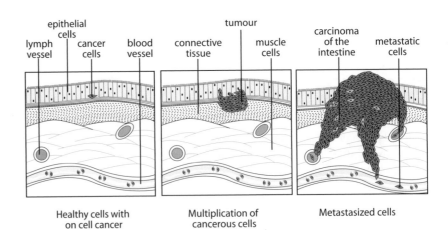

epithelial cells
lymph vessel | cancer cells | blood vessel | connective tissue | tumour | muscle cells | carcinoma of the intestine | metastatic cells

Healthy cells with on cell cancer   Multiplication of cancerous cells   Metastasized cells

Figure 243   Stages in the growth of a cancer

The duration of the cell cycle varies greatly between different cells. The cell cycle of bacteria is 20 minutes, beans take 19 hours and mouse fibroblasts take 22 hours. Also the different stages in interphase can last for different amounts of time. However, generally interphase lasts longer than mitosis. The cell division times quoted above are under ideal conditions.

2.5.4	Describe the events that occur in the four phases of mitosis.
	©IBO 2007

The behaviour of the chromosomes in each of the four phases is described below. The purpose of mitosis is to increase the number of cells without changing the genetic material, i.e. the daughter cells are identical to the parent cell in the number of chromosomes, the genes and alleles. Mitosis can occur in haploid, diploid or polyploid cells.

Mitosis is divided into four phases:
- prophase
- metaphase
- anaphase
- telophase

When a nucleus is not dividing it can be said that the cell is in interphase.

It is important to note that nuclear division is a continuous process although it is usually discussed as consisting of four stages. It is more important to know what typically happens in each stage than to be able to determine the stage of every cell in a microscope slide.

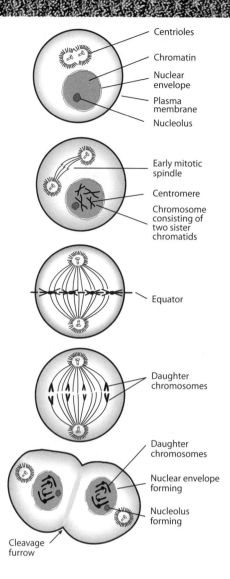

Figure 244   The process of mitosis

INTERPHASE
- DNA replication occurs.
- At this stage, the genetic material is in the form of chromatin: long strands of DNA with associated proteins.

PROPHASE
- Chromosomes become visible (supercoiling).
- Centrioles move to opposite poles.
- Spindle formation.
- Nucleolus becomes invisible.
- Nuclear membrane disappears.
- At this stage, each chromosome consists of two identical sister chromatids, held together by a centromere as shown in Figure 244.

METAPHASE
- Chromosomes move to the equator.
- Spindle microtubules attach to the centromeres.

ANAPHASE
- Centromeres separate.
- Chromatids separate and move to opposite poles - they are now called chromosomes.

TELOPHASE
- Chromosomes have arrived at poles.
- Spindle disappears.
- Centrioles replicate (in animal cells).
- Nuclear membrane reappears.
- Nucleolus becomes visible.
- Chromosomes become chromatin.

These headings correspond to the stages shown in Figure 244.

The division of the cell is sometimes included as the last stage of telophase; strictly speaking, however, cytokinesis is not a part of mitosis.

Mitosis can be summarised as the dispersing of the nuclear material, the movement of centrioles (if present) to opposite ends, microtubules developing into a spindle, the supercoiling of chromatin, its attachment to the spindle fibres at the centromere region, and the separation and movement of chromatids to opposite poles of the cell.

2.5.5	Explain how mitosis produces two genetically identical nuclei.
	©IBO 2007

The result of the process of mitosis is two nuclei. During S phase, each chromosome replicates (forms an exact copy of itself). These copies are called sister chromatids. These identical sister chromatids are separated during Anaphase, and are moved to each pole. When they are separated they are referred to as chromosomes. The result is two nuclei, identical to each other and to the original nucleus.

2.5.6	State that growth, embryonic development, tissue repair and asexual reproduction involve mitosis.
	©IBO 2007

The growth of tissue involves the production of similar cells. Muscle produces more muscle by the process of mitosis. Similarly, a wound requires the production of identical replacement cells to repair the damage.

A zygote, or fertilised egg cell is one cell. To grow out into a multicellular organism, repeated mitotic divisions increase the number of cells. As the number of cells increases, differentiation takes place by expressing some genes and not others (see also Topic 2.1.8).

Asexual reproduction involves the production of identical cells by mitosis. It is a means for a rapid and significant increase in the numbers of individuals. Plants that are called 'weeds', for example, are successful partly due to their capacity for vegetative reproduction which is a form of asexual reproduction.

EXERCISES

1. The resolving power of a light microscope is closest to:
   A   20 nm
   B   200 nm
   C   2000 nm
   D   2 mm

2. If it was desired to observe the true colour of a coral polyp of diameter 0.02 mm it would be best to use:
   A   the unaided eye
   B   a light microscope with staining
   C   a light microscope without staining
   D   an electron microscope

3. The membrane-bound structures within eukaryotic a cell are known as:
   A   cytoplasm
   B   nuclei
   C   granules
   D   organelles

4. The size of the nucleus of a typical cell is about:
   A   10 - 20 micrometer
   B   50 - 70 micrometer
   C   100 - 200 micrometer
   D   10 - 20 mm

5. Two cubes have side lengths in the ratio 1:3. Their surface areas are in the ratio:
   A   1:3
   B   1:6
   C   1:9
   D   1:27

6. Large fish need to have gills because:
   A   Their bodies have a large surface area through which they can exchange gases with the surrounding water.
   B   Their bodies have a small surface area compared with their volume. Gills provide additional surface area through which they can exchange gases with the surrounding water.
   C   Their bodies have a small surface area through which they can exchange gases with the surrounding water.
   D   They use them to adjust their buoyancy.

7. The DNA in the nucleus of eukaryotic cells is:
   A   linear but not contained in the nucleus
   B   linear and contained in the nucleus
   C   circular but not contained in the nucleus
   D   circular and contained in the nucleus

8. The largest cell organelle is generally the:
   A   Golgi apparatus
   B   rough endoplasmic reticulum
   C   nucleus
   D   ribosome

9. The main reserve food for animal cells is:
   A   glycogen
   B   DNA
   C   starch
   D   RNA

10. What is an important part of the structure of a cell membrane?
    A   a phospholipid layer
    B   a phospholipid bilayer
    C   a protein bilayer
    D   protein layer

11. Endocytosis is:
    A   the process by which the cell takes up a substance by surrounding it with membrane
    B   the process by which the cell takes up a substance by osmosis
    C   the process by which the cell takes up a substance by diffusion
    D   a disease of single celled animals

12. In the cell cycle, the interphase is:
    A   a passive phase between two active phases
    B   an active phase during which DNA replication and many other processes occur
    C   a period when mitosis occurs
    D   a period when cytokinesis occurs

13. Replicated DNA molecules (chromosomes) are moved to opposite ends of the cell by:
    A   diffusion
    B   osmosis
    C   the nucleus
    D   spindle fibres

14. One of the functions of the Golgi apparatus is to:
    A   prepare substances for exocytosis
    B   excrete waste
    C   synthesise proteins.
    D   respire

15. The passive movement of water molecules, across a partially-permeable membrane from a region of lower solute concentration to a region of higher solute concentration is known as:
    A   diffusion
    B   osmosis
    C   dilution
    D   extraction

16. The nuclear membrane disappears during the:
    A   prophase
    B   telophase
    C   anaphase
    D   interphase

17. The heart, liver and kidneys are examples of:
    A   organelles
    B   organs
    C   systems
    D   single tissues

18. Differentiation results in cells:
    A   transcribing some of their DNA
    B   using all of their DNA during replication
    C   changing type when they replicate
    D   mutating

19. Arrange the following by size. Start with the smallest.
    • atom
    • cell
    • organelle
    • DNA double helix
    • eukaryotic cell
    • prokaryotic cell
    • thickness of membranes

20. A chihuahua (small dog) was gently wrapped in a paper cylinder. Her surface area was estimated to be approximately 0.13 m². The volume was estimated (using a clay model) at 2 dm³.

    The same method was used to estimate the surface area and volume of a child. The child was estimated to have a surface area of 0.9 m² and a volume of 24 dm³.
    (a) State which organism has the largest surface area?
    (b) Calculate the surface area over volume ratio for the dog and the child.
    (c) Predict which organism would need the most food per kg bodyweight? Explain your answer.

21. (a) Draw and label a diagram of a prokaryotic cell as seen with the electron microscope.
    (b) Draw and label a diagram of a eukaryotic cell as seen with the electron microscope.
    (c) List the cell organelles found in eukaryotic cells but not in prokaryotic cells and outline their structure and functions..

22. (a) Describe the structure of a membrane according to the fluid mosaic model. Use a diagram to illustrate your answer.
    (b) Explain why integral proteins in the membrane are arranged so that their non polar amino acids are in the middle of the protein molecule.

23. Identify during which stage of the cell cycle (Interphase or Mitosis) each of the following occurs.
    • creation of two genetically identical nuclei
    • biochemical reactions
    • separation of sister chromatids
    • DNA replication
    • chromosomes moving to the equator
    • protein synthesis

24. Mitosis is used in several different processes. List as many as you can.

25. Explain why does the surface area to volume ratio decreases as a cell gets bigger?
    Outline why this causes problems for the cell.

26. A light microscope is used to take a photograph of a cell, using a magnification of 400 times. In the photograph, the nucleus measures 8 mm. Calculate the actual (real) size of the nucleus?

THE CHEMISTRY OF LIFE

CORE

3.1 CHEMICAL ELEMENTS AND WATER

> **3.1.1   State that the most frequently occurring chemical elements in living things are carbon, hydrogen, oxygen and nitrogen.**
>
> ©IBO 2007

> **3.1.2   State that a variety of other elements are needed by living organisms, including sulphur, calcium, phosphorus, iron and sodium.**
>
> **3.1.3   State one role for each of the elements mentioned in 3.1.2**
>
> ©IBO 2007

Pure substances that cannot be broken down any further are called elements and their particles are called atoms. When **atoms** combine chemically they form molecules. Some substances are made of two or more elements that are chemically combined to form a compound. All of the elements are listed in the periodic table. Some elements, e.g. chlorine and hydrogen, usually exist as molecules Cl_2 and H_2. In biological systems, atoms often combine by forming covalent bonds. In covalent bonds, atoms share electrons between them. Atoms can also combine to form ionic bonds. In ionic bonds, one or more electrons are transferred from one atom to another. The result is a positively charged particle and a negatively charged particle. These particles are called **ions**.

Living things consist largely of compounds containing the **element** carbon. The elements that most commonly associate with carbon are hydrogen, oxygen and nitrogen. The approximate proportions of these elements in living organisms are Oxygen (65%), Carbon (19%), Hydrogen (10%) and Nitrogen (3%). Carbon has the symbol C and forms 4 covalent bonds with other atoms, and can form long chains with other carbon atoms. Nitrogen has the symbol N and forms 3 covalent bonds with other atoms. Oxygen has the symbol O and forms 2 covalent bonds with other atoms. Hydrogen has the symbol H and forms 1 covalent bond with another atom.

SULFUR

Some amino acids contain sulfur and can form a bond with another amino acid which also contains sulfur. These connections are called **disulfide bridges**. They can occur within a polypeptide chain which causes folding of the chain. They can also occur between polypeptide chains and keep the chains together. *Refer to Figure 301.*

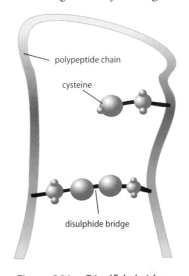

polypeptide chain

cysteine

disulphide bridge

Figure 301   Disulfide bridges

CORE

Element	Role in prokaryotes	Role in plants	Role in animals
sulfur	some prokaryotes use a chemical reaction involving sulfur as their source of energy (chemo-autotrophs)	plants and animals require sulfur to produce some of the amino acids that are part of enzymes they need. proteins often contain sulfur but never phosphorus	
phosphorus	prokaryotes, plants and animals all contain ATP and DNA phosphorus is part of the phosphate group in ATP and also in DNA DNA always contains phosphorus but never sulphur		
calcium	involved in maintaining the of cell structure and movement	component of cell walls and cell membranes	calcium makes our bones hard, lack of calcium can cause osteoporosis calcium also plays a role in releasing the neurotransmitter into the synapse when nerve messages are being transmitted
iron	some anaerobic bacteria use a chemical reaction involving iron as their source of energy	iron is needed to help the formation of chlorophyll	component of hemoglobin found in red blood cells; hemoglobin helps oxygen transport
sodium	indirectly helps move the flagellum	in some plants (C4 plants), sodium can help bind CO_2 for photosynthesis	involved in creating an action potential in neurons and aids glucose transport across membranes

Figure 302   Composition of living things

PHOSPHORUS

A schematic diagram of a molecule of ATP is shown in Figure 303. Note that the three phosphates have high-energy bonds between them. Each phosphate contains the elements phosphorus and oxygen.

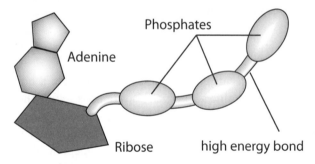

Figure 303   Adenosine Triphosphate (ATP)

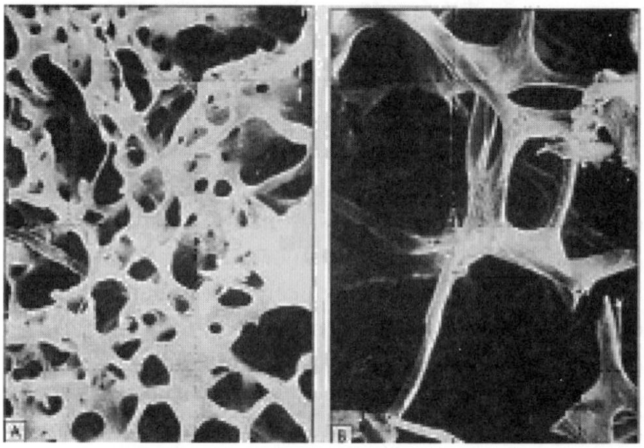

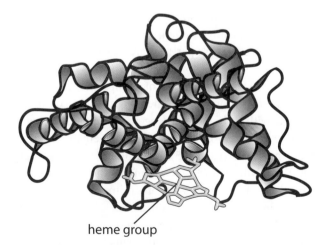

Figure 304   Calcium is needed to form bone

CALCIUM

Calcium is needed to form bone tissue. Figure 304 shows normal bone on the left and bone with osteoporosis on the right. Notice the decrease in bone material and hence in strength. *See Figure 304.*

IRON

Figure 305 shows the structure of one of the four polypeptide chains that makes up hemoglobin. Each chain has a 'heme' group containing iron associated with it. The heme group containing the iron is indicated by a pointer. Iron is also important in myoglobin and cytochromes.

heme group

Figure 305   Iron occurs in the heme group of hemoglobin

Figure 306 is taken from a photograph of an experiment that was done to test the effects of iron deficiency to the growth of plants. Note that the plants on the left have darker green leaves than the ones on the right. Iron is needed to help form **chlorophyll**.

Figure 306   *Iron deficiency in plants*

SODIUM

During a nerve impulse, in the first part of an action potential, sodium channels open across the plasma membrane and sodium will diffuse into the neuron as shown in Figure 307. *See also Topic 6.5.*

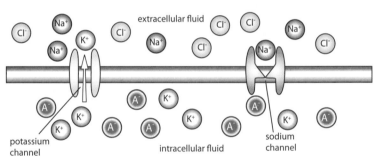

Figure 307   *Sodium-potassium pump*

Figure 308 suggests a mechanism for the co-transport of glucose and sodium ions across membranes.

3.1.4	Draw and label a diagram showing the structure of water molecules to show their polarity and hydrogen bond formation.

©IBO 2007

A molecule of water is made from one atom of oxygen and two atoms of hydrogen. Covalent bonds (sharing of electrons) keeps the atoms together. The structure of a water molecule is fixed: the (small) hydrogen atoms bond to the (larger) oxygen atom at a fixed angle as shown in Figure 309.

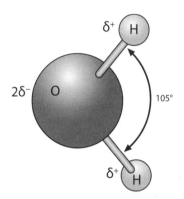

Figure 309   *A water molecule*

Although the electrons are shared, oxygen pulls harder at them than hydrogen. This results in a slightly negative oxygen atom and slightly positive hydrogen atoms. Since positive and negative charges attract, there will be an attraction force (hydrogen bond) between the (slightly positive) hydrogen of one water molecule and the (slightly negative) oxygen of the adjacent molecule.

Due to the water molecule having a (slightly) positive and a (slightly) negative side, we can say it has two poles: a positive and a negative pole. That means that water is polar and that polar solutes are likely to dissolve in it, whereas non-polar molecules will not. Hydrogen bonding in water is a result of its polarity. *Refer to Figure 310.*

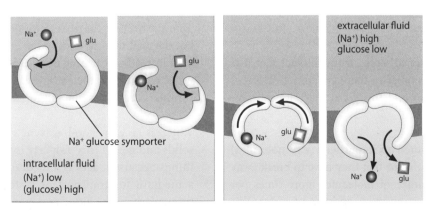

Figure 308   *A mechanism for co-transport of substances*

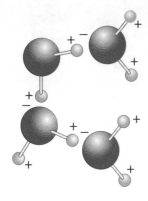

Figure 310   Hydrogen bonding

Hydrogen bonds are not complete chemical bonds. There is no sharing or transferring of electrons. Instead, it is an attraction force between a slightly positive hydrogen atom and a slightly negative oxygen atom. *See Figure 310.* Hydrogen bonds are much weaker than covalent or ionic bonds. They are significant though, because they are very common. A lot of hydrogen bonds together are quite strong. For example the bonds between the complementary bases keep the two strands of the DNA double helix together as shown in Figure 311.

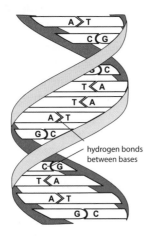

Figure 311   A DNA molecule

3.1.5	Outline the thermal, cohesive and solvent properties of water.

©IBO 2007

The properties of **water** all come from the fact that it is polar. As a result of its polarity, there are attraction forces between the molecules and this gives water its cohesive properties. *See Figure 312.*

When an object is warmed up, its particles (e.g. molecules) will move faster. This means that they have to break away from cohesion with adjacent molecules more times per minutes. Due to the cohesive properties of water, this

takes a lot of energy. The same goes for evaporation. A water molecule that evaporates, escapes from the liquid and the other water molecules with which it interacted. Again, due to cohesion, this requires a lot of energy.

TOK   Properties of water

Homeopathy relies on the concept that solutions containing active substances can be repeatedly diluted to the point that the active substances are theoretically no longer present but the water retains the 'memory' of the active substance. This 'memory' is reputed to produce an effect in an individual person. There continues to be scientific debate about this principle. The claim has some evidence to support it, yet the concept that there is no active ingredient present in the solution conflicts with current scientific belief. Some describe homeopathy as pseudoscience (where a testable belief is accepted without being put through the rigour of the scientific method), others argue that all scientific theories begin with observations that are eventually supported by a body of evidence and that homeopathy is at this stage of the scientific method.

3.1.6	Explain the relationship between the properties of water and its uses in living organisms as a coolant, medium for metabolic reactions and transport medium.

©IBO 2007

As outlined in Figure 312, the thermal properties of water are very important. The high 'specific heat capacity' means that water will not warm up much, even when the sun shines on it all day. You know that because when you go to the beach on a warm day, the water is much cooler than the sand. Water needs to take in a lot of energy to go from liquid to gas, this is called the 'latent heat of vaporisation'. That means that the water evaporating from the sea on a hot day will take up a lot of the energy of the sun shining on it instead of warming up the rest of the water. In winter, water will give off the energy as heat. So, near the sea, the summers are not as hot and the winters not as cold.

Water is a very good solvent and can dissolve many solids and gases. This property is very important in living things because it acts as a medium for reactions and also a medium for transport of materials around the body, particularly in the blood and lymph systems.

Outline of property		Use in living organism
COHESIVE PROPERTIES		
the attraction forces between molecules of the same kind		**transport**: cohesion helps water go up the xylem of plants
THERMAL PROPERTIES		
high specific heat	water requires a lot of energy to warm up and gives off a lot of energy when cooled down	**transport**: blood can carry heat to colder places in our body: your nose goes red when you are skiing or skating
high heat of vaporization	water requires a lot of energy to change from a liquid into a gas	**coolant**: both plants and animals evaporate water which has a cooling effect - a little water will take up a lot of energy to evaporate
SOLVENT PROPERTIES		
water is polar and will dissolve many polar solutes		**transport**: plants: xylem: water + minerals phloem: water + sugar animals: blood: oxygen, glucose, urea
		medium for metabolic reactions: reactions involving polar molecules can take place in water

Figure 312   The properties of water

3.2 CARBOHYDRATES, LIPIDS AND PROTEINS

3.2.1   Distinguish between *organic* and *inorganic* compounds.

©IBO 2007

ORGANIC COMPOUNDS

Organic compounds are produced by living things and include all compounds containing carbon that are found in living organisms except hydrogencarbonates (HCO_3^-), carbonates (CO_3^{2-}) and oxides of carbon (CO and CO_2).

INORGANIC COMPOUNDS

Inorganic compounds are all other compounds. There are many more different organic compounds than inorganic compounds.

The following few pages cover the material of Topic 3.2. The content is divided into three sections:
- CARBOHYDRATES
- LIPIDS
- PROTEINS

CARBOHYDRATES

3.2.2   Identify glucose and ribose from diagrams showing their structure.

©IBO 2007

Carbohydrates are compounds that contain carbon, hydrogen and oxygen (C, H, O). Monosaccharides are simple sugars, the building blocks of disaccharides and polysaccharides.

Glucose has the formula $C_6H_{12}O_6$ and is an example of a monosaccharide. A glucose molecule has the shape of a 6-sided ring (hexagon) as shown in Figure 313.

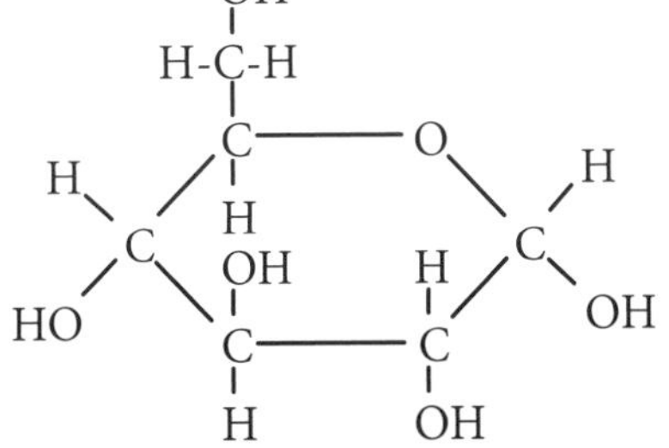

Figure 313   The structure of glucose

Ribose has the formula C5H10O5 and is another monosaccharide but with only 5 carbon atoms and is called a pentose sugar. Its structure is shown in Figure 314.

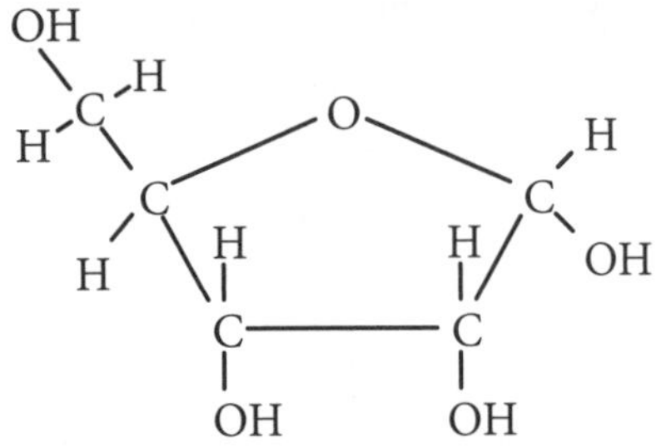

Figure 314   The structure of ribose

3.2.5	Outline the role of condensation and hydrolysis in the relationship bewteen monosaccharides, disaccharides and polysaccharides.
	©IBO 2007

Two monosaccharides can combine to form a disaccharide and a molecule of water.

glucose + glucose → maltose + water

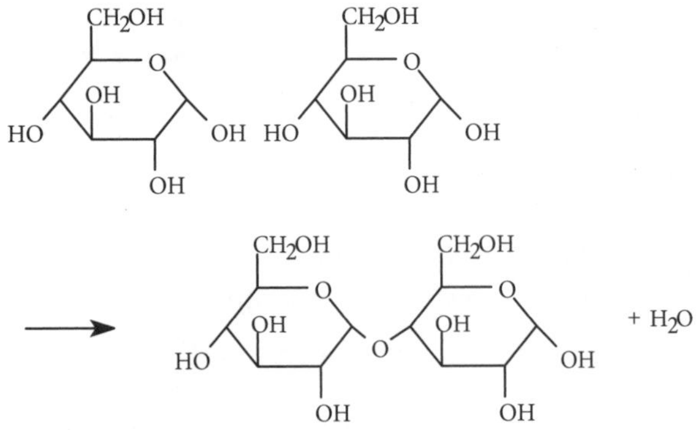

Figure 315   The condensation reaction

This is called a condensation reaction because it produces water. The reaction can be reversed and is then called a hydrolysis reaction. *(hydro - water, lysis - splitting)* as shown in this word equation:

$$\text{glucose + glucose} \underset{hydrolysis}{\overset{condensation}{\rightleftarrows}} \text{maltose + water}$$

$$\text{glucose + fructose} \underset{hydrolysis}{\overset{condensation}{\rightleftarrows}} \text{sucrose + water}$$

$$\text{glucose + galactose} \underset{hydrolysis}{\overset{condensation}{\rightleftarrows}} \text{lactose + water}$$

Two monosaccharides form a disaccharide plus water via a condensation reaction. Adding more monosaccharides, will produce a polysaccharide and more water molecules (depending on how many monosaccharides were added).

3.2.3	List three examples each of monosaccharides, disaccharides and polysaccharides.
	©IBO 2007

Examples of **monosaccharides** include:
- glucose
- fructose
- galactose

Examples of **dissaccharides** are:
- maltose
- sucrose
- lactose

Examples of **polysaccharides** are:
- starch
- glycogen
- cellulose

3.2.4	State one function of glucose, lactose and glycogen in animals and of fructose, sucrose and cellulose in plants.
	©IBO 2007

Functions of some of the above carbohydrates in animals are:
- Glucose is a source of energy.
  It can be broken down to produce ATP in the process called 'respiration' *(see Topic 3.7)*.
- Lactose is the sugar found in the milk of mammals.
  It provides a source of energy to the young drinking the milk.
- Glycogen is used for short term energy storage (between meals) in the liver.

Functions of some of the above carbohydrates in plants are:
- Fructose is very sweet and a good source of energy. It is found in honey and onions.
- Sucrose is used to transport and store energy, e.g. in sugarbeets and sugar cane.
- Cellulose fibres, arranged in layers, provide strength to the cell wall.

LIPIDS

CORE

3.2.2	Identify fatty acids from diagrams showing their structure.
	©IBO 2007

Lipids are a group of fats which generally come from animals and oils which are usually derived from plants. Lipids are made by a condensation reaction between glycerol and 3 fatty acids. Fatty acids are carboxylic acids. That means that they have a carboxylic group (-COOH) as shown on the right side in Figure 316.

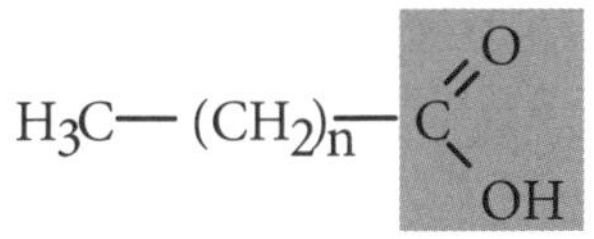

$$H_3C-(CH_2)_n-C\overset{O}{\underset{OH}{\Big\langle}}$$

Figure 316   A generalised fatty acid

The rest of the molecule is a chain (or ring) of carbon atoms with hydrogen atoms. If there are no double bonds in this chain, then the fatty acid is 'saturated'. If there are one or more double bonds between the carbon molecules of the chain, it is referred to as an 'unsaturated' fatty acid.

3.2.5	Outline the role of condensation and hydrolysis in the relationship between fatty acids, glycerol and triglycerides.
	©IBO 2007

Lipids are composed of glycerol and 1, 2 or 3 fatty acids. Triglycerides are a sub-group of lipids that are composed of glycerol and 3 fatty acids. Triglycerides are formed by the reaction of glycerol and three fatty acids as shown in Figure 317.

Again water is produced as a larger molecule is formed and this is a condensation reaction. The reverse reaction is hydrolysis, as shown in this simple word equation.

$$glycerol + 3\ fatty\ acids \underset{hydrolysis}{\overset{condensation}{\rightleftharpoons}} triglyceride + 3\ water$$

3.2.6	State three functions of lipids.
	©IBO 2007

The main functions of lipids are:
- energy storage because one gram of lipids contains twice as much energy as one gram of carbohydrates or proteins
- thermal insulation, for example a layer of lipids under the skin (subcutaneous layer) reduces the loss of heat from the organism
- cell membranes because the main component of cell membranes are phospholipids

3.2.7	Compare the use of carbohydrates and lipids in energy storage.
	©IBO 2007

One gram of lipid releases twice as much energy as one gram of carbohydrates (or proteins). Since most of the energy of a lipid is stored in its fatty acid chains, the lipids used to store energy are triglycerides.

Animals use glycogen to store the energy from a meal. This energy is likely to be used before the next meal. Overnight, we already need to use energy from triglycerides as the energy from glycogen stored in the liver is not enough for all our body processes (keeping warm, breathing, etc). Some birds use this stored fat for long flights and many animals store fat for the time spent in aestivation or hibernation.

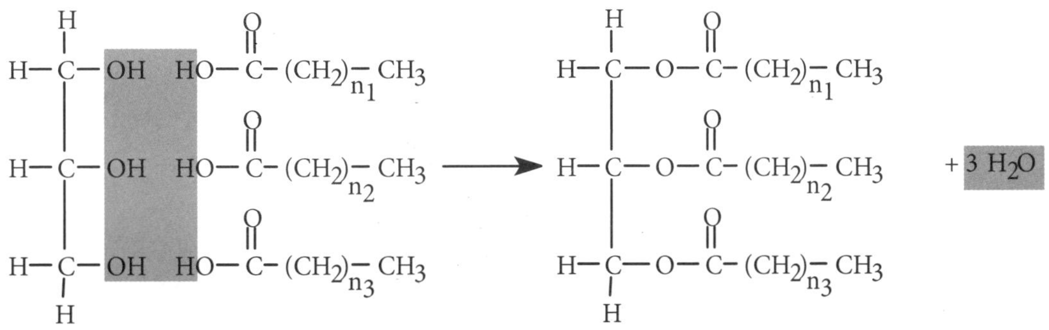

Figure 317   The formation of a triglyceride

CORE

Figure 318   Some animals store fat

Lipids (triglycerides) are used for the longer term storage of energy because storing the same amount of energy as carbohydrates, would involve more weight. As the animal moves, it would have to carry this weight. *See Figure 318.*

Plants use carbohydrates to store energy in parts of the plant that do not move. A good example are potato tubers, growing underground. They do not need to move anywhere so it does not matter if they are heavier. But if you consider vegetable oil, good examples are rapeseed oil or sunflower oil. These are seeds that need to store energy to germinate. But the seeds also need to move away from the parent plant so the lighter they are, the more distance they are likely to cover. Therefore, you find energy stored as lipids in the seeds of plants but not in other parts that do not need to move.

PROTEINS

3.2.2	Identify amino acids from diagrams showing their structure.
	©IBO 2007

Polypeptides are long chains of amino acids. There are many different amino acids but they have some structures in common:

- amino acids have a central C atom - as shown in Figure 319.

- there are four different groups attached to this central C atom:
  1. the amine group - NH_2
  2. the (carboxylic) acid group - COOH
  3. an simple -H group
  4. the 'R' group which is different in different amino acids

A generalised amino acid can be represented by the structure shown in Figure 319.

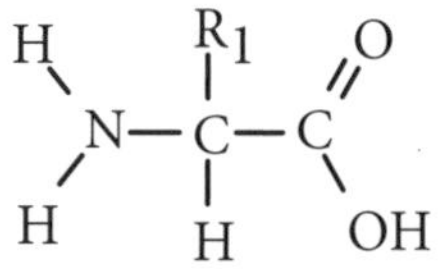

Figure 319   A generalized amino acid

3.2.5	Outline the role of condensation and hydrolysis in the relationship between amino acids and polypeptides.
	©IBO 2007

Two amino acids can combine to form a dipeptide. This, again, is a condensation reaction. *See Figure 320.*

The highlighted (thicker) bond in Figure 320 is called the peptide linkage or simply a peptide bond. It is a special bond between a C (with a double bonded O attached on one side) and an N (with an H attached) on the other side. Again the reverse of this reaction is hydrolysis as shown by this simple word equation.

$$\text{amino acid 1 + amino acid 2} \underset{\textit{hydrolysis}}{\overset{\textit{condensation}}{\rightleftarrows}} \text{dipeptide + water}$$

Again, as more amino acids are added they produce a polypeptide and more water (depending on how many amino acids were added). A polypeptide can be a protein by itself or it may need to combine with other polypeptide chains to form a functional protein. For example, hemeoglobin is made of 4 polypeptide chains, 2 alpha chains and 2 beta chains.

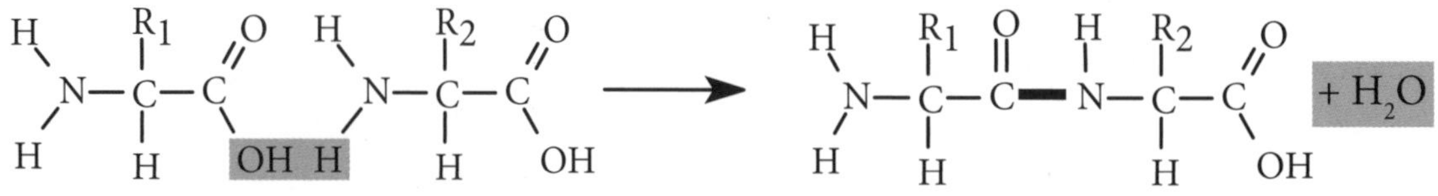

Figure 320   The formation of a peptide linkage

3.3 DNA STRUCTURE

CORE

3.3.1 Outline DNA nucleotide structure in terms of sugar (deoxyribose), base and phosphate.

©IBO 2007

Genetic information is stored by nucleic acids. There are two kinds of nucleic acids:

- deoxyribonucleic acid (DNA)
- ribonucleic acid (RNA)

For the majority of species genetic information is stored in **DNA** in the nucleus while **RNA** is found in the cytoplasm. Some viruses and prokaryotes store genetic information in RNA.

Nucleic acids are long-chain molecules (like proteins, but longer) and their building blocks are called nucleotides (like amino acids but, again, more complicated).

Nucleotides themselves are complex molecules consisting of three molecules linked together:

- a pentose sugar
- a phosphate
- an organic base

The nucleotide is usually schematically represented as shown in Figure 321.

Figure 321   The components of DNA

There are three components.

THE SUGAR
Two possibilities: ribose gives RNA and deoxyribose gives DNA.

THE PHOSPHATE
H_3PO_4 (P forms 5 bonds with other atoms.)

THE ORGANIC BASE
Also known as the nitrogenous base.

3.3.2 State the names of the four bases in DNA.

©IBO 2007

There are five different bases:
- Adenine
- Cytosine
- Thymine
- Guanine
- Uracil

A, C, T and G are found in DNA; A, C, U and G are found in RNA. The structural formulae of these nitrogenous bases are shown in Figure 322. You do not need to memorise these structures but you need to remember the names.

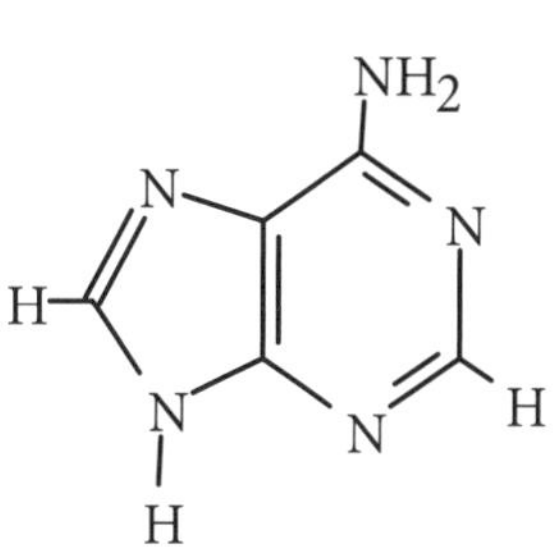

Figure 322 (a)   Adenine

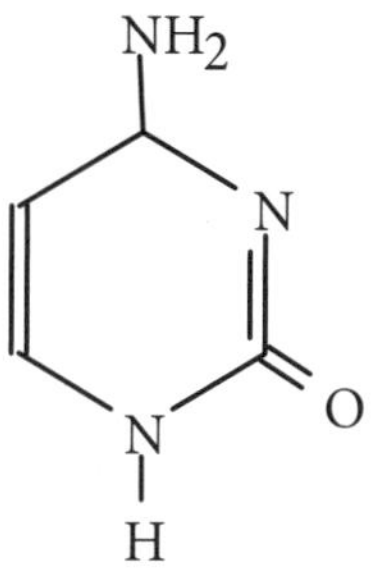

Figure 322 (b)   Cytosine

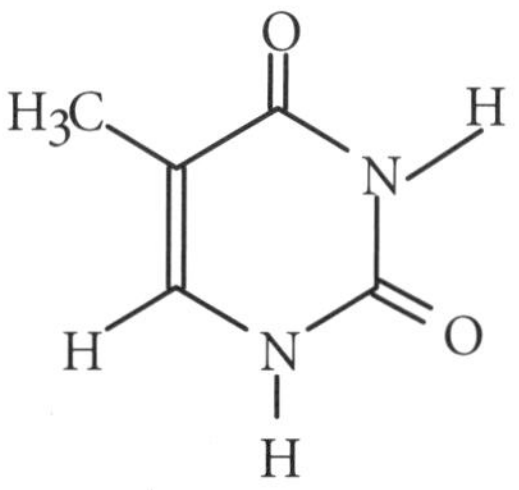

Figure 322 (c)   Thymine

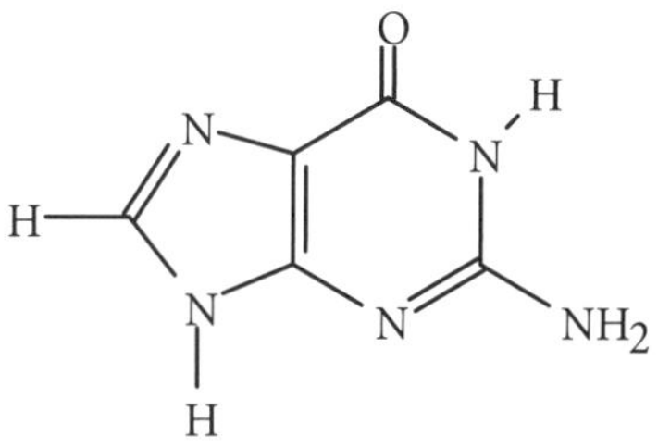

Figure 322 (d)   Guanine

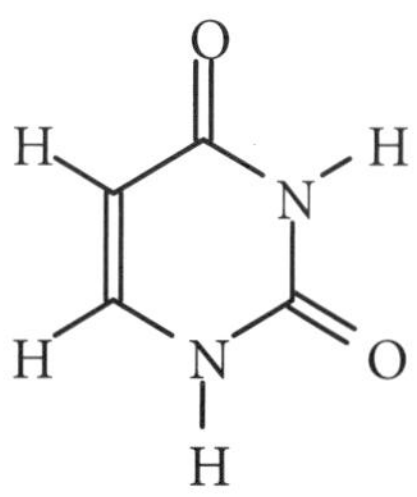

Figure 322 (e)   Uracil

COMPLEMENTARY BASE PAIRING

Adenine, Thymine and Uracil are capable of forming two Hydrogen bonds while Cytosine and Guanine can form three. So Adenine (A) can form a base pair with Thymine (T) (or uracil (U) in RNA) and Cytosine (C) can form a base pair with Guanine (G).

All organic bases have a complicated molecular structure involving ring compounds (see Figure 322). Adenine and Guanine are purines, 'big' 2-ring structures; Cytosine, Thymine and Uracil are pyrimidines, 'small' 1-ring structures.

3.3.3	Outline how DNA nucleotides are linked together by covalent bonds into a single strand.

©IBO 2007

Since the reactions involved are (again) condensation reactions, the equation becomes:

phosphate + sugar + organic base → nucleotide + 2 water

The nucleotides can be linked together to form a single chain by a condensation reaction between the phosphate of one nucleotide and the sugar of another. The sugar and phosphate form the 'backbone' of the nucleic acid with the organic bases sticking out.

Covalent bonds are formed between the phosphate and sugar and a single strand is made with a 'backbone' of phosphate and (deoxy)ribose and an organic base attached to every ribose. This is shown in Figure 323.

3.3.4	Explain how the DNA double helix is formed using complementary base pairing and hydrogen bonds.
3.3.5	Draw and label a simple diagram of the molecular structure of DNA.

©IBO 2007

Knowing that the structure of DNA is a 'double helix' (a twisted ladder) we need to fit two DNA molecules together. Since some of the organic bases can form bonds with certain others (Topic 3.3.2), we can combine the DNA strands this way. The sugar and phosphate 'backbones' run antiparallel forming the sides of the ladder with the organic base pairs as rungs in between.

Figure 324 shows DNA as it would look if we 'untwisted' it. The DNA molecules coil in such a way that approximately 10 nucleotides complete one turn of the helix.

In a DNA molecule, the backbone is made of alternating phosphate - sugar groups. The 'rungs' of the twisted ladder which DNA resembles are the organic base pairs. The available space for these rungs is the equivalent of three of the rings.

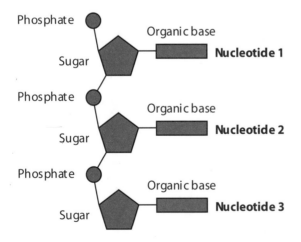

Figure 323 How nucleotides are joined together

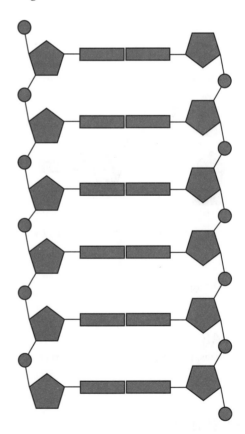

Figure 324   The structure of DNA

This means that to fill the space, an organic base pair must have a total of three rings. To allow them to have hydrogen bonding, they must be capable of forming the same number of bonds. Which, in DNA, makes A and T one of the possible base pairs and C and G the other. When the base pairing involves RNA, the pairs are A and U, C and G.

So the bonds between the components of a nucleotide are covalent bonds, formed by condensation reactions. The bonds between nucleotides are also covalent bonds, formed by condensation. However the bonds keeping the two strands of the DNA together are hydrogen bonds. Hydrogen bonds are much weaker than covalent bonds but there are so many hydrogen bonds between the two strands of DNA that they are kept together securely.

TOK   The structure of DNA

The story of the discovery of DNA illustrates how communication between scientists is critical in the growth of knowledge. The discovery of the structure of DNA was one of the most significant Biological milestones of the twentieth century, but it was not without controversy.

Chemist Rosalind Franklin began work on the structure of DNA in the early 1950's. Her area of expertise was making X-ray diffraction images that revealed the arrangement of atoms in molecules. Soon Franklin discovered key features of the structure of DNA such as the fact that there were two strands in DNA and that the bases were on the inside of the molecule. One X-ray diffraction image ('Photo 51') was shown by Franklin's colleague, Maurice Wilkins, to James Watson without her knowledge. Wilkins also shared Franklin's insights gained from X-ray diffraction images with Watson. This information was critical to Watson and Francis Crick developing their model for the structure of DNA. Watson later acknowledged that he was openly competitive in the search for the structure of DNA.

In acknowledgement of the discovery, Watson, Crick and Wilkins were all awarded the Nobel Prize for Medicine and Physiology in 1962. Franklin was not. She died from ovarian cancer at age 37 in 1956. Nobel prizes are not awarded posthumously, and no more than three people can be awarded a Nobel prize for a discovery. Whether Franklin would have received the prize had she been alive has been the cause of much debate. The cause of the cancer was most likely the radiation she used to produce her images.

3.4 DNA REPLICATION

3.4.1   Explain DNA replication in terms of unwinding the double helix and separating the strands by helicase, followed by the formation of the new complementary strands by DNA polymerase.

©IBO 2007

DNA replication requires several processes to take place and is illustrated in Figure 325. First the DNA double helix needs to unwind and the two strands need to separate (or 'unzip'). The enzyme 'helicase' is responsible for this process.

Free **nucleotides** which are 'floating around' in the nucleus form complementary pairs with the nucleotides of both of the DNA strands.

The nucleotides which have formed complementary base pairs with the nucleotides on the old strand now join to each other to form a new strand of DNA. The enzyme 'DNA polymerase' is responsible for this process. All these processes result in two identical DNA double helices, each consisting of one 'old' and one 'new' strand.

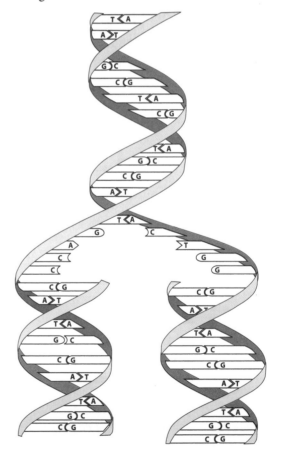

Figure 325   DNA replication

CORE

3.4.2 Explain the significance of complementary base pairing in the conservation of the base sequence of DNA.

©IBO 2007

Since every organic base will only 'fit' with one other one (complementary base pairing), the 'new' strand of DNA will be identical to one from which the 'old' strand just separated. So (theoretically) this process can continue forever without any change to the genetic material. Mistakes however do occur and these are called mutations.

3.4.3 State that DNA replication is semi-conservative.

©IBO 2007

When a DNA double helix replicates into 2 DNA double helices, one strand of each helix is an 'old' while the other is 'new'. This is illustrated in Figure 326.

When DNA replication is described as 'semi-conservative' it is meant that each of the two DNA molecules will have a 'new' strand and an 'old strand.

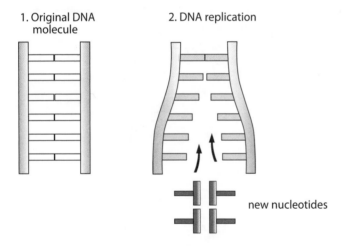

1. Original DNA molecule

2. DNA replication

new nucleotides

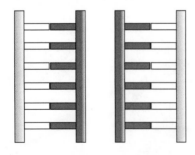

3. Two new DNA molecules

Figure 326   Replication is semi-conservative

3.5 TRANSCRIPTION AND TRANSLATION

3.5.1 Compare the structure of RNA and DNA.

©IBO 2007

As was mentioned in *Topic 3.3*, there are two different kinds of nucleic acids; **DNA** and **RNA**. They are compared in Figure 327.

	Deoxyribonucleic acid	**Ribonucleic acid**
Shape	double helix (2 strands)	Usually single strand
Sugar	deoxyribose	ribose
Bases	A, T, C and G	A, U, C and G

Figure 327   DNA - RNA

Three main kinds of RNA are commonly found in cells:
- ribosomal RNA (rRNA) which is a major component of ribosomes
- transfer RNA (tRNA) which is folded upon itself and carries amino acids to mRNA
- messenger RNA (mRNA) which consists of a sequence of nucleotides that determines the primary sequence of a polypeptide.

3.5.2 Outline DNA transcription in terms of the formation of an RNA strand complementary to the DNA strand by RNA polymerase.

©IBO 2007

The process of protein (or polypeptide) synthesis can be divided into two parts:
- **Transcription**: the process by which RNA is produced from a DNA template.
- **Translation**: the assembly of a polypeptide in a sequence specified by the order of nucleotides in the mRNA.

Transcription is similar to DNA replication in that it takes place in the nucleus and involves a section of DNA which needs to unzip. Then only one of the two strands of DNA is transcribed (the 'anti-sense' strand) and a complementary RNA strand to this strand is made. This is called messenger RNA (mRNA) and it has the same sequence of nucleotides, except for U instead of T, as the sense strand of the DNA (the strand that is NOT transcribed). After transcription, the mRNA leaves the nucleus through the pores in the nuclear envelope and goes into the cytoplasm. *Refer to Figure 328.*

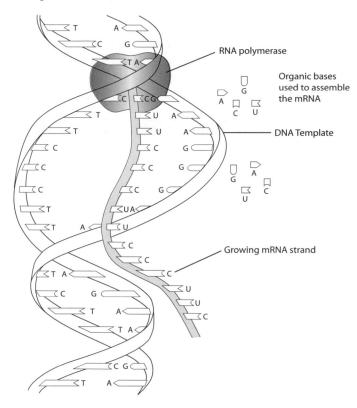

Figure 328   Transcription of DNA to Produce RNA

| 3.5.3 | Describe the genetic code in terms of codons composed of triplets of bases. |

©IBO 2007

The genetic code is based on sets of 3 nucleotides called codons. Since 20 amino acids are commonly found in cells, it is not possible to have 4 different nucleotide codes

for all of them. The possible permutations are $4^1 = 4$. If we tried using a set of 2 nucleotides, we could create $4^2 = 16$ different combinations, which is insufficient for the 20 different amino acids. So, therefore, we need to use a set of 3 nucleotides which will create $4^3 = 64$ possibilities. This is more than is required for the 20 different amino acids. As a result, the code is said to be degenerate, meaning that more than one codon can code for a single amino acid. The sequence of the codons in the mRNA determines the sequence of the amino acids in the polypeptide. This 'codon' table is shown in Figure 329. You may need to check the abbreviations of the amino acids names elsewhere although you do not need to know them.

| 3.5.4 | Explain the process of translation, leading to polypeptide formation. |

©IBO 2007

After the mRNA has reached the cytoplasm, translation takes place. In the cytoplasm, ribosomes attach to the mRNA. The ribosome covers an area of three codons on the mRNA. The first tRNA carrying an amino acid will come in and the anti-codon exposed on the tRNA will have complementary binding with the codon of the mRNA in the A site of the ribosome. The ribosome will move and the first tRNA will be in the P site on the ribosome.

The second tRNA with its own anti-codon, and consequently carrying a specific amino acid, will complementary bind to the second codon on the mRNA, filling the A site in the ribosome. The second amino acid will attach to the first (formation of a peptide bond by a condensation reaction) and the first amino acid will be released from the first tRNA. The ribosome will move in relation to the mRNA. The first tRNA (without amino acid) is now found in the E site of the ribosome. The second tRNA will be in the P site and the A site is empty.

UUU	phe	UCU	ser	UAU	tyr	UGU	cys
UUC	phe	UCC	ser	UAC	tyr	UGC	cys
UUA	leu	UCA	ser	UAA	stop	UGA	stop
UUG	leu	UCG	ser	UAG	stop	UGG	trp
CUU	leu	CCU	pro	CAU	his	CGU	arg
CUC	leu	CCC	pro	CAC	his	CGC	arg
CUA	leu	CCA	pro	CAA	gln	CGA	arg
CUG	leu	CCG	pro	CAG	gln	CGG	arg
AUU	ile	ACU	thr	AAU	asn	AGU	ser
AUC	ile	ACC	thr	AAC	asn	AGC	ser
AUA	ile	ACA	thr	AAA	lys	AGA	arg
AUG	start/met	ACG	thr	AAG	lys	AGG	arg
GUU	val	GCU	ala	GAU	asp	GGU	gly
GUC	val	GCC	ala	GAC	asp	GGC	gly
GUA	val	GCA	ala	GAA	glu	GGA	gly
GUG	val	GCG	ala	GAG	glu	GGG	gly

Figure 329   The mRNA codon table

CORE

The anticodon of the third tRNA will bind to the third codon of the mRNA in the A site of the ribosome. The anticodon of first tRNA (without its amino acid) will dissociate from the first codon of the mRNA in the E site of the ribosome. The second amino acid will form a peptide bond with the third amino acid and the second amino acid will be released from the second tRNA. The ribosome will move so that the second tRNA (without amino acid) will now occupy the first site of the ribosome. The second site is occupied by the third tRNA, which has a chain of three amino acids attached. The third site is free and the next tRNA will come in, carrying its own amino acid. A simplified diagram is shown in Figure 330.

This process continues until a STOP codon is reached. The STOP codon does not code for an amino acid but terminates translation.

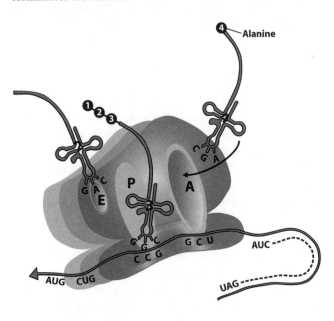

Figure 330 Translation

| 3.5.5 | Discuss the relationship between one gene and one polypeptide. |

©IBO 2007

The 'one gene – one polypeptide' concept means that every polypeptide chain is coded for by one gene. It also means that a gene only codes for one polypeptide chain. Hemoglobin contains four polypeptide chains, 2 alpha chains and 2 beta chains. To make a hemeoglobin therefore requires 2 genes: one for the alpha chains and one for the beta chains.

It can be assumed that every biological reaction is catalysed by enzymes and does not occur without them. The presence or absence of the enzyme will decide if the reaction takes place. So if you have the allele for brown eyes, it means that you have the allele that makes the

enzyme which catalyses the reaction which makes brown pigment. You therefore make the brown pigment. You do not have the allele for the enzyme which makes the blue pigment (*unless you are heterozygous, see Topic 4*).

There are exceptions to the 'one gene-one polypeptide' hypothesis: Transcription of certain genes will produce rRNA or tRNA rather than mRNA. Since neither rRNA nor tRNA is translated, these genes do not produce polypeptides. Eukaryotic RNA needs to have **introns** removed before

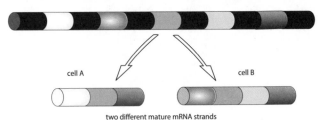

two different mature mRNA strands

Figure 331   Introns and Exons

translation (*Topic 7.3.4*); it is thought that in different cells, different parts of the RNA are selected as **exons**. Introns are therefore not part of the translated polypeptide even though they are transcribed.

TOK   A paradigm shift

Theories must be supported by new evidence as it comes to light to remain valid. When evidence contradicts a theory it must be rejected. In reality it takes time for repeated testing to demonstrate that a theory is no longer valid. What usually happens is that subsequent testing or observation reveals that a theory needs to be modified. A major change in direction of thought is called a paradigm shift.

The development of the theory of evolution through natural selection illustrates the most significant paradigm shift in Biology. Prior to the publication of Charles Darwin's The Origin of Species in 1859, it was widely assumed that life on earth had been specially and unchangingly created by a supernatural being. Human understanding of the world was tied inextricably to religious belief. Darwin proposed a theory, supported by evidence, which explained that the variety of life on Earth is not necessarily tied to a supernatural belief.

This process is illustrated in Figure 331 in which introns are black and exons are various other shades and colours.

3.6 ENZYMES

3.6.1	Define *enzyme* and *active site*.

©IBO 2007

An **enzyme** is defined as a globular protein molecule that accelerates a specific chemical reaction.

Enzymes are biological catalysts. A catalyst speeds up a reaction without changing it in any other way. Adding an enzyme to a reaction does not create different products and does not alter the reaction's equilibrium. It only helps to reach this equilibrium faster. Enzymes are not used

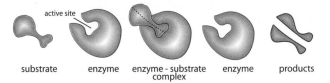

Figure 332   Enzyme action

up in the reactions they catalyse. This is illustrated in Figure 332.

After the product has formed, the enzyme may be used again and again.

The active site is the region of an enzyme's surface that binds the substrate (reacting substance) during the reaction catalysed by the enzyme.

3.6.2	Explain enzyme-substrate specificity.

©IBO 2007

Enzymes make it easier for a reaction to take place. The substrate will bind to a special area of the enzyme called the active site. In Figure 333, the enzyme is

phosphofructokinase, the substrates are fructose-6-phosphate and phosphate and the product is fructose-1,6-diphosphate.

Written as a word equation:

fructose-6-phosphate + phosphate $\xrightarrow{\text{phosphofructokinase}}$ fructose-1,6-diphosphate

As shown in Figure 333, the substrate fits into the active site of the enzyme as a key fits into a lock. This is called the **lock and key model** of enzyme action.

The three dimensional structure of the protein (*remember, enzymes are proteins*) determines the shape of the active site. The substrate fits into the active site and the reaction procedes. Another molecules with a different shape will not fit into the active site will not react with the enzyme. So, an enzyme only works with a specific substrate and only catalyses a specific reaction.

3.6.3	Explain the effects of temperature, pH and substrate concentration on enzyme activity.

©IBO 2007

The speed of a reaction can be measured in two ways: how fast does the substrate disappear and how fast is the product formed? Since both of these should give information about the speed of reaction, it is a matter of convenience which is chosen.

Generally, biological reactions are extremely slow at room temperature without the help of enzymes. Therefore the speed of reaction is a measurement of the enzyme activity.

A number of factors affect enzyme activity.

- *Temperature* - every enzyme has an optimum temperature where its activity is highest. The optimum temperature of our enzymes is mostly around 37°C.

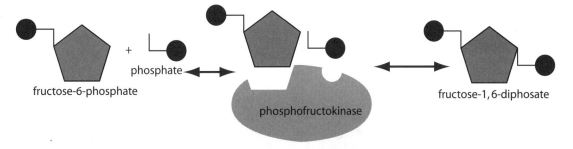

Figure 333   Phospho-fructo-kinase Reaction

Almost every enzyme will be denatured above 60°C although some bacteria live in hot springs at 80°C and have enzymes suitable for this environment.

- **pH** - every enzyme works best at a certain pH. Pepsin (in the stomach) works best at approximately pH 2 but trypsin (secreted from the walls of the small intestine) works best at approximately pH 8.
- **Concentration of substrate** - using a given amount of enzyme, the reaction will go faster if the substrate is more concentrated.

Research has been done into the effect of acid rain on the action of enzymes. A study from 1983 showed that if soil is exposed to very acidic precipitation (pH 2), the activity of many enzymes was seriously reduced in the top layer of the soil. Deeper layers were less affected. When less acid ic precipitation (pH 3) was used, many enzymes were not affected.

3.6.4 Define *denaturation*.

©IBO 2007

Denaturation refers to a structural change in a protein that results in a loss (usually permanent) of its biological properties.

High temperatures and extreme pH can denature a protein. If you think of a raw egg as an example of several proteins, you can think of a boiled egg as an example of denatured proteins. The fact that denaturation is permanent is shown by cooling down a boiled egg: it becomes a cold, boiled egg but does not change back to being a raw egg. Figures 334 and 335 show images of raw eggs and of boiled (denatured) eggs. This gives a good impression of the changes that denaturing can bring to proteins, including enzymes.

Enzymes depend on the shape of their active site to function (*see Figure 333*). The process of denaturation causes a structural change in the enzyme. This includes a change in the shape of its active site which means that it will not function anymore.

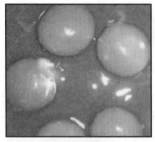

Figure 334
Raw eggs

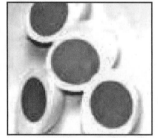

Figure 335
Cooked (denatured) eggs

3.6.5 Explain the use of lactase in the production of lactose-free milk.

©IBO 2007

Overall, around 70% of adult humans in the world are **lactose** intolerant. This means that they have lost the ability to produce lactase after early childhood. This commonly happens to mammals after weaning. The incidence of lactose intolerance is not evenly distributed: only 2% of Swedes but 75% of African Americans and nearly 100% of American Indians are lactose intolerant.

When a **lactose intolerant** person consumes a reasonable amount of milk (or ice cream), s/he will suffer from excess gas production and diarrhoea.

The food industry has found that it is possible to produce milk and milk products that contain (almost) no lactose. They do this by attaching the enzyme lactase to a large molecule and then bringing it into contact with milk. Any lactose present will be broken down into glucose and galactose by the lactase. This will make the milk taste sweet but neither of these products causes problems for lactose intolerant adults. It allows lactose intolerant people to drink milk and consume products that contain milk, such as cheese and ice-cream.

TOK Applications of biotechnology

Lactose intolerance has a genetic basis. Production of lactose-free milk was first engineered in Europe where the proportion of the adult population that are unable to produce lactase is approximately 20%. In Asia, Latin American and Africa well over half the population is lactose intolerant, so the benefit of lactose free milk to people these parts of the world far outweighs that to those in the part of the world where the product was first made.

In many cases in Science the eventual use is far removed from the original point of discovery. The antibiotic properties of Penicillin were first reported in 1897 by a French medical student, Ernest Duchesne, though he did not understand its potential. Penicillin was discovered again by Alexander Fleming in London in 1928. In 1939 a team of Scientists at Oxford University was able to produce a pure and stable form of penicillin, however in World War II Europe there were not the resources to mass-produce the first anti-biotic. Instead it was mass-produced at breweries in the United States and shipped back to Europe to assist war wounded recover from bacterial infections.

3.7 CELL RESPIRATION

CORE

> 3.7.1 Define *cell respiration*.
>
> 3.7.2 State that, in cell respiration, glucose in the cytoplasm is broken down by glycolysis into pyruvate, with a small yield of ATP.
>
> ©IBO 2007

CELL RESPIRATION

Cell respiration is the controlled release of energy from organic compounds in cells to form ATP.

The process of cell respiration can take place in the presence or in the absence of oxygen. In either case, the first stage of cell respiration is glycolyis.

GLYCOLYSIS

Glycolysis: glucose → 2 pyruvate + ATP

Glycolysis is the breakdown of one molecule of glucose (a six carbon compound) into two molecules of pyruvate (a three carbon compound), with a small net yield of ATP. This process takes place in the cytoplasm and does NOT require the presence of oxygen.

> 3.7.3 Explain that, during anaerobic cell respiration, pyruvate can be converted in the cytoplasm into lactate, or ethanol and carbon dioxide, with no further yield of ATP.
>
> ©IBO 2007

If there is no oxygen present, the cell needs to use the process of anaerobic cell respiration to obtain its energy. It will carry out glycolysis as described in *Topic 3.7.2*. In order to be able to continue with glycolysis which produces a small amount of ATP, the cell needs to change the pyruvate into another substance. Yeast cells will convert pyruvate (a three carbon compound) into ethanol (a two carbon compound) and carbon dioxide (a one carbon compound). Human cells will change pyruvate (a three carbon compound) into lactate (another three carbon compound). Neither of these equations requires the presence of oxygen. That is why they are part of **anaerobic cell respiration**.

We use the process of anaerobic cell respiration in our bodies when, for example, we run a sprint. The muscles suddenly require a lot of energy. The body can only supply a limited amount of oxygen to the muscles and there can only be a limited amount of aerobic respiration. This does not produce enough energy to contract the muscles at the rate required. So, in addition to aerobic respiration, the cells in the muscles will use anaerobic respiration to release the remaining amount of energy. This produces lactate which, under certain conditions, may cause muscle cramps.

Anaerobic respiration is also used with yeast in bread-making so that the dough will rise. The carbon dioxide produced will create bubbles in the dough which makes it rise. The alcohol produced will evaporate during baking.

> 3.7.4 Explain that, during aerobic cell respiration, pyruvate can be broken down in the mitochondrion into carbon dioxide and water with a large yield of ATP.
>
> ©IBO 2007

If oxygen is present, the pyruvate produced in the cytoplasm during glycolysis will move into the mitochondria. Inside the mitochondria, pyruvate will be broken down to carbon dioxide and water. This process yields much more ATP than glycolysis or anaerobic respiration. *For details see Topic 8.1.*

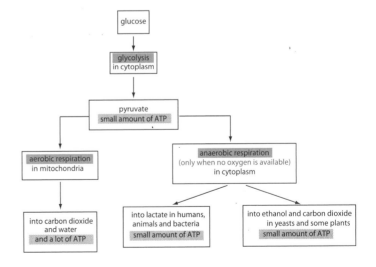

Figure 336 The aerobic and anaerobic respiration of glucose

3.8 PHOTOSYNTHESIS

CORE

3.8.1	State that photosynthesis involves the conversion of light energy into chemical energy.
	©IBO 2007

In the process of **photosynthesis**, light energy is converted into chemical energy. The substances needed for photosynthesis are carbon dioxide and water, which, in the presence of sunlight and **chlorophyll**, can produce glucose and oxygen. This is far from being a one-step reaction as you will see in *Topic 8.2*. Some of the energy of the light will be converted into chemical energy in glucose.

3.8.2	State that light from the Sun is composed of a range of wavelengths (colours).
	©IBO 2007

The most usual light for photosynthesis is sunlight. Sunlight is white light, made of all colours together. Different colours are actually different wavelengths of light. On one side of the **spectrum**, there is violet light with the shortest wavelength and the most energy, on the other side there is red light with the longest wavelength and the least energy. To one side of the visible spectrum (shorter wavelength), the electromagnetic radiation continues as ultraviolet, X rays, etc. To the other side (longer wavelength) are e.g. infrared, radio waves. *Refer to Figure 337.*

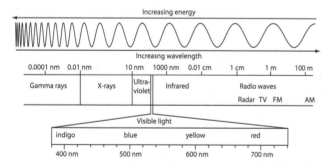

Figure 337   The spectrum

3.8.3	State that chlorophyll is the main photosynthetic pigment.
	©IBO 2007

Most plants are green. The green colour is caused by the presence of the pigment chlorophyll, found in chloroplasts. Chlorophyll is the main photosynthetic pigment. *Refer to Figures 338 and 339.*

 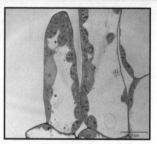

Figure 338
A green plant

Figure 339
An EM of plant cells

Chlorophyll is green, i.e. it reflects green light and absorbs all other colours. Several different kinds of chlorophyll exist, each with their own specific absorption spectrum *(See also Topic 3.8.4).*

3.8.4	Outline the differences in absorption of red, blue and green light by chlorophyll.
	©IBO 2007

Since chlorophyll appears to be green, green light is reflected. From this you can conclude that green light is not absorbed very well. An absorption spectrum can be determined in the following way:

If you shine white light through a chlorophyll solution, some frequencies will be absorbed, others will not. If the remaining light is directed through a prism, you will get the usual spectrum but with some colours 'missing'. These are the colours which were absorbed by the chlorophyll solution. *Refer to Figure 340.*

ABSORPTION SPECTRUM OF CHLOROPHYLL

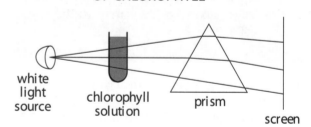

Figure 340   Determining the absorption spectrum

If you measure the intensity of the different colours, you can then draw a graph of the percentage absorption against the wavelength (colour) as shown in Figure 341.

This shows that orange-red light and blue light are mostly absorbed while green light is mostly reflected/transmitted. There is some variation between the different kinds of chlorophyll but this is generally true for all. *Refer to Figure 341.*

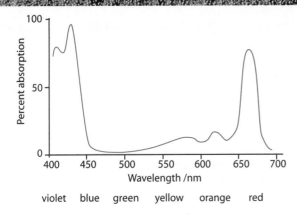

Figure 341   The absorption spectrum of chlorophyll

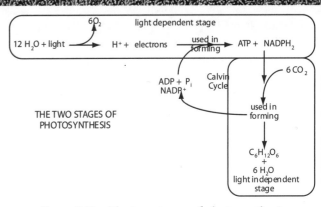

THE TWO STAGES OF
PHOTOSYNTHESIS

Figure 342   The two stages of photosynthesis

CORE

3.8.5	State that light energy is used to produce ATP, and to split water molecules (photolysis) to form oxygen and hydrogen.

©IBO 2007

Photosynthesis can be divided into two stages:
- the light dependent stage
- the light independent stage

In the light dependent stage, light energy is used to split water molecules (photolysis) into hydrogen ions (H^+) and oxygen (O_2) and electrons. This process also produces ATP.

3.8.6	State that ATP and hydrogen (derived from the photolysis of water) are used to fix carbon dioxide to make organic molecules.

©IBO 2007

In the light independent stage, the H^+ and ATP produced in the light dependent stage, are used to fix carbon dioxide to make organic molecules. This is shown in the Figure 342.

ATP (Adenosine Tri Phosphate) is an energy rich compound. It contains high energy bonds between the phosphate groups. It can release a phosphate, and with it a certain amount of energy, and become ADP (Adenosine Di Phosphate).

This reaction is reversible.

$$ATP \rightleftharpoons ADP + P + energy.$$

NADPH can do something similar in the reaction
$$NADPH \rightleftharpoons NADP^+ + H^+.$$

(*Note: SL students do not need to know about NADPH.*)

3.8.7	Explain that the rate of photosynthesis can be measured directly by the production of oxygen or the uptake of carbon dioxide, or indirectly by an increase in biomass.

©IBO 2007

If you want to measure how much photosynthesis is taking place per unit time (minute, hour, decade), you can measure one of the following factors.

Since photosynthesis utilises carbon dioxide, it is theoretically possible to place a plant in an enclosed space, then measure the available carbon dioxide before and after the experiment. This will tell you how much carbon dioxide was used for photosynthesis. This method allows the carbon dioxide to interact with water, producing bicarbonate and hydrogen ions. Hence the acidity of the resulting solution will indicate the amount of carbon dioxide present as shown in Figure 343 (a).

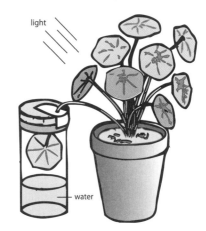

Figure 343 (a)   Measuring carbon dioxide consumption

It is easier to measure photosunthesis by looking at the other side of the equation. Photosynthesis produces oxygen and glucose. It is possible to measure how much oxygen a plant produces over time. Again, it is easier to use water plants such as *Elodea*. If you set up an experiment similar to Figure 343(b) and shine a bright light on it, it is possible to measure how much oxygen is produced in a certain amount of time.

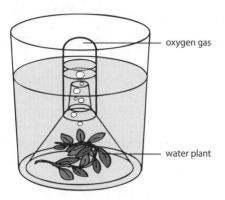

Figure 343 (b)   Measuring oxygen production

It is also possible to measure how much heavier a plant is after photosynthesis. We need to make sure that we measure the change in organic matter and not, for example, the change in water content. Therefore, we need to determine the biomass by completely dehydrating (drying) the plant before weighing it. Needless to say, the experiment would need to allow for the fact that no organism survives this treatment.

3.8.8	Outline the effect of temperature, light intensity and carbon dioxide concentration on the rate of photosyntheses.

©IBO 2007

To allow photosynthesis to take place the following criteria need to be fulfilled:
- presence of chlorophyll
- presence of light
- presence of carbon dioxide
- presence of water
- suitable temperature

In practical work, it is possible to determine if all the above (and maybe some other factors) are required for photosynthesis.

The basis of the experiment is the following set of observations:
- the glucose produced during photosynthesis is turned to starch;
- a plant can be 'destarched' by placing it in a dark cupboard for 2 days;
- during the experiment photosynthesis may or may not take place;

- the presence of starch can be tested for in a simple test involving the use of iodine (producing a blue/black colour in the presence of starch).

CHLOROPHYLL REQUIREMENT

- use a destarched plant with variegated leaves (green and white)
- test that the leaves contain no starch
- place it in the light
- after a day, the leaf will show that the white parts still contain no starch but the green parts show the presence of starch

This demonstrates the need for chlorophyll in the process of photosynthesis.

TEMPERATURE REQUIREMENT

The enzymes involved in photosynthesis have temperature ranges in which they are most effective. These vary from enzyme to enzyme. The rate is therefore highest at the optimum temperature and lower at both low and high temperatures. *Refer to Figure 344.*

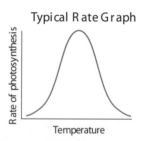

Typical Rate Graph

Figure 344   Effect of temperature

CO_2 REQUIREMENT

Two destarched plants are placed in the light but covered with a transparent plastic bag. Under the bag (with one of the plants), a small beaker of soda-lime (which contains NaOH) is placed (this absorbs carbon dioxide from the air). When the plants are tested for starch the next day, the plant with the soda-lime will have had no photosynthesis, while the other plant will show the presence of starch, indicating the need for carbon dioxide to allow photosynthesis. *Refer to Figure 345.*

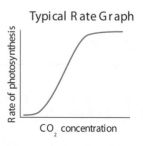

Typical Rate Graph

Figure 345   Effect of CO_2 concentration

CORE

LIGHT REQUIREMENT

A destarched plant left in a dark cupboard will contain no starch a day later, while a similar plant placed in the light will have photosynthesised and starch will be found. Alternatively we can cover part of a leaf of a green destarched plant which is placed in the light and show the absence of starch the next day. So, light is essential for photosynthesis. *Refer to Figure 346.*

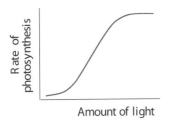

Figure 346   The effect of light intensity

The highest rate of photosynthesis will be reached by providing the plant with its optimum temperature, maximum light intensity and maximum carbon dioxide concentration.

The factor the furthest away from its optimum value will limit the amount of photosynthesis. This is then the **limiting factor**. If you improve this factor, the rate of photosynthesis will increase until another factor becomes the limiting factor. If you plot a graph of the rate of photosynthesis versus light intensity, the graph will go up until light is no longer the limiting factor. Then, the amount of photosynthesis will remain constant.

An example of this is found in greenhouses. In the Netherlands, people growing vegetables often do this in greenhouses (*see Figure 347*). They will heat these greenhouses to provide the plants with the optimum temperature. They may switch on lights at night to provide optimum lighting conditions.

Of course, water is readily available and will be provided to the plants. It has been found that adding carbon dioxide to the air in the greenhouse will increase the yield since all other factors are near optimum and carbon dioxide has become the limiting factor.

Figure 347   Greenhouses provide good growing conditions for plants

EXERCISES

1. The three most common elements in the 'molecules of life' are:
   A   carbon, hydrogen and sodium.
   B   iron, hydrogen and oxygen.
   C   carbon, nitrogen and oxygen.
   D   carbon, hydrogen and oxygen.

2. In addition to carbon, hydrogen and oxygen, nucleic acids contain the element:
   A   sodium.
   B   potassium.
   C   phosphorus.
   D   iron.

3. Sucrose and maltose are examples of
   A   monosaccharides.
   B   disaccharides.
   C   polysaccharides.
   D   inorganic molecules.

4. Which one of the following is NOT a major function of lipids in the human body?
   A   as a short term energy source.
   B   synthesis of hormones.
   C   long term energy storage.
   D   insulation.

5. An example of a structural protein in the human body is:
   A   hemoglobin.
   B   amylase.
   C   cellulose.
   D   collagen.

6. In the lock and key model for enzyme action, the enzyme:
   A   fits very closely onto a site on the substrate.
   B   has a hydrophobic head which dissolves in the substrate.
   C   has a hydrophilic head which dissolves in the substrate.
   D   attaches itself to the substrate by a chemical bond.

7. Which one of the following is not a component of a nucleotide molecule?
   A   a pentose sugar.
   B   a phosphate group.
   C   an organic base.
   D   an inorganic base.

CORE

8. The process by which RNA is produced from a DNA template is known as:

A transcription.

B translation.

C division.

D coding.

9 Which one of the following graphs best represents the reaction rate of an enzyme catalysed reaction.

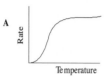

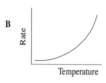

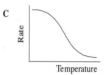

10 Which one of the following statements is NOT true?

A Light is necessary for every stage of photosynthesis.

B Photosynthesis will not occur without light.

C Some stages of photosynthesis do not require light.

D Photosynthesis is a multi-step reaction.

11. Explain the thermal, cohesive and solvent properties of water in terms of the structure of its molecules and the associated bonding.

12. Which elements are found in

(a) carbohydrates

(b) lipids

(c) proteins

13. Name and draw the molecular structure of the building blocks of:

(a) carbohydrates

(b) lipids

(c) proteins

14. How do the condensation reactions in forming disaccharides and lipids differ from those forming dipeptides?

15. Describe in terms of the lock and key model of enzyme action:

(a) the effect of temperature on enzyme activity

(b) the effect of substrate concentration on enzyme activity

(c) denaturation

16. Name the bonds between

(a) the sugar and the base in the nucleotide.

(b) the sugar and the phosphate in the nucleotide.

(c) the complementary bases in the nucleic acid.

(d) Which bonds are the strongest and why?

(e) Why does complementary base pairing only occur between A-T and C-G in a DNA molecule?

17. Compare DNA and RNA structure.

18. (a) Which factors can affect the rate of photosynthesis in a plant?

(b) State the products of the light-dependent reactions of photosynthesis.

19. (a) State the products of glycolysis

(b) State one product of anaerobic respiration

20. Explain how lactase is used to make lactose free milk.

GENETICS

CORE

4.1 CHROMOSOMES, GENES, ALLELES AND MUTATIONS

4.1.1	State that eukaryote chromosomes are made of DNA and proteins.

©IBO 2007

Prokaryotic chromosomes are circular. Prokaryotes also have some DNA in the form of small loops called plasmids. Prokaryotic DNA is found in the nucleoid area of the cell, not in a nucleus. Prokaryotic chromosomes contain DNA but no protein. *Refer to Figure 215.*

Eukaryotic chromosomes are found inside a nucleus. There are usually more than one chromosome and they are linear. Eukaryotic chromosomes contain DNA and proteins. *Refer to Figure 222.*

4.1.2	Define *gene, allele* and *genome.*
4.1.3	Define *gene* mutation.

©IBO 2007

A gene is a heritable factor that controls a specific characteristic (such as eye colour), consists of a length of DNA and occupies a position on a chromosome known as a locus.

The term **allele** refers to one specific form of a gene, differing from other alleles by one or a few bases only and occupying the same gene locus as other alleles of the gene. *Refer to Figure 401.* A **genome** is the total genetic material of an organelle, cell or organism. The **gene pool** refers to the total of the genes carried by the individual members

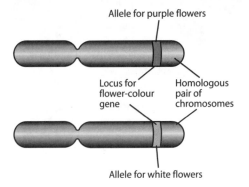

Figure 401   Alleles for flower colour

of a population. A gene **mutation** may be defined as a permanent change in the sequence of base pairs in the DNA that makes up a gene. A mutation may involve just one nucleotide or it may affect a large section of the gene.

An example of a mutation occurs in the Manx cat shown in Figure 402. Due to a mutation, some Manx cats were born without tails. This was selected for by breeders and a tailless breed of cats was created.

Figure 402   The Manx cat, an example of a mutation

4.1.4   Explain the consequence of a base substitution mutation in relation to the processes of transcription and translation, using the example of sickle-cell anemia.

©IBO 2007

It is often thought that a mutation which involves a smaller number of nitrogenous bases in the DNA will be less significant than one where a larger number of bases is changed. This is not necessarily true and a good example is found in the gene that controls sickle-cell **anemia** where a change of only one base leads to a protein with one amino acid changed and the resulting disease of sickle-cell anemia.

Hemoglobin is made of four polypeptide chains: two alpha chains and two beta chains. When an A to T base substitution occurs in the region of the gene coding for the 6th amino acid in the beta chain, the codon GAG (glutamic acid) becomes GTG (valine).

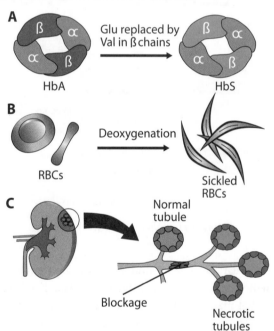

Figure 403   Sickle-cell anemia: cause and consequences

The resulting polypeptide is different and the hemoglobin formed is commonly known as HbS; the 'normal' hemoglobin is known as HbA.

The result of this is a slightly different structure, by one amino acid of the hemoglobin molecule which makes it crystallise at low oxygen levels (e.g. in the capillaries). The erythrocyte in which the hemoglobin can be found will then change from a biconcave shape into a sickle-cell

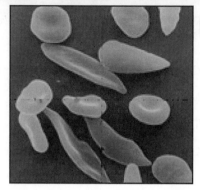

Figure 404   Sickle-cells and normal red blood cells

shape *(see Figure 404)* and can block the small capillaries, and is less efficient at transporting oxygen. Even when the oxygen concentration increases again, the cells keep their sickle shape.

The symptoms of sickle-cell anemia are acute anemia, which causes physical weakness. The lack of oxygen may be severe enough to cause damage to the heart and kidneys or even death (in **homozygous** individuals). The gene for sickle-cell anemia is codominant with the "normal" allele although the latter is expressed more strongly in the **heterozygous** individual. Heterozygous individuals (carriers) have some HbS but more normal hemoglobin. They may suffer from mild anemia. The selective advantage of being a carrier is found in malaria-infested areas. *Plasmodium* (the protist causing malaria) cannot reproduce in erythrocytes with HbS. This means that individuals heterozygous for the sickle-cell trait have a reduced chance of contracting malaria.

Natural selection has ensured that the sickle-cell trait is more common among people living in malaria-infested areas such as West Africa. As the African-American population largely originates from this area, the trait is found in frequencies higher than usual in this group. Carriers may not be aware of the fact that they possess the sickle-cell allele and are capable of passing it on to their children. If two carriers have a child, there is a 1 in 4 (25%) chance of the child having the disease. *See Figure 405.*

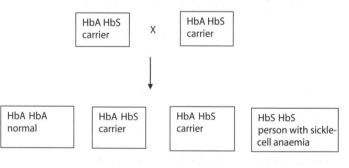

Figure 405   The inheritance of sickle-cell anemia

Therefore, it is important that people who may be carriers, are tested to confirm the presence or absence of the sickle-cell allele. If a female carrier is pregnant and the father is also a carrier, it is possible to test using amniocentesis or chorionic villi sampling (*refer to Topic 4.2.6*) to see if the child will have sickle-cell anemia. Should this be the case, then the parents may decide to discontinue the pregnancy. There are no easy answers to this problem. A great deal of research is being done about treating sickle-cell anemia including bone marrow transplant and/or blood stem cell treatment. Gene therapy is also a possibility but research is in an early stage. *Refer also to Topic 4.3.2 and D.2.11.*

TOK   Malaria and sickle-cell anemia

The incidence of sickle-cell anemia is correlated with the incidence of malaria in parts of Africa and South Asia. It is a case of heterozygote advantage, where those who are heterozygous for the sickle-cell anemia allele are better suited to the environment than homozygotes. Sickle-cell heterozygotes can be infected with malaria, but it does not effect them as severely as those who do not have the allele. Heterozygotes do not express sickle-cell disease. Those who are homozygous recessive for the allele do express the disease which is often fatal. A balance between the risk of death from malaria and death from the homozygous form of sickle-cell anaemia is played out in the population of individuals in the parts of the world where both these disease are present. This is a case of a causal link for the continuation of sickle-cell anemia alleles in the population.

In other cases causal links may be difficult to find or simply just not there. Making the decision that there is a causal requires a large body of evidence to support the link as in the incidence of sickle-cell disease and malaria. There was at one stage a suggested causal link between the Measles, Mumps and Rubella (MMR) Vaccine and autism. Several large-scale studies have since confirmed that there is no causal link between the MMR vaccine and autism.

4.2 MEIOSIS

CORE

4.2.1	State that meiosis is a reduction division of a diploid nucleus to form haploid nuclei.

©IBO 2007

Meiosis is called a "reduction division" because the daughter cells have only half of the number of chromosomes as the original parent cell.

The purpose of meiosis is to produce gametes. A (haploid) gamete (sex cell, sperm or egg cell) has half the number of chromosomes compared to a (diploid) somatic cell (body cell). A male and a female gamete may then fuse (fertilisation) to form a zygote, which will have the same number of chromosomes as a somatic cell.

The number of chromosomes in a haploid cell is often given as 'n'. The number of chromosomes in a diploid cell is usually given as '$2n$'. For example:

- in a human somatic cell $2n = 46$
- in a gamete of a camel $n = 35$
- in a somatic cell of an apple $2n = 34$

4.2.2	Define *homologous chromosomes*.

©IBO 2007

Homologous chromosomes (or a homologous pair) are two chromosomes, one from each parent, that look the same. They are the same size and they will show the same banding pattern in a karyotype (*see Figure 409*). They carry the same genes but not necessarily the same alleles, for example, both homologous chromosomes will carry the gene for eye colour but one may have the allele 'brown' while the other may have the allele 'blue'. Homologous chromosomes will pair up and split up during meiosis.

4.2.3	Outline the process of meiosis, including pairing of homologous chromosomes and crossing over, followed by two divisions, which results in four haploid cells.

©IBO 2007

The process of meiosis can be divided into two main stages:

- Meiosis I
- Meiosis II.

Both Meiosis I and II are subdivided into:
- Prophase
- Metaphase
- Anaphase
- Telophase

The key to the process of meiosis is the pairing of homologous chromosomes in Prophase I and the splitting of the homologues in Anaphase I. *See Figure 406.*

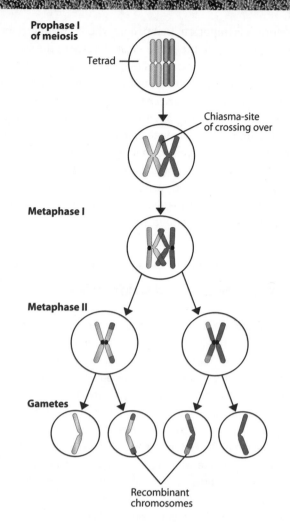

Figure 407   Crossing over

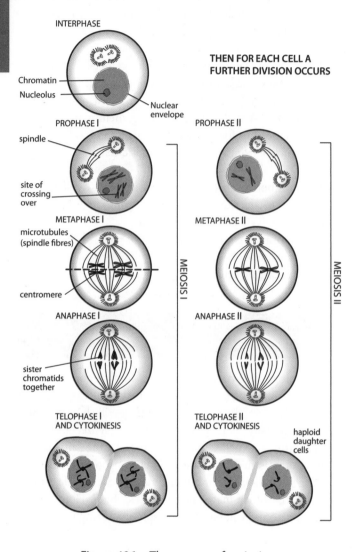

Figure 406   The process of meiosis

One event that can take place during meiosis is crossing over, as seen in Figure 407. Crossing over is the exchange of genetic material between two homologous chromosomes which have paired up during Prophase I. The result of crossing over is genetic recombination: an exchange of genes. The points where the homologous chromosomes cross over are called chiasmata.

| 4.2.4 | Explain that non-disjunction can lead to changes in chromosome number, illustrated by reference to Down syndrome (trisomy 21). |

©IBO 2007

The pairing up of homologous chromosomes during Prophase I is called synapsis. Each resulting pair of homologous chromosomes (both chromosomes consisting of two identical 'sister' chromatids) is called tetrad or bivalent. The separation of homologous chromosomes during Anaphase I is called disjunction. Failure of chromosomes to separate can lead to aneuploidy, which means having one extra chromosome or missing one chromosome. In extreme cases, all homologous pairs fail to separate. This is called total non-disjunction and will lead to polyploidy, where the organisms has one complete extra set of chromosomes and becomes, for example, 3n.

One of the best known examples of aneuploidy is **Down Syndrome**. If non-disjunction occurs in either parent, one of the two gametes will carry two copies of chromosome 21. When the zygote is formed, it will contain three copies of chromosome 21 and will be aneuploid. It is also referred to as trisomy 21. The resulting symptoms are called Down Syndrome and are accompanied by (varying degrees of) disability. The karyotype of a person with Down syndrome is illustrated in Figure 408.

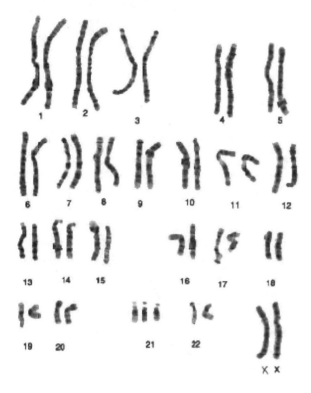

Figure 408   The cause of Down syndrome

Unlike the production of sperm cells in the male (which begins at puberty), the female gametes develop before birth. At birth, the future female gametes are present as primary oocytes in Prophase I of meiosis. They remain in this stage until ovulation. This means that for a twenty year old woman, her egg cells have collected twenty years of damage (chemicals, radiation, etc.). But for a forty year old woman, the cells have collected forty years of damage and the chance of non-disjunction, resulting in a baby with Down Syndrome is increased.

Since the sperm cells of the male are produced constantly, the age of the father seems to have less effect than the age of the mother. Genetic factors can play a role in either parent: generally if a person has a relative with Down Syndrome, this person may have an increased chance of having a baby with Down Syndrome.

4.2.5   State that, in karyotyping, chromosomes are arranged in pairs according to their size and structure.

©IBO 2007

Karyotyping is the process of finding the chromosomal characteristics of a cell. Chromosomes can be stained to show banding. This is used in the process of karyotyping. Chromosome structure and banding can be used to arrange the chromosomes in their pairs. Figure 409 shows an idealised picture of the human chromosomes. To make a karyotype, the chromosomes in the picture would be cut out and arranged in pairs, starting with the largest.

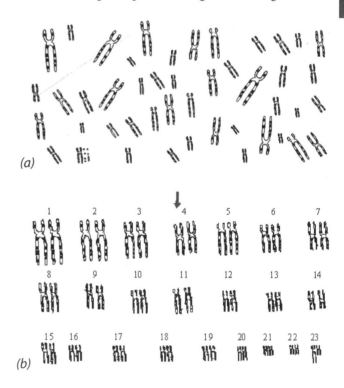

Figure 409 (a) and (b)   The process of karyotyping

4.2.6   State that karyotyping is performed using cells collected by chorionic villus sampling or amniocentesis, for pre-natal diagnosis of chromosome abnormalities.

©IBO 2007

One application of karyotyping can be found in an amniocentesis. The risk of having a child with Down's syndrome increases with the mother's age. Non-disjunction, which can cause Down syndrome, also seems to have a genetic component so that it can be said that people with relatives with Down syndrome have an increased chance of having a baby with this genetic disorder, as have mothers over the age of 35.

In either situation, it is possible to do pre-natal testing. There are two common tests:

- chorionic villus sampling
- amniocentesis

To explain both of these techniques, it is helpful to briefly outline human embryonic development.

Human fertilisation takes place in the oviduct. The zygote will travel to the uterus and undergo many divisions. When it arrives in the uterus, it is a ball which consists of an inner cell mass and an outer cell mass. The outer cells will come into contact with the mucus lining of the wall of the uterus and develop into chorionic villi. They will eventually become the placenta.

Chorionic villus sampling is a pre-natal test that can be done at 11-12 weeks of pregnancy. It involves taking a sample of the chorionic villi in order to obtain cells from tissue that originally came from the zygote. The cells will therefore have the same genetic composition as the cells of the unborn baby so a karyotype can be made. This should take fewer than two weeks. The risks associated with chorionic villus sampling (around 1%) are slightly larger than of amniocentesis (around 0.5%).

Figure 410 shows chorionic villus sampling (CVS) and where the tissue will be removed.

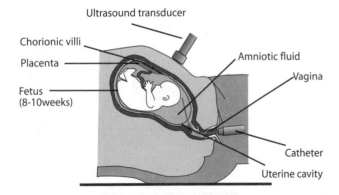

Figure 410   Chorionic villus sampling

Amniocentesis can be done around the 16th week of the pregnancy. A sample of the amniotic fluid (containing fetal cells) is taken and a culture is made. When sufficient cells have been obtained, a karyotype can be done to detect chromosome abnormalities. The dividing cells are photographed and, using these pictures, the chromosomes are arranged in homologous pairs. Some genetic disorders can be detected this way (e.g. Down syndrome). This process takes approximately 3 weeks. A diagram of the process of amniocentesis is shown in Figure 411.

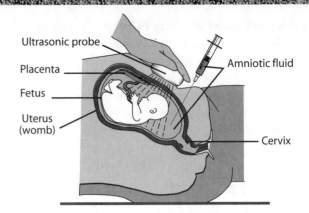

Figure 411   Amniocentesis

TOK   Karyotyping

All medical procedures involve some risk. Those who undergo procedures need to balance the risk against the benefit. Karyotyping increases the risk of miscarriage but can reveal the presence of major chromosomal abnormalities. Knowledge is power. The knowledge gained from karyotyping can be used to perform an abortion or allow life to continue. There are significant responsibilities and consequences in such decisions, so it is no surprise that there is disagreement as to who should have the power to authorise such testing and take action on the outcome of the test. Who should make such decisions: the individual (mother or father), the couple together, their wider family, health care professionals, government? There are cultural and religious opinions to consider. This will always be an area of significant debate.

4.2.7	Analyse a human karyotype to determine gender and whether non-disjunction has occurred.

©IBO 2007

When analysing a human karyotype to determine gender and the occurrence of non-disjunction, the karyotype must be carefully examined and pairs of chromosomes need to be identified and placed together. This can be done using pictures on paper or on a computer screen. If non-disjunction has occurred there will either be one, or three copies, of a particular chromosome. *See also Topic 4.3.5.*

4.3 THEORETICAL GENETICS

4.3.1	Define *genotype, phenotype, dominant allele, recessive allele, codominant alleles, locus, homozygous, heterozygous, carrier* and *test cross*.
	©IBO 2007

Genotype refers to the alleles of an organism. This is usually written using upper and lower case letters, e.g. Tt. **Phenotype** includes all the characteristics of an organism. This is written as a word, e.g. tall. A **dominant allele** is one which has the same effect on the phenotype whether it is present in the homozygous or heterozygous state. A **recessive allele** is one which only has an effect on the phenotype when present in the homozygous state. **Codominant alleles** are a pair of alleles that both affect the phenotype when present in a heterozygote. The terms 'incomplete' and 'partial' dominance are no longer used.

A **locus** is the particular position on homologous chromosomes of a gene. **Homozygous** means having the two identical alleles of a gene. **Heterozygous** means having two different alleles of a gene. A **carrier** is a heterozygous individual that has one copy of a recessive allele that causes a genetic disease in individuals that are homozygous for this allele. A **Test cross** refers to testing a suspected heterozygote by crossing with a known homozygous recessive. (*The term 'backcross' is no longer used.*)

4.3.2	Determine the genotypes and phenotypes of the offspring of a monohybrid cross using a Punnett grid.
	©IBO 2007

A Punnett grid is a way of finding the expected ratio of the offspring, given certain parental phenotypes.

We can study one of the characteristics *Gregor Mendel* (1822-1884) used in his experiments. He studied the size of pea plants and found that 'tall' is dominant over 'short'. If we start with 2 pure breeding (homozygous) plants of contrasting traits (tall and short), we will obtain an F1 (First filial generation) which has the dominant phenotype (tall) but is heterozygous. When self-fertilising the F1, we will obtain an F2 (Second filial generation) which will appear 3/4 dominant (tall) and 1/4 recessive (short).

Using a certain format will help to solve a question. Start by writing down what phenotypes exist for the relevant gene and what the corresponding genotypes are, as in Figure 412.

Possible phenotypes	Corresponding genotypes
Tall	TT or Tt
Short	tt

Figure 412   Table of phenotypes and genotypes

Then write out the cross. Make sure to include both genotype and phenotype of the parents (P), as well as the genotype and phenotype of the offspring (F_1).

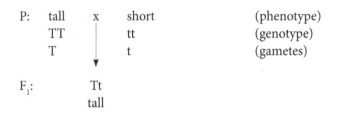

The next generation is called F_2 which could be created by self-fertilising the F_1.

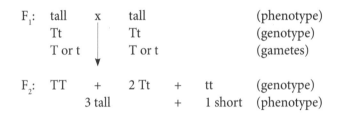

A Punnett grid (also known as a Punnett square) can be used to find the genotypes of the offspring. (*Figure 413*)

Punnett square		Tt		genotype parent
genotype parent	gametes	T	t	gametes
Tt	T	TT *tall*	Tt *tall*	genotype offspring phenotype offspring
	t	Tt *tall*	tt *short*	genotype offspring phenotype offspring

Figure 413   A Punnett square

CORE

4.3.3 State that some genes have more than two alleles (multiple alleles).

©IBO 2007

The example in *Topic 4.4.2* used the gene for size which had two alleles, tall and short. It is possible to have more than two alleles for one gene. A good example of this is found in blood groups. The gene is blood type and the alleles are I^A, I^B, and i.

4.3.4 Describe ABO blood groups as an example of codominance and multiple alleles.

©IBO 2007

The ABO **blood group** system is based on 4 different phenotypes (group A, B, AB and O) caused by different combinations of 3 different alleles (I^A, I^B and i). The alleles I^A and I^B are codominant so both will affect the phenotype. The allele i is recessive and will only affect the phenotype when homozygous. *Refer to Figure 414.*

The following possibilities exist:

Phenotypes	Genotypes
A	I^AI^A or I^Ai
B	I^BI^B or I^Bi
AB	I^AI^B
O	ii

Figure 414   Blood groups

Using a **Punnett square**, it can be worked out how a female with blood group A and a male with blood group B can have four children, each with a different blood group. *Refer to Figure 415.*

Punnett square		I^Ai		genotype parent
genotype parent	gametes	I^A	i	gametes
I^Bi	I^B	I^AI^B type AB	I^Bi type B	genotype offspring phenotype offspring
	i	I^Ai type A	ii type O	genotype offspring phenotype offpring

Figure 415   First blood group cross

Both parents would have to be heterozygous in order to produce a type O child.

It also explains why a female with blood group O and a male with blood group AB cannot have children with either of the parent's blood group. *Refer to Figure 416.*

Punnett square		ii		genotype parent
genotype parent	gametes	i	i	gametes
I^AI^B	I^A	I^Ai type A	I^Ai type A	genotype offspring phenotype offspring
	I^B	I^Bi type B	I^Bi type B	genotype offspring phenotype offpring

Figure 416   Second blood group cross

4.3.5 Explain how the sex chromosomes control gender by referring to the inheritance of X and Y chromosomes in humans.

©IBO 2007

Humans have 46 chromosomes in somatic cells. These cells are diploid, so there are pairs of homologous chromosomes which carry the same genes and look the same in a karyotype. This is indeed the case for chromosome pairs 1-22. The remaining two chromosomes are the **sex chromosomes**. Males have one X and one Y (XY) chromosome, while females have two X chromosomes (XX) as shown in Figures 417 and 418, respectively. A diagram of these chromosomes can be seen in Figure 419.

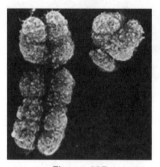

Figure 417
Male sex chromosomes
(XY)

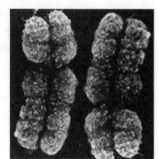

Figure 418
Female sex chromosomes
(XX)

As shown in Figures 417 to 419, the X chromosome is much larger than the Y chromosome. It contains some genes that are not found on the Y chromosome.

A Punnett square can be used to predict the chances of the gender of a child. So the gender-determining factors (the X and Y chromosomes) can be treated like any other trait and predictions can be made accordingly. *Refer to Figure 420.*

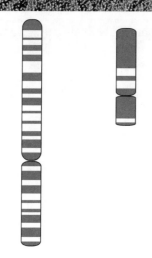

Figure 419   A diagram of the human sex chromosomes (X, Y)

Punnett square		XX		genotype parent
		X	X	gametes
XY	X	XX *female*	XX *female*	genotype offspring phenotype offspring
	Y	XY *male*	XY *male*	genotype offspring phenotype offpring
genotype of parent	gametes			

Figure 420   Using a Punnett square to determine gender

4.3.6   State that some genes are present on the X chromosome and absent from the shorter Y chromosome in humans.

©IBO 2007

The X chromosome is relatively large; the Y chromosome is much smaller. Several genes are located on the X chromosome such as the ability to see colours and hemophilia (also spelled haemophilia) but are absent from the Y chromosome. These genes are said to be 'X-linked'. This means that a male with one allele for colour blindness on the X chromosome, will be colour blind since there is no locus on the Y chromosome. The same applies for hemophilia. Both of these conditions are therefore found much more commonly in males than in females. Only a few genes are located exclusively on the Y chromosome (e.g. hairy ears).

4.3.7   Define *sex linkage*.

©IBO 2007

Conditions like colour blindness and hemophilia are much more common in men than in women and are said to be sex-linked.

Sex linkage occurs when the genes carried on the sex chromosomes, most often on the X chromosome.

An example of inheritance of a sex-linked trait is shown in Figure 421.

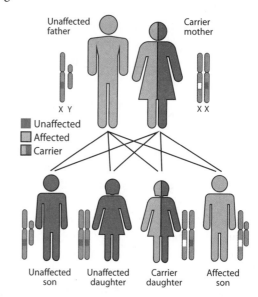

Figure 421   Inheritance of an X-linked, recessive characteristic

4.3.8   Describe the inheritance of colour blindness and hemophilia as examples of sex linkage.

©IBO 2007

COLOUR BLINDNESS

Colour blindness is a condition that can be caused by genetic factors. Human eyes contain cells with different pigments that absorb different wavelengths (colours) of light. If this pigment absorbs light, a message is sent to the brain and we see a colour. The ability to produce the different pigments is mainly found as genes on the X chromosome. The ability to make the pigment is a dominant allele; the recessive allele will not allow the pigment to be made.

A female has two X chromosomes. In order for a female to be colour blind, she would have to have two copies of the recessive allele. A male has only one X chromosome so will only have one copy of the gene. If this is the recessive allele, then the man is colour blind.

Existing alleles
X^B for normal vision, X^b for colour blindness.

A female can be
$X^B X^B$ or $X^B X^b$ or $X^b X^b$ (genotypes)
normal vision   colour blind   (phenotypes)

CORE

A male can be

$X^B Y$ or $X^b Y$ (genotypes)

normal vision   colour blind   (phenotypes)

HEMOPHILIA

Hemophilia is a blood disorder. Normally, there is a very fine balance for blood clotting. Blood should not clot when it is inside blood vessels or it will block the vessels (possibly causing a stroke) but it should clot when there is injury so that not too much blood is lost.

The process of blood clotting involves a number of different proteins, each having their own gene. If even one of these genes has an allele that does not code for the proper protein, the entire process of blood clotting can be disturbed and even very small wounds will not clot.

In humans the locus for the gene that controls the production of a blood clotting factor is on the X chromosome (i.e. and not on the Y chromosome). This means that if a male has one defective allele he will have the hemophilia condition. However a female will need to have two copies of the defective allele in order to have the condition. Statistically this is much less likely and with the advent of menstruation and child birth, a woman will need blood transfusions containing the clotting factors to survive. Prior to this technique hemophilia was thought to be homozygous lethal in all cases and some examples in some books are still based on this information.

Existing alleles

X^H for normal, X^h for hemophilia.

A female can be

$X^H X^H$ or $X^H X^h$ or $X^h X^h$ (genotype)

normal or carrier   hemophiliac, very rare   (phenotype)

A male can be

$X^H Y$ or $X^h Y$ (genotype)

normal   hemophiliac, rare   (phenotype)

> **4.3.9** State that a human female can be homozygous or heterozygous with respect to sex-linked genes.
>
> ©IBO 2007

Sex-linked genes are found on the X chromosome. Since females have two X chromosomes, they can have two dominant alleles (homozygous dominant), two recessive alleles (homozygous recessive) or one dominant and one recessive allele (heterozygous). Males only have one X chromosome. This means that the terms homozygous or heterozygous do not apply.

> **4.3.10** Explain that female carriers are heterozygous for X-linked recessive alleles.
>
> ©IBO 2007

In humans the locus for the gene that controls the production of a blood clotting factor is on the X chromosome (i.e. and not on the Y chromosome). This means that if a male has one defective allele he will have the hemophilia condition. However a female will need to have 2 copies of the defective allele in order to have the condition. Statistically this is much less likely and with the advent of menstruation and child birth a woman will need blood transfusions containing the clotting factors to survive. Women can be carriers for trait. In that case, they are heterozygous and will not show the trait but are capable of passing it on.

Since men only have one X chromosome, the allele on this chromosome will always be expressed. Men can have the allele for colour blindness and be colour blind or have the allele for normal vision and have normal vision. The same applies for hemophilia. Men cannot have the allele without expressing it so they can never be carriers for X-linked traits.

> **4.3.11** Predict the genotypic and phenotypic ratios of offspring of monohybrid crosses involving any of the above patterns of inheritance.
>
> ©IBO 2007

The accepted notation for the alleles for this characterisitc is shown in Figure 422.

Sickle-cell	Hb^A = normal	Hb^S = sickle-cell
Colourblindness	X^b = colour blindness	X^B = normal vision
Hemophilia	X^h = haemophilia	X^H = normal bloodclotting

Figure 422   Accepted notation

Codominance, the main letter should relate to the gene, while the superscript should relate to the allele. Both should be capital letters.

e.g. C^R = red flowers C^W = white flower

Drosophila melanogaster (vinegar fly)

         a+ = dominant allele   a = recessive allele

e.g.   vg+ = normal wing   vg = vestigial wing

Mendel's two laws are as follows:

Mendel's first law

Law of segregation

'Parental factors (genes) are in pairs and split so that one factor is present in each gamete.'

Mendel's second law

Principle of independent assortment

'Any of one pair of characteristics may combine with either one of another pair.' (dihybrid inheritance)

CORE

ABO Phenotypes	ABO Genotypes
A	$I^A I^A$ or $I^A i$
B	$I^B I^B$ or $I^B i$
AB	$I^A I^B$
O	ii
Rhesus Phenotypes	**Rhesus Genotypes**
Rhesus positive	$Rh^+ Rh^+$ or $Rh^+ Rh^-$
Rhesus negative	$Rh^- Rh^-$

Figure 423   Human blood groups

TOK   A paradigm shift

"Blending inheritance" was the most widely accepted explanation of inheritance in the nineteenth century. The offspring of parents usually seemed to display characteristics of both parents. Mendel's theories of inheritance involved a paradigm shift in the understanding of the basis of inheritance. Mendel proposed that inheritance was governed by discrete structures that he called *elemente*. Mendel's published results explaining patterns of inheritance but could not provide an explanation of the mechanism by which his *elemente* were passed from one generation to the next. Without a mechanism his model was forgotten.

Today we know Mendel's *elemente* as alleles. The reality of the existence of alleles and genes was not confirmed until the early twentieth century, more than twenty years after Mendel's death. It was only then that a mechanism was discovered that allowed an explanation of how Mendel's model of inheritance could take place. Mendel's place in genetics today stands upon the fact that his model was based on simple, easily reproducible experiments for which a large amount of data was collected, processed and analysed appropriately. His research was published allowing it to be re-discovered and stand up to scrutiny as is required according to the scientific method. Mendel's contemporaries did not carry out experiments that could withstand the scrutiny of the scientific community, so their theories are remembered as pre-scientific, if at all.

4.3.12   Deduce the genotypes and phenotypes of individuals in pedigree charts.

©IBO 2007

Pedigree charts are often used to record blood lines in royal families. Figure 424 is a pedigee showing Queen Victoria and her descendants. It is very likely that Queen Victoria was a carrier with respect to hemophilia because one of her sons was affected and two of her daughters were carriers.

The genotype of Queen Victoria must have been $X^H X^h$, while her husband was $X^H Y$. Leopold must have received Y from his father and X^h from his mother which caused him to have hemophilia. Alice received X^H from her father and X^h from her mother, making her a carrier. The same happened to Alice's daughter, Alexandra. She subsequently passed on her X^h to her son Alexis, who obviously received his Y chromosome from his father Czar Nicolas II of Russia. Alexis had hemophilia.

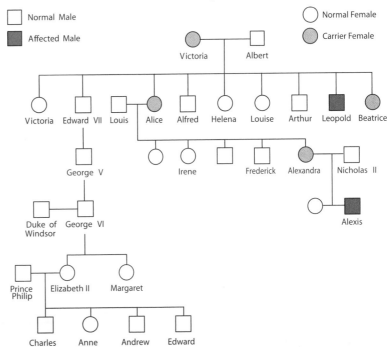

Figure 424   Part of the European royal family pedigree

4.4 GENETIC ENGINEERING AND BIOTECHNOLOGY

CORE

4.4.1 Outline the use of polymerase chain reaction (PCR) to copy and amplify minute quantities of DNA.

©IBO 2007

PCR stands for **polymerase chain reaction**. When researchers want to study a particular sequence of DNA, they need many (identical) copies of it. The traditional method of cloning (using plasmids) takes a lot of time and work.

Instead, a 'photocopier for DNA' is used, which is essentially what the PCR does. It uses enzymes to replicate DNA so no living organisms (e.g. bacteria or yeast) are required. The process for PCR was developed in 1983 by Kary Mullis who received the Nobel prize for Chemistry in 1993 for his work.

PCR is carried out in a thermal cycler which is shown in Figure 425.

Figure 425   A PCR machine

THE PRINCIPLE OF PCR

The desired DNA is heated which breaks the hydrogen bonds between the strands of the double helix so that they separate. Primers are added to start the process of DNA replication *(see Topic 7.2)*. As the mixture is cooled, the primers bond to the original, but now single stranded, DNA molecules (through hydrogen bonding between complementary base pairs). Nucleotides and a thermostable DNA polymerase are added.

The nucleotides will bond with the 'exposed' organic bases of the single stranded DNA (again through hydrogen bonding between complementary base pairs) and the DNA polymerase will then join them into a DNA strand. This way, each of the original strands has formed a new complementary strand. These strands can be heated and separated and will function as a template for more DNA strands to be formed. A large amount of identical copies of the original DNA can therefore be made quickly. The DNA is exponentially amplified. This is shown in Figure 426.

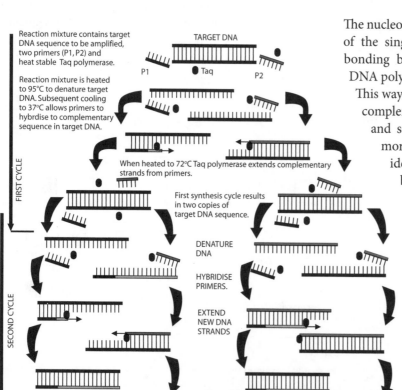

Figure 426   The PCR process

4.4.2 State that, in gel electrophoresis, fragments of DNA move in an electric field and are separated according to their size.

©IBO 2007

Gel electrophoresis is a process commonly used in biochemistry. Electrophoresis is a technique used to separate large molecules (nucleic acids or proteins) based on their different rates of movement in an electric field caused by a combination of their charge and their size.

A gel is prepared into a thin layer and placed in the container as shown in Figure 427. Then some holes are made on one side where the molecular biologist will place the samples. Often at least one of them will be an unknown sample. The others can contain (mixtures of) known molecules. Then the equipment is connected to a source of electricity. The gel will conduct electricity. Depending on the charge of the molecules, they will be attracted more or less to the other side. DNA fragments are slightly negative and will move towards the positive electrode (anode). So they will start to move through the gel. The speed with which they move will depend on how strong the attraction force is, but also on the size of the molecule. Larger molecules will move more slowly through the gel than smaller molecules.

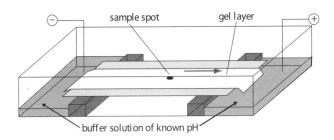

Figure 427 Gel electrophoresis

When the molecules have moved through the gel, the equipment is turned off and the gel removed. Sometimes the gel then needs to be stained to show the spots to where the molecules have travelled. If a spot of the unknown sample has travelled exactly the same distance as one of the known molecules, they are likely to be the same.

PCR can be used to increase the size of a sample and then gel electrophoresis can be used to compare the sections of DNA with the DNA of various suspects in an investigation.

4.4.3 State that gel electrophoresis of DNA is used in DNA profiling.

©IBO 2007

DNA profiling is also known as DNA fingerprinting. It is a technique that compares DNA from different sources without mapping the entire genome since that would take a long time.

DNA profiling is used to compare the DNA of a suspect with, for example, blood found at a crime scene or to compare the DNA of a child with that of an adult who could be the parent.

When a small amount of DNA is found, for example, in a spot of blood on a crime scene, the polymerase chain reaction (PCR) can be used to increase the amount of DNA. The two strands of the DNA double helix are separated. Restriction enzymes (or endonucleases, *see Topic 4.4.8*), which will cut between specific sequences of organic bases, are used to cut the DNA into sections. The sections will differ in size and charge and are separated using gel electrophoresis. The same treatment is used on every sample.

The gel electrophoresis will separate the sections of DNA according to size and charge. This creates a pattern of stripes and bands, detemined by the sequence of the organic bases. As every person's DNA is unique (except monozygotic or identical twins), it would be highly unlikely that two different people would produce the exact same pattern of DNA sections on the gel.

4.4.4 Describe the application of DNA profiling to determine paternity and also in forensic investigations.

©IBO 2007

PATERNITY PROFILING

DNA profiling to determine paternity uses the concept that all of the child's DNA comes from its parents. Each band shown on the DNA profile of a child must correspond with a band in the profile of the father or the mother. *See also Topic 4.4.5.*

FORENSIC INVESTIGTIONS

Compare DNA from the suspect with DNA from the crime scene sample

This technique breaks down DNA into sections which are separated by gel electrophoresis. If the DNA bands of a suspect are a match with those found in a sample (e.g. blood, semen, hairs) at the crime scene, then the suspect probably was at the scene although it is not always this simple. See http://en.wikipedia.org/wiki/Genetic_fingerprinting for some ideas of problems when using DNA profiling as evidence.

Use a relative's DNA to determine the identity of a victim

This technique has also been used to try to determine the identity of the remains of dead people. People claimed that the Tsar of Russia and his family were shot during the Russian Revolution and bodies were shown to prove this. However, not everyone believed that they were really the remains of the Romanovs. The identity of these bodies could not be proven until DNA fingerprinting was brought in. By taking blood samples of (distant) relatives of the Romanovs, DNA patterns could be established. Samples from the bodies showed similar DNA patterns and the conclusion was that the bodies were likely to be the Romanov family.

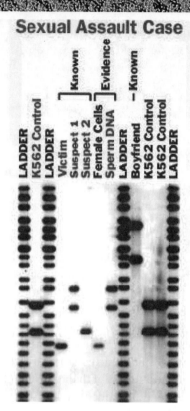

Figures 428   Evidence from a sexual assault case

TOK   DNA Profiles

Blood typing was used in paternity and forensic testing before the advent of DNA profiling. The outcome of tests using blood typing is so broad that it is only useful in excluding an individual (that is, it can say that the individual does not have the same blood type as the one searched for. To say that they do have the same blood type would not be useful unless the pool of possible suspects was very small and all with different blood types).

DNA profiling, on the other hand, compares parts of non-coding DNA that are unique to each individual (except identical twins). Profiles constructed using appropriate procedures have a statistically extremely high reliability rate and as such, are widely used in paternity and forensic cases with great success.

4.4.5	Analyse DNA profiles to draw conclusions about paternity or forensic investigations.

©IBO 2007

FORENSIC INVESTIGATION

A crime has been committed and two suspects are under investigation. DNA profiling has been carried out and the results are shown in Figure 428. It can be seen that the two bands visible in the "sperm DNA" match the DNA bands of Suspect 1 but not Suspect 2.

PATERNITY INVESTIGATION

When the paternity of a child is investigated, the bands found in the child's DNA are compared to those of the mother and the alleged father. Since all of the child's DNA comes from its parents, all bands should be found in either parent. Of course, a parent only gives half of its DNA to the child, so not all the parent's bands can be found in the child.

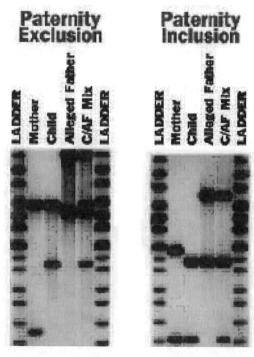

Figure 429 (a)   Exclusion   429 (b)   Inclusion

In Figure 429 (a), it can be seen that there are some DNA bands in the child's profile that cannot be attributed to either the father of the mother. Hence the alleged father is not the father of this child. In Figure 429 (b), you can see that both of the child's bands can be attributed to its parents; one to the mother and one to the alleged father. This person is likely to be the father of the child.

TOK   Human Genome Project

At one level the human genome project maps the DNA sequence of a human and could be seen as a recipe for what it is to be human. This reductionist view does not account for the complexity of life that stems from the myriad of interactions between our genes, the environment and our ability to transcend our genetic basis. Studies of identical and conjoined twins illustrate the limitations of this reductionist approach. Such twins have many similarities that stem from an identical genetic code, but are without doubt unique individuals. Conjoined twins have had an identical environment since conception. Clearly, to be human is more than simply the expression of genetic code and its interaction with our environment. How can this be? What makes us human?

4.4.6	Outline three outcomes of the sequencing of the complete human genome.

©IBO 2007

The **Human Genome Project** was a commitment undertaken by the scientific community across the world to determine the location and structure of all genes in the human chromosomes. Groups of scientists sequenced the genes of a particular (section of) a chromosome and all the information was pooled. It is part of the international Human Genome Organisation and an excellent example of how collaboration of scientists across the world can benefit all of us.

Mapping the human genome was first suggested in 1985 and the expected financial and time investment was staggering. Finally, in 1990, the project of sequencing all (approximately 3×10^9) base pairs in the human DNA was started. It was expected to take 15 years. Some new developments in DNA sequencing and software made the process faster and cheaper than originally expected and a "rough draft" was finished in 2000. In 2003, 50 years after Watson and Crick described the DNA double helix structure, the sequencing of the human DNA was 99.9% complete.

Having a map of the sequence of the nucleotides of the human DNA then lead to mapping the genes, i.e. listing and finding the locus of each human gene. They are not the same thing: knowing the sequence of A, T, C and G does not tell you if you are looking at a gene for eye colour or the ability to roll your tongue.

Outcomes of having sequenced the entire human genome are:

- an improved understanding of many genetic diseases: now many more genes causing disease are known than before the Human Genome Project;
- the production of medicines (based on DNA sequences) to cure diseases and/or genetic engineering to remove the genes which cause the disease;
- to determine fully which genetic diseases any individual is prone to (genetic screening leading to preventive medicine);
- research into a particular disease can now focus on only the gene(s) that are relevant to the disease;
- it can provide more information about evolutionary paths by comparing similarities and differences in genes between species.

This information could be valuable, but it could also be abused (e.g. by insurance companies or prospective employers) and society faces the challenge of coming to terms with these ethical issues.

4.4.7	State that, when genes are transferred between species, the amino acid sequence of the polypeptides translated from them is unchanged because the genetic code is universal.

©IBO 2007

Genetic engineering refers to the deliberate manipulation of genetic material. It is possible to move genetic material between species because **the genetic code is universal**. This means that, for every organism, the same RNA codon codes for the same amino acid in an mRNA strand, UUU and UUC both code for the amino acid phenylalanine while CUU, CUC, CUA and CUG all code for leucine, regardless of the species.

Since the genetic code is universal, it is possible to transfer genetic material from one species to another. Because the code is universal, it is possible to introduce a human gene for making insulin into a bacterium. The bacterium will then produce the human protein hormone insulin, which is responsible for making cells take up more glucose and convert it to glycogen.

CORE

4.4.8   Outline a basic technique used for gene transfer involving plasmids, a host cell (bacterium, yeast or other cell), restriction enzymes (endonucleases) and DNA ligase.

©IBO 2007

Gene transfer involves the following elements:

- a vector
- a host cell
- restriction enzymes
- DNA ligase.

The vector is what is needed to carry the gene into the host cell. Plasmids are often used as vectors.

Bacteria carry all the required genetic information on one large circular DNA. However, most bacteria also possess extra DNA in the form of plasmids. Plasmids are circular bits of genetic material carrying 2-30 genes. Plasmids may replicate at the time the chromosome replicates, or at other times. It is therefore possible for a cell to possess several identical plasmids.

Plasmids are used to clone a desired gene. This is illustrated in Figure 430. First, you splice or introduce the desired gene into a plasmid and transfer it into a bacterial cell. Then, culture these bacteria; many of them will have a plasmid with the desired gene. Use a section of nucleotides, complementary to the desired gene, but also attached to a (e.g. radioactive) label to find out which plasmids have the gene and which do not. Use restriction enzymes to cut the desired gene out of the plasmids and purify the gene using gel electrophoresis (see Topic 4.4.2). Refer to Figure 430.

The host cell is the cell which is to receive the genetic material. A bacterium may be the host cell and produce a protein desired by humans.

Restriction enzymes (endonucleases) are used to cut a desired section of the DNA. Bacteria produce these enzymes naturally as a defense against invading viruses. One commonly used restriction enzyme recognises the sequence GAATTC and cuts both strands of the DNA between G and A (see Figure 431). When preparing to transfer DNA, the same restriction enzyme is used for the host and the donor so the cuts are made in the same way. This way, the same 'sticky ends' are created so that the donor DNA can fit in between the host DNA. Refer to Figure 431.

Figure 431   Restriction sequence

The result is an uneven cut in the DNA and the ends of the DNA are referred to as "sticky ends". If the same sequence is found on another section of DNA and is cut in the same way, the two strands can be combined as shown in Figure 432.

To attach the two cut sections of DNA, the enzyme DNA ligase is used to create the required covalent bonds.

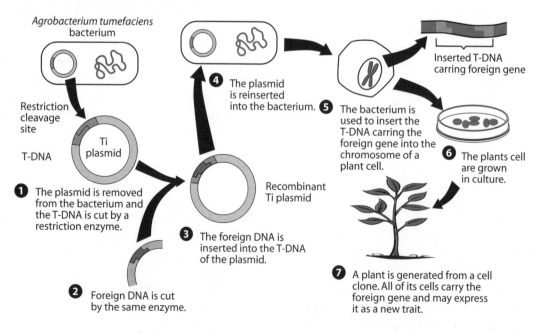

Figure 430   The general technique of gene transfer

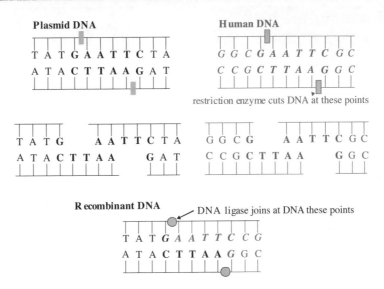

Figure 432   Recombinant DNA

4.4.9	State two examples of the current uses of genetically modified crops or animals.

©IBO 2007

GM crops and GM animals are referred to as Genetically Manipulated organisms (GMO's), also known as **transgenic** organisms. Their genetic material has been changed to include specific genes, usually from another species.

In 1994, the first genetically modified food sold commercially was introduced. It was the '**Flavr Savr**', a **tomato** that was genetically altered to stay fresh longer. This was achieved by adding another gene that blocked the gene for the production of an enzyme which caused rotting. Due to various commercial problems, the tomatoes are no longer available.

Bt corn is genetically modified maize. A gene from *Bacillus thuringiensis* (Bt) has been incorporated into the maize DNA. As a result, the plants produce a toxin that makes them resistant to insects. Bt corn crops are grown in the US.

There are also examples of genetically modified mice. Normally, mice do not contract polio because they do not have the receptor in their cell membranes that allows the polio virus to infect their cells. Adding this receptor, means that mice can be infected with polio and used for laboratory experiments in order to study the disease and its possible treatment and prevention. GM mice infected with polio will develop symptoms similar to humans with the disease.

Many people in the world who have rice as a very major part of their diet, suffer from vitamin A deficiency (VAD) which can lead to blindness. Countries most affected are in Africa and South America. *Refer to Figure 433.*

Rice plants store vitamin A in their leaves but not in the rice grains. **Golden rice** is genetically modified by adding genes from daffodils and from a bacterium. This allows the plant to store beta carotene, a precursor of vitamin A, in the grains, which causes the yellow colour. A new kind of Golden Rice has now been produced, using one gene from maize and a bacterium, which contains more than 20 times the amount of beta carotene compared to the first kind of Golden Rice.

This would provide a valuable source of vitamin A for many people but it has been met with a lot of opposition from environmentalists and anti-globalisationists.

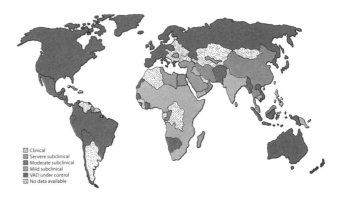

Figure 433   World map showing vitamin A deficiency

CORE

4.4.10 Discuss the potential benefits and possible harmful effects of one example of genetic modification.

©IBO 2007

Bt Corn

Bt corn *(Figure 435)* contains a gene from the *Bacillus thuringiensus* which produces a protein that is toxic to specific insects, in particular the European corn borer (ECB) *(Figure 434)*, which, despite its name, is also found in the US.

Figure 434
The European corn borer

Figure 435   Healthy corn

The ECB through stems and leaves of the corn plant and will damage vascular bundles and disrupt the transport of water and nutrients through the plant. It can also weaken the stems and leaves so that the plant or leaves may break. *See Figure 436.* Only a small part of the damage is caused by the ECB eating the corn directly.

Bt corn is already in commercial use.

Benefits of Bt corn

- The damage caused by the ECB is much reduced.
- Bt corn is slightly more expensive, but the difference is less than one extra application of insecticide.
- Non-Bt corn needs to be checked often for signs of ECB - less checking needed for Bt corn.

Figure 436   The effects of the beetle

Figure 437   The effects on a crop

- Less insecticide needed means less impact on the environment and lower health risks for the worker(s).
- Seems to reduce the infection with fungus so mycotoxin (poisons produced by fungi) levels are lowered. Mycotoxins are difficult to remove by cooking/freezing and may go into the food chain and be found in meat of animals which ate the infected corn. Mycotoxins can be a hazard to human and animal health.

Harmful effects of Bt corn

- Will also kill some other insects (though many are not affected).
- Insects may develop resistance to Bt toxin because they are exposed to it all the time.
- Resistant insects also make Bt spray useless as insecticide (Bt spray is considered to be relatively safe for humans and the environment).
- It is difficult to prevent pollen (with the Bt gene) from travelling outside the field where the Bt corn is grown
  - it may fertilise non-Bt corn e.g. organically grown corn which can then no longer be sold as organic corn.
  - it may fertilise wild relatives and make them more resistant to insects and have them dominate the niche they live in. This would result in loss of biodiversity.

4.4.11 Define *clone*.

©IBO 2007

A **clone** is a group of genetically identical organisms or a group of cells derived from a single parent cell.

TOK   Are GM crops safe?

One of the roles of natural science is to provide knowledge that may be used for informed decision-making. This leads to many questions. What decisions must be made by scientists to gain knowledge? What risks are involved in gaining knowledge? Do scientists have a special responsibility given the knowledge they gain? Who should be allowed to make decisions based on the knowledge gained through scientific research?

What is the role of education in society with regard to decision-making? Some argue that some science is too specialised for the public to understand and be able to make knowledgeable decisions. In this case the scientists should be entrusted with the ability to make decisions on behalf of the society in which they belong. Others argue that it the responsibility of

scientists to educate society so that it can gain knowledge, understanding and make corporate decisions. Should scientists be held morally responsible for the way their discoveries are applied or does the responsibility lie with the society that allowed research?

The case of genetically modified organisms raises all these questions and more. Genetic modification is illegal in some countries but widely encouraged in others. There are risks that must be carefully considered and weighed against the potential benefits. Would the more than 250,000 people who go blind each year from Vitamin A deficiency welcome genetically modified 'golden rice', in which each grain contains Vitamin A, or protest against its development? How seriously are the concerns of those opposed to genetic modification taken? Does protesting make the world a better place to live in? How should we decide how we use knowledge?

4.4.12   Outline a technique for cloning using differentiated animal cells.

©IBO 2007

Cloning is a controversial issue. The technique for cloning using differentiated cells is mostly **somatic** cell nuclear transfer (SCNT) but the use made of the produced cells can be quite different. Generally reproductive cloning and therapeutic cloning are discussed separately.

Figure 438   Dolly was the first cloned sheep

Figure 439   A mare and her cloned foal

REPRODUCTIVE CLONING

Reproductive cloning creates a new individual. The best known example is Dolly the sheep, shown in Figure 438. The technique used to create Dolly is known as **SCNT**. The concept is relatively simple and is illustrated in Figure 440. First you take a nucleus from a somatic (body) cell. In the case of Dolly, it was the nucleus from a cell in the udder of her "mother". The rest of the cell is no longer needed. The nucleus is then removed from an egg cell and replaced with the nucleus from the somatic cell. A small and brief electric shock is used to make the cell start dividing. Once it has grown into a group of cells, it can be implanted into a uterus where it will grow into a new individual, having the same genetic material in its nuclei as the individual who donated the

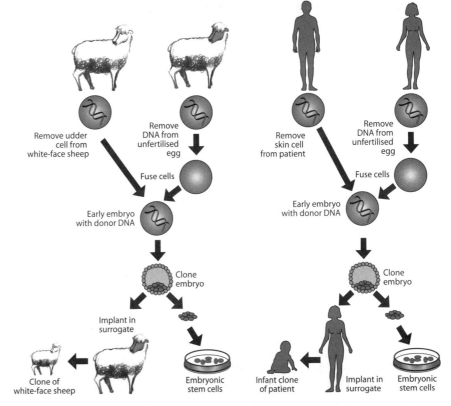

Figure 440   The method of cloning mammals

CORE

nucleus. The mitochondrial DNA will come from the donor of the egg cell.

As shown in Figure 439, it is theoretically possible to apply the same technique to cloning other species. Horses are an example of a species cloned successfully, but attempts with several other species have been less successful.

THERAPEUTIC CLONING

Therapeutic cloning involves stem cell research. In therapeutic cloning, human embryos are produced and allowed to grow for a few days into a small ball of cells. These cells are not yet specialised (totipotent or pluripotent) and when SCNT is used, the cells can grow into any of a large number different specialised tissues. Other sources of stem cells are cells from the umbilical cord or cells from aborted fetuses.

Therapeutic cloning often aims at cell therapy where diseased cells are replaced with healthy ones. Cell therapy is used for people suffering from Parkinson's disease but may also be possible when a patient has spinal cord injury.

Bone marrow transplants for patients with leukemia, new skin cells for burn victims and to grow new corneas for some forms of visual impairments are examples of therapeutic cloning already in use.

4.4.13	Discuss the ethical issues of therapeutic cloning in humans.
	©IBO 2007

A large number of websites can be found on the ethical issues of cloning.
Arguments in favour of therapeutic cloning focus on:
* the ability to cure serious diseases with cell therapy: currently leukemia and in the future possibly cancer and diabetes.

Some of the concerns raised about therapeutic cloning relate to :
* fears of it leading to reproductive cloning;
* use of embryonic stem cells involves the creation and destruction of human embryos (although it is possible to use embryos left over from IVF treatment which would be destroyed anyway);
* embryonic stem cells are capable of many divisions and may turn into tumours.

Ethical aspects of cloning are difficult to discuss since a lot of the benefits are currently not yet realised. They are potential benefits. Likewise, some of the disadvantages are

still unknown because we are not (yet?) cloning at a large scale. This could be an argument for carefully monitoring and regularly evaluating the results of any technological advances.

Many people have very clear opinions on the ethics of cloning and, as you can see from the websites, feel strongly about this issue. When trying to find some facts about cloning, it is not helpful that both sides accuse the other of misrepresenting the truth and/or selectively including or excluding information. It makes it very difficult for an outsider to have an informed opinion if you know that some of the information is incorrect and/or incomplete but you do not necessarily know which parts. Sometimes it helps to consider the source of the information : scientists may be more positive than justified, critics may be more negative. Overall, every person will have to come to his/her own conclusions but remember that 'other people, with their differences, can also be right' (*last part of the mission statement of IBO, http://www.ibo.org/mission*).

EXERCISES

1. Eukaryotic chromosomes are made of:
   A   DNA and lipids.
   B   DNA and protein.
   C   DNA and polysaccharides.
   D   lipids and protein.

2. A heritable factor that controls a specific characteristic, consisting of a length of DNA occupying a particular position on a chromosome known as a locus is a:
   A   chromosome
   B   gene
   C   allele
   D   genome

3. The total genetic material of an organelle, cell or organism is known as a:
   A   chromosome
   B   gene
   C   allele
   D   genome

4. A change in the base sequence of a gene is known as a:
   A   replication
   B   translation
   C   genome
   D   genetic mutation

5. The pairing up of the homologous chromosomes during Prophase I is known as:
   A   meiosis
   B   synapsis
   C   interphase
   D   telophase

6. Mendel's Law of Segregation is:
   A   The separation of the pair of parental factors, so that one factor is present in each gamete.
   B   The separation of the pair of parental factors, so that two factors are present in each gamete.
   C   Offspring resemble their parents.
   D   Offspring resemble the female parent.

7. The alleles possessed by an organism are known as the:
   A   Phenotype
   B   Dominant allele
   C   Genotype
   D   Recessive allele

8. An allele which has the same effect on the phenotype whether it is present in the homozygous or heterozygous state is known as a:
   A   Phenotype
   B   Dominant allele
   C   Genotype
   D   Recessive allele

9. The cells of an apple tree contain 34 chromosomes. What will the product of meiosis in the apple?
   A   2 cells, each with 34 chromosomes
   B   2 cells, each with 17 chromosomes
   C   4 cells, each with 34 chromosomes
   D   4 cells, each with 17 chromosomes

10. When identical twins marry *identical twins*, the children of both couples are genetically
    A   identical because of the low probability of random mutation
    B   different because of the high probability of random mutation
    C   identical unless crossing over takes place
    D   different because of random segregation of chromosomes during parental meiosis

11. If a tall garden pea is crossed with a dwarf garden pea, the F1 are all tall. Predict the result of self fertilisation of the F1, using a Punnett square.

12. In *Drosophila*, black body colour is recessive to wild type body colour. You have three sets of flies with wild type bodies designated A, B and C. You crossed A x B and obtained 112 wild type flies; A x C gave 78 wild type and 30 black-bodied; whilst B x C gave 86 wild type flies. Explain the expected genotypic and phenotypic ratios when flies A, B and C are crossed with flies having black bodies.
    w+ = wild type
    w = black

13. In a species of plant, petal colour is determined by one pair of alleles and stem length by another. The following experimental crosses were carried out.

Experiment A.
A yellow flowered plant was crossed with several white flowered plants. The F1 were all yellow flowered plants.

Experiment B.
A short stemmed plant was crossed with several long stemmed plants. The F1 were all short stemmed

Experiment C.

A different yellow flowered, short stemmed plant of the same species was crossed with several white flowered long stemmed plants.

The following F1 were grown.
  38 yellow flowered short stemmed
  35 white flowered short stemmed
  40 white flowered long stemmed
  37 yellow flowered long stemmed

(a) What are the dominant alleles?
(b) Give all genotypes in Experiment A and B.
(c) Explain the results of Experiment C using a Punnett square.

14 In mice, coat colour is controlled by several pairs of alleles, including the following:
A, wild type colour, dominant over a, black
C, coloured (i.e. pigmented), dominant over c, albino

(a) If a black individual, CCaa, is crossed with an albino, ccAA, what will be the appearance of the F1 generation?
(b) If an individual of the F1 generation is bred with another individual of the same genotype, what will be the appearance of the F2 generation?

Explain your answer using a Punnett square.

15 A baby has blood type B, his mother has blood type A, his paternal grandfather has blood type A, and his paternal grandmother has blood type B. Determine
(a) the genotype of the baby
(b) all possible genotypes

16 In shorthorn cattle the coat colour can be red, white or in the heterozygous condition, roan. In addition, the polled (without horns) condition is dominant to the horned condition.
(a) What will be the phenotypes and the genotypes of the F1 and F2 generations if homozygous polled red cattle are crossed with white horned cattle?
(b) How would you establish a pure breeding strain of red polled shorthorns from your F2 generation?

17 A boy called Mohammed and his sister Latifa have a brother who suffers from haemophilia. Their parents are normal.
(a) What are Mohammed's chances of having a haemophiliac child?
(b) What are Latifa's chances of having a haemophiliac child?

18 Compare the processes of mitosis and meiosis.

19 Photocopy the diagram below. Cut out the chromosomes. Find the homologous chromosome for each of the ones already given in the second diagram.

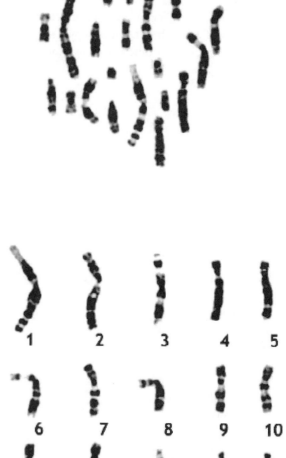

ECOLOGY AND EVOLUTION

5.1 Communities and ecosystems

5.2 The greenhouse effect

5.3 Populations

5.4 Evolution

5.5 Classification

5

CORE

5.1 COMMUNITIES AND ECOSYSTEMS

5.1.1 Define *species, habitat, population, community, ecosystem* and *ecology.*

©IBO 2007

SPECIES

A **species** is a group of organisms that can interbreed and produce fertile offspring.

HABITAT

A **habitat** is the environment in which a species normally lives or the natural location of a living organism.

POPULATION

A **population** is a group of organisms of the same species who live in the same area at the same time.

COMMUNITY

A (biological) **community** refers to a group of populations living and interacting with each other in an area.

ECOSYSTEM

An **ecosystem** is a community and its abiotic environment.

ECOLOGY

Ecology refers to the study of relationships between living organisms and organisms and their environment.

5.1.2 Distinguish between *autotroph* and *heterotroph.*

©IBO 2007

AUTOTROPH

An **autotroph** is an organism that synthesises its organic molecules from simple inorganic substances.

A **heterotroph** is an organism that obtains organic molecules from other organisms.

5.1.3 Distinguish between *consumers, detritivores* and *saprotrophs.*

©IBO 2007

Consumers, detritivores and saprotrophs are all heterotrophs.

CONSUMER

A (biological) **consumer** is an organism that ingests other organic matter that is living or has recently died.

DETRITIVORE

A **detritivore** is an organism that ingests dead organic matter (detritus).

SAPROTROPHS

A **saprotroph** is an organism that lives on, or in, dead organic matter, secreting digestive enzymes into it and absorbing the products of digestion.

5.1.4 Describe what is meant by a food chain, giving three examples, each with at least three linkages (four organisms).

©IBO 2007

A **food chain** describes the feeding relationships between species in a community. The arrows represent the molecules and energy as one organism is eaten by another. The first organism in a food chain is the producer, the second the primary consumer, the third the secondary consumer and so oon. *Refer to Figures 501, 502 and 503.*

5.1.5 Describe what is meant by a food web.

©IBO 2007

Very few animals feed on only one kind of organism and very few have only one predator. So a food chain often shows only a section of the feed relationships that exist. A **food web** will include more of these relationships and will show a more accurate representation of the very complex interactions between species. In reality, even food webs rarely show all relationships since this would make the web too complicated. An example of a marine food web is shown in Figure 504.

5.1.6 Define *trophic level*.

©IBO 2007

The trophic level is the position of the organism in a food chain. Producers are on the first trophic level, primary consumers on the second.

5.1.7 Deduce the trophic level of organisms in a food chain and a food web.

©IBO 2007

It is simple to deduce the trophic level of an organism from a food chain. In the Figures 501, 502 and 503, on the first trophic level (producers), we find phytoplankton, wheat and an oak tree respectively. Krill, locusts and wood mice are the second trophic level of these food chains.

Food webs are more complex. As shown in Figure 504, the fish can be on the third trophic level (phytoplankton → krill → fish) but also on the fourth trophic level (phytoplankton → other herbivorous zooplankton → squid → fish).

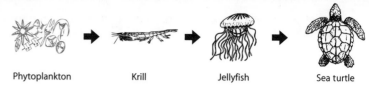

Phytoplankton   Krill   Jellyfish   Sea turtle

Figure 501   Marine food chain

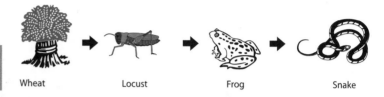

Wheat   Locust   Frog   Snake

Figure 502   Terrestrial food chain

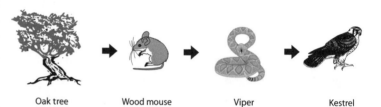

Oak tree   Wood mouse   Viper   Kestrel

Figure 503   Woodland food chain

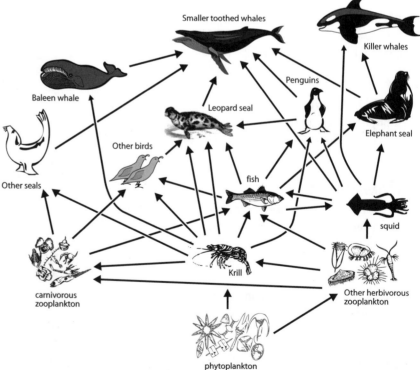

Figure 504   A marine food web

©IBO 2007

5.1.8 Construct a food web containing up to 10 organisms, using appropriate information.

Many of the species used in the food chains illustrated in Figures 501, 502 and 503 have been used to create the food web shown in Figure 505. Producers are usually shown at the bottom, full names of organisms should be used and the arrows show the movement of matter.

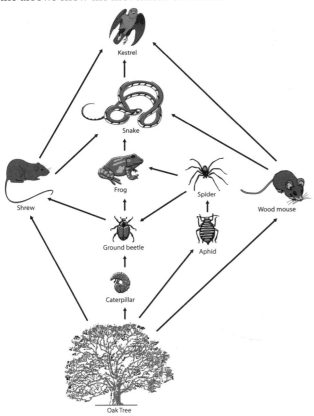

Figure 505   A sample food web

5.1.9 State that light is the initial energy source for almost all communities.

©IBO 2007

The first trophic level of any community consists of the producers or autotrophs. They use the energy from light to fix carbon dioxide, i.e. use light energy to produce (large) organic molecules from simple inorganic molecules such as carbon dioxide. Then it is used, directly or indirectly, by other organisms in the community as a source of energy.

5.1.10 Explain the energy flow in a food chain.

©IBO 2007

In order to obtain food, chew and digest it, energy is required. Animals also use energy to breathe, move and keep warm. So a lot of the energy that is taken into the

organism, will be used by this organism and will not be available to the next trophic level. As a very rough average, we can expect around 10% of the ingested energy to be available for the next trophic level; the other 90% is used by the organism itself.

This principle is illustrated in the Figure 506 assuming available input from sunlight of 7,283,333 kJ.

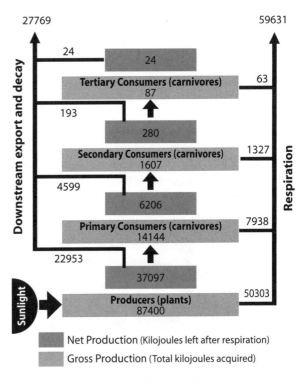

Figure 506   The flow of energy

Of course this is only an example. The figures are given in kilojoules per square metre per year (kJ/m²/yr).

It is easy to understand that, as the food chain becomes longer, more energy is needed at the first trophic level (producers) to sustain the top consumer(s).

5.1.11 State that energy transformations are never 100% efficient.

©IBO 2007

When energy is changed from one form into another, the transformation is never 100% efficient. This means that some energy will be changed into a form other than the intended form and will usually not be very useful.

An example would be the change of (potential) chemical energy in fuel (e.g. petrol) to kinetic energy when a car is moving. The bonnet of a car feels warm after it has been driven. The combustion of the fuel has produced heat which is a form of energy not useful for moving the car.

The same applies to organisms. Figure 507 shows the energy use in a mouse.

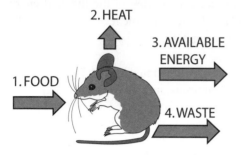

Figure 507   Energy use in a mouse

The efficiency of the **energy transformations** depend on a number of factors. Looking at Figure 508 of a snake eating a mouse, the difference in the amount of heat lost to the environment by the two animals becomes clear.

Figure 508   A snake eating a mouse

The energy lost to the environment as heat needs to come from the food that the organism eats. This helps to explain why birds and mammals, which have a constant body temperature, need to eat much more per kg body mass than, for example, reptiles which do not.

5.1.12	Explain the reasons for the shape of pyramids of energy.

©IBO 2007

A **pyramid of energy** is a graphical representation of the amount of energy of each trophic level in a food chain. The units are kJ/m²/yr. The pyramid will never be inverted since it is based on the amount of energy per unit area that flows through the trophic level of the food chain in a given amount of time.

In order to produce a pyramid of energy, it is necessary to find out how much energy an organism contains and how many organisms there are in a trophic level. The amount

of energy in an organism can only be found by burning (i.e. destroying) one of these organisms. *Refer Figure 509.*

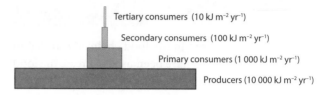

Figure 509   An example of an energy pyramid

5.1.13	Explain that energy enters and leaves ecosystems, but nutrients must be recycled.

©IBO 2007

As was shown in Figure 509, energy enters the system as sunlight. Some of it is absorbed and stored in products of photosynthesis by autotrophs. Then it is gradually used as these products make their way through the trophic levels. Finally all energy captured in chemical bonds will have been changed to other forms of energy which cannot be passed on.

So energy is NOT recycled through the **ecosystem**. The earth constantly receives energy from the sun and also constantly radiates out energy in the form of light and heat. The earth, however, does not receive nor send out matter on a regular basis. This means that nutrients must be recycled through the ecosystems. The process of recycling nutrients requires energy.

5.1.14	State that saprotrophic bacteria and fungi (decomposers) recycle nutrients.

©IBO 2007

All living things die sooner or later. For some, this may be sooner than anticipated if they are eaten, others may live out their full life span. Regardless of how long they live, however, all living things produce organic waste during their life. Somehow, the organic nutrients need to be returned to the soil as inorganic minerals to allow the cycling of elements to start again.

Various names are used relating to the group of organisms involved in this cyclical process. **Decomposers** are organisms that obtain their energy from dead organisms. Two main groups are **detritivores** (e.g. earthworms and dung beetles) and **saprotrophs** (e.g. fungi and bacteria). Saprotrophs absorb soluble organic compounds while detritivores ingest (parts of) dead plants or animals. These processes are essential for the cycling of nutrients.

5.2 THE GREENHOUSE EFFECT

> **5.2.1** Draw and label a diagram of the carbon cycle to show the processes involved.
>
> ©IBO 2007

The carbon cycle includes **photosynthesis**, cell respiration, combustion and fossilisation. Only the first of these processes removes carbon dioxide from the atmosphere; the other three add to levels of carbon dioxide.

Figure 510 shows a schematic diagram of the processes involved in the carbon cycle.

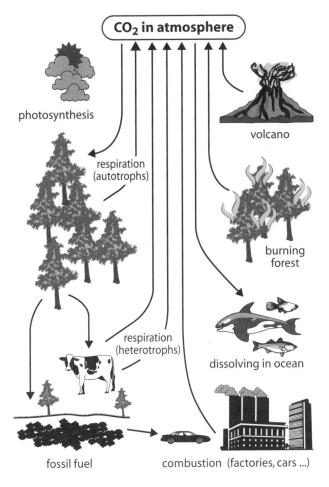

Figure 510 *The processes involved in the carbon cycle*

> **TOK   What are metaphors in science?**
>
> Metaphors are helpful in relating a concept that we are unfamiliar with to one that we are. Metaphors help us to connect ideas and develop new knowledge. Organelles are often related to body parts to introduce their function, for example the nucleus is like a brain of a cell. The Gaia hypothesis is a metaphor for ecosystems, stating that each is like a finely tuned machine, with the functioning of the whole dependent on the individual parts.
>
> Try to explain an ecosystem in terms of this metaphor. How helpful are metaphors in understanding the Biological principle? Should the 'Gaia hypothesis' really have the status of a hypothesis if it is a metaphor?

> **5.2.2** Analyse the changes in concentration of atmospheric carbon dioxide using historical records.
>
> ©IBO 2007

From Figure 511 (which relates to the Northern Hemisphere), it can be seen that the average carbon dioxide concentration has increased since 1960 from around 315 ppm (0.0315%) to 380 ppm (0.0380%). The graph is not smooth but goes up and down to reflect the changes in the amount of atmospheric carbon dioxide due to the seasons; in autumn, the leaves drop and plants no longer take up carbon dioxide. As a result, atmospheric carbon dioxide levels go up. In spring, when plants grow leaves again and start to photosynthesise, the levels drop.

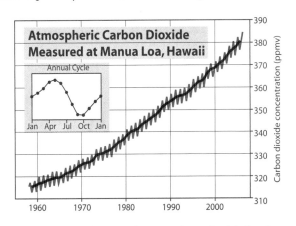

Figure 511 *Atmospheric carbon dioxide levels*

CORE

5.2.3 Explain the relationship between the rises in concentrations of atmospheric carbon dioxide, methane and oxides of nitrogen and the enhanced greenhouse effect.

©IBO 2007

Comparing the temperatures in Figure 512 with the carbon dioxide concentrations in Figure 511, it can be seen that both have been increasing since 1960. As was shown in *Topic 1.1.6*, the existence of a correlation does not establish a causal relationship, i.e. it does not mean that one causes the other. Yet, many factors suggest that the increase in average yearly temperatures is, at least in part, caused by the additional carbon dioxide in the air.

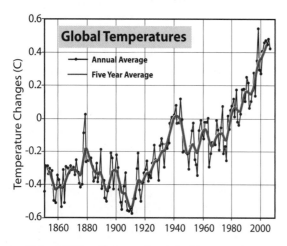

Figure 512   Changes in global temperatures

Longer term studies involve the use of ice from the polar regions. Scientists in Antarctica have taken samples of the ice, each which contain small amounts of air. Although the entire theory is complicated, in principle the idea is that the deeper you drill to get your ice, the "older" the air will be. When the ice is crushed, you can get the air and use a gas chromatograph to measure the level of carbon dioxide. The results found from this kind of measurement are shown in Figure 513.

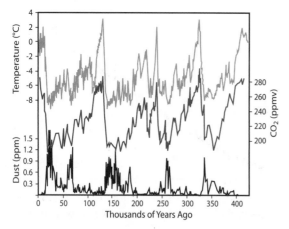

Figure 513   The results of historical atmospheric studies

The last Ice Age began around 70 000 years ago, reached it coldest time around 18 000 years ago and ended about 10 000 years ago. These data provide a longer perspective of atmospheric composition.

Most energy from the Sun reaches the Earth in the form of light radiation which has relatively short wavelengths. About 30% of this is reflected back into space. The remaining 70% warms up the Earth's surface and will eventually radiate out as infra red radiation, which has much longer wavelengths.

THE GREENHOUSE EFFECT

The **greenhouse effect** is the common name for the fact that some gases in the Earth's atmosphere (greenhouse gases) absorb some of the infra red radiation, with the longer wavelength, that would otherwise leave the Earth. As a result, the Earth is about 30°C warmer than it would be without any greenhouse gases in the atmosphere. That would be too cold to sustain life, so having some greenhouse gases has been very important to life on Earth. These naturally occurring greenhouse gases have been around for a long time but the enhanced or anthropogenic ("made by people") greenhouse effect is currently a cause for concern. *Refer to Figure 514.*

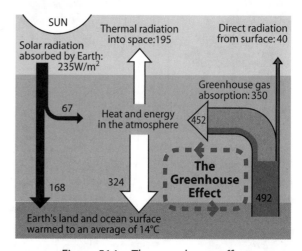

Figure 514   The greenhouse effect

The name "greenhouse effect" is based on the observation that the temperature inside a greenhouse (made of glass) is higher than outside. The heat seems to be trapped inside. This also happens on Earth but the mechanism that keeps the heat inside a greenhouse is actually quite different from the mechanism of absorption of infrared radiation by the Earth's atmosphere.

Most of the atmosphere is made of nitrogen (N_2) and oxygen (O_2). Neither of these gases absorbs much infra red radiation. None of the gases in the atmosphere really absorbs the shorter wavelength light radiation coming in from the Sun.

Carbon dioxide (CO_2), methane (CH_4) and oxides of nitrogen (NO_x) are the best known examples of greenhouse gases. Methane contributes much more (20 times) to the greenhouse effect than carbon dioxide but they all operate on the same principle. Greenhouse gases absorb the longer wavelength infrared radiation which prevents it from escaping into space. As a result of the radiation spending a longer time in the atmosphere, the temperature of the atmosphere is slightly increased as can be seen in Figure 515.

The Intergovernmental Panel on Climate Change produced a report about global warming in February 2007. It can found at http://www.ipcc.ch/SPM2feb07.pdf.

The report states the following:

"Global atmospheric concentrations of carbon dioxide, methane and nitrous oxide have increased markedly as a result of human activities since 1750 and now far exceed pre-industrial values determined from ice cores spanning many thousands of years [see Figure 515]. The global increases in carbon dioxide concentration are due primarily to fossil fuel use and land-use change, while those of methane and nitrous oxide are primarily due to agriculture."

One concern is that the increasing temperature will melt some of the frozen tundras in Siberia which could release a lot of methane gas. This would be a positive feedback cycle that might be difficult to break.

5.2.4   Outline the precautionary principle

©IBO 2007

The **precautionary principle** is the concept that someone wishing to take a certain kind of action should prove that the action does not cause serious or irreversible harm to the public if there is no scientific consensus about the outcome of the action.

In slightly simpler wording, it means that if we are not certain what the results of a change in our behaviour will be, the people wanting this change should prove that it will not be harmful.

The precautionary principle is often applied to situations involving the environment, our health, food and medicine. These are aspects that concern all of us and therefore need to be dealt with carefully. An application of the precautionary principle can be seen in legalisation of new medication; the producer needs to prove that the medicine

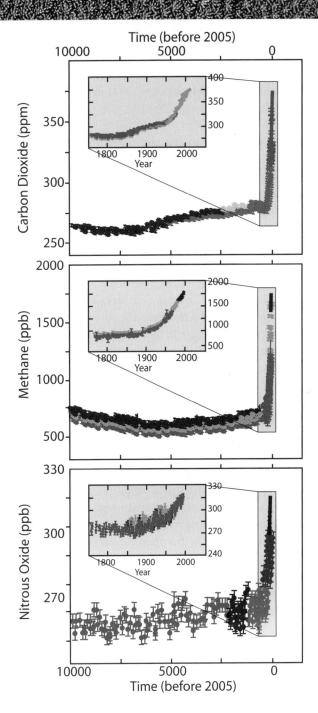

Figure 515   Changes in greenhouse gases

will do what it promises and that it has no serious and/or lasting side effects. The same is applied to food additives; they are not allowed unless they have been proven safe.

In many other situations, the proof needs to be given by the person who is resisting the change. They will then need to prove that the change will cause harm. Sometimes this is difficult to prove and putting the responsibility for proof with the other party (who needs to prove it will do NO harm) makes it less likely that the change will be approved.

CORE

Both the European Union and the United Nations have adopted the precautionary principle as a foundation for some of their policies. Examples are the Montreal Protocol (1987) and the Rio Declaration (1992) of the UN and the Maastricht Treaty (1993) of the EU.

Not everyone agrees with the precautionary principle as a basis for environmental policies. The principle is sometimes summed up as "do no harm". However, in environmental policies, this alternative does not always exist. Those opposing the principle also claim that the principle includes assumptions of consequences that have not been proven and that the principle is more concerned with the degree of seriousness of possible consequences than with the chance of them actually occurring. Most people do not plan their life for the event of winning a multi-million lottery. If they win, the consequence is likely to be a significant change in their life. Yet, this is not really considered when buying the ticket since the chance of this event occurring is so small.

Another criticism of the precautionary principle is that it is sometimes only applied to new technology and not to the technology it would replace. We do not know exactly what the effects of large scale construction of wind turbines, like the ones shown in Figure 516, will be. They are likely to include noise pollution, visual pollution of the landscape and the death of birds who collide with the wings. The precautionary principle would suggest that we do not include wind energy in our plans for the future. However, if that means we will continue to generate electricity, using coal, oil or other fossil fuels, without applying the precautionary principle, we might not have taken the best decision.

Figure 516   Wind turbines

A third criticism of the precautionary principle is that it is often used to scare people with doomsday scenarios because "fear is funding". This would benefit those involved in the research but not necessarily the rest of the population.

TOK   The precautionary principle

The legal presumption of innocence that is central to the operation of most societies has long been extended to natural science, that is, it is assumed that human actions are not detrimental to the environment unless proven otherwise. The precautionary principle is the reverse of this approach, i.e. that a proposal may proceed unless proven to be detrimental. It does not presume that all human impacts on the environment innocent. As humans, we often forget that we are unique in our far-reaching ability to change the natural world.

The precautionary principle is now applied to many activities in developed countries where governments increasingly insist that development of natural resources is conditional upon assurances that the environment will not be harmed and that fragile habitats or species will not be threatened.

The full impact of unchecked human activity upon the biosphere is now becoming obvious. Climate change and the degradation of fresh water supplies could be seen as a consequence of the precautionary principle not being applied as humans have developed the natural world over the last two decades. The application of the precautionary principle now is argued as essential by many in the scientific community in the areas of issues affecting climate change and fresh water. These are global issues that reach far beyond the borders of politics, culture and language. To take action in these areas requires a substantial economic cost. Should this cost be borne by developed countries that have had decades or centuries of economic benefit from their environmentally costly actions or should it be shared by all societies? Should economically developed countries assist the poor in developing countries who have been affected by the consequences of climate change?

The solution to these issues lies in international co-operation founded on the desire to protect the biosphere for all of its inhabitants, current and future, regardless of their species.

5.2.5	Evaluate the precautionary principle as a justification for strong action in response to the threats posed by the enhanced greenhouse effect.
	©IBO 2007

Since we are not sure what the exact effects of increasing carbon dioxide levels are, the precautionary principle could be applied. Countries could agree to reduce greenhouse emissions and boycott trade with countries that do not comply. However, in poorer countries, it may not be possible to reduce greenhouse emissions without delaying economic growth. This in itself may cause hunger and even cause large numbers of people to die. For some, the consequence of the precautionary principle might be worse than the consequence it is trying to avoid.

When trying to work out which action to take, it might make sense to prioritise some possibilities. For example, immediate danger should be dealt with before causes that are dangerous later on. Another one could be that human life comes before environmental concerns and the more likely it is that something can become a threat, the more we need to deal with it. If we agree with most of the previously mentioned priorities, however, we are putting off the effects of increasing carbon dioxide levels since they do not present a certain and immediate risk to human life.

On the other hand, we can look back to the fourth century BCE when Chinese philospher Lao Tzu wrote that 'small problems are easy to solve but, when not solved are likely to grow into big problems'.

5.2.6	Outline the consequences of a global temperature rise on arctic ecosystems.
	©IBO 2007

A global temperature rise would affect many ecosystems but the effects would be clearly visible on arctic ecosystems as shown in Figure 517.

The average temperature in the arctic region is rising at twice the speed compared to the rest of the world. This results in the polar cap shrinking. There used to be a fresh water lake on the Ward Hunt Shelf. The shelf started to melt, broke and this rare ecosystem drained into the ocean and disappeared forever.

The snow and ice covering the Arctic reflects a lot of the Sun's radiation. When this snow and ice melts, the Arctic will absorb more heat and warm up even faster. Melting permafrost in Siberia would release more methane which is a greenhouse gas. This is an example of positive feedback, which, in biology, usually has undesirable consequences.

Many species are changing their migration patterns to respond to changes in their feeding patterns. This includes caribou, polar bears and seals and as a result, Native People of the Arctic find it more difficult to hunt them. In addition, many villages have to move since their environment is turning into a swamp as a result of the permafrost disappearing.

Higher temperatures melt the snow in polar bears' (*shown in Figure 518*) dens sooner which shortens their hibernation. Thin ice, which is at times even absent, means that polar bears have to swim more often to reach their destination and/or prey. They are good swimmers but the process is slow and takes a lot of energy.

One possible advantage is that the melting the arctic ice will give us access to more oil and gas reserves but again this could lead to positive feedback.

Many of the plant species in the Arctic survive because there is little competition. A milder climate would enable other species to survive in the Arctic and they could possibly compete with the specialised native species which might disappear as a result of this competition. This would reduce biodiversity but also change the food available to herbivores like the caribou. However, overall, the plant productivity might increase which would increase the number of species (biodiversity) in this area.

Figure 517 (a) and (b)   Comparisons of sea-ice from (a) 1979 and (b)2003

Figure 518   Polar bears will be affected

5.3 POPULATIONS

CORE

5.3.1	Outline how population size is affected by natality, immigration, mortality and emigration.

©IBO 2007

Four factors exist which influence the size of a **population** (*refer to Figure 519*):

- natality (birth rate)
- mortality (death rate)
- immigration ('moving in')
- emigration ('moving out')

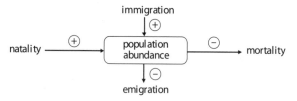

Figure 519   Factors influencing population size

5.3.2	Draw and label a graph showing a sigmoid (S-shaped) population growth curve.

©IBO 2007

Figure 520 is a graph which is known as a sigmoid (S-shaped) growth curve.

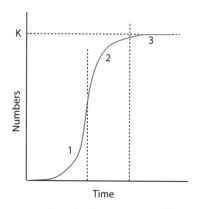

Figure 520   The sigmoid growth curve

5.3.3	Explain reasons for the exponential growth phase, the plateau phase and the transitional phase between these two phases.

©IBO 2007

Figure 520 shows the number of individuals in a population over time. Any population has the potential to increase its numbers quickly. In most natural situations, this increase in numbers is controlled by limiting factors.

Limiting factors are factors that will place restrictions on the amount a population can grow (*see Topic 5.3.4*).

In Figure 520, a typical sigmoidal curve, three stages are indicated:

1. Exponential growth phase.
2. Transitional phase.
3. Plateau phase.

EXPONENTIAL GROWTH PHASE

In this stage, there is unlimited growth of the population due to the absence of limiting factors. The growth could follow the pattern 1, 2, 4, 8, 16, 32 etc if we talk about bacteria where each bacterium divides into two every twenty minutes.

TRANSITIONAL PHASE

In this stage, limiting factors start influencing the rate of increase of the population. The number of individuals is still increasing but no longer at an exponential rate. It is the transition from exponential growth to no growth.

PLATEAU PHASE

In this stage, the number of individuals of the population no longer increases, due to limiting factors. Natality + immigration = mortality + emigration. Natural selection (survival of the fittest) is taking place. The population has reached the carrying capacity of the environment.

Carrying capacity refers to the maximum number of individuals of a species that can be sustainably supported by the environment. This is shown by 'K in Figure 520.

5.3.4	List three factors that set limits to population increase.

©IBO 2007

Limiting factors are those factors that control a process such as population growth.

Examples of limiting factors for animal populations are:
- amount of food available
- presence of parasites and/or disease
- amount of predation
- available nesting sites

Examples of limiting factors for plant populations are:
- amount of light available
- temperature
- amount of carbon dioxide
- amount of water available

5.4 EVOLUTION

Although there seems to be a lot of evidence to support **evolution**, there are also people who doubt the evidence and make a case against evolution. Many websites can be found supporting the concept of evolution. Equally there are many websites that do not support the concept of evolution.

IB students are expected to gain knowledge about many aspects of Biology. Since evolution is one of these aspects, students are expected to be familiar with the concepts presented in this section. At a personal level, students may choose to accept or reject the possibility of evolution.

5.4.1	Define *evolution*.

©IBO 2007

Evolution is the cumulative change in the heritable characteristics of a population.

For evolution to take place, it is necessary to have two separate processes taking place:
1. a source of variation between individuals of one species
2. a change in the frequency of the genes in the gene pool of a population

The source of variation can be mutation, crossing over and/or independent assortment *(see Topic 5.4.6)*. A change in the gene frequency can be caused by natural selection. Natural selection assumes that if certain (combinations of) alleles will make the individual better adapted to its environment, then that individual is likely to have a larger number of offspring survive to reproductive age. Since the individual will pass on its genetic material, the offspring will have some of the successful alleles which are then likely to become more frequent in the population over time.

5.4.2	Outline the evidence for evolution provided by the fossil record, selective breeding of domesticated animals and homologous structures.

©IBO 2007

FOSSIL RECORD

The fossil record consists of all fossils, discovered and undiscovered that exist. Fossils are the mineralised remains of organisms. Fossilisation is the process that produces fossils. Normally, dead organisms decompose quickly, leaving little trace. However, if they are covered by sediment soon after they die, they may, totally or in part, become fossils. Fossilisation does not happen very often so we only have an incomplete fossil record of, for example, human evolution.

One of the most complete fossil records found has shown us the evolution of the horse. The study of fossil skeletons allows inferences about form and function and clearly suggests a process of gradual change over time as shown in Figure 521.

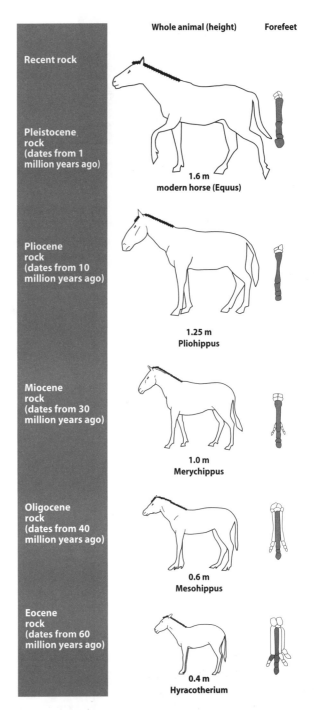

Figure 521   The evolution of the horse

CORE

SELECTIVE BREEDING OF DOMESTICATED

ANIMALS

Humans and dogs share a long history. It is very likely that dogs were the first animals to be domesticated by humans. In the early days of the partnership, dogs must have looked like wolves and were probably used for hunting and pulling sledges. Dogs may also have played a role in magic or religious rituals.

Figure 522   A Dalmatian dog

As breeding started, selection must have taken place. By selecting the best hunters for hunting, the strongest dogs for pulling sledges and the most unusual for rituals, humans made the start to the many different breeds of dog we know today.

Figure 522 shows a Dalmatian breed of dog, originally bred as a hunting dog and now a popular pet.

HOMOLOGOUS STRUCTURES

Evolution suggests that many different species may have originated from a common ancestor. This pattern of divergence would then suggest that they should still have some things in common. These structures do exist and are called **homologous structures**. Their existence supports the concept of evolution.

Human arms are similar in structure to the front paws of a dog, the wings of a bat and the flipper of a dolphin. The structure is called the pentadactyl limb (="five fingered") and it is common to all tetrapods. They all have the same bones, although the relative size of the bones may differ. *Refer Figure 523.*

5.4.3	State that populations tend to produce more offspring than the environment can support.

©IBO 2007

Most species are capable of producing many more offspring than the environment can support. Even elephants with a gestation time of 22 months can produce a large population over time if there are no factors limiting the growth of the population.

5.4.4	Explain that the consequence of the potential overproduction of offspring is a struggle for survival

©IBO 2007

Individuals in a population are not identical. The differences between them will make some more suited to their particular environment at a particular time than others. Where there are too many individuals in a population, there will be competition for resources such as food (for animals) or light (for plants). This competition between individuals in a population will allow the more successful individuals to grow faster and they will be able to produce more offspring (or seeds). In the case of some animals, they may also be able to provide more nourishment and/ or care for their offspring so that a greater number of them

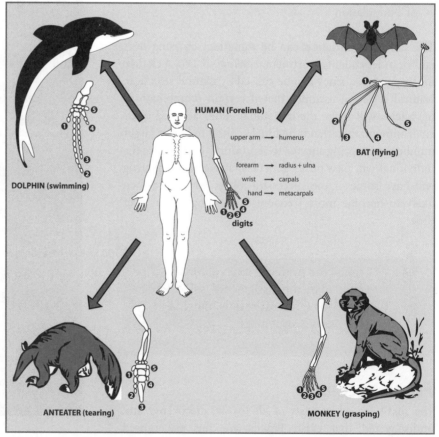

Figure 523   Homologous forelimbs in mammals

will survive. The offspring will carry some of the genes that made the parents better adapted so the offspring may also be more successful and pass on their genes more successfully. This struggle for survival between individuals of the same species (or even between species sharing the same habitat) is called **natural selection**.

5.4.5   State that the members of a species
         show variation.
                                              ©IBO 2007

Due to independent assortment and crossing over in meiosis, the gametes produced by one individual are not identical. In sexual reproduction, two gametes need to fuse to produce a new individual. As a results, individuals are different from each other. This is called variation.

5.4.6   Explain how sexual reproduction
         promotes variation in a species.
                                              ©IBO 2007

In *Topic 4.2.3*, meiosis is discussed in detail. There are two processes in meiosis that can cause variation:

- independent assortment
- crossing over

INDEPENDENT ASSORTMENT

Independent assortment occurs during Metaphase I when the homologous pairs of chromosomes (also known as bivalents or tetrads) move to the equator of the cell and line up. In Figure 524 an example is given of an imaginary organism (2*n* = 4). There are two possibilities for the homologous pairs to arrange themselves on the equator and each will result in the formation of different gametes. One cell undergoing meiosis might go through the process as drawn under Possibility 1 whereas the next cell might go through Possibility 2. So an individual could produce all four kinds of gametes.

CROSSING OVER

Crossing over occurs during Prophase I when the homologous chromosomes pair up (and form bivalents or tetrads). Each chromosome consists of

two identical sister chromatids. When the non-sister chromatids overlap, they may break and re-attach to the other chromosome, exchanging genetic material as is shown in *Figure 407 in Chapter 4*.

Both of these processes will cause the gametes to differ from each other resulting in variation between the offspring of one set of parents.

5.4.7   Explain how natural selection leads to
         evolution.
                                              ©IBO 2007

When a population produces more offspring than the environment can support, the individuals of the population will compete with each other for resources such as food and shelter. The variation between the individuals (resulting from independent assortment and crossing over during gametogenesis before the process of sexual reproduction) will make some more successful in this struggle for survival than others. The more successful ones are likely to also be more successful in reproduction, passing on the genes that made them successful. After one generation, there will be slightly more of the advantageous genetic traits than the others. The situation will repeat itself and after many generations, the advantageous genetic traits will be very common. As the process continues, the other genetic traits may disappear completely from the gene pool of the population and all individuals will be the kind that is more successful. As this process describes "the cumulative change in the heritable characteristics of a population", we call it evolution (*see Topic 5.4.1*).

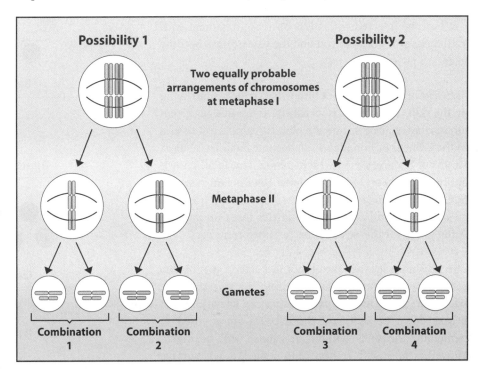

Figure 524   Independent assortment of chromosomes

CORE

5.4.8   Explain two examples of evolution in response to environmental change; one must be antibiotic resistance in bacteria.
©IBO 2007

If a species cannot adapt to the changing environment, then the species will die out. As the dinosaurs did not find a way to deal with the climate becoming colder, they did not survive. Their place was taken by the homeothermic (warm-blooded) mammals.

ANTIBIOTIC RESISTANCE IN BACTERIA

Antibiotic resistance means that bacteria can survive in the presence of an antibiotic.

Penicillin, one of the first antibiotics discovered, is not effective over the entire field of microorganisms pathogenic to humans. During the 1950s, the search for antibiotics to fill this gap resulted in a steady stream of them, some with a much wider antibacterial range than penicillin (the so-called *broad-spectrum* antibiotics) and some capable of coping with those microorganisms that are inherently resistant to penicillin or that have developed resistance through long-term exposure to penicillin.

Many diseases caused by bacteria have been successfully treated with penicillin and other antibiotics. However, since the Second World War, when the use of antibiotics became widespread, many disease-causing bacteria have developed resistance against antibiotics. There are strains of bacteria that cause tuberculosis which are resistant to all known antibiotics. Cholera is almost the same, as there is only one effective antibiotic available. This means that if you become infected with these bacteria, treatment with antibiotics will not cure you and the disease may become fatal.

Staphylococcus aureus is a common bacterium found living on the skin. This species is usually harmless but, in certain circumstances, can invade the bloodstream, infect tissues in the kidneys or bones and can become fatal. These days, strains of *S. aureus* exist which are resistant to all known antibiotics. These MRSA bacteria (methicillin-resistant *Staphylococcus aureus*) are of grave concern to hospitals all over the world and some countries insist on patients being tested for this strain of bacteria before surgery.

The resistance against antibiotics in bacteria is probably caused by a spontaneous mutation. As a result, the bacterium produces e.g. penicillinase, an enzyme which breaks down penicillin. If the bacteria are exposed to penicillin, the ones without resistance will be killed. However, those with resistance to penicillin, will survive and, due to a lack of competition, grow rapidly. The genetic information for antibiotic resistance is often found on plasmids which can be spread rapidly over a population and can even cross over into other species of bacteria.

Antibiotic resistance is more likely to occur when a small dose of antibiotics is used for a short time. It will kill some of the bacteria but not all and may lead to the creation of bacteria that have some resistance. An example of this is depicted in Figure 525. The next time antibiotics are used, these bacteria are less vulnerable and some more of them may survive. Repeated use of small doses of antibiotics can produce very resistant strains. This explains why doctors always insist on patients finishing the course of antibiotics even if they feel better much before that time.

Antibiotics are sometimes considered 'wonder drugs'. They are certainly very powerful and very effective and we must take measures to keep them this way.

Antibiotics do not work against viral disease and will not cure the flu or the common cold. It may be difficult (and time consuming) for a doctor to explain this to a patient asking for antibiotics to cure his cold and sometimes it is easier to give the patient what he or she wants!

In the USA, half the livestock is fed antibiotics. This happens not because they are ill, but to increase the growth of the animals. As can be expected, this has led to strains of antibiotic-resistant bacteria being discovered in the gut of these animals. The same genes for antibiotic resistance have since been discovered in human guts and this may also be attributed to over-use of antibiotics.

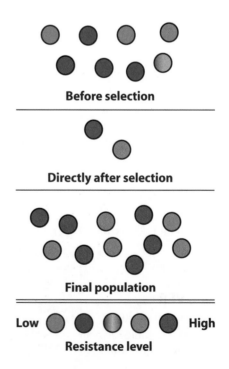

Figure 525   How antibiotic resistance arises

Bacteria may pass on the gene for antibiotic resistance to other bacteria, even of a different species. So harmless bacteria living in our gut that posses antibiotic resistance could pass on the resistance to pathogenic (disease causing) bacteria, which could have serious consequences.

PEPPERED MOTH

Another example of evolution in response to environmental change can be found in the case of the peppered moth and is shown in Figure 526. *Biston betularia* (peppered moth) is found near Manchester, England and elsewhere in the UK. Before 1848, trees on which the moths rested were covered with off-white lichen. The moths were speckled and therefore camouflaged from predation by birds. Occasionally a black moth would appear. It, of course, was highly visible on the lichen-covered trees and would have a very high chance of being eaten by a bird before reproducing.

Due to (coal-based) industry, the trees became covered with soot and the white moths were easily spotted and eaten. The dark (melanic) form now had the advantage and became predominant (95%) in certain areas in 1850. Reduced use of coal has now made the trees green (covered in algae) and both forms are common. This is called balanced polymorphism.

The environment before 1848 was such that the white moth was the best adapted. However, when the environment changed, the black moth became the best adapted. This is a simple and short-term example of evolution.

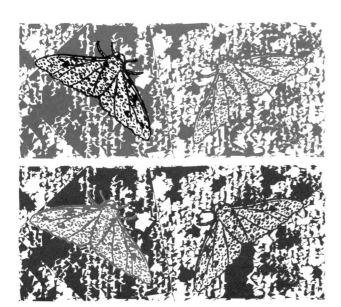

Figure 526   Changes in the peppered moth population

5.5 CLASSIFICATION

5.5.1	Outline the binomial system of nomenclature.

©IBO 2007

CORE

The **binomial system** of nomenclature was designed by Carolus Linneaus, also known as Carl von Linné, in the 18th century *(Figure 527)*. Linneaus' idea is still the basis of the binomial system today. It is based on the idea that every species has a Latin name, made up of two parts.

Figure 527   Carolus Linnaeus

TOK   Social context

Carolus Linnaeus is best known as the scientist who devised binomial classification. When Linnaeus classified humans he defined four subgroups within the human species based on observation and understanding of physical and social traits. For example, he described Europeans as "changeable, clever, and inventive, ... putting on tight clothing ... governed by laws." These descriptions were made within a specific historical and cultural context. It is important to consider knowledge claims in the light of the social context in which they are made. Today differences within the human species would be acknowledged but treated according to the current social context. This context, however, will still differ from culture to culture.

The first part is the name of the genus, the second part specifies the species. The name should be printed in italics (or underlined when handwritten) and the first part (but not the second) is capitalised. Humans are *Homo sapiens*.

CORE

> 5.5.2 List seven levels in the hierarchy of taxa—kingdom, phylum, class, order, family, genus and species—using an example from two different kingdoms for each level.
>
> ©IBO 2007

A kingdom is the largest group in the system of classification. A kingdom consists of one or more phyla (singular: phylum) which is divided into one or more classes, which is divided into one or more orders, which is divided into one or more families, which is divided into one or more genera (singular: genus), which is divided into one or more species.

The classifications of *Homo sapiens* and *Taraxacum officinale*, the dandelion, are illustrated in Figure 528. Images are shown in Figures 529 and 530.

taxa (=level of hierarchy)	dandelion	human
KINGDOM	Plantae	Animalia
PHYLUM	Tracheophyta	Chordata
CLASS	Angiospermae	Mammalia
ORDER	Asterales	Prima
FAMILY	Asteraceae	Hominidae
GENUS	Taraxacum	Homo
SPECIES	*Taraxacum officinale*	*Homo sapiens*

Figure 528   The classification of two species

Figure 529   A dandelion

Figure 530   Two humans on horses (all mammals)

> 5.5.3 Distinguish between the following phyla of plants, using simple external recognition features: *bryophyta, filicinophyta, coniferophyta* and *angiospermophyta*.
>
> ©IBO 2007

BRYOPHYTA

Mosses and liverworts *(Figure 531)*

- small terrestrial plants
- do not have true roots, stems or leaves but they might have structures resembling them
- leaf-like structures are often arranged in a spiral
- usually live in clusters which act like sponges holding water

Figure 531
A cluster of moss plants

Figure 532
A fern plant

FILICINOPHYTA

Ferns *(Figure 532)*

- have true leaves
- new leaves unroll
- have an underground creeping stem (rhizome)

CONIFEROPHYTA

Conifers *(Figure 533)*

- all conifers are woody plants, most are trees with a single wooden trunk with side branches
- leaves are long thin needles, often arranged in spirals, often a dark green colour
- produce seeds found in cones

ANGIOSPERMOPHYTA

Flowering plants *(Figure 534)*

- have flowers, although they may be small in wind-pollinated angiospermophyta
- seeds are in ovaries which become the fruit
- leaves usually as leaf blade and leaf stalk, with veins visible on the lower surface

Figure 533
A conifer

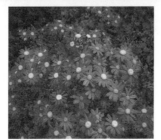

Figure 534
A flowering plant

Figure 535
A sponge

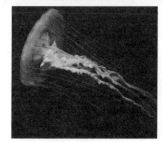

Figure 536
A jellyfish

Figure 537
A flatworm

Figure 538
An earthworm

Figure 539
A clam

Figure 540
A ladybird beetle is an
arthropod

> 5.5.4 Distinguish between the following phyla of animals, using simple external recognition features: *porifera, cnidaria, platyhelminthes, annelida, mollusca* and *arthropoda*.
>
> ©IBO 2007

All of these groups are invertebrates - animals without backbones.

PORIFERA

Sponges *(Figure 535)*

- most primitive animals with a simple body
- live in water
- do not move around
- no mouth, but many small holes through which water is pumped into body
- filter water for food and pump it out through larger holes

CNIDARIA

Jellyfish *(Figure 536)* and sea anemones

- have stinging cells (cnidocytes)
- radially symmetrical
- have a gastro-vascular cavity (hollow space in the centre of the body)
- one opening to cavity
- often have tentacles around the opening

PLATYHELMINTHES

Flatworms *(Figure 537)*

- soft flattened body, definite head region
- bilateral symmetry
- gastro-vascular cavity (hollow space in the centre of the body)
- usually one opening to cavity
- live in water or damp environment
- can be free-living but often are parasitic

ANNELIDA

Worms *(Figure 538)* and leeches

- bodies of ring-like segments
- have mouth and anus
- live in water/moist earth
- may be free-living or parasitic
- no legs
- bristles from body which help movement

MOLLUSCA

Snails, squids, clams, slugs *(Figure 539)*

- soft unsegmented bodies
- may have shell

ARTHROPODA

Animals with jointed legs *(Figure 540)*

- exoskeleton made of chitin (a polysaccharide)
- segmented body
- appendages to each segment
- at least 3 pairs of jointed legs
- many free-living but also some parasitic

5.5.5	Apply and design a key for a group of up to eight organisms.

©IBO 2007

In Biology, a key is used to identify an organism. Imagine that you are taking someone to a farm who does not know the appearance of a cow, a horse, a chicken or a pig. You could give this person the following key:

1. Animal is taller than 1.5 metres   go to 2
   Animal is smaller than 1.5 metres   go to 3

2. Animal is black and white   cow
   Animal is brown   horse

3. Animal has feathers   chicken
   Animal is pink with curly tail   pig

You can make a key to identify items of any group of things. If there are two choices at each stage it is called a **dichotomous key**. The important thing is that it works.

In Biology, keys are most commonly used to identify plants, insects and birds. These are often area specific, for example, the Plants of Northern Europe.

This statement is best addressed in an Investigation which your teacher may arrange for the class.

EXERCISES

1   A community and its abiotic environment is known as:
A   a population.
B   an ecosystem.
C   a habitat.
D   a community.

2   A species is a group of organisms that:
A   live in a community.
B   do not eat each other.
C   share the same habitat and look similar to one another.
D   can interbreed, producing fertile offspring.

3   The food chain:
    leaf litter → earth worm → sparrow
implies that:
A   earthworms eat leaf litter.
B   sparrows feed on leaf litter.
C   leaf litter is essential food for earthworms.
D   sparrows eat only earthworms.

The next two questions refer to the following Figure:

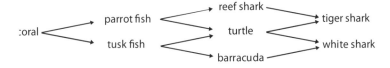

4   The diagram is best described as:
A   a food pyramid.
B   a food chain.
C   a food web.
D   a species diagram.

5   The diagram indicates that:
A   turtles are occasionally eaten by tiger sharks.
B   barracuda eat coral.
C   tusk fish eat noting but coral.
D   white sharks will eat anything.

6   The level of the food chain at which an organism is found is known as its:
A   consumer level.
B   producer level.
C   web level.
D   trophic level.

7   Seaweed and grass are known as
A   autotrophs.
B   saprotrophs.
C   heterotrophs.
D   detritivores.

8   Parrots and eagles are known as:
A   autotrophs.
B   saprotrophs.
C   heterotrophs.
D   detritivores.

9   Which one of the following graphs best represents the rate of photosynthesis in a green plant as light levels are altered?

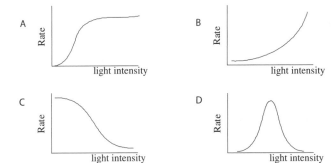

The next two questions refer to the following diagram:

10 The diagram is known as

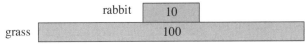

A   a food pyramid.
B   a food chain.
C   a food web.
D   a species diagram.

11 The diagram indicates if a rabbit eats 50 grams of grass, this will be turned into:
A   0.5 grams of rabbit.
B   1 gram of rabbit.
C   5 grams of rabbit.
D   10 grams of rabbit.

12 Which one of the following activities is not a part of the carbon cycle?
A   photosynthesis.
B   burning wood.
C   rain.
D   burning oil.

13 The main cause of the greenhouse effect is:
   A   global warming.
   B   pollution.
   C   burning of fossil fuels.
   D   increased human population.

14 Fire coral, *Millepora platyphylla* is of the genus:
   A   coral.
   B   Millepora.
   C   platyphylla.
   D   Millepora platyphylla.

15 Unicellular organisms lacking distinct nuclei and other membrane bound organelles are known as:
   A   Prokaryotes.
   B   Protoctista.
   C   Fungi.
   D   Plantae.

16 The largest grouping in the classification system is the:
   A   genus.
   B   species.
   C   class.
   D   kingdom.

17 Design a key for the following imaginary insects.
   There are many possibilities here but one example is given below:

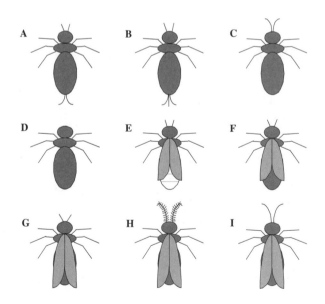

18 (a) Define the term species
   (b) Distinguish between habitat and ecosystem

19 Study the graph below.

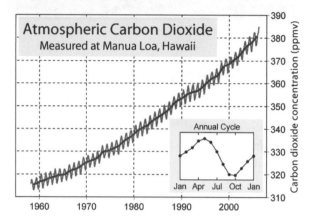

(a) Outline how carbon dioxide levels change between 1960 and 2000.
(b) Suggest reasons for these changes.

20 (a) Carbon dioxide is a greenhouse gas. Name two others.
   (b) Explain how greenhouse gases cause an increase in temperatures.

21 (a) Outline the precautionary principle
   (b) How is the precautionary principle applied to conservation?

22 Draw a food web of the following organisms:
   grass, daisies, dandelions, hawks, foxes, insectivorous birds, snakes, herbivorous insects, spiders, seed eating birds, rabbits, squirrels, mice.

23 Explain the relationship between sexual reproduction and variation in a species.

24 Use the example of the Peppered Moth to explain how changes in the environment lead to evolution.

25 (a) What is the official name of humans?
   (b) List the levels of hierarchy of taxa. Start with the biggest.

26. Compare coniferophyta and angiospermophyta.

27. Consider the following invertebrate phyla:
   porifera, cnidaria, platyhelminthes, annelida, mollusca and *arthropoda.*
   (a) In which of the above phyla do the animals have a mouth?
   (b) In which of the above phyla do the animals have an anus?
   (c) In which of the above phyla are the animals bilateral symmetry?
   (d) In which of the above phyla are the animals radial symmetry?

HUMAN HEALTH AND PHYSIOLOGY

6.1   Digestion

6.2   The transport system

6.3   Defence against infectious disease

6.4   Gas exchange

6.5   Nerves, hormones and homeostasis

6.6   Reproduction

6

6.1 DIGESTION

6.1.1 Explain why digestion of large food molecules is essential.
©IBO 2007

Food contains starch, proteins and lipids. These molecules are very large as was shown in *Topic 3.2*. Large food molecules need to be digested before being absorbed. The process of **absorption** of food molecules requires them to pass into a cell lining the gut. To do so, molecules must be small and soluble. Therefore large molecules like polysaccharides, proteins and lipids need to be broken down into their building blocks before they can be absorbed.

Even if we could absorb the food as large molecules, many of these molecules would not be useful to us as such. Plants may contain a lot of starch which is useful for releasing energy, but only after it has been digested down to glucose. Steak contains proteins but probably not the exact same ones we need. If we break the proteins down into amino acids, we can use them as monomers or 'building blocks' and then used to produce exactly the right proteins.

6.1.2 Explain the need for enzymes in digestion.
©IBO 2007

Like many other biological reactions, the breakdown of starch, proteins and lipids is a slow process at body temperature. **Enzymes** lower the required activation energy and make this process sufficiently fast. The action of enzymes is discussed in detail in *Topic 3.6*.

6.1.3 State the source, substrate, products and optimum pH conditions for one amylase, one protease and one lipase.
©IBO 2007

The three kinds of macronutrients are carbohydrates, lipids and proteins. Since enzymes are highly specific, each molecule has at least one enzyme to break it down into its building blocks. But as we can recognise three kinds of macronutrients, we can recognise three groups of enzymes:

- the amylases digest most carbohydrates
- the proteases digest proteins
- the lipases digest lipids

Examples of some common digestive enzymes are given in Figure 601.

type of enzyme	example of enzyme	source	substrate	product	optimum pH
amylase	salivary amylase	saliva	starch	maltose	pH 7
protease	pepsin	gastric juice	protein	shorter polypeptide chains	pH 2
lipase	pancreatic lipase	pancreatic juice	lipids (triglycerides)	glycerol and fatty acids	pH 8

Figure 601   Some common digestive enzymes

CORE

Saliva is produced by the salivary glands.

Gastric juice is produced by cells in the wall of the stomach; the pepsin-producing cells are called 'chief' cells.

Pancreatic lipase is produced by the exocrine cells of the pancreas.

6.1.4	Draw and label a diagram of the digestive system.
	©IBO 2007

Figure 602 shows the major organs in the human digestive system.

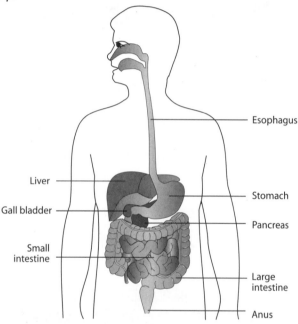

Figure 602   The human digestive system

6.1.5	Outline the function of the stomach, small intestine and large intestine.
	©IBO 2007

Functions of the stomach:
- temporarily store food
- chemically digest proteins
- kill pathogens

The stomach receives the food from the mouth via the esophagus and will pass it on to the small intestine. Food is eaten in less time than it can be digested by the small intestine so it is stored in the stomach for a while. It is then moved along by waves of muscular contraction of the intestinal wall called **peristalsis**.

Pepsin is the best known enzyme in the stomach. Pepsin chemically digests proteins and breaks them down into

shorter polypeptides. Pepsinogen is the inactive precursor of pepsin. It is produced by chief cells in the wall of the stomach and activated by the presence of hydrochloric acid (HCl). The hydrochloric acid necessary to activate pepsinogen is produced by the parietal cells in the wall of the stomach. Due to the hydrochloric acid, the pH in the stomach is very low (pH 2). The very acidic condition protects us from disease as it will kill most pathogens.

Functions of the small intestine are:
- digestion
- absorption of products of digestion

Enzymes are secreted into the small intestine from two sources: the wall of the small intestine and the exocrine part of the pancreas (via the pancreatic duct). These enzymes are responsible for a large part of the digestion of food. A third fluid is secreted into the small intestine: bile. Bile is NOT an enzyme. Bile contains bile salts which break drops of fat into smaller droplets (emulsification) so that the enzyme (pancreatic lipase) has more surface area to work on.

Absorption of digested food takes place in the small intestine. To ensure enough surface area for absorption, the small intestine is long (6 metres in humans) and has folds on its inner surface. The surface also has villi (finger-like projections into the hollow centre) and microvilli on these villi to further increase surface area.

Functions of the large intestine:
- absorption of liquids
- absorption of minerals

In the process of digestion, a lot of fluid is added to the "food" as it moves through the alimentary canal. Glucose is actively absorbed in the small intestine and minerals are actively absorbed in the large intestine and water follows by osmosis.

6.1.6	Distinguish between *absorption* and *assimilation*.
	©IBO 2007

ABSORPTION

Absorption means taking in substances through cell membranes or layers of cells, in particular from the lumen of the gut into the blood or lymph capillaries.

ASSIMILATION

Assimilation involves the conversion of nutrients into fluid or solid parts of the organism. Assimilation can only occur after absorption has taken place.

6.1.7   Explain how the structure of the villus is related to its role in absorption and transport of the products of digestion.

©IBO 2007

The small intestine is a very important place for chemical digestion but it is also the major site of absorption. For this reason the wall of the small intestine is not just simply a smooth inner surface of a tube, as you may have imagined from the schematic and simplified diagrams, but covered with villi (singular: villus), which are small finger-like projections made of many cells. The cells of the villus often also have projections into the lumen of the gut: microvilli (similar in function to plant root hairs). The structure of the small intestine is shown in Figure 603. The purpose of villi and microvilli is to increase the surface area of the small intestine.

As the function of the small intestine is absorption, the relationship of its role to its structure is the increased surface area of the villi. More products of digestion can be absorbed at the same time due to the larger surface area. Inside the villi, a capillary bed can be seen. Small carbohydrates (such as glucose) and amino acids are absorbed into the blood and transported to the liver. Lipids are absorbed in the lacteals, which are part of the lymphatic system. The absorbed fat is transported with the lymph to drain into the circulatory system at the subclavian vein.

So the relationship of structure and function of the villi, with regards to transport, is found in the presence of blood capillaries to remove water, small carbohydrates and amino acids from the small intestine. The lacteals remove fats from the small intestine. Absorbed products of digestion need to be moved away from the area where they are absorbed as soon as possible in order to maintain the concentration gradient which helps the absorption process.

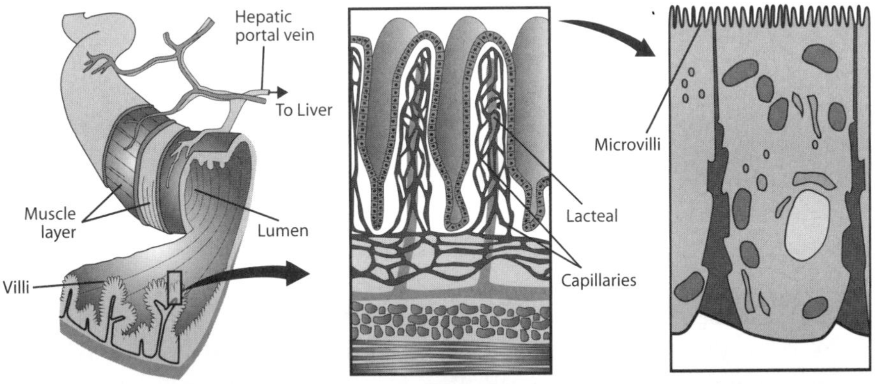

6.2 THE TRANSPORT SYSTEM

6.2.1   Draw and label a diagram of the heart showing the four chambers, associated blood vessels, valves and the route of blood through the heart.

©IBO 2007

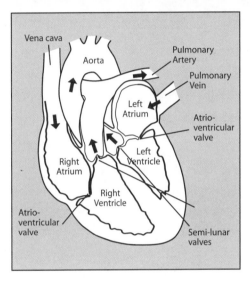

Figure 604   The structure of the human heart

The human **heart** (Figure 604) is a very specialised organ that pumps blood through the body. It is divided into a left and right atrium (plural: atria) and a left and right ventricle, each of which has specific characteristics defined by its role in moving the blood through the body.

The atria have thin walls since they only have to put enough pressure on the blood to move it into the ventricles, which are next to the atria. The wall of the ventricles is thicker because they need to move the blood further. The wall of the left ventricle is thicker than that of the right ventricle since the left ventricle pumps the blood around the entire body and the right ventricle only pumps the blood to the lungs. The thicker the wall, the more pressure can be put on the blood and the further it can be pumped.

SMALL INTESTINE   VILLI   EPITHELIUM

Figure 603   The structure of the small intestine

CORE

6.2.2 State that the coronary arteries supply heart muscle with oxygen and nutrients.

©IBO 2007

Since the heart is an active muscle, it needs food (glucose) and oxygen in order to release the energy (in cellular respiration) to contract. The heart cannot readily absorb oxygen and nutrients from the blood passing through its chambers, so coronary arteries *(Figure 605)* supply the heart muscles with its requirements.

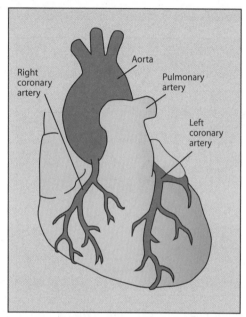

Figure 605   The coronary arteries

6.2.3 Explain the action of the heart in terms of collecting blood, pumping blood, and opening and closing of valves.

©IBO 2007

A major component of the heart is muscle tissue. The heart collects blood from the body and lungs in the right and left atria, respectively. The blood is then pumped into the right and left ventricles, which are found directly below the atria. The right ventricle will pump the blood to the lungs. The wall is thicker than that of the atria but thinner than that of the left ventricle. The left ventricle pumps the blood into the aorta and from there it goes to the rest of the body. Since this is the longest distance that the blood must travel, it needs to be pushed out of the heart with some force. This explains why the wall of the left ventricle is the thickest wall of all the chambers of the heart.

Mammals have a double circulation, this means the blood coming from the body goes through the heart, to the lungs, back to the heart and then to the body. The heart is therefore divided into a right and a left side. Each side has an atrium and a ventricle. The atria collect the blood

and their walls are thin; the walls of the ventricles are thick and muscular since they pump the blood into the arteries. The left ventricle has a thicker wall than the right ventricle since it has to pump the blood through the entire body.

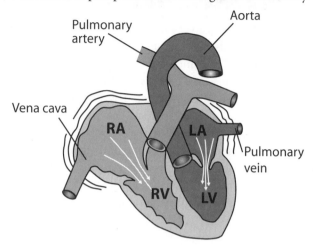

Figure 606 (a)   Atria contracting

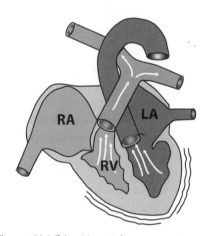

Figure 606 (b)   Ventricles contracting

Figure 606 is simplified, if you look at a more detailed diagram of the heart, you will find that the vena cava really exists as two vessels: the vena cava superior, from above the heart, and the vena cava inferior, coming from below the heart. The pulmonary vein is really four veins, two from each lung.

The direction of the blood flow is controlled by the valves. **Valves** are flaps of tissue without muscle. Valves are opened and closed by the flow of blood. As long as the blood flows in the right direction, the valves remain pushed open. As soon as the blood starts to flow in the wrong direction, they are pushed shut. Figure 606 shows the opening and closing of valves as the atria or ventricles contract.

It may help to consider valves as doors. If a group of people are pushing against an outward opening door, the door will be pushed open. However, if these people suddenly turn around and try to go back, they will only push the door shut.

The atrio-ventricular valve between the right atrium and the right ventricle is called the tricuspid valve; the one between the left atrium and left ventricle is called the bicuspid valve. The valves in the pulmonary artery and in the aorta are semi-lunar valves. The valves have some strings of connective tissue attached to them. This prevents them from opening to the wrong side.

6.2.4	Outline the control of the heartbeat in terms of myogenic muscle contraction, the role of the pacemaker, nerves, the medulla of the brain and epinephrine (adrenaline).

©IBO 2007

The contractions of the cardiac muscles are **myogenic** which means they originate from within the heart muscle. They are brought about by nerve impulses which originate not from the brain but from inside the heart from a specific region of the right atrium: the Sino-Atrial Node (SA node) also known as the cardiac **pacemaker**. The SA node is made from specialised muscle cells. The SA node releases an impulse at regular intervals which spreads across the walls of the atria, causing simultaneous contractions.

The impulse cannot spread to the muscles of the ventricles except in the region of the Atrio-Ventricular Node (AV node). The AV node is connected to the 'bundle of His' (specialised cardiac fibres) which branches out into the Purkinje tissue. From the AV node, the impulse travels through the bundle of His down to the apex of the heart and from there spreads up through the Purkinje tissue. This causes the ventricular contractions to start at the apex and push the blood up into the arteries. *Refer to Figure 607.*

Although the heart is largely autonomous in its contractions, the brain and some hormones influence the frequency of the heartbeats. Impulses from the lower part of the brain stem (the medulla oblongata) via the parasympathetic part of the autonomous nervous system (controls mainly involuntary actions), decrease the cardiac frequency. Impulses from the brain, via the sympathetic nerves, will also increase cardiac frequency (heart rate).

Some **hormones** also have an effect on the heart rate. For example adrenaline (epinephrine) from the adrenal glands near the kidneys, increases cardiac frequency.

If the SA node does not function properly, it is quite possible to implant an artificial pacemaker to carry out this function. With a well-adjusted pacemaker, a person with a malfunctioning SA node can live a long and active life.

6.2.5	Explain the relationship between the structure and function of arteries, capillaries and veins.

©IBO 2007

Blood is circulated through the body by the contractions of the heart. Mammals (unlike, for example, insects) have a closed circulatory system, this means the blood is confined to blood vessels. There are three kinds of blood vessels as can been seen in Figure 608.

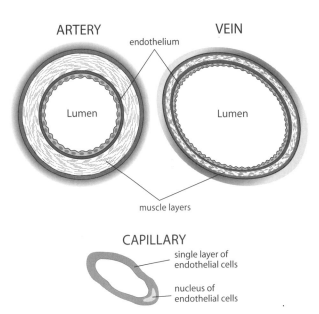

Figure 608   Different types of blood vessels

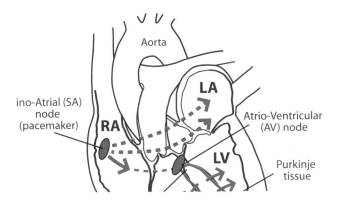

Figure 607   The control of heartbeat

CORE

ARTERIES

- transport blood away from the heart
- carry oxygenated blood (except Pulmonary Artery)
- have thick muscular walls but no valves
- move blood at high speed (10-40 cm/s)
- contain blood at high pressure (80-120 mmHg)

CAPILLARIES

- small numerous blood vessels in tissue
- very thin walls to allow easy exchange of materials e.g. respiratory gases
- move blood at low speed (< 0.1 cm/s)
- contain blood at moderate pressure (15 mmHg)

VEINS

- transport blood towards the heart (except hepatic portal vein)
- carry de-oxygenated blood (except Pulmonary Vein)
- have quite thin walls and valves
- move blood at moderate speed (5-20 cm/s)
- contain blood at low pressure (< 10 mmHg)
- have valves to prevent blood from flowing back

Figure 609 shows how valves in veins stop the backflow of blood.

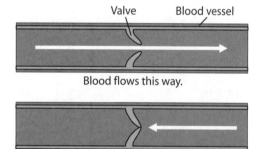

Figure 609   The function of valves in vessels

6.2.6	State that blood is composed of plasma, erythrocytes, leucocytes (phagocytes and lymphocytes) and platelets.
	©IBO 2007

By weight, about 8% of the human body is blood. It has the following composition; plasma (50-55%) and cells (45-50%).

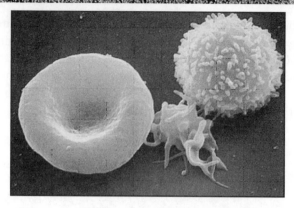

Figure 610   Types of blood cells

The plasma is 90% water and dissolved in it are:
- proteins (e.g. fibrinogen, globulins, albumins)
- dissolved nutrients
- hormones
- waste materials

The cells are:
- erythrocytes (red blood cells) (90%)
- leucocytes (white blood cells)
  - phagocytes (70%):
    non-specific defence: phagocytosis of antigens
  - lymphocytes (30%):
    specific defense: production of antibodies
- thrombocytes (platelets)

Figure 610 shows from left to right: an erythrocyte, a thrombocyte, and a leucocyte.

6.2.7	State that the following are transported by the blood: nutrients, oxygen, carbon dioxide, hormones, antibodies, urea and heat.
	©IBO 2007

The function of the circulatory system is transport. The following are transported by the blood:
- nutrients e.g. glucose
- oxygen
- carbon dioxide
- hormones e.g. insulin
- antibodies
- waste products e.g. urea
- heat

Transport of oxygen and carbon dioxide is associated with the erythrocytes; all the other substances listed are dissolved in the blood.

6.3 DEFENCE AGAINST INFECTIOUS DISEASE

6.3.1	Define *pathogen*.
	©IBO 2007

A **pathogen** is an organism or virus that causes a disease in any other organism. Common pathogens include bacteria, fungi and viruses.

6.3.2	Explain why antibiotics are effective against bacteria but not against viruses.
	©IBO 2007

Antibiotics, such as the aminoglycosides, chloramphenicol, erythromycin, and clindamycin, block protein synthesis in bacteria but not in eukaryotic cells. Bacteria and animal cells synthesise proteins in a similar manner, though the proteins involved are not the same. Those antibiotics that are useful as antibacterial agents use these differences to bind to or inhibit the function of the bacterial proteins. In this way, they prevent the synthesis of new proteins and new bacterial cells without damaging the 'patient'.

Most bacteria have a cell wall. Antibiotics may disrupt this cell wall which will interfere with the life cycle of the bacteria. Eukaryotic animal cells do not have cell walls so are not affected by the antibiotic. Viruses do not have a cell wall so are also not affected by antibiotics. Viruses *(such as the example seen in Figure 611)* invade a cell and get this host cell to produce the protein and DNA that the virus needs to reproduce. As the virus uses it host's processes, antibiotics do not hurt them. If they did, the antibiotic would also disrupt the process of protein synthesis in the host (which would be a serious problem).

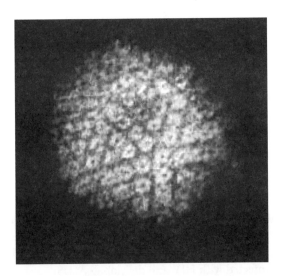

Figure 611   An example of a virus

Many anti-viral drugs focus on disrupting the protein coat of a virus and will therefore not usually cause harm to the host.

6.3.3	Outline the role of skin and mucous membranes in defence against pathogens.
	©IBO 2007

The best way to prevent disease is to prevent the pathogens from entering the body. The skin plays a major role in this. When unbroken, it is almost impossible for any micro-organism to penetrate the skin. Weak points are those where we are not protected by skin. Most of these areas have defences of their own. Mucus is an often-used barrier. It traps micro-organisms and prevents further entry.

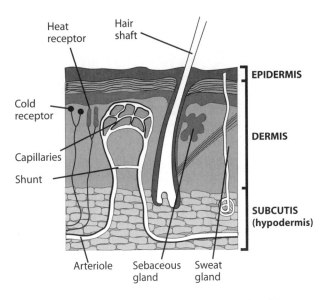

Figure 612   The main structures in the skin

Figure 612 shows the main structures in the human skin.

Lungs are protected by mucus and cilia which transport the mucus to the throat.

The stomach contains a very acidic environment.

Glands above the eyes produce tears that contain lysozymes (enzymes which destroy bacterial cell walls).

The vagina produces mucus and has an acidic environment.

CORE

6.3.4 Outline how phagocytic leucocytes ingest pathogens in the blood and in body tissues.

©IBO 2007

Despite all of the measures (*Topic 6.3.3*) to keep pathogens out of the body, many do manage to get in. This is called **infection** (a successful invasion of the body by pathogens) but does not always lead to disease. Leucocytes (white blood cells) are the body's defence against pathogens after they have entered. They can be found in the blood but also in the body's tissues, e.g. lungs. Several different kinds of leucocytes exist, some of which are phagocytic, i.e. they simply will 'eat' (phagocytosis) any cell which is not recognised as 'body own' (determined by the 'code' on the outside of the cell surface membrane).

Figure 613 depicts blood stained to show the nucleus of the cells. Red blood cells (erythrocytes) lack a nucleus, while leucocytes have a nucleus which shows up purple. The type of leucocyte in Figure 613 has a nucleus that is in lobes.

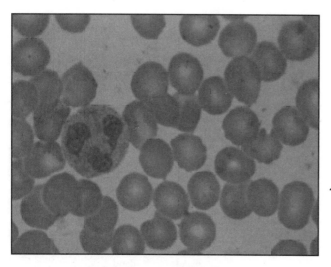

Figure 613   A photograph of blood cells

6.3.5 Distinguish between *antigens* and *antibodies*.

©IBO 2007

An **antigen** is a molecule that is recognised by the organism as foreign. It will cause an immune response.

An **antibody**, also known as "immunoglobulin", is a soluble protein produced by a plasma cell. It is produced by the immune system as a response to the presence of an antigen.

An antibody will recognise an antigen and neutralise it.

6.3.6 Explain antibody production.

©IBO 2007

There are many different kinds of antibodies. They are produced by different kinds of lymphocytes. Each different **lymphocyte** will recognise a particular kind of antigen and produce antibodies that work against that kind of antigen.

When an antigen enters the organism, the lymphocyte that produces the right kind of antibody will recognise the antigen. The lymphocyte will divide many times, forming a clone. This clone is a group of lymphocytes, all producing the same kind of antibody. They will produce a lot of this antibody which will attach itself to the antigen that has entered the organism and make it harmless. Further details can be found in *Topic 11.1*.

6.3.7 Outline the effects of HIV on the immune system.

©IBO 2007

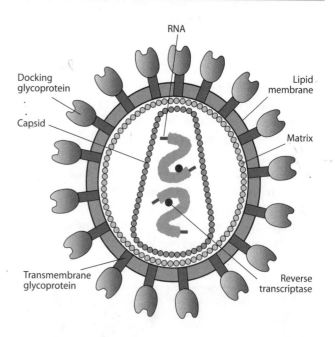

Figure 614   The HIV virus

The Human Immunodeficiency Virus (**HIV**), shown in Figure 614, is a virus that infects cells of the immune system. It reduces the number of lymphocytes that are actively involved in the production of antibodies. As a result, the infected person makes a much lower number of antibodies and is therefore much more likely to develop a disease. These diseases are called opportunistic diseases and they are the major cause of death of people who have been infected with HIV and developed **AIDS**.

6.3.8 Discuss the cause, transmission and social implications of AIDS.

©IBO 2007

AIDS is an acronym for 'Acquired Immune Deficiency Syndrome'. AIDS is not a disease but rather a collection of symptoms and/or opportunistic diseases. AIDS is **caused** by the weakening of the immune system by the HIV virus. A person is diagnosed with AIDS when s/he shows one or more "indicator illnesses" or based on the results of a blood test in which the number of certain lymphocytes are counted.

Transmission of the HIV virus can take place via:
- blood
- semen
- vaginal secretions
- breast milk

Blood and semen contain the highest concentration of the HIV virus.

The most common transmission of the HIV virus occurs during:
- unprotected sexual contact (no condom), either vaginal or anal contact
- sharing injection needles (usually by people addicted to intravenously-used drugs)
- mother to child during birth or breastfeeding

Some statistical information shows the extent of the problem. In 2006, nearly 40 million people were estimated to be living with HIV/AIDS, of whom 4.3 million had been newly infected. More than 60% of the people infected with HIV/AIDS were living in Sub-Saharan Africa. Nearly 3 million people died in 2006 of AIDS-related diseases and 2 million of these lived in Sub-Saharan Africa.

In North America and Western Europe, the number of new infections has remained the same. In many other countries, the decrease in the number of new infections has slowed or in other countries the number of new infections has increased. It is believed that this is caused by a reduction in HIV prevention programmes.

The social implications of AIDS are many and can be found on any of numerous websites. Some of these implications are listed below:
- People with HIV/AIDS can suffer from stigma and discrimination.

- Women are more likely to contract HIV from sex with an infected partner than men. This further increases the inequality between men and women in some countries.

- People who die as a result of HIV/AIDS are often at an age where they are the most productive members of society. In countries were AIDS causes many deaths, a relatively large proportion of the work force may be removed, delaying economic growth.

- If both parents die because of AIDS, the country will need to spend resources on caring for the **orphans**.

- If one adult in a household suffers from HIV/AIDS, s/he may face unemployment and not be able to earn an income. This may push the entire household into **poverty**, further reducing the chances of obtaining anti-viral drugs.

- Poverty in itself increases the chances of contracting HIV/AIDS due to a lack of information (no school) and/or being forced to have sex in exchange for food/money. Also the incidence of rape may increase, which is also a factor in spreading HIV/AIDS.

- It is expensive to treat people with HIV/AIDS so obtaining insurance might be a problem.

- Use of condoms increases.

TOK   The spread of HIV

After the discovery of the cause of AIDS, it quickly became clear that HIV transmission could be eliminated through education as to the modes of its transmission as well as the provision of preventative resources such as needle exchange programmes and condoms. In many cultures, education regarding AIDS and provision of condoms has been thought to encourage early sexual activity and was prohibited. A similar argument has been made about needle exchange programmes. HIV infection is spreading in societies where such prohibitions are found and decreasing where education and preventative resources are available. The form of effective AIDS education differs from culture to culture and the greatest success has been obtained where the type of education has been culturally sensitive.

Although the spread of HIV can be eliminated, world-wide the number of people infected continues to grow. In many cases this is because of lack of education and resources, but in others it is because people knowingly ignore knowledge of how to stop the spread of HIV and choose to practice activities that place themselves and others at risk of infection. To what extent should an individual be held accountable for their actions when they place others at risk?

CORE

6.4 GAS EXCHANGE

6.4.1 Distinguish between *ventilation, gas exchange* and *cell respiration*.

©IBO 2007

Breathing is the act of inhaling and exhaling which allows ventilation of the lungs.

Gas exchange is the intake of oxygen and excretion of carbon dioxide which takes place at the (specialised respiratory) surface of an organism. *Refer to Figure 615.*

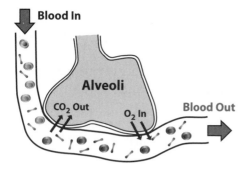

Figure 615   Gas exchange in the lungs

Cell respiration is the process of releasing energy from food (large organic molecules), often using oxygen as the ultimate electron acceptor.

Ventilation is the process of moving air into and out of lungs. It involves muscular movement and as such requires energy (released by cell respiration). Ventilation is required to maintain a concentration gradient so that gaseous exchange can occur. Oxygen will diffuse from the air in the lungs into the blood only if the concentration of oxygen in the air in the lungs is higher than that in the blood. As the oxygen diffuses into the blood, the concentration of oxygen in the air of the lungs decreases. By refreshing the air in the lungs, the concentration gradient is maintained. The mechanism of ventilation is described in *Topic 6.4.5.*

Gas exchange is the movement of oxygen from the air in the lungs into the blood and carbon dioxide in the

opposite direction. First, the oxygen dissolves in the film of water around the cells that make the walls of the alveoli. The dissolved oxygen then diffuses through the alveoli cells and through the walls of the capillaries into the erythrocytes in the blood. The circulation of the blood will take the oxygen away from the area of gas exchange, which also serves to maintain the concentration gradient.

The movement of carbon dioxide, produced in the tissues, takes place in the opposite direction. The blood carries carbon dioxide to the lungs. Here, it diffuses from the blood, across the walls of the capillaries and the walls of the alveoli into the air in the lungs. The circulatory system will continue to bring blood carrying carbon dioxide to the lungs and ventilation of the lungs will refresh the air so that the concentration gradient is maintained.

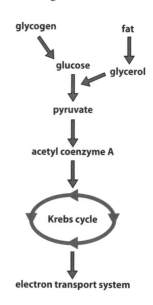

Figure 616   Cellular respiration

Cell respiration, shown in Figure 616, is the release of energy from large organic molecules. Every living cell requires energy for its metabolic processes, which means that cell respiration takes place in all living cells. Cell respiration can use oxygen as its ultimate electron acceptor. This is called aerobic respiration and this process releases more energy per molecule glucose than anaerobic respiration.

	Ventilation	Gas exchange	Cell respiration
where	involves muscles to move ribs and move air into and out of lungs	at the exchange surface where alveoli are next to blood capillaries	in cytoplasm (glycolysis) and mitochondria (Krebs cycle and oxidative phosphorylation)
energy	muscle movements require energy	diffusion is a passive process, no energy needed	converts energy into a useable form
physical or chemical process	physical	physical	chemical

Figure 617   Ventilation, gas exchange and respiration

Ventilation, gas exchange and cell respiration are all dependent on each other. Ventilation requires energy provided by cell respiration. Gas exchange depends on a concentration gradient of respiratory gases, which is maintained by ventilation. Cell respiration is more efficient when using oxygen as its electron acceptor. The oxygen needed and the carbon dioxide produced are exchanged with the environment via gas exchange in the lungs.

Ventilation moves air into and out of lungs. Gas exchange removes carbon dioxide from the blood and takes oxygen into the blood. Cellular respiration uses oxygen to release energy from food and produces carbon dioxide. These processes are compared in Figure 617.

6.4.2	Explain the need for a ventilation system.

©IBO 2007

One of the characteristics of life is respiration. Respiration in this case has the biological meaning of the release of energy. This means that cellular respiration goes on in every living cell. Since anaerobic respiration releases about 5-7% of the energy that aerobic respiration releases *(see Topic 8.1)*, most cells require a constant supply of oxygen to function properly. A few species of bacteria, living in the mud at the bottom of ponds and lakes, cannot tolerate oxygen; they employ alternative pathways to release energy.

Unicellular organisms and small multicellular organisms have few problems in gaseous exchange. The required gases will easily diffuse into and out of their system. For larger organisms this is not possible due to their smaller surface area over volume ratio. The decrease of the surface area over volume ratio is quite rapid as the size of an organism increases.

Two examples will illustrate this important point.

Example 1

If you examine the cubes in Figure 618, you can see the 4 shaded sides.

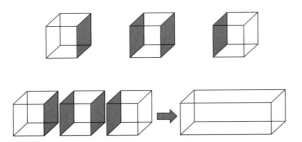

Figure 618   Surface area over volume ratio

This is the amount of surface area which is 'lost' if you change these 3 small cubes into 1 larger structure, whilst no volume is lost.

Example 2

Again examine the cubes in Figure 619.

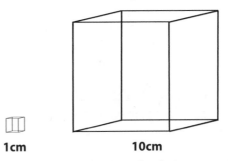

1cm   10cm

Figure 619   Large and small cells (not to scale)

The smaller cube:
The surface area is 6 x 1 x 1 cm² = 6 cm²
The volume is 1 x 1 x 1 cm³ = 1 cm³
The surface area over volume ratio is 6/1 = 6

The larger cube:
The surface area is 6 x 10 x 10 cm² = 600 cm²
The volume is 10 x 10 x 10 cm³ = 1 000 cm³
The surface area over volume ratio is 600/1000 = 0.6

This means that the smaller cube has 6 cm² of surface for every cm³ of volume, whereas the larger cube has 0.6 cm² of surface for every cm³ of volume. (The mathematical explanation is that when increasing size of factor y, the surface increases with y^2 but the volume increases with y^3.)

So, when organisms become larger, there is simply not enough surface for gaseous exchange. An added problem is that the oxygen, once inside the organism, has to travel a long way to reach some cells. Since diffusion in liquids is a fairly slow process, this is unsatisfactory. The same principle applies to other organs that exchange material with the internal or external environments e.g. intestine and kidney.

When the size of the organism is limited, the problems outlined in the previous paragraph can be solved by flattening the body (e.g. flatworms). This increases the surface area and decreases the diffusion distance. However, in larger organisms, even this measure is insufficient and a need for a respiratory surface exists.

Insects have a system of tracheal tubes. These many tubes run from the exoskeleton throughout the insect's body. They are partially air-filled, which ensures much faster diffusion.

Larval amphibians often have external gills. These are thin structures with a large surface area especially suited for gaseous exchange. Due to their position, however, they are easily damaged.

CORE

Fish have internal gills. These are similar to external gills but safely inside the body. A fine capillary network transports the gases around the body. Many terrestrial animals have lungs. A ventilation movement refreshes the air in these sacs, which have a large surface area, are moist, and have an excellent blood supply.

6.4.3	Describe the features of alveoli that adapt them to gas exchange.
	©IBO 2007

Four features of alveoli *(shown in Figure 620)* allow efficient gas exchange:
- large surface area
- thin (short diffusion distance)
- moist (gases need to dissolve before passing through membranes)
- good blood supply (maintains the concentration gradient)

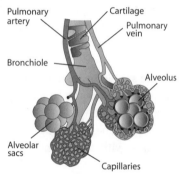

Figure 620   The structure of alveoli

6.4.4	Draw and label a diagram of the ventilation system, including trachea, lungs, bronchi, bronchioles and alveoli.
	©IBO 2007

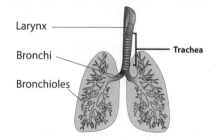

Figure 621   The ventilation system

The lungs are found in the chest cavity (or **thorax**) with the heart. The air enters the body through the nose or mouth. From there it passes the **trachea** (or windpipe), into the bronchi which branch into many smaller bronchioles. Finally, the air ends up in the air sacs; the alveoli. Alveoli, *(see Figure 621)*, are small thin-walled sacs in which most of the gaseous exchange takes place. The oxygen diffuses across the wall of the alveolus, through the capillary cells,

across the membrane of the erythrocytes to bind with hemoglobin. The blood then transports it to the tissues. Carbon dioxide from the tissues is carried back to the lungs, diffuses into the alveoli and is breathed out.

6.4.5	Explain the mechanism of ventilation of the lungs in terms of volume and pressure changes caused by the internal and external intercostal muscles, the diaphragm and abdominal muscles.
	©IBO 2007

VENTILATION OF THE LUNGS

The air in the lungs constantly needs to be refreshed. Since the lungs only have one connection with the atmosphere, the 'old' air needs to be exhaled before fresh air can be taken in.

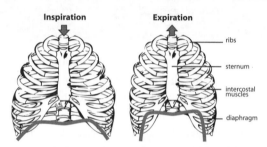

Figure 622   Inspiration and expiration

Inspiration

The external intercostal muscles contract and move the rib cage up and outward. The diaphragm contracts, flattening it downward *(refer to Figure 622)*. Both actions have the effect of increasing the volume of the chest cavity. If the volume increases, the pressure decreases and the air will flow into the lungs.

Expiration

The relaxation of the intercostal muscles and the diaphragm will bring them back into their original position *(refer to Figure 622)*. The volume decreases and the resultant increase in pressure will make the air leave the lungs. In forced expiration, the abdominal muscles and the internal intercostal muscles contract, which increases the pressure in the abdominal cavity to expel the air from the lungs.

. A normal breath will move approximately 500 cm³ of air into and out of the lungs. This is called the tidal volume. After breathing in normally, you can breathe in an extra 3000 cm³ of air: the inspiratory reserve volume or complemental air. If you then breathe out as much as you can, you expire approximately 4500 cm³. This is your vital capacity. All you have left now is approximately 1200 cm³ of residual air which you cannot force out or your lungs would collapse. The air which you can exhale after breathing out normally is approximately 1100 cm³ of expiratory reserve volume or supplemental air.

6.5 NERVES, HORMONES AND HOMEOSTASIS

> **6.5.1** State that the nervous system consists of the central nervous system (CNS) and peripheral nerves, and is composed of cells called neurons that can carry rapid electrical impulses.
>
> ©IBO 2007

The **nervous system** can be divided into the Central Nervous System (CNS) and the Peripheral Nervous System (PNS). The CNS is the brain and spinal cord, the other nerves are peripheral nerves. The peripheral nerve cells are called neurons. Their function is to transport messages in the form of electrical impulses to specific sites. This is done very quickly by local depolarisations of the cell membrane of the neuron.

> **6.5.2** Draw and label a diagram of the structure of a motor neuron.
>
> ©IBO 2007

A motor neuron is a nerve cell which transmits impulses from the brain to a muscle or gland. Its structure is shown in Figure 623.

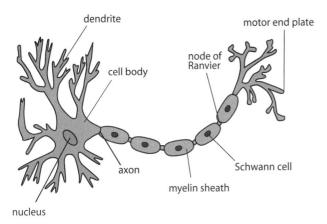

Figure 623   The structure of a motor neuron

The cell body contains the following cell organelles:

- nucleus
- rER and sER
- Golgi apparatus
- ribosomes
- lysosomes
- mitochondria; mitochondria are also found in the axon

> **6.5.3** State that nerve impulses are conducted from receptors to the CNS by sensory neurons, within the CNS by relay neurons, and from the CNS to effectors by motor neurons.
>
> ©IBO 2007

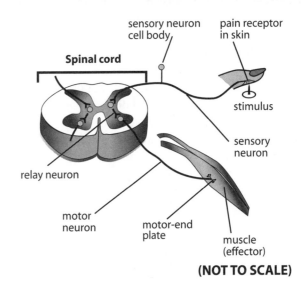

(NOT TO SCALE)

Figure 624   Parts of the CNS

Figure 624 shows a **reflex arc**. This is a neural pathway that allows a quick reaction. If a person puts his or her finger on a pin, the pain receptors will send out an impulse. The impulse is carried to the CNS by a **sensory neuron**. Inside the spinal cord (part of the CNS), the impulse is passed to a **relay neuron** and then from the CNS to the muscle by a **motor neuron.**

> **6.5.4** Define *resting potential* and *action potential* (depolarization and repolarization).
>
> ©IBO 2007

RESTING POTENTIAL

The electrical potential (measured in millivolts, mV) across a cell membrane when not propagating an impulse.

ACTION POTENTIAL

The localised reversal and then restoration of the electrical potential (measured in mV) across the membrane of a neuron as the impulse passes along it.

CORE

6.5.5 Explain how a nerve impulse passes along a non-myelinated neuron.

©IBO 2007

The nature of nerve impulses is discussed in this section.

At rest, there is a potential difference between the outside of the membrane of an axon and the inside. *Refer to Figure 625.* This resting potential varies a little in different species and different parts of the nervous system but the usual (average) value used is -70 mV. This means that the outside is positive compared to the inside.

It has been found that the concentration of Na^+ is higher outside, while K^+ concentration is higher inside the axon. Since both have a charge of +1, this does not create a potential difference. The distribution of Cl^- and negatively charged organic ions are responsible for the resting potential. The situation is maintained by the properties of the selectively permeable membrane.

value has reached +40 mV, the sodium pores shut and the potassium pores open.

The K^+ moves through the potassium channels out of the axon. *Refer to Figure 626 (b).*

The forces behind this are diffusion and electrical forces. As a result the potential difference across the membrane will start to decrease (repolarization) and as soon as it falls below zero, K^+ is only driven out by forces of diffusion.

The potassium pores will shut when the potential difference is restored to approximately –70 mV.

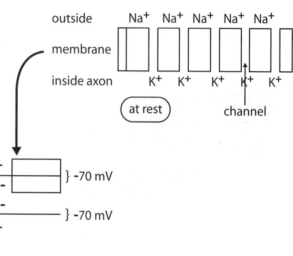

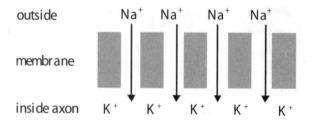

Figure 625   The transmission of a nerve impulse

ACTION POTENTIAL

Information travels down a neuron as an action potential. An **action potential** is generated by a stimulus of a receptor or from an action potential from another neuron.

Initially, in an action potential, the sodium pores suddenly open.

Due to the difference in concentration of sodium outside and inside, the sodium diffuses in. Also the electrical forces will cause Na^+ to go from a positively charged environment into a negatively charged environment. This influx of positive ions reduces the potential difference and is called depolarization. *Refer to Figure 626 (a).*

As soon as the potential difference is above zero, the Na^+ is now only driven by diffusion forces. The inside of the axon is now more positive than the outside and the movement of Na^+ is into the more positively charged area. When the

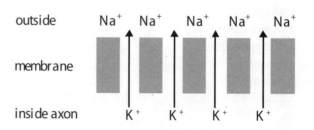

Figure 626 (a)   Depolarization

Figure 626 (b)   Repolarization

Although the potential difference is back at its original value, the Na⁺ and K⁺ ions are in the 'wrong' place. The sodium/potassium pump will return them to their original positions by active transport.

The action potential, shown in Figure 627, is the time of depolarization (1 msec). Repolarization is the refractory period and is divided into the absolute refractory state (1 msec), followed by the relative refractory state (up to 10 msec). During the absolute refractory state, no new impulse is possible. During the relative refractory state, the potential is below the resting potential of –70 mV and a stronger stimulus is required to generate an action potential.

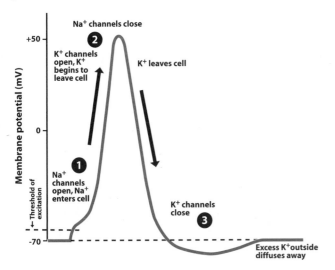

Figure 627   The action potential

The refractory period is followed by the action of the Na/K pump which returns the ions to their original sides of the membrane. A neuron can generate thousands of action potentials before the change in concentration of Na⁺ and K⁺ ions affects the cell.

THRESHOLD POTENTIAL

An action potential is not generated by every impulse. A threshold potential needs to be reached (which means a depolarisation to –40 to –50 mV) or the impulse fades out; it is called an 'all or nothing response'.

So, for a certain neuron, all action potentials are identical. The strength of the stimulus is conveyed by the frequency of the action potentials. Using the ear as an example: sounds of a different frequency (pitch) will stimulate different neurons and end up in slightly different places in the brain. Sounds of the same frequency but different loudness will have a different frequency of action potentials in the same neuron.

6.5.6   Explain the principles of synaptic transmission.

©IBO 2007

ELECTRICAL SYNAPSES (Not in the syllabus)

Two neurons may have membranes pressed close together with minute pores through them called gap junctions. An impulse can travel from one membrane to another causing an action potential in the second neuron. Electrical synapses are faster than chemical ones. They occur in invertebrates' giant axons and are related to escape responses. Vertebrate fish have electrical synapses to activate the tail flip which is used in quick starts for escape or in catching prey.

CHEMICAL SYNAPSES

In the **synapse**, the arrival of an action potential causes a change in membrane permeability for Ca²⁺. As a result, Ca²⁺ flows into the synaptic knob. The consequence of this is exocytosis of a transmitter substance in vesicles. This neurotransmitter then diffuses across the synaptic cleft (20 nm) and attaches to receptors in the post-synaptic membrane. A chemical synapse is shown in Figure 628. In an excitatory synapse, the receptor sites change their configuration and open the Na⁺ channels which causes an action potential in the neuron. In an inhibitory synapse, the configuration change in the receptors opens the K⁺ and Cl⁻ channels; K⁺ moves out and Cl⁻ moves in, increasing polarisation of the neuron and increasing the distance from the threshold value.

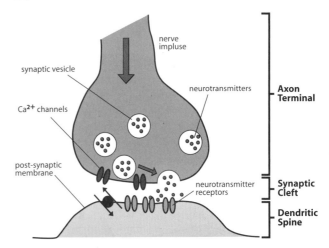

Figure 628   Chemical synapses

After the post-synaptic membrane has been affected, enzymes break down the neurotransmitter. (Acetyl) cholinesterase (found on the post-synaptic membrane) changes acetylcholine into choline and ethanoic acid. These diffuse back to the synaptic knob, then are absorbed and recycled into acetylcholine.

CORE

Acetylcholine is a common neurotransmitter found in synapses all through the nervous system. Noradrenaline is found in synapses of the sympathetic nervous system; dopamine and serotonin are two examples of neurotransmitters found in the brain.

> 6.5.7 State that the endocrine system consists of glands that release hormones that are transported in the blood.
>
> ©IBO 2007

The **endocrine system** consists of endocrine glands which produce hormones and secrete them into the blood. Endocrine glands are ductless glands; they do not release their product into a duct, as exocrine glands (e.g. sweat glands) do. Instead, endocrine glands secrete their product (hormones) into the blood which transports it around the body. As the hormone passes cells, only those with special receptors will react to the presence of the hormone. These cells are called target cells.

> 6.5.8 State that homeostasis involves maintaining the internal environment between limits, including blood pH, carbon dioxide concentration, blood glucose concentration, body temperature and water balance.
>
> ©IBO 2007

Homeostasis refers to the maintenance of the internal environment within acceptable limits, despite possible fluctuations in the external environment. The internal environment consists of blood and tissue fluid. The maintenance of fairly constant temperatures in water baths and air conditioning systems are two examples of homeostasis in non-biological systems.

Examples of biological homeostasis are, the maintenance of:
- blood pH
- carbon dioxide concentration
- blood glucose concentration
- body temperature
- water balance

Blood pH is maintained within narrow limits, around pH 7.4. The blood plasma contains buffers to minimise the fluctuations in the pH, caused by e.g. dissolving carbon dioxide.

Oxygen and carbon dioxide concentrations are maintained with the aid of a system of chemoreceptors in the walls of certain blood vessels (see Topic H.6).

The maintenance of the blood glucose level is described in *Topic 6.5.11*.
The maintenance of the body temperature is described in *Topic 6.5.10*.
The maintenance of the water balance is described in *Topic 11.3*.

> 6.5.9 Explain that homeostasis involves monitoring levels of variables and correcting changes in levels by negative feedback mechanisms.
>
> ©IBO 2007

Negative feedback is the control of a process by the result or effect of the process in such a way that an increase or decrease in the results or effects is always reversed.

The process of negative feedback requires certain elements to be present. It requires sensors to measure the current situation. The sensors need to pass on the information to

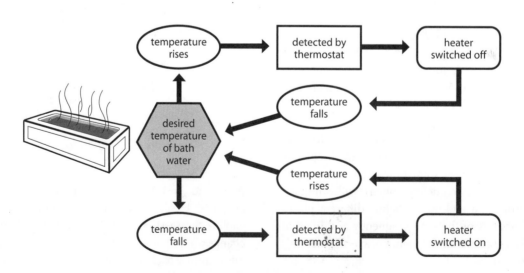

Figure 629   Homeostasis in a non-biological system

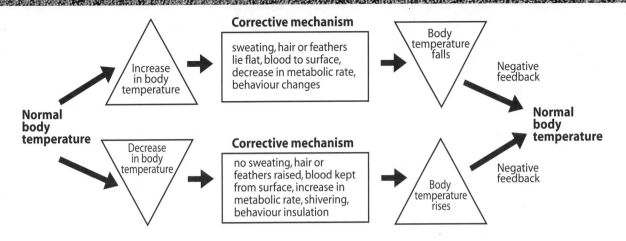

Figure 630   The regulation of body temperature

CORE

a centre which knows the desired value (the norm) and compares the current situation to the norm. If these two are not the same, then the centre activates a mechanism to bring the current value closer to the norm. When this has happened, the centre will turn off the mechanism. This is the key to negative feedback. The action taken aims at changing a situation so that the action is no longer required. In Figure 629, a change in temperature is detected. When the water in the bath becomes too cold, the heater is switched on. This will result in the water warming up and the heater being switched off. So the action will result in a change which will cancel the action.

> 6.5.10 Explain the control of body temperature, including the transfer of heat in blood, and the roles of the hypothalamus, sweat glands, skin arterioles and shivering.
>
> ©IBO 2007

THERMOREGULATION

The body of a mammal/bird has thermoreceptors in the skin and in the heat centre in the hypothalamus of the brain. This way, it monitors temperature changes in the environment as well as changes in the blood temperature. An example of how a mammal/bird can correct temperature change is shown in Figure 630.

If the organism is too hot, it can cool down using one or more of the following mechanisms:

- vasodilation
- sweating
- decreased metabolism
- behaviour adaptations

Vasodilation

The blood vessels in the skin become wider which increases the flow of blood to the skin. As a result, the skin becomes warmer which increases heat loss to the environment. Convection and radiation are increased.

Sweating

Evaporation of fluid from the skin; change of phase (liquid to gas) requires energy which is taken from the body. Panting has the same effect.

Decreased metabolism

Many reactions produce heat as a by-product.

Behaviour adaptations

For example:

- birds - bathing
- desert rodents - retreat into humid burrows
- dogs - dig holes and allow cool earth to absorb heat from belly

If the organism is too cold, it can warm up using one or more of the following mechanisms:

- vasoconstriction
- shivering
- Increased metabolism
- 'fluffing' of hair or feathers
- thick layer of brown fat or of blubber
- special structures e.g. polar bears have hairs which absorb UV light

Vasoconstriction

The blood vessels in the skin contract which decreases the flow of blood to the skin. As a result, the skin becomes colder, reducing the heat loss to the environment. Convection and radiation are decreased.

CORE

Shivering

Any reaction will produce heat as a by-product. Muscular contractions produce a lot of heat.

Increased metabolism

Increased production of heat in some organs e.g liver.

'Fluffing' of hair or feathers

This increases the thickness of the insulating layer of air.

Thick layer of brown fat or of blubber

This is a good insulator and reduces radiation and convection and also generates heat.

Special structure hair

Hair which absorbs UV light (polar bears).

Heat is not produced equally in all parts of the body, neither is it lost equally. The blood, moving round all parts of the body, will carry heat around. When you are out in the cold, your nose may go red. It is losing a lot of heat and the cells are in danger of being damaged. To compensate for the rapid loss of heat, dilating the blood vessels increases the blood supply to your nose, which brings in more warm blood and turns your nose red.

6.5.11	Explain the control of blood glucose concentration, including the roles of glucagon, insulin and α and β cells in the pancreatic islets.
	©IBO 2007

The pancreas is both an exocrine and an endocrine gland. The pancreas is found below the stomach, as can be seen in Figure 631. The exocrine cells in the pancreas produce digestive enzymes which are released into the small intestine via the pancreatic duct *(see Topic 6.1.4 and H.2)*.

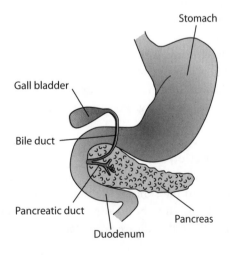

Figure 631   Location of the pancreas

The endocrine cells are clustered together in groups called the islets of Langerhans, which are shown in Figure 632. They produce hormones, which help in regulating the blood glucose levels.

Cells in the islets of Langerhans in the pancreas have chemoreceptors which are sensitive to levels of glucose in the blood.

In Figure 632 the islets of Langerhans are the light cells near the centre. The darker cells around them are exocrine pancreatic cells.

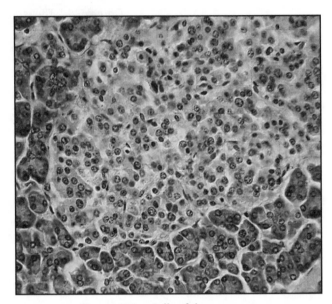

Figure 632   Cells of the pancreas

Glucose is absorbed from digested food and is used in cellular respiration. It can also be converted to glycogen and stored. Levels of glucose could go up after a meal and down after exercise if not carefully regulated.

If blood glucose levels are too low, the α cells in the islets of Langerhans in the pancreas will secrete glucagon. **Glucagon** is a protein hormone and is secreted into the blood. It will travel to all parts of the body but the liver is the main target organ. Hepatocytes (cells in the liver) will respond to the presence of glucagon by converting glycogen to glucose and releasing it to the blood. They also convert amino acids into glucose (indirectly). *See Figure 633.*

If blood glucose levels are too high, the β cells in the islets of Langerhans in the pancreas will secrete insulin. **Insulin** is a protein hormone and is secreted into the blood. It will travel to all parts of the body. The presence of insulin will make the muscle cells absorb more glucose and the muscle

CORE

cells and hepatocytes convert glucose into glycogen. In adipose tissue (fat tissue), glucose is converted to fat in the presence of the hormone insulin. *See Figure 633.*

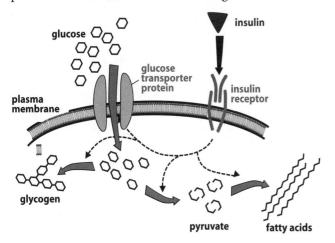

Figure 633   How insulin works

6.5.12	Distinguish between *type I* and *type II* diabetes.

©IBO 2007

Diabetes (diabetus mellitus) is a metabolic disorder where the person does not produce enough insulin or the body does not react properly to insulin. As a result, the person is likely to have hyperglycemia (too much glucose in the blood) from time to time. Hyperglycemia can cause damage to nerves and to the retina in the eye, causing blindness, damage to bloodvessels, renal failure and when acute can cause a coma and even result in death. Diabetes cannot be cured but it can be treated.

TYPE I DIABETES

No insulin, or insufficient levels of insulin, are produced by the beta (β) cells in the islets of Langerhans.

Causes
Usually caused by the body producing antibodies against insulin and/or the β cells in the islets of Langerhans.

Treatment
- Regularly injecting insulin (it is a protein so would be digested in the stomach if taken orally).
- Pancreas transplantation or β cell transplantation.

TYPE II DIABETES
Combination of two causes:
- insufficient amounts of insulin are produced
- cells of the body have become less sensitive to insulin

Causes
Causes are unknown, but factors that increase the likelyhood of type II diabetes are:
- obesity (especially with fat around the waist)
- increasing age
- family history; a person is more likely to develop type II diabetes if other people in the family have it too

Treatment
- reduced carbohydrate intake (diet) and increase physical activity (exercise)
- weight loss
- medication
    - to increase production of insulin
    - to lower blood glucose levels

TOK   What is the cause of diabetes?

The risk of type II diabetes is multi-faceted. Risk factors include lack of physical activity, being overweight, high blood pressure, high triglyceride levels as well as an age relationship. There are also genetic predispositions, for example the Pima, a group of Native American Indians, are of extreme risk of type II diabetes when removed from their ancestral diet and introduced to a Western diet of processed foods. Cases such as this indicate clearly that culture has a genetic role in the development of the disease.

Incidence of obesity is also thought to have a genetic link, with various genes having been identified that contribute to the incidence of obesity. Most studies in this area also conclude that there are significant environmental and lifestyle choice factors that also significantly contribute to the incidence of obesity in the world today.

CORE

6.6 REPRODUCTION

6.6.1	Draw and label diagrams of the adult male and female reproductive systems.

©IBO 2007

The male and female reproductive systems are shown in Figures 634 and 635, respectively.

6.6.2	Outline the role of hormones in the menstrual cycle, including FSH (follicle stimulating hormone), LH (luteinizing hormone), estrogen and progesterone.

©IBO 2007

In the female, there are four hormones involved in the control of the monthly cycle. These four hormones are outlined in Figure 636. They are:

- Follicle Stimulating Hormone (FSH)
- Luteinizing Hormone (LH)
- Estrogen
- Progesterone

FSH and LH are produced by the anterior lobe of the pituitary gland in the brain. Estrogen and progesterone are produced in the ovaries.

The cycle starts with the release of FSH from the pituitary gland, which is about the size of a pea and deep within the brain. As its name suggests FSH stimulates the ripening of a follicle. The growing follicle releases estrogen. Estrogen increases the thickness of the endometrium and inhibits the production of FSH, but stimulates the production of LH. LH stimulates ovulation and the formation of the

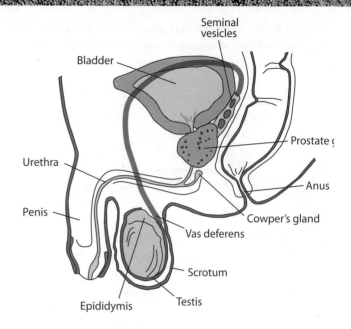

Figure 634   Male reproductive system

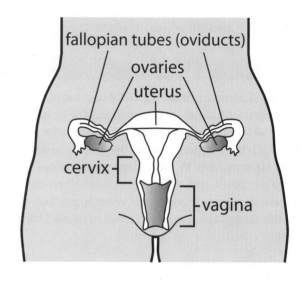

Figure 635   Female reproductive system

	Produced by	**Function**
FSH	pituitary gland	stimulates follicle growth stimulates estrogen secretion stimulates progesterone secretion a surge in FSH concentration stimulates ovulation
LH	pituitary gland	a surge in LH concentration stimulates ovulation stimulates formation of corpus luteum
Estrogen	ovary - growing follicle	stimulates thickening of endometrium promotes secondary sexual characteristics e.g. growth of breasts, widening of hips inhibits secretion of FSH stimulates secretion of LH
Progesterone	ovary - corpus luteum (placenta during pregnancy)	inhibits ovulation maintains endometrium inhibits FSH inhibits LH

Figure 636   The hormones involved in the menstrual cycle

corpus luteum. The corpus luteum produces progesterone which keeps the endometrium intact and inhibits both FSH and LH. If fertilisation does not occur, the corpus luteum degenerates and the pituitary will start producing FSH again to stimulate another follicle. *Refer to Figure 637*.

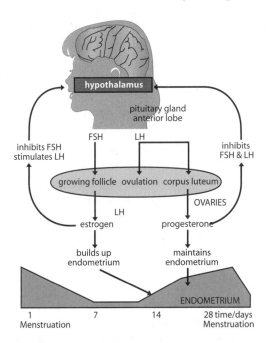

Figure 637   A diagram of the menstrual cycle

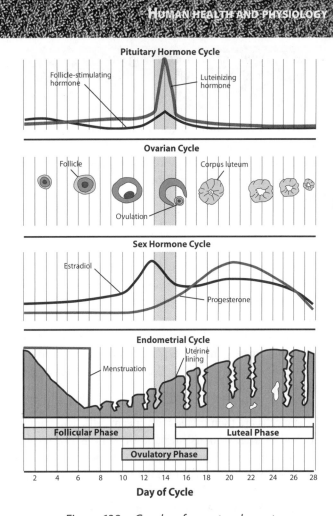

Figure 638   Graphs of menstrual events

> **6.6.3   Annotate a graph showing hormone levels in the menstrual cycle, illustrating the relationship between changes in hormone levels and ovulation, menstruation and thickening of the endometrium.**
>
> ©IBO 2007

The graphs shown in Figure 638 illustrate various aspects of the menstrual cycle.

> **6.6.4   List three roles of testosterone in males.**
>
> ©IBO 2007

Testosterone is a hormone produced by the testes. It has a variety of functions in the male body, these include:

- promotion of male secondary sexual characteristics, e.g. facial and chest hair *(see Figure 639)*, extra muscles, deeper voice
- growth and activity of the male reproductive organs
- spermatogenesis
- enhanced sexual desire (libido)
- enhances immune function
- protection against osteoporosis

Figure 639   Facial hair is an effect of testosterone

6.6.5 Outline the process of in vitro fertilization (IVF)

©IBO 2007

IVF is *in vitro* fertilization ('*in vitro*' - 'in glass'). In this procedure, the egg and sperm cells 'meet' outside the female's body. A successful procedure results in a so-called 'test tube baby'. The first test tube baby was Louise Brown, born in 1978.

IVF is used for women who have blocked **fallopian tubes** (oviducts), usually due to an earlier infection, or who cannot sustain a pregnancy. Depending on the reasons for the IVF procedure, it may be possible to use the egg cells of the woman who wants to get pregnant. If not, donor egg cells can be used. In either case, the woman generating the egg cells is treated with hormones so that more than one follicle will ripen. A needle is placed in the follicle and the egg cell is carefully removed. This is repeated until all egg cells are harvested.

The egg cells are then mixed with sperm cells. This can be supplied by the woman's husband or, if he is not fertile, by a sperm donor. If the quality of the sperm is poor, a sperm cell may be injected into the egg cell. The fertilised egg cells are cultivated and either placed inside the uterus or frozen so that they can be used later. The number of embryos placed in the uterus depends on several factors and policies about this depend on the country and even the opinion of the doctor involved. It is important to consider that, if all embryos were to implant successfully, that a multiple pregnancy may result in a premature delivery and a reduced chance of survival for the babies.

6.6.6 Discuss the ethical issues associated with IVF.

©IBO 2007

There are a lot of ethical issues associated with IVF. A search on the Internet will provide many sites explaining arguments for and against.

When looking for information on the Internet, make sure you check when the information was posted and the nature of the organisation managing the website. This is particularly important for something like IVF where information, such as the statistics, have changed considerably over the past few years.

Some issues with IVF are:
- the creation of life in a laboratory
- freezing embryos and keeping them in case they are needed
- discarding surplus embryos or using them for (stem cell) research
- the possibility of creating embryos for research
- the possibility of selecting embryos
- the potential possibility to modify embryos
- the birth mother may not be genetic mother
- elderly women can have babies (using egg cell donors)

TOK   What are the risks of IVF?

As with all medical procedures, IVF brings risk to the patient, the mother, and in this case, the potential offspring. As IVF bypasses the natural selection process through which the 'fittest' sperm reaches the egg in the oviduct there has been some suggestion that the incidence of abnormality in IVF offspring is higher than in naturally conceived children. At present there is no conclusive evidence for this argument.

Technologies are routinely employed to examine an IVF embryo by removing one or two cells soon after conception and examining them for chromosomal or other abnormalities. The discovery of abnormalities would lead to a discussion with the parents as to whether or not the embryo would be destroyed.

The stimulation of the mother's ovaries ahead of the IVF procedure can adversely affect the ovaries and the overall health of the mother. IVF therapy usually involves implanting multiple embryos to increase the chance of a successful pregnancy. This has led to an increase in multiple pregnancies, leading to a greater risk to the mother and to the offspring in multiple deliveries.

Of course there is also the ethical issue to consider that reproductive technologies such as IVF are available to a relatively small proportion of the world's population who are unable to conceive naturally at a time of their choice, while more than ten million children under five die each year from lack of basic needs such as clean water or diseases for which vaccines exist but are unavailable in their community.

EXERCISES

1 Salivary amylase works best at a pH of:
   A 5-6
   B 6-7
   C 7-8
   D 8-9

The diagram below shows a schematic representati on of the digestive tract. Questions 2-4 refer to the labels on this diagram.

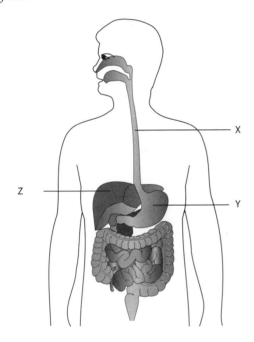

2 Label X points to the:
   A liver.
   B esophagus.
   C stomach.
   D colon.

3 Label Y points to the:
   A liver.
   B esophagus.
   C stomach.
   D colon.

4 Label Z points to:
   A liver.
   B esophagus.
   C stomach.
   D colon.

5 The process by which the body takes up the substances that it needs is known as:
   A digestion.
   B absorption.
   C excretion.
   D respiration.

6 Carbohydrates and proteins are known as:
   A micronutrients.
   B macronutrients.
   C dietary fibre.
   D minerals.

7 The part of the heart labelled X in the schematic diagram is the:

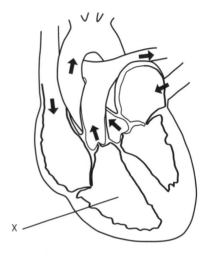

   A tricuspid valve.
   B aorta.
   C right ventricle.
   D right atrium.

8 The electrochemical impulses that trigger the contractions of the heart originate in the:
   A sino atrial node.
   B brain.
   C spinal cord.
   D atrio ventricular node

9 The main blood vessels are the arteries, veins and capillaries. In order of decreasing blood pressure, these should be arranged:
   A arteries, veins, capillaries.
   B veins, capillaries, arteries.
   C capillaries, arteries, veins.
   D arteries, capillaries, veins.

10 Approximately 90% of blood cells are:
   A erythrocytes.
   B leucocytes.
   C thrombocytes.
   D plasma.

11 The main mechanism by which the body restricts infections of the stomach is its:
   A   alkalinity.
   B   acidity.
   C   large surface area.
   D   mucous secretions.

12 A globular protein that recognises an antigen is known as:
   A   a virus.
   B   a bacterium.
   C   an antigen.
   D   an antibody.

13 Which one of the following are features of alveoli that allow them to carry out gas exchange efficiently?
   A   small surface area.
   B   their thinness.
   C   their very high moisture content.
   D   limited blood supply.

14 Very small organisms such as algae do not need gills or lungs because:
   A   they have a comparatively small surface area to volume ratio that allows them to exchange nutrients and waste products with their environment.
   B   they have a comparatively large surface area to volume ratio that allows them to exchange nutrients and waste products with their environment.
   C   they have a comparatively small surface area to volume ratio which means that they need very little food to survive.
   D   they have a comparatively small mass which allows them to exchange nutrients and waste products with their environment.

15 The ribs are moved by the:
   A   intercostal muscles.
   B   diaphragm.
   C   alveoli.
   D   thorax.

16 The process of temperature regulation in the human body is an example of:
   A   homeostasis.
   B   respiration.
   C   excretion.
   D   dilation.

17 The control of a process by the result or effect of the process in such a way that an increase or decrease in the results or effects is always reversed is known as:
   A   convection.
   B   negative feedback.
   C   positive feedback.
   D   shivering.

18 (a)   Describe the structure of the villus
   (b)   Explain how this structure makes it suitable to absorb and transport nutrients.

19 (a)   Why do arteries have thick walls?
   (b)   Why does the blood in capillaries flow at a relatively low speed?
   (c)   Why do many veins have valves?

20 List what is transported by the blood.

21 Outline the process of antibody production.

22 Outline the effect of the HIV virus on the immune system and on antibody production

23 (a)   Draw a diagram of the human respiratory system.
   (b)   What features of alveoli make them suitable for gaseous exchange?
   (c)   How does the structure of alveoli affect its function?
   (d)   Why do lungs need to be ventilated?

24 Compare resting potential and action potential

25 (a)   List the elements that are involved in thermoregulation in humans.
   (b)   Outline how the organism can reduce heat loss.

26 Birth control pills contain substances resembling estrogen and progesterone. Explain how keeping these hormones in the blood at a high level prevents pregnancy.

27 Outline the role of the skin and mucous membranes in preventing pathogens from entering the organism.

NUCLEIC ACIDS AND PROTEINS

7.1 DNA structure

7.2 DNA replication

7.3 Transcription

7.4 Translation

7.5 Proteins

7.6 Enzymes

7

AHL

7.1 DNA STRUCTURE

> 7.1.1 Describe the structure of DNA, including the antiparallel strands, 3' - 5' linkages and hydrogen bonding between purines and pyrimidines.
>
> ©IBO 2007

The **DNA** double helix is made of two antiparallel strands, kept together by hydrogen bonds between the organic bases *(see also Topic 3.3.4).*

Each DNA strand is made up of a chain of nucleotides. Each nucleotide is composed of a sugar (deoxyribose), a phosphate group and a nitrogenous base.

It is possible to assign numbers to the carbon atoms in deoxyribose. By convention, the numbering of the Carbon atoms is done as shown in Figure 701.

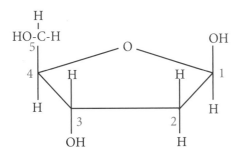

Figure 701   Deoxyribose sugar

If we then draw in the phosphate (circle) and the nitrogenous base (rectangle), the result is a **nucleotide**, as shown in Figure 702.

Figure 702   A nucleotide

The phosphate is covalently attached to C_5 of the deoxyribose. In a single strand of DNA, the phosphate of the next nucleotide will attach to C_3. This is called a 3' - 5' (phosphodiester) bond or linkage.

A DNA strand therefore, ends on one side with a phosphate on the 5 prime (5') end of the deoxyribose and on the other with a deoxyribose at the 3 prime (3') end. Since there are two strands which are antiparallel, the result is shown in Figure 703. The sequence of the nucleotides is customarily given in the 5' to 3' direction.

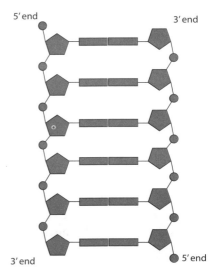

Figure 703   The DNA double strand

7.1.2   Outline the structure of nucleosomes.
©IBO 2007

Analysis of chromosomes has shown that they are made of DNA and protein and a small amount of chromosomal RNA. (The 'chromosomes' of prokaryotes, like bacteria, are made of only DNA.)

DNA has negative charges along the strand and positively charged proteins are bonded to this by electrostatic forces. These basic proteins are called histones. The complex of DNA and protein is known as chromatin.

There are different opinions on the total length of DNA in a eukaryotic cell. The values given range from 2 m to 3 m for the total length of the DNA in a human cell. This means that an average chromosome is around 4 – 6 cm long.

A typical eukaryotic nucleus is between 11 and 22 μm $= 22 \times 10^{-6}$ m in size. {1 millimetre=1000 micrometres (μm)}

This means that the length of the DNA needs to be reduced 2000 to 6000 times. You can imagine that this requires good organisation to prevent the DNA from getting tangled. The answer to how this packing ration is accomplished is found in the existence of nucleosomes. The structure of a nucleosome is shown in Figure 704.

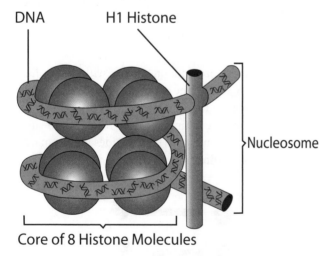

Figure 704   The structure of a nucleosome

High resolution EM images of DNA have shown that the genetic material looks like beads on a string. This is caused by the DNA helix combining with eight small histone molecules with an additional histone (H1) keeping it all together. These structures are called **nucleosomes**.

Figure 705 illustrates how the nucleosomes interact with each other and achieve a high degree of organisation in the process of shortening the DNA to a more manageable length.

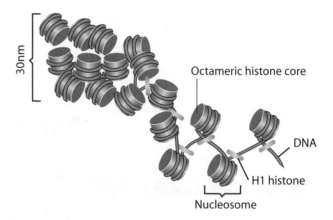

Figure 705   The arrangement of nucleosomes along the DNA helix

7.1.3   State that nucleosomes help to supercoil chromosomes and help to regulate transcription.
©IBO 2007

Nucleosomes are important in two ways. The first was illustrated in Figure 705, that is nucleosomes help to organise the DNA so that it can fit into a nucleus. When they are in this compact arrangement, the chromosomes are described as supercoiled. The second role of nucleosomes is to prevent transcription.

Transcription is the process in which the antisense strand of the DNA is used as a template for producing a strand of RNA *(see Topics 3.5 and 7.3)*. In order for transcription to occur, RNA polymerase needs to be able to attach to the promotor region of the 3' end of the structural gene on the DNA. If the DNA is organised into nucleosomes, the promotor region is usually not accessible to RNA polymerase and therefore, transcription will not occur.

When the cell requires transcription to occur, enzymes will alter the shape of the nucleosomes to allow RNA polymerase to attach to the promotor region of the DNA strand and to start the process of transcription.

7.1.4 Distinguish between *unique or single-copy genes* and *highly repetitive sequences* in nuclear DNA.

©IBO 2007

Nuclear DNA contains sequences for genes, sequences that regulate genes and sequences that have no currently-known function.

Unique genes are also called single-copy genes or codable genes. They make up only about 1.5% of the human genetic material. These are the genes that carry our genetic information as outlined in Mendelian genetics *(see Topic 4.3)*.

The remainder of the human genetic material includes repetitive sequences of DNA that seem to have no known function for the individual. It has been suggested that they play a role in genetic control processes, but the details are not yet understood. Some repetitive sequences are used in DNA research, for example determining parentage or crime forensics.

TOK   What is meant by 'junk' DNA?

Interpretation of information is influenced by the labels that are associated with it. Labels allow us to quickly categorise the importance or relevance of information.

It is now known that most of a eukaryote's genome is made up of repetitive sequences of DNA that appear to be non-coding.

At first this genetic material was labelled 'junk' DNA. This arrogantly emotive label suggested that this DNA was useless. Such an idea runs contrary to evolutionary theory which would predict that a useless code would not persist in the genome. The sheer size of the genome that is repetitive and the fact that it is found in all eukaryotes has led scientists to change the label.

What is becoming increasingly obvious is that repetitive DNA sequences are likely to have a significant role in organisms that is beyond current human knowledge and understanding.

Think of some other examples in which labels used in the pursuit of knowledge affect the knowledge we obtain.

7.1.5 State that eukaryotic genes can contain exons and introns.

©IBO 2007

While in prokaryotes, genes are uninterrupted sections of DNA, it appears that in eukaryotic cells, coding sections of DNA are interrupted with long non-coding intervening sequences. In other words, many genes are discontinuous. The intervening sequences are called **introns**, while the coding sequences are called **exons** (since they are **ex**pressed). *Refer to Figure 706.*

(a) EUKARYOTES

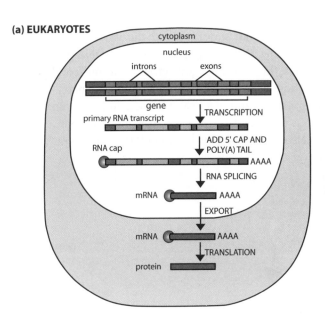

(b) PROKARYOTES

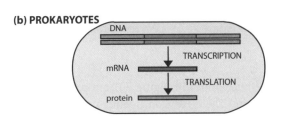

Figure 706   Only eukaryotic DNA contains introns

AHL

7.2 DNA REPLICATION

7.2.1 State that DNA replication occurs in a 5′ → 3′ direction.

©IBO 2007

As described in *Topic 3.5*, **DNA replication** is a semi-conservative mechanism. This was demonstrated by Meselson and Stahl in 1958.

Semi-conservative essentially means that in the process of DNA replication, the DNA double helix 'unzips' and new hydrogen bonds are formed with the organic bases of DNA nucleotides 'floating around' in the cell. DNA polymerase creates the 3'-5' linkages between the nucleotides thus creating a new DNA strand, complementary to the original one and identical to the one that was 'unzipped'. DNA polymerase creates the covalent bonds between the nucleotides of the growing strand. *Refer to Figure 707.*

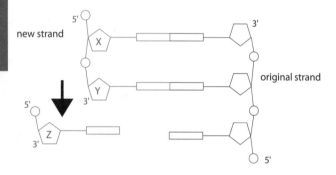

Figure 707   DNA replication

The 'black' nucleotides in Figure 707 are part of the old, existing chain. The 'green' nucleotides are part of the new, growing chain. Nucleotide X is in place. Nucleotide Y has just been added and nucleotide Z is in the process of forming hydrogen bonds between its organic base and the complementary base on the existing chain. The DNA polymerase will catalyse the formatin of a covalent bond between the 3' end of nucleotide Y (the nucleotide that has just been added) and the 5' end of nucleotide Z (the nucleotide that is being added). So if you draw in an arrow pointing in the direction of the most recently added nucleotide, the arrow will point from the 5' end to the 3' end. This means that DNA replication occurs in a 5' to 3' direction.

7.2.2 Explain the process of DNA replication in prokaryotes, including the role of enzymes (helicase, DNA polymerase, RNA primase and DNA ligase), Okazaki fragments and deoxynucleoside triphosphates.

©IBO 2007

DNA replication is a semi-conservative process. This means that the two "old" DNA strands that form the helix will unwind and unzip (separate), and a new complementary strand is formed for each "old" strand. So this process results in two complete new molecules of DNA and each of these will be made of an "old" strand and a "new" strand. *(Note that all of the enzymes involved end with –ase.)*

Prokaryotic DNA replication is illustrated in Figure 708. It involves the following steps:

- The DNA is a double helix (like a twisted ladder) which needs to be unwound by the enzyme helicase.

- Helicase also breaks the hydrogen bonds between the two strands (between the base pairs) separating the strands. One of the old strands will be 3'→5' while the other strand will be 5'→3'.

- Present in the cell are deoxyribonucleoside triphosphates which are composed of an organic base, a deoxyribose sugar and three phosphate groups. They are sometimes referred to as dATP, dCTP, dGTP and dTTP.

- Before a new strand of DNA can be formed, it is necessary to start with an RNA primer. The RNA primer is a few RNA nucleotides which bind to the old DNA strand (hydrogen bonding between the organic bases). The enzyme RNA primase will bind these RNA nucleotides together (covalent bonds).

- Now that the RNA primer is in place, the deoxyribonucleoside triphosphates will form hydrogen bonds between their organic bases and the complementary base on the exposed strand of the old DNA, i.e. A with T and C with G.

- In the new strand that is forming in the 5'→3' direction, the 'leading strand', DNA polymerase III will bind the new nucleotides to the growing strand by covalent bonds formed via condensation reactions. DNA polymerase III only works in a 5'→3' direction.

- As it attaches to the growing DNA strand, the second and third phosphate groups are removed from the deoxyribonucleoside triphosphate, changing it into deoxyribonucleotide (organic base, deoxyribose sugar, phosphate).

- The other new strand, the lagging strand, would have to grow in a 3'→5' direction to keep up. However, DNA polymerase III cannot work in this direction. As a result, the lagging strand is formed in short segments of 100 – 200 nucleotides (called Okazaki fragments) in a 5'→3' direction. The process is the same:

  - RNA primer formed from RNA nucleotides by RNA primase.

  - Deoxyribonucleoside triphosphates form hydrogen bonds with the exposed organic bases of the old DNA strand.

  - DNA polymerase III, working in a 5' to 3' direction (i.e. away from the direction in which the DNA unwinds and unzips), binds the DNA nucleotides to form an Okazaki fragment.

- DNA polymerase I will then remove the RNA primer of the Okazaki fragment and replace the RNA nucleotides with DNA nucleotides.

- DNA ligase then catalyses the formatin of the bonds attaching the DNA segments to create one strand.

7.2.3   State that DNA replication is initiated at many points in eukaryotic chromosomes.

©IBO 2007

The rate of replication in fruit flies *(Drosophila)* is 2600 nucleotides/minute. The largest chromosome of *Drosophila* is 6.5×10^7 nucleotides. If DNA replication started at both ends of the chromosome, it would take 8.5 days to replicate the chromosome. In fact, it only takes 3-4 minutes. In order to explain this discrepancy, scientists have determined that replication must start at many points along the same DNA helix at the same time. *Refer to Figure 709.*

AHL

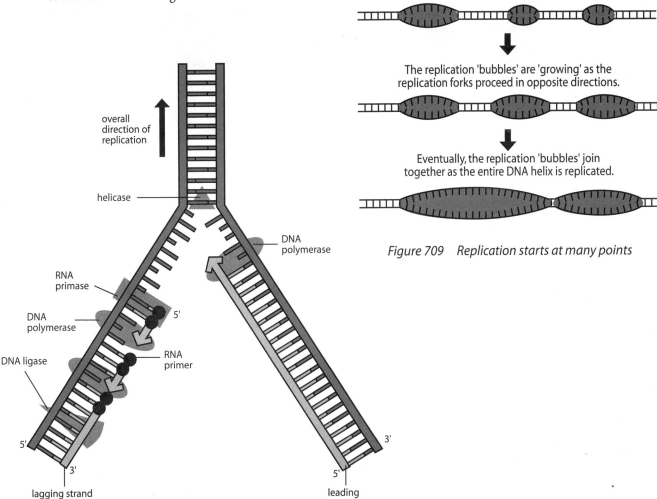

Replication 'bubbles' begin at different points along the DNA helix.

The replication 'bubbles' are 'growing' as the replication forks proceed in opposite directions.

Eventually, the replication 'bubbles' join together as the entire DNA helix is replicated.

Figure 709   Replication starts at many points

overall direction of replication

helicase

DNA polymerase

RNA primase

DNA polymerase

DNA ligase

RNA primer

5'

3'

5'

3'

5'

3'

lagging strand with Okazaki fragments

leading strand

Figure 708   DNA replication

123

7.3 TRANSCRIPTION

AHL

> **7.3.1** State that transcription is carried out in a 5'→3' direction.
>
> ©IBO 2007

Transcription is the enzyme-controlled process of synthesising RNA from a DNA template. It is carried out in a 5' to 3' direction (of the new RNA strand). This means that new RNA nucleotides are added to the 3' end of the growing RNA strand. The process involves RNA polymerase. mRNA, tRNA and rRNA all need to be transcribed for protein synthesis to take place.

> **7.3.2** Distinguish between the *sense* and *antisense* strands of DNA.
>
> ©IBO 2007

DNA is a double helix. Only one of the strands is transcribed into mRNA, which is translated into a polypeptide with the aid of tRNA. The DNA strand, which is transcribed, is called the **antisense strand**. The strand that is not transcribed is called the **sense strand.** The mRNA is complementary to the antisense strand. This makes it an "RNA version" of the sense strand, i.e. they have the same base sequence but RNA has uracil (U) instead of thymine (T).

In the process of **translation**, the tRNA anticodons are complementary to mRNA.

That makes the sequence of tRNA anticodons, as they associate with the ribosomes, the same as the DNA antisense strand, again replacing Thymine with Uracil.

An example of how the amino acid histidine is coded for is shown in Figure 710. There is no need to memorise this example.

> **7.3.3** Explain the process of transcription in prokaryotes, including the role of the promoter region, RNA polymerase, nucleoside triphosphates and the terminator.
>
> ©IBO 2007

Transcription in prokaryotic cells *(see Figure 711)* involves a promoter region. This is the site for binding RNA polymerase which will attach the individual nucleotides together to form a single strand of RNA. At the (5') end of the gene, a terminator site is found which will stop the transcription process.

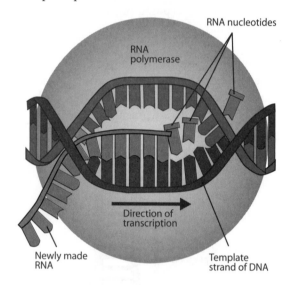

Figure 711   The process of transcription

RNA polymerase is similar to DNA polymerase and works in almost the same way, however, it can also function in a 3' to 5' direction. RNA nucleotides, in the form of ribonucleoside triphosphates, form hydrogen bonds with the complementary nucleotide of the DNA strand.

The only difference between ribonucleoside triphosphate and deoxyribonucleoside triphosphate is one hydroxyl group (-OH group) on C_2 in the pentose sugar. This changes the deoxyribose into ribose.

DNA		mRNA	tRNA	amino acid
sense strand	anti-sense strand (this is transcribed)	codon (this is translated)	anticodon	
CAT	GTA	CAU	GUA	histidine

Figure 710   The flow of genetic information from DNA to amino acid

As in DNA replication, the ribonucleoside triphosphate will attach (by a covalent bond) to the 3' hydroxyl group of the growing strand. The second and third phosphate groups will be removed, providing the energy required to drive this reaction.

> **7.3.4** State that eukaryotic RNA needs the removal of introns to form mature mRNA.
>
> ©IBO 2007

Whilst in prokaryotes, genes are uninterrupted sections of DNA, it appears that in eukaryotic cells, coding sections of DNA are interrupted with long non-coding intervening sequences. In other words, many genes are discontinuous. The intervening sequences are called introns, while the coding sequences are called exons since they are expressed.

It appears that the entire section of the DNA (introns and exons) is transcribed into RNA. Before the RNA leaves the nucleus, a 'cap', which is a single altered nucleotide added to the 5' end (the front) which will protect the mRNA from degradation by phosphatases and nucleases and assist in protein synthesis. A 'tail' (e.g. AAAAA) is added to the 3' end. The 'tail' will increase the stability of the mRNA, but is not required for translation or for transport to the cytoplasm.

Before the mRNA leaves the nucleus, enzymes will very precisely cut the bond between exon and intron nucleotides and attach the remaining exon nucleotides to each other. (The introns are taken out.) This process is called splicing. The RNA is now ready to be transported to the cytoplasm and called mature DNA.

It now seems that one gene can make different polypeptides by cutting out different sections of the mRNA. E.g. if a gene (DNA) has five sections which we label V, W, X, Y and Z, it is possible to splice out of the mRNA W and Y on one occasion (leaving mRNA V-X-Z to be translated) and on another occasion, to remove V and X, leaving mRNA section W-Y-Z to be translated into a different protein. *See Topic 3.5.5. Refer to Figure 706.*

7.4 TRANSLATION

> **7.4.1** Explain that each tRNA molecule is recognized by a tRNA-activating enzyme that binds a specific amino acid to the tRNA, using ATP for energy.
>
> ©IBO 2007

The structure of **tRNA** has the typical clover shape as shown in Figure 712.

At the 3' end, the amino acid will bind to the tRNA. Each amino acid has its own tRNA with a unique anticodon.

The amino acid is bound to the tRNA in a two step process catalysed by its own tRNA-activating enzyme:

1. The amino acid will react with ATP and become activated. The ATP loses its energy in this process.

2. The activated amino acid will then bind to the acceptor stem of its own tRNA.

AHL

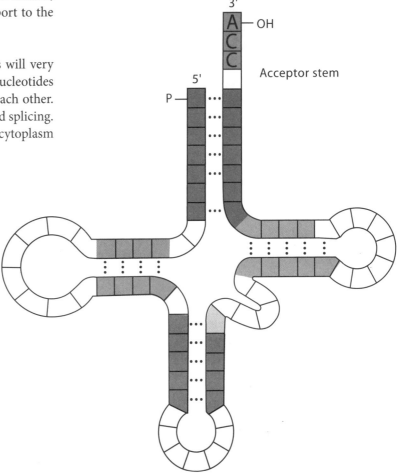

Figure 712   The transfer RNA (tRNA) molecule

AHL

As there are 20 different amino acids, there also will be 20 different tRNA-activating enzymes. The different tRNA-activating enzymes will recognise the correct tRNA to bind to the correct amino acid. The structure of each tRNA is unique, allowing only the correct tRNA (with the correct anticodon) to be matched with the correct amino acid.

The CCA sequence at the 3' end of the tRNA molecule *(see Figure 712)* forms a covalent bond with the appropriate amino acid (which is determined by the anticodon) by a condensation reaction. The -OH of the -COOH group of the amino acid will react with the -OH of adenine at the 3' end of the tRNA, forming water and leaving an oxygen to connect the two molecules. During translation, the bond between the tRNA and the amino acid is broken when the amino acid forms a peptide link with the growing polypeptide chain.

> **7.4.2** Outline the structure of ribosomes, including protein and RNA composition, large and small subunits, three tRNA binding sites and mRNA binding sites.
> ©IBO 2007

tRNA will not bind to mRNA, unless ribosomes are present. **Ribosomes** are the most numerous cell organelle. Cells can have thousands of ribosomes- eukaryotic cells even tens of thousands. Ribosomes measure approximately 25 nm in diameter. Ribosomes are sometimes clustered together on the mRNA, simultaneously creating several copies of the same polypeptide. They are then called a polyribosome or polysome.

Ribosomes are found in both prokaryotic and eukaryotic cells but have a slightly different structure in each and are larger in eukaryotic cells than in prokaryotic cells. Ribosomes are measured by their size and density in units called 'Svedberg' or 'S'. Prokaryotic ribosomes and ribosomes of chloroplasts and mitochondria are 70S, whereas eukaryotic ribosomes are 80S. *Refer to Figure 714.*

All ribosomes are made of protein and ribosomal RNA (rRNA). The nucleolus contains (many copies of) the information on how to make rRNA. Ribosomes consist of two subunits, a small and a large unit. The smaller subunit is made of one molecule of rRNA and some proteins, the larger subunit is made of two molecules of rRNA and some proteins, including the enzyme peptidyl transferase which links together the amino acids brought in by tRNA. The smaller subunit has the binding site for mRNA, the larger subunit has the binding sites (known as the A, P and E sites) for tRNA.

> **7.4.3** State that translation consists of initiation, elongation, translocation and termination.
> ©IBO 2007

The process of protein synthesis consists of several parts:

- transcription:
  The information is transcribed from the DNA to mRNA.

- Processing of the mRNA to remove introns.

- translation:
  The information is translated from mRNA codons into a polypeptide sequence.

- post translation modification:
  Example 1:
  Addition of functional groups such as carbohydrate groups to produce a glycoprotein. This happens in the ER or Golgi.

  Example 2:
  Proteolytic cleavage to remove a section of the polypeptide chain which can change, for example, an inactive enzyme into an active enzyme.

Translation takes place in a 5' to 3' direction of the mRNA and can be divided into three stages:

- initiation
- elongation
- termination

The polypeptide sequence is produced starting with the amino acid on the N terminus and finishing with the amino acid on the C terminus.

> **7.4.4** State that translation occurs in a 5'→3' direction.
> ©IBO 2007

The 'start' codon, which marks the beginning point of translation, is found at the 5' end of the mRNA. This means that translation takes place in a 5' to 3' direction (of the mRNA).

7.4.5 Draw and label a diagram showing the structure of a peptide bond between two amino acids.

©IBO 2007

Two amino acids participate in a condensation reaction and form a dipeptide and water. The condensation reaction takes place between the -OH of the -COOH of one amino acid and the -NH$_2$ of the next amino acid. The peptide bond (peptide linkage) is formed between N (with one H attached) and C (with a double bonded O attached). An example of a condensation reaction between two amino acids is shown in Figure 713.

7.4.6 Explain the process of translation, including ribosomes, polysomes, start codons and stop codons.

©IBO 2007

INITIATION

In order to start the process of translation, the ribosome needs to attach to the mRNA. There is a set sequence of events that eventually attach the ribosome to the mRNA:

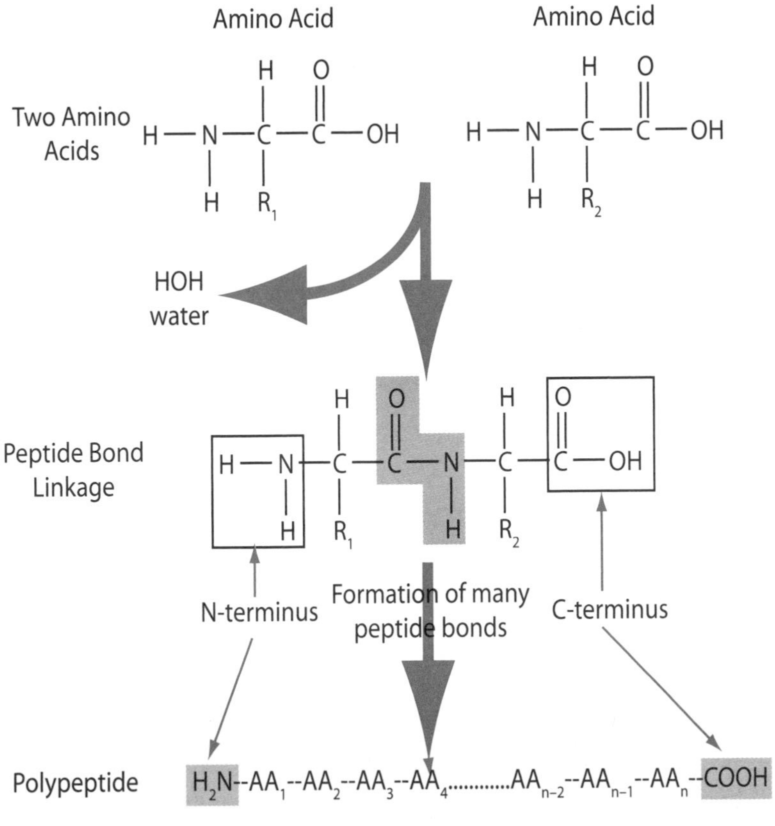

before initiation

1. tRNA + amino acid + ATP $\xrightarrow{\text{tRNA-activating enzyme}}$ activated tRNA-amino acid complex + AMP

initiation (in prokaryotes)

2. The start codon on the mRNA is AUG, so the first tRNA must have the anti-codon UAC and carry the amino acid methionine (met).

3. The tRNA will bind to the base of the P site on the small subunit of the ribosome with the aid of an ATPase enzyme (see Figure 714).

4. The rRNA of the small subunit will recognise and attach to the ribosomal binding site on the mRNA. This site is found near the 5' end of the mRNA.

5. The small subunit of the ribosome will slide along the mRNA until the base of the P site reaches the start codon (AUG).

6. The large subunit, containing the binding sites for tRNAs joins the complex.

ELONGATION

7. With the first tRNA attached to the P site, a slight change in the shape of the ribosome occurs, opening up the A site for the next tRNA to bind.

8. The second tRNA will bind to the A site.

9. The amino acid (met) of the first tRNA will be released from the tRNA and form a peptide link with the amino acid attached to the second tRNA (in the A site). This process is catalysed by peptidyltranferase which is part of the ribosome.

10. The ribosome now moves three nucleotides (one codon) along the mRNA (towards the 3' end).

11. This means that the first tRNA (minus its amino acid met) can now be found in the E binding site, the second tRNA (with the growing polypeptide chain attached) is now in the P site and the A site is available for the third tRNA (with amino acid) to bind.

Figure 713   Formation of a peptide bond

TERMINATION

12. The stop codons on the mRNA are found near the 3' end of the mRNA.

13. When the A site moves over one of the three stop codons, this is a signal to stop protein synthesis since there is no tRNA available that has an anti-codon complementary to a stop codon. Instead, a protein release factor comes in to break the bond between the polypeptide chain and the last tRNA (in the P position) by hydrolysis.

14. The polypeptide is released from the ribosome.

15. The tRNAs are released and the ribosome will dissociate into a large and a small subunit. All of these elements may be used again.

> 7.4.7 State that free ribosomes synthesize proteins for use primarily within the cell, and that bound ribosomes synthesize proteins primarily for secretion or for lysosomes.
>
> ©IBO 2007

The distribution of ribosomes depends on the function of the protein they make; if the proteins are to be used inside the cell, the ribosomes tend to be found throughout the cytoplasm; if the protein is to be exported (secretion) or used by lysosomes, the ribosomes are generally associated with the endoplasmic reticulum. These proteins will then enter the lumen of the RER as they are produced and from there move to the Golgi apparatus where they are packaged into vesicles (see Figure 239).

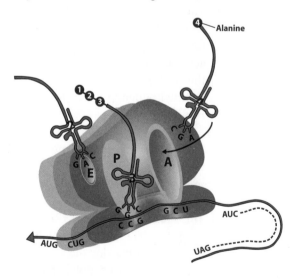

Figure 714   Translation and the ribosome

7.5 PROTEINS

> 7.5.1 Explain the four levels of protein structure, indicating the significance of each level..
>
> ©IBO 2007

Four 'levels' are distinguished in the structure of a protein:

- primary
- secondary
- tertiary
- quaternary.

PRIMARY STRUCTURE

The primary structure of a protein is the sequence of the amino acids in the chain. *Refer to Figure 715.* The linear sequence of amino acids with peptide linkages affects all the subsequent levels of structure since these are the consequence of interactions between the R groups of the amino acids. Each amino acid can be characterised by its R group. Polar R groups will interact with other polar R groups further down the chain and the same goes for non-polar R groups.

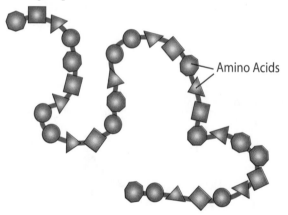

Figure 715   Primary structure

SECONDARY STRUCTURE

The secondary structure of a protein consists of the coils of the chain, for example α helix and β pleated sheet. *Refer to Figure 716.* α helix structures are found in the proteins of hair, wool, horns and feathers; β pleated sheet structures are found in silk. Hydrogen bonds are responsible for the secondary structure. Fibrous proteins like collagen and keratin are in helix or pleated sheet form which is caused by a regular repeated sequence of amino acids. They are structural proteins.

Beta pleated sheet   Alpha helix

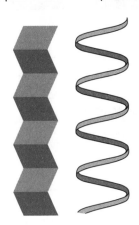

Figure 716   Secondary structure

TERTIARY STRUCTURE

The tertiary structure of a protein refers to the way the chain is folded. *Refer to Figure 717.* This is caused by the interactions between the R groups of the amino acids in the polypeptide chain. Hydrophobic groups cluster together on the inside of the protein (away from the water) while hydrophilic groups cluster together on the outside of the protein (near the water). Several amino acids have a sulfur atom in their R group. Two adjacent sulfur atoms may come together, under enzyme control and form a covalent bond called a disulfide bridge.

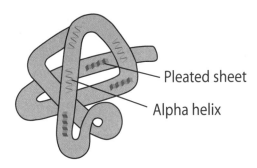

Pleated sheet

Alpha helix

Figure 717   Tertiary structure

Hydrogen bonds are also involved in the formation of the tertiary structure. Bonds between an ion serving as a cofactor *(see Topic 8.6)* and the R group of a certain amino acid may also be responsible for the folds in the polypeptide. Proteins which have a globular (folded) shape, such as hemoglobin, are called globular proteins. Microtubules are globular proteins but they have a structural function. Enzymes are globular proteins. The precise and unique folding of the polypeptide creates the 'active site', i.e. the location where the substrate binds to the enzyme so that the reaction can take place. *(see Topic 8.6).*

QUATERNARY STRUCTURE

The quaternary structure of a protein involves the combination of different polypeptide chains. *Refer to Figure 718.* Many proteins (especially large globular proteins) are made of more than one polypeptide chain. Together, with the greater variety in amino acids, this causes a greater range of biological activity. The different polypeptide chains are kept together by hydrogen bonds, attraction between positive and negative charges, hydrophobic forces and disulfide bridges or any combination of the above.

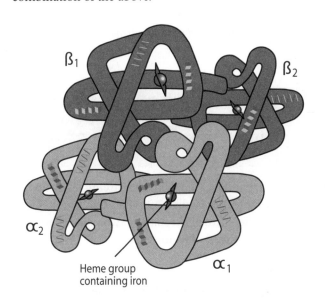

β_1 β_2

α_2

Heme group
containing iron

α_1

Figure 718   Quaternary structure of a globular protein

Another example of the quaternary structure is the binding of prosthetic groups such as the heme group of hemoglobin. Figure 718 shows a hemoglobin molecule.

It can seen that it is made of 4 polypeptide chains:
- two α chains
- two β chains

Each of these four chains is also combined with a prosthetic group, the heme group. This is not a polypeptide but an iron-containing molecule. In Figure 718, the heme groups are shown as rectangles with (iron) spheres in the middle.

Proteins with a prosthetic group are called conjugated proteins. Chlorophyll and many of the enzymes in the electron transport chain are conjugated proteins.

AHL

	Fibrous proteins	Globular proteins
Shape	long	tightly folded
Solubility	insoluble in water	soluble in water
Main level of organisation	secondary structure is the most important	tertiary structure is the most important
Function	structural (they *are* something)	function (they *do* something)
Examples	collagen keratin myosin	hemoglobin (*Figure 718*) enzymes antibodies hormones

Figure 720   Fibrous and globular proteins

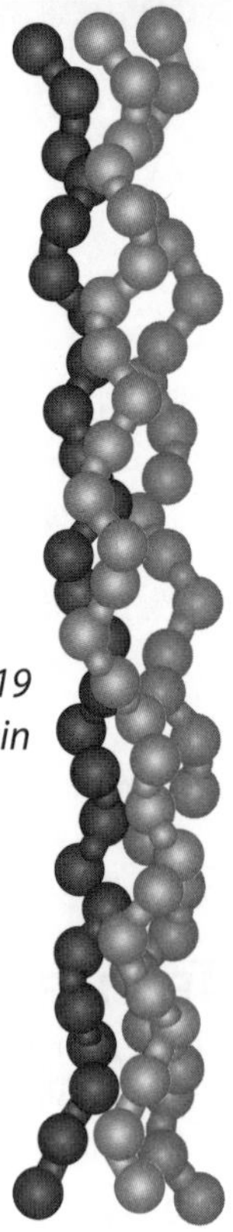

*Figure 719
A fibrous protein*

7.5.2   Outline the difference between fibrous and globular proteins, with reference to two examples of each protein type.

©IBO 2007

Proteins can be fibrous or globular. An example of a fibrous protein is shown in Figure 719. There are a number of important differences between these two types of proteins and they are outlined in Figure 720.

7.5.3   Explain the significance of polar and non-polar amino acids.

©IBO 2007

Of the 20 amino acids commonly used to build proteins, 8 have non-polar (hydrophobic) R groups. The others have polar R groups and are soluble in water. The non-polar amino acids in the polypeptide chain will cluster together in the centre of the molecule and contribute to the tertiary structure of the molecule. In general, the more non-polar amino acids a protein contains, the less soluble it is in water. In membranes, proteins are found in between phospholipids. The phospholipid layer is polar on the outside and non-polar in the centre. The protein will often arrange itself so that it exposes hydrophilic portions to the outside of the membrane and hydrophobic sections to the centre. *Refer to Figure 721.*

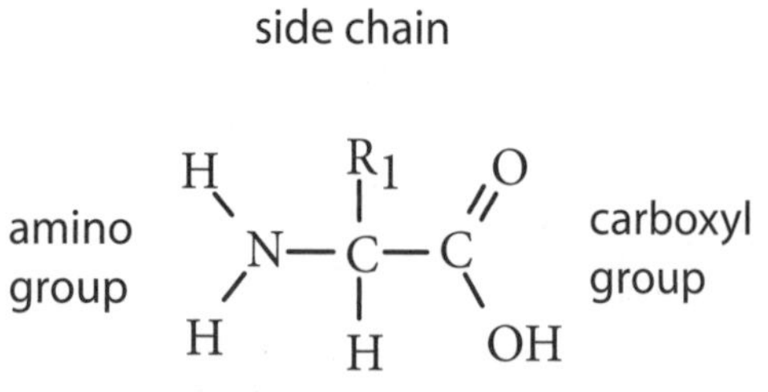

side chain

Figure 721   The structure of an amino acid

7.5.4   State four functions of proteins, giving a named example of each.

©IBO 2007

Functions of proteins include:

- enzymes
- hormones
- defense
- structure
- transport

ENZYMES

All enzymes are (globular) proteins, for example amylase which catalyses the following reaction:

starch $\longrightarrow$ maltose.

HORMONES

Some hormones are proteins, others are steroids. An example of a protein hormone is insulin.

DEFENSE

Antibodies or immunoglobulins are globular proteins assisting in the defense against foreign particles (antigens).

STRUCTURE

Collagen is a fibrous, structural protein which builds tendons and is an important part of your skin.

TRANSPORT

Hemoglobin is a globular conjugated protein which readily and reversibly binds to oxygen due to the heme group attached to it.

7.6 ENZYMES

7.6.1   State that metabolic pathways consist of chains and cycles of enzyme-catalysed reactions.

©IBO 2007

Very few, if any, chemical changes in a cell result from a single reaction. Metabolic pathways are chains and cycles of enzyme-catalysed reactions.

The reactions will rarely occur spontaneously at a measureable rate at room temperature. Therefore **enzymes** are used to speed up a reaction. You may safely assume that biological reactions only occur at measureable rates in the presence of enzymes.

Examples of metabolic pathways are photosynthesis and cellular respiration *(see Topic 8).*

7.6.2   Describe the induced-fit model.

©IBO 2007

As discussed in *Topic 3.6* the 'lock-and-key' model exists to explain the very high specificity of enzymes. The lock and key model was first suggested by Emil Fischer in 1894. Soon after, it appeared that certain enzymes can catalyse several (similar) reactions. The 'induced-fit' model *(Figure 722)*

was proposed in 1958 and suggests the following: The active site may not be as rigid as orginally was thought. Its shape will adapt somewhat to allow several slightly different substrates to fit. The active site will interact with the substrate and adapt to make the perfect fit. It is like a glove which will fit on several hands but not on a foot.

7.6.3   Explain that enzymes lower the activation energy of the chemical reactions that they catalyse.

©IBO 2007

Enzymes speed up a biochemical reaction without changing the nature of it but also without being used up.

The presence of an enzyme will speed up a reaction because the active site will facilitate the chemical change. This happens by a means of lowering the activation energy (E_a). Every reaction requires a certain amount of activation energy. If two molecules are going to react with each other, they need to collide with a certain speed. The higher the activation energy, the higher the speed required. At a low temperature, only a few molecules will have this speed, which means that the rate of reaction is low.

The active site of the enzyme assists in the chemical reaction by lowering the required activation energy. This means that more molecules are able to react and the rate of reaction will increase.

AHL

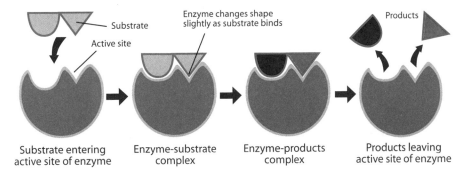

Figure 722   The induced fit model

TOK   How do enzymes work?

The lock and key model as proposed by Emil Fischer late in the nineteenth century neatly described the mechanism of enzyme action. The model's simplicity made it effective and it remained in popular use for nearly a century until a more accurate and detailed one, Koshland's model of induced fit, replaced it.

The development of knowledge in the natural sciences is usually stepwise, with one scientist standing on the shoulders of previous scientists' knowledge, ideas, and models. In rare cases there is a complete change of thinking (a paradigm shift), but most advances are gradual and measured.

Figure 723 shows what happens to the energy level during an exothermic biochemical reaction and what happens when a enzyme is added to this reaction.

It is apparent that the enzyme has reduced the required **activation energy** (E_a).

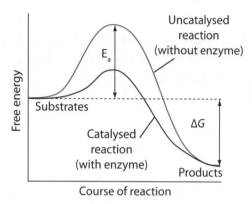

Figure 723   Energy of activation graph

7.6.4   Explain the difference between competitive and non-competitive inhibition, with reference to one example of each.

©IBO 2007

A number of molecules exist which can reduce the rate of an enzyme-controlled reaction. These molecules are called **inhibitors**. There are two kinds of inhibitors:
*   competitive inhibitors
*   non-competitive inhibitors

COMPETITIVE INHIBITORS

The structure of the inhibiting molecule is so similar to the structure of the substrate molecule that it competes and binds to the active site of the enzyme and prevents the substrate from binding. Adding more substrate will reduce the effect of the inhibitor. *Refer to Figure 724.*

Example

Prontosil (an antibacterial drug) inhibits the synthesis of folic acid (vitamin B, which acts as a co-enzyme) in bacteria. The drug will bind to the enzyme which makes folic acid. Folic acid is needed in nucleic acid synthesis. With Prontosil, the folic acid will no longer be made and the bacterial cell dies. Animal cells are not affected because they do not make folic acid but absorb it from food. Animal cells therefore lack the enzyme and the drug has no effect.

NON-COMPETITIVE INHIBITORS

The inhibiting molecule binds to the enzyme in a place which is NOT the active site. As a result, the shape of the active site of the enzyme changes and the substrate molecule will no longer fit. Adding more substrate has no effect on the reaction rate. *Refer to Figure 725.*

Example

Cyanide ions (CN^-) will attach thenselves to the - SH groups in the enzyme cytochrome c oxidase. By doing this, it destroys the disulfide bridges (-S-S-) and changes the tertiary structure of the enzyme. The shape of the active site of cytochrome c oxidase is irreversibly changed and the enzyme will no longer function.

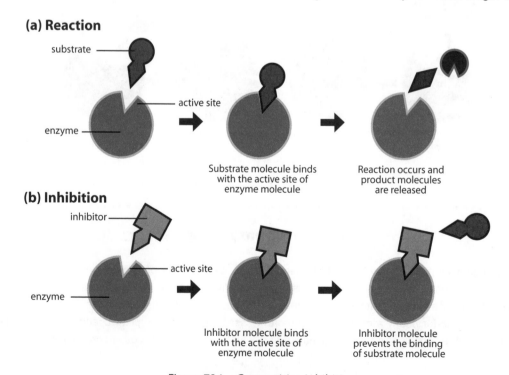

Figure 724   Competitive inhibition

AHL

(a) Reaction

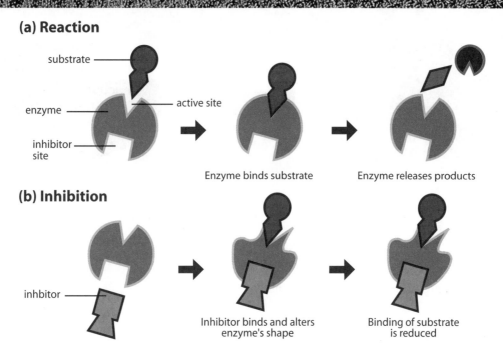

(b) Inhibition

Figure 725   Non-competitive inhibition

Example (continued)

The function of cytochrome c oxidase is to catalyse the reduction of oxygen to water. Without the enzyme, the reaction will not proceed sufficiently quickly and the process of releasing energy via cellular respiration stops and the organism dies.

> 7.6.5   Explain the control of metabolic pathways by end-product inhibition, including the role of allosteric sites.
>
> ©IBO 2007

A special kind of non-competitive inhibition is **allostery**. Allosteric enzymes are made of two or more polypeptide chains. The activity of allosteric enzymes is regulated by compounds which are not their substrates and which bind to the enzyme at a specific site, well away from the active site. They cause a reversible change in the shape of the active site.

The compounds are called allosteric effectors and are divided into two categories:

- allosteric activators (which speed up a reaction) and
- allosteric inhibitors (which slow down a reaction).

End products of a metabolic pathway can act as allosteric inhibitors. An example is found in glycolysis *(see also Topic 8.1)*.

In glycolysis *(see also Topic 8.1)*, one molecule of glucose is broken down into two molecules of pyruvate.

The first few steps in glycolysis *(see Figure 726)* involve adding a phosphate to glucose, then changing glucose-6-phosphate into fructose-6-phosphate and adding a second phosphate to make fructose-1,6-diphosphate. The fructose-1,6-diphosphate is then changed, in a series of enzyme-controlled reactions, into two molecules of

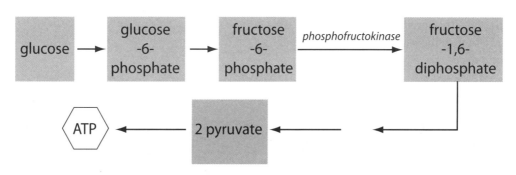

Figure 726   Glycolysis reactions

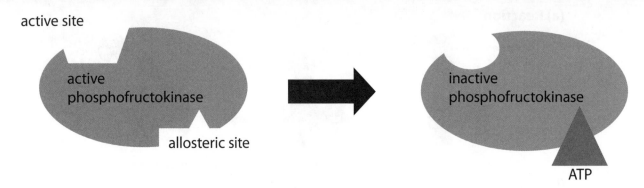

Figure 727   Active and allosteric sites

pyruvate. In the process of respiration, pyruvate is broken down and some of its energy is used to convert ADP into ATP.

End-product inhibition by allostery takes place in the reaction where fructose-6-phosphate is changed into fructose-1,6-diphosphate. This reaction is catalysed by the enzyme phosphofructokinase. *Refer to Figure 333.*

As the above reactions proceed, fructose-1,6-diphosphate is produced. The metabolic pathway from there will eventually yield a number of ATP molecules. ATP is an allosteric inhibitor. It will fit into the allosteric site of the phosphofructokinase molecule, changing the shape of the active site.

Because of the change of shape of the active site, fructose-6-phosphate does not fit anymore and the reaction will not take place. Without fructose-1,6-diphosphate, pyruvate will not be produced and no new ATP will be formed.

So if there is a sufficient amount of ATP, the production of new ATP will be reduced due to end-product inhibition. When levels of ATP are reduced, the ATP bound to the enzyme will be released from the enzyme. This changes the shape of the active site again and the enzyme will be able to catalyse the production of fructose-1,6-diphosphate, which will eventually yield ATP.

End-product inhibition is the concept that the presence of a high concentration of end-product of a metabolic pathway will inhibit the production of one of the metabolites somewhere in the pathway and no more end-product will be produced. *See Figure 727.*

Allosteric inhibition is the concept that a molecule can bind to the allosteric site of an enzyme and change the shape of the active site so that the substrate no longer fits and reaction is no longer catalysed.

EXERCISES

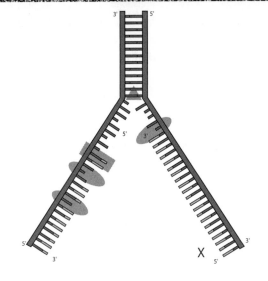

1. The complex of DNA and protein found in eukaryotic nuclei is known as:
   A   a histone.
   B   a nucleosome.
   C   genes.
   D   chromatin.

2. The units of genetic information are called:
   A   histones.
   B   nucleosomes.
   C   genes.
   D   chromatin.

3. The diagram shows a section of DNA. The point labelled X is the:

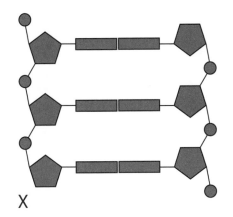

   A   3' end.
   B   5' end.
   C   gene.
   D   chromosome.

4. DNA replication occurs in a
   A   random direction.
   B   helical direction.
   C   3' → 5' direction.
   D   5' → 3' direction.

5. The following diagram illustrates DNA replication. The point marked X is the:
   A   lagging strand.
   B   leading strand.
   C   DNA polymerase molecule.
   D   Okazaki fragment.

6. Which of the following is not an enzyme involved in DNA replication?
   A   helicase.
   B   DNA ligase.
   C   DNA polymerase.
   D   amylase.

7. Transcription is carried out in a:
   A   random direction.
   B   helical direction.
   C   3' → 5' direction.
   D   5' → 3' direction.

8. Initiation, elongation and termination are the main stages in:
   A   transcription.
   B   translation.
   C   replication.
   D   decomposition.

9. Which of the four levels of organisation in proteins may involve a non-protein molecule?
   A   primary structure
   B   secondary structure
   C   tertiary structure
   D   quaternary structure

10. If a competitive inhibitor is added to an enzyme catalysed reaction, the rate of reaction will always decrease unless
    A   more substate is added
    B   the inhibitor is added in excess
    C   the temperature is increased
    D   the temperature is kept constant

AHL

135

11 Explain the structure of double stranded DNA. Use a drawing of a segment of 6 linked nucleotides to enhance your explanation.

12 What is the function of each of the following enzymes in DNA replication?
(a) helicase
(b) RNA primase
(c) DNA polymerase III
(d) DNA polymerase I
(e) DNA ligase

13. Outline the differnces and similaries between transcription and translation.

14 What is the role of the following in the process of translation?
(a) mRNA
(b) ribosomes
(c) codons and anticodons
(d) tRNA

15 Which types of bonds are involved in each of the four levels of protein structure?

16. State four functions of proteins. Give an example of each.

17 Explain why both polar and non-polar amino acids are used in protein that are part of the cell membrane.

18 (a) Where does the competitive inhibitor bind to the enzyme?
(b) Where does the non-competitive inhibitor bind to the enzyme?
(c) Give an example of each.

19 Explain end product inhibition.

20. Explain why an exothermic reaction may need to have energy added in order to proceed and what the effect of enzymes can be.

CELL RESPIRATION AND PHOTOSYNTHESIS

8.1 Cell respiration

8.2 Photosynthesis

AHL

8.1 CELL RESPIRATION

8.1.1 State that oxidation involves the loss of electrons from an element, whereas reduction involves a gain of electrons; and that oxidation frequently involves gaining oxygen or losing hydrogen, whereas reduction frequently involves losing oxygen or gaining hydrogen.

©IBO 2007

In cell respiration, as in photosynthesis (*see Topic 8.2*), reactions often involve the enzyme controlled transfer of electrons. This type of reaction is called a redox reaction. In these *red*uction-*ox*idation reactions, one compound loses some electrons and the other compound gains them.

Here is a useful mnemonic to help you remember this:

OIL RIG

Oxidation **I**s **L**oss (of electrons),

Reduction **I**s **G**ain (of electrons).

The process of oxidation often involves gaining oxygen (hence its name) or losing hydrogen while reduction often involves losing oxygen or gaining hydrogen.

A substance which has been reduced, now has the power to reduce other substances (and becomes oxidised in the process); e.g. NADH (respiration) and NADPH (photosynthesis).

	oxidation	reduction
electrons	loss	gain
oxygen	gain	loss
hydrogen	loss	gain

If a molecule, atom or ion is oxidised, then it loses electrons. These electrons have to be accepted by another molecule, atom or ion which is reduced. Therefore, oxidation and reduction reactions always take place together, hence the name '**redox' reactions**.

8.1.2 Outline the process of glycolysis, including phosphorylation, lysis, oxidation and ATP formation.

©IBO 2007

Glycolysis takes place in the cytoplasm and produces two pyruvate molecules from every glucose according to the following reaction:

Glucose + 2ADP + 2P$_i$ + 2NAD$^+$ $\longrightarrow$
$\qquad$ 2Pyruvate + 2ATP + 2NADH + 2H$^+$ + 2H$_2$O

Glycolysis is anaerobic and does not require oxygen and produces a small amount of ATP and NADH and H$^+$.

One molecule of glucose contains sixatoms of carbon; one molecule of pyruvate contains three atoms of carbon. The structural formula for pyruvate is shown in Figure 801.

137

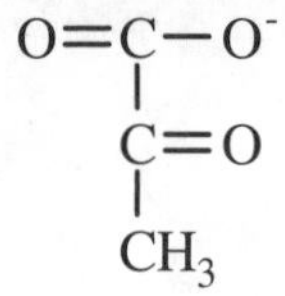

$$O=C-O^-$$
$$|$$
$$C=O$$
$$|$$
$$CH_3$$

Figure 801   Pyruvate

Glycolysis uses glucose, a hexose sugar, with six carbon atoms to eventually produce two molecules of pyruvate, a triose, i.e. a monosaccharide with 3 carbon atoms.

The first step of glycolysis involves **phosphorylation**. In this step, ATP is used (invested) to add a phosphate group to glucose. It is followed by a second phosphorylation reaction, again using ATP and producing hexose biphosphate.

The hexose biphosphate still contains 6 carbon atoms. It is split in a lysis reaction, producing 2 triose phosphate molecules with 3 carbon atoms each.

The next step is a combined oxidation phosphorylation reaction. The enzyme involved first oxidises the triose

phosphate into a different triose phosphate (for those taking Chemistry HL: glyceraldehyde to glycerate or, in general, aldehyde to carboxylic acid). The oxidation has to occur because in the overall reaction, it was shown that glycolysis produces 2 NADH and $2H^+$. NAD^+ has been reduced to NADH, i.e. it has gained electrons. The electrons were supplied by a triose phosphate which is oxidised into a different triose phosphate.

After the oxidation reaction, the enzyme will attach an inorganic phosphate from the cytoplasm to the triose phosphate to form a triose biphosphate. So this phosphorylation reaction does not involve ATP.

Finally, each triose biphosphate gives up one of its phosphate groups. This phosphate is taken up by ADP to form ATP. This is repeated in the last step of glycolysis, again forming one ATP, but now also producing pyruvate.

The process of glycolysis is shown in Figure 802 and can be summarised by the following overall equation:

Glucose + 2ADP + $2P_i$ + $2NAD^+$ ⟶
    2Pyruvate + 2ATP + 2NADH + $2H^+$ + $2H_2O$

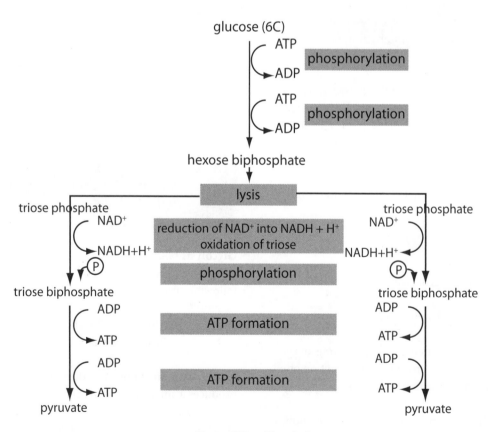

Figure 802   Glycolysis

8.1.3 Draw and label a diagram showing the structure of a mitochondrion as seen in electron micrographs.

©IBO 2007

Mitochondria (singular: mitochondrion) are large organelles found in eukaryotic cells. They are surrounded by an outer membrane and an inner membrane. The inner membrane is folded and these folds, cristae (singular crista), project into the matrix of the mitochondrion. The matrix of the mitochondrion is a watery fluid which contains many molecules and enzymes. In the matrix of the mitochondrion, we also find ribosomes and DNA. The space between the outer and inner membrane of the mitochondrion is called the inter-membrane space. Figure 803 is an electron micrograph showing several mitochondria.

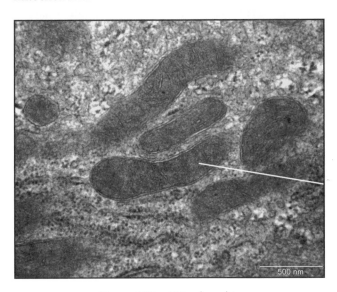

500 nm

Figure 803   Mitochondria

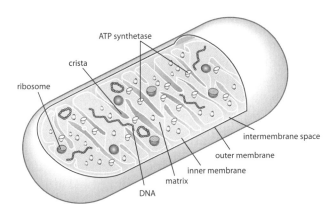

Figure 804   Structure of a mitochondrion

Mitochondria are often drawn as a two-dimensional cross-section to show the internal structure. *Refer to Figure 804.*

8.1.4 Explain aerobic respiration, including the link reaction, the Krebs cycle, the role of NADH + H⁺, the electron transport chain and the role of oxygen.

©IBO 2007

When oxygen is NOT present in the cell, pyruvate will stay in the cytoplasm and be converted into lactate (in animals) or ethanol and carbon dioxide (in plants and yeasts) in the process of anaerobic respiration (*see Topic 3.7*). Glycolysis releases a small amount of energy but conversion of pyruvate to lactate or ethanol and carbon dioxide does not yield more ATP. Therefore, anaerobic respiration releases only a small amount of the energy in glucose and is only used in the absence of oxygen, when aerobic respiration is not possible.

If oxygen is present, a series of reactions take place which result in pyruvate being broken down to produce carbon dioxide and a relatively large amount of energy in the form of ATP.

The first of these reactions is called the link reaction because it forms the link between glycolysis (*see Topic 3.7.3*) and the Krebs cycle. Pyruvate, produced in the cytoplasm during glycolysis, is transported to the mitochondrial matrix according to the following equation:

$$\text{Pyruvate} + \text{CoA} + \text{NAD}^+ \longrightarrow \text{Acetyl CoA} + \text{CO}_2 + \text{NADH} + \text{H}^+$$

This process is known as *decarboxylation* of pyruvate because a molecule of carbon dioxide is removed from pyruvate.

The Krebs cycle, (also known as the tricarboxylic citric acid cycle or TCA cycle), occurs in the matrix of the mitochondria and produces 2CO_2, $3\text{NADH} + 3\text{H}^+$, 1FADH_2 and 1ATP from 1 molecule of acetyl CoA. As the name suggests, it is a cyclic process. The logical place to start studying the Krebs cycle is at the point where acetyl CoA, a compound containing 2 carbon atoms and produced from pyruvate in the link reaction, enters the cycle.

Acetyl CoA will combine with a four carbon compound, forming a six carbon compound. This six carbon compound will then be decarboxylated, producing a five carbon compound and carbon dioxide. The same sequence of reactions will happen again, producing a four carbon compound and another carbon dioxide. We are now back to the 4 carbon compound that originally reacted with acetyl CoA.

AHL

Figure 805 shows a simple diagram of the Krebs cycle.

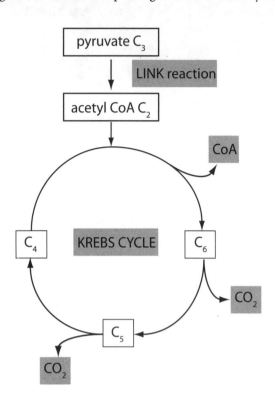

Figure 805   The Krebs cycle

One turn of the cycle will require the input of one acetyl CoA and produce one CoA molecule and two carbon dioxide molecules. However, the purpose of the Krebs cycle is to produce energy and so one turn of the cycle also produces 3 NADH + 3H$^+$, 1 FADH$_2$ and 1 ATP. FADH$_2$ is like NADH + H$^+$ in that it has accepted hydrogen ions so it has become reduced. It now has reducing power - the ability to reduce another compound.

8.1.5   Explain oxidative phosphorylation in terms of chemiosmosis.

©IBO 2007

In glycolysis, one glucose is split into two pyruvate, 2 ATP and 2 NADH + 2H$^+$.

In the link reaction, one pyruvate is changed into one acetyl CoA, one carbon dioxide and 1 NADH + H$^+$.

In the **Krebs cycle**, one acetyl CoA is changed into 2 carbon dioxide, 3 NADH + 3H$^+$, 1 ATP and 1 FADH$_2$.

This means that overall, one molecule of glucose has been changed into 6 molecules of carbon dioxide and, so far, no oxygen has been used and only a little ATP has been produced. The final stage of aerobic respiration will use the

energy stored in NADH + H$^+$ and in FADH$_2$ to produce more ATP. The last step of this stage involves the use of oxygen. In the absence of oxygen, none of the reactions will occur. This will prevent the Krebs cycle from taking place and, instead, the process of anaerobic respiration will be carried out (*see Topic 3.7*).

The last stage of aerobic respiration involves the electron transport chain and takes place on the cristae, the folds of the inner membrane of the mitochondrion. A series of protein complexes (electron carriers) are arranged in a specific order in the phospholipid bilayer of the inner membrane of the mitochondrion. These protein complexes pass electrons along, from one complex to the next. As the electrons move through the membrane, some hydrogen ions (protons) are pumped from the matrix into the intermembrane space. Finally the last member of the electron transport chain promotes the reduction of oxygen to form water.

The proton gradient, which is the result of the movement of hydrogen ions from the matrix into the intermembrane space, drives the production of ATP (from ADP and P$_i$) by the enzyme, ATP synthetase. This is the chemiosmotic theory, proposed by a British biochemist, Peter Mitchell in 1961. **The chemiosmotic theory explains how the synthesis of ATP is coupled to electron transport and proton movement.**

Initially, not many scientists accepted Mitchell's idea, but as more information became available, the chemiosmotic theory gained credibility and Peter Mitchell was awarded a Nobel Prize for Chemistry in 1978.

The net result of this process is that 1 NADH + H$^+$ supplies enough energy to produce 3 ATP from 3 ADP + 3 P$_i$ and 1 FADH$_2$ supplies enough energy to produce 2 ATP from 2 ADP + 2 P$_i$. During these reactions, NADH + H$^+$ and FADH$_2$ are returned to the ir oxidised forms NAD$^+$ and FAD. The mechanism of this series of reactions is that the energy from NADH + H$^+$ and FADH$_2$ is transferred to ATP through a series of electron carriers.

This series of electron carriers finally yields H$^+$ and electrons to oxygen (O$_2$) to form water (H$_2$O). However if no oxygen is present, this reaction cannot take place. As a consequence, no NAD$^+$ or FAD is formed and hence the Krebs cycle cannot operate. This will cause acetyl CoA to accumulate and, as a result, it will no longer be produced from pyruvate. Glycolysis will continue to operate however, since, even without oxygen, it is possible to break down pyruvate and release some energy. This process is less efficient though, since the amount of energy produced is much lower in anaerobic than aerobic respiration.

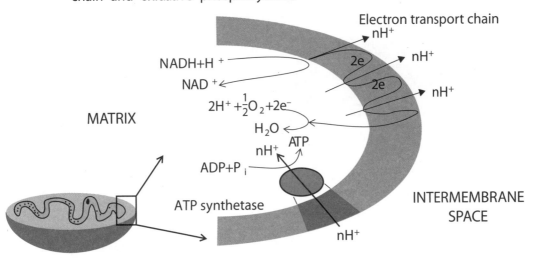

Chemiosmotic coupling of electron transport chain and oxidative phosphorylation

Figure 806   Chemiosmosis

The chemiosmotic theory of *Peter Mitchell*

It had already been obvious for some time that a link existed between the electrons being passed down the electron transport chain and the production of ATP. *Peter Mitchell* discovered that during the passing of the 'high energy' electrons down the electron transport chain, protons were being pumped across the inner mitochondrial membrane.

There is a build up of H^+ ions in the intermembrane space. The concentration gradient (known as the proton motive force) will drive H^+ through the ATP synthetase molecule which has chemiosmotic channels. As the H^+ ions go through the ATP synthetase molecule, the potential energy they possess will be used to drive ATP synthesis. *Refer to Figure 806.*

8.1.6	Explain the relationship between the structure of the mitochondrion and its function.

©IBO 2007

Keeping in mind all of the information presented in the previous sections, it is useful to return to the structure of the mitochondrion. *Refer to Figures 803 and 804.*

The outer membrane is a regular membrane, separating the mitochondrion from the cytoplasm. Its structure is based on the fluid mosaic model.

The inter-membrane space has a higher concentration of H^+ ions (hence a lower pH) because of the electron transport chain.

The inner membrane is folded into cristae to provide maximum space and surface area for the electron carriers and ATP synthetase. It is impermeable to H^+ ions. Its structure is based on the fluid mosaic model with the electron carriers and the ATP synthetase embedded among the phospholipid molecules. The ATP synthetase molecules can be seen on the cristae.

The inter-membrane space has a small volume so that the movement of even a limited number of hydrogen ions (protons) will greatly affect the concentration. The matrix contains the enzymes which enable the Krebs cycle to proceed.

Glycolysis takes place in the cytoplasm. Pyruvate is transported to the matrix of the mitochondrion and decarboxylated to acetyl CoA which enters the Krebs cycle. The resulting NADH and H^+ and $FADH_2$ give their electrons to the electron carriers in the inner membrane. The electrons move through the membrane as they are passed from one electron carrier to another in a series of redox reactions. During this process, H^+ ions are pumped from the matrix into the intermembrane space, creating a potential difference. A concentration gradient drives the H^+ ions back to the matrix through the ATP synthetase which uses the energy released to combine ADP and P_i into ATP, which is released into the matrix.

8.2 PHOTOSYNTHESIS

> 8.2.1 Draw and label a diagram showing the structure of a chloroplast as seen in electron micrographs.
>
> ©IBO 2007

Photosynthesis occurs in the chloroplasts. Cells in the palisade layer often have a large number of chloroplasts because the main function of these cells is photosynthesis.

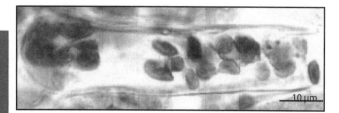

Figure 807   Light microscope view of chloroplasts

Chloroplasts found in cells of green plants are 2 - 10 μm in diameter and ovoid in shape when found in higher plants (in green algae their shape varies). As you can see in Figure 807, chloroplasts can be seen with the light microscope.

Pictures of the chloroplast, taken with the electron microscope, allow its structure to be seen and studied in sufficient detail. See Figure 808 (a), (b) and (c), the approximate magnifications are shown.

Figure 808 shows several electron micrographs showing the location and detail of a chloroplast. From similar EMs, a three-dimesional impression of the structure has been deduced. A diagram of the structure of a chloroplast is shown in Figure 809.

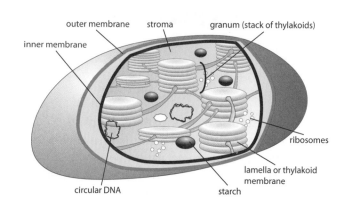

Figure 809   Diagram of a chloroplast

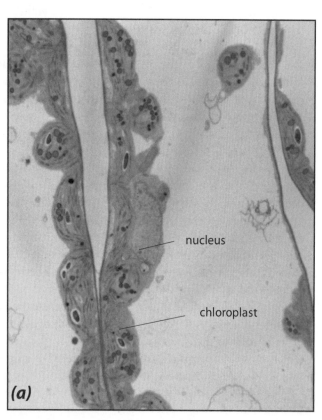

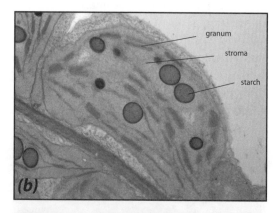

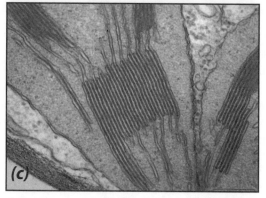

Figure 808   (a) A leaf cell (x400)   (b) A chloroplast (x1200)   (c) Granum and stroma (x5000)

8.2.2 State that photosynthesis consists of light-dependent and light-independent reactions.

©IBO 2007

As was shown in *Topic 3.8,* photosynthesis is NOT a simple one-step reaction. It consists of a series of reactions which can be grouped into a light-dependent stage and a light-independent stage. These two stages are shown in Figure 810. The light-dependent stage will only take place in the light. However, the light-independent stage can occur at any time, if the required materials are available. Outside the laboratory, these materials are provided (ATP and NADPH) come from the light-dependent stage.

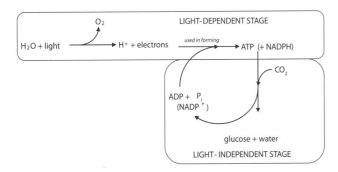

Figure 810   *The two stages of photosynthesis*

Some texts will still use the terms 'light stage' and 'dark stage'. These are incorrect since they imply that light is required for one stage and darkness for the other. This is not the case. Indeed light is needed for the light-dependent stage but the light-independent stage can take place in the presence or absence of light - which makes the name 'dark stage' misleading.

8.2.3 Explain the light-dependent reactions.

©IBO 2007

OUTLINE

In the light-dependent reaction, light energy is used (indirectly) to split water molecules into hydrogen ions, oxygen molecules and electrons. The oxygen is a waste product and will leave the chloroplast. The H^+ and electrons will be used to produce energy-rich ATP and NADPH.

In the light-independent stage, the ATP and NADPH are used to combine 3 carbon dioxide molecules into 1 triose phosphate (TP) (C3) in the Calvin Cycle. Once two molecules of TP are produced, they are combined to form one molecule of glucose (C6).

DETAILS OF THE LIGHT-DEPENDENT STAGE

The light-dependent stage takes place on the membrane of the grana, the stacks of thylakoid membrane in the chloroplast. There are two possible processes which will produce ATP:

- non-cyclic photophosphorylation *(Figure 811)*
- cyclic photophosphorylation *(Figure 812)*

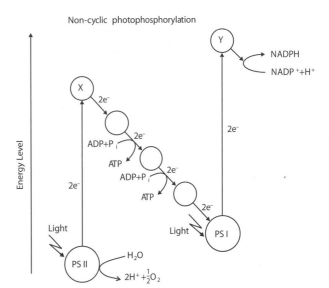

Figure 811   *Non-cyclic photophosphorylation in the light-dependent stage*

Non-cyclic photophosphorylation

As can be seen in Figure 811, the light is absorbed by the pigments of photosystem II (PS II), which are mainly found in the grana of the chloroplast. Absorbing this light energy excites some electrons which, as a result, leave their normal position (circling the nucleus of the atom) and move away from the nucleus of the atom. This is called photoactivation of PS II. The electrons are taken up by an electron acceptor X, resulting in a chlorophyll 'a' molecule with a positive charge. The electrons are then passed through a number of electron carriers in the membrane via oxidation-reduction reactions (*see Topic 8.1*) and will end up at photosystem I (PS I). This is a system of electron tranport.

The presence of chlorophyll a+ (Chl a+) will induce the lysis of water so that oxygen, hydrogen ions and electrons are released. Chl a+ is the strongest biological oxidant known. Since the lysis of water is the direct result of the photoactivation of PS II, the process is known as photolysis of water.

The light is also absorbed by PS I which, like PS II, is found in the membranes of the grana. Again, the electrons absorb the light energy and move away from the nucleus.

AHL

This is called photoactivation of PS I. The electrons leave the chlorophyll a molecule and are taken up by electron acceptor Y. They are then passed on and taken up by NADP$^+$ which combines with an H$^+$ and is reduced to form NADPH. The Chl a$^+$ of PS I receives electrons from the electron carrier chain (ultimately from PS II) and becomes an uncharged Chl a molecule.

Cyclic photophosphorylation

In cyclic photophosphorylation (see Figure 812), the electrons from PS I go to electron acceptor Y, but instead of being used to produce NADPH, they go through the membrane via several electron carriers (electron transport) (redox reactions) and are returned to PS I. PS II is not involved. This process is cyclic, as its name suggests. It does not produce NADPH but it does produce ATP. For this reason, cyclic photophosphorylation is a useful process, but as it does not produce NADPH, it is not able to drive the Calvin cycle and will not produce complex carbohydrates for long term energy storage.

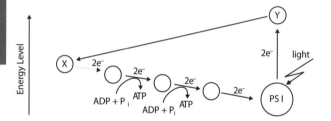

Figure 812   Cyclic photophosphorylation in the light-dependent stage

8.2.4   Explain photophosphorylation in terms of chemiosmosis.

©IBO 2007

The electrons from photolysis of water are taken up by Chl a$^+$ in PS II. The following happens:

- Chl a$^+$ will be converted to Chl a
- oxygen is released as a waste product
- H$^+$ ions (protons) are pumped to the inside of the grana (the lumen). They accumulate there until the concentration gradient drives them through chemiosmotic proton channels in the ATP synthetase, driving the phosphorylation reaction ADP + P$_i$ $\longrightarrow$ ATP (see Topic 8.1). This is shown in Figure 813.

Since the formation of ATP is indirectly caused by light energy, the process is often described as photophosphorylation.

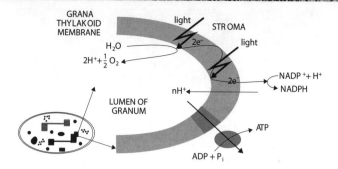

Figure 813   Photophosphorylation

8.2.5   Explain the light-independent reactions.

©IBO 2007

The light-dependent stage uses light to produce the energy-rich compounds ATP and NADPH and H$^+$ which are used to drive the **Calvin cycle** (see Figure 814) in the light-independent reactions. In the Calvin cycle, three molecules of carbon dioxide are combined to form the 3C compound triose phosphate (TP). TP will leave the Calvin cycle and be subsequently combined to larger, more complex, carbohydrates such as glucose and, eventually, starch.

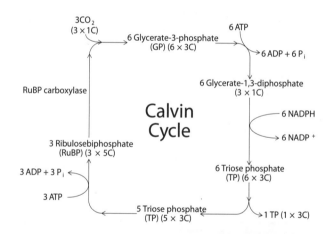

Figure 814   The Calvin cycle

The Calvin cycle takes place in the stroma of the chloroplast. ATP provides the energy and NADPH provides the reducing power needed for biosynthesis using carbon dioxide. RuBP is the carbon dioxide acceptor and (catalysed by RuBP carboxylase which is also known as RuBisCo) will take up CO_2, forming GP. GP will be reduced to TP but this conversion needs energy from ATP and reducing power from NADPH. TP can be converted to glucose, sucrose, starch, fatty acids and amino acids and other products. Of course, RuBP is regenerated from TP to keep the cycle going. This process requires energy from ATP.

AHL

AHL

TOK   Is research science or art?

For the series of experiments from which the mechanism of the Calvin cycle was determined, new procedures were devised and equipment designed. This is often the case when new knowledge is revealed. Melvin Calvin's team of scientists displayed amazing creativity and imagination in their investigation of the mechanism of photosynthesis. One device they designed and built was called the lollipop because of its shape. It was made from clear glass with light sources on both sides to illuminate the unicellular green algae, *Chlorella*, which was suspended in a watery solution. In this environment, substantial photosynthesis occurred and *Chlorella* could quickly and easily be removed from the lollipop and examined for the presence of chemicals involved in the stages of what is now known as the Calvin cycle.

To some, the lollipop is just a machine. Perhaps it is viewed in this way because it was built for a specific purpose, to reveal knowledge. It can also be seen as the result of the creative minds of scientists. The development of new scientific protocols and devices have many parallels with the development of works of art.

8.2.6   Explain the relationship between the structure of the chloroplast and its function.

©IBO 2007

The light-dependent reactions of photosynthesis involve photoactivation, followed by a series of redox reactions during electron transport by electron carriers. The reactions need to take place in a certain order so the electron carriers are fixed in positions in the membrane of the grana thylakoid. Since the thylakoid membrane has a large surface area inside the chloroplast, many of light-dependent reactions can take place at the same time. *Refer to Figures 808 and 809.*

Another process during the light-independent reactions is the movement of hydrogen ions (H^+) or protons. As the electrons move from the stroma through the membrane into the lumen of the grana, hydrogen ions are actively transported across the thylakoid membrane, into the lumen of the grana. Since the lumen of the granum is a small space, it has a small volume and even a limited change in the number of hydrogen ions will have a significant effect on the H^+ concentration. (*The same situation occurs in the intermembrane space of mitochondria, refer Topic 8.1.6.*)

The light-independent reactions of the Calvin cycle take place in the stroma of the chloroplast. The concentration of the required enzymes, particularly RuBisCo, in the stroma of the chloroplast is much higher than would be possible in the cytoplasm. Also the concentration of magnesium ions (Mg^{2+}) in the stroma increases in light. Magnesium ions are needed for the proper functioning of Rubisco. Also, due to the fact that protons are pumped from the stroma into the lumen of the grana, the pH of the stroma slightly increases making it slightly alkaline (pH around 8). This facilitates the reactions of the Calvin cycle. Again, in the much larger volume of the cytoplasm, the effect of removing some protons would be much smaller.

8.2.7   Explain the relationship between the action spectrum and the absorption spectrum of photosynthetic pigments in green plants.

©IBO 2007

For a person to see an object, the object needs to reflect light which then enters the person's eye. The colour of the object is the colour of the light that is reflected. All other colours are absorbed.

Chlorophyll is green. That means that it will absorb other colours better than the colour green, which will be reflected. An absorption spectrum can be produced from measurements of the percentage of the light of a certain colour that is absorbed. An absorption spectrum of chlorophyll 'a' (one of the types of chlorophyll) is shown in Figure 815. It can be seen that the absorption of green light (500 nm) is nearly zero, indicating that this colour is reflected and will therefore enter a person's eye, creating the image of a green leaf.

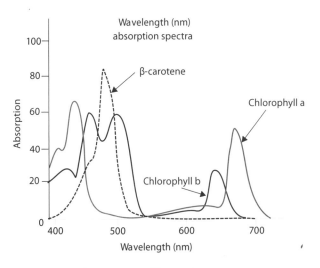

Figure 815   Absorption spectra

AHL

Chlorophyll needs to absorb light before it can use it in the light-dependent reactions. However, not all absorbed wavelengths (colours) of light are equally well used in photosynthesis. This is where an action spectrum is different from an absorption spectrum. An action spectrum will show how well the light of different wavelengths is used in photosynthesis. The amount of photosynthesis can be measured, for example, by the amount of oxygen produced (which is easiest to measure in water plants).

In Figure 815, you can see that the different kinds of chlorophyll have different absorption spectra (you do not need to know the differences). You can also see that these different pigments (chlorophyll a, b, and carotenoid) work together in photosynthesis as can be seen from the **absorbtion spectrum** in Figure 815.

> 8.2.8 Explain the concept of limiting factors in photosynthesis, with reference to light intensity, temperature and concentration of carbon dioxide.
>
> ©IBO 2007

The factor the furthest away from its optimum value will limit the amount of photosynthesis. This is the limiting factor. If you improve this factor, the rate of photosynthesis will increase until another factor becomes the limiting factor.

Limiting factors for photosynthesis are:
- light intensity
- temperature
- concentration of carbon dioxide.

As can be seen in Figure 816 , graph (a), light intensity can be a limiting factor in photosynthesis. If the intensity of the light is increased, the rate of photosynthesis will increase to a certain level, at which point further increases will not affect the rate of photosynthesis. At this point, light intensity is no longer a limiting factor in photosynthesis.

The same applies for the concentration of carbon dioxide. Increasing the concentration of carbon dioxide will increase the rate of photosynthesis until a point when carbon dioxide concentration is no longer the limiting factor for photosynthesis and further increases do not affect the rate. *See Figure 816 (b).*

However, the shape of the graph for temperature versus the rate of photosynthesis is different. When the temperature is low, it can be a limiting factor for the rate of photosynthesis. Increasing the temperature will increase the rate of photosynthesis until the optimum temperature is reached. A further increase in temperature will decrease the rate of photosynthesis because the enzymes will start to denature. *See Figure 816 (c) which is only approximate.*

TOK Does correlation mean causation?

In experimental design, to be sure of the link between cause and effect, one must control all factors that could influence the outcome apart from one. Calvin's experiments were meticulously designed to achieve this outcome in an environment almost totally removed from the world in which most organisms live and interact. In the every day world, it is impossible to control all factors and draw definitive 'cause and effect' conclusions.

Epidemiology is an attempt by Scientists to study factors affecting health. It acknowledges at its foundation that humans cannot control all factors when we study health. Epidemiologists are quick to point out that they determine a correlation between a factor and a disease and that this is very different to proof that the factor is the cause of the disease. We can say that there is a correlation between longer life and vegetarianism as opposed to meat-eating. This does not prove that eating meat lowers life expectancy. What experiment would you have to perform to make such an assertion?

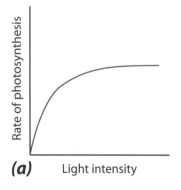 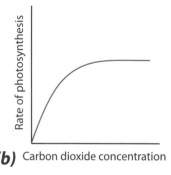 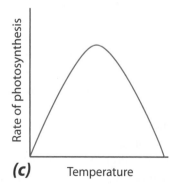

(a) Light intensity   *(b)* Carbon dioxide concentration   *(c)* Temperature

Figure 816   Limiting factors for photosynthesis

EXERCISES

1   In a redox reaction:
   A   both compounds lose electrons.
   B   both compounds gain electrons.
   C   electrons are not involved in the reaction.
   D   one compound loses electrons and the other compound gains them:

2   Oxidation involves:
   A   loss of electrons.
   B   gain of electrons.
   C   removal of oxygen.
   D   removal of hydrogen.

3   If glycolysis is written as a one step equation, what are the reactants and the products?

	reactants	products
A	glucose, oxygen	carbon dioxide, water
B	glucose, ADP, Pi, NAD+	pyruvate, ATP, NADH, H2O
C	glucose, ATP	pyruvate, ADP
D	glucose	lactate

Questions 4 and 5 refer to the schematic diagram of a mitochondrion.

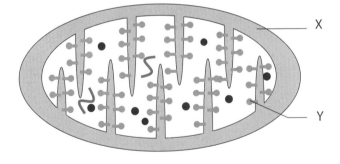

4   X is the:
   A   intermembrane space
   B   DNA
   C   matrix
   D   ATP synthetase

5   Y is the:
   A   crista
   B   DNA
   C   matrix
   D   ATP synthetase

6   A leaf is exposed to sunlight. Which colours are absorbed and which are reflected?
   A   all colours are reflected
   B   all colours are absorbed except red which is reflected
   C   green is absorbed and all other colours are reflected
   D   all colours are absorbed except green which is reflected

7   The Calvin cycle is a part of:
   A   the light dependent stage of photosynthesis.
   B   the light independent stage of photosynthesis.
   C   fermentation.
   D   respiration.

8   Which one of the following is not a limiting factor for photosynthesis?
   A   light intensity.
   B   temperature.
   C   concentration of carbon dioxide.
   D   concentration of oxygen.

9   (a)   Where in the cell does glycolysis take place?
   (b)   Where in the cell does the Krebs cycle take place?
   (c)   Where in the cell is the electron transport chain found?

10   Draw a diagram of the structure of a mitochondrion as seen with the electron microscope.

11   (a)   How does the structure of the site for the Krebs cycle relate to its function?
   (b)   How does the structure of the site for the electron transport chain relate to its function?
   (c)   What would happen to aerobic respiration if the outer membrane of the mitochondrion became permeable to protons (hydrogen ions)?

12   Draw a diagram of the structure of a chloroplast as seen with the electron microscope.

13   Outline how the light-independent reaction depends on the light dependent reaction.

AHL

14 (a) What are the functions of the ATP and NADPH produced in non-cyclic photophosphorylation?

(b) What would be the purpose of cyclic photophosphorylation?

(c) What is the advantage of non-cyclic photophosphorylation over cyclic photophosphorylation for the plant?

(d) What is the purpose of the Calvin cycle?

15 Explain how the structure of the chloroplast is suited to its function.

16 Compare and contrast the process of ATP production in chloroplasts and mitochondria.

AHL

PLANT SCIENCE

9.1   Plant structure and growth

9.2   Transport in angiospermophytes

9.3   Reproduction in angiospermophytes

9.1 PLANT STRUCTURE AND GROWTH

AHL

9.1.1   Draw and label plan diagrams to show the distribution of tissues in the stem and leaf of a dicotyledonous plant.

©IBO 2007

The root, stem and leaf of a dicotyledon contain many different tissue types. These are outlined in Figures 901, 902 and 903, respectively.

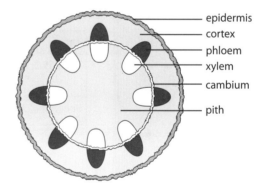

Figure 902   Tissues in the stem of a dicotyledon

Figure 901   Tissue distribution in the root of a dicotyledon

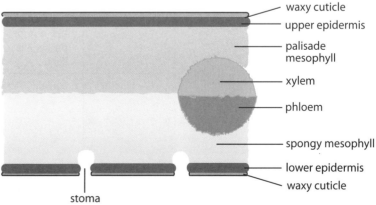

Figure 903   Tissues in the leaf of a dicotyledon

9.1.2 Outline three differences between the structures of dicotyledonous and monocotyledonous plants.

©IBO 2007

Several differences between monocotyledonous and dicotyledonous plants are outlined in Figure 904. Figure 905 shows a germinating monocotyledonous plant on the left and a dicotyledonous plant on the right.

9.1.3 Explain the relationship between the distribution of tissues in the leaf and the functions of these tissues.

©IBO 2007

Please refer to Figure 903 in conjunction with Figure 906.

Structure	monocotyledonous plants	dicotyledonous plants
veins in leaf	parallel	reticulate (net-like)
distribution of vascular tissue	scattered	in a ring
number of cotyledons in seed	one	two
floral organs	multiples of three	four or five
roots	unbranched	branched
examples	grass, onion, lily and tulip	daisy, oak tree and rose

Figure 904   Differences between monocotyledons and dicotyledons

Figure 905   Monocotyledon and dicotyledon seedlings

Tissue	Structure	Function
upper cuticle	• THIS IS NOT A TISSUE but a waxy layer covering the outside of the leaf	• reduces water loss by reducing transpiration
upper epidermis	• one layer of cells • no chloroplasts • transparent	• reduces water loss • prevents gas exchange • allows light to pass • secretes cuticle • barrier against infection
palisade layer	• long cells lined up with short side facing top • has a large number of chloroplasts • near top of leaf to receive most light	• photosynthesis
spongy layer	• irregularly shaped cells with air spaces in between • has chloroplasts but fewer than the palisade layer since it receives less light	• allows rapid diffusion of oxygen and carbon dioxide through air spaces • photosynthesis
lower epidermis	• contains stomata	• stomata open/close to allow gas exchange but reduce water loss • secretes cuticle • barrier against infection
lower cuticle	• THIS IS NOT A TISSUE but a waxy layer covering the outside of the leaf	• reduces water loss by reducing transpiration

Figure 906   Structures of the leaf

9.1.4 Identify modifications of roots, stems and leaves for different functions: bulbs, stem tubers, storage roots and tendrils.

©IBO 2007

Bulbs, stem tubers and storage roots are geophytes, which are storage organs for water and/or food. Storage organs often grow underground for protection against animals.

BULBS

A bulb is a stem that grows underground and has modified leaves for storing food to allow the plant to grow again after it has been dormant. The stem is shortened so that the leaves are together rather than spaced apart. The leaves do not have chloroplasts but are thickened to store food. Only monocotyledons form true bulbs. Onions, which are commonly used as food, are a good example. *See Figure 907.*

STEM TUBERS

Stem tubers are stems, modified for food storage, which can form roots. The buds on the stem can grow out to form stems and roots. The stem contains a lot of parenchyma tissue for storing food. Potatoes are a good example. *See Figure 908.*

STORAGE ROOTS

Some plants, such as carrots, have storage roots that may be modified to store water or food. Storage roots are typical of biennials. *See Figure 909.*

TENDRIL

A tendril is a specialised stem or leaf which will attach the plant to something. When the tendril touches something, the other side will grow faster, making it wrap around the object. An example is the sweet pea. *See Figure 910.*

9.1.5 State that dicotyledonous plants have apical and lateral meristems.

©IBO 2007

Dicotyledonous plants have apical and lateral meristems. Meristem is undifferentiated tissue and generates new cells for growth of the plant. It is found in growth areas of the plants.

AHL

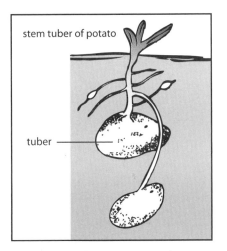

Figure 907   An onion bulb

Figure 909   A carrot is a storage root

Figure 911   An apical meristem

stem tuber of potato

tuber

Figure 908   A potato tuber

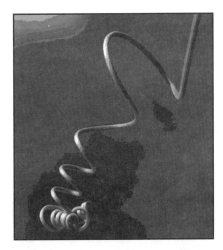

Figure 910   A sweet pea tendril

Figure 912   An example of phototropism

AHL

> 9.1.6   Compare growth due to apical and lateral meristems in dicotyledonous plants.
> ©IBO 2007

APICAL MERISTEM

Apical **meristem** is found in buds and tips of shoots and is responsible for primary growth. During primary growth, plants produce new organs and grow into the basic shape of that plant. *See Figure 911.*

LATERAL MERISTEM

Lateral meristem is responsible for secondary growth and will make a stem grow thicker. This includes growing new vascular bundles. Lateral meristem is found in the cambium as shown in Figure 902.

> 9.1.7   Explain the role of auxin in phototropism as an example of the control of plant growth.
> ©IBO 2007

Phototropism is a growth response (or growth movement) of a plant in response to light coming from a specific direction. A positive phototropism is often thought of as "plants growing towards the light". *Refer to Figure 912.*

Auxins are a group of plant hormones. The best known auxin is IAA (indole-3-acetic acid). Auxins work together with other plant hormones.

Auxin is produced by the apical bud (tip) of a growing plant and from there it is transported down to the stem. Auxin accumulates at the shaded side of the plant and it functions by stimulating growth (both cell division and cell stretching). As a result, the plant grows towards the light.

This has been shown in a well-known experiment involving shoots and an agar block. *Refer to Figure 913.*

First, two shoots were compared. The control was kept in the dark and the other plant was exposed to (blue) light coming from one side. The control grew straight and the other plant grew towards the light.

The second experiment was a repeat of the first except that the tips were covered with foil that allowed no light to pass. The plant in the dark grew straight and so did the plant in the light. This shows that the light is perceived at the tip of the shoot.

Then the tips were cut off the plants and the experiment was repeated with a piece of mica between the plant and the tip. Mica is impermeable and both plants grew straight. This shows that for phototropism, a chemical produced in the tip needs to be distributed down to the stem. Mica was blocking this movement, so both plants grew straight.

When this was repeated but, instead of mica, a block of agar was used, the plant in the light grew towards the light, showing phototropism. The plant responded to the light because auxin was able to diffuse through the agar.

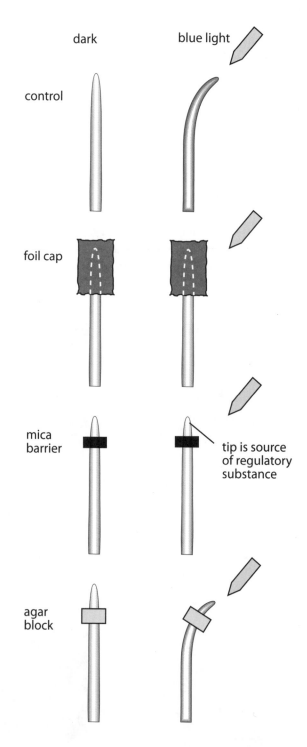

Figure 913   An experiment on phototropism

9.2 TRANSPORT IN ANGIOSPERMOPHYTES

> 9.2.1 Outline how the root system provides a large surface area for mineral ion and water uptake by means of branching and root hairs.
>
> ©IBO 2007

Plants take up water (and minerals) via their roots. As we have seen in other systems, materials need a certain amount of time to cross a barrier. Therefore, to allow an adequate uptake of these molecules, a large surface area is needed. In, for example, the small intestine, villi and microvilli greatly increase the surface area. Roots are branched and have root hairs to further increase their surface area. The structure of the cortex is such that it also facilitates water uptake. *Refer to Figure 914.*

Figure 914   Roots provide a large surface area for absorption

> 9.2.2 List ways in which mineral ions in the soil move to the root.
>
> ©IBO 2007

Minerals that need to be taken up from the soil are:

- N as NO_3^- or NH_4^+
- K as K^+
- P as PO_4^{3-}
- Ca as Ca^{2+}

There are three main methods for the absorption of minerals from the soil into roots:

- diffusion
- via Fungal hyphae
- mass flow.

DIFFUSION

Some minerals are more concentrated in the soil than in the root and when dissolved in water will diffuse into the root. This happens when the mineral touches the membrane protein which is responsible for the transport into the cell.

FUNGAL HYPHAE

Many plant species work together with a fungus to help absorb minerals. The threads of the fungus (hyphae) grow through the soil and absorb minerals. They also grow into the plant roots and transport these minerals to the roots. This helps the plant obtain the minerals they would not be able to absorb without the fungus. The fungus receives sugars from the plant so both species benefit. This is an example of mutualism.

MASS FLOW OF WATER

The third way of obtaining minerals is via the water. The plant takes up large volumes of water which contains some dissolved minerals. This is called mass flow.

> 9.2.3 Explain the process of mineral ion absorption from the soil into roots by active transport.
>
> ©IBO 2007

ACTIVE TRANSPORT

Since it has been found that the concentration of some minerals inside the root may exceed that of a specific mineral in the soil water, it can be concluded that these minerals are taken up by active transport. This is supported by the fact that uptake of some minerals requires energy.

In experiments, mineral uptake has been brought to a halt by depriving the roots of oxygen or adding a substance that blocks cellular respiration. This will happen when the soil becomes waterlogged.

The mechanism of active transport for the uptake of minerals is based on the fact that roots can actively pump out H^+ causing an electrochemical gradient. It will make the inside of the cell more negative than the soil outside. This helps positively charged mineral ions enter the cells of the root. It also allows negatively charged mineral ions to enter by accompanying H^+ as it diffuses back into the cell.

AHL

9.2.4 State that terrestrial plants support themselves by means of thickened cellulose, cell turgor and lignified xylem.

©IBO 2007

Plants do not have a skeleton to keep them upright. Herbaceous plants depend mainly on turgor for their support. As the vacuole takes up water, the cell swells up. This will stretch the cell wall to its limit. The vacuole will still have a lower water potential than the fluid surrounding the cell. It will continue to draw in water. However, the force of the cell wall will force water out at the same rate. The result is like a water-filled balloon in a cardboard box. The structue is quite firm and a number of these cells on top of each other will not need external support.

The movement of water in and out of a cell is called **osmosis** and is shown in Figure 915.

hypertonic

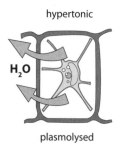

plasmolysed

isotonic

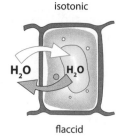

flaccid

hypotonic

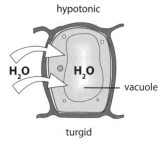

turgid

Figure 915   Osmosis in cells

Trees and shrubs have woody stems that support them. In these plants, xylem vessels and tracheids have lignin which is a supporting tissue and which will assist in the process of keeping the plant upright. More than 25% of the mass of dry wood can be lignin. *See Figure 917.*

9.2.5 Define *transpiration*.

©IBO 2007

Transpiration is the loss of water vapour from the leaves and stems of plants.

Water generally moves into plants through their roots, upwards through the vascular system and out of the stomata in the leaves.

9.2.6 Explain how water is carried by the transpiration stream, including the structure of xylem vessels, transpiration pull, cohesion, adhesion and evaporation.

©IBO 2007

The specialisation of different parts of the plant means that it is necessary to move substances from one place to the next. Water and minerals are absorbed by the roots and need to be moved to other parts, while sugar is produced by the leaves and therefore also requires distribution.

The transpiration stream (*see Figure 916*) is the movement of water and minerals from the roots to the leaves. The water is carried up to the leaves in the xylem vessels. Xylem vessels are dead.

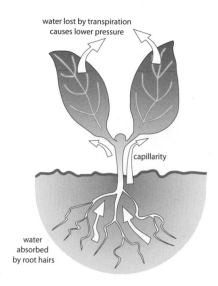

Figure 916   The transpiration stream

Xylem vessels are large. They are originally made of columns of cells but, when the cells die, the walls in between them disappear partly or completely. Xylem vessels have a fairly wide diameter. This makes the xylem vessel efficient in water transport. The walls on the side are reinforced with lignin so that xylem also plays a role in supporting the stem. Xylem vessels are generally only found in angiosperms.

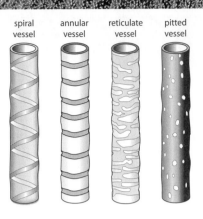

Figure 917
Patterns of lignin in xylem vessels

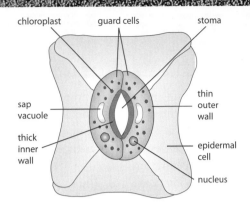

Figure 918
The structure of a stoma

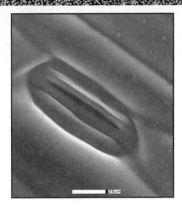

Figure 919
A stoma

The structure of xylem vessels somewhat resembles a drainpipe with walls reinforced with lignin. The lignin can be deposited in various patterns as indicated in Figure 917. All patterns are similar in that there are spaces between the lignin. This allows the water to leave the xylem vessels and move into the tissue. The walls of the xylem will also have pits, to further facilitate the movement of water out of the vessel.

Water moves up the plants in the transpiration stream but it does not run up a drainpipe without assistance. Several forces cooperate in getting the water from the roots of a plant up to the leaves, which may be 20 metres higher.

A tree has many leaves exposed to direct sunlight. The leaves are thin and large, so that they can catch a lot of light and perform a lot of photosynthesis. The shape of the leaves also creates a lot of surface area from which water can (and will) evaporate. On a hot, dry day, a medium-sized tree can evaporate more than 1000 litres of water.

Inside the leaf, the water will evaporate from the spongy mesophyll cells into the airspaces. From there, it will diffuse out through the pores of the stomata. New water molecules will then evaporate from the cells to replace the molecules lost by diffusion.

As the water evaporates from the mesophyll cells, the concentration of dissolved particles increases which will make water from the vascular bundle move into the mesophyll cells by osmosis. The xylem vessels of the vascular bundle are filled with water. The water molecules have strong cohesion forces. Cohesion is the attraction between molecules of the same kind resulting from intermolecular forces.

Moving some water molecules out of the xylem vessel will mean that others will tend to move up. It is like pulling a cord. So all the water molecules in the vessel will move up a bit and at the other end, in the roots, some water will move from the soil into the plant. This is called transpiration pull. Transpiration pull would not work if water molecules did not have strong forces of cohesion. Water molecules also have adhesion with molecules in the walls of the xylem.

Adhesion is the attraction between different kinds of molecules. Adhesion explains why the water level in a glass tube is higher at the wall than in the middle. There is adhesion between the water in the xylem and the cellulose in the wall of the xylem. This supports the water movement up the xylem.

| 9.2.7 | State that guard cells can regulate transpiration by opening and closing stomata. |

©IBO 2007

It is vital for a plant to be able to exchange gases with its environment. A plant also needs to expose a large surface area to the (sun)light. Both of these are needed for the plant to have efficient photosynthesis. However, this creates a problem as it puts the plant at risk of drying out. A large surface area with the ability to exchange respiratory gases is likely to allow enormous amounts of transpiration.

The solution to this problem lies in the existence of guard cells around the **stomata**. The plant maintains its large surface area required for capturing (sun)light energy, but to avoid excessive water loss, the surface is covered with a waxy cuticle that is impermeable to water. However, this cuticle is also impermeable to respiratory gases. Pores, known as stomata, in the cuticle and (lower) epidermis allow the respiratory gases to diffuse into and out of the air spaces in the spongy mesophyll where the gas exchange with the cells takes place. When the plant is at risk of drying out, the guard cells lose turgor and sag together, closing the stomata. This is efficient in reducing water loss but it also stops photosynthesis so it only happens when the plant is at risk. See Figures 918 and 919.

AHL

> **9.2.8** State that the plant hormone abscisic acid causes the closing of stomata.
>
> ©IBO 2007

When there is not enough water, the plant loses more water from its leaves than it can absorb from the soil. When the roots find a lack of water in the soil, they will produce abscisic acid which is transported to the leaves. In the leaves, the abscisic acid will change the concentration of dissolved particles in the guard cells of the stomata. As a result, these cells will lose water through osmosis and become flaccid. They will sag together, closing the pore and reducing water loss.

> **9.2.9** Explain how the abiotic factors light, temperature, wind and humidity, affect the rate of transpiration in a typical terrestrial plant.
>
> ©IBO 2007

A mesophyte is a plant adapted to conditions of average water supply, i.e. not a xerophyte or a hydrophyte.

A typical terrestrial mesophytic plant could be an oak tree or a dandelion.

The rate of transpiration depends on several factors:
- light
- temperature
- wind
- humidity

LIGHT

Plants generally open their stomata in the light to allow diffusion of carbon dioxide into the leaf and hence allow photosynthesis to take place. However, this will also greatly increase evaporation.

TEMPERATURE

The rate of evaporation is doubled for every 10°C increase in temperature.

WIND

Air currents will take water vapour away from the leaf. This will maintain the concentration gradient and as a result water will continue to diffuse out of the leaf.

HUMIDITY

Evaporation is much higher in dry air than in air which is already (partly) saturated with water vapour.

> **9.2.10** Outline four adaptations of xerophytes that help to reduce transpiration.
>
> ©IBO 2007

Xerophytes are plants that can tolerate dry conditions. The advantage of being a xerophyte is that there is less competition in these very dry areas but special adaptations are needed to survive under these conditions.

These adaptations can include:
- reduced leaves
- rolled leaves
- spines
- thickened waxy cuticle
- low growth form
- reduced number of stomata
- stomata in pits surrounded by hairs

REDUCED LEAVES

Reducing the surface area of the leaf to a stem-like structure will reduce the area for transpiration and cut down on water loss. For example, *Salicornia virginica* or Virginia pickleweed. *Refer to Figure 920.*

ROLLED LEAVES

Rolling up the leaves with the lower surface inside, reduces the exposure of the stomata to the air and reduces transpiration. For example, *Erica cinerea* or Bell heather. *Refer to Figure 921.*

Figure 920
Reduced leaves

Figure 921
Rolled leaves

SPINES

Many plants have their leaves reduces to spines so that there is less surface area for evaporation. For example, many species of cactus. *Refer to Figure 922.*

THICKENED WAXY CUTICLE

The thicker the waxy cuticle, the less water will escape. For example, the leaves on a rhododendron. *Refer to Figure 923.*

Figure 922   Spines

Figure 923   Thickened cuticle

Figure 924   Low growth

LOW GROWTH FORM

Small plants, near to the ground, will be less exposed to the wind. As the wind takes away evaporated water, maintaining a high concentration gradient, reducing the air flow will reduce evaporation. *Refer to Figure 924.*

REDUCED NUMBER OF STOMATA

Having a smaller number of stomata will reduce the amount of water that can evaporate at any one time.

STOMATA IN PITS SURROUNDED BY HAIRS

When stomata are in pits, the water vapour will stay in the pit near the pore, reducing the concentration gradient. Surrounding the pit with hairs will further reduce the movement of air, reinforcing this effect.

> 9.2.11 Outline the role of phloem in active translocation of sugars (sucrose) and amino acids from source (photosynthetic tissue and storage organs) to sink (fruits, seeds, roots).
>
> ©IBO 2007

Translocation refers to the movement of sugars and amino acids from source to 'sink'.

The sugars are mainly sucrose. A source is either a photosynthetic organ, such as a leaf where food is made, or a storage organ, such as a root, when the food is taken out of storage. A sink is a place where food is used e.g. a fruit, or stored e.g. root.

Translocation occurs through the phloem by a mechanism called the pressure flow hypothesis. The fluid in the phloem is called sap. The phloem is made of living cells which take up sugar by active transport in a source area. Water will follow by osmosis, causing a high pressure in that part of the phloem and the sap will flow away from that area. In a sink area, phloem cells will move sugar out of the cells and again, water will follow by osmosis. This creates an area of lower pressure so the sap will flow towards this area, bringing new sugar.

9.3 REPRODUCTION IN ANGIOSPERMOPHYTES

AHL

> 9.3.1 Draw and label a diagram showing the structure of a dicotyledonous animal-pollinated flower.
>
> ©IBO 2007

The general structure of a dicotyledonous animal-pollinated flower is shown in Figure 925.

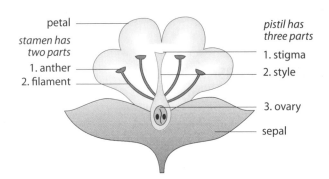

Figure 925   The general structure of a flower

> 9.3.2 Distinguish between *pollination, fertilization* and *seed dispersal.*
>
> ©IBO 2007

POLLINATION

Pollination refers to the tranfer of pollen grains from the anther to the carpel, usually in another flower. This is usually done by insects, wind or water movement.

Bees transfer pollen when they are collecting nectar. *Refer to Figure 926.*

AHL

Figure 926   Pollination

Figure 927   Fruit formation

Figure 928   Seed dispersal of dandelions

FERTILIZATION

Fertilization is the fusion of male and female gametes to form a new organism.

After fertilization, the blackberry plant begins to form the fruit, as shown in Figure 927.

Pollination does not always lead to fertilization. It is possible to pollinate a flower with pollen of a different species but, in this case, fertilization usually does not happen.

SEED DISPERSAL

Seed dispersal is the moving of seeds away from the parent plant to reduce competition. *See Figure 928.*

> 9.3.3   Draw and label a diagram showing the external and internal structure of a named dicotyledonous seed.
>
> ©IBO 2007

The external and internal structure of a pea seed is shown in Figure 929.

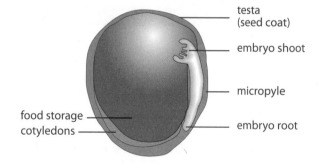

Figure 929   Diagram of a pea seed (Pisum sativum)

> 9.3.4   Explain the conditions needed for the germination of a typical seed.
>
> ©IBO 2007

After dispersal, seeds are likely to be dormant for some time. To allow **germination** to take place, the seed's dormancy must be broken. Different species of plants have different ways of achieving this, depending on the circumstances under which they live.

For successful germination, seeds need:
- oxygen
- water
- suitable temperature

OXYGEN

Oxygen is needed to act as a final electron acceptor in the process of aerobic respiration which releases the required energy for germination to take place.

WATER

Water is taken up by the seed and will make it swell up. As a result, the testa will crack and hydrolytic enzymes are activated which will start to break down large molecules e.g. starch to maltose.

TEMPERATURE

The temperature needs to be suitable. This varies between plants, depending on their natural environment. Some plants need a period of low temperature followed by higher temperatures to break dormancy; this ensures that the seed does not germinate until the winter has passed.

9.3.5 Outline the metabolic processes during germination of a starchy seed.

©IBO 2007

A seed has very few metabolic processes occurring. The seed grew in the parent plant and became dormant when it left the parent. After dormancy has been broken, germination can begin. Germination is the resumption of growth or development from a seed.

The first step in the process of germination is the absorption of water. As the water content of the seed is very low, a large amount of water, sometimes as much as the mass of the seed itself, needs to be absorbed to allow metabolic processes to start. The presence of water will activate hydrolytic enzymes such as amylase.

Amylase breaks down the stored starch into maltose. The maltose will be moved to the embryo and it will be used in cellular respiration to provide energy but also to make cellulose for cell walls of new cells.

The stored proteins and lipids will also be hydrolysed (broken down by adding water, see *Topic 3.2*). The amino acids thus produced will be used to make new proteins which the growing embryo can use in cell membranes or as enzymes. The fatty acids and glycerol from the stored lipids are used in cell membranes (phospholipids) and for energy.

Germination uses the food stored in the cotyledons to grow until it reaches light when it will start to photosynthesise. The plant will grow leaves as soon as possible after that to make the best use of the light available. *Refer to Figure 930.*

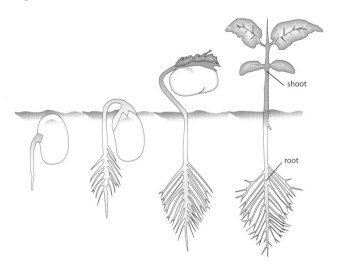

Figure 930   The process of germination

9.3.6 Explain how flowering is controlled in long-day and short-day plants, including the role of phytochrome.

©IBO 2007

Some plants need a minimum number of hours of darkness before they can flower. This means they often flower during spring and autumn when the days are shorter. They are therefore called short-day plants. Coffee and strawberry are short-day plants.

Some other plants have a maximum number of hours of darkness that they can have if they are to produce flowers. They flower in summer, when the days are long, and are called long-day plants. Carnations and clover are long-day plants.

Both of these names can be misleading because the number of hours of darkness is the deciding factor, rather than the amount of daylight.

Some plants are not much affected by the number of hours of darkness and are said to be day neutral.

Photoperiodicity is the name for the plants' responses to the length of the night. Many plants use phytochrome to regulate their photoperiodism.

Phytochrome is a photoreceptor, a protein that can absorb light. It exists in two states, P_r and P_{fr}. P_r absorbs red light and changes quickly into P_{fr}. P_{fr} absorbs far-red light and changes into P_r. In the absence of light, P_{fr} slowly changes back to P_r.

$$P_r \xrightleftharpoons[\textit{far-red light or darkness}]{\textit{red light}} P_{fr}$$

Far-red light has a slightly longer wavelength than red light (but shorter than infra-red).

Daylight contains a lot of red light so after many hours of daylight, plants will have most of their phytochrome as P_{fr}. After a night of uninterrupted darkness, most phytochrome will be in the state of P_r. As the conversion of P_r into P_{fr} in red light is very quick, even a flash of light during the night can disrupt the slow process of changing P_{fr} back into P_r.

Plants are sensitive to the amount of P_{fr}. In long-day plants, P_{fr} is required for flowering. In short-day plants, P_{fr} inhibits the formation of flowers.

AHL

EXERCISES

1. The diagram shows a cross section of a root. The xylem is labelled:

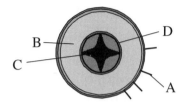

A   A
B   B
C   C
D   D

2. The diagram shows a section through a flower. The part labelled X is:

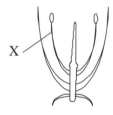

A   a stamen.
B   a sepal.
C   a petal.
D   a bud.

3. Plants that are able to live in dry environments are called:
A   Hydrophytes.
B   Algae.
C   Xerophytes.
D   Mesophytes.

4. Roots take up water from the soil by:
A   evaporation.
B   suction.
C   diffusion.
D   osmosis.

5. The loss of water vapour from the leaves and stems of living plants is known as:
A   transpiration.
B   diffusion.
C   dessication.
D   osmosis.

6. The movement of organic substances from one part of a plant to another in the phloem is known as:
A   diffusion.
B   osmosis.
C   evaporation.
D   translocation.

7. Palms and grasses are examples of:
A   monocotyledons.
B   dicotyledons.
C   conifers.
D   hydrophytes.

8. (a) Draw an annotated diagram of the distribution of tissues in the leaf.
   (b) List the functions of each tissue.
   (c) For each tissue, explain how the structure of this tissue is suited to its function.

9. List the differences between dicotyledenous and monocotyledonous plants.

10. Explain the role of auxin in plants.

11. Explain the process of water uptake in the roots.

12. Outline the role of phloem in active translocation of sugars (sucrose) and amino acids.

13. Draw a labelled diagram of a dicotyledenous animal pollinated flower.

14. Outline the metabolic processes during germination of a starchy seed.

15. (a) List the conditions that are always required for germination.
    (b) Explain why these conditions are necessary.

16. Explain how flowering is controlled.

GENETICS

10.1   Meiosis

10.2   Dihybrid crosses and gene linkage

10.3   Polygenic inheritance

10.1 MEIOSIS

10.1.1 Describe the behaviour of the chromosomes in the phases of meiosis.

©IBO 2007

The behaviour of chromosomes in the various phases of meiosis is described below. Figure 1001 gives a visual summary of the process, as previously shown in Figure 406.

Interphase
- Cell growth and DNA replication.

Prophase I
- Chromosomes condense.
- Nucleolus becomes invisible.
- Spindle formation.
- Synapsis: homologous chromosomes pair up side by side (the pair is now called a **bivalent**, the crossover points are called **chiasmata**).
- Nuclear membrane disappears (sometimes considered as early metaphase).

Metaphase I
- Bivalents move to the equator.

Anaphase I
- Homologous pairs split up, one chromosome of each pair goes to each pole.

Telophase I
- Chromosomes arrive at poles.
- Spindle disappears.

Prophase II
- New spindle is formed at right angles to the previous spindle.

Metaphase II
- Chromosomes move to the equator.

Anaphase II
- Chromosomes separate, chromatids move to opposite poles.

Telophase II
- Chromosomes have arrived at poles.
- Spindle disappears.
- Nuclear membrane reappears.
- Nucleolus becomes visible.
- Chromosomes become chromatin.

Again cell division (**cytokinesis**), strictly speaking, is not a part of meiosis but is often considered to be the last stage of telophase II. The nett result of meiosis is that from one diploid cell, four haploid cells are produced and these are usually sperm or eggs (**gametes**). This enables the chromosome number of a sexually reproducing species to be kept constant from one generation to the next.

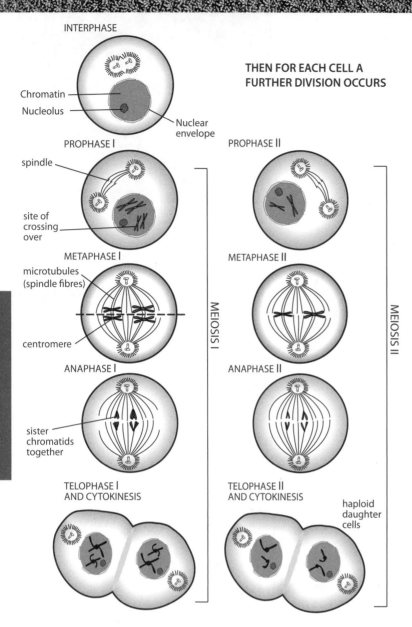

INTERPHASE

Chromatin

Nucleolus

Nuclear envelope

THEN FOR EACH CELL A FURTHER DIVISION OCCURS

PROPHASE I

spindle

site of crossing over

PROPHASE II

METAPHASE I

microtubules (spindle fibres)

centromere

METAPHASE II

MEIOSIS I

ANAPHASE I

sister chromatids together

ANAPHASE II

MEIOSIS II

TELOPHASE I AND CYTOKINESIS

TELOPHASE II AND CYTOKINESIS

haploid daughter cells

Figure 1001   The process of meiosis

> **10.1.2 Outline the formation of chiasmata in the process of crossing over.**
>
> ©IBO 2007

The importance of meiosis as a source of genetic variation is not only found in creating new combinations of the parent chromosomes. New combinations of genes within the chromosome are also possible through a process called **crossing over**. When, during prophase I, synapsis occurs, the chromatids of the bivalent are close together. It is then possible that parts of two chromatids overlap, break at the chiasmata and reattach to the other chromatid. This is illustrated in Figure 1002. Chromatids a and b are sister chromatids, which means that they are identical. One is made as a copy of the other during DNA replication during interphase. The same applies for chromatids c and d. Chromosome a/b is homologous (but not identical) to chomosome c/d.

Each of the chromatids a, b, c, d will end up in a gamete. In the example shown in Figure 1002, the chromosomes carry the genes for hair colour and eye colour. Before crossing over, two gametes would have contained the alleles for H and E (e.g. brown hair and brown eyes) and the other two would have contained genetic information h and e (e.g. blond hair and blue eyes).

After crossing over is complete, each gamete would contain:

gamete a: H and E   (brown hair, brown eyes)
gamete b: H and e   (brown hair, blue eyes)
gamete c: h and E   (blond hair, brown eyes)
gamete d: h and e   (blond hair, blue eyes)

Gametes b and c are therefore new combinations. They are called recombinants.

The points at which two non-sister chromatids overlap during prophase I of meiosis forms a cross shaped structure. This structure is known as a **chiasma** (plural chiasmata). This is the point where crossing over occurs and the segments of the non-sister chromatids will break and reattach to the other chromatid.

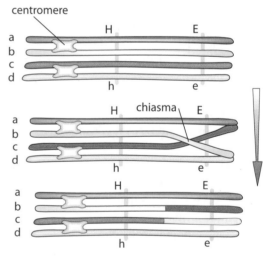

Figure 1002   Crossing over

> **10.1.3 Explain how meiosis results in an effectively infinite genetic variety in gametes through crossing over in prophase I and random orientation in metaphase I.**
>
> ©IBO 2007

Crossing over takes place during prophase I. The number of chiasmata may differ. Chiasmata can occur between any non-sister chromatids. It is even possible to have multiple chiasmata on two non-sister chromatids as illustrated in Figure 1003.

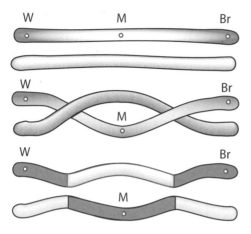

Figure 1003   Multiple chiasma (chiasmata)

The number of different types of gametes produced by random orientation alone is 2^n where n = haploid number. Add to this the effect of crossing over and the resulting variation is almost infinite. Figure 1004 shows this random orientation diagrammatically.

10.1.4   State Mendel's law of independent assortment.
©IBO 2007

Mendel's law of independent assortment (second law) states that 'any one of a pair of characteristics may combine with either one of another pair'.

The provision with Mendel's law of independent assortment is that the two characteristics must be on different chromosomes.

TOK The importance of Mendel's laws

Mendel's laws of inheritance explained the basis of inheritance: genes occur in pairs that are separated in meiosis. However, over time it became obvious that his laws did not account for all cases of inheritance. These cases made it clear that inheritance was more complex than Mendel's laws implied. Without Mendel's laws though, scientists would not have been aware of the exceptions. Study of these exceptions led to a deeper knowledge of the factors at play in inheritance and revealed gene linkage as a variation to Mendel's laws.

10.1.5   Explain the relationship between Mendel's law of independent assortment and meiosis.
©IBO 2007

AHL

Mendel's second law applies to traits carried on different chromosomes. Since any combination of chromosomes is possible in metaphase I, any one of a pair of characteristics may combine with either one of another pair.

Example
pea plants

gene: shape of pea	alleles: wrinkled, round
gene: colour of pea	alleles: yellow, green

When crossing two plants which are heterozygous for both traits (genes), the offspring will show all combinations: green-round, green-wrinkled, yellow-round and yellow-wrinkled. This shows that the genes for shape and colour are inherited independently. Exceptions to Mendel's law will be described in *Topic 10.2*.

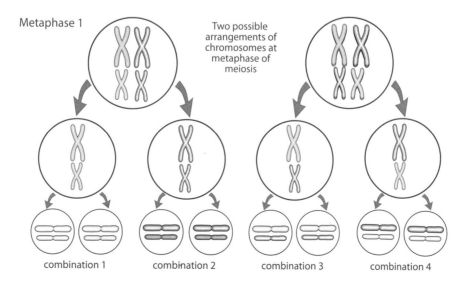

Metaphase 1

Two possible arrangements of chromosomes at metaphase of meiosis

combination 1   combination 2   combination 3   combination 4

Figure 1004   Random orientation

10.2 DIHYBRID CROSSES AND GENE LINKAGE

10.2.1 Calculate and predict the genotypic and phenotypic ratio of offspring of dihybrid crosses involving unlinked autosomal genes.

©IBO 2007

A classic example of a **dihybrid cross** is illustrated using Mendel's peas. The two genes involved are those for shape and colour. Figure 1005 examines each gene separately.

Possible phenotypes	Corresponding Genotypes
Yellow	YY or Yy
green	yy
Round	RR or Rr
wrinkled	rr

Figure 1005   Phenotypes and genotypes of Mendel's peas

If we start off with two homozygous sets of parents (P generation), we will obtain a heterozygous first filial generation (F1). If we then either interbreed or self-fertilise the F1, we obtain the second filial (F2) generation. This is shown diagrammatically in Figure 1006.

```
P      Yellow-Round   x    green-wrinkled      (phenotype)

          YYRR        x        yyrr            (genotype)

           YR                   yr             (gametes)

                        |
                        v

F1             Yellow-Round                    (phenotype)

                   YyRr                        (genotype)

                        |
                        v

      YR  or  Yr  or  yR  or  yr               (gametes)
```

Figure 1006   A dihybrid cross

In order to establish the result of self-fertilising the F1, it is recommended to put the possible gametes into a Punnett square as shown in Figure 1007.

From Figure 1007 the phenotypes appear in the following ratios:

Yellow-Round	9
Yellow-wrinkled	3
green-Round	3
green-wrinkled	1

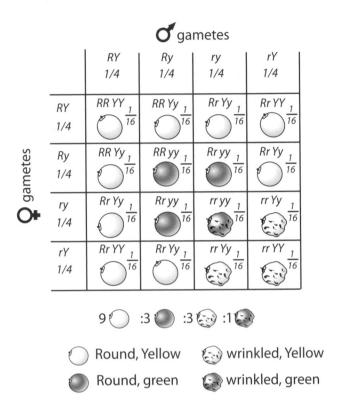

♂ gametes

9 :3 :3 :1

Round, Yellow   wrinkled, Yellow
Round, green   wrinkled, green

Figure 1007   Punnett square outlining a dihybrid cross

10.2.2 Distinguish between *autosomes* and *sex chromosomes*.

©IBO 2007

Autosomes are all chromosomes which are not sex chromosomes. Sex chromosomes are those chromosomes which help to determine the sex of an individual.

Humans have 22 pairs of autosomes and 2 sex chromosomes. Females have XX and males have XY sex chromosomes.

X chromosomes are larger than Y chromosomes and carry more genes. Female gametes (egg cells) always contain an X chromosome; male gametes (sperm cells) contain either an X chromosome or a Y chromosome.

10.2.3 Explain how crossing over between non-sister chromatids of a homologous pair in prophase I can result in an exchange of alleles.

©IBO 2007

Refer back to Topic 10.1.3.

AHL

AHL

©IBO 2007

10.2.4 Define *linkage group*.

LINKAGE GROUP

A **linkage group** refers to a group of genes whose loci are on the same chromosome.

Mendel's law of independent assortment does not apply to linked genes. Because linked genes are found on the same chromosome, they will often be inherited together. However, if crossing over takes place, with the chiasma between the linked genes, these genes will not be inherited together.

The closer the loci of the two genes on a chromosome, the smaller the chance that crossing over will occur with a chiasma between the genes, so the smaller the percentage of recombinants. The reverse is also true, the larger the number of recombinants, the further the loci of the genes will be apart.

If no information is given about the genes (linked or not), it is best to assume that they are not linked. If the percentage of recombinants is lower than expected with this assumption, then it might be prudent to investigate the possibility of the genes being linked.

10.2.5 Explain an example of a cross between two linked genes.

©IBO 2007

An example of a cross between two linked genes will now be examined. The notation AaBb, that was used for the non-linked dihybrid crosses, will be modified to represent crosses involving linkage. The letters representing linked genes will be represented as vertical pairs, as shown in Figure 1008.

$$\frac{A \qquad B}{a \qquad b}$$

Figure 1008

Drosophila (fruit flies) only possess 8 chromosomes and are easy to breed. They mature quickly and have been found to be useful for studying genetics. When studying dihybrid crosses in fruit flies, scientists found that the results did not always correspond with the expected ratio. For example, a pure breeding fruit fly with a tan body and long wings was crossed with a mutant having a black body and short wings. As expected, the F1 generation all had tan bodies and long wings.

However, the F2 generation was 75% tan with long wings and 25% black with short wings. If this cross followed typical Mendelian genetics, the F2 generation would have displayed the ratio of phenotypes shown in Figure 1007. The only possible explanation for the unexpected results of this cross is that body colour and wing length are found on the same chromosome. They are linked.

b^+: tan body   b: black body
w^+: long wings   w: short wings

$$\frac{b^+ \qquad w^+}{b^+ \qquad w^+}$$

Figure   1009

Using the above notation, a wild type *Drosophila* with a tan body and long wings can be represented by Figure 1009.

A mutant *Drosophila* with a black body and short wings could be represented by Figure 1010.

$$\frac{b \qquad w}{b \qquad w}$$

Figure   1010

Therefore, the cross of a fly with a tan body and long wings with the mutant fly with a black body and short wings would be represented by Figure 1011. 75% of the F2 offspring have a tan body with long wings and 25% will have a black body with short wings (a 3:1 ratio). This is very different from the ratio of offspring produced dihybrid cross between non-linked genes shown in Figure 1007.

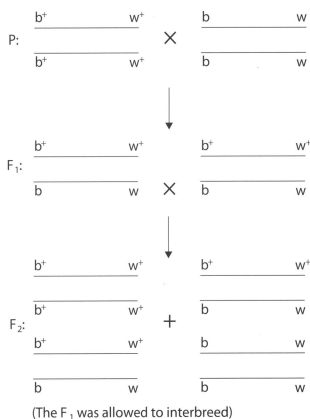

(The F₁ was allowed to interbreed)

Figure 1011   A dihybrid cross between two linked genes

AHL

10.2.6 Identify which of the offspring are recombinants in a dihybrid cross involving linked genes.

©IBO 2007

Recombinants in linked genes are those combinations of genes which the parents did not possess. So for the example shown in Figure 1011, recombinants are shown in Figure 1012.

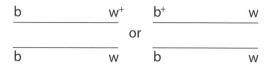

Figure 1012

10.3 POLYGENIC INHERITANCE

10.3.1 Define *polygenic inheritance*.

©IBO 2007

POLYGENIC INHERITANCE

Polygenic inheritance concerns the inheritance of a characteristic which is controlled by more than one gene. Many conditions are thought to be polygenic, including human skin colour, obesity, cancer, autism and diabetes. Polygenic inheritance can lead to continuous variation (e.g. skin colour in humans) or discontinuous variation (e.g. shape of the comb in chickens). Often, variation can also be caused by environmental factors. Human skin colour is affected by the amount of UV light (tanning) and milk yield in cows is affected by the type of food and the environment under which the animal is kept.

Polygenic inheritance is the same as 'multifactorial' inheritance described by Mendel.

10.3.2 Explain that polygenic inheritance can contribute to continuous variation using two examples, one of which must be human skin colour.

©IBO 2007

GENES FOR OBESITY

In mice, several genes have been identified that affect obesity. Leptin is a protein hormone involved in regulating appetite and metabolism. In humans, the *Ob(Lep)* gene (Ob for obese and Lep for leptin) is located on chromosome 7. However, it is known that other genes for obesity are located on several other chromosomes.

HUMAN SKIN COLOUR

Human skin colour involves the interaction of at least three independent genes. If we assume that A, B and C will each represent alleles for dark skin, then a, b and c will represent alleles for light skin. Each person will have two alleles per gene, so six alleles in total (or more if more than three genes are involved).

We can symbolise the alleles for darker skin by ● and the alleles for light skin by ○. The phenotype of darkest skin would then be caused by ●● ●● ●●. The phenotype of the lightest skin would be caused by ○○ ○○ ○○. If these two produced offspring, they would have the genotype ●○ ●○ ●○ with an intermediate skin colour. If one of these

---

TOK   How is skin colour important?

The difference in skin colour in humans results from varying amounts of a pigment, melanin, found in the skin. Pigment absorbs light and melanin is found in highest concentration in the skin of people whose ancestors came from the parts of the world receiving the most light (equatorial regions of Central Africa, South Asia and Australia). This is thought to protect these people from absorbing high amounts of light which would interfere with the production of vitamin D in the skin. Conversely melanin is found in lowest concentration in the skin of people whose ancestors came from the parts of the world receiving the least light (those closest to the Arctic Circle). Light is required for the production of one of the D vitamins in the skin, so the presence of melanin would be a disadvantage for these people.

The large-scale migration of humans that occurred as modern transportation developed resulted in people moving to parts of the world where the presence or absence of melanin in their skin could become a biological disadvantage. The development of vitamin supplements and sun-block creams has largely overcome this disadvantage. Sadly, the amount of melanin in the skin has also been used by some to create social disadvantage, giving the genes involved in its production a place in human history that they do not deserve. Are any genes in the genome more important than others?

offspring produced offspring with someone with the same genotype, the possibilities for skin colour of their offspring are as shown in Figure 1013.

As can be seen fin Figure 1013, human skin colour shows a normal distribution with the highest numbers in the middle range. This is typical for continuous variation.

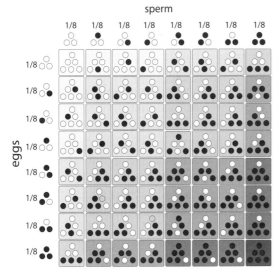

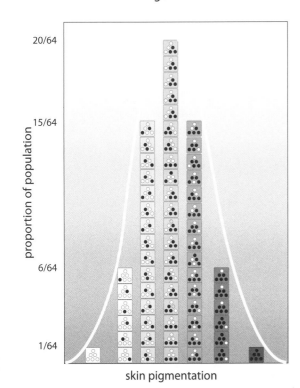

Figure 1013   Inheritance of skin colour

EXERCISES

1   The reassortment of genes or characters into different combinations from those from of the parents is known as:
    A   meiosis.
    B   recombination.
    C   chiasma.
    D   interphase.

2. A human cell contains 46 chromosomes. After meiosis is completed, the result is:

	number of cells	number of chromosomes per cell
A	2	46
B	2	23
C	4	46
D	4	23

3   Two bean plants are crossed. The flowers of this type of bean are either white or yellow. The pods are either short or long. The plant that is crossed could not have:
    A   white flowers and long pods.
    B   white flowers and short pods.
    C   red flowers and short pods.
    D   yellow flowers and long pods.

4   During meiosis, DNA replication occurs during:
    A   Prophase I
    B   Anaphase I
    C   Interphase
    D   Telophase I

5. A man who does not have haemophila marries a women who is a carrier.
    What is the chance of one of their sons having haemophilia?
    A   0%
    B   25%
    C   50%
    D   100%

6   A man who does not have haemophila marries a women who is a carrier.
    What is the chance of one of their daughters having haemophilia?
    A   0%
    B   25%
    C   50%
    D   100%

AHL

7. A diagram of a bivalent in Prophase I is given below. Deduce the correct answer.

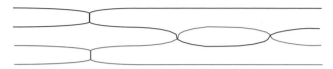

	no. of homologous pairs	no. of chromatids	no. of chiasmata
A	2	4	4
B	1	4	2
C	2	2	2
D	1	2	4

8 A group of genes whose loci are on the same chromosome is known as a:
A linkage group
B gene.
C chromosome.
D cross.

9 Draw a complete diagram of the stages of meiosis and explain what happens in each stage.

10 (a) Write down Mendel's second law.
(b) How does Mendel's second law apply to linked genes.

11 A *Drosophila* (fruit fly) with white eyes and vestigial wings was mated to an individual that showed wild type for both characteristics (red eyes, normal wings). The offspring were all wild type.
(a) Which are the dominant alleles?
(b) List the possible genotypes and phenotypes of the parents and offspring. Use the correct notation.
(c) Use a Punnett square to predict the genotypes and phenotypes of the F2 if the F1 is allowed to interbreed. Assume that both parents are homozygous for both traits.
(d) Give the expected ratios of the genotypes and phenotypes of the F2.

12. Queen Victoria was probably a carrier for the disease haemophilia. Several of her daughters were married to princes of other European royal families. Why did this introduce haemophilia into some of these families but did it not persist in the English royal family?

13 In *Drosophila* (fruit flies) the allele for grey colour is dominant over black. Straight wings are dominant over curly wings.
A heterozygous grey-straight winged fly was crossed with a black-curly winged fly. The offspring were as follows:
43 grey straight
12 grey curly
39 ebony curly
10 ebony straight

(a) If these genes are not linked, which phenotypes would you expect in the F1?
(b) Give the expected numbers of the phenotypes.
(c) Based on these results, would you expect the genes to be linked?

14 In rabbits, having coloured fur is dominant over producing no pigment (albino). Grey fur is dominant over black. A homozygous completely recessive albino rabbit is mated with a homozygous grey rabbit. The F1 are allowed to interbreed.
(a) What are the genotype and phenotype of the F1?
(b) Predict the genotypes of the F2
(c) What are the expected ratios?
(d) Predict the phenotypes of the F2
(e) What are the expected ratios?

HUMAN HEALTH AND PHYSIOLOGY

11.1   Defence against infectious disease

11.2   Muscles and movement

11.3   The kidney

11.4   Reproduction

11

11.1   DEFENCE AGAINST INFECTIOUS DISEASE

11.1.1   Describe the process of blood clotting.

©IBO 2007

Blood is too precious a fluid to allow it to escape in large amounts. As a result, blood clots when there is a cut. It is equally important that blood does not clot at other times and obstruct the blood vessels. The finely-regulated process of blood clotting involves the following processes.

Blood from a cut will react with air and substances from damaged cells and platelets. Damaged cells will release the enzyme thrombokinase (or thromboplastin) which, together with factor X and factor VII and Ca^{2+} ions, will change prothrombin into thrombin. Thrombin will hydrolyse soluble fibrinogen into smaller insoluble fibrin molecules. These will form a network which captures erythrocytes and becomes a clot. See Figure 1101 for a schematic representation of this process.

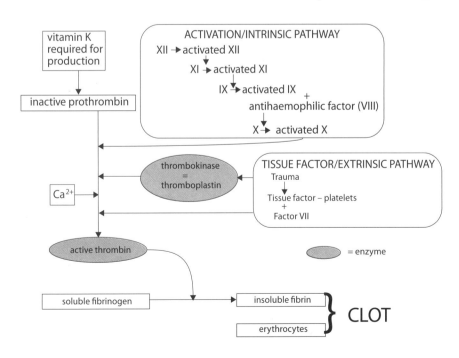

Figure 1101   The process of blood clotting

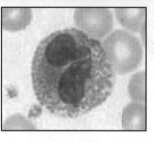

Figure 1102
A granulocyte

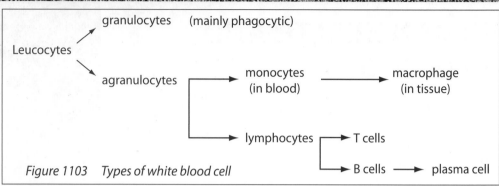

Figure 1103   Types of white blood cell

Figure 1104
A macrophage

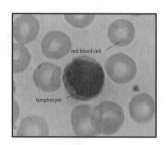

Figure 1105
A lymphocyte (SEM)

Figure 1106
A lymphocyte (stained)

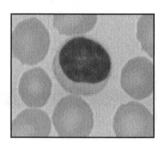

Figure 1107
A plasma cell

AHL

11.1.2   Outline the principle of challenge and response, clonal selection and memory cells as the basis of immunity.

©IBO 2007

The blood contains red cells (**erythrocytes**), platelets (**thrombocytes**) and white cells (**leucocytes**). The **leucocytes** play a role in the immune system. There are many different kinds of leucocytes and these are shown in Figure 1103.

Leucocytes have a nucleus. They can be seen under the light microscope after staining of the slide. Based on their appearance, the leucocytes are divided into granulocytes (see Figure 1102) and agranulocytes.

The role of granulocytes can be phagocytic and/or to release chemicals found in the granules that gave the cells their name to destroy the pathogens near them.

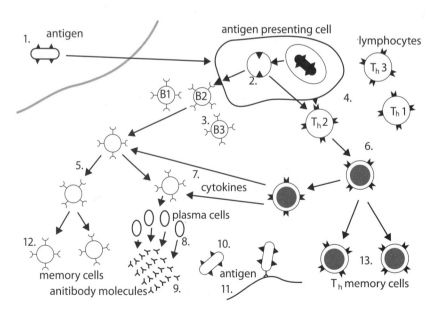

1-2 antigen presentation, 3-4 clonal selection, clonal expansion, 7 T$_h$ secrete cytokines
8 plasma cells secrete antibodies, 9 antibody molecules in blood and lymph
10 antibody coats bacteria, 11 phagocytosis, 12-13 memory cells remain

Figure 1108   Clonal selection and expansion

When a pathogen invades the organism, the immune system is challenged and will produce antibodies against the invading pathogen as a response. The macrophages *(see Figure 1104)*, which are the first to encounter a pathogen, will ingest the pathogen (phagocytosis) but do so incompletely. Parts of the bacterial cell wall and cell membrane will be displayed on the outside of the cell membrane of the macrophage. It will then travel to the lymph node.

The lymph node contains cells known as lymphocytes *(see Figures 1105 and 1106)*. Once inside the lymph node, the macrophage displaying the antigen will select a helper-T (T_h) cell which has receptors on its membrane complementary to the antigen that the macrophage carries. As a result, these T_h cells will divide by mitosis, forming a clone. The cloned T_h cells will activate B-cells which also have surface receptors complementary to the antigen. The B-cells will also form a clone. The B-cells will then differentiate into plasma cells *(see Figure 1107)* and memory cells. The plasma cells will make large amounts of antibodies.

Clonal selection refers to the process of the macrophage selecting which T-cells and B-cells have the required surface receptor.

Clonal expansion describes the process of T-cells and B-cells forming clones by mitosis to produce the large numbers of cells required to deal with the infection. Figure 1108 shows this process diagrammatically.

11.1.3 Define *active* and *passive* immunity.
©IBO 2007

ACTIVE IMMUNITY

Active immunity is immunity due to the production of antibodies by the organism itself after the body's defence mechanisms have been stimulated by antigens.

PASSIVE IMMUNITY

Passive immunity refers to immunity that is due to the acquisition of antibodies from another organism in which active immunity has been stimulated, including via the placenta, colostrum, or by injection of antibodies.

11.1.4 Explain antibody production.
©IBO 2007

As stated in *Topic 11.1.2*, the B-cells can be found in the lymph nodes. They will form a clone and then differentiate into plasma cells (and memory cells) producing one kind of antibody. The general structure of an antibody, with its antigen-binding sites, is shown in Figure 1109. MHC (major histocompatability complex) proteins are membrane proteins found on macrophages. T-cell receptors do not respond to antigens unless the antigens are associated with MHC proteins (on the macrophages).

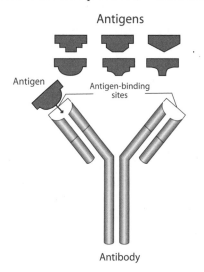

Figure 1109   An antibody with two antigen-binding sites

The macrophage will present the antigen to the T-helper cell. The T-helper cell will secrete a substance which activates nearby B-cells. The B-cells will divide, form a clone and differentiate into plasma cells producing specific antibodies.

Cytotoxic T-cells are involved in the cell mediated response. In response to substances secreted by the T-helper cell, cytotoxic T-cells will kill pathogens and viruses which have invaded cells. A cell which contains viruses or other pathogens will be detected (these cells display special proteins on their cell surfaces) and destroyed.

B-cells can form memory cells. This means that the second response to exposure of the antigen is much faster and stronger than the first response *(refer to Figure 1110)*. It has been argued that T-helper cells can also form memory cells but their existence has not yet been proven.

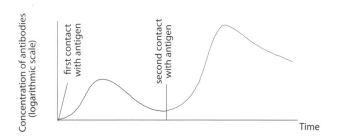

Figure 1110   The antibody response

AHL

11.1.5 Describe the production of monoclonal antibodies and their use in diagnosis and in treatment.

©IBO 2007

Monoclonal antibodies are obtained from single B-cell clones. You inject a mammal (e.g. a mouse) with the antigen (e.g. human red blood cells - type A). The mouse plasma cells will produce antibodies against the human red blood cells. You can extract the mouse plasma cells and fuse them with B-cell tumour cells. The resulting hybridoma cells will grow in culture and will all produce identical antibodies (anti-A) as the original plasma cells extracted from the mouse injected with the human type A red blood cells.

If you add human blood to the antibodies produced by the hybridoma cells and you see clotting, then you know that the blood you added contained type A cells. This method is used to determine a patient's blood type.

Monoclonal antibodies are also commonly used to diagnose pregnancy. The method is as follows:

• Obtain monoclonal antibodies against the HCG (human chorionic gonadotropin), a hormone produced in pregnancy.
• Fix the antibodies in place on a testing stick/strip.
• Add urine to the testing stick/strip.
• If the HCG is present in the urine (as it will be if the woman is pregnant), it will attach to the antibodies.
• The test has been designed so that this will produce a specific colour indicating a positive test.

There is enormous potential in the application of monoclonal antibody technology. However such technologies remain relatively expensive so research and development is usually only carried out where there is a market opportunity. In reality this means that a substantial financial benefit from a potential product must be foreseen before a company will commit to develop such technologies. In other words, the product must have a market in the economically developed world. Because of economies of scale, it often becomes feasible to distribute them cheaply in the economically underdeveloped world at a later time through the action of various aid agencies.

Some medical conditions, such as tropical diseases and parasitic infections, are rare in the economically developed world, but common in the economically underdeveloped world. Therefore, there is no market incentive to produce treatments for them. River blindness is a disease that causes permanent blindness to tens of millions of people in Latin America, Central Africa and Yemen. A scientist in the pharmaceutical company, Merck, discovered that a drug being developed to prevent parasitic infection in pets

could be modified to kill the parasite that causes River blindness in humans. In 1987, Merck made the decision to develop and manufacture the drug, Ivermectin, and provide it free to aid agencies to distribute for as long as was needed. Today 50 million people are provided free Ivermectin and the incidence of River blindness has been substantially reduced. The programme has since been expanded to treat other parasitic diseases. Merck's decision was unusual but the benefit has been enormous to those who could never afford to pay for the necessary medicine.

11.1.6 Explain the principle of vaccination.

©IBO 2007

As explained in *Topic 11.1.4*, the secondary response to an antigen is much faster and stronger than the first response. This fact is used in **vaccination**. By deliberately exposing someone to a weakened/dead/related pathogen, this person develops memory cells against the antigen. If the disease is very serious (bacterial diseases: diphtheria, whooping cough, tetanus; viral diseases: measles, polio, rubella) you may want to vaccinate against it. If the person then comes into contact with the pathogen after being vaccinated, the body will have a much faster and stronger response and the person is unlikely to become ill.

Vaccination involves a deliberate exposure (often by injection, *see Figure 1111*) to the pathogen in order to produce memory cells. To avoid becoming ill as a result of this, the pathogen is killed, weakened or a related strain is used (e.g. cowpox for smallpox).

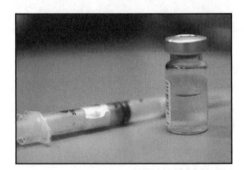

Figure 1111   The vaccine with applicator

11.1.7 Discuss the benefits and dangers of vaccination.

©IBO 2007

Vaccination has helped to reduce the incidence of many diseases. However, there are also possible dangers associated with vaccination.

BENEFITS OF VACCINATION

- Eradication of some diseases (e.g. smallpox).

- Fewer people get certain diseases
  For example, measles, polio and diphtheria because when they come into contact with the pathogen, they will have a secondary response rather than a primary response *(see Topic 11.1.6)*.

- Prevents disability
  For example, polio can cause paralysis and when pregnant women get rubella, the baby's vision may be affected. Christina, the youngest sister of Queen Beatrix of the Netherlands, has eye problems due to her mother (Juliana) contracting rubella during pregnancy.

- Herd immunity
  If many people in a population are vaccinated, the disease will not spread and even the individuals not vaccinated will be protected because they probably will not come into contact with the disease.

DANGERS OF VACCINATION

- Overloading the immune system with an antigen will reduce the ability to handle other infections (Gulf War syndrome?).

- Other pathogens could grow in the solution with the vaccine.

- The vaccine could contain other harmful substances e.g. although no evidence has been found of harmful effects of mercury in vaccinations, as a precaution, it is now used less and less.

- In tests, vaccines are studied when administered individually, but usually the effect of a mixture of antigens (as in MMR vaccination) is not considered.

- Artificial immunity is less effective; childhood diseases avoided as a child may cause a more serious disease as an adult (e.g. measles).

- Side effects of vaccination:
  - in 1998 Dr. Wakefield *et al* suggested a possible link between MMR vaccination and an increased chance of autism; studies carried out since have failed to confirm this link and most of Dr. Wakefield's co-authors have retracted the interpretation of the results.
  - vaccination against whooping cough, using a whole cell vaccine, may increase the chances of brain damage; again, further studies have not shown a link.

- Malnourished individuals may not be able to make the antibodies (which are proteins) because they do not have enough amino acids.

TOK Is vaccination safe?

Vaccination programmes have had the most significant positive effect on human health of any preventative treatment apart from sanitation. They have rid the world of diseases such as smallpox and substantially reduced the risk of infections that were once major causes of death or disease.

Vaccines, like other drugs, are developed through a series of stages that culminate in human testing. Double blind trials involve testing both a drug and an inactive substance (a placebo, which acts as a control) where neither the patient nor the researcher knows who is in the experimental or control group. Such testing removes any bias that may come from knowledge about the nature of treatment.

Data gathered is analysed to determine the effectiveness of the drug. Interestingly, sometimes those receiving the inactive substance receive a psychological benefit called the placebo effect, but there is no evidence of any clinical benefit in receiving a placebo.

Poor education about the benefits of health initiatives, such as vaccination programmes, sometimes allows ignorance and misinformation to flourish. How can society be better educated about public health initiatives?

For vaccination to be most effective, all members of a community at risk must be vaccinated to deny the pathogen a host. This has led to questioning as to whether or not the individual right to decide whether or not to be vaccinated is more important than the society's right to be protected. In some countries vaccination is optional, in others there are financial incentives to become vaccinated and in yet others vaccination is compulsory. How should decisions be made about vaccination policy?

AHL

11.2 MUSCLES AND MOVEMENT

AHL

11.2.1	State the roles of bones, ligaments, muscles, tendons and nerves in human movement.
	©IBO 2007

When an animal moves, the signals pass along the nerves to the muscle, causing it to contract. The **muscles** are connected to the bones by **tendons**. The contraction causes the bones to move. In the case shown in Figure 1112, the leverage of the bones causes the hand at the end of the lower arm bone to move much more than the amount by which the muscle has contracted. The movement is usually reversed by the contraction of a muscle on the opposite side of the bone. An example of an opposed pair of muscles is the bicep at the front of the upper arm and the tricep at the back. The bicep bends the arm and the tricep straightens it. *Refer to Figure 1112.*

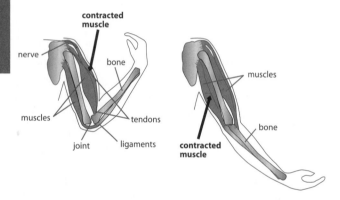

Figure 1112   Muscles and bones of the arm

The musculo-skeletal system consists of various organs and tissues which have different roles. The role of bones is to provide rigid structure for anchorage of muscles. The role of **ligaments** is to connect bones together so they do not move apart. The vital role of muscles is to attach to two bones.

Muscles can alter the position of the bones relative to each other only by contracting (becoming shorter). Tendons serve to attach bone to muscle; they do not stretch or contract. The role of nerves is twofold, they sense the contraction and relative position of limbs and they also provide the impulse that makes muscles contract.

11.2.2	Label a diagram of the human elbow joint, including cartilage, synovial fluid, joint capsule, named bones and antagonistic muscles (biceps and triceps).
	©IBO 2007

A diagram of a human elbow joint is shown in Figure 1113. The opposed, or antagonistic muscles, are the biceps and triceps. The joint is held together by ligaments.

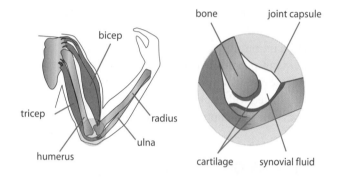

Figure 1113   The elbow joint

11.2.3	Outline the functions of the structures in the human elbow joint named in 11.2.2.
	©IBO 2007

At a joint, two bones can move relative to each other. The end of each bone is made of spongy bone which is light but strong. A cartilage covering helps produce smooth movement as well as absorb shocks. The structures and functions are summarised in the table below.

Synovial fluid contains the required food and oxygen to maintain cartilage and acts as a lubricant for the joint. The synovial membrane keeps the synovial fluid in place.

Structure	Function
Bone	Rigid structure for anchoring muscles
Tendons	Attach biceps to scapula (shoulder blade) near the humerus (bone of the upper arm) and radius (one of two bones in the lower arm)
	Attach triceps to the scapula and humerus near the shoulder and to the ulna (other bone of the lower arm)
Spongy bone	Provides great strength without too much mass
Ligaments	Keep bones in the correct relative position

Structure	Function
Biceps	Bend the arm
Triceps	Straighten arm
Cartilage	Allows easy movement because of smooth surface Absorbs shock and distributes load
Synovial membrane	Secretes synovial fluid and keeps it within the joint
Synovial fluid	Provides food, oxygen and lubrication to cartilage

11.2.4 Compare the movements of the hip joint and the knee joint.

©IBO 2007

There are several similarities between the hip joint and knee joint:

- Both joints are synovial joints.
- Both are involved in the movement of the leg.
- Both are required for the process of walking.

There are also several differences. These are outlined in Figure 1114.

	Hip joint	Knee joint
Type of joint	Socket and ball	Hinge joint
Axes of movement	Multiaxial	Movement only in one axis
Kinds of movement	Flex and extend Abduction and adduction Rotation	Flex and extend Small amount of rotation

Figure 1114   Differences between hip joint and knee joint

The term "flex and extend" refers to the kind of movement that moves the leg back and forth. "Abduction and adduction" means the leg will move sideways (away from the centre of the body), whereas "rotation" will point toes in and out. A combination of these movements will create a "wind-milling" effect. Refer to Figures 1115 and 1116 which show X-rays of these joints.

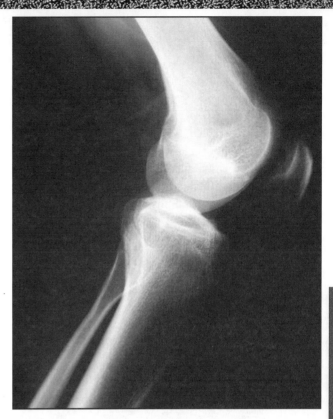

Figure 1115   An X-ray of a knee joint

AHL

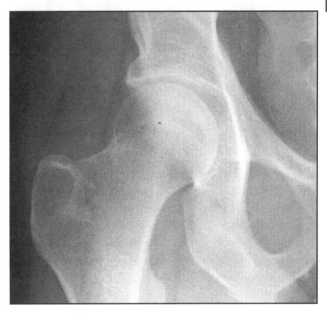

Figure 1116   An X-ray of a hip joint

11.2.5 Describe the structure of striated muscle fibres, including the myofibrils with light and dark bands, mitochondria, the sarcoplasmic reticulum, nuclei and the sarcolemma.

©IBO 2007

Muscles are groups of cells working together. Each muscle cell originally was many cells which fused and therefore the resulting cell contains many nuclei. The sarcolemma is the membrane surrounding the muscle cell. *Refer to Figure 1117.*

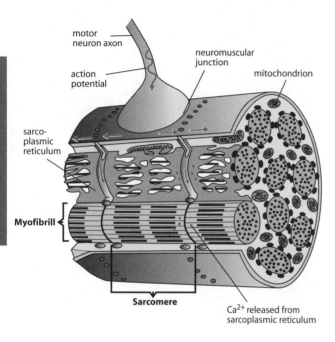

Figure 1117   The structure of a muscle cell

Inside the muscle cell, there is cytoplasm which is called sarcoplasm. The internal membrane within the sarcoplasm is called the sarcoplasmic reticulum. The function of the sarcoplasmic reticulum is to store and release calcium ions (Ca^{2+}) into the sarcoplasm to trigger a muscle contraction. *Refer to Figures 1117 and 1118 for schematic representations.*

Inside a muscle cell, there are many thin myofibrils. These thin fibres cause the typical striated (striped) pattern of light and dark bands of skeletal muscles. Myofibrils contain two types of myofilaments, myosin and actin. They are made of a protein-like substance. As muscle contractions require a lot of energy, many mitochondria are found inside the sarcolemma, in between the myofibrils. The **sarcomere** is the functional unit of the muscle.

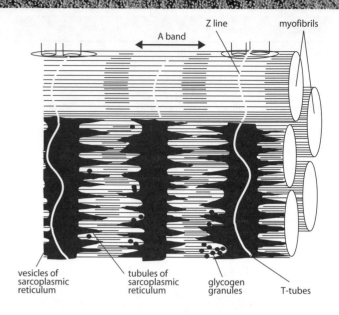

Figure 1118   The structure of a sarcomere

11.2.6 Draw and label a diagram to show the structure of a sarcomere, including Z lines, actin filaments, myosin filaments with heads, and the resultant light and dark bands.

©IBO 2007

The 'unit' within a myofibril is the sarcomere. It contains from one side to the other:

- a light section
- a dark section
- an intermediate section
- a dark section
- a light section.

The thin actin filaments are attached to the Z line and form the light section, the I band. They partly overlap with the thick myosin filaments which appears as a dark section, the A band. In the middle between the two Z lines, you find only myosin, shown as a gray section, the H zone. *Refer to Figure 1118.*

Across the fibres, you find the sarcoplasmic reticulum which regulates the movement of calcium ions (Ca^{2+}) to and from the sarcoplasm. Since the Ca^{2+} concentration determines the activity of ATPase (which hydrolyses ATP, releasing its energy), this essentially determines the activity of the muscle.

> **11.2.7** Explain how skeletal muscle contracts, including the release of calcium ions from the sarcoplasmic reticulum, the formation of cross-bridges, the sliding of actin and myosin filaments, and the use of ATP to break cross-bridges and re-set myosin heads.
>
> ©IBO 2007

Contraction of skeletal muscle can be explained by the sliding filament theory and is shown diagrammatically in Figure 1119.

It was discovered that the A band is the same length in contracted and relaxed muscles. The A band is **actin** and **myosin** *(see Topic 11.2.8)*. This led to the sliding filament theory. Essentially this theory says that the actin and myosin filaments slide over each other to make the muscle shorter. Little 'hooks' on the myosin filaments attach to the actin and pull them closer. Then they release and repeat futher down the actin. This can be referred to as the ratchet mechanism. ATP provides energy by being hydrolysed to ADP by the enzyme ATPase.

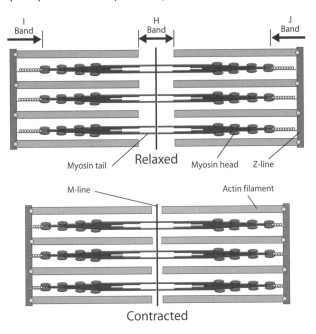

Figure 1119   The mechanism of muscle contraction

Actin filaments contain actin as well as two proteins: tropomyosin and troponin. Tropomyosin forms two strands which wind around the actin filament, covering the binding site for the myosin hooks. As such, the muscle cannot contract.

When a nerve impulse arrives at the muscle, the depolarisation of the motor end plate is passed on to the sarcoplasmic reticulum which causes it to release calcium ions (Ca^{2+}) into the sarcoplasm. The calcium ions attach to troponin which is attached to tropomyosin. This uncovers the binding sites on the actin for the myosin hooks. The muscle can now contract.

When no more nerve impulses arrive, calcium ions are moved back into the vesicles of the sarcoplasmic reticulum by active transport. The binding sites on the actin will then be covered again and the muscle will relax.

> **11.2.8** Analyse electron micrographs to find the state of contraction of muscle fibres.
>
> ©IBO 2007

If the skeletal muscle is relaxed, it is possible to see several shades of gray on an EM of a muscle. Immediately next to the Z line, there is a very light (white) band of only actin (I band). Further to the centre of the sarcomere is the darkest band, the A band which is myosin and actin. In the centre of the dark A band, there is a gray H zone of only myosin.

When the muscle is contracted, the distance between the Z lines becomes shorter because the myosin and actin have slid over each other. Both the I band and the H zone have become smaller. When there is maximum contraction, both these sections may be difficult to see. Refer to Figure 1120 for details of a relaxed muscle.

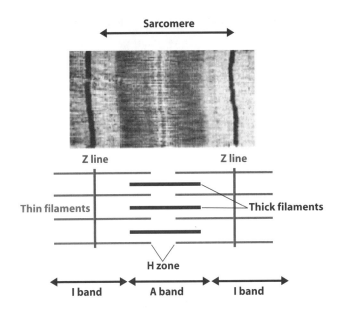

Figure 1120   Details of a relaxed muscle

11.3 THE KIDNEY

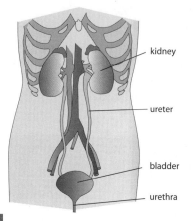

Figure 1121
The urinary system

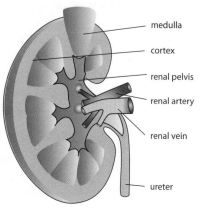

Figure 1122
The structure of the kidney

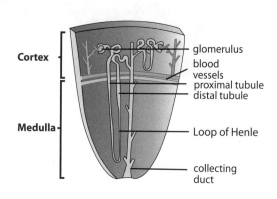

Figure 1123
The structure of the nephron

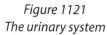

11.3.1 Define *excretion*.

©IBO 2007

Excretion refers to the removal of the waste products of metabolic pathways from the body. This can occur in a number of ways but is mainly through the lungs, skin and kidney and urinary system.

11.3.2 Draw and label a diagram of the kidney.

©IBO 2007

Humans have two **kidneys**, situated low in the abdominal cavity, near the back *(Figure 1121)*. Each kidney has a renal artery leading to it and a renal vein and a ureter leading away from it *(Figure 1122)*. The renal vein takes the 'clean' blood away from the kidney while the ureter leads the urine to the bladder.

When a kidney is examined, the cortex on the outside and the medulla on the inside can be seen. In the centre is the renal pelvis. *Refer to Figure 1122.*

11.3.3 Annotate a diagram of a glomerulus and associated nephron to show the function of each part.

©IBO 2007

The functional unit in the kidney is the **nephron**. Figure 1123 is a schematic representation of a nephron and Figure 1124 provides a summary of structures and functions. *Refer also to Figures 1125 and 1126.*

Structure	Function
Renal artery	takes blood to kidney
Renal vein	takes blood away from kidney
Afferent vessel	takes blood to glomerulus
Efferent vessel	takes blood away from glomerulus
Vasa recta (blood vessels around nephron)	take away reabsorbed materials
Glomerulus (extensive capillary bed)	ultra-filtration
Bowman's capsule (first part of the nephron)	receives filtrate from glomerulus
Proximal convoluted tubule	most reabsorption of glucose, salt and water takes place here
Loop of Henle	reabsorption of water reabsorption of salts
Distal convoluted tubule	reabsorption of salt
Collecting duct	reabsorption of urea reabsorption of salt reabsorption of water regulated by ADH

Figure 1124   *Structures of the nephron and their functions*

AHL

11.3.4 Explain the process of ultrafiltration, including blood pressure, fenestrated blood capillaries and basement membrane.

©IBO 2007

The activity of the nephron is based on the principles of ultrafiltration, reabsorption and secretion. In ultrafiltration, part of the fluid in the blood is pushed out of the glomerulus into the nephron. Further in the nephron, the substances which the body does not want to lose, such as glucose, are reabsorbed into the blood. Finally some substances, for example ammonia, are secreted into the **filtrate**, by the cells of the nephron, to be removed with the urine.

The renal artery supplies the kidney with blood. It splits into many smaller blood vessels and each nephron has an afferent vessel which carries the blood to the glomerulus. From the glomerulus, the efferent vessel carries the blood around the other parts of the nephron. After this, the blood passes into larger blood vessels which eventually become the renal vein.

The diameter of the afferent vessel is larger than that of the efferent vessel, so in the glomerulus, the blood is under a high pressure and ultrafiltration takes place. This means that some of the liquid and dissolved particles are pushed out of the blood vessel and into Bowman's capsule; the cells and the larger molecules (e.g. proteins) are too big to pass through and therefore will not be found in Bowman's capsule. All the blood in the body passes through the kidney every 5 minutes. Approximately 15 - 20% of the fluid in the blood will pass into Bowman's capsule which is about 200 litres a day!

The filtrate needs to pass a 'barrier' made of three different layers:
- the wall of the glomerulus,
- the basement membrane and
- the inner wall of Bowman's capsule.

The wall of the glomerulus contains small pores. It is said to be 'fenestrated' and allows blood plasma to pass through. The basement membrane is a protein membrane outside the cells; it contains no pores and serves as a filter during the ultrafiltration process (it acts as a dialysis membrane) and stops the blood cells and large proteins from entering. The cells of the inner wall of **Bowman's capsule** are called podocytes; they have many extensions, called pedicels, which fold around the blood vessels and have a network of filtration slits that hold back the blood cells. *Refer to Figure 1125.*

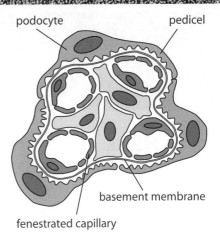

Figure 1125   The structure of the glomerulus

11.3.5 Define *osmoregulation*.

©IBO 2007

Osmoregulation refers to the regulation and control of the water balance of the blood, tissue and cytoplasm of a living organism.

11.3.6 Explain the reabsorption of glucose, water and salts in the proximal convoluted tubule, including the roles of microvilli, osmosis and active transport.

©IBO 2007

The first part of the nephron is Bowman's capsule. This is where the filtrate from the glomerulus enters the nephron. Bowman's capsule joins onto the proximal convoluted tubule. The fluid in the proximal convoluted tubule is similar to plasma and contains glucose, amino acids, vitamins, hormones, urea, salt ions and, of course, water. Most of the reabsorption in the nephron occurs here: all the glucose, amino acids, vitamins, hormones and most of the salt (sodium chloride) and water are reabsorbed into the blood vessels (peritubular capillaries). Osmosis drives the reabsorbtion of water as it follows the active transport of glucose and Na^+. Cl^- passively follows the actively transported Na^+.

All of these substances need to move across the wall of the proximal convoluted tubule. To facilitate all this transport, the cells lining the lumen of the proximal convoluted tubule have a brush border: a row of microvilli (finger-like extensions of the cell) which greatly increase the available surface area. Mitochondria are also prominent in these cells, providing the energy needed for active transport.

AHL

11.3.7   Explain the roles of the loop of Henle, medulla, collecting duct and ADH (vasopressin) in maintaining the water balance of the blood.

©IBO 2007

THE LOOP OF HENLE

In the descending limb of the loop of Henle, water leaves the nephron by osmosis due to the increasing concentration (of salt). This water immediately passes into the blood capillaries and is removed from the area. Some salt diffuses into the filtrate inside the loop. The tubule and the capillaries provide a very large surface area for the exchange of materials in the nephrons of the kidney.

The ascending limb is impermeable to water and salt is lost from the filtrate by active transport. (The amount of salt actively transported from the ascending limb is greater than the amount which diffuses into the descending limb.) The salt remains near Henle's loop (it is not immediately removed by the blood) and helps to maintain a concentration gradient in the medulla. The fluid which leaves Henle's loop is less concentrated than the tissue fluid of the medulla around it.

MEDULLA

The concentration gradient in the **medulla** is maintained by the vasa recta countercurrent exchange. The vasa recta are the blood vessels running along Henle's loop. There is no direct exchange between the filtrate and the blood, but substances pass through the interstitial region of the medulla. The blood entering the medulla will, in the descending capillary, lose water to the region by osmosis and absorb salt and urea by diffusion. In the ascending capillary the reverse happens. The advantage is that the blood leaving the area is in a constant state, irrespective of the osmotic concentrations of the blood entering the medulla. Since the movements are caused by osmosis and diffusion, there is no energy required. *Refer to Figure 1126.*

COLLECTING DUCT

The wall of the distal convoluted tubule is permeable (permeability regulated by ADH) and water can pass from the ultrafiltrate into the blood vessels to be carried away. The same happens in the collecting duct.

ADH

ADH (anti-diuretic hormone) increases the permeability of the walls of the distal convoluted tubule and the **collecting duct**. ADH is released from the posterior lobe

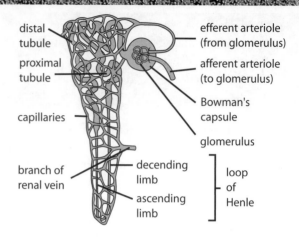

Figure 1126   How the nephron works

of the pituitary gland when the concentration of dissolved particles in the blood is too high. The dilute filtrate coming from Henle's loop can then lose water (by osmosis) in the distal convoluted tubule and again in the collecting duct. The water is reabsorbed by the blood so it is not lost to the system. When ADH is absent and the walls are impermeable, water is not removed from the filtrate in the distal convoluted tubule and the collecting duct and ends up in the bladder as dilute urine.

11.3.8   Explain the differences in the concentration of proteins, glucose and urea between blood plasma, glomerular filtrate and urine.

©IBO 2007

BLOOD PLASMA

Blood plasma in the renal artery is rich in oxygen and contains more **urea**, more salt and possibly more water than the required value.

Blood plasma in the renal vein contains carbon dioxide, the optimum amounts of water and salts, the same amount of proteins and glucose as when it was in the renal artery, and very little urea. (Since the amount of water may have decreased, the concentration of glucose and protein may have gone up compared to the renal artery.)

GLOMERULAR FILTRATE

Glomerular filtrate found in Bowman's capsule, is similar to blood plasma but without large proteins. The selection process that occurred to produce glomerular filtrate was based on size of the molecules only, not on any other criteria.

AHL

URINE

Urine contains less water, less salt, no glucose, no proteins or amino acids but a lot more urea than glomerular filtrate.

> **11.3.9** Explain the presence of glucose in the urine of untreated diabetic patients.
>
> ©IBO 2007

Due to the absence of insulin in **diabetics** (or the lack of sensitivity of the cells), glucose is not absorbed into cells or subsequently changed into glycogen. As a result, high levels of glucose in blood occur after a meal. This means that the blood arriving at the kidneys will have a higher glucose content than normal.

The renal threshold for glucose is 9 - 10 mmol/dm^3 (or 1620 - 1800 mg/dm^3), although there is some variation between people. If the blood in the renal artery contains a higher level of glucose, some of the glucose will not be reabsorbed into the blood. It will stay in the filtrate and become part of the urine.

11.4 REPRODUCTION

> **11.4.1** Annotate a light micrograph of testis tissue to show the location and function of interstitial cells (Leydig cells), germinal epithelium cells, developing spermatozoa and Sertoli cells.
>
> ©IBO 2007

The **testis**, when studied under the light microscope, is seen to consist of many seminiferous tubules. *See Figure 1127.*

In between the seminiferous tubules, which have a length of over 100 m per testis, are found interstitial cells (some of which are Leydig cells) and blood capillaries. The seminiferous tubules have an outer layer of germination epithelium cells which is surrounded by the basement membrane.

Development of **spermatozoa** takes places from the outside of the tubule and developing spermatozoa are nourished by Sertoli cells. Spermatozoa will eventually leave the tubule via the lumen. *Refer to Figure 1128 (a) and (b).*

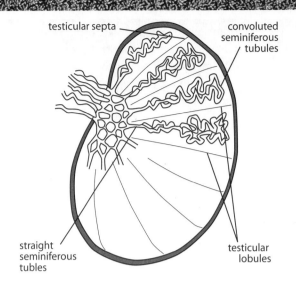

Figure 1127   The structure of the testis

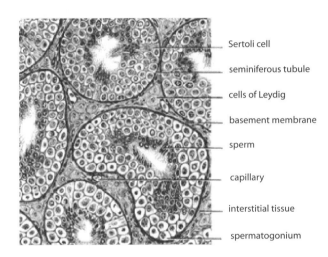

Figure 1128 (a)   Where sperm are produced

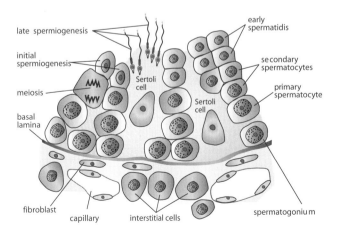

1128 (b)   The production of spermatozoa

AHL

11.4.2 Outline the processes involved in spermatogenesis within the testis, including mitosis, cell growth, the two divisions of meiosis and cell differentiation.

©IBO 2007

Spermatogenesis is the process of producing sperm cells. It involves mitosis, meiosis I and II, and cell differentiation. **Mitosis** produces the germ cell layer and the spermatogonia. Growth then produces primary spermatocytes which undergo meiosis I and II. The spermatids have the correct amount of genetic material (haploid) but need to differentiate into spermatozoa. The process is illustrated in Figure 1129.

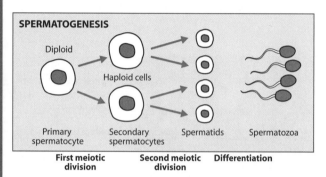

Figure 1129   How sperm are produced

11.4.3 State the role of LH, testosterone and FSH in spermatogenesis.

©IBO 2007

Three hormones play a role in spermatogenesis:
- Follicle Stimulating Hormone (FSH)
- Luteinizing Hormone (LH)
- Testosterone

FSH and **LH** are produced in the pituitary gland. **Testosterone** is produced by the Leydig cells in the testis as shown in Figure 1128.

FSH
- Stimulates sperm production in seminiferous tubules.
- Stimulates division and maturation of Sertoli cells.

LH
- Stimulates the interstitial cells (Leydig cells) to produce testosterone.

TESTOSTERONE
- Promotes spermiogenesis (maturation of spermatids into spermatozoa).

11.4.4 Annotate a diagram of the ovary to show the location and function of germinal epithelium, primary follicles, mature follicle and secondary oocyte.

©IBO 2007

The **ovaries** contain follicles in different stages of development, containing developing oocytes (*see Figure 1130*). The function of the germinal epithelium is not, as once was thought, to provide cells that may become oocytes. The germinal epithelium functions as does any epithelial layer, it keeps the tissues of the organ together and separates them from the rest of the body.

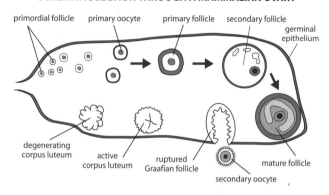

Figure 1130   The development and production of eggs

The mature follicle is also known as a Graafian follicle. The developing oocytes are surrounded by a zona pellucida. During development, meiosis I occurs, followed by an unequal cell division. This results in a secondary oocyte and a polar body (sometimes referred to as a secondary oocyte). Ovulation then takes place and meiosis II will occur after fertilisation.

The function of the follicle cells is to support the growth of the oocyte into a very large secondary oocyte and eventually an ovum. The ovum will fuse will a sperm cell and become the zygote.

11.4.5 Outline the processes involved in oogenesis within the ovary, including mitosis, cell growth, the two divisions of meiosis, the unequal division of cytoplasm and the degeneration of polar body.

©IBO 2007

Oogenesis is the development of egg cells (ova). It includes mitosis, cell growth, meiosis I and II, and the unequal division of cytoplasm leading to the formation of polar bodies.

Mitosis produces the germ cell layer and the oogonia. Growth then produces primary oocytes which undergo meiosis I and II. Unequal divisions remove excess genetic material while allowing the maximum amount of cell material to stay with the future ovum. The polar bodies contain genetic material that is no longer wanted and very little cytoplasm. They will degenerate. *Refer to Figure 1131.*

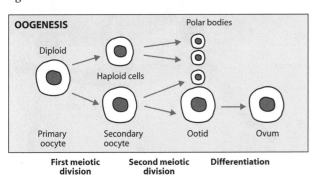

Figure 1131   *How egg cells are produced*

11.4.6   Draw and label a diagram of a mature sperm and egg.

©IBO 2007

The structure of the mature sperm cell can be seen in Figure 1132. The sperm cell has three parts:

- a head
- a midpiece
- a tail

The head carries the enzymes necessary to penetrate the zona pellucida of the egg cell as well as the genetic information. The midpiece contains mitochondria which provide the energy for the tail to move and propel the sperm cell.

The structure of the egg cell is shown in Figure 1133. Figure 1136(b) shows a sperm about to enter the egg cell. This EM gives an idea of the difference in size between sperm and egg.

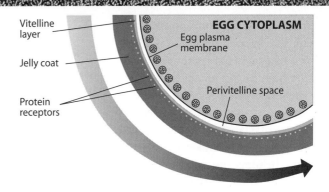

Figure 1133   *The structure of an egg cell*

11.4.7   Outline the role of the epididymis, seminal vesicle and prostate gland in the production of semen.

©IBO 2007

The sperm cells produced in the seminiferous tubules travel to the head of the epididymis (via the vasa efferentia). Here they mature and become somewhat motile. Fluid from the Sertoli cells in the seminiferous tubules, which carried the sperm cells to the epididymis, is reabsorbed, concentrating the sperm. *Refer to Figure 1134.*

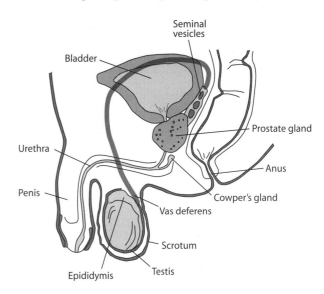

Figure 1134   *The male reproductive organs*

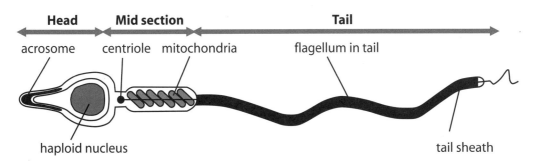

Figure 1132   *The structure of a sperm cell*

183

During one ejaculation, approximately 3 cm³ of semen is produced. Only 10 % of this consists of sperm cells. Most of the fluid in the semen is produced by the seminal vesicles. The fluid they produce contains fructose for energy and prostaglandins which cause contractions in the female reproductive system helping the sperm to move towards the egg cell. *Refer to Figure 1136.*

The fluid from the prostate is alkaline and helps to neutralise the normally acidic environment of the female reproductive tract. Normal pH is around 4, but the presence of prostate fluid will make it around pH 6 which is the optimum pH for sperm motility.

Cowper's glands (or the bulbo-urethral glands) produce a clear fluid which will lubricate the penis and facilitate copulation (the female secretions play a more important role in this).

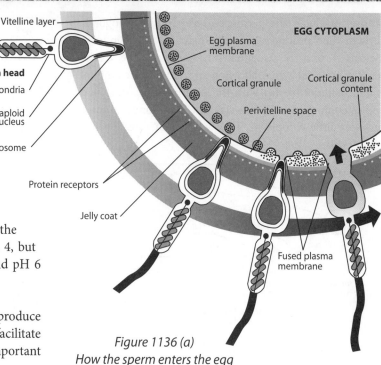

Figure 1136 (a)
How the sperm enters the egg

> **11.4.8** Compare the processes of spermatogenesis and oogenesis, including the number of gametes and the timing of the formation and release of gametes.
>
> ©IBO 2007

Comparing spermatogenesis and oogenesis, some similarities as well as some differences become obvious.

Similarities include:
- both produce haploid gametes by meiosis
- both take place in the gonads
- both start during puberty
- both are controlled by hormones

A comparison is shown in Figure 1135.

	Spermatogenesis	Oogenesis
number of gametes produced	large number of sperm cells	limited number of ova
number of gametes produded from one germ cell	four	one
time of formation (from puberty)	continuously	once a month
until when	does not stop	stops at menopause
release of gametes	any time	monthly cycle

Figure 1135   Differences between spermatogenesis and oogenesis

> **11.4.9** Describe the process of fertilization, including the acrosome reaction, penetration of the egg membrane by a sperm and the cortical reaction.
>
> ©IBO 2007

Fertilization refers to the fusion of male and female gametes.

For male and female gametes to fuse in humans, the sperm cell needs to penetrate the egg cell. At the moment of ovulation, the secondary oocyte is surrounded by a zona pellucida and a corona radiata.

Zona pellucida refers to the amucoprotein (a complex of protein and polysaccharide) membrane surrounding the secondary oocyte of mammals. It is secreted by the ovarian follicle cells.

Corona radiata is the name of the layer of follicle cells surrounding the zona pellucida.

The acrosome of the sperm cell contains proteolytic enzymes. As the sperm touches the cells of the corona radiata, the membrane around the acrosome fuses with the membrane of the cells, releasing the proteolytic enzyme and digesting the cell. The is called the acrosome reaction. The head of the sperm cell can now penetrate this layer. This process is shown in Figure 1136 (b).

The **sperm** cell then reaches the zona pellucida (a thick jelly-like layer surrounding the secondary oocyte). The

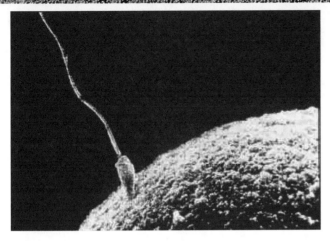

Figure 1136 (b)   An EM of sperm and egg (~x1000)

zona pellucida has special receptors to bind the sperm cell and the sperm will pass through.

The head of the sperm cell will fuse with the membrane of the secondary oocyte and special lysosomes, the cortical granules, will release enzymes to thicken the zona pellucida so that it becomes a fertilization envelope. This cannot be penetrated by other sperm cells. The ovum is therefore fertilized by only one sperm cell. The reaction of the cortical granules is called the cortical reaction.

11.4.10 Outline the role of HCG in early pregnancy.
©IBO 2007

Approximately eight days after fertilization, the blastocyst will embed itself into the **endometrium**. The outer cells, the trophoblastic cells, start to secrete human chorionic gonadotrophin (HCG). This hormone sustains the corpus luteum which therefore will continue to produce progesterone, maintaining the endometrium. Gradually the placenta will start to produce progesterone and at approximately ten weeks of pregnancy, the corpus luteum is no longer necessary.

HCG is excreted in the urine and can be detected with a pregnancy test. A specially manufactured stick is placed in urine. The urine will flow through the stick (by capillary action) and reach an area of antibodies against HCG which have a pigment attached to them. HCG will attach to the antibodies and the complex will travel further, with the movement of fluid. A second group of antibodies is found higher up in the stick. These antibodies are fixed. The HCG-antibody complex will attach to these antibodies, appearing as a blue line.

If no HCG is present, the first group of antibodies (with pigment) cannot bind to it. Therefore no HCG complex is formed. As a result the second group of (fixed) antibodies cannot bind to an HCG complex, so the coloured pigment will not concentrate in one line.

11.4.11 Outline early embryo development up to the implantation of the blastocyst.
©IBO 2007

After fertilization, the (haploid) chromosomes of the male and female gametes line up at the equator and prepare for the first mitotic division. This is a division, which is not followed by cell growth and is therefore called a cleavage division. Several of these cleavage divisions occur, which leads to the formation of a solid ball of cells called the morula. In humans, the morula reaches the uterus about four days after fertilization. Then, slightly unequal divisions cause a fluid filled space to form in the middle. The structure is now called a **blastocyst** and will implant in the endometrium. This happens approximately seven days after fertilization.

The cells on the outside of the blastocyst are called the **trophoblast**. The trophoblast will embed in the endometrium in the process of implantation. The trophoblast will grow trophoblastic villi into the endometrium and absorb nutrients from it. This is sufficient as the nutrient supplier for about two weeks after which the placenta takes over. *Refer to Figure 1137.*

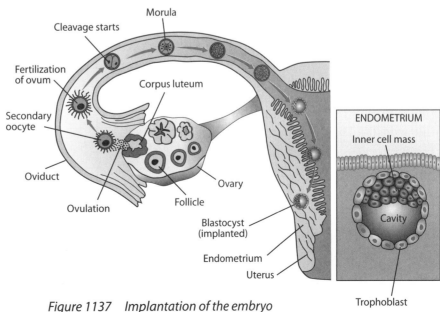

Figure 1137   Implantation of the embryo

AHL

185

AHL

11.4.12 Explain how the structure and functions of the placenta, including its hormonal role in secretion of estrogen and progesterone, maintain pregnancy.

©IBO 2007

The **placenta** is the place where oxygen and food from the mother's blood diffuse into the baby's blood and carbon dioxide and other waste diffuse from baby to mother. This way, the baby will receive the necessary materials for cell respiration and growth and the waste products from metabolism will not accumulate.

In the very early stages of pregnancy, progesterone is produced by the corpus luteum. Later, the production is taken over by the placenta. **Progesterone** is important in maintaining the pregnancy by reducing coordinated contractions of uterus. It also reduces the immune response so that the mother's body does not create antibodies against the baby.

A drop in the level of progesterone occurs during the time of birth and allows lactation which was previously inhibited by higher levels of progesterone.

Estrogen stimulates the growth of the muscles of the uterus and stimulates the growth of the mammary glands. Estrogen levels also drop near the time of birth.

11.4.13 State that the fetus is supported and protected by the amniotic sac and amniotic fluid.

©IBO 2007

A mass of cells within the trophoblast will eventually form the baby and its surrounding membranes.

A **fetus** is surrounded by amniotic fluid which, in turn, is surrounded by the amniotic sac. The amniotic sac keeps the fluid from leaking out and protects the fetus against infections. The amniotic fluid buffers shocks and protects the baby from mechanical harm. Also, babies drink amniotic fluid and, as a result, urinate in it. It is constantly made and filtered by the mother. *Refer to Figure 1138.*

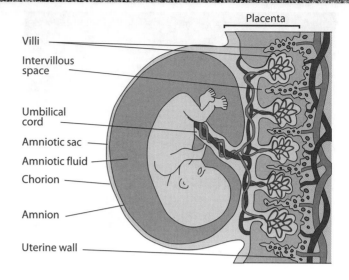

Figure 1138   *The structure of the fetus and placenta*

11.4.14 State that materials are exchanged between the maternal and fetal blood in the placenta.

©IBO 2007

This fast growing fetus needs a good supply of nutrients and also needs to excrete waste products. Both of these functions are carried out by the placenta. The placenta is fetal tissue which invades maternal uterine tissue. The baby's blood runs through blood vessels which go through blood spaces filled with maternal blood. An exchange of substances takes place by diffusion. The fetal blood returns to the fetus enriched with nutrients and oxygen. The maternal blood has taken up the carbon dioxide and other metabolic waste products from the fetus, which it will excrete. Refer to the photograph shown in Figure 1139.

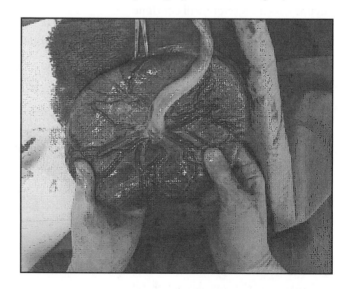

Figure 1139   *A human placenta*

Mother and fetus each have their own blood and circulation. Materials are exchanged but the blood does not mix. Many babies have blood groups different from their mothers.

> 11.4.15 Outline the process of birth and its hormonal control, including the changes in progesterone and oxytocin levels and positive feedback.
>
> ©IBO 2007

Normally, approximately 38 weeks after conception, the fetus is ready to be born. Around that time, progesterone levels will drop so that the uterus can have coordinated contractions. The baby will send a signal to the extra-embryonic membranes (like the amniotic sac) which leads to a secretion of prostaglandins. These locally-produced hormones will initiate contractions of the uterine wall. These contractions push the baby's head against the cervix, causing it to dilate. Nerve endings in the uterus and cervix will report to the brain that they are pushing against something (the baby!) and the posterior lobe of the pituitary gland will release oxytocin. Oxytocin causes the contractions to become longer and stronger which will push the baby's head against the cervix more resulting in a release of more oxytocin. This is positive feedback and results in increasing the strength and duration of the contractions.

When the cervix is fully dilated, the first stage of **birth** (labour) is over and the second stage (expulsion) begins. While the first stage can take many hours, the second stage usually does not take more than one hour. Powerful contractions push the baby out of the uterus.

Now that the uterus is no longer pushing against something, the positive feedback loop is broken and contractions soon reduce. However, a few contractions are needed to expel the placenta from the uterine wall. This is the last stage of birth.

AHL

EXERCISES

1. Large numbers of B-cells can be found in the:
   A   blood.
   B   urine.
   C   heart.
   D   lymph nodes.

2   Chai has just received a second vaccination against hepatitis B. His body's reaction to this is most likely to be to:
   A   produce fewer antibodies than on the first vaccination.
   B   produce more antibodies than on the first vaccination.
   C   give Chai a mild attack of the disease.
   D   produce complete immunity to the disease

3   The movement of the knee joint is achieved by:
   A   a single muscle in the upper leg.
   B   flexing of the knee joint.
   C   a pair of opposed muscles in the upper leg,
   D   a single muscle in the back of the lower leg.

4   The digram shows a joint. The synovial fluid is contained in the part labelled:

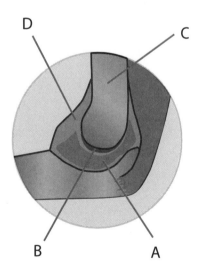

   A   A.
   B   B.
   C   C.
   D   D.

5   Muscles are joined to bones by:
   A   ligaments.
   B   tendons.
   C   cartilage.
   D   fibres.

6   The cytoplasm in a myofibril is known as:
   A   Sarcolemma.
   B   Sarcomere.
   C   Sarcoplasm.
   D   Sarcoplasmic reticulum.

7   Bird droppings (guano) is a useful fertilizer because it contains the element:
   A   oxygen.
   B   hydrogen.
   C   nitrogen.
   D   iron.

8   Waste products are removed from the kidney by the:
   A   ureter
   B   urethra
   C   inferior vena cava
   D   aorta

Questions 9 refers to the diagram of a human kidney.

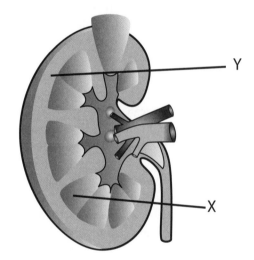

9   X and Y are

	X	Y
A	cortex	medulla
B	medulla	cortex
C	pelvis	medulla
D	bladder	cortex

10 The functional unit in the kidney is the:
   A   aorta.
   B   ureter.
   C   cortex.
   D   nephron.

AHL

11 In the descending limb of Henle's loop water leaves the nephron by:
   A diffusion.
   B osmosis.
   C evaporation.
   D condensation.

12 Kidney dialysis machines remove waste products from:
   A the urine using a partially permeable membrane.
   B the blood using a partially permeable membrane.
   C the blood by replacing it with fresh blood.
   D the bladder directly.

13 The function of Sertoli cells is to:
   A nourish developing spermatozoa.
   B produce testosterone.
   C produce ova.
   D produce spermatozoa.

14 Oogenesis is:
   A the production of oestrogen.
   B the production of spermatozoa.
   C the development of egg cells.
   D birth.

Questions 15 and 16 refer to the diagram of a sperm cell.

15 Point X is the:
   A tail sheath.
   B acrosome.
   C haploid nucleus.
   D centriole.

16 Point Y is the:
   A tail sheath.
   B acrosome.
   C haploid nucleus.
   D centriole.

17 The prostate gland produces:
   A a neutral fluid.
   B a slightly acidid fluid.
   C a slightly alkaline fluid.
   D a strongly alkaline fluid.

18 Which one of the following statements is not true?
   A spermatogenesis produces large numbers of gametes, oogenesis produces few.
   B spermatogenesis produces 4 sperm cells from 1 primary spermatocyte.
   C oogenesis produces 1 ovum from 1 primary oocyte.
   D males produce gametes continuously, from birth until old age.

19 The fusion of male and female gametes is known as:
   A pregnancy.
   B fertilisation.
   C menstruation.
   D birth.

20 Pregnancy is often detected by testing the level of:
   A human chorionic gonadotropin (HCG) in the urine.
   B human chorionic gonadotropin (HCG) in the blood.
   C testosterone in the urine.
   D progesterone in the urine.

21 Progesterone is needed throughout pregnancy:
   A to maintain correct blood pressure.
   B to prevent the release of oestrogen.
   C to initiate ovulation.
   D to sustain the endometrium.

22 (a) What is the role of helper T cells in the antigen/antibody response?
   (b) What is the role of B-cells in the antigen/antibody response?

23 (a) Discuss the benefits of vaccination.
   (b) Discuss the dangers of vaccination.

24 Explain the role of the following in muscle contractions.
   (a) Ca^{2+} ions
   (b) troponin and tropomyosin
   (c) actin and myosin
   (d) ATP

25 Describe how nerves, muscles and bones work together to cause movement.

26 Compare the composition of blood in the renal artery with that of the renal vein.

27 (a) What is oogenesis?
    (b) What is the function of mitosis in oogenesis?
    (c) What is the function of meiosis in oogenesis?
    (d) Why does a spermatogonia yield 4 spermatozoa while an oogonia yields one ovum and 2 or 3 polar bodies?

28 (a) Which structure secretes HCG?
    (b) What is the function of HCG to the embryo?
    (d) Why is HCG only produced early in pregnancy?
    (d) How can HCG be used in pregnancy testing?

HUMAN NUTRITION AND HEALTH

A1   Components of the human diet

A2   Energy in human diets

A3   Special issues in human nutrition

A1   COMPONENTS OF THE HUMAN DIET

A.1.1   Define *nutrient*.

©IBO 2007

A **nutrient** is a chemical substance found in foods that is used in the human body. Some examples of foods containing helathy nutrients are shown in Figure 1201.

Figure 1201   Some healthy food

A.1.2   List the type of nutrients that are essential in the human diet, including amino acids, fatty acids, minerals, vitamins and water.

©IBO 2007

Some, but not all, **amino acids** are essential in the human diet. Examples of essential amino acids are Threonine and Valine.

Similarly, some, but not all, **fatty acids** are essential in the human diet. There are two groups of essential fatty acids:

- omega-3
- omega-6.

An example of an omega-3 essential fatty acid is alpha-linoleic acid, an omega-6 essential fatty acid is linoleic acid.

Example of essential **minerals** are Iodine and Calcium.

Examples of essential **vitamins** are vitamin A (retinol) and vitamin C (ascorbic acid).

Water is also essential in the diet and has several major roles inlcuding transport, cooling and lubrication.

A.1.3   State that non-essential amino acids can be synthesized in the body from other nutrients.

©IBO 2007

As essential nutrients are defined as those that cannot be synthesized by the body, non-essential nutrients therefore are those nutrients that can be synthesized by the body from other nutrients. Examples of non-essential amino acids are Alanine and Proline.

OPTION

OPTION

A.1.4   Outline the consequences of protein deficiency malnutrition.

©IBO 2007

There are several different kinds of **malnutrition**:
- not enough food
- too much food
- food lacking in some minerals and/or vitamins.

Protein deficiency malnutrition is caused by not enough of one or more essential amino acids. As a result, there are not enough proteins in the blood which means that tissue fluid is not returned to the blood as well as it should. This causes fluid retention, typically the swollen belly of the child in the picture below. In the longer term, it may also cause a retardation of mental and physical growth. *See Figure 1202.*

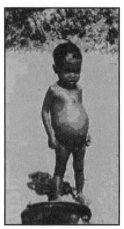

Figure 1202   A result of protein deficiency

A.1.5   Explain the causes and consequences of phenylketonuria (PKU) and how early diagnosis and a special diet can reduce the consequences.

©IBO 2007

Phenylketonuria (PKU) is a genetic disorder. People who suffer from this disorder are not capable of producing the enzyme phenylalanine hydroxylase. This enzyme catalyses the reaction from phenylalanine (an essential amino acid) to tyrosine (another amino acid). Without this enzyme, phenylalanine will be converted to phenylpyruvic acid which causes retardation and siezures.

Babies in many countries are tested soon after birth for PKU which is characterised by phenylketones in the blood. If they are found to have this condition, they can grow up normally provided they keep to a strict diet. The diet focusses on avoiding most protein since levels of phenylalanine must be kept low. With low levels of phenylalanine in the diet, the affected children lead normal lives.

PKU is caused by a recessive autosomal gene and is therefore not sex-linked. Two people who are carriers would not be aware of this, but would have a 25% chance of having a child with PKU.

A.1.6   Outline the variation in the molecular structure of fatty acids, including saturated fatty acids, *cis* and *trans* unsaturated fatty acids, monounsaturated and polyunsaturated fatty acids.

©IBO 2007

Fatty acids are carboxylic acids, often with a long hydrocarbon chain attached.

There are many different kinds of fatty acids, however all fatty acids are either:
- saturated
- unsaturated

SATURATED FATTY ACIDS

These have **no carbon-carbon double bonds** in the chain For example, arachidic acid: $CH_3(CH_2)_{18}COOH$ Their general structure is shown in Figure 1203.

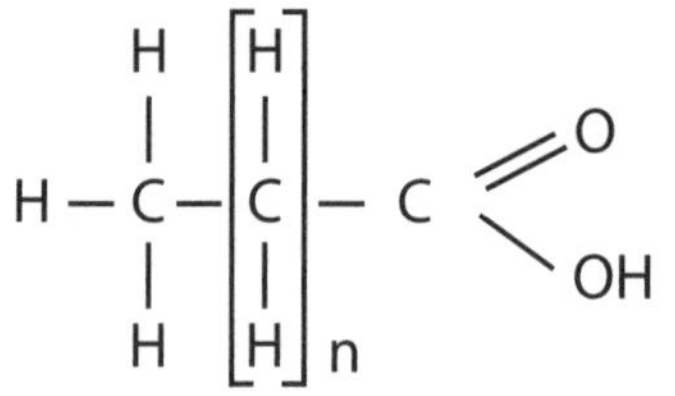

Figure 1203   General formula for fatty acids

UNSATURATED FATTY ACIDS

These have **one or more carbon-carbon double bonds** in the chain.

In unsaturated fatty acids, a distinction is made between
- *cis* fatty acids:
  the carbon atoms attached to the carbons that have the double bonds, are on the <u>same side</u>.
- *trans* fatty acids:
  the carbon atoms attached to the carbons that have the double bonds are on <u>opposite sides</u>.

The distinction may seem relatively unimportant until we look at the entire fatty acid molecule as drawn in Figure 1205. Where the *trans* molecule is more or less straight, the *cis* molecule has a kink. The structure of the *trans* fatty acid is more like that of a saturated fatty acid and, as a result, *trans* fatty acids are more unhealthy than *cis* fatty acids.

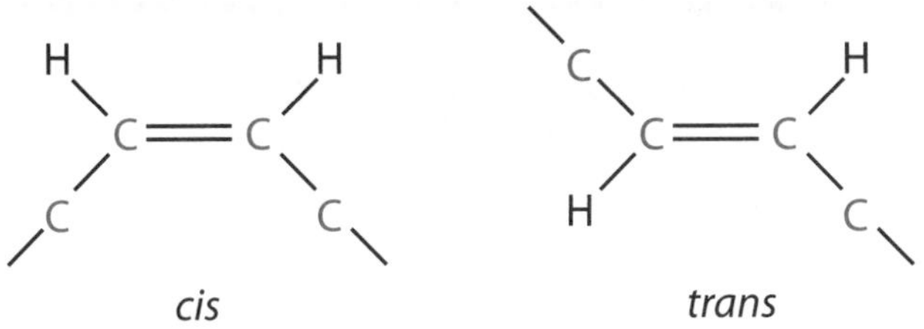

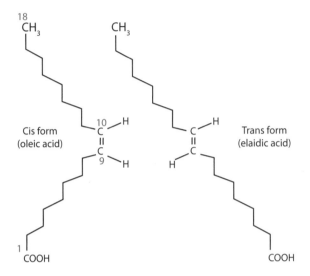

Figure 1204   General structure of cis and trans fatty acids

Figure 1205   An example of cis and trans forms

There are two different kinds of unsaturated fatty acids:
- mono unsaturated fatty acids
- poly unsaturated fatty acids

Mono unsaturated fatty acids
Mono unsaturated fatty acids have only one double bond.

Poly unsaturated fatty acids
Poly unsaturated fatty acids have more than one double bond as shown in Figure 1206.

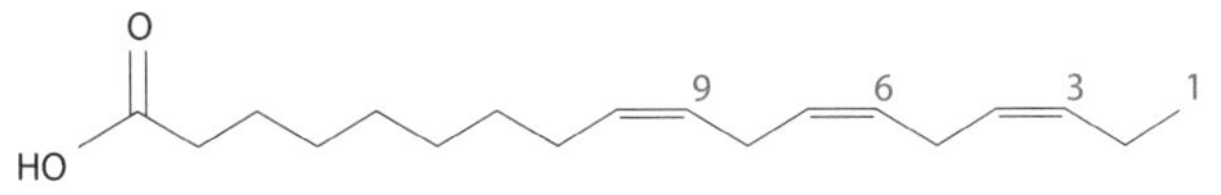

Figure 1206   Omega-3 - a polyunsaturated fatty acid

Omega-3 fatty acids are examples of polyunsaturated fatty acids. These fatty acids are called omega-3 (or ω-3) because the first double bond is found after the third carbon, counting from the side of CH_3. (*This can be confusing because Chemists usually number the Carbons starting at the end of the carboxylic acid.*)

A.1.7   Evaluate the health consequences of diets rich in the different types of fatty acid.

©IBO 2007

High density lipoproteins (HDL) carry cholesterol from the tissue to the liver where it is broken down. HDL attached to cholesterol (HDL-C) is known as "good cholesterol" whereas low density lipoprotein attached to cholesterol (LDL-C) is "bad cholesterol".

Monounsaturated fatty acids and (*cis*) polyunsaturated fatty acids do not increase cholesterol levels and may even reduce them. Both saturated and *trans* unsaturated fatty acids are likely to increase cholesterol levels and are therefore considered to be more unhealthy. Olive oil is rich in mono unsaturated fatty acids. People in Mediterranean countries tend to eat a lot of olive oil. In these countries, there is a lower incidence of heart disease. However this information alone does not prove that monounsaturated fatty acids result in a decreased incidence of heart disease.

People in Japan generally eat a lot of fish and rice and generally consume a low fat and cholesterol diet. It has been concluded that this diet is the cause of the lower rate of heart disease in Japan compared to many other western countries. However, it has been found that people living in France also have a lower rate of heart disease, despite the fact that the French eat a lot of meat.

The study done in Japan in 1958 that led to the above conclusion, was repeated in 1989 in the same area. It was found that the Japanese were eating less rice and more meat and dairy products, greatly increasing their intake of fats. High blood pressure became more common and average cholesterol levels went up. Despite all this, the number of heart attacks and deaths from heart attacks did not change during this time. However, it has been suggested that, in Japan, there is a stigma attached to dying as a result of a heart attack and that it is possible that some deaths reported as being a result of a stroke may have been caused by heart attacks. This information has not been confirmed.

It has also been found that people who ate large amounts of fresh fish were less likely to develop lung cancer than those who ate less fish. This may be caused by the high levels of Vitamin A and omega-3 fatty acids in fresh fish. Although a correlation between dieat and disease was shown in one group, the "cause and effect relationship" has not been proven. It would also not be correct to assume (without testing) that this correlation would exist in other parts of world.

OPTION

In 2002, The British Journal of Psychiatry reported a study of *Gesch, Hammond, Hampson, Eves* and *Crowder*. Their findings suggest that antisocial behaviour, including violence, in prisons is reduced by increasing the amounts of vitamins, minerals and essential fatty acids in the diet.

TOK   Correlation or cause?

Epidemiology is a field of science where factors affecting heath are studied. Epidemiologists acknowledge that correlation between a factor and a disease does not mean that that factor is the cause of the disease. A link between high saturated fat intake and heart disease is widely understood to exist. However Maasai (an African tribe) people have a very high intake of saturated fat and extremely low incidence of cardiovascular disease, contradicting this observation. This reinforces the nature of epidemiology, that correlation is not the same as cause. Carefully controlled experiments can determine cause, but this is extremely difficult in the area of human health we must therefore rely on epidemiological studies to determine risk of illness.

A.1.8	Distinguish between minerals and vitamins in terms of their chemical nature.
	©IBO 2007

Minerals are elements in ionic form such as calcium (Ca^{2+}) and vitamins are organic compounds.

A.1.9	Outline two of the methods that have been used to determine the recommended daily intake of vitamin C.
	©IBO 2007

The Recommended Daily Intake (RDI) of vitamin C is the amount of vitamin C required to meet the needs of almost all healthy individuals for a given age group and gender. The older method to calculate the RDI of Vitamin C was to determine the amount necessary in the diet to prevent scurvy. A more recent method is to determine how much Vitamin C is needed in the diet for general protection, without excreting it in the urine.

TOK   What are appropriate levels for the intake of nutrients?

Determining appropriate levels of nutrient intake in humans is fraught with difficulty. Such information ultimately relies on humans to act as experimental volunteers. In such cases the subject should be advised of the risk involved so that they can consider if they should take part. In some cases, participants in trials are paid, especially where there could be some health risk in participating in the trial. This raises the question as to whether or not financial benefit may cloud the ability of the volunteer to make an objective decision about whether or not to take part in a trial.

Recommended doses for nutrients are published in some countries. Such recommendations are a result of limited human trials and epidemiological studies, however these recommendations vary from country to country. In part these recommended doses reflect differences in bias of scientists in different countries. Such variations also reflect the difficulty in determining generic optimal levels of any medication given the huge variation in human physiology.

A.1.10	Discuss the amount of vitamin C that an adult should consume per day, including the level needed to prevent scurvy, claims that higher intakes give protection against upper respiratory tract infections, and the danger of rebound malnutrition.
	©IBO 2007

Three common sources of vitamin C are:
- Citrus fruit -*Figure 1207 (a)*
- Vitamin C tablets - *Figure 1207 (b)*
- Orange juice - *Figure 1207 (c)*

Figure 1207 (a)   Figure 1207 (b)   Figure 1207 (c)
Citrus fruit   Vitamin C tablets   Orange juice

OPTION

VITAMIN	RDI	1968 RDA	1974 RDA	1980 RDA	1989 RDA	DRIs
Vitamin C	60 mg	60 mg	45 mg	60 mg	60 mg	90 mg

Figure 1208   The recommendations for Vitamin C

Ideas about the desired amount of Vitamin C (or other vitamins or minerals) do not remain constant. Figure 1208 shows the changing recommendations over the last 40 years or so.

RDI

RDI refers to the Recommended Daily Intake which is based on the highests RDAs in 1968 to ensure no person was at risk of deficiency disease (scurvy in the case of vitamin C).

RDA

RDA refers to the Recommended Daily Allowance which is the amount needed to avoid deficiency diseases (scurvy in the case of vitamin C).

DRI

DRI stands for Dietary Reference Intake which means the amount needed to avoid deficiency or (chronic) diseases.

DRI for Vitamin C is usually suggested at around 40 mg for males and 30 mg for females but recommendations vary in different countries.

In 2007, Harvard School of Public health stated the current RDI for Vitamin C is 90 mg for men and 75 mg for women but based on recent evidence suggests 200-300 mg might be a better dose.

It is clear that the amount of vitamin C needed to be taken in can change over time so amounts listed should specify age, gender and level of activity. However, the changes in the amounts stated over the years are due to changes in thinking about the effects of vitamin C. At any one time, different official organisations will list different amounts.

MEGAVITAMIN THERAPY

Megavitamin therapy involves taken doses larger then the RDI in order to achieve a beneficial effect. The RDI for vitamin C is 90 mg.

In the case of vitamin C, two (controversial) reasons for initiating the use of high dosage of vitamin C are:
* to stop upper respiratory tract infections (URTIs), including the common cold, from developing
* to prevent cancer

Several opinions exist, especially regarding the use of Vitamin C megatherapy to stop colds:
a. there is no strong evidence that suggests that adding 1-3 g of vitamin C per day to stop a cold is effective
b. there is a suggestion that there may be some benefit
c. to be really effective, the dose would need to be up to 100 g per day

While vitamin C is water-soluble and most of the surplus will leave the body with the urine, there is a chance of developing 'rebound malnutrition'. The body will have adjusted to a large intake (and therefore excretion) of vitamin C. Should the level then drop to normal intake level, the body may continue to excrete too much and as a result not enough Vitamin C will be available.

TOK   Linus Pauling and vitamin C

Linus Pauling was one of the most significant Chemists of the twentieth century, winning a Nobel Prize in 1954 for his research into chemical bonds. Later in life he advocated the use of Vitamin C for prevention of the common cold, some cardiovascular diseases and some cancers. Such recommendations were not endorsed by the wider scientific community and made Pauling a figure of controversy. Consumption of Vitamin C increased in the community largely because of his personal recommendation rather than scientific evidence of its benefit. To what extent do public figures have a responsibility to limit public comment on issues until the scientific community validates their findings?

A.1.11   List the sources of vitamin D in human diets.

©IBO 2007

Unlike vitamin C, vitamin D is fat-soluble. It plays a role in maintaining the correct levels of calcium in the blood. Vitamin D is made in the skin under the influence of UV light.

Food rich in vitamin D includes fish oil (cod liver oil), fatty fish (salmon, tuna and eel) and eggs.

OPTION

Figure 1209
A case of rickets

Figure 1210   Iodine
deficiency causes goitre

A.1.12   Discuss how the risk of vitamin D deficiency from insufficient exposure to sunlight can be balanced against the risk of contracting malignant melanoma.

©IBO 2007

In children, deficiency of vitamin D causes a disease known as **rickets**. Rickets can also be caused by a insufficient amounts of calcium. Either way, the bones do not harden and as the child becomes heavier, the bones will bend. *(Refer to Figure 1209)*

In adults, vitamin D deficiency will cause osteoporosis (brittle bones) or osteomalacia (minerals in the bones are not maintained, leading to backpain). *Refer to Figure 304.*

To prevent diseases such as rickets and osteoporosis, it is important to have sufficiently high levels of vitamin D. However, as most people are aware, exposing skin to sunlight for long stretches of time increases the risk of skin cancers such as malignant melanoma, especially if sunburnt often. Lighter skin tends to be more at risk than darker skin but this is only a general trend and does not predict anything for an individual.

A.1.13   Explain the benefits of artificial dietary supplementation as a means of preventing malnutrition, using iodine as an example.

©IBO 2007

Iodine is a mineral needed to make thyroxine. If a person does not have in enough iodine in the diet, the thyroid gland (in the throat region) will grow larger *(see Figure 1210)*. This disease is called **goitre**. In some communities, most people had goitre. Sea fish contains iodine, so goitre was more common in inland areas where people did not eat fish from the sea.

TOK   The inevitability of risk

There is a correlation between high exposure to sunlight and increased risk of the skin cancer, melanoma. However this must be balanced against the risk of vitamin D deficiency that is correlated with low exposure to sunlight. In this case, a vitamin deficiency is easier to treat than a cancer so it would be most reasonable to err on the side of low exposure to sunlight.

Risk is inevitable and one can only try to minimise it. In the case of risk of disease, epidemiology is helpful in examining the correlation between risk factors and disease, but is never definitive.

Iodine deficiency may also lead to cretinism (mental retardation and impaired physical growth). Both goitre and cretinism are deficiency diseases caused by **malnutrition**.

In order to address this, many countries started adding iodide to salt (iodized salt). This greatly reduced the incidence of goitre and cretinism. In India where iodized salt is not always available, it is estimated that over 50 million people suffer from goitre and about 2 million from cretinism.

A.1.14   Outline the importance of fibre as a component of a balanced diet.

©IBO 2007

There are two categories of fibre:
*   soluble fibre e.g. pectin
*   insoluble fibre e.g. cellulose

The total daily recommended amount of fibre is at least 18.g.

SOLUBLE FIBRE

Soluble fibre is found in beans and peas. It seems to slow down the uptake of sugar and is useful for controlling some types of **diabetes**. It may also slightly reduce blood cholesterol levels.

INSOLUBLE FIBRE

Insoluble fibre acts as a laxative. It causes peristalsis of the gut which will make the food move faster through the large intestine. Therefore the stools (faeces) are softer and the incidence of constipation and hemaroids is reduced.

Increasing the amount of fibre is likely to help with weight loss as people feel full sooner on a high fibre diet. It has not yet been clearly shown that fibre lowers cholesterol levels

A2 ENERGY IN HUMAN DIETS

> **A.2.1** Compare the energy content per 100 g of carbohydrate, fat and protein.
>
> ©IBO 2007

Energy content of
carbohydrates: 1760 kJ per 100 g
proteins: 1720 kJ per 100 g
fats: 4000 kJ per 100 g

Animals tend to store their energy reserves as fat. It would take twice the weight to store the energy in the form of carbohydrates or protein. In plants, lipids (fats) are found in seeds which need a certain amount of energy stored but also need to be light in order to be transported away from the parent plant.

> **A.2.2** Compare the main dietary sources of energy in different ethnic groups.
>
> ©IBO 2007

Worldwide, rice, maize and wheat provide 60% of the energy in our diet. In an average African diet, about half of the energy comes from plant roots and tubers and less than 10% comes from animal products.

In a Western diet, a third of the energy comes from animal products and about a quarter from cereals. Roots and tubers supply less than 5% of the energy. Figure 1211 shows a hamburger which is part of the Western diet.

In a Chinese-Japanese diet, **rice** and soybean provide a lot of the energy. Japanese people also eat a lot of **fish** which provides energy. *See Figures 1212 and 1213.*

Maize is an important source of energy in Central American diets. *See Figure 1214.*

Cassava provides a large amount of energy in South American diets. *See Figures 1215 (a) and (b).*

Wheat is a staple food in a Mediteranean diet. It is harvested mechanically and used to make pasta. *See Figures 1216 (a) and (b).*

> **A.2.3** Explain the possible health consequences of diets rich in carbohydrates, fats and proteins.
>
> ©IBO 2007

A diet rich in carbohydrates provides a lot of energy. Some people will eat carbohydrates, e.g. pasta, before entering in an endurance event (Elf Steden Tocht, the Eleven Cities Tour, a rare one day 200 km skating event on frozen canals in the North of the Netherlands), believing it will help provide them with energy.

A diet rich in protein can also be beneficial. In the *Journal of Clinical Nutrition, Dr. Weigle* described that protein would make people feel full sooner and for longer than

OPTION

Figure 1211
A hamburger

Figure 1212
Brown rice

Figure 1213
Japanese dish with fish

Figure 1214
Different varieties of maize

Figure 1215 (a)
Unprocessed cassava tubers

Figure 1215 (b)
Cooked cassava

Figure 1216 (a)
Wheat being harvested

Figure 1216 (b)
A plate of pasta

carbohydrates of fats. Hence, a high protein diet was likely to cause people to eat less and lose weight. It was not mentioned that using proteins for energy, requires the kidneys to excrete larger amounts of urea and also more water.

A diet rich in fats (and low in fibre) has been shown to increase the amount of cancer-causing substances in the stool (faeces). Although it has not been proven, many people believe that this diet is more likely to cause cancer of the large intestine. A diet rich in fat is also likely to contain more energy so might cause obesity.

TOK   What is a diet?

In the developed world, colloquial use of the term diet has change from "the food that is consumed by an individual" to "the food that is consumed by an individual that will help them lose weight". This change of meaning reflects a social issue in such countries where physical appearance sometimes becomes more important than the health of the individual. Many so-called "diets" are not based on sound scientific research and the outcome of following them is questionable. This raises a broader social question: should an individual's self-worth be linked to their physical appearance? To what extent is this issue of concern in societies today?

| A.2.4 | Outline the function of the appetite control centre in the brain. |

©IBO 2007

The **appetite control centre** is found in the **hypothalamus** in the brain. After eating, the digestive tract and the pancreas produce **hormones** that travel via the blood to the brain. Their presence is interpreted by the hypothalamus as having eaten enough. The adipose tissue (storing fat) also can send chemical messages (leptin) to the brain, indicating that enough fat is stored. This also should make the mouse (or person) stop eating. This matter has been researched in mice as shown in Figure 1217. The obese mouse shown doesn't have the leptin gene. Because the mouse doesn't have the leptin gene, it never gets the signal of satiety, so continues to eat and eat and eat.

Sometimes the appetite control function seems to have become less sensitive to the levels of hormones. In other words, the person secretes the right hormones but the hypothalamus still does not send out signals to stop eating.

Figure 1217   An obese and a normal mouse

| A.2.5 | Calculate body mass index (BMI) from the body mass and height of a person. |

©IBO 2007

The body mass index indicates whether someone is underweight, normal weight, overweight or obese.

$$\text{BMI} = \text{Body mass index} = \frac{\text{body mass (kg)}}{(\text{height (m)})^2}$$

| A.2.6 | Distinguish, using the body mass index, between being *underweight, normal weight, overweight* and *obese*. |

©IBO 2007

Having calculated the body mass index, an individual can now be (approximately) classified: *See Figure 1218.*

BMI	category
< 18.5	underweight
18.5 - 24.9	normal weight
25 - 29.9	overweight
≥ 30	obese

It is most important to recognise that people vary. It would be a mistake to conclude that any person is the wrong weight either on the basis of this calculation or fashion.

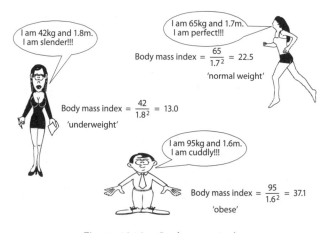

Figure 1218   Body mass index

A.2.7   Outline the reasons for increasing rates of clinical obesity in some countries, including availability of cheap high-energy foods, large portion sizes, increasing use of vehicles for transport, and a change from active to sedentary occupations.

©IBO 2007

The World Health Organisation has a website on obesity http://www.who.int/topics/obesity/en/. This webiste provides information and allows a user to choose certain comparisons.

In some countries, the diet of many of its inhabitants has changed over the last few decades. Snacks, which are often high energy-food, are eaten more since they are easily available and often cheap. In many cultures, families do not eat together as much as they used to do which also encourages people to eat more snacks.

Many restaurants providing snacks, encourage people to take larger portions by making them financially attractive.

However, people only gain weight when the amount of energy consumed is more than the amount of energy used in physical activity. As stated above, the amount of food energy consumed has gone up but the amount of physical activity has decreased. People walk or cycle less than they used to because so many have a car. This is particularly effecting the weight of children. Whereas 40 years ago, we would walk/cycle to school and play out on the street or in the park with friends in the evenings, nowadays this is no longer safe. The increase in traffic has forced children back into the homes where playstations, computers and tv provide sedentary entertainment and most parents will take their children to school by car. The result is an increase in **obesity** as shown in Figure 1219.

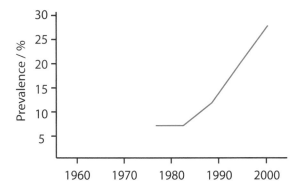

Figure 1219   Trends in obesity in the United Kingdom

A.2.8   Outline the consequences of anorexia nervosa.

©IBO 2007

Anorexia nervosa is the name for the condition where the person is obsessive about his (but usually her) weight. To this person, it is very important to be slim but unfortunately, the condition is accompanied by a distortion of their self-image. People who suffer from anorexia are generally very thin but, when the look in the mirror, they will see themselves as overweight.

Consequences/symptoms of anorexia nervosa are:
* obsessive about weight
* depression
* mood swings
* poor performance at school
* deteriorating personal relationships
* extreme weight loss
* (girls) menstrual period will stop
* feeling cold (due to lack of body fat)
* growth of body hair (to compensate for lack of fat)
* poor immune functions
* thinning of hair
* bruised and dry skin

In 2006, at a Madrid fashion show, models with a BMI of less than 18 were not accepted. It was felt that too many girls were developing anorexia in order to look like a model. Some time ago, a particular brand of soap started a campaign to sell their new firming cream. They decided to avoid using superslim women as they wanted to appeal to all women that the cream would work for "normal" thighs too.

A lot of media coverage was given to two sisters who were models from Uruguay. They died in August 2006 and February 2007 at the ages of 22 and 18. Both died of a heart attack, possibly due to malnutrition.

Anorexia nervosa is a serious, life-threatening physical and psychological disorder. Most research on the condition has been done in developed countries where it appears to be strongly linked to environments where there is strong social pressure to be thin. The Theory of Natural Selection clearly shows that organisms vary in many characteristics and human body shape is just one area where variation is found. How can we build a society where healthy body shape is valued?

OPTION

199

A3 SPECIAL ISSUES IN HUMAN NUTRITION

> A.3.1 Distinguish between the composition of *human milk* and *artificial milk* used for bottle-feeding babies.
>
> A.3.2 Discuss the benefits of breast-feeding.
>
> ©IBO 2007

There are many advantages to breast-feeding, for the baby, the mother and for the bond between them. Information about the advantages in breast feeding can be found on numerous websites. In the Western world, breast feeding is promoted so much that it is difficult for some mothers to decide to use artificial milk, e.g when taking medication for a serious illness.

Benefits of breast feeding:

- breast milk contains antibodies which help the baby fight infections
- proteins in breast milk are easier digested than those in artificial milk
- calcium and iron in breast milk are better absorbed
- breast feeding helps the uterus contract so that the bleeding after delivery will be shorter
- breast feeding reduces the risk of breast cancer
- breast feeding improves the bond between mother and child
- breast feeding is cheaper - very important in some parts of the world
- mother usually does not ovulate while breast feeding (natural contraception)

Component	Human milk	Artificial milk
disaccharide	rich in lactose	no or little lactose
protein	more whey, less casein	less whey, more casein
antibodies	present	absent
fats	rich in omega-3 fatty acids (DHA)	some brands add DHA but usually less than in human milk
enzyme	contains lipase	no lipase
minerals	most iron absorbed	most iron not absorbed

Figure 1220   A comparison of human and artificial milk

Figure 1221
Artificial milk

Figure 1222
An infant breastfeeding

TOK   Human milk and artificial milk

The best way to feed a new-borne child is with breast milk. This is possible in all but a small minority of cases. Children in developing countries that are not breast-fed have a significantly higher mortality rates, usually from gastrointestinal infection, than those who are breast-fed. There has been significant controversy surrounding the sale of infant formula milk in developing countries. Concern about this issue was so great that in 1981 the World Health Organization developed an International Code of Marketing of Breast-milk Substitutes. The code was developed in response to the aggressive marketing of infant formula in developing countries by companies from developed countries. The code is voluntary though and sadly, there is evidence that it is widely ignored by the companies that develop such products and benefit from their ongoing sale.

The introduction of breast milk supplements in developing countries often starts with free samples provided by the companies. Use of these free samples as an alternative to breast-feeding reduces or stops the production of the mother's breast-milk and produces a dependency on the product. The dependency is both physical, (because the mother can no longer breast feed) and financial. As breast-feeding inhibits the mother's reproductive cycle, once she stops feeding she can quickly become pregnant again and the cycle of dependence continues.

OPTION

" ... *commercial infant formulas provide a satisfactory alternative sole source of nutrition to young infants up to about 6 months of age.*"

source: http://www.euro.who.int/document/WS_115_2000FE.pdf; document page 157; read in April 2007

In the past, companies producing artificial milk have marketed their product as being better than human milk. They targetted women who, often due to lack of education, were not able to reject the advertising but could not really afford the artificial milk, nor provide the necessary hygiene required for preparing and supplying the milk to the baby. It is clear that human milk in many situations (but not all) is the best and most suited food for a baby.

> A.3.3 Outline the causes and symptoms of type II diabetes.
>
> ©IBO 2007

The incidence of Type II **diabetes** in America over the period from 1997 to 2004 is shown in Figure 1223.

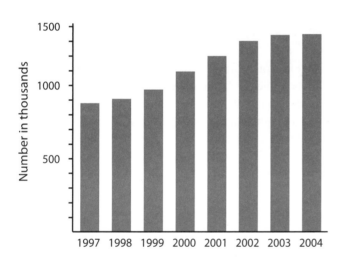

Figure 1223   The increasing incidence of diabetes

People may be born with diabetes (type I) or it may occur later in their life (type II). In type II diabetes, either the body no longer produces enough insulin and/or the receptors in the target cells (liver and muscle) are less sensitive to the presence of insulin.

CAUSES
- genetic factors
- obesity
- sedentary lifestyle

SYMPTOMS
- elevated levels of insulin
- hyperglycemia (high blood sugar):
  - frequent hunger and thirst
  - frequent and excessive urination
  - blurred vision
  - fatigue
  - weight loss

Type II diabetes is more common in Native Australians (Aboriginal Australians) and Maoris, African Americans, Native Americans and Latinos. In general older people are more likely to develop type II diabetes than younger people.

> ### TOK   Diabetes - nature or nurture?
>
> There are clear differences in the incidence of type II diabetes between different ethnic populations suggesting a genetic link. Research suggests that Australian aborigines and New Zealand Maoris have amongst the world's highest incidence of type II diabetes. However there is a more significant variation in incidence of the disease within similar populations living in environments of different economic development.
>
> Singaporean Indians have a much higher incidence of diabetes than those living in rural Bangladesh. Africans living in Jamaica have a much higher incidence than those living in rural Tanzania. This pattern, that type II diabetes is much more prevalent in economically developed societies than rural societies, illustrates that although there are genetic differences between human populations, these are often not as significant as environmental differences.

> A.3.4 Explain the dietary advice that should be given to a patient who has developed type II diabetes.
>
> ©IBO 2007

Initially, people with type II diabetes are recommended to increase their amount of exercise and reduce their weight. A reduction in weight might increase the sensitivity of the insulin receptors in the target cells.

The diet that currently seems very successful is the 'HCF' diet. It involves eating a lot of fibre and a lot of complex carbohydrates. Complex carbohydrates (e.g. pasta, beans) are

OPTION

digested and absorbed slowly. Fibre slows down the digestion and absorption of carbohydrate. The diet should also contain fruit since the sugar in fruit is fructose which is usually tolerated by patients with diabetes.

A.3.5	Discuss the ethical issues concerning the eating of animal products, including honey, eggs, milk and meat.

©IBO 2007

There can be many reasons for not wishing to eat (some) animals and/or animal products. These reasons relate directly to what animals/products are part of the diet and which are excluded.

RELIGIOUS REASONS

Islam and Judaism do not permit eating certain kinds of meat (e.g. pork) and animals need to be slaughtered in specified ways.

Hindus are often vegetarians in order to avoid violence to animals as well as not indulging in eating meat.

ENVIRONMENTAL REASONS

It takes a lot of grain to feed the cow that produces the beef for the human. More humans would have more to eat if they ate the grain rather than the beef.

ETHICAL REASONS

- Bio-industry does not give animals a decent life.
- The transport of animals causes them a lot of stress.
- Procedures before slaughter cause them stress.

HEALTH REASONS

Some people believe it is healthier to avoid animal products.

ECONOMIC REASONS

Meat is relatively expensive in some countries compared with vegetables.

A.3.6	Evaluate the benefits of reducing dietary cholesterol in lowering the risk of coronary heart disease.

©IBO 2007

Cholesterol is a lipid that can be part of our food but is also made by the human body. Cholesterol is needed as part of cell membranes (making them less fluid) and

as a precursor for steroid hormones (e.g. testosterone). Cholesterol is transported by the blood and can form plaque on the walls of blood vessels which restricts blood flow. This can cause a heart attack or a stroke.

Some years ago, it was common to assume that reducing dietary cholesterol would reduce serum levels of cholesterol. This is now compared to thinking that eating oil will lubricate your joints.

It has since been discovered that cholesterol is transported by lipoproteins. Low densisty lipoprotein (LDL) transports cholesterol from the liver (where it is formed). LDL seems to increase the chance of coronary heart disease (CHD) and is known as "bad cholesterol". High density lipoprotein (HDL) transports cholesterol to the liver where it is broken down. HDL may reduce the chance of CHD so is called "good cholesterol".

In order to reduce LDL and increase HDL, the focus is on the human metabolism. Exercise, not smoking and weight loss seem to change the metabolism and increase the production of HDLs. Omega-3, mono-unsaturated fatty acids also seem to increase HDL levels but *trans* fatty acids are to be avoided as they increases LDL levels. A lot of fibre and a limited amount of fat are beneficial too.

The effect of dietary cholesterol on blood serum cholesterol levels is unclear. Using the precautionary principle *(Topic 5.2.4)*, many doctors recommend limiting cholesterol intake. Some studies have shown a correlation between moderate use of alcohol and higher HDL levels but have been unable to explain why alcohol would cause an increase in HDL.

A.3.7	Discuss the concept of food miles and the reasons for consumers choosing foods to minimize 'food miles'.

©IBO 2007

'**Food miles**' are a measure of how far a food item has been transported from its site of production to its site of consumption. In other words, it reflects the distance from field to plate. Agriculture and food account for about one third of goods transported. Transport of food causes air pollution, traffic congestion and greenhouse gas emissions.

As a result of centralisation and a need for increased efficiency, it is possible that the milk produced by the farm next door is moved quite a distance to the milk factory, returned to a supermarket in a city only to be brought back to the same street after having been bought by the farmer's neighbour. Consumers add to food miles by travelling

OPTION

further to larger supermarkets for economic reasons or convenience ("it has everything I need"). Consumers may wish to choose local food in order to support the local economy .

Another aspect of 'food miles' is that it may involve live animals. The further the distance they need to travel, the greater the stress.

To complicate matters further, it has been calculated that to grow tomatoes in the UK will cause more pollution than to transport them from Spain. More energy would be used to heat the greenhouse in the UK than for transport from Spain. Shifting to tomatoes that grown under cooler conditions and/or using more environmentally friendly forms of energy could reverse the outcome of the calculation.

Consumers can choose to buy at local shops and/or make fewer trips to a supermarket. Information about the country of origin of the product may be supplied, although, given the above example, that may not necessarily inform consumers as to the environmental impact of the food.

Although some foods have many food miles, the continuity of supply and the increased choice are valuable to most consumers.

TOK   What are 'food miles'?

'Food miles' provide a new perspective on where we source our food, and an interesting insight into how globalised food supply in the 'developed world' has become, but probably little more.

'Food miles' do not take into account agricultural practise that is far more significant in the production of greenhouse gasses than transportation costs. Is a tomato that has travelled five kilometres from a hydroponic greenhouse more environmentally friendly than one that has travelled fifty kilometres from a traditional farm?

EXERCISES

1 Outline the consequences of protein deficiency malnutrition

2 (a) What is PKU?
  (b) Explain the causes of PKU.
  (c) Explain the consequences of PKU.
  (d) How is PKU tested?
  (e) Explain how a special diet can reduce the consequences of PKU.

3 (a) Describe the function of vitamin C.
  (b) Suggest how much vitamin C an adult should take in every day.
  (c) Discuss what benefits an increased amount of vitamin C could have.
  (d) Explain rebound malnutrition.

4 (a) List the factors that affect the amount of energy a person needs.
  (b) Explain what the effect of each of these factors is on the energy requirements.

5 Outline the importance of fibre in the diet.

6 (a) Compare the composition of breast milk and artificial milk
  (b) Discuss the advantages and disadvantages of breast feeding and bottle feeding

PHYSIOLOGY OF EXERCISE

B1   Muscles and movement

B2   Training and the pulmonary system

B3   Training and the cardiovascular system

B4   Exercise and respiration

B5   Fitness and training

B6   Injuries

B1 MUSCLES AND MOVEMENT

This section is identical to *Topic 11.2 page 174*.

B2 TRAINING AND THE PULMONARY SYSTEM

> **B.2.1**   Define *total lung capacity, vital capacity, tidal volume* and *ventilation rate*.
>
> ©IBO 2007

There are a number of important terms that are involved in the discussion of lung function, including:
- total lung capacity
- vital capacity
- tidal volume
- ventilation rate

TOTAL LUNG CAPACITY
Total lung capacity refers to the volume of air in the lungs after a maximum inhalation.

VITAL CAPACITY
Vital capacity indicates the maximum volume of air that can be exhaled after a maximum inhalation.

TIDAL VOLUME
Tidal volume refers to the volume of air taken in or out with each inhalation or exhalation.

VENTILATION RATE
Ventilation rate means the number of inhalations or exhalations per minute.

> **B.2.2**   Explain the need for increases in tidal volume and ventilation rate during exercise.
>
> ©IBO 2007

Exercise involves contracting (and relaxing) muscles which requires energy. The muscles will use **aerobic respiration** as much as possible to release the required amounts of energy. Aerobic respiration requires oxygen (to be the ultimate electron acceptor) so the supply of oxygen to the muscles needs to increase. Aerobic respiration also produces carbon dioxide which needs to be excreted via the lungs.

To maintain a concentration gradient of high oxygen levels and low levels of carbon dioxide in the lungs, the air in the lungs needs to be refreshed more often. This increases the ventilation rate. The tidal volume increases so that there is more air in the lungs, hence a larger amount of oxygen.

Ventilation rate and tidal volume are controlled by the levels of carbon dioxide in the blood. Higher levels of carbon dioxide will decrease the pH of the blood, increasing ventilation rate.

Increasing tidal volume is more efficient than increasing ventilation rate. During one ventilation cycle, not all air in the lungs is refreshed. There is a constant amount of "dead air". Increasing the tidal volume increases the amount of air that is refreshed- the dead air remains the same so the percentage of dead air decreases. Increasing the ventilation rate does not affect the percentage of dead air.

> **B.2.3**   Outline the effects of training on the pulmonary system, including changes in ventilation rate at rest, maximum ventilation rate and vital capacity.
>
> ©IBO 2007

Physical training will have only a small effect on the structure of the pulmonary system. As a result of training, the ventilation rate at rest may go down from 14 to 12 breaths per minute (bpm) (decrease of 14%) and maximum ventilation rate may go from 40 to 45 bpm (increase of 13%). Vital capacity may increase slightly.

B3   TRAINING AND THE CARDIOVASCULAR SYSTEM

> **B.3.1**   Define *heart rate, stroke volume, cardiac output* and *venous return*.
>
> ©IBO 2007

HEART RATE

Heart rate refers to the number of contractions of the heart per minute.

STROKE VOLUME

Stroke volume refers to the volume of blood pumped out with each contraction of the heart.

CARDIAC OUTPUT

Cardiac output is the volume of blood pumped out by the heart per minute.

VENOUS RETURN

Venous return refers to the volume of blood returning to the heart via the veins per minute.

> **B.3.2**   Explain the changes in cardiac output and venous return during exercise.
>
> ©IBO 2007

During exercise, the muscles require oxygen in order to release energy using aerobic cellular respiration ($C_6H_{12}O_6 + 6 O_2 \rightarrow 6 CO_2 + 6 H_2O$ + energy). Aerobic respiration releases much more energy per molecule glucose than anaerobic respiration ($C_6H_{12}O_6 \rightarrow 2 C_3H_6O_3$ + energy).

Muscles will use aerobic respiration to release energy but are limited by the amount of oxygen that can be provided. In order to maximise the amount of oxygen going to the muscles, the heart will contract more strongly and more frequently. This means that **cardiac output** increases during exercise.

The signal for increasing cardiac output comes from the brain. An increased amount of carbon dioxide (produced in the muscles) in the blood causes a decrease in pH ($CO_2 + H_2O \rightarrow H_2CO_3 \rightarrow HCO_3^- + H^+$). *Refer to Figure 1301.*

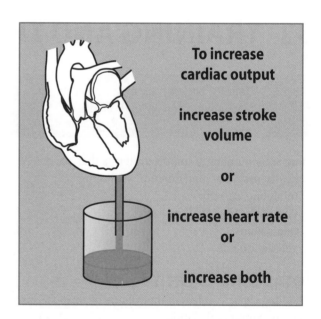

To increase cardiac output

increase stroke volume

or

increase heart rate

or

increase both

Figure 1301   How to increase heart output

The **respiratory centre**, found in the medulla oblongata, is sensitive to the drop in pH and will increase cardiac output as well ventilation rate.

Many of the deeper veins which carry most of the blood back to the heart are found near muscles. When the muscles contract, they become shorter and fatter, squeezing the vein against the bone. This will help move blood in the vein. Because veins have valves, the blood can only flow towards the heart. This way, muscle contractions assist in increasing venous return.

On long intercontinental flights, people are advised to walk around or at least move their feet and toes regularly. This will help the bloodflow and reduce the chance of developing deep vein thrombosis (D.V.T.).

> **B.3.3** Compare the distribution of blood flow at rest and during exercise.
>
> ©IBO 2007

Blood flow to the brain is unchanged during exercise because the amount activity and hence the amount of oxygen required by the brain does not really change.

As muscles are more active, they need significantly more oxygen. So blood flow to skeletal muscles is increased. *See Figure 1302.*

In order to make the blood flow faster, cardiac frequency goes up. So the muscles in the wall of the heart (ventricles) are more active and they also need more oxygen. Hence the bloodflow to the muscles in the wall of the heart is increased.

Moving muscles generates a lot of heat. A lot of heat is lost by the skin so the bloodflow to the skin is increased in order to increase heat loss.

Blood flow to kidneys, stomach, intestines and other abdominal organs is reduced because processes such as digesting food are not a priority. Instead, the blood is mostly diverted to muscles, heart and skin.

Figure 1302
A weightlifter competing at the Commonwealth Games in 2006

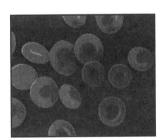

Figure 1303
Erythrocytes (red blood cells)

> **B.3.4** Explain the effects of training on heart rate and stroke volume, both at rest and during exercise.
>
> ©IBO 2007

Training that increases the heart rate, will make the heart grow larger. This increases stroke volume, both at rest and during exercise. At rest, cardiac output should not change, so with an increased stroke volume, heart rate will decrease. During exercise, heart rate will increase and cardiac output will be greater than before training.

A trained heart will also recover faster, i.e. it will take less time to return to a resting rate than an untrained heart.

> **B.3.5** Evaluate the risks and benefits of using EPO (erythropoietin) and blood transfusions to improve performance in sports.
>
> ©IBO 2007

One of the factors that places limits on physical activity is the amount of oxygen that can be transported to the tissues. With more oxygen, the muscles could release more energy and the athlete could e.g. run faster. This is particularly important in sports where a lot of energy is required for a longer time such as in endurance sports. Since erythrocytes (red blood cells) are responsible for the transport of oxygen, it is to be expected that some athletes (and coaches) haveconsidered increasing the number of erythrocytes in the blood. *See Figure 1303.*

There are two main methods of achieving an increase in the number of erythrocytes:
- blood doping
- EPO

BLOOD DOPING

In **blood doping**, blood is taken from the athlete (or from someone else) some time before a competition. The erythrocytes are separated from the plasma and frozen. Just before an event, the erythrocytes are injected. During the competition, the athlete has extra erythrocytes which will help provide more oxygen to the muscles.

EPO

Erythropoietin is a naturally occurring hormone, produced in the kidney, that stimulates the bone marrow to produce more erythrocytes. Taking EPO would increase the amount of erythrocytes in the blood.

The risks of either blood doping or the use of EPO are that with more erythrocytes, the blood is more viscous (thicker) so more difficult to move. This may lead to heart failure. Blood doping is also risky if the erythrocytes have not been stored properly. More viscous blood may increase the chances of thrombosis and/or embolism. Using blood from another person involves the risk of transmitting diseases such as AIDS and hepatitis.

EPO is listed as a forbidden substance and blood doping as a forbidden practice in the 2007 Prohibited List of the World Anti-Doping Code. This list is updated every year and used, for example in the Olympic Games.

The 2007 Tour de France was, once again, associated with the use of drugs. The cyclist leading the race until then had turned out to have missed some doping tests earlier and was dropped by his team. Several other riders were also accused of doping (EPO, blood doping and other kinds of doping) although some of the accusations were later retracted.

Testing for EPO or blood doping involves a comparison of the amount of mature vs immature erythrocytes. If doping is involved, then the number of mature cells will be much larger than usual but the number of immature cells will be normal or even lower. Also, according to the regulations, athletes are only allowed a certain percentage of cells in their blood. Should they naturally have a higher percentage, this needs to be confirmed by a number of official tests over a long time.

TOK What is performance enhancement?

Sports allow people to socialise in the context of a specific physical activity. They bring physical, social and emotional wellbeing to participants. Spectators also benefit socially and emotionally from watching sports. Sporting competitions operate on the basis of equality of opportunity for all the participants. Use of performance-enhancing drugs or treatments such as transfusions undermines the egalitarian nature of sports competition and their use is widely considered to be unethical. Their use may also bring unnecessary risk to the athlete.

How does an athlete taking performance enhancing drugs justify their action? Is it possible for an individual athlete to act morally if the sport or organization they participate in tolerates or encourages the use of performance enhancing drugs? To what extent do ethical decisions regarding performance-enhancing drugs have a social, cultural or historical context? What responsibility do scientists developing performance enhancing drugs or doctors administering them have? What responsibility does knowledge of unethical behaviour bring to the knower?

B4 EXERCISE AND RESPIRATION

B.4.1	Define VO_2 and $VO_2\,max$.
	©IBO 2007

VO_2 is the oxygen uptake at any particular time.

$VO_2\,max$ is the highest possible oxygen uptake for an individual.

The units for VO_2 and $VO_2\,max$ are $dm^3\,min^{-1}$ or $dm^3\,min^{-1}\,kg^{-1}$

B.4.2	Outline the roles of glycogen and myoglobin in muscle fibres.
	©IBO 2007

The energy requirement of many muscles fibres fluctuates depending on the amount of work the muscle does. The range is from very little to very high and the transition may be very abrupt. This means that the muscle fibre may suddenly need to have a lot of respiration to fill the need for energy. Aerobic respiration requires glucose and oxygen.

GLYCOGEN

Glycogen is stored in muscle fibres in order to have a reserve of glucose. Glycogen is easily broken down into glucose (under the influence of glucagon). It is better to store glycogen than glucose because glucose would cause a lot of water to enter the cell by osmosis. *See Figure 1305.*

MYOGLOBIN

Myoglobin is a protein made of one polypeptide chain. It has the ability to bind oxygen, similar to haemoglobin. However, myoglobin has a greater affinity for oxygen than haemoglobin so the oxygen will not be released from oxymyoglobin until the levels of oxygen around the protein are very low. This makes it a useful way of storing oxygen in the muscles: the oxygen will not be released until almost all the oxygen in the muscle fibres has been used up.

As can be seen in Figure 1304, at the very low partial pressure of e.g. 10 mm Hg of oxygen, myoglobin is still around 70% saturated with oxygen, i.e. has only given up 30% of its oxygen. By contrast, at a similar pressure haemoglobin released about 90% of its oxygen.

OPTION

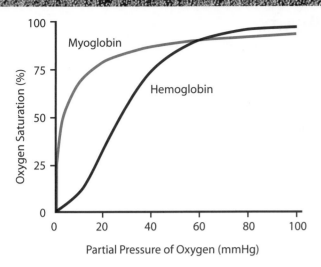

Figure 1304   *The dissociation of myoglobin and hemoglobin*

B.4.3   Outline the method of ATP production used by muscle fibres during exercise of varying intensity and duration.

©IBO 2007

During contractions, muscles use up ATP at a very fast rate. Creatine, found in food (meat) is changed into creatine phosphate by attaching a phosphate via a high energy bond. When ATP in the muscle releases its energy and changes into ADP, it can be remade quickly using high enery phosphate group from creatine phosphate. There is only enough creatine phosphate to generate ATP for less than 10 seconds of intense exercise.

If the exercise lasts beyond this time, all ATP is generated via cell respiration. Very intense exercise which lasts a short time (e.g. running a sprint) will use mainly anaerobic respiration. Less intense exercise which takes longer (e.g. running a marathon) will use mainly aerobic respiration as anaerobic respiration would reduce the pH too much by producing lactic acid. It would also require too much glucose to release the required amount of energy.

B.4.4   Evaluate the effectiveness of dietary supplements containing creatine phosphate in enhancing performance.

©IBO 2007

Humans break down a small amount of creatine every day. Taking creatine supplements is likely to reduce the amount of creatine synthesized by the body. There does not seem a clear consensus about the effectiveness of dietary supplements containing creatine phosphate.

The university of California reports that performance might be slightly enhance the initial performance of maximum effort trials. Opinions differ about whether, and to what extent creatine phosphate enhances performance.

B.4.5   Outline the relationship between the intensity of exercise, VO₂ and the proportions of carbohydrate and fat used in respiration.

©IBO 2007

It is possible to generate energy from breaking down fats or carbohydrates. To metabolise fats and obtain a certain amount of energy, the body needs more oxygen than to obtain the same amount of energy from carbohydrate metabolism. So if exercising below 50% of VO_2 max, fats are utilised for energy but at higher intensity carbohydrates need to be used. Beyond VO_2 max, the body will go to anaerobic respiration to release the required extra energy.

B.4.6   State that lactate produced by anaerobic cell respiration is passed to the liver and creates an oxygen debt.

©IBO 2007

Lactate is produced in anaerobic respiration when more energy is needed than can be released via aerobic respiration using the available amount of oxygen. Large amounts of lactate can be produced in skeletal muscles during intense exercise. The lactate produced is transported to the liver where it is metabolised. Some of the lactate is broken down to carbon dioxide and water. This process requires oxygen and produces enough energy to resynthesize glucose from the remaining lactate whilst creating an oxygen debt..

This process occurs in the liver and is outlined in The **Cori cycle** as shown in Figure 1305.

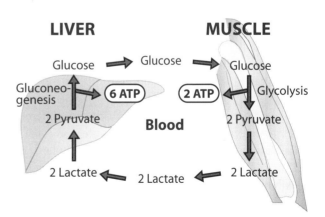

Figure 1305   *The Cori Cycle*

OPTION

| B.4.7 | Outline how oxygen debt is repaid. |
| | ©IBO 2007 |

During exercise, an **oxygen debt** is created which is repaid after exercise by breathing longer and deeper than normal.

There are several aspects responsible for this oxygen debt.
- lactate metabolism:
  - breaking down lactate in mitochondria by aerobic respiration requires oxygen and releases energy
  - the remainder of the lactate will be converted back into glucose
- restoring myoglobin to oxymyoglobin requires oxygen
- restoring creatine phosphate requires energy (from aerobic respiration)

B5   FITNESS AND TRAINING

| B.5.1 | Define *fitness*. |
| | ©IBO 2007 |

In the context of fitness and training, fitness is the physical condition of the body which suits it to the particular exercise which it performs. (For ecological fitness, see option G)

There are two generally recognised types of fitness:
- health-related fitness that reflects an individual's ability to resist infection and also the absence of conditions such as obesity and high blood pressure, strength of the muscles and skeleton etc.
- performance-related fitness which is more related to the fitness needed to complete specific tasks such as climbing a mountain, sprinting 100 metres or winning a tennis match.

All fitness can be improved by training.

There are different aspects to fitness which have different degrees of relevance depending on the exercise (sport) that the person is involved in. These aspects include:
- agility
- flexibility
- speed
- stamina
- strength

AGILITY
The ability to change direction efficiently

FLEXIBILITY
Suppleness, the ability to carry out a range of movement without stiffness or pain

SPEED
How much distance is covered in a certain time

STAMINA
Endurance: the ability to sustain an effort over a longer time

STRENGTH
The amount of force than can be exerted

| B.5.2 | Discuss speed and stamina as measures of fitness. |
| | ©IBO 2007 |

SPEED
Speed is particularly important when in a race but also when playing in a team sport such as a soccer match or in athletics. *See Figure 1306.*

Figure 1306   Athletes competing at the Commonwealth Games in 2006

STAMINA
A sprint athlete requires high speed but not necessarily stamina. His body needs to be able to release a lot of energy over a very short time. This usually involves anaerobic respiration in fast muscle fibres. The endurance athlete needs to be able to release a reasonable amount of energy over a very long time. This involves aerobic respiration in

OPTION

Type of muscle fibre	Slow muscle fibres	Fast muscle fibres
other name	type I	types II a and II b
speed of repeated contractions	slow - more time needed between contractions	fast - one contraction can be followed quickly by the next
type of work performed	work for a long time without getting tired (stamina)	produce a lot of work in a short period (strength)
found predominantly in	marathon runners	sprinters
fibres are suited for	endurance activities	rapid movements
type of respiration	aerobic respiration	II a: aerobic and anaerobic II b: anaerobic respiration
blood supply	a lot of blood vessels (dark meat in chicken)	fewer blood vessels (white meat in chicken)
energy release	release a large amount of energy slowly	release a small amount of energy quickly
no. of mitochondria	more mitochondria	fewer mitochondria
amount of myoglobin	more myoglobin	less myoglobin

Figure 1309   A comparison of the different types of muscle fibres

slow muscle fibres and an efficient cardiovascular system to take oxygen to the muscles and remove carbon dioxide. Stamina is needed when involved in endurance sports, e.g. the Tour de France. *See Figure 1307.*

Figure 1307   Cyclists compete in the Tour de France

Figure 1308   Endurance riding requires slow muscle fibres in horse and rider

B.5.3   Distinguish between *fast* and *slow* muscle fibres.

©IBO 2007

There are two different types of muscle fibres found in skeletal muscle. Fast muscle fibres which are involved in the speed sports and slow muscle fibres that are more important in endurance events. *Refer to Figure 1308.* Everyone has both types in most muscles but not necessary in the same proportion. *See Figure 1309.*

B.5.4   Distinguish between the effects of *moderate-intensity* and *high-intensity* exercise on fast and slow muscle fibres.

©IBO 2007

Although there seems to be a genetic component in the composition of our muscles (how many fast muscle fibres and how many slow muscle fibres), it also seems possible to influence the composition by training.

Moderate-intensity exercise stimulates the development of slow muscle fibres.

High-intensity exercise stimulates the development of fast muscle fibres.

OPTION

211

B.5.5 Discuss the ethics of using performance-enhancing substances, including anabolic steroids.

©IBO 2007

Competing in a sport involves wanting to win. Often winning is not only about honour and personal achievement but also about money. The gentlemen's single winner at the Wimbledon Tennis Championships in 2006 won GBP 655 000. In addition to prize money, there may be scholarships and/or sponsoring and/or commercial opportunities for those who perform very well in a sport. So the temptation to use performance-enhancing drugs is easily understood.

Performance-enhancing drugs may do any of the following:

- reduce pain (local anaesthetics)
- increase the size and strength of muslces (anabolic steroids)
- improve oxygen transport to the muscles (EPO and blood doping)
- hide the presence of other drugs

However, there are a number of negative aspects which also need to be considered. Anabolic steroids increase the size and strength of muscles. Anabolic steroids are similar to the male hormone testosterone. Known side effects are liver damage (the liver needs to break all these substances down) and infertility for both males and females. In females, it also causes them to become more masculine with hair growth on face and body and deepening voice. Males may find that they develop breasts, baldness and a higher voice.

B6 INJURIES

B.6.1 Discuss the need for warm-up routines.

©IBO 2007

In general, people believe that warming up will enhance performance and reduce injuries.

Some benefits of warming-up:

- increasing heart rate
- increasing temperature of the muscle
- increasing release of oxygen from oxyhaemoglobin
- decreasing the viscosity of the blood
- greater elasticity of muscles and tendons

TOK   Is warming-up important?

Double blind trials involve testing both something active (e.g. warming-up before exercise) and something inactive (a placebo, which acts as a control such as not warming-up before exercise) where neither the patient nor the researcher knows who is in the experimental or control group. Such testing removes any bias that may come from knowledge about the treatment. Data gathered is analysed to determine the effectiveness of the activity. Interestingly, sometimes patients in the control group receive a psychological benefit called the placebo effect, but there is no evidence of any clinical benefit in receiving a placebo.

There is dispute about the need for warm-up or down activities, with little evidence to allow for an objective decision to be made as to their value, yet they have high status in the sporting community. Controlled trials are difficult if not impossible to conduct in this field. What is the status of such exercises if their validity cannot be confirmed through scientific methodology? How does the willingness of athletes to continue to complete such exercises without question play a role in the maintenance of their status?

It is now thought that warming-up should not be too prolonged. It should consist of three stages:

- cardiovascular warm up
- stretching
- sports specific exercises

B.6.2 Describe injuries to muscles and joints, including sprains, torn muscles, torn ligaments, dislocation of joints and intervertebral disc damage.

©IBO 2007

Sports injuries can be divided into two categories:

- injuries caused by over-use (e.g. tennis elbow)
- injuries with a specific cause (e.g. a sprained ankle caused by a soccer tackle)

SPRAINS

A **sprain** is the over-stretching of a ligament in a joint.

Since the ankle is a complicated joint made of many bones, it also involves a number of ligaments which are prone to sprains. Sprains mostly require rest to heal.

OPTION

One of the most common way to sprain an ankle is shown in Figure 1310.

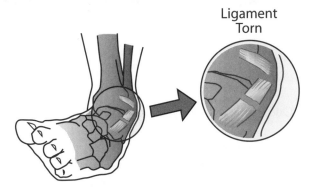

Figure 1310   A torn ankle ligament

TORN LIGAMENTS

When a **ligaments** is stretched, it may tear. Depending on the severity of the tear, it may need surgery to repair. *See Figure 1311.*

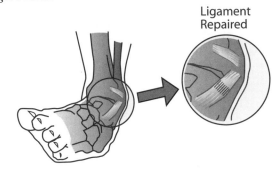

Figure 1311   A repaired ankle ligament

TORN MUSCLE

A torn muscle is the most severe case of muscle strain. Due to an incorrect movement, too much pressure is put on one section of a muscle. Then, it is possible to tear a muscle. The muscle may tear partly or completely, often at the point where it is attached to the tendon. *See Figure 1312.*

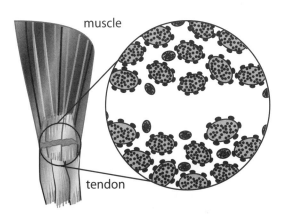

Figure 1312   A torn muscle

DISLOCATION OF JOINTS

A **dislocation** occurs when the bones in the joint are moved, relative to each other, and do not return to their original position. *See Figures 1313 and 1314.*

Ligaments in the joint are usually damaged in dislocation. Dislocations are very painful and should be corrected as soon as possible, to reduce pain but also to limit the amount of damage done to the ligaments.

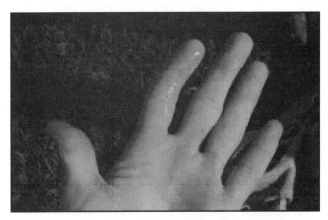

Figure 1313   A dislocated index finger

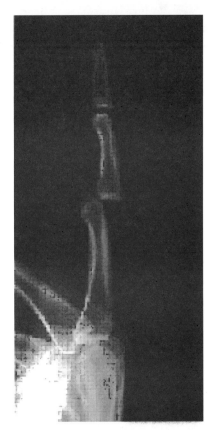

Figure 1314   An X-ray of a dislocated finger

OPTION

INTERVERTEBRAL DISC DAMAGE

Cartilage discs are found between the vertebrae made of bone. The discs work as a cushion and facilitate movement of the vertebrae. Due to a movement or carrying heavy loads, one of the discs may bulge out and put pressure on the nerves in the spinal cord. *See Figure 1315.* Sometimes this injury will recover with time but often it requires corrective surgery.

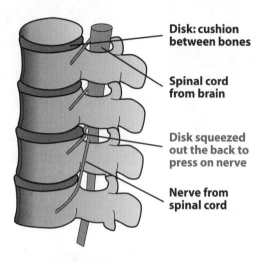

Lower part of BACKBONE (SPINE)
Sideview of 4 vertebral bones

Disk: cushion between bones

Spinal cord from brain

Disk squeezed out the back to press on nerve

Nerve from spinal cord

Figure 1315   Damage to the vertebrae

EXERCISES

1. Outline the role of glycogen in muscles during exercise.

2. Outline the role of myoglobin in muscles.

3. (a) Evaluate the risks and benefits of using EPO or blood transfusions to enhance performance.
   (b) Discuss the ethical aspects of using performance enhancing substances.

4. Describe injuries that can occur to muscles and joints.

CELLS AND ENERGY

C1   Proteins   (same as 7.5)

C2   Enzymes   (same as 7.6)

C3   Cell respiration   (same as 8.1)

C4   Photosynthesis   (same as 8.2)

C1   PROTEINS

> C.1.1   Explain the four levels of protein structure, indicating the significance of each level..
>
> ©IBO 2007

Four 'levels' are distinguished in the structure of a protein:

- primary
- secondary
- tertiary
- quaternary.

PRIMARY STRUCTURE

The primary structure of a protein is the sequence of the amino acids in the chain. *Refer to Figure 1401*. The linear sequence of amino acids with peptide linkages affects all the subsequent levels of structure since these are the consequence of interactions between the R groups of the amino acids. Each amino acid can be characterised by its R group. Polar R groups will interact with other polar R groups further down the chain and the same goes for non-polar R groups.

SECONDARY STRUCTURE

The secondary structure of a protein consists of the coils of the chain, for example α helix and β pleated sheet. *Refer to Figure 1402*. α helix structures are found in the proteins of hair, wool, horns and feathers; β pleated sheet structures are found in silk. Hydrogen bonds are responsible for the secondary structure. Fibrous proteins like collagen and

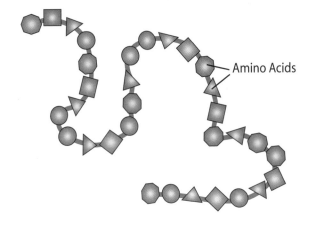

Figure 1401   Primary structure

Beta pleated sheet   Alpha helix

Figure 1402   Secondary structure

OPTION

keratin are in helix or pleated sheet form which is caused by a regular repeated sequence of amino acids. They are structural proteins.

TERTIARY STRUCTURE

The tertiary structure of a protein refers to the way the helix chain is folded. *Refer to Figure 1403.* This is caused by the interactions between the R groups of the amino acids in the polypeptide chain. Hydrophobic groups cluster together on the inside of the protein (away from the water) while hydrophilic groups cluster together on the outside of the protein (near the water). Several amino acids have a sulfur atom in their R group. Two adjacent sulfur atoms may come together, under enzyme control and form a covalent bond called a disulfide bridge.

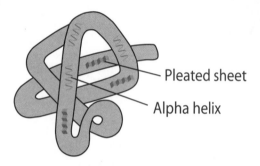

Figure 1403   Tertiary structure

Hydrogen bonds are also involved in the formation of the tertiary structure. Bonds between an ion serving as a cofactor *(see Topic 8.6)* and the R group of a certain amino acid may also be responsible for the folds in the polypeptide. Proteins which have a globular (folded) shape, such as hemoglobin, are called globular proteins. Microtubules are globular proteins but they have a structural function. Enzymes are globular proteins. The precise and unique folding of the polypeptide creates the 'active site', i.e. the location where the substrate binds to the enzyme so that the reaction can take place. *(see Topic 8.6).*

QUATERNARY STRUCTURE

The quaternary structure of a protein involves the combination of different polypeptide chains. *Refer to Figure 1404.* Many proteins (especially large globular proteins) are made of more than one polypeptide chain. Together, with the greater variety in amino acids, this causes a greater range of biological activity. The different polypeptide chains are kept together by hydrogen bonds, attraction between positive and negative charges, hydrophobic forces and disulfide bridges or any combination of the above.

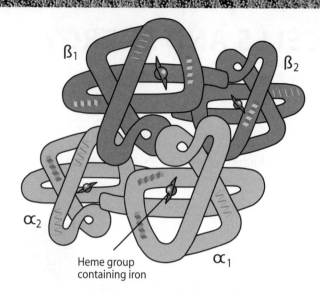

Figure 1404   Quaternary structure of a globular protein

Another example of the quaternary structure is the binding of prosthetic groups such as the heme group of hemoglobin. Figure 1404 shows a hemoglobin molecule.

It can seen that it is made of 4 polypeptide chains:
- two α chains
- two β chains

Each of these four chains is also combined with a prosthetic group, the heme group. This is not a polypeptide but an iron-containing molecule. In Figure 1404, the heme groups are shown as rectangles with (iron) spheres in the middle.

Proteins with a prosthetic group are called conjugated proteins. Chlorophyll and many of the enzymes in the electron transport chain are conjugated proteins.

> C.1.2   Outline the difference between fibrous and globular proteins, with reference to two examples of each protein type.
>
> ©IBO 2007

Proteins can be fibrous or globular. An example of a fibrous protein is shown in Figure 1405. There are a number of important differences between these two types of proteins and they are outlined in Figure 1406.

	Fibrous proteins	Globular proteins
Shape	long	tightly folded
Solubility	insoluble in water	soluble in water
Main level of organisation	secondary structure is the most important	tertiary structure is the most important
Function	structural (they *are* something)	function (they *do* something)
Examples	collagen keratin myosin	hemoglobin *(Figure 1404)* enzymes antibodies hormones

Figure 1406   Fibrous and globular proteins

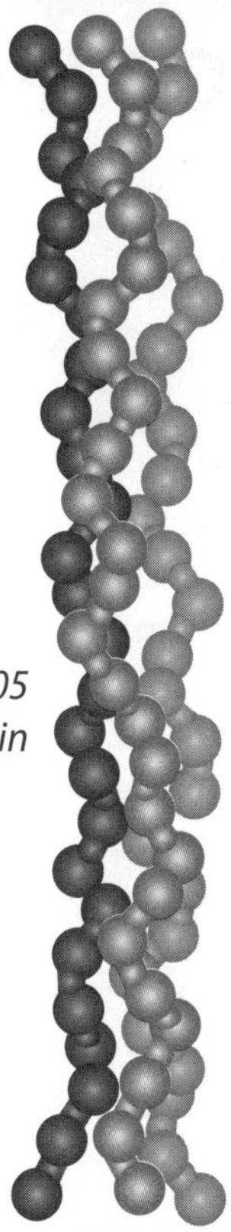

*Figure 1405
A fibrous protein*

C.1.3   Explain the significance of polar and non-polar amino acids.

©IBO 2007

Of the 20 amino acids commonly used to build proteins, 8 have non-polar (hydrophobic) R groups. The others have polar R groups and are soluble in water. The non-polar amino acids in the polypeptide chain will cluster together in the centre of the molecule and contribute to the tertiary structure of the molecule. In general, the more non-polar amino acids a protein contains, the less soluble it is in water. In membranes, proteins are found in between phospholipids. The phospholipid layer is polar on the outside and non-polar in the centre. The protein will often arrange itself so that it exposes hydrophilic portions to the outside of the membrane and hydrophobic sections to the centre. *Refer to Figure 1407.*

C.1.4   State four functions of proteins, giving a named example of each.

©IBO 2007

Functions of proteins include:
- enzymes
- hormones
- defense
- structure
- transport

ENZYMES

All enzymes are (globular) proteins, for example amylase which catalyses the following reaction:

starch ⟶ maltose.

HORMONES

Some hormones are proteins, others are steroids. An example of a protein hormone is insulin.

DEFENSE

Antibodies or immunoglobulins are globular proteins assisting in the defense against foreign particles (antigens).

STRUCTURE

Collagen is a fibrous, structural protein which builds tendons and is an important part of your skin.

TRANSPORT

Hemoglobin is a globular conjugated protein which readily and reversibly binds to oxygen due to the heme group attached to it.

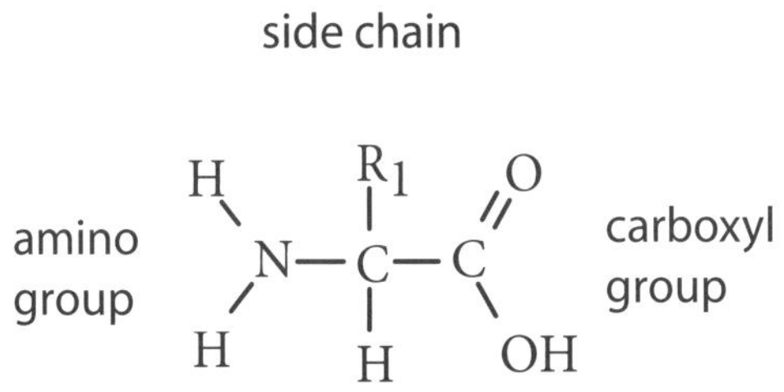

Figure 1407   The structure of an amino acid

217

C2 ENZYMES

C.2.1   State that metabolic pathways consist of chains and cycles of enzyme-catalysed reactions.

©IBO 2007

Very few, if any, chemical changes in a cell result from a single reaction. Metabolic pathways are chains and cycles of enzyme-catalysed reactions.

The reactions will rarely occur spontaneously at a measureable rate at room temperature. Therefore **enzymes** are used to speed up a reaction. You may safely assume that biological reactions only occur at measureable rates in the presence of enzymes.

Examples of metabolic pathways are photosynthesis and cellular respiration *(see Topic 8)*.

C.2.2   Describe the induced-fit model.

©IBO 2007

As discussed in *Topic 3.6* the 'lock-and-key' model exists to explain the very high specificity of enzymes. The lock and key model was first suggested by Emil Fischer in 1894. Soon after, it appeared that certain enzymes can catalyse several (similar) reactions. The 'induced-fit' model *(Figure 1408)*

was proposed in 1958 and suggests the following: The active site may not be as rigid as orginally was thought. Its shape will adapt somewhat to allow several slightly different substrates to fit. The active site will interact with the substrate and adapt to make the perfect fit. It is like a glove which will fit on several hands but not on a foot.

C.2.3   Explain that enzymes lower the activation energy of the chemical reactions that they catalyse.

©IBO 2007

Enzymes speed up a biochemical reaction without changing the nature of it but also without being used up.

The presence of an enzyme will speed up a reaction because the active site will facilitate the chemical change. This happens by a means of lowering the activation energy. Every reaction requires a certain amount of activation energy. If two molecules are going to react with each other, they need to collide with a certain speed. The higher the activation energy, the higher the speed required. At a low temperature, only a few molecules will have this speed, which means that the rate of reaction is low.

The active site of the enzyme assists in the chemical reaction by lowering the required activation energy. This means that more molecules are able to react and the rate of reaction will increase.

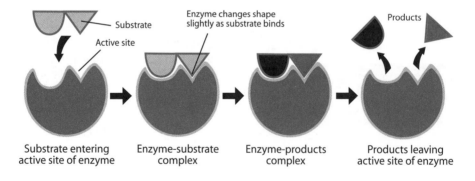

Figure 1408   The induced fit model

TOK   How do enzymes work?

The lock and key model as proposed by Emil Fischer late in the nineteenth century neatly described the mechanism of enzyme action. The model's simplicity made it effective and it remained in popular use for nearly a century until a more accurate and detailed one, Koshland's model of induced fit, replaced it.

The development of knowledge in the natural sciences is usually stepwise, with one scientist standing on the shoulders of previous scientists' knowledge, ideas, and models. In rare cases there is a complete change of thinking (a paradigm shift), but most advances are gradual and measured.

Figure 1409 shows what happens to the energy level during an exothermic biochemical reaction and what happens when a enzyme is added to this reaction.

It is apparent that the enzyme has reduced the required **activation energy**.

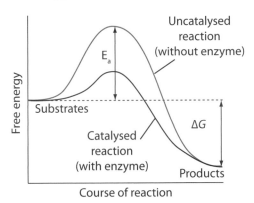

Figure 1409   Energy of activation graph

C.2.4   Explain the difference between competitive and non-competitive inhibition, with reference to one example of each.

©IBO 2007

A number of molecules exist which can reduce the rate of an enzyme-controlled reaction. These molecules are called **inhibitors**. There are two kinds of inhibitors:
- competitive inhibitors
- non-competitive inhibitors

COMPETITIVE INHIBITORS

The structure of the inhibiting molecule is so similar to the structure of the substrate molecule that it competes and binds to the active site of the enzyme and prevents the substrate from binding. Adding more substrate will reduce the effect of the inhibitor. *Refer to Figure 1410.*

Example

Prontosil (an antibacterial drug) inhibits the synthesis of folic acid (vitamin B, which acts as a co-enzyme) in bacteria. The drug will bind to the enzyme which makes folic acid. Folic acid is needed in nucleic acid synthesis. With Prontosil, the folic acid will no longer be made and the bacterial cell dies. Animal cells are not affected because they do not make folic acid but absorb it from food. Animal cells therefore lack the enzyme and the drug has no effect.

NON-COMPETITIVE INHIBITORS

The inhibiting molecule binds to the enzyme in a place which is NOT the active site. As a result, the shape of the active site of the enzyme changes and the substrate molecule will no longer fit. Adding more substrate has no effect on the reaction rate. *Refer to Figure 1411.*

Example

Cyanide ions (CN^-) will attach thenselves to the - SH groups in the enzyme cytochrome c oxidase. By doing this, it destroys the disulfide bridges (-S-S-) and changes the tertiary structure of the enzyme. The shape of the active site of cytochrome c oxidase is irreversibly changed and the enzyme will no longer function.

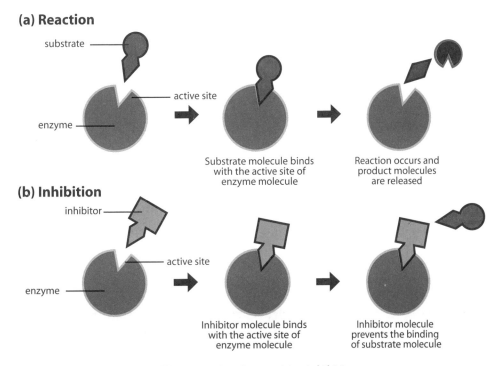

Figure 1410   Competitive inhibition

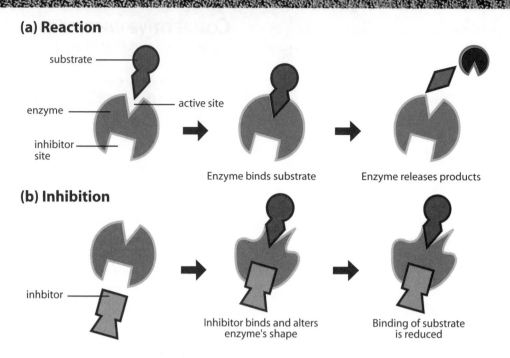

(a) Reaction

substrate

enzyme

active site

inhibitor site

Enzyme binds substrate

Enzyme releases products

(b) Inhibition

inhbitor

Inhibitor binds and alters enzyme's shape

Binding of substrate is reduced

Figure 1411   Non-competitive inhibition

OPTION

The function of cytochrome c oxidase is to catalyse the reduction of oxygen to water. Without the enzyme, the reaction will not proceed sufficiently quickly and the process of releasing energy via cellular respiration stops and the organism dies.

> C.2.5   Explain the control of metabolic pathways by end-product inhibition, including the role of allosteric sites.
>
> ©IBO 2007

A special kind of non-competitive inhibition is **allostery**. Allosteric enzymes are made of two or more polypeptide chains. The activity of allosteric enzymes is regulated by compounds which are not their substrates and which bind to the enzyme at a specific site, well away from the active site. They cause a reversible change in the shape of the active site.

The compounds are called allosteric effectors and are divided into two categories:

- allosteric activators (which speed up a reaction) and
- allosteric inhibitors (which slow down a reaction).

End products of a metabolic pathway can act as allosteric inhibitors. An example is found in glycolysis (see also Topic C3).

In glycolysis (see also Topic C3), one molecule of glucose is broken down into two molecules of pyruvate.

The first few steps in glycolysis (see Figure 1412) involve adding a phosphate to glucose, then changing glucose-6-phosphate into fructose-6-phosphate and adding a second phosphate to make fructose-1,6-diphosphate. The fructose-1,6-diphosphate is then changed, in a series of enzyme-controlled reactions, into two molecules of pyruvate.

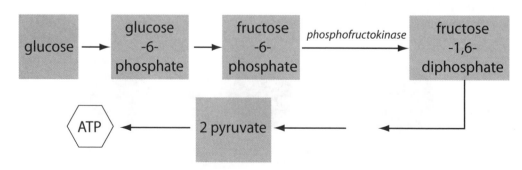

glucose → glucose -6- phosphate → fructose -6- phosphate → *phosphofructokinase* → fructose -1,6- diphosphate

ATP ← 2 pyruvate ←

Figure 1412   Glycolysis reactions

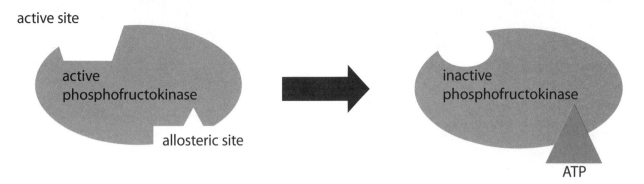

active site

active phosphofructokinase

allosteric site

inactive phosphofructokinase

ATP

Figure 1413   Active and allosteric sites

pyruvate. In the process of respiration, pyruvate is broken down and some of its energy is used to convert ADP into ATP.

End-product inhibition by allostery takes place in the reaction where fructose-6-phosphate is changed into fructose-1,6-diphosphate. This reaction is catalysed by the enzyme phosphofructokinase. *Refer to Figure 333.*

As the above reactions proceed, fructose-1,6-diphosphate is produced. The metabolic pathway from there will eventually yield a number of ATP molecules. ATP is an allosteric inhibitor. It will fit into the allosteric site of the phosphofructokinase molecule, changing the shape of the active site.

Because of the change of shape of the active site, fructose-6-phosphate does not fit anymore and the reaction will not take place. Without fructose-1,6-diphosphate, pyruvate will not be produced and no new ATP will be formed.

So if there is a sufficient amount of ATP, the production of new ATP will be reduced due to end-product inhibition. When levels of ATP are reduced, the ATP bound to the enzyme will be released from the enzyme. This changes the shape of the active site again and the enzyme will be able to catalyse the production of fructose-1,6-diphosphate, which will eventually yield ATP.

End-product inhibition is the concept that the presence of a high concentration of end-product of a metabolic pathway will inhibit the production of one of the metabolites somewhere in the pathway and no more end-product will be produced. *See Figure 1413.*

Allosteric inhibition is the concept that a molecule can bind to the allosteric site of an enzyme and change the shape of the active site so that the substrate no longer fits and reaction is no longer catalysed.

C3 CELL RESPIRATION

> C.3.1 State that oxidation involves the loss of electrons from an element, whereas reduction involves a gain of electrons; and that oxidation frequently involves gaining oxygen or losing hydrogen, whereas reduction frequently involves losing oxygen or gaining hydrogen.
>
> ©IBO 2007

In cell respiration, as in photosynthesis (*see Topic C4*), reactions often involve the enzyme controlled transfer of electrons. This type of reaction is called a redox reaction. In these *red*uction-*ox*idation reactions, one compound loses some electrons and the other compound gains them.

Here is a useful mnemonic to help you remember this:

OIL RIG

Oxidation **I**s **L**oss (of electrons),

Reduction **I**s **G**ain (of electrons).

The process of oxidation often involves gaining oxygen (hence its name) or losing hydrogen while reduction often involves losing oxygen or gaining hydrogen.

A substance which has been reduced, now has the power to reduce other substances (and becomes oxidised in the process); e.g. NADH (respiration) and NADPH (photosynthesis)

	oxidation	reduction
electrons	loss	gain
oxygen	gain	loss
hydrogen	loss	gain

OPTION

221

If a molecule, atom or ion is oxidised, then it loses electrons. These electrons have to be accepted by another molecule, atom or ion which is reduced. Therefore, oxidation and reduction reactions always take place together, hence the name '**redox**' reactions.

C.3.2   Outline the process of glycolysis, including phosphorylation, lysis, oxidation and ATP formation.

©IBO 2007

Glycolysis takes place in the cytoplasm and produces two pyruvate molecules from every glucose according to the following reaction:

$$\text{Glucose} + 2\text{ADP} + 2\text{P}_i + 2\text{NAD}^+ \longrightarrow$$
$$2\text{Pyruvate} + 2\text{ATP} + 2\text{NADH} + 2\text{H}^+ + 2\text{H}_2\text{O}$$

Glycolysis is anaerobic and does not require oxygen and produces a small amount of ATP and NADH and H^+.

One molecule of glucose contains six atoms of carbon; one molecule of pyruvate contains three atoms of carbon. The structural formula for pyruvate is shown in Figure 1414.

Glycolysis uses glucose, a hexose sugar, with six carbon atoms to eventually produce two molecules of pyruvate, a triose, i.e. a monosaccharide with 3 carbon atoms.

The first step of glycolysis involves **phosphorylation**. In this step, ATP is used (invested) to add a phosphate group to glucose. It is followed by a second phosphorylation reaction, again using ATP and producing hexose biphosphate.

The hexose biphosphate still contains 6 carbon atoms. It is split in a lysis reaction, producing 2 triose phosphate molecules with 3 carbon atoms each.

The next step is a combined oxidation phosphorylation reaction. The enzyme involved first oxidises the triose phosphate into a different triose phosphate

(for those taking Chemistry HL: glyceraldehyde to glycerate or, in general, aldehyde to carboxylic acid). The oxidation has to occur because in the overall reaction, it was shown that glycolysis produces 2 NADH and 2H$^+$. NAD$^+$ has been reduced to NADH, i.e. it has gained electrons. The electrons were supplied by a triose phosphate which is oxidised into a different triose phosphate.

After the oxidation reaction, the enzyme will attach an inorganic phosphate from the cytoplasm to the triose phosphate to form a triose biphosphate. So this phosphorylation reaction does not involve ATP.

Finally, each triose biphosphate gives up one of its phosphate groups. This phosphate is taken up by ADP to form ATP. This is repeated in the last step of glycolysis, again forming one ATP, but now also producing pyruvate.

The process of glycolysis is shown in Figure 1415 and can be summarised by the following overall equation:

$$\text{Glucose} + 2\text{ADP} + 2\text{P}_i + 2\text{NAD}^+ \longrightarrow$$
$$2\text{Pyruvate} + 2\text{ATP} + 2\text{NADH} + 2\text{H}^+ + 2\text{H}_2\text{O}$$

Figure 1414   Pyruvate

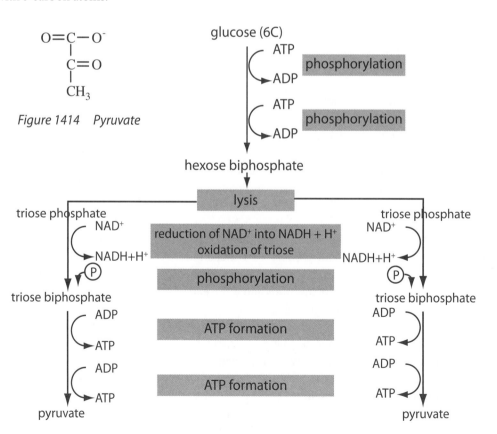

Figure 1415   Glycolysis

C.3.3 Draw and label a diagram showing the structure of a mitochondrion as seen in electron micrographs.

©IBO 2007

Mitochondria (singular: mitochondrion) are large organelles found in eukaryotic cells. They are surrounded by an outer membrane and an inner membrane. The inner membrane is folded and these folds, cristae (singular crista), project into the matrix of the mitochondrion. The matrix of the mitochondrion is a watery fluid which contains many molecules and enzymes. In the matrix of the mitochondrion, we also find ribosomes and DNA. The space between the outer and inner membrane of the mitochondrion is called the inter-membrane space. Figure 1416 is an electron micrograph showing several mitochondria.

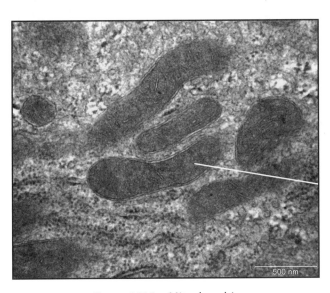

500 nm

Figure 1416 Mitochondria

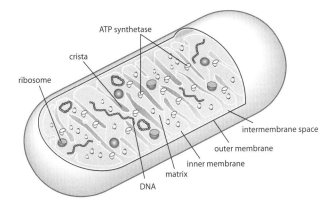

Figure 1417 Structure of a mitochondrion

Mitochondria are often drawn as a two-dimensional cross-section to show the internal structure. *Refer to Figure 1417.*

C.3.4 Explain aerobic respiration, including the link reaction, the Krebs cycle, the role of NADH + H$^+$, the electron transport chain and the role of oxygen.

©IBO 2007

When oxygen is NOT present in the cell, pyruvate will stay in the cytoplasm and be converted into lactate (in animals) or ethanol and carbon dioxide (in plants and yeasts) in the process of anaerobic respiration (*see Topic 3.7*). Glycolysis releases a small amount of energy but conversion of pyruvate to lactate or ethanol and carbon dioxide does not yield more ATP. Therefore, anaerobic respiration releases only a small amount of the energy in glucose and is only used in the absence of oxygen, when aerobic respiration is not possible.

If oxygen is present, a series of reactions take place which result in pyruvate being broken down to produce carbon dioxide and a relatively large amount of energy in the form of ATP.

The first of these reactions is called the link reaction because it forms the link between glycolysis (*see Topic 3.7.3*) and the Krebs cycle. Pyruvate, produced in the cytoplasm during glycolysis, is transported to the mitochondrial matrix according to the following equation:

$$\text{Pyruvate} + \text{CoA} + \text{NAD}^+ \longrightarrow \text{Acetyl CoA} + \text{CO}_2 + \text{NADH} + \text{H}^+$$

This process is known as *decarboxylation* of pyruvate because a molecule of carbon dioxide is removed from pyruvate.

The Krebs cycle, (also known as the tricarboxylic citric acid cycle or TCA cycle), occurs in the matrix of the mitochondria and produces $2CO_2$, $3NADH + 3H^+$, $1FADH_2$ and $1ATP$ from 1 molecule of acetyl CoA. As the name suggests, it is a cyclic process. The logical place to start studying the Krebs cycle is at the point where acetyl CoA, a compound containing 2 carbon atoms and produced from pyruvate in the link reaction, enters the cycle.

Acetyl CoA will combine with a four carbon compound, forming a six carbon compound. This six carbon compound will then be decarboxylated, producing a five carbon compound and carbon dioxide. The same sequence of reactions will happen again, producing a four carbon compound and another carbon dioxide. We are now back to the 4 carbon compound that originally reacted with acetyl CoA.

OPTION

223

Figure 1418 shows a simple diagram of the Krebs cycle.

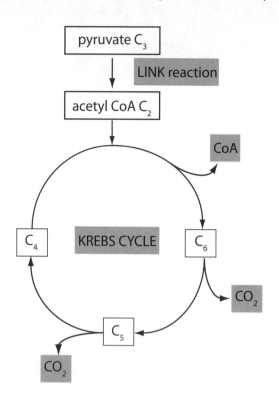

Figure 1418   The Krebs cycle

One turn of the cycle will require the input of one acetyl CoA and produce one CoA molecule and two carbon dioxide molecules. However, the purpose of the Krebs cycle is to produce energy and so one turn of the cycle also produces 3 NADH + $3H^+$, 1 $FADH_2$ and 1 ATP. $FADH_2$ is like NADH + H^+ in that it has accepted hydrogen ions so it has become reduced. It now has reducing power - the ability to reduce another compound.

C.3.5   Explain oxidative phosphorylation in terms of chemiosmosis.

©IBO 2007

In glycolysis, one glucose is split into two pyruvate, 2 ATP and 2 NADH + $2H^+$.

In the link reaction, one pyruvate is changed into one acetyl CoA, one carbon dioxide and 1 NADH + H^+.

In the **Krebs cycle**, one acetyl CoA is changed into 2 carbon dioxide, 3 NADH + $3H^+$, 1 ATP and 1 $FADH_2$.

This means that overall, one molecule of glucose has been changed into 6 molecules of carbon dioxide and, so far, no oxygen has been used and only a little ATP has been produced. The final stage of aerobic respiration will use the energy stored in NADH + H^+ and in $FADH_2$ to produce more ATP. The last step of this stage involves the use of oxygen. In the absence of oxygen, none of the reactions will occur. This will prevent the Krebs cycle from taking place and, instead, the process of anaerobic respiration will be carried out (*see Topic 3.7*).

The last stage of aerobic respiration involves the electron transport chain and takes place on the cristae, the folds of the inner membrane of the mitochondrion. A series of protein complexes (electron carriers) are arranged in a specific order in the phospholipid bilayer of the inner membrane of the mitochondrion. These protein complexes pass electrons along, from one complex to the next. As the electrons move through the membrane, some hydrogen ions (protons) are pumped from the matrix into the intermembrane space. Finally the last member of the electron transport chain promotes the reduction of oxygen to form water.

The proton gradient, which is the result of the movement of hydrogen ions from the matrix into the intermembrane space, drives the production of ATP (from ADP and P_i) by the enzyme, ATP synthetase. This is the chemiosmotic theory, proposed by a British biochemist, *Peter Mitchell* in 1961. **The chemiosmotic theory explains how the synthesis of ATP is coupled to electron transport and proton movement.**

Initially, not many Scientists accepted Mitchell's idea, but as more information became available, the chemiosmotic theory gained credibility and Peter Mitchell was awarded a Nobel Prize for Chemistry in 1978.

The net result of this process is that 1 NADH + H^+ supplies enough energy to produce 3 ATP from 3 ADP + 3 P_i and 1 $FADH_2$ supplies enough energy to produce 2 ATP from 2 ADP + 2 P_i. During these reactions, NADH + H^+ and $FADH_2$ are returned to the ir oxidised forms NAD^+ and FAD. The mechanism of this series of reactions is that the energy from NADH + H^+ and $FADH_2$ is transferred to ATP through a series of electron carriers.

This series of electron carriers finally yields H^+ and electrons to oxygen (O_2) to form water (H_2O). However if no oxygen is present, this reaction cannot take place. As a consequence, no NAD^+ or FAD is formed and hence the Krebs cycle cannot operate. This will cause acetyl CoA to accumulate and, as a result, it will no longer be produced from pyruvate. Glycolysis will continue to operate however, since, even without oxygen, it is possible to break down pyruvate and release some energy. This process is less efficient though, since the amount of energy produced is much lower in anaerobic than aerobic respiration.

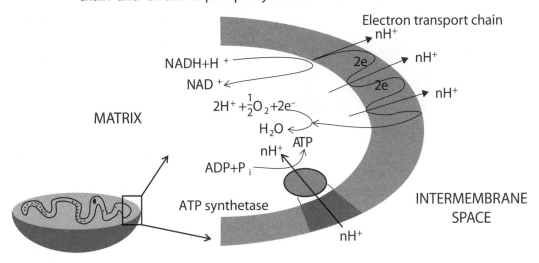

Chemiosmotic coupling of electron transport chain and oxidative phosphorylation

Figure 1419   Chemiosmosis

The chemiosmotic theory of *Peter Mitchell*

It had already been obvious for some time that a link existed between the electrons being passed down the electron transport chain and the production of ATP. *Peter Mitchell* discovered that during the passing of the 'high energy' electrons down the electron transport chain, protons were being pumped across the inner mitochondrial membrane.

There is a build up of H^+ ions in the intermembrane space. The concentration gradient (known as the proton motive force) will drive H^+ through the ATP synthetase molecule which has chemiosmotic channels. As the H^+ ions go through the ATP synthetase molecule, the potential energy they possess will be used to drive ATP synthesis. *Refer to Figure 1419.*

> C.3.6   Explain the relationship between the structure of the mitochondrion and its function.
>
> ©IBO 2007

Keeping in mind all of the information presented in the previous sections, it is useful to return to the structure of the mitochondrion. *Refer to Figures 1416 and 1417.*

The outer membrane is a regular membrane, separating the mitochondrion from the cytoplasm. Its structure is based on the fluid mosaic model.

The inter-membrane space has a higher concentration of H^+ ions (hence a lower pH) because of the electron transport chain.

The inner membrane is folded into cristae to provide maximum space and surface area for the electron carriers and ATP synthetase. It is impermeable to H^+ ions. Its structure is based on the fluid mosaic model with the electron carriers and the ATP synthetase embedded among the phospholipid molecules. The ATP synthetase molecules can be seen on the cristae.

The inter-membrane space has a small volume so that the movement of even a limited number of hydrogen ions (protons) will greatly affect the concentration. The matrix contains the enzymes which enable the Krebs cycle to proceed.

Glycolysis takes place in the cytoplasm. Pyruvate is transported to the matrix of the mitochondrion and decarboxylated to acetyl CoA which enters the Krebs cycle. The resulting NADH and H^+ and $FADH_2$ give their electrons to the electron carriers in the inner membrane. The electrons move through the membrane as they are passed from one electron carrier to another in a series of redox reactions. During this process, H^+ ions are pumped from the matrix into the intermembrane space, creating a potential difference. A concentration gradient drives the H^+ ions back to the matrix through the ATP synthetase which uses the energy released to combine ADP and P_i into ATP, which is released into the matrix.

C4 PHOTOSYNTHESIS

C.4.1 Draw and label a diagram showing the structure of a chloroplast as seen in electron micrographs.

©IBO 2007

Photosynthesis occurs in the chloroplasts. Cells in the palisade layer often have a large number of chloroplasts because the main function of these cells is photosynthesis.

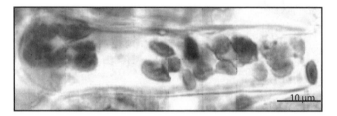

Figure 1420   Light microscope view of chloroplasts

Chloroplasts found in cells of green plants are 2 - 10 μm in diameter and ovoid in shape when found in higher plants (in green algae their shape varies). As you can see in Figure 1420, chloroplasts can be seen with the light microscope.

Pictures of the chloroplast, taken with the electron microscope, allow its structure to be seen and studied in sufficient detail. See Figure 1421 (a), (b) and (c), the approximate magnifications are shown.

Figure 1421 shows several electron micrographs showing the location and detail of a chloroplast. From similar EMs, a three-dimesional impression of the structure has been deduced. A diagram of the structure of a chloroplast is shown in Figure 1422.

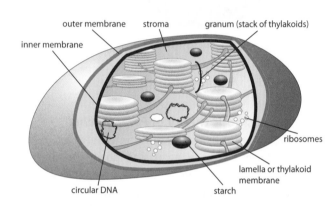

Figure 1422   Diagram of a chloroplast

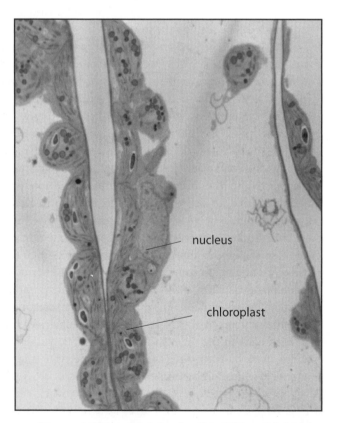

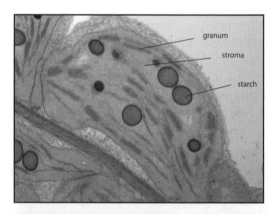

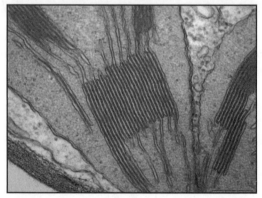

Figure 1421   (a) A leaf cell (x400)   (b) A chloroplast (x1200)   (c) Granum and stroma (x5000)

C.4.2 State that photosynthesis consists of light-dependent and light-independent reactions.

©IBO 2007

As was shown in *Topic 3.8*, photosynthesis is NOT a simple one-step reaction. It consists of a series of reactions which can be grouped into a light-dependent stage and a light-independent stage. These two stages are shown in Figure 1423. The light-dependent stage will only take place in the light. However, the light-independent stage can occur at any time, if the required materials are available. Outside the laboratory, these materials are provided (ATP and NADPH) come from the light-dependent stage.

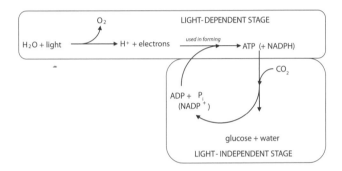

Figure 1423   The two stages of photosynthesis

Some texts will still use the terms 'light stage' and 'dark stage'. These are incorrect since they imply that light is required for one stage and darkness for the other. This is not the case. Indeed light is needed for the light-dependent stage but the light-independent stage can take place in the presence or absence of light - which makes the name 'dark stage' misleading.

C.4.3 Explain the light-dependent reactions.

©IBO 2007

OUTLINE

In the light-dependent reaction, light energy is used (indirectly) to split water molecules into hydrogen ions, oxygen molecules and electrons. The oxygen is a waste product and will leave the chloroplast. The H^+ and electrons will be used to produce energy-rich ATP and NADPH.

In the light-independent stage, the ATP and NADPH are used to combine 3 carbon dioxide molecules into 1 triose phosphate (TP) (C3) in the Calvin Cycle. Once two molecules of TP are produced, they are combined to form one molecule of glucose (C6).

DETAILS OF THE LIGHT-DEPENDENT STAGE

The light-dependent stage takes place on the membrane of the grana, the stacks of thylakoid membrane in the chloroplast. There are two possible processes which will produce ATP:

- non-cyclic photophosphorylation *(Figure 1424)*
- cyclic photophosphorylation *(Figure 1425)*

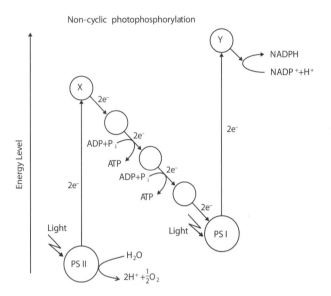

Figure 1424   Non cyclic photophosphorylation in the light-dependent stage

Non-cyclic photophosphorylation

As can be seen in Figure 1424, the light is absorbed by the pigments of photosystem II (PS II), which are mainly found in the grana of the chloroplast. Absorbing this light energy excites some electrons which, as a result, leave their normal position (circling the nucleus of the atom) and move away from the nucleus of the atom. This is called photoactivation of PS II. The electrons are taken up by an electron acceptor X, resulting in a chlorophyll 'a' molecule with a positive charge. The electrons are then passed through a number of electron carriers in the membrane via oxidation-reduction reactions *(see Topic C3)* and will end up at photosystem I (PS I). This is a system of electron tranport.

The presence of chlorophyll a^+ (Chl a^+) will induce the lysis of water so that oxygen, hydrogen ions and electrons are released. Chl a^+ is the strongest biological oxidant known. Since the lysis of water is the direct result of the photoactivation of PS II, the process is known as photolysis of water.

The light is also absorbed by PS I which, like PS II, is found in the membranes of the grana. Again, the electrons absorb the light energy and move away from the nucleus. This is called photoactivation of PS I. The electrons leave

OPTION

227

the chlorophyll a molecule and are taken up by electron acceptor Y. They are then passed on and taken up by NADP+ which combines with an H+ and is reduced to form NADPH. The Chl a+ of PS I receives electrons from the electron carrier chain (ultimately from PS II) and becomes an uncharged Chl a molecule.

Cyclic photophosphorylation

In cyclic photophosphorylation (see Figure 1425), the electrons from PS I go to electron acceptor Y, but instead of being used to produce NADPH, they go through the membrane via several electron carriers (electron transport) (redox reactions) and are returned to PS I. PS II is not involved. This process is cyclic, as its name suggests. It does not produce NADPH but it does produce ATP. For this reason, cyclic photophosphorylation is a useful process, but as it does not produce NADPH, it is not able to drive the Calvin cycle and will not produce complex carbohydrates for long term energy storage.

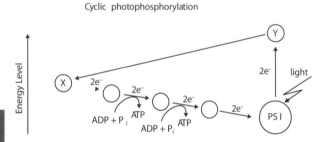

Figure 1425   Cyclic photophosphorylation in the light-dependent stage

C.4.4   Explain photophosphorylation in terms of chemiosmosis.

©IBO 2007

The electrons from photolysis of water are taken up by Chl a+ in PS II. The following happens:

- Chl a+ will be converted to Chl a
- oxygen is released as a waste product
- H+ ions (protons) are pumped to the inside of the grana (the lumen). They accumulate there until the concentration gradient drives them through chemiosmotic proton channels in the ATP synthetase, driving the phosphorylation reaction ADP + P$_i$ $\longrightarrow$ ATP (see Topic C3). This is shown in Figure 1426.

Since the formation of ATP is indirectly caused by light energy, the process is often described as photophosphorylation.

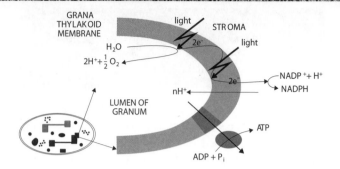

Figure 1426   Photophosphorylation

C.4.5   Explain the light-independent reactions.

©IBO 2007

The light-dependent stage uses light to produce the energy-rich compounds ATP and NADPH and H+ which are used to drive the **Calvin cycle** (see Figure 1427) in the light-independent reactions. In the Calvin cycle, three molecules of carbon dioxide are combined to form the 3C compound triose phosphate (TP). TP will leave the Calvin cycle and be subsequently combined to larger, more complex, carbohydrates such as glucose and, eventually, starch.

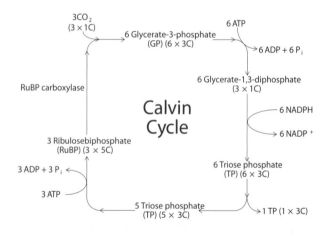

Figure 1427   The Calvin cycle

The Calvin cycle takes place in the stroma of the chloroplast. ATP provides the energy and NADPH provides the reducing power needed for biosynthesis using carbon dioxide. RuBP is the carbon dioxide acceptor and (catalysed by RuBP carboxylase which is also known as RuBisCo) will take up CO_2, forming GP. GP will be reduced to TP but this conversion needs energy from ATP and reducing power from NADPH. TP can be converted to glucose, sucrose, starch, fatty acids and amino acids and other products. Of course, RuBP is regenerated from TP to keep the cycle going. This process requires energy from ATP.

OPTION

TOK   Is research science or art?

For the series of experiments from which the mechanism of the Calvin cycle was determined, new procedures were devised and equipment designed. This is often the case when new knowledge is revealed. Melvin Calvin's team of scientists displayed amazing creativity and imagination in their investigation of the mechanism of photosynthesis. One device they designed and built was called the lollipop because of its shape. It was made from clear glass with light sources on both sides to illuminate the unicellular green algae, *Chlorella*, which was suspended in a watery solution. In this environment, substantial photosynthesis occurred and *Chlorella* could quickly and easily be removed from the lollipop and examined for the presence of chemicals involved in the stages of what is now known as the Calvin cycle.

To some, the lollipop is just a machine. Perhaps it is viewed in this way because it was built for a specific purpose, to reveal knowledge. It can also be seen as the result of the creative minds of scientists. The development of new scientific protocols and devices have many parallels with the development of works of art.

> **C.4.6**   Explain the relationship between the structure of the chloroplast and its function.
>
> ©IBO 2007

The light-dependent reactions of photosynthesis involve photoactivation, followed by a series of redox reactions during electron transport by electron carriers. The reactions need to take place in a certain order so the electron carriers are fixed in positions in the membrane of the grana thylakoid. Since the thylakoid membrane has a large surface area inside the chloroplast, many of light-dependent reactions can take place at the same time. *Refer to Figures 1421 and 1422.*

Another process during the light-independent reactions is the movement of hydrogen ions (H^+) or protons. As the electrons move from the stroma through the membrane into the lumen of the grana, hydrogen ions are actively transported across the thylakoid membrane, into the lumen of the grana. Since the lumen of the granum is a small space, it has a small volume and even a limited change in the number of hydrogen ions will have a significant effect on the H^+ concentration. (*The same situation occurs in the intermembrane space of mitochondria, refer Topic C.3.6.*)

The light-independent reactions of the Calvin cycle take place in the stroma of the chloroplast. The concentration of the required enzymes, particularly RuBisCo, in the stroma of the chloroplast is much higher than would be possible in the cytoplasm. Also the concentration of magnesium ions (Mg^{2+}) in the stroma increases in light. Magnesium ions are needed for the proper functioning of Rubisco. Also, due to the fact that protons are pumped from the stroma into the lumen of the grana, the pH of the stroma slightly increases making it slightly alkaline (pH around 8). This facilitates the reactions of the Calvin cycle. Again, in the much larger volume of the cytoplasm, the effect of removing some protons would be much smaller.

> **C.4.7**   Explain the relationship between the action spectrum and the absorption spectrum of photosynthetic pigments in green plants.
>
> ©IBO 2007

For a person to see an object, the object needs to reflect light which then enters the person's eye. The colour of the object is the colour of the light that is reflected. All other colours are absorbed.

Chlorophyll is green. That means that it will absorb other colours better than the colour green, which will be reflected. An absorption spectrum can be produced from measurements of the percentage of the light of a certain colour that is absorbed. An absorption spectrum of chlorophyll 'a' (one of the types of chlorophyll) is shown in Figure 1428. It can be seen that the absorption of green light (500 nm) is nearly zero, indicating that this colour is reflected and will therefore enter a person's eye, creating the image of a green leaf.

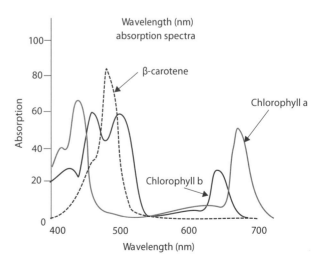

Figure 1428   Absorption spectra

Chlorophyll needs to absorb light before it can use it in the light-dependent reactions. However, not all absorbed wavelengths (colours) of light are equally well used in photosynthesis. This is where an action spectrum is different from an absorption spectrum. An action spectrum will show how well the light of different wavelengths is used in photosynthesis. The amount of photosynthesis can be measured, for example, by the amount of oxygen produced (which is easiest to measure in water plants).

In Figure 1428, you can see that the different kinds of chlorophyll have different absorption spectra (you do not need to know the differences). You can also see that these different pigments (chlorophyll a, b, and carotenoid) work together in photosynthesis as can be seen from the **absorbtion spectrum** in Figure 1428.

C.4.8	Explain the concept of limiting factors in photosynthesis, with reference to light intensity, temperature and concentration of carbon dioxide.

©IBO 2007

The factor the furthest away from its optimum value will limit the amount of photosynthesis. This is the limiting factor. If you improve this factor, the rate of photosynthesis will increase until another factor becomes the limiting factor.

Limiting factors for photosynthesis are:
- light intensity
- temperature
- concentration of carbon dioxide.

As can be seen in Figure 1429, graph (a), light intensity can be a limiting factor in photosynthesis. If the intensity of the light is increased, the rate of photosynthesis will increase to a certain level, at which point further increases will not affect the rate of photosynthesis. At this point, light intensity is no longer a limiting factor in photosynthesis.

The same applies for the concentration of carbon dioxide. Increasing the concentration of carbon dioxide will increase the rate of photosynthesis until a point when carbon dioxide concentration is no longer the limiting factor for photosynthesis and further increases do not affect the rate. *See Figure 1429 (b).*

However, the shape of the graph for temperature versus the rate of photosynthesis is different. When the temperature is low, it can be a limiting factor for the rate of photosynthesis. Increasing the temperature will increase the rate of photosynthesis until the optimum temperature is reached. A further increase in temperature will decrease the rate of photosynthesis because the enzymes will start to denature. *See Figure 1429 (c) which is only approximate.*

TOK   Does correlation mean causation?

In experimental design, to be sure of the link between cause and effect, one must control all factors that could influence the outcome apart from one. Calvin's experiments were meticulously designed to achieve this outcome in an environment almost totally removed from the world in which most organisms live and interact. In the every day world, it is impossible to control all factors and draw definitive 'cause and effect' conclusions.

Epidemiology is an attempt by Scientists to study factors affecting health. It acknowledges at its foundation that humans cannot control all factors when we study health. Epidemiologists are quick to point out that they determine a correlation between a factor and a disease and that this is very different to proof that the factor is the cause of the disease. We can say that there is a correlation between longer life and vegetarianism as opposed to meat-eating. This does not prove that eating meat lowers life expectancy. What experiment would you have to perform to make such an assertion?

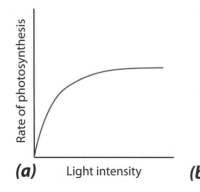
(a) Light intensity

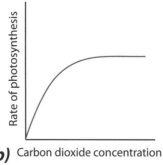
(b) Carbon dioxide concentration

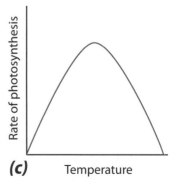
(c) Temperature

Figure 1429   Limiting factors for photosynthesis

EXERCISES

1 Which of the four levels of organisation in proteins may involve a non-protein molecule?
   A primary structure
   B secondary structure
   C tertiary structure
   D quaternary structure

2 If a competitive inhibitor is added to an enzyme catalysed reaction, the rate of reaction will always decrease unless
   A more substate is added
   B the inhibitor is added in excess
   C the temperature is increased
   D the temperature is kept constant

3 In a redox reaction:
   A both compounds lose electrons.
   B both compounds gain electrons.
   C electrons are not involved in the reaction.
   D one compound loses electrons and the other compound gains them:

4 Oxidation involves:
   A loss of electrons.
   B gain of electrons.
   C removal of oxygen.
   D removal of hydrogen.

5 If glycolysis is written as a one step equation, what are the reactants and the products?

	reactants	products
A	glucose, oxygen	carbon dioxide, water
B	glucose, ADP, Pi, NAD+	pyruvate, ATP, NADH, H2O
C	glucose, ATP	pyruvate, ADP
D	glucose	lactate

Questions 6 and 7 refer to the schematic diagram of a mitochondrion.

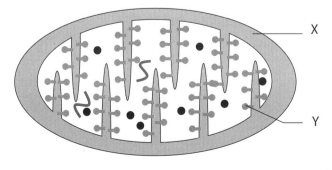

6 X is the:
   A intermembrane space
   B DNA
   C matrix
   D ATP synthetase

7 Y is the:
   A crista
   B DNA
   C matrix
   D ATP synthetase

8 A leaf is exposed to sunlight. Which colours are absorbed and which are reflected?
   A all colours are reflected
   B all colours are absorbed except red which is reflected
   C green is absorbed and all other colours are reflected
   D all colours are absorbed except green which is reflected

9 The Calvin cycle is a part of:
   A the light dependent stage of photosynthesis.
   B the light independent stage of photosynthesis.
   C fermentation.
   D respiration.

10 Which one of the following is not a limiting factor for photosynthesis?
   A light intensity.
   B temperature.
   C concentration of carbon dioxide.
   D concentration of oxygen.

11 Which types of bonds are involved in each of the four levels of protein structure?

12. State four functions of proteins. Give an example of each.

13 Explain why both polar and non-polar amino acids are used in protein that are part of the cell membrane.

14 (a) Where does the competitive inhibitor bind to the enzyme?
    (b) Where does the non-competitive inhibitor bind to the enzyme?
    (c) Give an example of each.

15 Explain end product inhibition.

16. Explain why an exothermic reaction may need to have energy added in order to proceed and what the effect of enzymes can be.

17 (a)   Where in the cell does glycolysis take place?
    (b)   Where in the cell does the Krebs cycle take place?
    (c)   Where in the cell is the electron transport chain found?

18 Draw a diagram of the structure of a mitochondrion as seen with the electron microscope.

19 (a)   How does the structure of the site for the Krebs cycle relate to its function?
    (b)   How does the structure of the site for the electron transport chain relate to its function?
    (c)   What would happen to aerobic respiration if the outer membrane of the mitochondrion became permeable to protons (hydrogen ions)?

20 Draw a diagram of the structure of a chloroplast as seen with the electron microscope.

21 Outline how the light-independent reaction depends on the light dependent reaction.

22 (a)   What are the functions of the ATP and NADPH produced in non-cyclic photophosphorylation?
    (b)   What would be the purpose of cyclic photophosphorylation?
    (c)   What is the advantage of non-cyclic photophosphorylation over cyclic photophosphorylation for the plant?
    (d)   What is the purpose of the Calvin cycle?

23 Explain how the structure of the chloroplast is suited to its function.

24 Compare and contrast the process of ATP production in chloroplasts and mitochondria

EVOLUTION

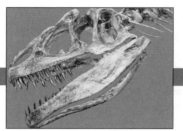

D1 ORIGIN OF LIFE ON EARTH

> **D.1.1** Describe four processes needed for the spontaneous origin of life on Earth.
>
> ©IBO 2007

The following processes are needed for the spontaneous origin of life on Earth.

The non-living synthesis of simple organic molecules

The early Earth is presumed to have provided all of the elements and chemical compounds needed for life to begin. It was believed that the early oceans contained a mixture of simple inorganic molecules that were converted into simple organic molecules *(see Topic 3.2.1.)* The organic chemicals may have been generated on the Earth *(see Topic D.1.2)* or introduced from space *(see Topics D.1.3 and D.1.4)*.

The assembly of these molecules into polymers

The simple organic molecules present in the oceans would have needed to undergo a process of polymerisation to form the larger more complex organic chemicals needed by cells. A variety of different environments, both hot and cold, have been proposed where this may have occurred *(see Topic D.1.4)*.

The origin of self-replicating molecules made inheritance possible

Self-replicating molecules are molecules that are able to undergo replication, that is, act as a template for copies of themselves to be made. The only biological molecules capable of self-replication are DNA and RNA. DNA can only replicate in the presence of protein enzymes, but certain RNA sequences are capable of self-replication: it can catalyse its formation from nucleotides in the absence of proteins. This is an example of an RNA-based catalyst or ribozyme *(see Topic D.1.5.)*. Only self replicating molecules are capable of undergoing evolution by natural selection *(see Topic D.1.5)*.

The packaging of these molecules into membranes with an internal chemistry different from their surroundings

The formation of closed membranes is believed to be an early and important event in the origin of cellular life. Closed membrane vesicles form spontaneously from lipids and can maintain different chemical compositions between the intracellular compartment and the extra cellular compartment (surroundings). This allowed for the development of an internal cellular metabolism *(see Topic D.1.6)*.

OPTION

TOK   Can the investigation of the origin of life be scientific?

Although experiments have been done to investigate the history of the evolution of life on Earth, it can be argued that these are purely speculative and have little value. The difficulty of the enormity of the time that has passed since life began, leads to countless critical presumptions being made in such investigations. The philosopher Karl Popper argued that a hypothesis is not scientific if it cannot be shown to be false. This concept of a case where the hypothesis is not supported leads scientists to modify or change their hypothesis in the light of data generated. This criterion is helpful in determining the difference between science and pseudo-science. Some investigations into the history of life on Earth run the risk of not being falsifiable, making their Scientific value questionable.

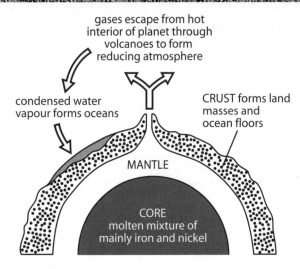

Figure 1501   Structure of the planet Earth

> **D.1.2**   Outline the experiments of Miller and Urey into the origin of organic compounds.
>
> ©IBO 2007

A variety of Scientific evidence strongly suggests that the Earth was formed about five thousand million years ago from a cloud of dust particles surrounding the Sun. As the mass of the developing planet increased, heat generated by the force of gravity and radioactive decay caused the interior to melt, producing a dense metallic core, composed of iron and nickel. This was surrounded by a cooler liquid mantle. On top of the mantle is the crust which has solidified and formed the continents and the sea floor. During the cooling of the crust gases from the hot interior escaped through volcanoes, forming an atmosphere that probably contained hydrogen, water vapour, methane, ammonia, nitrogen and hydrogen sulfide. This mixture of gases lacked oxygen and was termed a **reducing atmosphere.** The term reducing atmosphere refers to the atmospheric condition on Earth prior to the origin of life when molecular oxygen was absent and reducing agents (hydrogen containing compounds) were present.

Many of the chemicals needed as monomers for the synthesis of biological molecules are thought to have been formed in the shallow waters of the oceans as the products of chemical reactions between simple inorganic compounds present in the atmosphere and water. This mixture of chemicals believed to be present in the oceans is known as primeval soup or simply 'chemical soup'.

Miller and Urey's experiments conducted in 1953 simulated the conditions, believed at the time, to be present on the early Earth. They attempted to establish whether **chemical evolution** could occur in primeval soup. Chemical evolution refers to the pre-biological changes that transformed simple atoms and molecules into the more complex chemicals needed for the origin of life.

The experiments used water, H_2O, methane, CH_4, ammonia, NH_3 and hydrogen, H_2. The chemicals were sealed inside sterile glass tubes and flasks connected together in a loop, with one flask containing water and another with a pair of electrodes. The water was heated to produce steam and sparks were produced between the electrodes to simulate lightning. The mixture was cooled so that the water could condense and trickle back into the first flask in a continuous cycle.

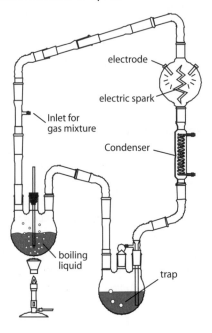

Figure 1502   Miller and Urey's Apparatus

At the end of a week of continuous operation Miller and Urey observed that up to fifteen percent of the carbon was present in the form of organic compounds. Thirteen of the twenty naturally occurring amino acids were detected. Later other researchers found that amino acids could be synthesised from hydrogen cyanide, HCN. They also detected a high concentration of the nucleotide base, adenine.

TOK   Did molecules arise like this naturally?

The Urey-Miller experiments demonstrated that organic compounds could be produced in conditions thought to have been present on the pre-biotic Earth. The experiments were falsifiable, in that they tested Oparin and Haldane's hypothesis that organic compounds were produced in the pre-biotic Earth's atmosphere. If the experiments were unsuccessful, a new explanation for the production of organic compounds on the early Earth would have to have been found. However, a demonstration that they could have been produced under such conditions is not evidence that they were. The experimental conclusions stand because they have not been falsified, though many presumptions were made in their design, some of which have since been questioned. These experiments, do however act as a stepping-stone upon which other investigations may be built.

> **D.1.3   State that comets may have delivered organic compounds to Earth.**
>
> ©IBO 2007

Panspermia is the hypothesis that life on Earth may have originated by the introduction of complex organic chemicals or even bacteria via comets.

A comet is a small body in the solar system that orbits the Sun and occasionally exhibits a tail resulting from solar radiation upon the comet's nucleus, which itself is composed of rock, dust, and ice. Recent evidence suggests that some bacteria and archaebacteria *(see Topic F.1.4)* are very resistance to extreme conditions and may be able to survive for long periods of time, even perhaps in deep space. Semi-dormant bacteria found in ice cores deep beneath Antarctica suggest that bacterial endospores might survive on the surface of icy comets.

Cosmic radiation in deep space may provide the energy to form complex organic molecules. Spectra of comets reveal the presence of hydrocarbons, amino acids and peptides. Comets are covered by a dark tar-like layer formed when simple carbon compounds are exposed to ultraviolet radiation. A shower of comets about four thousand million years ago could have introduced complex organic molecules and water to the Earth and initiated chemical evolution.

> **D.1.4   Discuss possible locations where conditions would have allowed the synthesis of organic compounds.**
>
> ©IBO 2007

One of the difficulties faced by the chemical soup theory is to explain how amino acids and nucleotides polymerised to form proteins and nucleic acids. In an aqueous environment hydrolysis of polymers is favoured. In addition, the Miller-Urey experiment produces many substances that would prevent polymerisation.

Some researchers believe that the first cellular organisms evolved inside black smokers located on seafloors. They are a type of **hydrothermal vent** where superheated water from the Earth's crust enters the ocean floor. It is rich in dissolved sulfides which crystallise to form a black chimney around each vent. The vents may have provided a suitable environment for the formation and concentration of biological polymers.

Figure 1503   A 'black smoker"

Volcanoes may have also played an important role in the origin of life by fixing nitrogen *(see Topic F.2.1.)*. Researchers have measured the composition of gases above hot lava lakes and found that there was a higher than average level of fixed nitrogen. Volcanoes may have been as important as lightning in fixing nitrogen for use by the earliest bacteria. Volcanoes under the sea bed or on land may have also provided a suitable environment for chemical evolution to occur.

An alternative to **abiogenesis** (generation of life from chemicals) on Earth is the hypothesis that primitive life may have originally formed extra terrestrially, either in space or on a nearby planet, for example, Mars. Organic compounds are relatively common in space, especially in the outer solar system where they are not evaporated by solar heating.

An alternative hypothesis is the suggestion that life originated on Mars. Due to its smaller size Mars cooled down more quickly which might have allowed **prebiotic evolution** to occur while the Earth was too hot. Crustal material was later blasted from the surface of Mars by the asteroid and comet impacts. Evolution on Mars may have stopped when it lost its atmosphere due to low volcanic activity. There is little direct evidence for this extraterrestrial hypothesis, but Martian meteorites (possibly containing remains of fossilised bacteria) have been found in Antarctica.

The extraterrestrial hypothesis does not address the issue of how life first originated but shifts it to a planet or comet. However, the advantage is that primitive life or complex organic compounds are only required to have occurred once in a single location and then spread through the galaxy by comets or meteorites.

| D.1.5 | Outline two properties of RNA that would have allowed it to play a role in the origin of life. |
| | ©IBO 2007 |

A number of researchers believe that RNA may have played an important role in the origin of life by acting as the first molecule capable of replication. The **RNA World hypothesis** is supported by RNA's ability to behave like DNA and store, transmit, and replicate genetic information.

Ribozymes are naturally occurring small sequences of RNA that can act as enzymes, either on themselves or other RNA molecules. A range of artificial ribozymes have been chemicallly synthesised and some have been shown to perform some of the reactions of RNA replication such as polymerising nucleotides using ATP. Artificial or modified naturally occurring ribozymes can also be made to cleave chemical bonds including peptide bonds.

The ribosome (*see Topic 7.4.2.*) itself appears to be a ribozyme: the formation of the peptide bond is catalysed

by the ribosomal RNA. The function of the proteins in the ribosome appears to be purely structural. These findings suggest that RNA molecules were perhaps capable of generating the first proteins. Eventually RNA was replaced by DNA and enzymes to take over the storage of genetic information and enzymatic functions.

Evolution via natural selection can only occur on molecules that exhibit the properties of variation and heredity. Variation means that in a population of RNA molecules there are a number of molecules with different base sequences. Heredity, in this context, refers to the process by which an RNA molecule can undergo replication and produce copies or slightly modified copies of itself. Mutation refers to the situation where a mistake occurs during heredity and a mutated RNA molecule with a different base sequence is generated. Figure 1504 illustrates the concepts of heredity and variation due to mutation, where A, B and C represent different RNA sequences.

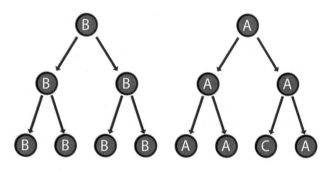

Figure 1504   Concepts of heredity and variation

| D.1.6 | State that living cells may have been preceded by protobionts, with an internal chemical environment different from their surroundings. |
| | ©IBO 2007 |

Over millions of years, the complexity of organic compounds in the primeval soup gradually increased. In warm concentrated solutions the amino acids, monosaccharides and nucleotides would have undergone a process of polymerisation. This may have occurred in shallow rock pools, particularly those where organic compounds had accumulated by adsorption on to the surface of clay particles. A more radical suggestion originating with A. G. Cairns Smith is that silicates were capable of replication and heredity. They were later replaced with nucleic acids, most likely RNA.

It is also believed that large aggregations of polymeric molecules called coacervate droplets occurred spontaneously. They can be prepared by dissolving gelatin (a protein) and gum arabic (a polysaccharide) in water. They can also be prepared from proteins and nucleic acids. When protein **coacervates** are heated in water to 130 - 180 °C they form a boundary which resembles a cell membrane, although it lacks phospholipids. They can also grow by absorbing protein from the surrounding solution and then splitting when a certain size is reached.

Experiments have shown that artificially prepared coacervate droplets containing enzymes could absorb and concentrate substrate molecules and release the products into the external solution. For example, phosphorylase has been shown to catalyse the polymerisation of glucose phosphate to form starch *(see Figure 1506)*. Later experiments showed that chlorophyll could be incorporated into coacervate droplets. They were able to absorb an oxidised dye and return it in a reduced form to the surrounding solution. However, the lack of any Biological mechanism by which coacervates can reproduce prevents them being classified as cells.

The first precursors to cells, known as **protobionts**, may have evolved from coacervate droplets which contained polynucleotides (DNA or more likely RNA). RNA molecules may have evolved the ability to direct the assembly of amino acids into proteins. Once a simple genetic code was established this allowed the coacervate to perform the major processes of life. Presumably, a primitive process of enzyme-controlled binary fission evolved. The first true cells are believed to have been heterotrophic and anaerobic.

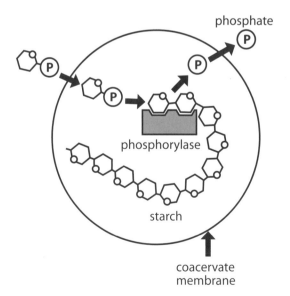

Figure 1505   The formation of starch in a coacervate

Microspheres are related to coacervates. They are formed in the laboratory when mixtures of pure, dry amino acids are heated at about 175 °C for six hours. The product is stirred

with hot water and the insoluble material removed. When the solution cools small protein globules form composed of peptides. Microspheres exhibit catalytic properties and like coacervates can undergo simple division and split to form two coacervates. Microspheres and coacervates may represent an important link or intermediate between the primordial chemical environment and true cells.

D.1.7   Outline the contribution of prokaryotes to the creation of an oxygen-rich atmosphere.

©IBO 2007

Small amounts of oxygen were first produced by the action of ultraviolet radiation on water vapour. Atmospheric oxygen is also indirectly damaging since it reacts with water to form traces of hydrogen peroxide. This is a strong oxidising agent and degrades lipids and nucleic acids. The gradual accumulation of oxygen selected for organisms which synthesised protective enzymes, for example, catalase which converts hydrogen peroxide into water and oxygen.

A major transition in evolution occurred when bacteria evolved containing a form of chlorophyll that allowed a simple form of oxygenic photosynthesis to occur. There was then an explosive rise in oxygen levels known as the oxygen catastrophe. Geological evidence suggests that oxygenic photosynthesis, such as that in cyanobacteria *(see Topic F.5.5)* became important around two billion years ago.

The release of oxygen by cyanobacteria had an irreversible effect on the subsequent evolution of life. The remaining organic chemicals in the 'chemical soup' in the oceans were broken down into carbon dioxide and oxidised sediments. In addition a layer of ozone, O_3, began to form in the upper atmosphere. This acted as a barrier to the penetration of ultra-violet radiation from the Sun. The production of new organic chemicals in the 'chemical soup' was thereby blocked.

D.1.8   Discuss the endosymbiotic theory for the origin of eukaryotes.

©IBO 2007

The differences between eukaryotes and prokaryotes were discussed in *Topics 2.2 and 2.3*. Eukaryotes have a considerably more complex structure and appear much later in the fossil record than prokaryotes. However, despite structural differences they share many biochemical pathways, for example, glycolysis *(see Topic 3.7.2)* and the light reactions of photosynthesis.

OPTION

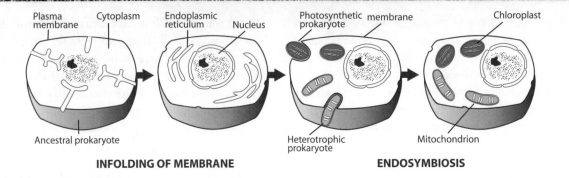

Figure 1506   The endosymbiosis theory

The **endosymbiotic theory** suggests that chloroplasts and mitochondria are derived from free living prokaryote ancestors. They were engulfed by larger prokaryotes but survived inside the cytoplasm and gradually evolved into the chloroplast and mitochondrion.

Mitochondria are believed to have evolved from **proteobacteria** and chloroplasts from cyanobacteria *(see Topic F.5.5.). See Figure 1506.*

Listed below is the main evidence that supports the endosymbiotic theory:

- Both organelles contain DNA that is different from the nucleus and is similar to bacteria.
- Both organelles are surrounded by two membranes which resemble the composition of a prokaryote cell.
- New organelles are formed by a process that resembles bacterial binary fission *(see Topic 1).*
- The internal structure and biochemistry of chloroplasts is very similar to that of cyanobacteria.

Age / years x 10⁶	Animal groups	Plant groups
2	Origin of humans	
	Adaptive radiation of mammals	
	Extinction of dinosaurs; origin of modern fish and placental mammals	Dominance of flowering plants (angiosperms)
195	Dinosaurs dominant; origin of birds and mammals; insects abundant	Origin of flowering plants
225	Dinosaurs appear; adaptive radiation of reptiles	Abundance of conifers and cycads
280	Adaptive radiation of reptiles; extinction of trilobites	Origin of conifers
350	Origin of reptiles and insects; adaptive radiation of amphibians	Ferns, club mosses and horsetails
400	Origin of amphibians; spiders appear, adaptive radiation of fish (bony and cartilaginous eg sharks)	Earliest mosses and ferns
440	Origin of jawed fish; earliest coral reefs	Earliest spore-bearing plants with vascular tissue
500	Origin of vertebrates, jawless fish, trilobites abundant, adaptive radiation of molluscs	
570	Origin of all non-vertebrate phyla	
1000	Primitive sponges	
2000	Primitive eukaryotes	
3000	Blue-green bacteria, eubacteria	
3500	Origin of life	
5000	Origin of Earth	

Figure 1507 (a)   Geological time scale and history of life

- DNA sequence analysis suggests that plant nuclear DNA contains genes that had previously been part of the chloroplast.

- Some proteins encoded in the nucleus are transported to the two organelles. The two organelles have smaller genomes than bacteria. This is consistent with an increased dependence on the eukaryotic host after forming an endosymbiosis. The majority of genes on the genomes of the chloroplast and mitochondria have been lost or transferred to the nucleus. Most of the proteins that comprise these organelles are encoded by genes in the nucleus.

- The ribosomes of the organelles closely resemble those found in bacteria (70S).

Figures 1507 (a) shows the geological time scale and Figures 1507 (b) shows the summary of the major events that may have occured during the origin of life on Earth.

TOK   Is the hypothesis falsifiable?

It could be argued that scientific theories should only be applied to explanations of current events, not those of the past, upon which we may speculate, but never know what occurred. Some experiments to investigate support for Oparin and Haldane's hypothesis could possibly be carried out elsewhere in the universe. The planet Mars may used to test some simple hypotheses in this area in the not too distant future. Results from such experiments may give insight into our understanding of the possible origin of life on Earth, but they would not be conclusive. On their own, they may be falsifiable and valid, allowing further predictions to be made. In this sense, they are scientific, but we must limit the conclusions that we draw from their results.

Atmosphere of carbon dioxide, methane, hydrogen, ammonia and water on the Earth soon after its formation. Lighter gases, for example, hydrogen are gradually lost.

↓

Simple organic molecules such as amino acids, adenine and ribose are formed by chemical synthesis

↓

The primordial 'soup' of organic molecules floating on the oceans is concentrated in various possible locations, for example, hydrothermal vents

↓

Simple organic molecules are polymerised and coacervates and microspheres are formed

↓

Enzymes catalyse further polymerisation and coacervates increase in size, and then break up into smaller coacervates

↓

Lipid layers form around coacervates which contain self-replicating molecules, initially RNA and then later DNA. Protein synthesis develops.

↓

Primitive anaerobic prokaryotic cells evolve

↓

Oxygen producing anaerobic autotrophs evolve; the ozone layer forms and chemical evolution ceases

↓

Aerobic prokaryotic cells develop

↓

Eukaryotic cells develop via a process of endosymbiosis

↓

Colonial forms, for example, slime moulds develop

↓

Multicellular organisms evolve from colonial organisms

↓

Adaptive radiation gives rise to numerous different species including some capable of colonising land

Figure 1507 (b)   Summary of the major events that may have occured during the terrestrial origin of life

OPTION

D.2 SPECIES AND SPECIATION

D.2.1	Define allele frequency and gene pool.
	©IBO 2007

The physical characteristics in an organism are influenced by one or more genes together with the effects of the environment. Several forms of each gene may exist and these are termed alleles. The **allele frequency** is a measurement of the proportion of all copies of that gene that exist in that allelic form in that population.

A **gene pool** is the total collection of alleles present in a sexually reproducing population. Gene pools constantly change: mutations are always occurring and introducing new genes into the gene pool. Alleles that confer a disadvantage are removed from the gene pool by natural selection.

For example, in humans the frequency of a dominant allele is 99%. The recessive allele (at the same locus) has a frequency of 1%. Hence the dominant allele frequency is 0.99 and the recessive allele frequency is 0.01. Since the total population represents 100% or 1.0 it can be seen that:

dominant allele frequency + recessive allele frequency = 1
(This expression is only true if there are only two alleles in the population).
0.99 + 0.01 = 1

The convention in Mendelian genetics is that the dominant allele would be represented by A and the recessive allele represented by a. In this example, the frequency of A equals 0.99 and a equals 0.01.

D.2.2	State that evolution involves a change in allele frequency in a population's gene pool over a number of generations.
	©IBO 2007

A population whose gene pool shows directional change from one generation to the next is undergoing an evolutionary process.

New combinations of alleles produce unique genotypes which, when expressed as phenotypes, experience natural selection which determines which genes are passed on to the next generation.

There are three main types of selection: stabilising selection, directional selection and disruptive selection *(see Topic D.2.9.).*

D.2.3	Discuss the definition of the term species.
	©IBO 2007

The term **species** may be defined in a number of ways and a number of these are summarised in Figure 1508 However, the most widely used definition is the genetic definition where the individuals of a species form a single gene pool.

Biological aspect	Definition
Breeding	A group of organism capable of interbreeding and producing fertile offspring
Ecological	A group of organisms sharing the same ecological niche; no two species can share the same ecological niche
Genetic	A group of organisms showing identical genetic karyotype
Evolutionary	A group of organisms sharing a unique collection of structural and functional characteristics
Cladistic	A group of organisms that shares an ancestor (see Topic D.5.5.). At some point in the progress of such a group, members may diverge from one another: when such a divergence becomes sufficiently clear, the two populations are regarded as separate species.

Figure 1508   Definitions of a species

It should be noted that, unlike other groups used for classification *(see Topic D.5.),* for example, class and genus, species are real biological units. The individuals which form a species have a relationship which is different from that between other taxonomic groups, for example, genus and kingdom.

Many extinct organisms are known only as fossils *(see Topic D.3.7)* which generally only preserve some features. Fossils cannot indicate which organisms bred with which other organism, and cannot suggest whether any of the resulting offspring would have been fertile. Hence Biologists generally use either the morphological or the cladistic definition of species. Biologists also have to cope with the evolution of species: a species may gradually or rapidly evolve into one or several species via a series of intermediate forms.

The genetic definition of species applies well to many multicellular organisms, but there are situations where it is not applicable.

- It only applies to sexually reproducing organisms and cannot be applied to single-celled organisms *(see Topic F.1.9.)*.

- Some hybrids, for example, mules and tigrons *(see Topic D.2.4.)*, cannot mate with one of their own kind, for example, a mule with a mule, but sometimes produce offspring when mated with members of one of the parent species, for example, a ligron with a liger.

- In a **ring species** members of adjacent populations interbreed successfully but members of widely separated populations do not. A ring species has an almost continuous set of intermediates between two distinct species, and these intermediates happen to be arranged in a ring. At most points in the ring, there is only one species; but there are two where the end-points meet. The variation within a single species has produced differences as large as those between two separate species.

  For example: the herring and lesser black-backed gulls in northern Europe: while they are two reproductively isolated species, there is a continuous set of interbreeding forms between them.

  The existence of ring species is a powerful argument against the belief that members of one species can not evolve to become different from other individuals via natural selection to form two separate non-interbreeding species.

- It may be a physically impossible for members of the same species to mate, for example, large and small breeds of the dog (*Canis familiaris*).

D.2.4	Describe three examples of barriers between gene pools.

©IBO 2007

GENETIC ISOLATION

Genetic isolation is the commonest requirement for speciation. Geographical isolation of two populations of individuals may result in the accumulation of different allele frequencies and they may eventually behave as a separate species because of genetic incompatability. The mechanisms for maintaining genetic isolation between populations of one species are known as reproductive isolating mechanisms. **Prezygotic isolation** means that zygotes are not formed because gametes do not meet and fertilise. However, if zygotes are formed, they may not develop as a result of **postzygotic isolation**. A summary classification of isolating mechanisms is shown in Figure 1509.

Prezygotic mechanisms (barriers to the formation of hybrids)	
Temporal isolation	Occurs where two species mate or flower at different times of the year
Ecological isolation	Occurs where two species inhabit similar regions, but occupy different habitats.
Behavioural isolation	Occurs where animals exhibit courtship patterns, mating only results if courtship display by one sex results in acceptance by the other sex.
Mechanical isolation	Occurs in animals where differences in the genitals prevent successful copulation and in plants where related species of flowers are pollinated by different animals.
Postzygotic mechanisms (barriers affecting hybrids)	
Hybrid inviability	Hybrids are produced but fail to develop to maturity
Hybrid infertility	Hybrids fail to produce functional gametes
Hybrid breakdown	The F1 hybrids are fertile but the F2 generation and backcrosses between hybrids and parental stocks fail to develop or are infertile.

Figure 1509   A summary of isolating mechanisms

TEMPORAL ISOLATION

In California in the United States *Pinus radiata* (Monterey pine) flowers in February, whereas *Pinus attenuata* (knob cone pine) flowers in April. The Knobcone pine may hybridise with the Bishop pine and the Monetery Pine. In North America, four frog species of the genus Rana differ in the time of their peak breeding activity, *see Figure 1510*.

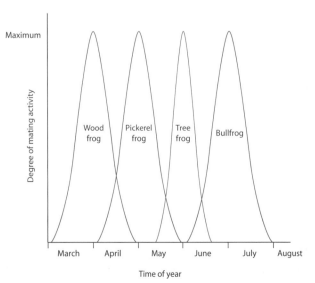

Figure 1510   Seasonal reproductive isolation

ECOLOGICAL ISOLATION

This is not very common in animals but is widespread among plants. Closely related species often differ significantly in their flowering seasons, or in their requirements for soil type or climate. For example, the sea campion, *Silene maritima*, grows on rocky beaches, while the bladder campion, *Silene vulgaris*, grows in meadows. Breeding between the species is rare, even though the hybrids formed are fertile. Another example of ecological isolation is provided by the genus Viola: *Viola arvensis* grows on soils rich in calcium carbonate, whereas *Viola tricolor* prefers acidic soils. The lion and tiger had overlapping ranges in India until 150 years ago, but the lion lived in open grassland and the tiger in forest. Consequently, the two species did not hybridise in nature (although they sometimes do in zoos to form 'tigrons' and 'ligers').

BEHAVIOURAL ISOLATION

A wide range of behavioural mechanisms have evolved which help to keep species separate. A number of animals utilise chemical stimuli to bring the mating partners together. Many female moths release small amounts of sexual pheromones. These secretions are released into the air and are detected by the antennae of the males. Each species of moth produces its own distinctive pheromone.

Auditory and visual signals may also play an important role in maintaining reproductive isolation. A number of insects, for example, crickets and cicadas, seek out males, which produce characteristic species-specific songs. The sounds are produced when one part of the body is rubbed rapidly against another. Bird songs also serve similar functions, but are also involved in defending territory.

HYBRID INVIABILITY

Hybrids formed from the fusion of gametes from different species are often sterile because they cannot produce gametes. For example, in a cross between a male horse (2n=64) and a female donkey (2n=62), the resulting mule has 63 chromosomes. The chromosomes do not pair up during meiosis and the mule is sterile.

Geographical isolation is also thought to have played an important role as a powerful isolating mechanism and hence a force for speciation *(see Topic D.2.6)*. Darwin observed the effects of geographical isolation when he visited the Galapagos Islands which lie in the Pacific Ocean several hundred kilometres to the west of South America.

John Gould (Ornithologist at London Zoo) noted from Darwin's specimens that there were thirteen birds called finches, a number of which are unique and not found on the mainland of South America. The species of birds, now known as **Darwin's finches**, can be distinguished by their feeding habits and the shape of their beaks. Some species eat seeds, others feed on cacti, some feed on insects and some on a mixture of foods. *See Figure 1511.*

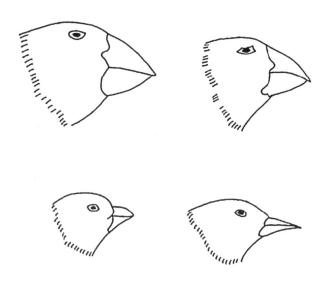

Figure 1511   Types of Darwin's finches

Darwin suggested that soon after the Galapagos Islands were formed by an undersea volcanic eruption, seed-eating finches flew across from South America and small groups colonised the islands. The finch population then experienced mutation and natural selection. A number of different species evolved which are adapted to the different environments of the islands. The ancestral finches were geographically isolated from the South American finches and from each other. Eventually, fourteen new species evolved from a single species which originally migrated to the islands. This is called adaptive radiation *(see Topic D.2.7)*.

> **D.2.5   Explain how polyploidy can contribute to speciation.**
>
> ©IBO 2007

POLYPLOIDY

Polyploidy is the condition of some organisms whose cells contain more than two homologous sets of chromosomes. Polyploid types are termed according to the number of chromosome sets in the nucleus: triploid (three sets; 3×), tetraploid (four sets; 4×), pentaploid (five sets; 5×), hexaploid (six sets; 6×) and so on. Polyploidy is well tolerated in many species of plants.

OPTION

Polyploidy is a form of sympatric speciation *(see Topic D.2.6.)*. Polyploidy does not add new genes to the gene pool, but gives rise to new combinations of genes. Polyploidy may involve a single organism or a process of hybridisation between organisms of different species. Polyploidy is common in higher plants and between one third to half of all angiosperms (flowering plants) are polyploid. Molecular biology studies have revealed that after polyploidy formation very rapid changes in gene structure and gene expression can occur.

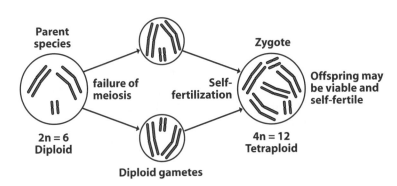

Figure 1512 (a)   The process of polyploidisation

The relatively rare survival of polyploids among animals is because the increased number of chromosomes in polyploids makes normal gamete formation during meiosis extremely improbable. In addition polyploidy would disrupt the pairing of the sex chromosomes which occurs in insects, birds and mammals. This is not an issue in plants since they lack separate sexes. In addition, most animals cannot self fertilise (exceptions include nematodes) or reproduce asexually (exceptions include ciliates) and hence it is a relatively rare form of speciation in animals. However, polyploidy occurs in some animals, such as goldfish, salamaders and salmon. *See Figure 1512 (a).*

Since many plants are capable of asexual reproduction they are able to reproduce despite being polyploid. Polyploidy

is often associated with increased size, hardiness and resistance to disease. This is termed **hybrid vigour**. Many cultivated forms, for example, wheat, are polyploids producing large fruits, storage organs, leaves and flowers. Many species of common garden flowers, for example, tulips, crocuses, irises and primroses have been created by an artificial process of fertilisation. The chemical colchicine is used to induce polyploidy by blocking formation of the spindle.

There are two forms of polyploidy:

- autopolyploidy
- allopolyploidy

Autopolyploidy

Autopolyploidy may occur naturally or artificially as a result of an increase in the number of chromosomes within the same species. For example, if chromosomes undergo replication and the chromatids separate but the cytoplasm fails to cleave, a tetraploid (4n) cell is produced from a diploid cell. The amount of cytoplasm in the tetraploid cells increases to maintain the ratio of the nucleus to the cytoplasm size. This leads to an increase in the size of the entire plant or a specific part of it. Colchicine, extracted from the corm of the autumn crocus (*Colchicum*), can be used to induce autopolyploidy. *See Figure 1512 (b).*

Autopolyploids that have an odd number of sets of chromosomes, for example triploid or pentaploid, are usually sterile because during prophase I of meiosis, three homologues may pair up (synapsis). Disjunction at anaphase can result in variable numbers of chromosomes in the gametes. Another possibility is two of the three homologues synapse and the third does not synapse at all. This also leads to unbalanced gametes.

Those organisms that have an even number of sets, for example tetraploid or hexaploid, will have an even number

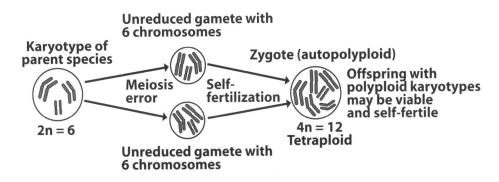

1512 (b)   Autopolyploidy

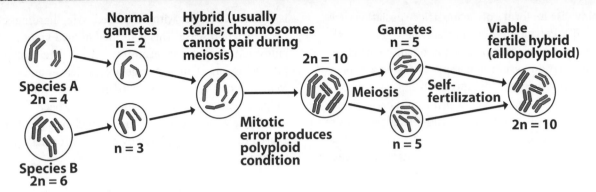

1512(c)   Allopolyploidy

of homologues synapsis, and have a better probability of introducing the same number of chromosomes to each gamete.

A modified form of polyploidy can occur in animals and give rise to tissues and cells which are polyploidy. This process is termed **endomitosis** and involves chromosome replication without cell division.

Allopolyploidy

This form of polyploidy arises when the chromosome number in a sterile hybrid becomes doubled and produces fertile hybrids. F_1 hybrids produced from different species are usually sterile since their chromosomes cannot form homologous pairs during meiosis. This is termed hybrid sterility. However, if multiples of the original haploid number of chromosomes for example, 2 ($n_1 + n_2$), 3 ($n_1 + n_2$) etc, (where n_1 and n_2 represent the haploid numbers of the parent species) occur, a new species is produced which is fertile with polyploids that genetically resemble itself. However, it is infertile with both parental species. *See Figure 1512 (c).*

D.2.6	Compare allopatric and sympatric speciation

©IBO 2007

Speciation is the process by which one or more species arise from previously existing species. A single species may give rise to a new species (intraspecific speciation), or two different species may give rise to a new species (inter-specific hybridisation). If intraspecific speciation occurs whilst the populations are physically separated it is termed allopatric speciation. If the process of speciation occurs while the populations are occupying the same geographical area or range it is termed sympatric speciation.

Allopatric speciation occurs when a geographical barrier, for example, a mountain range, sea or river produces a barrier to gene flow because of spatial separation. The

inability of organisms to meet and reproduce leads to reproductive isolation *(see Topic D.2.4).* Adaptations to a new environment (or random drift in small populations) leads to changes in allele and genotype frequencies. Prolonged separation of populations for many generations may result in two sub-populations becoming genetically isolated even if the barrier was removed. In other words, speciation can occur through random forces, rather than through the action of natural selection.

Parapatric speciation is discussed in *Topic D.2.9.* It is a form of speciation in which the new species is formed within a single population which is within the ancestral

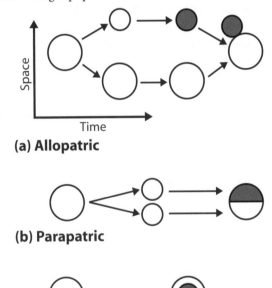

(a) Allopatric

(b) Parapatric

(c) Sympatric

Figure 1513   The three main types of speciation

species' geographical range. Figure 1513 illustrates the three main types of speciation (a) allopatric, (b) parapatric and (c) sympatric speciation.

OPTION

D.2.7 Outline the process of adaptive radiation.

©IBO 2007

When a group of organisms share a homologous structures *(see Topic D.5.6)* which are differentiated to perform a variety of different functions, it illustrates a principle known as **adaptive radiation.** Homologous structures have the same genetic determinants. They should be contrasted with structures which may superficially resemble each other but have risen through convergence; these are 'analogues' *(see Topic D.2.8)* Adaptive radiation occurs within all taxonomic groups, except at the level of the species *(see Topic D.2.3).*

For example, all organisms that belong to a particular taxonomic class share a number of modified features. These variations in shared features adapt them to particular ecological habitats.

For example, the mouthparts of insects consist of the same basic structures: a labrum (upper lip), a pair of mandibles, a hypopharynx (floor of mouth), a pair of maxillae. Insects are able to feed on a variety of different food sources, as shown below, because some of the mouth part structures are enlarged and modified, but others are reduced or even lost. The high degree of adaptive radiation in the insects *(insecta)* has allowed the class to occupy a huge range of ecological niches.

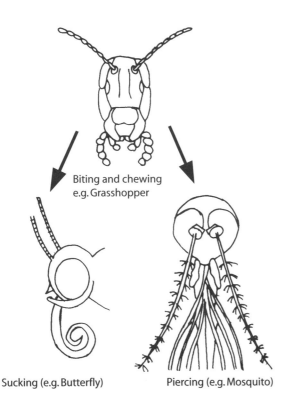

Figure 1514 Adaptive radiation of insect mouthparts

D.2.8 Compare convergent and divergent evolution

©IBO 2007

CONVERGENT EVOLUTION

Convergent evolution describes the process where distantly related organisms evolve similar traits as they adapt to similar environments or ecological niches. Biological adaptations that are the result of convergent evolution are termed analogous structures.

For example, a number of mammals have developed claws and sticky, long tongues that allow them to open ant and termite nests and eat them. These include the four species of ant eater, the African aardvark, the echidna and the Australian numbat.

DIVERGENT EVOLUTION

Divergent evolution occurs when two or more adaptations have a common evolutionary origin, but have diverged over evolutionary time. This is also known as adaptive evolution *(see Topic D.2.7).*

Divergent evolution and convergent evolution are distinct. In the case of divergent evolution, similarity is due to the common origin. In contrast, convergent evolution arises when there is pressure from natural selection toward a similar 'solution', even though the structure or function has evolved independently.

PARALLEL EVOLUTION

Parallel evolution is a type of evolution in which two species maintain the same degree of similarity while each undergoes evolutionary change along an independent path.

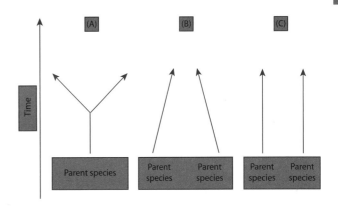

Figure 1515 (A) divergent, (B) convergent and (C) parallel evolution

245

For example, the vertebrate limb is an example of divergent evolution. The limb in many different species has a common origin, but has diverged somewhat in overall structure and function. For example, the forelimbs of a whale are used as paddles, the forelimbs of birds for flight and the hand of humans for grasping and manipulating objects. However, the limbs of all vertebrates develop from the same embryonic tissue and fit a 'common plan' known as the pentadactyl limb *(see Figure 1516)*.

(a)

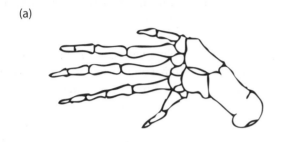

(b)

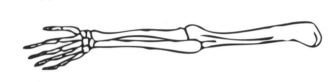

(c)

Figure 1516   The forelimbs of (a) whale, (b) human and (c) bird

D.2.9	Discuss ideas on the pace of evolution including gradualism and punctuated equilibrium.

©IBO 2007

PUNCTUATED EQUILIBRIUM

Punctuated equilibrium claims that many species will show stasis, that is, little or no evolutionary change through much of their geological history. This theory was an attempt to account for many observed gaps in the fossil record.

Punctuated equilibrium claims that rapid evolutionary change occurs during speciation when a species splits into two species. During these punctuation events the rate of change is relatively high.

GRADUALISM

Punctuated equilibrium is contrasted with phyletic **gradualism** which suggests that most evolutionary change at a relatively slow, but not necessarily uniform rate and that one species is gradually transformed into another species.

The theory of punctuated equilibrium suggests that evolution and hence speciation is more likely to occur in a small portion of the population located at the edge of its geographical range. Selective pressure may be higher in the peripheral populations. Favourable genetic variations would spread rapidly in the peripheral populations. These organisms would then spread and replace the other members of the original species. This form of speciation is known as parapatric speciation *(see Topic D.2.6)*.

Consider the fossil record for such an evolutionary event. At the extremes of the geographical range, the complete history, including transitional fossils, might be recorded. However, in the much larger main region the parent species would be observed abruptly followed by a new species. The probability of excavating for fossils in the extremes of the geographical range of the extinct species is remote, hence the chance of finding the transitional fossils is very low.

Figure 1517 shows phylogenetic trees based on the (a) Gradualistic model and (b) Punctuated equilibrium model.

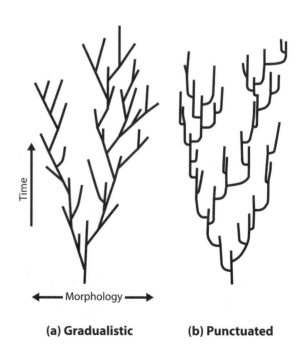

(a) Gradualistic   **(b) Punctuated**

Figure 1517   Models of evolution

The stasis observed in some fossil records may be explained by normalising for a fixed optimum via stabilising selection and punctuation by periods of directional selection.

STABILISING SELECTION

Stabilising selection may operate when environmental conditions are favourable to a particular phenotype and competition is not severe. This form of selection occurs in all populations and tends to eliminate extreme phenotypes from populations. Stabilising selection does not promote evolutionary change but maintains phenotypic stability within a population.

DIRECTIONAL SELECTION

Directional selection operates in response to gradual changes in the environment *(see Topic D.2.10.)*. It exerts selective pressure to move the mean phenotype towards a new mean. However, once the mean phenotype coincides with the new optimum environmental conditions then stabilising selection will operate.

DISRUPTIVE SELECTION

Disruptive selection occurs when fluctuating conditions within an environment, for example, season and climate, may favour the presence of two phenotypes within a population. Natural selection acting within the population may push the population mean towards the two extremes of the character. This may have the effect of splitting a population into two sub-populations and this may later result in speciation.

The evolution of Darwin's finches *(see Topic D.2. 4.)* on the Galapagos Islands provides an example of disruptive selection. Finches with long beaks and those with short beaks exploited different food sources and gradually evolved into populations of different species. *See Figure 1518.*

Selected fossil records have been carefully examined to establish whether punctuated equilibrium or phyletic gradualism predominate. Punctuated equilibrium patterns of evolution are common in the fossil record, but this may simply be due to the incompleteness of the fossil record *(see Topic D.3.7)*. Hence, the fossil records to be examined should consist of sediments that have been laid down continuously and differences in traits should be measured. Examples of both types of evolutionary change have been found with the punctuated equilibrium model being more common.

Studies of snails in thirteen lineages from Lake Turkana, Kenya showed no change for prolonged periods, with occasional periods of rapid (punctuational) change. The periods of change coincided with changes in the water level. As the level lowered, larger lakes would have fragmented

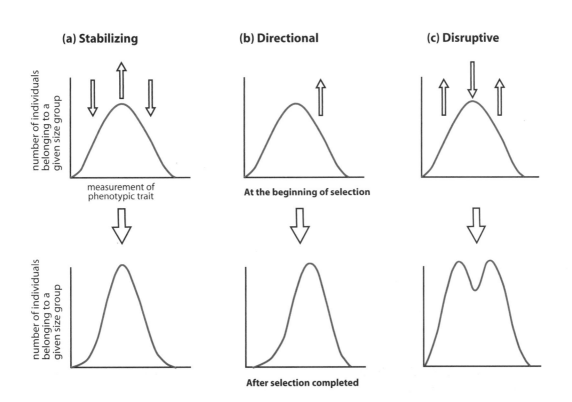

Figure 1518   Actions of stabilising, directional and disruptive selection

into groups of smaller lakes, and the snails would be in many smaller isolated populations.

Specimens of eight lineages of trilobites from Wales have been examined. The average number of pygidial ribs (a feature of the exoskeleton) increased from ten to fourteen and the evolution was gradual and some forms had full ribs and some partially developed ribs. At any given time a population was usually intermediate between the fossil samples before and after it. *See Figure 1519.*

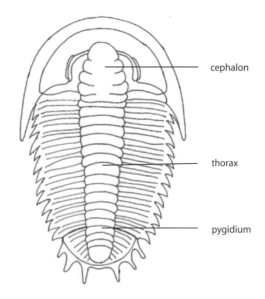

Figure 1519   Trilobite (an extinct arthropod)

However, it should noted that punctuated equilibrium and phyletic gradualism represent extreme models of a continuum.

Figure 1520 shows that Punctuated equilibrium and Phyletic gradualism are two extremes of a continuum.

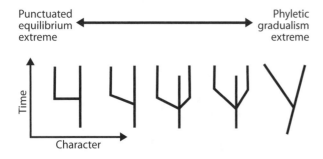

Figure 1520   Extremes of a continuum

The punctuations or rapid periods of evolutionary change, may have been greatly accelerated by major environmental changes in such factors as pressure from predators or parasites, food supply and global climate.

During these times when the environment changes rapidly, natural selection can favour genetic varieties that were previously at a disadvantage. This can result in a high rate of change in the gene pool of gene frequencies that adapt organisms to the new conditions. Strikes by meteors or comets, volcanic eruptions or the beginnings or ends of Ice Ages may have acted as 'triggers' for punctuational events.

A mass extinction even occurs when there is a sharp decrease in the number of species in a relatively short period of time. It may be caused by the extinction of large number of species and/or a dramatic decrease in the rate of speciation. If the numbers of marine animals are plotted against geological time six major extinction events can be observed *(see Figure 1521).*

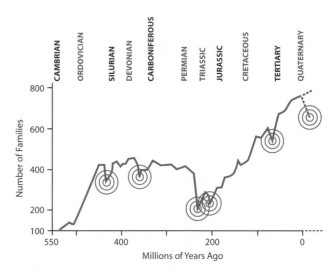

Figure 1521   Plant and animal family loss in six mass extinction events

The most well known of these mass extinction events is the Cretaceous-Tertiary extinction event (K/T event) when about half of all known species became extinct. It may have played an important role in human evolution *(see Topic D.3.5)* since the dinosaurs became extinct which may have allowed mammals to become the dominant vertebrates on land.

In 1980 a team of Physicists discovered that sedimentary rocks at several places around the world laid down at the Cretaceous-Tertiary boundary contain relatively high concentrations of the metal iridium. Meteorites contain

OPTION

a higher level of iridium than the Earth's crust. One consequence of the impact would be a huge dust cloud which would block sunlight and prevent photosynthesis for a number of years. This would account for the extinction of marine and terrestrial plants and the animals that depended on them.

D.2.10   Describe one example of transient polymorphism.

©IBO 2007

Polymorphism or genetic polymorphism plays a significant role in the process of natural selection. It is defined as the existence of two or more forms of the same species within the population. The concept can be applied to biochemical, morphological and behavioural characteristics. There are two forms of genetic polymorphism: transient polymorphism and balanced polymorphism.

A transient polymorphism refers to a polymorphism in which one allele is in the process of displacing another. A polymorphism that is maintained by selection in favor of the heterozygote phenotype, is called a balanced polymorphism.

One of the most famous examples of evolutionary change is the response of moth species to natural selection produced by the atmospheric pollution during the Industrial Revolution. This is known as **industrial melanism** and the most closely studied species is the British peppered moth *Biston betularia*. Until around 1840, all individuals of the species of the moth were creamy-white with black dots and darkly shaded areas.

In 1848 a black form or variety was recorded in Manchester and by 1895, most of the peppered moth population was black. The black or melanic form had presumably occurred in previous populations, due to recurring mutation. However, with the change in the environment it had a strong selective advantage in industrial areas due to its phenotype. The melanic form is due to the presence of a single dominant allele.

The moths fly at night and during the day they rest on the trunks of trees. The wild type form of the moth is very well camouflaged and it merges with the lichens that grown on the trunks. However, the Industrial Revolution resulted in acid rain produced from the sulfur dioxide released from the burning of coal. This killed off the lichens growing on trees in industrial areas. The exposed bark was darkened further by black soot deposits. *Refer to Figure 526* showing peppered moths against various tree trunks.

However, in 1956 Britain passed the Clean Air Act which led to a large reduction in the burning of coal in houses, hence leading to a decrease in air pollution. The numbers of the melanic form have decreased since the passing of the act.

Industrial melanism is an example of selective predation by birds that lie at an extreme of a colour type. It is an example of disruptive selection *(see Topic D.2.9.)* and hence an example of evolutionary change. However, as the two populations overlap and interbreed they are still one species. In order for speciation to occur the two populations would need to become reproductively *(see Topic D.2.4.)* isolated from one another.

To find out if natural selection was the cause of the changed gene frequency, Dr HBD Kettlewell bred a large stock of the two varieties of the peppered moth, which were marked and then released in two areas.

- in a polluted town where over 90% of the indigenous peppered moth population was the black variety, and
- in an unpolluted area in the countryside where none of the peppered moths was black

He observed and filmed insect-eating birds feeding in the two localities. The birds heavily predated the on the variety of the moth which was not camouflaged by its background. Kettlewell also recaptured the surviving marked moths *(see Figure 1522)*. The carefully conducted experimental fieldwork confirmed that natural selection was the cause of the increase in frequency of the gene for melanism or blackness among peppered moths in industralised areas. Industrial melanism has also been observed in many other species of moth in Britain, Europe and the United States.

	Non-melanic	Melanic
Unpolluted		
Released	496	473
Recaptured	62	30
Percentage recaptured	13%	6%
Polluted		
Released	137	447
Recaptured	18	123
Percentage recaptured	13%	28%

Figure 1522   Data for the peppered moth in two localities in the United Kingdom

249

Strong natural selective pressures have also been observed in populations of pathogenic bacteria and malarial mosquitoes. Mutation and natural selection have favoured strains of bacteria resistant to antibiotics and malarial mosquitoes resistant to insecticides, such as DDT *(See Topic F).*

> D.2.11 Describe sickle-cell anemia as an example of balanced polymorphism.
>
> ©IBO 2007

Balanced polymorphism occurs when two different forms or varieties coexist in the same population in a stable environment. The human condition of **sickle-cell anaemia** is an example of a mutation that causes substitution. The mutation affects a single base in one of the genes encoding hemoglobin. Specifically, the base sequence of the codon for a single amino acid in the beta protein chains gives rise to the production of sickle-cell hemogobin (denoted by HbS). The amino acid sequences for the normal and abnormal beta chains differ in the substitution of the amino acid valine for glutamic acid in the abnormal or mutant polypeptide chains of hemogobin S.

However, the replacement of a polar or hydrophilic amino acid by a non-polar or hydrophobic amino acid causes hemoglobin S to crystallise at low oxygen concentrations. Red blood cells containing hemogobin-S are distorted and appear sickle-shaped. The physiological consequence is that the red blood cells carry less oxygen leading to **anaemia**. Homozygous patients (Hb^S Hb^S) suffer from physical weakness and have a higher risk of heart and kidney failure at an early age. They have a lower life expectance.

In the heterozygous condition (Hb Hb^S) patients exhibit a condition called sickle-cell trait. The red blood cells appear normal and only about half of the hemoglobin is abnormal. However, they become sickle-shaped during heavy exercise. This produces only mild anameia and in Africa and Asia it prevents carriers of the trait from contracting malaria. This is because *Plasmodium*, a protozoan (see Topic F. 6.9.), does not have time to complete its life history inside the short lived red blood cells containing the mutant or abnormal hemoglobin (Hb^S). *Refer to Figure 1524.*

Sickle-cell anaemia is an example of **balancing selection** and **balanced polymorphism**. The allele frequency of sickle-cell anaemia is maintained by a mechanism known as heterozygote advantage. The wild type homozygotes suffer malaria and some die. The other homozygotes are severe anaemics and die. The heterozygotes survive and necessarily will produce more of each homozygote in the next generation.

Balancing selection refers to forms of natural selection which work to maintain genetic polymorphisms (or multiple alleles) within a population. A balanced polymorphism occurs when balancing selection within a population is able to maintain stable frequencies of two or more phenotypic forms.

Individuals who are homozygous for the recessive allele at this locus have sickle-cell disease. An individual heterozygous at this locus will not suffer from sickle-cell disease and is resistant to malaria. This resistance is favored by natural selection in tropical regions where malaria is present and so the heterozygote is selected for. Natural selection thus maintains both alleles in the population.

Genotype	Hb^{A}Hb^A	Hb^{A}Hb^S	Hb^{S}Hb^S
Phenotype	Normal	Sickle-cell trait	Sickle-cell anaemia
Type of hemoglobin	Normal	50% normal; 50% mutant	Mutant
Type of red blood cell	Normal	Usually normal, but sickle-shaped at low oxygen concentrations	Sickle-shaped
Oxygen carrying capacity	Normal	Reduced (mild anaemia)	Poor (severe anaemia)
Resistance to malaria	None	Moderate	High

Figure 1524   Comparison of different genotypes of the gene for hemoglobin

D3 HUMAN EVOLUTION

D.3.3	Define half-life.
	©IBO 2007

In 3.1 it was explained that the atoms of some elements exist in a number of **isotopes**, some of which are radioactive. The atoms of radioactive elements release energy in the form of radiation. This process is called radioactive decay and takes place at a constant rate which is independent of physical conditions, such as temperature and pressure. Each radioactive isotope undergoes a different rate of decay. The decay rates of different radioactive isotopes are measured in terms of the **half life**. The half life is the time for half of the radioactive atoms in a sample to undergo decay.

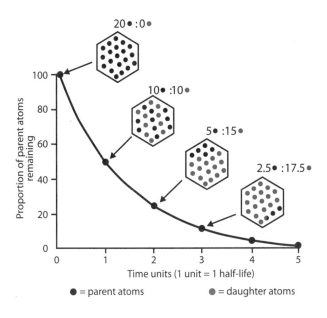

Figure 1525   The concept of half-life for a radioactive isotope

D.3.1	Outline the method for dating rocks and fossils using radioisotopes, with reference to ^{14}C and ^{40}K.
	©IBO 2007

RADIOACARBON DATING

Carbon-12, ^{12}C, is an abundant and non-radioactive isotope of carbon. Carbon-14, ^{14}C, is a radioactive isotope and occurs in trace quantities in air, surface water and living organisms. Carbon-14 is constantly being produced in the atmosphere by the action of cosmic rays on nitrogen and oxygen nuclei.

$^{1}n + {}^{14}N \rightarrow {}^{14}C + {}^{1}p$, where n represents a neutron and p represents a proton

An equilibrium exists between the production of carbon-14 and the loss of carbon-14 by radioactive decay. Carbon-14 is found occurring freely as $^{14}CO_2$ and the ratio of ^{14}C:^{12}C compounds remains constant.

Plants absorb carbon-14 as carbon dioxide and animals absorb carbon-14 containing compounds in their diet. However, at death more carbon is taken in and the carbon-14 continues to decay according to the rate determined by the half life. By calculating the amount of carbon-14 in the dead organism and comparing it with the amount of carbon-14 in a living organism, the age of the dead organism can be estimated.

For example, if the amount of carbon-14 in a fossil mammalian bone was found to be one eight that in the same bone from a recently killed mammal and the half life is 5.6×10^3 years, the estimated age of the fossil bone would be 22.4×10^3 years. Radiocarbon dating can be used to date organic remains fairly accurately for up to 10.0×10^4 years.

Radiocarbon labs generally report an uncertainty, for example, 3000±30BP indicates a standard deviation (see Chapter 1) of 30 radiocarbon years. The maximum range of radiocarbon dating appears to be about 50,000 years, after which the amount of ^{14}C is too low to be distinguished from background radiation. The potassium-argon (K-Ar) decay series is used in dating older objects.

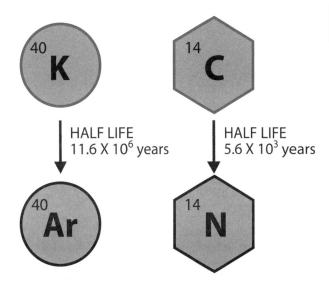

Figure 1526   Radiometric dating techniques

In the potassium-argon dating method, the element potassium (K) contains a small proportion of a radioactive isotope potassium-40. The radioactive isotope decays to give argon-40, a stable isotope of the element argon. The isotope potassium-40 is released in lava from active volcanoes, though at this temperature any argon released at the same time would be lost as gas. The eruption of the volcano effectively sets the clock to zero. The potassium-40 is incorporated into sedimentary deposits where it slowly decays to 40-argon.

The ratio of 40-potassium to 40-argon in the fossil under examination gives an indication of its age. Calculation of the actual age of the fossil is based on the half life of potassium-40 (1.3×10^9 years). Potassium-argon dating has been used mainly for dating materials in volcanic rocks older than one million years. The accuracy of potassium-argon dating is about 50,000 years.

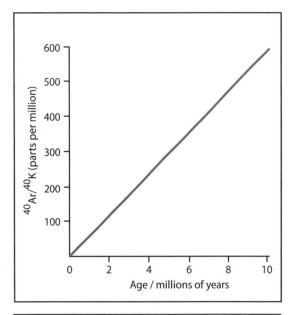

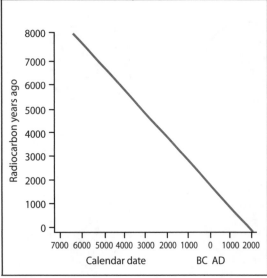

Figure 1527   (a) Potassium argon dating
(b) Radiocarbon dating

D.3.4   Describe the major anatomical features that define humans as primates.

©IBO 2007

Humans belong to the order known as the **primates**. Primates include humans, lemurs, monkeys, gibbons and the apes: orang-utans, gorillas, chimpanzees. Apes and humans are distinguished from the rest of the primates by being tailless and by having the ability to swing their arms freely, around and up and over their heads. Primates exhibit adaptations to life in a forest environment. (However, it should be noted that primates are generalists and hence difficult to define).

FEATURE	DESCRIPTION
Grasping limbs	Opposable thumb with grip for power and precision
Rotating forelimb	The hand can rotate through one hundred and eighty degrees
Stereoscopic vision	Eyes close together on face with parallel optical axes
Visual acuity	Increased numbers of rods/cones with own nerve cells
Reduced olfaction (sense of smell)	Reduced snout allowing flatter face
Enlarged skull	Expanded area for cerebrum, ventral foramen magnum
Large brain	Increased sensory/motor areas, deeply fissured
Few offspring	Longer gestation
Social dependency	Corporate activities, group cohesion

Figure 1528   Characteristics of the order Primates

Primates are adapted to an arboreal or tree dwelling life in a forest environment. However, these also served to pre-adapt human ancestors to exploit the new ecological niches which appeared when the African forests gave way to drier grassland savannas about five million years ago. The term pre-adaptation refers to organisms that have characteristics or traits that fortuitously (that is, by chance) fit an organism for a different habitat or ecological niche.

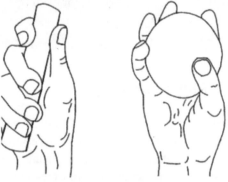

Figure 1529   (a) The power grip and
(b) The precision grip of humans

D.3.5   Outline the trends illustrated by
         the fossils of *Ardipithecus ramidus*,
         Australopithecus including *A. afarensis*
         and *A. africanus,* and *Homo* including
         H. habilis, H. erectus, H. neanderthalensis
         and *H. sapiens.*

©IBO 2007

The study of **human evolution** is an active area of research and is performed by studying fossils and where appropriate the tools of hominids. Few complete skeletons have been found and often only skulls and teeth are left, due to their thickness and hardness. The tools and bones are dated from the age of the rocks they are found in (**relative dating**) and dating the tools and bones directly (absolute dating) *(see Topic D.3.1)* using radioactive dating methods. The summary of hominid evolution shown in Figure 1530 must be regarded as tentative and subject to future revision.

SUMMARY OF THE TRENDS AND

FEATURES DURING HOMINID EVOLUTION

Skulls and brain size

Humans have the largest skull size (in relation to body mass) to other hominids. The enlarged cranium accommodates a larger brain. There has been a relatively rapid increase in cranium size during hominid evolution. The human skull has a protruding jaw and a shortened face. Brow ridges present in other hominids are not present in modern humans (***Homo sapiens***).

In modern humans the eyes are located at the front and the foramen magnum (hole through which the spinal cord goes) is located further forward than in apes. In humans, the **foramen magnum** is located further underneath the head than in the great apes (for example, the gorilla). Hence in humans, the neck muscles do not need to be as

Genus of hominid	Age of appear-ance/ million years ago	Skull and jaws	Brain capacity /cm³	Teeth	Diet	Posture	Distribution	Significance
Ardipithecus ramidus	4.4	Flat jaw	375 - 550	Large upper and lower canines	Fruit, leaves and insects	Possibly bipedal	Specimens found in Ethiopia	Currently the oldest known hominid.
Australopithecus afarensis	4.0	Large jaws	450	Small canines, small incisors, moderately large molars	Herbivore but some meat	Fully erect	South and East Africa	Lived in trees and savanna
Australopithecus africanus	2.5	Ventral foramen	450	Small canines	Carnivore	Fully erect	South and East Africa	Small game hunter
Homo habilis	2.0	Lighter jaw	700	Small canines	Carnivore	Fully erect	South and East Africa	Stone tools, major increase in brain size
Homo erectus	1.5	Thick skull bones, low forehead brow ridges	880	Small canines	Omnivore	Fully erect	Migrated out of Africa about 2.2 million years ago to Asia and Europe	Beginning of cultural evolution, use of fire, rudimentary language *(see Topics D.3.9 and D.3.10).*
Homo neanderthalensis	0.08	Face long and narrow, brow ridges, enlarged nasal cavity	1500	Heavier than modern teeth, wisdom teeth	Omnivore	Fully erect	Europe and Western Asia	Cave dweller, buried their dead, used flint flake tools
Homo sapiens	0.03	Large cranium, shorter skull; reduced jaws	1440	Teeth closer together, wisdom teeth	Omnivore	Fully erect	Earliest specimens found in South Africa, migrated to Asia and Europe	Polyphyletic origin giving rise to geographical races by migration and isolation, cave painting and primitive religion

Figure 1530   A simplified summary of hominid evolution

OPTION

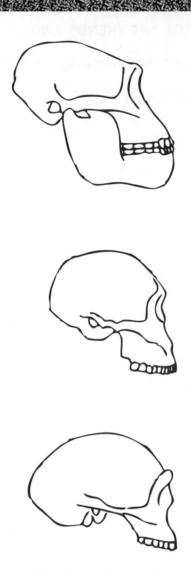

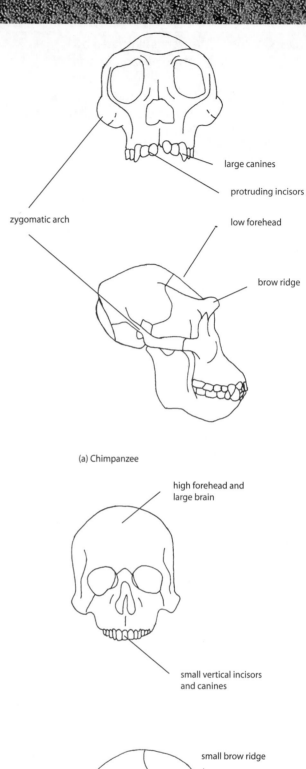

Figure 1531   Skulls showing the transition from
A. Africanus to H.Erectus

robust in order to hold the head upright. Comparisons of the position of the foramen magnum in early hominid species are useful to determine the degree of **bipedality** (the ability to walk upright on two legs).

The evolution of bipedalism is believed to have occurred early in hominid evolution and is believed to have facilitated the enlargement of the brain. Bipedalism also allowed hominids to carry objects and gave them increased height and range of vision.

Teeth and jaws

The U-shaped jaw of ancestral hominids has been replaced by a more V-shaped jaw in modern humans. The large conical canines have been lost and the molars have been reduced.

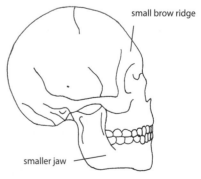

Figure 1532   Comparing the skulls and jaws of chimpanzees and humans

OPTION

254

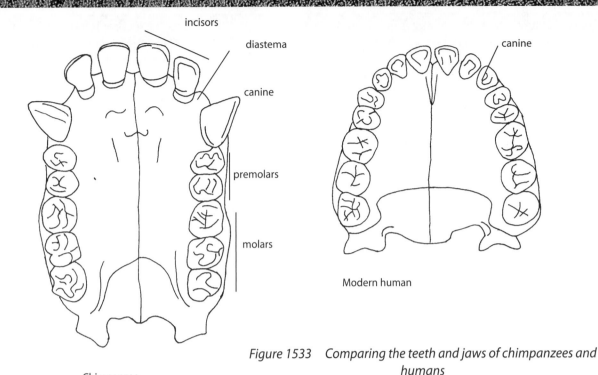

Figure 1533   Comparing the teeth and jaws of chimpanzees and humans

Hands

The modern human hand is prehensile and able to grasp and pick up objects between the thumb and the finger tips. The thumb is opposable so that its tip can touch other fingers, making the thumb joint highly mobile. Humans have relatively long fingers, but gorillas have shorter fingers which allows knuckle walking. The ability of the thumb to rotate, the mobility of the fingers and the ability of the wrist to rotate allow humans to perform a wide variety of precision movements. The palms of the modern human hand are very sensitive and convey large amounts of sensory and tactile information to the brain.

Skeleton, locomotion and posture

The human rib cage is more barrel-shaped than the great apes, because human arms are not used for locomotion. Compared to great apes, the human vertebral column has additional forward curves in the neck and lower back. These help to bring the head and trunk (chest, back and abdomen) above the centre of mass in the upright position.

The human pelvis is broader and lower than that of the great apes. Human legs are longer than their arms so a greater proportion of their body mass and hence their centre of mass is lower. The broad flexible shoulder blade allows free arm rotation during walking. The human femur is angled out towards the knee which allows the knee to be brought under the body. Humans extend their legs fully when walking and the bones of the leg form a straight line.

The big toe is opposable in apes, but non-opposable in humans. This means that humans cannot grasp objects with their big toe. This gives the humans a characteristic footprint an arched foot.

Neoteny

Neoteny is the retention, by adults in a species, of traits seen only in juveniles. In neoteny, the development of an animal or organism is slowed or delayed. This process results in the retention, in the adults of a species, of juvenile physical characteristics well into maturity. Neoteny is believed to have played a role in human evolution and has some support from the fossil record.

Selected list of possible juvenile human characteristics
* Flat face and thin skull bones
* Lack of body hair and pigmentation
* Small teeth
* Prolonged growth period
* Long life span

OPTION

D.3.6   State that, at various stages in hominid evolution, several species may have coexisted.

©IBO 2007

D.3.7   Discuss the incompleteness of the fossil record and the resulting uncertainties about human evolution.

©IBO 2007

Although distinct evolutionary trends can be observed in hominids it does not imply that one hominid evolved directly into the succeeding type. *Homo habilis* co-existed with the various species and forms of australopithecines for approximately 2 million years, before the australopithecines became extinct. *Homo erectus* also co-existed with the later australopithecines. *Homo erectus* was probably a common ancestor to both *Homo sapiens* and to the Neanderthals *(see Figure 1525)*. The co-existence of various hominids is probably due to the different species occupying different ecological niches.

The Neanderthals were probably a side branch of hominid evolution. They were stocky and muscular, with short legs and powerful hands. They were apparently adapted to the cold climate of the Ice Age in Europe. They used a wide range of tools and probably had limited speech. They lived in caves, but also constructed tents with animal skins. They wore skins and used fire. Neanderthals hunted large animals, such as the woolly mammoth, bears, reindeers and horses. Archaeological evidence suggests the presence of community living and the beginnings of religious practices from their burial sites.

The majority of Neanderthals became extinct relatively suddenly perhaps because of competition with *Homo sapiens*. Neanderthal man and *Homo sapiens* overlapped in Europe for half a million years but about forty five thousand years ago the numbers began to decrease significantly. It is possible that there was gene flow and the Neanderthals were absorbed into the *Homo sapiens* linage. Neanderthals are not regarded as a full species by some researchers.

Palaeontology is the study of fossils. Fossils are any form of preserved remains derived from a living organisms. They may include the following: entire organisms, hard skeletal structures, moulds and casts, petrifications, impressions, imprints and coprolites.

The fossil record forms part of the evidence for evolutionary change and supports Darwin's idea that species were not immutable, that is, they undergo change over geological time.

In the fossil record many species appear at an early level or strata of rock and disappear, often abruptly, at a later level. This is interpreted in evolutionary terms at which the species originated and became extinct *(see Topic D.2.9)*. Ecological considerations also match the fossil record, for example, plants appeared on land before animals, and insects appeared before insect-pollinated flowers.

One of the criticisms of using fossils in support of the concept of evolutionary change is the lack of a continuous record and the many gaps or 'missing links'. Punctuated equilibrium *(see Topic D.2.9)* asserts that these 'gaps' are real and to be expected from the speciation process. However, note punctuated equilibrium does not suggest that these intermediate fossils do not exist, simply that will exist in small numbers away from the main site of fossil discovery. In addition, many more 'missing links' are being discovered. For example, the discovery of well preserved fossils of the amphibious bird (*Gansus yumenensis*) in northwest China.

However, there are many explanations to account for the incompleteness:
- Dead organisms decompose rapidly
- Dead organisms are eaten by scavengers
- Soft-bodied organism do not fossilise easily
- Only a small fraction of living organisms will have died in conditions favourable for fossilisation
- Only a tiny fraction of the fossils have been unearthed

The summary of hominid evolution presented in Figure 1525 is simplified, tentative and probably incomplete. Very few complete fossils of hominids have been discovered. Bones, other than the teeth and the cranium, tend to be softer and disintegrate. In particular, there is a large gap in our knowledge of hominid evolution between eight to four million years ago.

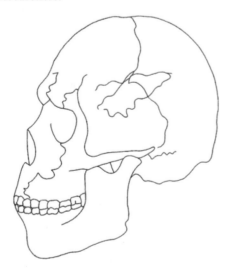

Figure 1534   Structure of a Neanderthal skull

Fossil	Fossilisation process
Entire organism	Frozen into ice Encased in amber Encased in tar
Hard skeletal materials	Trapped by sedimentary sand and clay which form sedimentary rock
Moulds and casts	Hard materials trapped above. The skeleton dissolves leaving its impression as a mould of the organism. This is infilled with fine material which hardens.
Petrification	Gradual replacement by water-carried mineral deposits.
Impressions	Impressions of remains of organisms in fine-grained sediments on which they died.
Imprints	Footprints, trails, tracks and tunnels of organisms made in mud. Rapid baking and filled in with sand and covered by sediments.
Coprolites	Faecal pellets prevented from decomposing, later compressed in sedimentary rock

Figure 1535   Types of fossils and examples

Every major new hominid discovery can potentially falsify previously held theories in human evolution. For example, fossil skulls and jaws were found in Dmanisi, Georgia, which appear intermediate between *Homo habilis* and *Homo erectus*. The brain volume is relatively small at 600 cm³ and may contradict the 'Out of Africa' theory (*see Topic D.3.9*) which suggests that *Homo erectus*, with its relatively large brain, was the first hominid to migrate from Africa.

TOK   The importance of new data

Paleoanthropology is a data-poor science, that is, a relatively small amount of data is used to draw conclusions. Many of the conclusions that have been drawn on limited data have not stood for long. New discoveries regularly come to light, leading scientists to re-interpret previous assumptions in the light of the new data. The discoveries of the Dmanisi site in Georgia have led to a re-evaluation of previous theories of human evolution, calling into question the view that *Homo erectus* was the first hominid to leave Africa. Falsification of earlier explanations is the hallmark of dynamic science and paleoanthropology is certainly that!

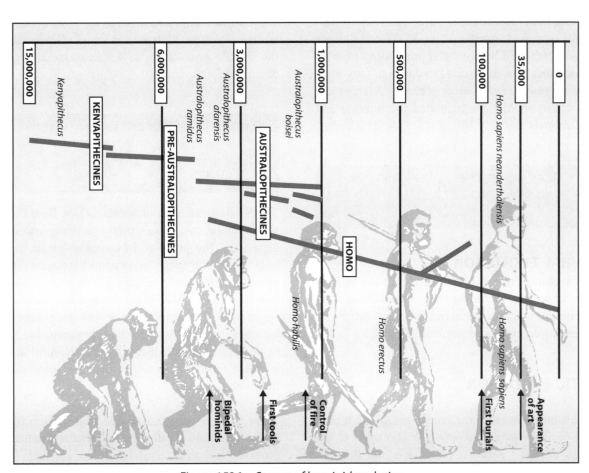

Figure 1536   Stages of hominid evolution

OPTION

OPTION

D.3.8 Discuss the correlation between the change in diet and increase in brain size during hominid evolution.

©IBO 2007

There are obvious advantages to the increase in brain capacity *(see Topic D.3.5)*. The increasing size of the brain meant hominids had greater behavioural flexibility to adapt to different environmental circumstances. These would include the ability to make more complex tools, construct stronger and longer lasting shelters, and use fire for warmth, protection from animals and cooking. It also helped in the transmission of cultural behaviour from one generation to the next *(see Topic D.3.9)*.

However, large brains also have costs. A longer gestation period and extension of the period of care for the infant following birth is required. Much of the development of the human brain occurs after birth. There is a period of critical care for a human infant for a period of two years after birth. The growth of the brain requires a high level of energy intake for the mother not only during the longer gestation, but for a relatively long period following birth.

Hominids with greater brain size and effective energy intake for infant development and care may have been better able to survive and reproduce. Therefore, the trend for increased brain capacity may have been coupled with a trend for increased nutritional intake. This is thought to have been achieved by hominids progressing from an omnivorous diet to a more carnivorous diet: fatty meat and bone marrow are rich sources of energy. A large more complex brain would have facilitated the hunting and killing of animals.

D.3.9 Distinguish between genetic and cultural evolution.

©IBO 2007

CULTURAL EVOLUTION

Cultural evolution refers to the changes in the actions, and ideas of society, including their transmission from one generation to another. Cultural evolution occurs via the written word, the spoken word and images. I

GENETIC EVOLUTION

Genetic evolution refers to the genetic changes that have occurred during hominid evolution. It also refers to the differences observed between individuals and different racial or cultural groups.

Studies of proteins and later DNA sequences *(see Topic D.5.3)* of people have allowed Biologists to produce a human 'family tree' for the past hundred thousand years. In addition the study of mitochondrial DNA and the Y chromosome, have been used to trace human migration patterns.

Considerable genetic evidence has accumulated to support the Out of Africa hypothesis which states that modern humans evolved in Africa before 200,000 to 100,000 years ago, with members of one branch leaving Africa about 80,000 years ago. These emigrants spread to the rest of the world replacing but not interbreeding with other Homo species already there, such as *Homo erectus* and the Neanderthals.

Recent research is focusing on identifying the genetic changes and natural selection occurring in modern human populations. In addition researchers are comparing the human genome to the recently sequenced chimpanzee genome. Researchers have recently identified the first gene (presumably one of many) that are involved in brain and speech development in humans. The gene, FOXP2, is believed to influence the ability to control facial movements. The gene exists in closely related primates and possibly all vertebrates, but the sequence has a few small differences in DNA sequence compared to primates. These small changes occurred in the last 200,000 years of human evolution. Mutations in human families involving the FOXP2 gene causes severe language and grammar difficulties.

D.3.10 Discuss the relative importance of genetic and cultural evolution in the recent evolution of humans.

©IBO 2007

The physical evolution of hominids *(see Topic D.3.5)* was accompanied by changes in the development of social behaviour. The process of becoming human is known as hominisation and is believed to have been due to the evolution of manipulative skills *(see Topic D.3.4)* and speech *(see Topic D.3.9)*. In addition changes in sexual behaviour encouraged the formation of life long relationships between men and women, who began to live together in communities with their children. **Hominisation** also included food sharing which benefited individuals and the community.

These changes were transmitted from person to person by communication, rather than inherited genetically. This process is known as cultural evolution and includes many different aspects of the life of modern day humans and their ancestors: customs, art, rituals, shared knowledge, language, beliefs, laws and religions.

The increased brain size of *Homo habilis* led to the development of stone tools. The earliest cultural artifacts were chopping tools, hammer stones and flakes of lava or quartz used for scraping meat off bones. *Homo erectus* produced hand held axes which had two cutting edges leading to a point. More sophisticated tools made from flint, bone and wood were produced by *Homo sapiens* about 35,000 years ago.

Spoken and written language is unique to humans and requires the coordinated action of the lips, tongue, larynx and three areas of the brain: the speech motor cortical area (controlling the delivery of speech) and two further areas in the left side of the cerebrum. Studies of fossil skulls shows that there was significant development in both *Australopithecus africanus* and *Homo habilis*.

The recent history of modern human cultural evolution has clearly been dominated by cultural evolution. Science and technology are products of cultural evolution. The gene pool of modern humanity is assumed to be little different from our first *Homo sapiens* ancestors, Cro-Magnon man, who lived 20, 000 years ago in France.

TOK   Is it nature or nurture?

There is much debate about the interaction of role of genes (nature) and the environment (nurture) on the evolution of modern humans. In some cases, there is a clear genetic reason for the presence and continuation of a characteristic in the population. This is most obvious in less complex organisms where an innate difference in the ability to detect a source of food or danger can have a profound effect on survival rate. The genes responsible for such advantage are most likely to be inherited and increase in the population over time.

Cultural factors are far more complex. Some cultural factors more than likely have a genetic origin. Determining the extent to which a cultural factor originates genetically is extremely difficult, if not impossible. Studies of behavioural patterns in identical twins offer some insight in this area, suggesting that many complex habits and preferences have a genetic component. Where such behaviours are involved in survival or sexual selection and reproduction they are likely to be passed on to future generations.

D4 THE HARDY-WEINBERG PRINCIPLE

D.4.1   Explain how the Hardy–Weinberg equation is derived.

©IBO 2007

Many characteristics of an individual organism are influenced by a pair of genes. Many of these gene pairs or alleles occur in simple dominant and recessive forms. When a population breeds at random it contains homozygous dominant, homozygous recessive and heterozygous individuals.

Consider an allele represented by A and its recessive allele represented by a. Individuals of genotypes AA, Aa and aa are present in the population and contribute their genes to the gene pool *(see Topic D.2.1)*. If the probability that a gamete contains A is p and the probability that it contains a is q, the proportions of genotypes among the offspring can be calculated as shown below.

	Male gametes A(p)	Male gametes A(q)
Female gametes A(p)	AA (p^2)	Aa (pq)
Female gametes A(q)	Aa (pq)	Aa (q^2)

Figure 1537   The Hardy Weinberg principle table

Because there is a 100% probability that a gamete contains A or a then p + q equals one hundred per cent or 1.0. There is also a 100% probability that the offspring are the genotypes AA, two Aa and aa.

Hence, $p^2 + 2pq + q^2 = 1.0$ or 100%

This algebraic expression is termed the Hardy-Weinberg equation. The **Hardy–Weinberg principle** is an expression of the concept of a population in genetic equilibrium and is a basic principle of population genetics.

Figure 1538 shows a graphical illustration of the Hardy–Weinberg principle for two alleles: the horizontal axis represents the two allele frequencies p and q, the vertical axis represents the genotype frequencies and the three possible genotypes.

OPTION

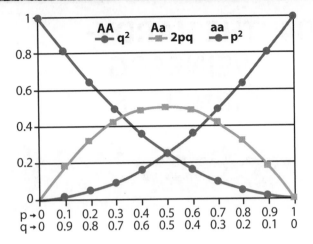

Figure 1538   A graphical illustration of the Hardy–Weinberg principle

The Hardy-Weinberg equation shows that a large proportion of the recessive alleles in a population exist as carriers in heterozygotes. The heterozygous genotypes are responsible for most of the genetic variation in a population. Only the alleles present in the homozygous recessive organisms will be expressed in the phenotype and hence exposed to natural selection and hence possible elimination from the population. Many recessive alleles are eliminated because they are disadvantageous to the organism's phenotype. These deleterious alleles may cause the death of the organism before breeding or genetic death, that is, the failure to reproduce.

However, not all recessive alleles are disadvantageous. For example, the sickle-cell *(see Topic 4.1.4)* frequency has remained relatively stable in regions of the world where malaria is endemic. The maintenance of a constant frequency for a recessive allele which may be harmful is known as heterozygote advantage *(see Topic D.2.11).*

If the Hardy-Weinberg assumptions are not met then deviations from the expected genotype frequencies will occur. When random mating does not occur, the population will not have Hardy-Weinberg frequencies:

- Inbreeding will cause an increase in **homozygosity** for all genes

- A small population size may cause random changes in genotype frequencies, especially if the population is relatively small. This is due to a sampling effect and is termed **genetic drift.**

- Assortative mating, which causes an increase in homozygosity only for those genes involved in the trait that is assortatively mated. (Assortative mating takes place when sexually reproducing organisms tend to mate with individuals that are like themselves in some respect (positive assortative mating) or dissimilar (negative assortative mating).

- Natural selection causes allele frequencies to change, often quite rapidly. While directional selection leads to the loss of alleles except the favoured one, some forms of natural selection, such as balancing selection, lead to genetic equilibrium without loss of alleles *(see Topic D.2.11).*

- Mutation rates are generally low and usually similar to changes in allele frequency. Hence, recurrent mutation can maintain alleles in a population, even if there is strong natural selection acting against them.

D.4.2	Calculate allele, genotype and phenotype frequencies for two alleles of a gene, using the Hardy–Weinberg equation.

©IBO 2007

Although the Hardy-Weinberg equation *(see Topic D.4.1.)* provides a simple mathematical model of how genetic equilibrium can be maintained in a gene pool, its major use in population genetics is calculating allele, genotype and phenotype frequencies. In simple algebraic terms the Hardy-Weinberg equation is given by the expression:

$$p^2 + 2pq + q^2 = 1$$

where, p represents the dominant allele frequency, q represents the recessive allele frequency, p^2 represents the homozygous dominant genotype, 2pq represents the heterozygous genotype and q^2 represents the homozygous recessive genotype.

Allele and genotype frequencies can be calculated using the following expressions:

$$p + q = 1, \text{ and } p^2 + 2pq + q^2 = 1$$

However, in populations it is only possible to visually estimate the frequency of the two alleles from the percentage or proportion of organisms which are homozygous recessive, since this is the only genotype that can be identified directly from its genotype.

For example, one person in 10,000 is albino and lacks skin pigmentation. The albino condition is homozygous recessive.

Hence $q^2 = 0.0001$; $q = \sqrt{0.0001} = 0.01$. The frequency of the recessive albino allele in the population is therefore 1%.

Since $p + q = 1$; $p = 1 - q = 1 - 0.001 = 0.99$. The frequency of the dominant allele in the population is therefore 99%.

$p = 0.99$; $p^2 = (0.99)^2 = 0.9801$

The frequency of the homozygous dominant genotype in the population is therefore approximately 98%.

$2pq = 2 \times (0.99) \times (0.01) = 0.0198$

The frequency of the heterozygous genotype is approximately 2%. This includes people who carry the albino allele as heterozygotes (carriers) or albino homozygotes.

Here is another worked example of a problem involving the Hardy-Weinberg equation:

Some people are unable to taste the chemical PTC, others experience a bitter taste. The allele for tasting (T) is dominant to non-tasting (t). Here is some sample data:

Phenotype	Percentage	Frequency
Taster	71.3	0.713
Non-taster	28.7	0.287
Total	100	1.000

Figure 1539   An Example of the Hardy-Weinberg principle

$p^2 + 2pq = 0.713$; $q^2 = 0.287$; $q = \sqrt{0.287} = 0.536$

$p + q = 1.0$; $p + 0.536 = 1.0$; $p = 0.464$

The probability of a person having the genotype TT (p^2) is therefore: $(0.464)^2 = 0.215 = 21.5\%$

The probability of a person having the genotype Tt ($2pq$) is therefore $2 \times (0.464 \times 0.536) = 0.497 = 49.7\%$

D.4.3   State the assumptions made when the Hardy–Weinberg equation is used.

©IBO 2007

The following assumptions are made when the Hardy-Weinberg equation is used in population genetics:
- The organism is diploid and sexually reproducing
- The trait under consideration is autosomal, that is, it is not located on a sex chromosome
- The organism has discrete generations

The three assumptions shown above are required for the mathematics involved.
- Random mating occurs within a single population
- The population is of infinite size, or sufficiently large that the effect of genetic drift is minimised
- No natural selection, mutation or immigration or migration (gene flow) occurs

The three assumptions shown above are inherent in the Hardy-Weinberg equation.

GENETIC DRIFT

Consider an allele which occurs in 2% of the members of a species. In a population of one million individuals, 20,000 individuals may be expected to possess this allele. Even if some of these fail to pass it on to their offspring, the majority are likely to do so. Hence, the proportion of the individuals with the allele will not be significantly altered in the next generation. If, however, if the population were considerably smaller, for example, 1000 individuals, only 20 will carry the allele. The effect of a few of these individuals to fail to pass on the allele will have a marked effect on its frequency in the next generation. This drift in the frequency of an allele is greater the smaller the population. In very small populations the allele is likely to be lost from the population.

OPTION

D.5 PHYLOGENY AND SYSTEMATICS

D.5.1 Outline the value of classifying organisms.

©IBO 2007

The study of the classification of living organisms into groups is termed systematics or taxonomy. The best taxonomic schemes are based on natural relationships due to common ancestry, rather than incidental similarities. Biological classification based on evolutionary relationships is termed phylogenetic.

A natural classification is one in which the members of a group resemble one another not only in the characters that define the group but also for many other non-defining characters too. The advantage of natural classification is that it is possible to predict the distribution of other characters from the groups alone.

Identification keys *(see Topic D.5.5)* are used to unambiguously identify an organism from a group of organisms. However, taxonomists have to be more careful when selecting distinguishing characteristics when devising a phylogenetic classification scheme. They need to select homologous structures *(see Topic D.5.6)* and avoid including analogous structures *(see Topic D.5. 6)*.

The taxonomist has to carefully distinguish between homologues and analogues in so that organisms can be grouped together to illustrate their evolutionary relationship. One approach to achieving this aim is termed cladistics *(see Topic D.5.5.)*

The aims of cladistics and other natural classifications is to organise data to assist in identifying organisms, suggest evolutionary links and allow the prediction of characteristics shared by members of a taxonomic group.

Unlike the traditional Linnaean system cladistics does not attempt to 'rank' groups of organisms artificially into kingdoms, phyla, orders, etc. This can be misleading as it seems to suggest that different groupings with the same rank are equivalent. For example, the cats (*Felidae*) and the orchids (*Orchidaceae*) are both family level groups in Linnaean classification. However, the two groups are not comparable since the two groups have very different levels of diversity and evolutionary histories. In addition many orchids of different genera can hybridise.

D.5.2 Explain the biochemical evidence provided by the universality of DNA and protein structures for the common ancestry of living organisms.

©IBO 2007

Most organisms use a nearly universal genetic code referred to as the standard genetic code *(see Topic 3.5.5.)*. Even viruses *(see Topic F.1.8.)*, which are acellular have proteins synthesised in their host cells using the standard genetic code.

For many years the genetic code was thought to be universal, but there are a few exceptions. For example, protein synthesis in mitochondria, yeast and ciliated protozoans *(see Topic F.1.9)* show slight deviations from the standard genetic code.

Despite the small variations that exist, the genetic codes used by all living organisms on Earth are very similar. Since there are many possible genetic codes that are thought to have similar efficiency to the one used by living organisms, the theory of evolution by natural selection suggests that the genetic code was established very early in the history of life and was present in the last common ancestor of all living organisms *(see Figure 1526)*.

Biochemical studies also reveals similarities between organisms of different species. For example, the metabolism of very different organisms is based on protein cytochrome c, an electron carrier essential for aerobic respiration *(see Topic 8.1.)*.

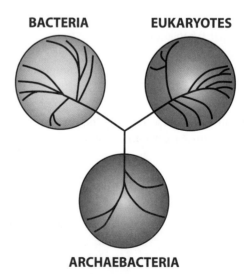

BACTERIA   **EUKARYOTES**

ARCHAEBACTERIA

Figure 1540   All living things have a common ancestor

OPTION

The universality of cytochrome c is strong evidence that all aerobic organisms probably descended from a common ancestor that utilised a precursor of this enzyme for respiration. Since cytochrome c is a complex metal containing enzyme it is very unlikely that proteins with very similar sequences would have evolved independently in a range of very different organisms.

Figure 1540 shows that all living organisms probably share a common ancestor and can be represented in a single tree.

TOK   Bound together by DNA?

Studies in genetics in the mid twentieth century made clear the common bond between all organisms: the universal genetic code. Humans could no longer justify a special, more important place for our species as compared to others, on scientific grounds. However, the discovery of the code opened up the future possibility, now realised, to modify it.

Marshall Nirenberg, whose team discovered the genetic code in the 1960's understood the implications of such knowledge. In an article published in the journal *Science* in 1967, he commented that "decisions concerning the application of this knowledge must ultimately be made by society, and only an informed society can make such decisions wisely." Nirenberg understood that this knowledge opened possibilities which were previously unimaginable and knew that as a scientist he had a responsibility not only to reveal knowledge but to educate others as to the possibilities and responsibilities that come with such knowledge.

D.5.3   Explain how variations in specific molecules can indicate phylogeny.

©IBO 2007

Automated sequencing techniques can be used to deduce the sequences of amino acids in proteins or bases in DNA. Comparisons have been made of the alpha and beta chains of hemoglobin from a range of very different species. The alpha chain is composed of 141 amino acid residues and the beta chain is composed of 146 residues.

Humans and chimpanzees are identical in both chains, but orangutans differ from humans in two amino acids. These results suggest that humans are more closely related to chimpanzees than to orangutans.

Figure 1526 shows a probable history or phylogeny of the alpha-hemoglobin molecules of several vertebrate species. The numbers on the branches of the phylogenetic tree are the minimum number of substitutions required to produce a new molecule from the one at the previous branching point, each substitution is the result of a single gene mutation affecting one base pair in the DNA sequence coding for the protein.

The relationships shown in Figure 1526 are confirmed by studying other conserved proteins, for example, cytochrome c *(see Topic D.5.2)* and histones *(see Topic 4.1.1.)*. The same relationship is also suggested by the fossil record and other taxonomic data. This molecular phylogenetic approach is based upon the concept termed the evolutionary clock *(see Topic D.5.4.)*.

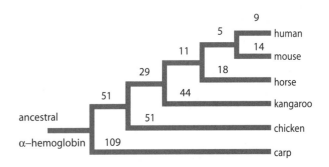

Figure 1541   Probable evolutionary history of alpha-hemoglobin

---

D.5.4   Discuss how biochemical variations can be used as an evolutionary clock.

©IBO 2007

The concept of an **evolutionary clock** is a technique in molecular genetics, which is used to date when two species diverged. It calculates the time since their common ancestor from examining the number of differences between their DNA or protein sequences.

The concept was first proposed when it was noticed that the number of amino acid differences in hemoglobin between species correlates with divergence times, as estimated from the fossil record. It was then generalised to suggest that the rate of evolutionary change of any protein or DNA sequence was approximately constant over time and over different lineages.

The concept of an evolutionary clock assumes that the DNA replication rate is constant over time and across all species. This assumption initially seemed plausible since the enzymes involved in DNA replication are very conserved in eukaryotes. Recent evidence suggests that the constant-rate assumption should not be universally

OPTION

assumed, hence introducing an element of uncertainty into molecular phylogenetic trees *(see Topic D.5.3.).*

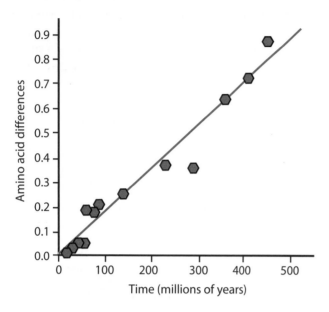

Figure 1542   A graph showing the constant rate of evolution of the alpha-globin gene

---

TOK   Mutation is a random process

Variation in the genetic code is a useful tool in understanding phylogeny. However, the changes in the genetic code that are due to mutation must be interpreted with caution. Mutations are most often random events that cannot be predicted or assumed to occur at invariable rates. Given this understanding, we must be careful how we interpret data based on differences in genetic codes. Given the huge time-frames involved in phylogenic trees there are most likely factors that we will never know that have influenced the rate of mutation and whether or not these mutation have persisted in the genome of an organism or removed from it.

D.5.5   Define clade and cladistics.

©IBO 2007

Cladistics is a method of taxonomy based on constructing groups, or clades, comprising organisms which share a unique homologous characteristic. Each clade is set off by a series of characteristics that appear in its members, but not in the other forms from which it diverged. These identifying characteristics of a clade are called shared, derived characters. In cladistics, a clade is a group of organisms consisting of a single common ancestor and

all the descendants of that ancestor. Cladists use DNA sequences, biochemical data and morphological data.

There are three basic assumptions made by cladists:
*   Change in characteristics occurs in lineages over time. The assumption that characteristics of organisms change over time is the most important one in cladistics. It is only when characteristics change that Biologists are able to recognise different lineages or groups.

*   Any group of organisms is related by descent from a common ancestor.
    This assumption is supported by a considerable amount of biochemical evidence (see Topic D.5.2.) and means that all life on Earth today is related and shares a common ancestor.

*   There is a branching pattern of lineage-splitting. This assumption suggests that when a lineage splits, it typically divides into exactly two groups.

D.5.6   Distinguish, with examples, between analogous and homologous characteristics.

©IBO 2007

A **homologous characteristic** is a structural or biochemical feature which is shared between two or more organisms because of a common ancestor. Examples of homologous structures in vertebrates are the vertebral column (backbone) and the pentadactyl limb *(see Topic D.2.8.).*

An **analogous characteristic** is a structural or biochemical feature which are shared by unrelated organisms. Analogous structures have the same basic function but their basic structure is fundamentally different. Analogous structures develop by a process of convergent evolution *(see Topic D.2.8.).*

Figure 1543 shows that the wings of a butterfly (a) and a bird (b) are analogous structures.

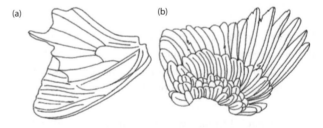

Figure 1543   The wings of a (a) butterfly and (b) bird

D.5.7 Outline the methods used to construct cladograms and the conclusions that can be drawn from them.

D.5.8 Construct a simple cladogram.

©IBO 2007

The relationships of clades to each is expressed in a **cladogram**. The simple cladogram shown below in Figure 1528 is based upon the list of shared features given in the table below in Figure 1529. The joints, or nodes, of the cladogram represent shared homologous characteristics. Moving across the cladogram left to right, the clades become smaller and the more homologous characteristics they have in common.

On the cladogram below the camel and the bat have four homologous features in common (jaws, lungs, fur and mammary glands); the camel and the eagle have two (jaws and lungs), while the camel and catfish have one feature in common (jaws).

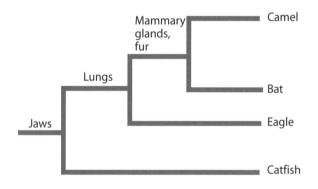

Figure 1544   A simple cladogram for four vertebrates

	Bat	Eagle	Camel	Catfish
Fur	√		√	
Jaws	√	√	√	√
Lungs	√	√	√	
Mammary glands	√		√	

Figure 1545   Shared homologous characteristics of vertebrate animals table

The cladogram drawn above provides the maximum number of shared homologous characteristics. To be as accurate as possible a whole range of approaches are employed: structural, as illustrated above, in addition to physiological and biochemical *(see Topic D.5.3.).* Computer algorithms have been developed that can process raw data and generate cladograms.

The validity of the cladistic approach to classification depends upon the assumption that if two organisms share a homologous characteristic, they must be related. In addition it is assumed that the greater the number of homologous characteristics shared, the more closely related two clades must be. The nodes of a cladogram should therefore represent the common ancestry, or phylogeny, of the organisms, and the branching should reflect their divergent evolutionary history.

The important components of a cladogram are evolutionary steps, such as the loss of one character, or the modification or gain of another. Each cladogram will have a certain number of evolutionary steps. When two possible cladograms for the same set of organisms are compared, the one with the least number of evolutionary steps is chosen. Because the cladogram with the least number of steps is the simplest, it is considered the most parsimonious and is the preferred choice.

D.5.9 Analyze cladograms in terms of phylogenetic relationships.

©IBO 2007

There are three nodes: 1, 2 and 3. Node 1 occurred earliest in time and Node 3 occurred latest in time. Node 2 represents the most recent common ancestor of taxa B and C. Node 1 represents the most recent common ancestor of taxa A and B. This can inferred since B shares a more recent common ancestor with C, represented by node 2, than it does with A: their most recent common ancestor is represented by node 1.

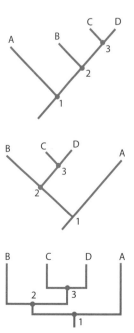

Figure 1546   Different representations of a simple cladogram

OPTION

265

D.5.10. Discuss the relationship between cladograms and the classification of living organisms.

©IBO 2007

Birds form a clade sharing the unique homologous characteristics, feathers, and mammals because they possess mammary glands (breasts) and suckle their young with milk. Both mammals and birds belong to a larger clade, vertebrates, due to the possession of a vertebral column (backbone).

Fish, however, do not form a clade because although they possess many features in common, such as gills, scales, fins and a tail, none of these features are unique to fish. Fish appear to consist of three clades: hagfishes, rays and sharks and bony fishes. Reptiles are another Linnean group that does not form a clade.

Cladistics recognises only **monophyletic** groups, that is, groups that include a single ancestor and all of its descendants. Birds, mammals and amphibians form clades. Groups that do not include the common ancestor of all of its members are called **polyphyletic**; groups that include the common ancestor but not all of its descendants are called **paraphyletic**.

Another clade is all animals whose eggs or developing young are held within a membrane termed the amnion. This clade is the **amniotes**, and includes reptiles, birds, dinosaurs and mammals. Clades can be nested within each other as with birds and vertebrates, for example the birds clade lies within the amniotes - thus, all birds are amniotes.

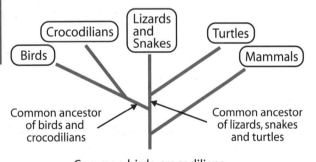

Figure 1547   Cladogram of the vertebrate chordates

OPTION

EXERCISES

D1 ORIGIN OF LIFE ON EARTH

1   What elements and compounds did the Chemists Miller and Urey place into their apparatus to simulate conditions on the pre-biotic Earth?
    A   methane, ammonia, water, hydrogen
    B   nitrogen, hydrogen, carbon, water
    C   oxygen, water, hydrogen, carbon dioxide
    D   methane, carbon dioxide, hydrogen, water

2   What term is used to describe an organism that has a *mutually beneficial symbiotic* relationship with a host organism while living inside the host?
    A   methanogen
    B   prokaryote
    C   epiphyte
    D   endosymbiont

3   How are the current living organisms on the Earth's surface protected from the harmful effects of ultraviolet radiation?
    A   by the carbon dioxide present in the lower atmosphere
    B   by the ozone layer in the stratosphere
    C   by the presence of clouds containing water vapour
    D   by the high levels of nitrogen present in air

4   Which one of the following conditions was **not** thought to be present in the *pre-biotic Earth?*
    A   an oxidising atmosphere
    B   high levels of ultra-violet radiation
    C   high temperature due to volcanic activity
    D   extensive lightning

5   Which organic molecules are believed by many molecular biologists to have been the first to be able to undergo replication?
    A   RNA
    B   DNA
    C   a polypeptide
    D   a clay

6   Which of the following chemical substances is not required to reproduce the experiments of Miller and Urey?
    A   ammonia
    B   carbon dioxide
    C   oxygen
    D   water

7   Many Biologists strongly believe that the ancestors of some eukaryotic organelles, such as the chloroplast and the mitochondria, were originally free-living prokaryotes. What is this theory termed?
    A   the panspermia theory
    B   the exosymbiotic theory
    C   the endosymbiotic theory
    D   the endomutalistic theory

8   Which of the following ideas is **not** being discussed as a possible explanation for the origin of life on Earth?
    A   life originated in a warm primordial 'soup' - possibly in tide pools
    B   life originated several kilometres beneath the surface of the Earth or at the bottom of the oceans near hydro-thermal vents
    C   life on Earth came from the planet Mars
    D   life on Earth originated on the Moon

9   Which is a *universal feature* of all known living organisms on Earth?
    A   They require oxygen
    B   They are multicellular
    C   They reproduce sexually
    D   They contain nucleic acids

10 Which of these gases was probably **not** present in the Earth's early pre-biotic atmosphere?
    A   oxygen, O_2
    B   nitrogen, N_2
    C   carbon dioxide, CO_2
    D   hydrogen, H_2

11. The geological age of the Earth generally accepted during Darwin's lifetime was later demonstrated to be incorrect. What is the current estimate of the Earth's age?
    A   1.5 billion years old
    B   4.5 billion years old
    C   1.5 million years old
    D   4.5 million years old

12 Which of the following molecules has been proposed by the Biochemist Graham Cairns Smith as having played a critical role in the catalysis of organic polymers during the early Earth's period of chemical evolution?
    A   Iron(III) oxide
    B   Clays
    C   Carbohydrates
    D   Adenine

13 Which one of the following observations is **not** strong and direct evidence for an *endosymbiotic* origin for the mitochondrion?

A   Mitochondria can divide and replicate independently of cell division

B   Mitochondria contain their own DNA, in the form of a plasmid

C   Mitochondria are enclosed by a double plasma membrane and contain 70S ribosomes

D   DNA in the eukaryotic nucleus codes for many of the enzymes in mitochondria

14 Which one of the following statements is **not** true about Sidney Fox's research work on *proteinoid microspheres* which may have played an important role in the evolution of the cell?

A   They are formed by a process of spontaneous self assembly under appropriate conditions

B   They are formed by the condensation of amino acids at low temperatures

C   Microspheres do not utilise energy

D   Microspheres can demonstrate catalytic activity

15 Which one of the following is **not** a correct statement about the *autogenous model* for the evolutionary origin of membranes?

A   The membrane bound organelles of eukaryotic cells arose through enfolding of the cell's plasma membrane

B   Enfolding of the plasma membrane could be favoured by natural selection because it allows compartmentalisation of the cell so that different regions have different specialised functions

C   The evolutionary process was driven by an increase in the efficiency of the cell's metabolism

D   There was a mutualistic relationship between a prokaryote and a prokaryotic endosymbiont

16 Which one of the following statements is **incorrect** about *prokaryotes*?

A   Numerous lysosomes and a large Golgi apparatus are present in the cytoplasm

B   A cross-linked cell wall protects the cell from osmotic lysis

C   Protein synthesis occurs within 70S ribosomes

D   Reproduction occurs via binary fission

17 Some Biologists believe that life on Earth was initiated by the arrival of organic molecules and perhaps even bacteria on asteroids and meteorites. What is this theory termed?

A   Lamarckism

B   special creation

C   panspermia

D   artificial selection

18 Discuss the evidence for an *endosymbiotic* origin for mitochondria and chloroplasts

19 Briefly outline the experiments conducted by Miller and Urey into the origin of organic compounds.

20 Outline the concept of *panspermia* and state evidence supporting its postulate.

21 Briefly outline some of the evidence that RNA might have been the genetic and enzymatic material of the first living organisms (the so-called RNA World hypothesis).

D2 SPECIES AND SPECIATION

1   The Galapagos islands contain thirteen species of finches which resemble each other closely, but differ markedly in their feeding habits and in the shape of their beaks.
What is the most likely explanation for this observation, assuming that an ancestral stock of finches came from the South American mainland?

A   The ancestral finches colonised the habitats for which they were already adapted

B   The ancestral finches underwent convergent evolution to produce a number of very similar species

C   The ancestral finches evolved separately due to the different habitats colonised

D   The ancestral finches from the mainland bred and hybridised with a resident population of a closely related species and produced a variety of new varieties of finch

2   The fossil record of trilobites, an extinct species of mollusc, shows the relatively sudden appearance of a number of new species, without numerous intermediates. What term may be used to describe the type of evolution pattern being exhibited?

A   phyletic gradualism

B   stasis

C   Lamarckism

D   punctuated equilibrium

OPTION

3 In which of the following situations would evolution by natural selection be **slowest** for an inter-breeding population of organisms?

	Migration	Selection pressure	Variation due to gene mutation
A	absent	low	low
B	absent	high	high
C	high	low	high
D	high	high	high

4 What is term used to describe the alleles present in the gametes of a sexually reproducing population?
A gene complex
B gene pool
C genomic library
D genotype

5 Researchers once regarded two birds A and B as distinct species, but more now consider them as northern and southern forms of a single species. What must have been observed by the researchers studying birds A and B?
A Birds A and B always live together in the same physical area
B Birds A and B successfully interbreed and produce viable offspring
C Birds A and B resemble each other very closely
D Birds A and B are allopatric and are reproductively isolated from each other

6 What does the term 'Gradualism' in Darwin's theory of evolution refer to?
A Evolution always proceeds at a slow and constant rate
B It took Darwin thirty years to develop his theory
C Complex Biological adaptations evolve in many small incremental steps
D Evolution is being driven by natural selection

7 There is no universal consensus the definition of the species concept, but the majority of Biologists would agree that there are three important criteria. Select the statement below that is not one of these criteria.
A Descent, via natural selection of all members from a common ancestral population
B Reproductive compatibility within a species and reproductive incompatibility between species
C The maintenance within species of genotypic and phenotypic cohesion
D Members of species cannot vary in phenotype

8 What term is given to Biological features that prevent different species from successfully interbreeding?
A Phenotypic barriers
B Reproductive barriers
C Systematic barriers
D Evolutionary barriers

9 There is strong evidence in the fossil record for periodic, sometimes catastrophic, events in which extinction rates increase dramatically. What are these events called?
A Mass extinction events
B Macroevolution
C Punctuated equilibria
D Microevolution

10 What is the term used to describe the production of ecologically diverse, but evolutionary related species, from a common ancestral stock or population?
A Adaptive radiation
B Balanced polymorphism
C Ecological diversification
D Genetic drift

11 Which statement describes the concept of microevolution?
A The mutation of genes in response to rapid environmental change
B Definite trends in the frequencies of alleles within a gene pool
C The existence of two more alleles for a gene locus
D The creation of large and complex organs in a relatively small number of steps

12 Because of a difference in peak breeding time, two species of closely related frogs do not produce interspecific hybrids. What term describes this isolating mechanism?
A Mechanical isolation
B Ecological isolation
C Spatial or temporal isolation
D Geographical isolation

13 Which of the following is **not** characteristic of evolutionary change by *punctuated equilibrium*?
A Co-evolution and the formation of macromutational intermediates
B Periods of rapid evolutionary change followed by long periods of little or no   change (stasis)
C Strong directional selection on small populations
D The presence of few intermediate species in the fossil record

OPTION

14 Two sub-groups within a population of a single species of frog gradually begin using separate mating rituals. What would this be an example of?
A   allopatric speciation
B   parapatric speciation
C   postzygotic isolation
D   behavioual isolation

15 Which of the following would be a pre-zygotic isolating mechanism?
A   A mature sperm being unable to penetrate an ovum
B   A hybrid born alive but unable to produce gametes at sexual maturity
C   Two individuals producing fertile offspring
D   A hybrid being born but dying immediately after birth

16 The lesser snow goose exists in two morphs or forms with light and dark plumage. This occurred when two populations came into contact with each other about 100 years ago. The two morphs mate randomly and both have equal fitness or reproductive success.

What type of phenomenon is most likely being exhibited?
A   Balanced polymorphism
B   Co-evolution
C   Sexual selection
D   Transient polymorphism

17 Which statement correctly describes balanced polymorphism?
A   The maintenance of the same number of organisms in a population in the same geographical range over many successive generations
B   The maintenance of dominance from one generation to another by exclusively selecting for dominant genes
C   The maintenance of recessives from one generation to another by exclusively selecting for recessive genes
D   The maintenance of the frequency of both dominant and recessive genes over a number of generations by selecting for the heterozygotes

18 Two forms of the peppered moth, *Biston betularia*, namely, the dark melanic and a pale form are found in Western Europe. The melanic form was first observed in 1848 and its frequency subsequently increased until the 1950's. This is thought to be the result of
A   adaptive radiation
B   convergent evolution
C   natural selection
D   an increasing mutation rate

19 Sufferers of sickle-cell anemia are homozygous for an allele, Hb^S, which codes for abnormal hemoglobin. Normal hemoglobin is coded for by the allele, Hb^A. The heterozygotes, Hb^AHb^S are healthy and can be detected by the characteristic shape of their red blood cells.
(a) In an area of Central Africa, where malaria is common, 2.6% of new born babies have sickle-cell anemia. Calculate the frequency of the Hb^S allele in this population.
(b) Calculate the number of babies expected to be heterozygous in a population of 600.
(c) What type of polymorphism is being exhibited?
(d) What is responsible for maintaining this polymorphism?

20 A species of moth exhibits industrial melanism. The dark colour of the melanic form is inherited as a simple dominant to the pale form.
(a) In a population where the two alleles M and m are in equal frequency, what will be the ratio of melanic to pale phenotypes at equilibrium?
(b) If 2000 moths in Hardy-Weinberg equilibrium are placed into a heavily polluted environment, where all the pale form are eaten by birds but all the melanics survive, what will be the frequency of M and m in the survivors?
(c) If 2000 moths in Hardy-Weinberg equilibrium are placed into a clean environment where all the melanics are eaten by birds, but all the pale forms survive, what will be the frequency of M and m in the survivors?
(d) Which alleles are being selected against in the polluted and clean environments, respectively?
(e) What type of polymorphism is being exhibited when m decreases relative to M, but is maintained in the population?

D3 HUMAN EVOLUTION

1 Which one of the following is not a species of Australopithecus?
   A *afarensis*
   B *erectus*
   C *africanus*
   D *robustus*

2 In which part of the world does anatomical and biochemical evidence, especially mitochondrial DNA analysis, strongly suggests where modern humans evolved?
   A Europe
   B Asia
   C Africa
   D Australia

3 Arrange the species of Homo into order of evolutionary appearance in the fossil record.
   A *H. habilis, H. erectus, H. neanderthalensis* and *H. sapiens.*
   B *H.erectus, H. habilis, H. neanderthalensis* and *H. sapiens.*
   C *H. neanderthalensis, H.erectus, H. habilis* and *H. sapiens.*
   D *H.erectus, H. neanderthalensis, H. habilis* and *H. sapiens.*

4 Which one of the following statements is incorrect as a description of a modern human in comparison to apes?
   A the head is kept in position by powerful neck muscles
   B the rib cage is barrel-shaped
   C the pelvis is lower and broader
   D the legs are longer than the arms

5 What does the term cultural evolution refer to?
   A learned behaviour which is passed from generation to generation via non-genetic processes
   B the innate or inherited behaviour of our species
   C universal behaviour patterns found in all primates
   D all of the above

6 Approximately how old are the first Australopithecene fossils?
   A 20 million years ago
   B 5 million years ago
   C 1 million years ago
   D 0.25 million years ago

7 Which of the following is not a characteristic of the order primates?
   A finger nails and toe nails
   B opposable thumbs
   C monocular vision
   D flexible shoulder and hip joints

8 For how long did the genus Homo live with the genus Australopithecus in East Africa?
   A 4 million years
   B 2.5 million years
   C 2.0 million years
   D 1.0 million years

9 Which of the following hominid species made the most sophisticated tools?
   A *Homo erectus*
   B *Australopithecus africanus*
   C *Homo sapiens*
   D *Homo habilis*

10 Which of the following hominid skeletons shows anatomic evidence of bipedalism?
   A *Homo erectus*
   B *Homo habilis*
   C *Australopithecus afarensis*
   D All of the above

11 Which of the following hominids was the first tool user?
   A *Australopithecus africanus*
   B *Homo habilis*
   C *Homo erectus*
   D *Homo sapiens neanderthalensis*

12 Modern humans and apes are presently classified in the taxonomic category as all of the following levels except
   A order
   B kingdom
   C class
   D genus

13 Of the living genera of apes, the one most closely related to humans is
   A chimpanzees
   B gibbons
   C gorillas
   D orangutans

OPTION

14 Which of the following is a feature that sets most primates apart from all other mammals?
  A   Placental embryonic development
  B   Bodies covered in hair
  C   The presence of opposable thumbs
  D   The ability to produce milk from breasts

15 What are the characteristics of the first hominids?
  A   bipedal locomotion, relatively large brains
  B   bipedal locomotion, relatively small brains
  C   quadrupedal locomotion, relatively large brains
  D   monogamous social groups

16 Where did the earliest hominids live?
  A   Africa, Asia, North America, Europe
  B   Africa, Asia
  C   Africa
  D   North America and Europe

17 Why are early hominids dating to between 6 and 3 million years ago generally considered to be primitive?
  A   they were not bipedal
  B   they possessed many ancestral characteristics common to all hominids
  C   they were not as complex as later hominids
  D   they had larger brains than the common ancestor

18 The fossil specimen nicknamed "Lucy" by Don Johnanson is an example of what species?
  A   *Ardipithecus ramidus*
  B   *Australopithecus afarensis*
  C   *Australopithecus aethiopicus*
  D   *Kenyanthropus platyops*

19 The fossil hominid footprints at Laetoli in Tanzania, Africa show clear bipedal characteristics. What would these include?
  A   non-divergent big toe
  B   heel strike
  C   well-developed arch on the foot
  D   all of the above

20 The hypothesis explaining the origin of bipedalism proposed by Darwin states that standing upright allowed hominids to carry tools with their hands. What is the problem with this theory?
  A   bipedalism evolved 3.5 million years before tool use
  B   bipedalism evolved as a strategy for carrying food back to the group
  C   hominids developed containers to carry tools
  D   bipedalism evolved as a means for efficient locomotion in searching for food

21 Which one of the following characteristics of homo sapiens is perhaps a consequence of neoteny?
  A   Bipedalism and repositioning of the *foramen magnum*
  B   Support of the organs by the pelvic girdle
  C   The retention of juvenile characteristics and the slow maturational processes (in brain and behaviour). These lead to prolonged periods of learning in offspring and increased parental care
  D   A high ratio of body surface to volume is favoured in hot areas so that body heat can be dispersed. A low ratio is favoured in cold areas so that heat is conserved

22 Which one of the following statements is false?
  A   The *australopithecines* were probably evolving when African forests were progressively shrinking and seasonally dry grasslands, or savannas, were advancing
  B   Chimpanzees and gorillas, our nearest evolutionary ancestors, are only found in Africa
  C   *A. afarensis* lived 4.2 – 3.9 million years ago in East Africa
  D   Fossils of *Homo erectus* have only been found in tropical Africa

23 Which is likely to be a correct statement about cultural versus genetic evolution in populations of modern humans?
  A   Genetic evolution is very rapid
  B   Cultural evolution is a rapid and powerful force
  C   Genetic evolution does not occur
  D   Cultural evolution is weak compared to the effects of genetic evolution

24 When fossils are unearthed, it is generally found that the bones or shells of the dead organism have been replaced by another substance. What is this substance?
  A   Water or ice
  B   Cross-linked proteins
  C   Hard minerals
  D   Bubbles of methane gas

25 Which one of the following environments provides a poor preservation medium for the remains of animals and plants?
  A   amber (solidified tree resin)
  B   water with dissolved oxygen
  C   tar
  D   ice

26 Which of the following statements is an incorrect statement about the technique of radio carbon –dating using carbon-14?

A Cosmic rays from the sun strike nitrogen -14 atoms in the atmosphere and cause them to turn into radioactive carbon-14, which combines with oxygen to form radioactive carbon dioxide.

B Living organisms are in equilibrium with the atmosphere, and the radioactive carbon dioxide is absorbed and used by plants. The radioactive carbon dioxide enters the food chain and the carbon cycle.

C The half life of carbon-14 is so long it can only be used to date organic remains that are over 70,000 years old

D At death, carbon-14 exchange ceases and any carbon-14 in the tissues of the organism begins to decay to nitrogen-14, and is not replenished by new carbon-14.

27 In 2004 researchers led by Dr Peter Brown of New England University, Australia excavating in Liang Bua cave on the Indonesian island of Flores uncovered a new species of human, *Homo floresiensis*, barely a metre tall, that lived until 13,000 years ago. The hominid is known partly from a partial skeleton known as LB1 whose body and brain proportions are comparable to much older *Australopithecines*, but the features such as walking and tool making align it with modern humans.

(a) (i) State the species and genus of *Homo floresiensis*.
   (ii) Why is it important that the researchers uncover further specimens?

(b) (i) Suggest why the evolution of dwarf forms of large animals on relatively small islands appears to be a relatively common phenomenon.
   (ii) What has the been general trend in body size and brain size during the lineage that gave rise to modern humans?

(c) What does the discovery of *Homo floresiensis* suggest about brain size?

(d) What discovery suggests that *Homo floresiensis* had developed cultural evolution?

28 DNA hybridisation is one method for comparing DNA from different closely related species. Purified samples from two different species are gently heated to break the hydrogen bonds and separate the strands - the process is termed 'melting'. The mixture of separated strands is then mixed and allowed to slowly cool together. A number of the newly formed double helices or duplexes are hybrid, that is, they consist of one strand from each of the two species.

The strands in the hybrid DNA separate or 'melt' at a lower temperature than in DNA from a single species. The more closely related, in genetic terms, the two species, the smaller the difference between the separation or 'melting' temperatures of hybrid DNA and the DNA from a single species.

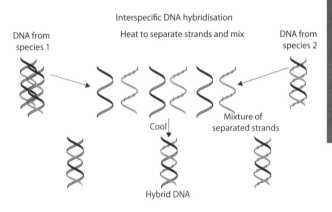

(a) Suggest why the strands in hybrid DNA separate or 'melt' at a lower temperature than those in DNA from a single species.
(b) Suggest why the separation or 'melting' temperature of hybrid DNA from distantly genetically related species is lower than that of hybrid DNA from closely related species.

The table below shows the difference between the average separation temperatures of hybrid DNA and single-species DNA for a number of primate species or groups.

Sources of hybrid DNA	Average separation or 'melting' temperature/ °C
Human/chimpanzee	1.9
Gorilla/chimpanzee	2.3
Human/gorilla	2.4
Human/orang-utan	3.7
Gorilla/orang-utan	3.7
Chimpanzee/orang-utan	3.7
Gibbon/other apes	4.9
Old World monkeys/apes	7.3

(The Old World monkeys occupy a wide variety of environments in South and East Asia, the Middle East and Africa).

It is assumed that the difference in separation or 'melting' temperature is directly proportional to the time since the evolutionary lineages of the two groups diverged.

(c) The evolutionary lineage of the Old World monkeys are believed to have diverged 30 million years ago. Use this figure to calculate the time represented by a difference of 1 °C.

(d) Calculate when the evolutionary lineages of humans and chimpanzees diverged, according to DNA hybridisation studies.

(e) Fill in the names of the missing species in boxes A and B. Complete the family tree or cladogram from the branching point marked X. Give two alternative techniques that have been used to establish divergences in primate evolution.

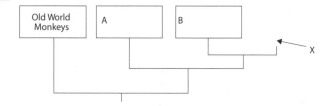

D4   THE HARDY-WEINBERG PRINCIPLE

1   In which of the following situations would evolution by natural selection be slowest for an inter-breeding population of organisms?

	Migration	Selection pressure	Variation due to gene mutation
A	low	low	low
B	absent	high	high
C	high	low	high
D	high	high	high

2   Which of the following is the conventional algebraic representation of the Hardy-Weinberg equation?
A $p^2 + 2pq + q^2 = 1$
B $p = q^2$
C $p^2 + q^2 = 1$
D $p + 2q = 1$

3   In the Hardy-Weinberg equation, what does the symbol p represent?
A   the frequency of individuals which are heterozygous for the dominant and recessive alleles
B   the frequency of a recessive allele
C   the frequency of individuals homozygous for the dominant allele
D   the frequency of a dominant allele

4   In the Hardy-Weinberg equation, what does the symbol q represent?
A   the frequency of individuals which are heterozygous for the dominant and recessive alleles
B   the frequency of a recessive allele
C   the frequency of individuals homozygous for the dominant allele
D   the frequency of a dominant allele

OPTION

5 What assumption does the Hardy-Weinberg principle not make about a population of organisms?
A the population is diploid and sexually reproducing
B immigration or emigration is not occurring within the population
C the population is experiencing mutation
D the mating between individuals is random

6 In a large population of cats, the probability that a gamete carries the dominant allele A for a long tail is 0.7. The probability that a gamete carries the recessive allele is 0.3.

Apply the *Hardy-Weinberg principle* and calculate the probability of a heterozygous *Aa* zygote being produced.
A 0.09
B 0.42
C 0.21
D 0.49

7 What may significant deviations from the frequencies predicted by the Hardy-Weinberg principle indicate to a Biologist studying a population of organisms?
A speciation is not likely to occur in the near future
B the mutation rate is zero
C the population under study is too large for the Hardy-Weinberg principle to be applied
D natural selection is occurring

8 In a population of white cats, the genotype for blue eyes is homozygous recessive, bb. If 9% of the cat population have blue eyes, calculate the frequency of the gene b.
A 0.7
B 0.18
C 0.0081
D 0.3

9 In a population of white cats, the genotype for blue eyes is homozygous recessive, bb. If 9% of the population have blue eyes, calculate the frequency of the heterozygous genotype Bb.
A 0.09
B 0.42
C 0.49
D 0.1638

10 Which is an incorrect statement about the application of the Hardy-Weinberg principle to a very large population?
A It predicts that allele and genotype frequencies remain constant from generation to generation
B It predicts a simple relationship between the allele frequencies and expected genotype frequencies
C It cannot be applied to three alleles
D It allows Biologists to detect natural selection

11 Which of the following conditions will maintain the proportion of dominant to recessive characteristics in a population will not change from generation to generation?
A random mating occurs
B mutations occur
C emigration occurs
D natural selection occurs

12 A breeding population of *Drosophila* is maintained in a large container in a laboratory. The frequency of the allele for black body (*b*) is 0.2 and the frequency of the normal allele (*B*) is 0.8. Calculate the expected proportions of the genotypes *BB*, *Bb* and *bb*.

13 Albinism, the complete lack of pigment, is determined in humans by a recessive allele. The frequency of albinos in a population is 1 in 20000 births. Calculate the proportion of the population that is heterozygous for this condition.

14 The ability to taste phenylthiocarbamide (PTC) is dominant to inability to taste. 252 people were tested and the following results were obtained.

	Tasters	Non-tasters	Total
Male	99	30	129
Female	103	20	123
Total	202	50	252

(a) Calculate the frequency of the recessive allele amongst males and females.
(b) The gene is **not** sex-linked. What is the most probable explanation to account for the sex difference in this *small* sample?

15 Phenylketonuria is an inherited disease of humans. Phenylketonurics are homozygous recessive and occur at a frequency of one in 10,000 births.
(a) In a population of 2000, how many people would be expected to be heterozygous?

OPTION

(b) A normal couple have already had one phenylketonuric child. What is the probability that their second child will be heterozygous for the condition?

16 The rat poison 'warfarin' was introduced into a rat infested town. Genetically determined resistance was later detected in the population. Resistance to warfarin is conferred by a dominant allele R. In a study 53% of rats in one area were found to be resistant to the poison.

(a) Calculate the frequency of the R allele in this rat population.

(b) Calculate the expected numbers of RR, Rr and rr genotypes in a population of 100 rats.

(c) If all the non-resistant rats in this population are killed by warfarin before reproducing, calculate the frequency of non-resistant rats born in the next generation.

D5 PHYLOGENY AND SYSTEMATICS

1 Which of the following is strong evidence for a single or unitary origin of life on Earth?

A   Analogous anatomical structures
B   Homologous anatomical structures
C   The universality of the genetic code
D   The fossil record

2 The trait of segmentation evolved before two groups of organisms branched from each other. What term is used to describe its presence in both groups of organisms?

A   Evolutionary divergence
B   Analogy
C   Homology
D   Co-evolution

3 The amino acid sequences of large protein common to a group of diverse organisms show a regularity in the rate of amino acid sequence change with time. What is the term applied to this phenomenon?

A   Phylogeny
B   Neutrality
C   Balanced polymorphism
D   Evolutionary or molecular clock

4 Which one of the following represents a pair of homologous evolutionary structures?

A   an insect wing and a bat wing
B   a human hand and a crab claw
C   a sperm tail and a tadpole tail
D   a human hand and a whale fin

OPTION

NEUROBIOLOGY AND BEHAVIOUR

16

- E1 Stimulus and response
- E2 Perception of stimuli
- E3 Innate and learned behaviour
- E4 Neurotransmitters and synapses
- E5 The human brain
- E6 Further studies of behaviour

E1 STIMULUS AND RESPONSE

> **E.1.1** Define the terms *stimulus, response* and *reflex* in the context of animal behaviour.
> ©IBO 2007

STIMULUS

A **stimulus** is a change in the environment (internal or external) that is detected by a receptor and elicits a response.

RESPONSE

A **response** is an action resulting from the perception of a stimulus. It is a reaction to a change perceived by the nervous system. The total of **responses** to stimuli is often called behaviour.

REFLEX

A **reflex** is a rapid, unconscious response.

> **E.1.2** Explain the role of receptors, sensory neurons, relay neurons, motor neurons, synapses and effectors in the response of animals to stimuli.
> ©IBO 2007

NEURON

Neuron is the medical name for a nerve cell (sometimes spelled neurone).

RECEPTORS

Receptors receive information from the (internal or external) environment. This information is in the form of energy, e.g. light, sound or the concentration of glucose in the blood. The information is changed into one or more action potentials and transmitted to the brain where the action potential is received and the information it contains is "decoded", for example an action potential from the eye is perceived as light and an action potential from the ear as sound. Examples of receptors are photoreceptors, chemoreceptors and thermoreceptors.

SENSORY NEURONS

Sensory neurons receive action potentials from receptors and conduct them towards the Central Nervous System (CNS brain and spinal cord). There they connect to relay neurons.

RELAY NEURONS

Relay neurons receive action potentials from sensory neurons and pass them to other parts of the CNS or to motor neurons in the case of a reflex arc. *(Refer to Topic E.1.3)*

MOTOR NEURONS

Motor neurons take action potentials from the CNS to muscles or glands. The result of an action potential conducted by a motor neuron is the contraction of a muscle or the release of product from a gland.

OPTION

277

SYNAPSE

A **synapse** is the connection between two neurons. In chemical synapses, the electrical impulse is changed into a chemical signal which crosses the synapse and changes back into one or more action potentials in the next neuron.

EFFECTOR

An **effector** is the muscle or gland that produces the response to a stimulus.

> E.1.3 Draw and label a diagram of a reflex arc for a pain withdrawal reflex, including the spinal cord and its spinal nerves, the receptor cell, sensory neuron, relay neuron, motor neuron and effector.
>
> ©IBO 2007

The elements listed in *Topic E.1.2* are part of reflex arc, found in, for example, a pain withdrawal reflex. *See Figure 1601*.

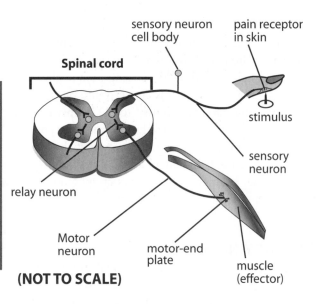

Figure 1601   The reflex arc

> E.1.4 Explain how animal responses can be affected by natural selection, using two examples.
>
> ©IBO 2007

Animal responses can only be affected by natural selection when the responses are caused by genetic factors.

BLACKCAP

The bird *Sylvia atricapilla* (blackcap) breeds during the summer in Germany and, until recently, migrated to Spain or other Mediterranean areas for winter. However, studies show that 10% of blackcaps now migrate to the UK instead. *See Figure 1602*.

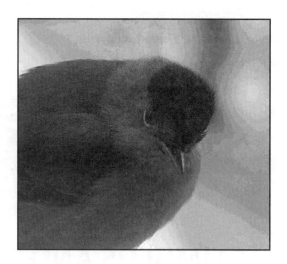

Figure 1602   The blackcap

To test whether this change is genetically determined or not (and, therefore, whether it was a consequence of natural selection or not), eggs were collected from parents who had migrated to the UK in the previous winter as well as from parents who had migrated to Spain. The young were reared and the direction in which they set off, when the time for migration came, was recorded. Birds whose parents had migrated to the UK tended to fly west, wherever they had been reared, and birds whose parents had migrated to Spain tended to fly south-west. Despite not being able to follow their parents at the time of migration, all the birds tended to fly in the direction that would take them on the same migration route as their parents.

This and other evidence suggests that blackcaps are genetically programmed to respond to stimuli when they migrate so that they fly in a particular direction. The increase in the numbers of blackcaps migrating to the UK for the winter may be due to warmer winters and greater survival rates in the UK.

In other words, when winters were colder, there was a lot of natural selection against the genes that caused birds to fly west: they were less successful in surviving the winter. Now, with warmer winters, the survival rate in the UK has increased, reducing the natural selection against these genes and hence against the behaviour.

HEDGEHOG

Hedgehogs roll into a ball when threatened. This behaviour is genetically determined and successful against most predators. Hedgehogs are nocturnal animals and travel one or two kilometers a night which is likely to involve crossing roads. Approaching cars are treated as predators but the spines are not effective protection in these cases. Hedgehogs that continue to display this behaviour, are likely to be killed earlier and produce less offspring.

Figure 1603   The hedgehog

It has been suggested that some hedgehogs run away when they sense the approach of a car. This is more likely to remove them from the road and extend their lifespan which could result in producing more offspring and passing on the gene(s) that cause the different response to cars. *See Figure 1603.*

TOK   How does behaviour affect survival?

Natural selection is complex process that is affected by many factors. Animal behaviour is often equally complex. As a result, it is difficult to determine relationships between animal responses or behaviour and natural selection. To determine links, carefully controlled investigations or observations must take place. In most cases, the conclusions drawn must be limited to the specific organism and location of the study, though wider implications may be inferred for further investigation. This can cause difficulties for us as humans often instinctively draw conclusions based on our own observations of behaviour, which can lead to incorrect conclusions.

E2 PERCEPTION OF STIMULI

E.2.1	Outline the diversity of stimuli that can be detected by human sensory receptors, including mechanoreceptors, chemoreceptors, thermoreceptors and photoreceptors.

©IBO 2007

CHEMORECEPTORS

Chemoreceptors have special proteins in their membranes. These proteins can bind to a particular substance and this will result in a depolarisation of the membrane leading to an action potential being sent to the brain. Chemoreceptors are responsible for our sense of smell and taste but also detect the blood pH. taste buds on the tongue contain chemoreceptors. *See Figure 1604.*

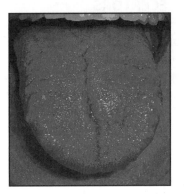

Figure 1604   The human tongue

ELECTRORECEPTORS

Electroreceptors are found, for example, in sharks. Muscle contractions generate electrical fields which are conducted by the water. The shark can sense these fields with its electroreceptors and detect its prey. As air is a poor conductor, terrestrial organisms would not have much use for this sense organ. *See Figure 1605.*

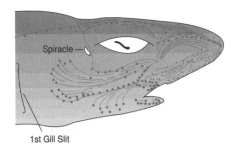

Spiracle —

1st Gill Slit

Figure 1605   Sharks have electro-receptors

MECHANORECEPTORS

Mechanoreceptors are those that are sensitive to some kind of movement. In fish, they are found in the 'lateral line system', which detects vibrations in the environment.

We have a similar system in our inner ear to inform us of our body's position and movement. Three fluid filled semicircular canals are connected to the area. At the end of the canals, as well as in the common area, we find a system of hair cells. Any change in speed or direction will move the fluid in at least one of the semicircular canals, bending the hairs. This causes action potentials to be sent to the brain.

PHOTORECEPTORS

Photoreceptors are the rods and cones in our eyes *(Topic E.2.2)*. Rods and cones contain photopigments that are broken down when exposed to light. This causes the cells to send an action potential to the brain.

THERMORECEPTORS

Thermoreceptors are found, for example, in the skin. Cold receptors, just under the surface of the skin, will send an action potential when the temperature drops. Warm receptors, located a little deeper, will send an action potential when the temperature increases. The temperature centre in the hypothalamus of the brain also contains thermoreceptors to monitor the temperature of the blood.

TOK   How does technology help us to 'know' the biological world?

Our perception of the physical world is based on the data received through our senses. This data is filtered both by the sense organs and the brain. As a result of this filtering our perception of the world around us is flawed. We do not perceive the world as it really is. Each organism differs in its sensing of the physical world, leading to a different perception of the world. Dogs, for example, cannot see colour, bats hear sounds outside of the human range of perception and some insect pollinators detect wavelengths beyond the range visible to humans. Our human instinct is to assume that the perception that we have of the world is the way it is, whereas it is really the way that our body perceives it. Our perception of the physical world is enhanced by technologies that allow us to detect radiation that our bodies cannot and display them is ways that we can perceive to aid in understanding of our world.

| E.2.2 | Label a diagram of the structure of the human eye. |

©IBO 2007

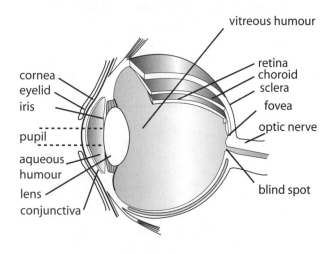

Figure 1606   The structure of the human eye

| E.2.3 | Annotate a diagram of the retina to show the cell types and the direction in which light moves. |

©IBO 2007

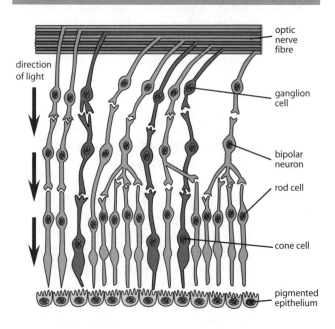

Figure 1607   The structure of the retina

The light enters from above *(in Figure 1607)* and passes in between various neurons. It finally hits the rods or cones. The light that is not absorbed by the rods or cones, hits a layer of pigmented epithelium to prevent it reflecting back into the eye land producing yet another set of images.

Light enters the eye and is refracted by the cornea and the lens. It passes through the clear vitreous humour and then reaches the retina. The light must pass between the nerve cells (ganglion cells and bipolar neurons) to reach the rods and cones which form the layer of light-sensitive cells.

The rods and cones contain photosensitive pigments which are broken down under the influence of light. This causes one or more impulses to be sent to the brain. In the absence of light, the pigments are rapidly reformed.

> **E.2.4   Compare rod and cone cells.**
>
> ©IBO 2007

ROD CELLS

Rods are found all through the retina except in the fovea. The pigment in rods is called rhodopsin or visual purple. Several rods are linked to one bipolar neuron. This means that their impulses are 'added up' and this explains their higher light sensitivity. However it also reduces accuracy.

When the light has caused an action potential in the rods or cones, it is passed on to the bipolar neurons. Here, the presence of action potentials of other cells may inhibit or further excite the bipolar cell. An action potential may then be passed on to the ganglion cell and from here to the optic nerve.

CONE CELLS

The **cones** are mostly found in the fovea. Cones contain three different pigments which are sensitive to different colours of light. Cones are individually linked to the bipolar neurons and are therefore less sensitive to lower light intensities but give a more accurate picture in bright light. Refer to Figure 1608 for a comparison of the structure and function of rods and cones.

> **E.2.5   Explain the processing of visual stimuli, including edge enhancement and contralateral processing.**
>
> ©IBO 2007

Processing visual stimuli already starts in the eye. It has been found that ganglion cells send impulses to the brain, even when light is completely absent. Adding diffuse, low intensity light, does not affect this process.

However, when a small spot of light shines on the retina, ganglions may greatly increase the number of impulses sent to the brain or may stop sending impulses, depending on where the light shines.

Rods are grouped together in receptive areas. Those in the centre of a receptive area are excitatory and will respond to light by sending an impulse to the ganglion. Those near the outside of the receptive area are inhibitory and will stop the ganglion from sending impulses to the brain.

If the light shines on the excitatory photoreceptors in the centre of a receptive area, the ganglions send more impulses. If the light shines on the inhibitory photoreceptors, the ganglion will stop sending impulses. If the light shines on both, there will be no change in the frequency of sending impulses, i.e. it remains the same as in the dark.

The explanation for this is that the nerves are not just passing information about the light intensity perceived to the brain. They are processing the details about light and dark and informing the brain about contrast which tells us a lot about shapes.

TVs and cameras use this concept and can do the same thing. This is called **edge enhancement**. It makes the edge of something dark even darker and creates a "halo" of light around it, enhancing the contrast. Edge enhancement occurs within the retina (and is also known as lateral

OPTION

	Rods	Cones
Where in the retina?	found outside the fovea	found in the fovea
Works best in which light conditions?	used in dim light ("night vision")	used in bright light ("day vision")
Connected to bipolar neurons	several rods are attached to one bipolar neuron	one cone is attached to one bipolar neuron
Accuracy	less accurate since signals of several rods are added up	very accurate (if enough light is available)
How many types?	only one type	three different types
Sensitive to which colours?	sensitive to all colours light	sensitive to red, green or blue light
Type of vision?	achromatic vision (black and white)	colour vision
How many?	many more than cones	fewer than rods

Figure 1608   Comparing rods and cones

inhibition) and can be demonstrated by looking at the **Hermann grid illusion**.

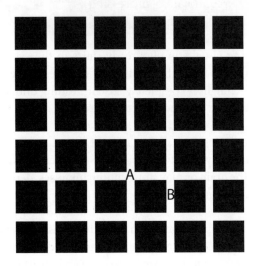

Figure 1609   The Hermann grid illusion

When glancing at the Figure 1609, there seem to be grey spots in the middle of the white intersections. These grey spots fade out when looking at them directly. The explanation lies in the receptive areas of the retina.

When glancing at an intersection, for example A, the excitatory photoreceptors are stimulated but, as there are four white lines around A, several inhibitory photoreceptors also receive light. When glancing at a line, for example at B, only a few of the inhibitory receptors will receive light. As a result, the brain will receive information that the contrast at A is less than at B. So we see B as a white spot and A as a more grey spot. When focussing on the spot, we use the photoreceptors in the fovea where the receptive areas are much smaller. As a result, the grey spots disappear when we look at them directly.

Contra-lateral processing refers to fact that some of the nerve fibres in the optic nerve will cross before reaching the brain (optic chiamsa). As is shown in Figure 1610, the information from the left half of the visual field, arrives on the right side of the retina in the left eye. The nerves from this section are processed by the right side of the brain. Information from the right half of the visual field, arrives on the left side of the retina in the left eye. The nerves from this section are processed by the left side of the brain. Vice versa occurs for the right eye.

Overall, it means that information of the right side of the visual field is processed by the left hemisphere of the brain and information from the left side of the visual field is processed by the right hemisphere.

Contralateral processing is arranged per visual field per eye. It is **NOT** true that all information from the right eye is processed by the left hemisphere (and vice versa).

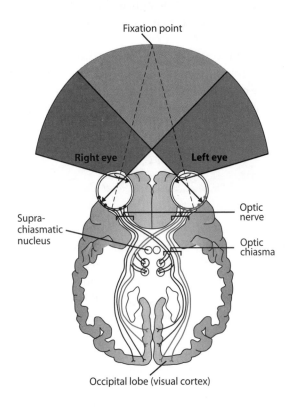

Figure 1610   Contra-lateral processing

E.2.6   Label a diagram of the ear.

©IBO 2007

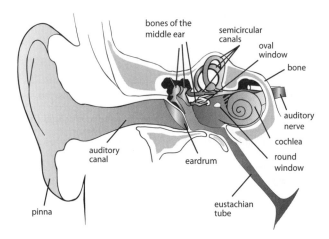

Figure 1611   The structure of the human ear

OPTION

E.2.7   Explain how sound is perceived by the ear, including the roles of the eardrum, bones of the middle ear, oval and round windows, and the hair cells of the cochlea.

©IBO 2007

Sound is caused by vibrations of air molecules. Sound travels through air because one vibrating air molecule collides with the next, passing on the vibrations. The function of the pinna is to direct sound towards the eardrum. The eardrum separates the outer ear from the middle ear.

When the sound reaches the **eardrum**, it starts to vibrate. The movement of the vibrating eardrum will cause the three small **bones** (auditory ossicles) to vibrate. The movement is passed from the hammer to the anvil to the stirrup and the vibrations are amplified. The stirrup is attached to the oval window. The oval window separates the middle ear from the inner ear.

The vibrations of the **oval window** create vibrations in the fluid filled cochlea to which it is attached. Inside the cochlea, the vibrating fluid causes movement of little hairs. As these hairs move, they create action potentials that are passed to the auditory nerve and transmitted to the brain. Different frequencies cause different parts of the cochlea to vibrate and causes action potentials in different neurons. This way, the brain can interpret the pitch of the sound which is identified by which particular nerve cells pass on the information.

The **round window** allows the vibrations of the fluid inside the cochlea to occur without an increase in pressure which could cause damage to the tissues.

E3 INNATE AND LEARNED BEHAVIOUR

E.3.1   Distinguish between *innate* and *learned* behaviour.

©IBO 2007

INNATE BEHAVIOUR

Innate behaviour develops independently of the environmental context. It is behaviour which normally occurs in all members of a species, including in young and inexperienced animals. Innate behaviour is controlled by genes which makes it subject to natural selection (*Refer to Topic E.1.4*). Taxes and kineses are examples of innate behaviour.

LEARNED BEHAVIOUR

Learned behaviour develops as a result of experience. When the experience is beneficial, the animal may repeat the behaviour as it has learned that this behaviour brings about a positive consequence.

E.3.2   Design experiments to investigate innate behaviour in invertebrates, including either a taxis or a kinesis.

©IBO 2007

As *Euglena* is a photosynthetic motile unicellular organism, it will display a positive phototaxis, i.e. it will move towards the light. The following experimental investigation should confirm the phototaxis. *See Figure 1612.*

Cover the sides and top of a Petri dish with aluminium foil. Cut out a few small sections of the foil from the top. Put 15 mL of concentrated *Euglena* solution in the petri dish, place under a light source and on top of a white sheet and leave for 15 minutes. Switch off the light and open the Petri dish. If *Euglena* is phototaxic, then the areas where the light came through the holes in the foil should be greener due to a high concentration of *Euglena*.

Woodlice are known to show kinesis to humidity because they have gills for respiration and are likely to dry out if they remain in dry conditions for too long. *See Figure 1613.*

OPTION

283

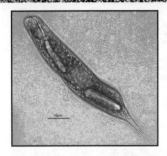

Figure 1612   Euglena   Figure 1613   Wood lice

Woodlice move faster and turn more often in dry conditions than in damp conditions. As a result, they are more likely to leave a dry area and remain in a damp area. An experiment could be done to investigate this kinesis.

Cut a filter paper in half. Place one half in a Petri dish. Wet the other half and also place it in the Petri dish. Put 5 woodlice in the dish and record their positions every minute for 10 minutes. They should spend more time on the wet paper than on the dry paper.

Another experiment could be to place one woodlouse in the dish and to mark its position every 30 seconds for 5 minutes. The trail should indicate more movement and more turning on dry paper than on damp paper.

E.3.3	Analyse data from invertebrate behaviour experiments in terms of the effect on chances of survival and reproduction.
	©IBO 2007

The above experiment on *Euglena* should indicate that this species shows a postive phototaxis, i.e. it travels towards the light. This increases the amount of photosynthesis, the process by which photoautotrophs produce glucose (and other organic molecules from glucose). In order to reproduce, *Euglena* must produce sufficient organic molecules.

The experiment on woodlice should indicate kinesis to humidity. Woodlice should move faster and turn more in dry conditions. This increases their chance of leaving the potentially dangerous dry conditions as woodlice are prone to dehydration as they breathe through gills. In damp conditions, woodlice move less and do not change direction as frequently, which is more likely to cause them to remain in the damp conditions which enhances their chances of survival and reproduction.

E.3.4	Discuss how the process of learning can improve the chance of survival.
	©IBO 2007

Innate behaviour is suited to conditions that do not change. Bees display innate behaviour of searching for nectar in brightly coloured flowers. A positive experience in one flower will cause the bee to actively look for this kind of flower next time (a concept the plants use in order to improve their chances of being pollinated with pollen of the same species). The bee will also have learned that it is vital to memorise the way home.

E.3.5	Outline Pavlov's experiments into conditioning of dogs.
	©IBO 2007

In the 1920, the Russian psychologist *Ivan Pavlov* did the first studies into conditioning. Dogs, like most mammals, will start to produce saliva at the smell or taste of food. When Pavlov for some time rang a bell before feeding the dog, eventually the dog began to produce saliva at the sound of the bell. Pavlov called the food the unconditioned stimulus. The bell became the conditioned stimulus: the dog had been conditioned to associate it with food. The conditioned response is producing saliva before there is any evidence of food. *Refer to Figure 1614.*

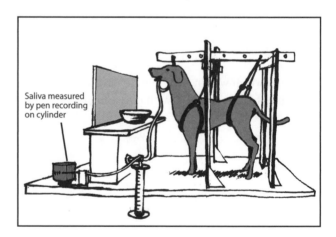

Saliva measured by pen recording on cylinder

Figure 1614   Pavlov's experimental set-up

E.3.6	Outline the role of inheritance and learning in the development of birdsong in young birds.
	©IBO 2007

Birdsong has a genetic component in all birds. In some species of birds young raised in isolation will be able to sing the song. For species like the *Phoebe*, their song is completely innate.

OPTION

Songbirds will sing a simplified song if not taught by older birds. Example of these birds that have an innate component to their song and expand it by learning from others are warblers.

Figure 1615   A Warbler

Figure 1616   A starling

Some birds, for example the starling, may incorporate sounds it has heard into its song. It has been said that the sounds of mobile telephones can now be heard as part of certain birds' songs.

TOK   How can Pavlov's theory be applied?

Pavlov's conditional reflex experiments are helpful in understanding learning in that they describe how many organisms respond to stimuli, in particular, the fact that association plays a role in many responses to stimuli. John Watson's *Little Albert* experiment demonstrated that humans could be conditioned to fear something that would not normally cause concern. Albert B, a child under the age of one was exposed to loud sounds causing distress in association with objects that had previously caused no concern to him. After the association with the loud sounds, these objects caused distress for Albert without the presence of the sounds.

This experiment demonstrated that humans could be conditioned just as other animals. Today such an experiment would be considered unethical for several reasons. Conditioning is used to assist people in aversion therapies to break an association that is harmful and in other behavioural therapies.

E4 NEURO-TRANSMITTERS AND SYNAPSES

E.4.1	State that some presynaptic neurons excite postsynaptic transmission and others inhibit postsynaptic transmission.

©IBO 2007

In *Topic 6.5.5*, Figure 1617 was used to explain how a nerve impulse is passed along a nerve fibre.

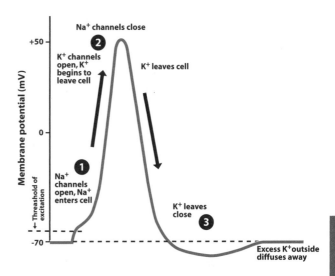

Figure 1617   The Action potential

It can be seen that the resting potential (the potential difference across the membrane of the nerve fibre when no impulse is being conducted) is -70 mV. During an action potential, the membrane potential goes from -70 mV to +50 mV.

As it is described in *Topic 6.5.6*, in order to transfer an impulse from one neuron to another via a chemical synapse, the neurotransmitter must cause a reaction in the post synaptic membrane. If the reaction in the post-synaptic membrane is to open sodium channels and let in sodium, the membrane potential will become closer to zero. This is called an **excitatory post-synaptic potential (EPSP)** which will depolarise the post-synaptic membrane. If enough signals come through this (or similar) synapses, an action potential will result.

It is also possible that the reaction of the post-synaptic membrane is to open chloride channels so that chloride ions can diffuse into the neuron. This will bring the membrane potential further away from zero and will

OPTION

285

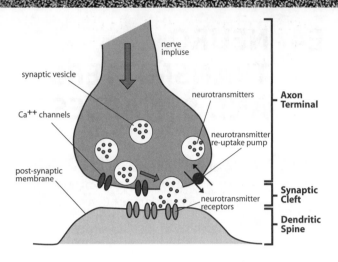

Figure 1618   Transmission across a synapse

make it more difficult to generate an action potential on the post-synaptic membrane. This is called an **inhibitory post-synaptic potential (IPSP)** which will hyperpolarize the post-synaptic membrane. If a number of signals come through inhibitory synapses, then one or more signals from an excitatory synapse will still not be enough to cross the threshold potential and will not generate an action potential in the next neuron. This means that the impulse will not be transmitted.

E.4.2   Explain how decision-making in the CNS can result from the interaction between the activities of excitatory and inhibitory presynaptic neurons at synapses.

©IBO 2007

Decision making can be based on the **summation** of EPSP and IPSP signals. If the EPSP are capable of depolarising the post-synaptic membrane beyond the treshold, despite the hyperpolarising effect of the IPSP, then the post-synaptic membrane will send an action potential. If the IPSPs hyperpolarise the membrane enough so that the EPSPs cannot cause a sufficent depolarisation, then the signal will fade out.

E.4.3   Explain how psychoactive drugs affect the brain and personality by either increasing or decreasing postsynaptic transmission.

©IBO 2007

Psychoactive drugs influence the brain by affecting it at the level of the neurotransmitters. They can increase or decrease post-synaptic transmission.

Psychoactive drugs can:
- release the neurotransmitter (Ecstacy)
- mimic its effect (LSD, morphine and heroin)
- reduce or delay the re-uptake of the neurotransmitter which will increase postsynaptic transmission in excitatory synapses and decrease transmission in inhibitory synapses. (atomoxetine, sold under the brand name Strattera)
- block the receptors of the neurotransmitter on the postsyntaptic membrane which will stop the depolarisation or hyperpolarisation (PCP, known as Angel Dust)

Some drugs bind to the neurotransmitter receptors but will have the opposite effect of the neurotransmitter, (naloxone, used to treat morphine or heroin overdose). If the neurotransmitter causes depolarisation, the drug will cause hyperpolarisation and vice versa.

E.4.4   List three examples of excitatory and three examples of inhibitory psychoactive drugs.

©IBO 2007

EXCITATORY DRUGS

Nicotine
Nicotine, found in cigarettes *(see Figure 1619)* stimulates receptors that usually respond to acetyl choline, causing an increase in adrenaline, which increases heart rate, blood pressure and blood sugar levels.

Cocaine
Cocaine stimulates the CNS and creates a sense of euphoria (happiness); it blocks the re-uptake of dopamine which therefore accumulates. Dopamine is part of the brain's reward system: it makes us feel good and any activity that increases the effect of dopamine is potentially addictive. Figure 1620 shows the Coca plant which is used to make cocaine.

Figure 1619   Nicotine is as addictive drug

Figure 1620 The Coca plant

Amphetamines

Amphetamines stimulate the CNS, release nor-adrenaline and dopamine into synapses and inhibit re-uptake. This leads to increased concentration and performance.

For many drugs, after some use, the number of receptors in the post-synaptic membrane are reduced, which leads to a decrease in the effect of the drug. Increasing doses are needed to obtain the same effect.

INHIBITORY DRUGS

Benzodiazepines

Benzodiazepines are tranquilizers which slow down the CNS, e.g. valium. They are used to treat anxiety, insomnia and muscle spasms. These drugs work because they hyper-polarise the post-synaptic membrane so that many impulses are not transmitted but "fade out".

Alcohol

Alcohol is a drug that also depresses the CNS. It reduces inhibitions and makes the person feel cheerful and relaxed. However at a later stage alcohol may cause the individual to flaunt legal or moral rules. It causes a receptor of a neurotransmitter (GABA) to remain open longer so further hyperpolarising the postsynaptic membrane. *See Figure 1621.*

Alcohol is a dangerous combination with many other drugs such as benzodiazepines because both drugs reinforce each other.

Figure 1621
Alcohol is an inhibitory drug

Figure 1622   The chemical structure of THC

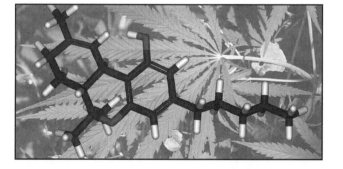

Tetrahydrocannabinol (THC)

Tetrahyrocannabinol (THC) is a psychoactive drug found in the *Cannabis* plant. It causes relaxation and is a pain killer. THC functions by binding to endorphin receptors. Figure 1622 shows the schematic formula of THC, an active component in *Cannabis*.

E.4.5	Explain the effects of THC and cocaine in terms of their action at synapses in the brain.

©IBO 2007

TETRAHYROCANNABINOL (THC)

THC is a psychoactive drug found in the *Cannabis* plant. It causes relaxation and is a pain killer by binding to endorphin receptors. It increases appetite and has been used for those who suffer from anorexia. THC is reported to be addictive or non-addictive, depending on the source of the research. THC impairs memory and decision making and students using THC statistically gain lower grades than those not using the drug. Workers using THC are more likely to have problems at work than those not using it.

COCAINE

Cocaine stimulates the CNS and creates a sense of euphoria (happiness). It is a very powerful drug because it gives a very intense "high" which users wish to repeat often. It blocks the re-uptake of dopamine which therefore accumulates. Cocaine also makes the user feel less tired or hungry and enhances endurance.

Dopamine is part of the brain's reward system. It makes us feel good and any activity that increases the effect of dopamine is potentially addictive.

Unfortunately, the "high" that (crack) cocaine provides, is usually followed by a "crash" when the effect of the drug wears off. Users experience depression, irritability and paranoia which are in great contrast with the "high" provided by the drug. This leads to further cocaine use. However, the brain will reduce the number of dopamine receptors when overloaded with cocaine so that when the drug has worn off, users indeed experience less joy out of every day events which further reinforces cocaine use.

At this stage, users often are not capable of holding a job and will finance their habit by lying and cheating, often stealing. Relations with family become insignificant compared to the ability to obtain cocaine and relatives are often the first victims of the user's changed behaviour. Addicts are willing to go to great length, including crime, in order to obtain money to buy more cocaine.

OPTION

OPTION

E.4.6 Discuss the causes of addiction, including genetic predisposition, social factors and dopamine secretion.

©IBO 2007

Addiction, in this context, refers to the repeated and compulsive use of psychoactive drugs.

GENETIC PREDISPOSITION

It is argued that genetic factors may increase the chance of a person becoming addicted. However, it is argued equally that this is not the case. The controversy over a genetic component to addiction has existed for many years. It is common to find more than one addicted person in a family. It could be argued that this just as likely to be caused genetically as by social factors. Native Americans are much more likely to die of alcoholism than Americans in general. This concept support the existence of a genetic factor in addiction but so far the data has been inconclusive.

SOCIAL FACTORS

Statistically, people from environments where there is substance abuse, people who suffered childhood trauma and/or neglect are more at risk of developing addictions. It has been suggested that psychoactive drugs are a way of dealing with an unpleasant situation. Every person experiences many unpleasant situations in his/her life, but some people respond by taking drugs while others do not. The reasons for this is not clear.

DOPAMINE SECRETION

Dopamine is produced by the brain, it makes us feel good and any activity that increases the effect of dopamine is potentially addictive. Many drugs interfere with dopamine and extend the time this substance is found at the synapse which makes us feel good.

The brain will reduce the number of dopamine receptors when overloaded with some drugs so that when the drug has worn off, users indeed experience less joy out of every day events which further reinforces drug use.

E5 THE HUMAN BRAIN

E.5.1 Label, on a diagram of the brain, the medulla oblongata, cerebellum, hypothalamus, pituitary gland and cerebral hemispheres.

©IBO 2007

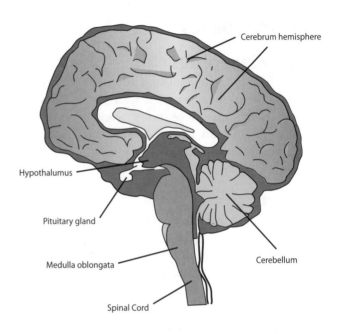

Figure 1623   The structure of the human brain

E.5.2 Outline the functions of each of the parts of the brain listed in E.5.1.

©IBO 2007

MEDULLA OBLONGATA

The medulla oblongata controls automatic and homeostatic activities, such as swallowing, digestion and vomiting; breathing and heart activity.

CEREBELLUM

The cerebellum coordinates unconscious functions, such as movement and balance.

HYPOTHALAMUS

The hypothalamus maintains homeostasis, coordinating the nervous and endocrine systems, secreting hormones from the posterior pituitary, and releasing factors regulating the anterior pituitary.

PITUITARY GLAND

The posterior lobe stores and releases hormones produced by the hypothalamus and the anterior lobe. It also produces and secretes hormones regulating many body functions.

CEREBRAL HEMISPHERES

Cerebral hemishperes act as the integrating centre for high complex functions such as learning, memory and emotions.

> E.5.3   Explain how animal experiments, lesions and FMRI (functional magnetic resonance imaging) scanning can be used in the identification of the brain part involved in specific functions.
>
> ©IBO 2007

ANIMAL EXPERIMENTS

There is now evidence that suggests that the brain is more capable of adapting to changes than we used to think. Research has been done where the optic nerve was rerouted into an auditory area of the brain. The animals developed the ability to process the visual information in what was considered to be an auditory part of the brain. Ethical issues are clearly a concern here but some claim that experiments on animal brains with the intention to extrapolate to human brians are not valid since the human brain is very different from those of animals. Others do not agree and claim that primate brain research has provided important information.

LESIONS

When humans suffer brain damage and develop lesions, it is possible to study the effects of the damage to certain areas and the resulting loss of functions. In animal experiments, it is possible to create these lesions and compare the effects with intact animal brains and also with humans who have lesions in the same areas.

Elisabeth Bates was a leading research scientist who in 2003 published that her team had developed a functional **brain imaging.** They applied their technique to study the damage to the brain and correlated this information with the abilities of a group of left-hemisphere-damaged aphasic patients. (Aphasia is the impairment to use and/or understand language due to brain damage.) The images were compared with those produced in "normal" brains. This way, the damage shown could be correlated to the impairment found.

fMRI

It has been known for many years that when a certain part of the brain is active, it requires more oxygen. Oxygen is carried in the erythrocytes (red blood cells) attached to haemoglobin. Hemoglobin with oxygen is referred to as oxyhemoglobin and when the oxygen has been removed, it is called de-oxyhemoglobin.

It has been shown that oxyhaemoglobin will respond differently to a magnetic field than de-oxyhaemoglobin. These differences can be measured using Magnetic Resonance Imaging (MRI). The bigger the difference is in the oxygenation levels of the blood, the more oxygen has been used and the more active the part of the brain is. These differences are then expressed as different colours.

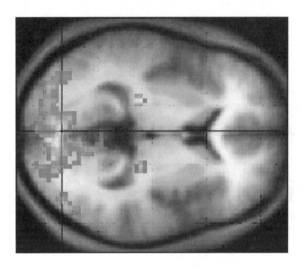

Figure 1624   An fMRI image of a brain

By comparing the responses of a person with an undamaged brain to that of someone who has suffered brain lesions (any kind of damage), the extent of the damage can be assessed. Figure 1624 shows an fMRI image of a brain which indicates activity in the visual area.

Researchers tested a young woman who fulfilled the existing criteria for "vegetative state" (not responding) due to a severe head injury in a traffic accident, for brain activity. They asked her questions and monitored her brain using fMRI. When they compared her results with those of a fully-functioning person being asked the same questions, the images were identical. The patient's brain showed the same increases in oxygen use in the same areas as that of a fully conscious person. Although the researches stress that this is (so far) an isolated case, the information is very startling.

OPTION

OPTION

TOK   Investigating the human mind

Functional magnetic resonance imaging (fMRI) is used to investigate how the human brain operates. Such investigation is based upon the observation that oxygenated blood flow to a region of the brain correlates with neural activity in that region and the fact that oxygenated blood has a different magnetic property to deoxygenated blood. As such, fMRI is an indirect tool to investigate brain activity. Observations made with this technique must be viewed with caution as many other factors could influence the production of images produced with fMRI and some scientists argue that many experiments using fMRI data are not falsifiable and should not be considered science. There is also the complication that many brain activities are based on conditioned reflexes and as such are thought to demand little extra blood supply to the region of the brain involved in the response. As with many technologies fMRI data is only valuable if it is generated from a well-designed experiment.

E.5.4   Explain sympathetic and parasympathetic control of the heart rate, movements of the iris and flow of blood to the gut.

©IBO 2007

The **autonomic nervous system** is the part of the nervous system that is (normally) not under voluntary control. It is divided into a sympathetic and a parasympathetic part.

The sympathetic nervous system is involved in action, for example fighting or running away. Impulses via the sympathetic nervous system will increase heart rate, contract the dilatory muscles in the iris, dilating the pupil in order to improve vision and decrease the flow of blood to the gut so that it can go to other tissues such as the muscles instead, which need more glucose and oxygen. Digesting food has a low priority in emergencies.

The parasympathetic nervous system is involved in processes that occur at rest. So messages via the parasympathetic system will reduce heart rate, cause the circular muscles in the iris to contract which constricts the size of the pupil, reducing the amount of light on the retina which limits damage to the retina (by too much light)and increases blood flow to the gut to facilitate digestion.

E.5.5   Explain the pupil reflex.

©IBO 2007

The **pupil reflex** is a cranial reflex. When bright light is perceived by the ganglion cells in the retina, an impulse is created which passes to the midbrain and from there to a nerve going to the eye. As a result, the circular muscle in the iris will immediately contract, reducing the amount of light upon the retina so that it will not be damaged. Dilating the iris is not such a fast response since there is a less urgent need to allow more light into the eye.

It is very important for enough light to fall on the retina so that the individual can see well. However, too much light can cause damage to the retina. In order to satisfy both conditions, the pupil will be dilated in dim light, allowing more light into the eye and constricted in bright light, reducing the chance of damage.

To achieve the changing diameter of the pupil, there are two sets of muscles in the iris: the circular and the radial muscles. When the circular muscle contracts and the radial muscles relax, the pupil becomes smaller. When the circular muscle relaxes and the radial muscles contract, the pupil becomes larger. Figure 1625 shows the muscles involved in the pupil reflex of the eye.

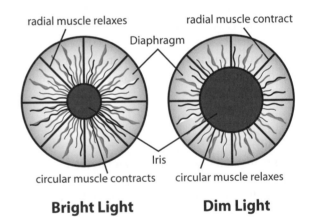

Figure 1625   The pupil reflex

E.5.6   Discuss the concept of brain death and the use of the pupil reflex in testing for this.

©IBO 2007

Brain death is the permanent absence of measurable brain activity. Due to technical advances in life support equipment, it became possible to maintain processes such as a heart beat for a long time without the patient responding to any signals. If no activity in the brain can be measured for some time, it is presumed that there is no longer is any form of conciousness and doctors are allowed to declare the patient dead and switch off the life support equipment.

The absence of a pupillary reflex is taken as an indication that cranial reflexes are absent. It is one of the list of checks (including no response to pain and no gag-reflex) that doctors perform before declaring a person brain dead.

Do not confuse brain dead with a coma or the vegetative state. In either of those, there is a measurable amount of brain activity.

E.5.7   Outline how pain is perceived and how endorphins can act as painkillers.

©IBO 2007

Pain is a very important sensation. It informs us that there is a problem somewhere and that we might be able to take action to reduce further damage. Pain receptors are nerve endings in the skin and other organs. They respond to chemicals released by blood vessels, macrophages and cells in connective tissue when they are damaged.

When the **pain receptors** detect the chemicals, an impulse is generated which travels, via the spinal cord, to the sensory areas of the cerebral cortex where the pain is experienced. The experience of pain is closely related to emotional factors as well as to the severity of the trauma causing the pain. When pain has alerted the individual to a problem, it is then desirable that the intensity of the pain is reduced so that it does not take up too much of the individual's attention (which might reduce its chances of survival). The brain produces endorphins, which are natural pain killers.

Encephalins are one example of endorphins. They are small polypeptide chains which act by inhibiting association neurons that transmit pain to the brain.

A sensory neuron, relaying impulses from a pain receptor, forms a synapse with an associate neuron. Near this synapse, another synapse is found, coming from the pain control centre in the brain. When the pain control centre sends out an impulse, the synapse will release endorphins which will interfere with the transmission of the impulse by attaching to receptors and blocking them, preventing a pain impulse from being passed on. Enkephalins will block calcium channels which stop calcium from flowing into the presynaptic knob. Without calcium, the vesicles containing neurotransmitters will not move to the presynaptic membrane, so the impulse will fade out.

E6   FURTHER STUDIES OF BEHAVIOUR

E.6.1   Describe the social organization of honey bee colonies and one other non-human example.

©IBO 2007

HONEY BEES

The honey bee lives in groups that often exceed 20,000 individuals. Most individuals in the colony are workers and there is one queen. The queen will lay fertilised diploid eggs that hatch into larvae. If the larvae are fed a special diet (more protein), they develop into queens. Otherwise they develop into workers. After about a week, a larva will become a pupa and two weeks later will emerge as an adult bee. Figure 1626 shows a queen bee, the light spot (*just above centre*) was added so that she is easier to identify.

— Queen Bee

Figure 1626   A Queen Bee and her Helpers

The various tasks in the colony are divided according to the age of the worker. Young workers start off as nurses, taking care of the larvae for about two weeks. They then are assigned house keeping duties, cleaning and guarding the hive and removing sick or dead bees. They gradually start to go outside, making short trips and will finally, for about 6 weeks, go out to collect honey and pollen.

When the colony gets too big, the queen will prepare to leave. As a result, some of her larvae will be fed the special diet and they will become queens. Some unfertilised eggs will hatch into drones (males). The old queen will leave with half the colony and soon after the new queen will fly out. She will be followed by the drones. She will be fertilised and store the sperm to use over the next few years. The new queen returns and starts laying eggs, fertilising them with the stored sperm. She will not fly again and she is looked after by the workers. The drones also return. They have no further role and when food becomes scarce, they will be driven out or killed.

NAKED MOLE RAT

Naked mole rats have a social structure that is unusual for mammals. *Refer to Figure 1627.*

They live in colonies underground in a series of burrows and tunnels. Only the queen will reproduce with a few males. Other females are workers with a specific task: tunnelers, defenders or food-gatherers.

The queen will nurse the young for a little while but after they are weaned, the workers will look after them until they are capable of playing a role in the colony. Should the queen die, the larger female workers will fight until it is clear who will become the new queen. The sterility of the workers is therefore not genetic but maintained by the queen, possibly using pheromones.

E.6.2	Outline how natural selection may act at the level of the colony in the case of social organisms.
	©IBO 2007

For social organisms, **natural selection** may act at the level of the colony, rather than at the level of the individual member of the colony. For example, in case of a food shortage, a worker could feed the queen but starve herself. As the queen and the worker are very closely related, this behaviour is still likely to spread, because the queen is likely to survive and spread the genes that caused the worker's behaviour in the first place.

E.6.3	Discuss the evolution of altruistic behaviour using two non-human examples.
	©IBO 2007

Altruism is a behaviour which benefits another individual but at cost to the performer. *Hamilton's rule* says that if the benefit to the individual multiplied by the degree of relatedness to the performer is greater than the cost to the

performer, the behaviour will spread by natural selection. This means that animals are more likely to perform altruistic acts that benefit those closely related to them than for members of the species that are not related, or are less closely related.

SIDE-BLOTCHED LIZARD

A model has been worked out that could explain altruistic behaviour in side-blotched lizards which live for one year. This study was done recently in California in the USA.

There are three different throat colours found in side-blotched lizards: orange, yellow and blue. Those with orange throats are very aggressive and will take territory from other lizards and those with yellow throats will sneak in and mate with females of other males.

Unrelated males with blue throats form partnerships to defend their territories. In general, the orange throated lizards will defeat the blue ones, which will defeat the yellow ones. However, the yellow throated lizards will not confront the orange ones but sneak in and mate with their females.

Often, both blue throated males will benefit (mutualism) and produce more offspring but when there are a lot of orange throated (aggressive) males, one of the blue-throated males may end up spending his time defending the territory and not reproducing (much) while the other blue throated male is able to reproduce. In those years, one of the males will display altruistic behaviour and will not pass on his genes.

So the behaviour may be mutualistic and be passed on in some years but altruistic in others. As the strategy is very successful in the 'mutualistic' years, it is sufficient to maintain the behaviour, even if it does not benefit all of them all the time.

VAMPIRE BATS

Vampire bats are nocturnal mammals found in Central and South Americas (*Refer to Figure 1628*). They live on blood that they obtain from other mammals or birds. They need to feed every few days and if they have not been able to obtain blood, they will be given some by another member of the group. This will be a 'cost' to the one providing the food but it seems that members who refuse to provide, will not receive food when they are in need. This tit-for-tat mechanism is sufficiently successful that it improves the survival of those individuals who participates and overall reduces the chance of survival of those who do not.

Figure 1627
A naked mole rat

Figure 1628
A vampire bat

E.6.4 Outline two examples of how foraging behaviour optimizes food intake, including bluegill fish foraging for *Daphnia*.

©IBO 2007

Predators cannot forage in the same area all the time. It would the deplete the numbers of the prey too much which would also not benefit the predator.

Krebs et al 1974 provided black-capped chickadees *(Parus atricapillus)* with different amounts of mealworms on pine cones, mimicking the different amounts of food in an area. They found that the birds will leave the area to go elsewhere when they have searched for food for a certain amount of time without being successful. This means that the birds do not spend too much time searching for food but also minimises the time spend travelling to a new area. Figure 1629 shows a black-capped chickadee which is native to northern USA and Canada.

The **foraging behaviour** of Bluegill fish foraging on *Daphnia* (waterfleas) has been investigated in several studies. Figure 1630 shows a bluegill fish and Figure 1631 shows *Daphnia magna* which is a common prey.

In 1976, *O'Brien, Slade* and *Vinyard* found that in their experiment bluegill fish chose the largest prey when given a choice. In more natural circumstances, the fish will select the prey that appears largest. This means that, when prey is abundant, they will choose the largest but when prey is scarce, they may select a smaller prey which is nearer since it appears larger. Larger prey is more desirable since it provides more food but if the bluegill fish needs to swim longer distances to catch it, it might be more profitable to catch several smaller prey.

In 1985, *Kao, Wetterer* and *Hairston* found that larger bluegill will select larger prey because their vision is better than that of smaller fish. As a result, the smaller fish will not actively choose the smaller prey but simply not be able to assess the size of the prey in relation to the distance. Therefore they will select the apparently largest prey

whereas the larger fish, with better vision, will be able to make a better assessment and go for the absolute largest prey.

If the above is indeed the case, it challenges the concept that the foraging behaviour of bluegill fish will optimise their food intake. In 1998, *Kolar* and *Wahl* investigated bluegill's choice of prey. The fish were presented with two species of *Daphnia*: *D. lumholtzi* and *D. pulex*.

The following observations were made:
- bluegill fish ate more *D. pulex* than *D. lumholtzi* when given either species alone.
- bluegill fish did not eat *D. lumholtzi* when both species were offered together.

D. lumholtzi has a large helmet and a long tail spine. This makes them more difficult to eat, especially for smaller bluegill fish. The fish take considerably more time to eat *D. lumholtzi* than to eat *D. pulex*. The selection against *D. lumholtzi* means that the fish can eat more prey in the same amount of time. The smaller the bluegill fish, the stronger the selection again *D. lumholtzi*. This is an example of foraging behaviour that optimizes food intake.

E.6.5 Explain how mate selection can lead to exaggerated traits.

©IBO 2007

There are many aspects to mate selection:
- females often choose their mate
- males need to attract females in order to mate
- males may fight other males to establish dominance

Females often choose their mate
- Females usually choose the mate with the best genes. This will enhance the chances of the survival of the offspring which also carry the genes of the female. *Refer to Figure 1632.*
- Males with ornaments are more likely to attract the attention of a predator. In order to survive, they must have very good genes to compensate.

OPTION

Figure 1629
The black-capped chickadee

Figure 1630
A bluegill fish

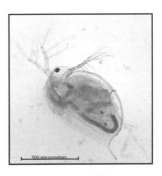

Figure 1631
Daphnia

Figure 1632
A male peacock

Males need to attract females in order to mate

- Males need to attract the attention of a female in order to be selected. He needs to make her pay attention to him.

Males may fight other males to establish dominance

- Males may fight to establish dominance if it is the dominant male that gets to mate with the female(s).
- Fighting may harm both males so if dominance could be established differently (e.g. by who has the most extravagant ornaments), then neither male gets hurt and the most extravagant male will pass on his (extravagant) genes.

E.6.6	State that animals show rhythmical variations in activity.

©IBO 2007

Many animals show rhythmical variations in their activities. Common rhythms are daily or yearly changes in activity. Examples are hummingbirds which slow down their metabolism at night in order to use less energy and egg-laying in spring.

E.6.7	Outline two examples illustrating the adaptive value of rhythmical behaviour patterns.

©IBO 2007

Many species of coral, in different parts of the world, have mass spawning where males and females release their gametes at the exact same time. The advantages are obvious: the male and female gametes are much more likely to meet when they are all released at the same time. Each coral has its own time window and in some species they can be predicted within 5 minutes each year. The spawning is probably triggered by a combination of temperature, (moon)light and chemical signals between the individuals.

Deer, as most mammals, need to give birth to their young in spring so that it is not too cold and food is plentiful. Many species of deer have a gestation time of about 7 months so the rut (fertile period) tends to be in November (i.e. Northern hemisphere). Roe deer are the only even-toed hoofed animal that has delayed implantation of the embryo. The rut takes place in July/August when the females are well fed and likely to be fertile. The embryo will travel to the uterus and "float" there until December. During this time, it grows slowly, not taking a lot of food from its mother who will be able to take advantage of the last easily available food at the end of summer and autumn

to increase her reserves. Once the embryo implants and starts growing, the mother should have stored enough food to see them both through the winter and still give birth in spring. *Refer to Figure 1633.*

*Figure 1633
Roe deer fawn*

EXERCISES

1. (a) State the name of the light sensitive layer in the eye.
    (b). State the names of the light sensitive cells in this layer.
    (c) Which of these kinds of cells will work better in low light conditions? Explain.
    (d) Outline how light is perceived and changed into an action potential.

2. (a) Define innate behaviour
    (b) State the cause of innate behaviour.
    (c) Give an example of innate behaviour.

3. Explain how learning can increase the individual's chances of survival.

4. Describe how psychoactive drugs affect the brain and personality. Give examples.

5   (a) Outline is the general effect of the sympathetic system.
    (b) Describe the result of sympathetic stimulation of the heart, the iris and the flow of blood to the gut.
    (c) Explain the survival value of the above described responses.

6   (a) Define by altruistic behaviour
    (b) Give 2 examples of altruistic behaviour in different situations.
    (c) Discuss the motivation for atruism

OPTION

MICROBES AND BIOTECHNOLOGY

F1   Diversity of microbes

F2   Microbes and the environment

F3   Microbes and biotechnology

F4   Microbes and food production

F5   Metabolism of microbes

F6   Microbes and disease

F1   DIVERSITY OF MICROBES

F.1.1   Outline the classification of living organisms into three domains.

©IBO 2007

In *Topic 2 Cells,* cells were divided into two fundamental types: eukaryotes *(see Topic 2.3)* and prokaryotes (bacteria). Eukaryotes include protists (unicellular organisms and algae), fungi, plants and animals. The grouping of all bacteria as prokaryotes *(see Topic 2.3)* was based on microscopic observations.

However, in 1978 the American Biologist Carl Woese proposed a three **domain** classification. He suggested that there are three distinct types of cellular organisms: the eukaryotes *(see Topic 2),* the **eubacteria** ('true bacteria') and the **archaebacteria** (from *archaios,* meaning ancient). In effect this is a sub-division of the prokaryotes.

F.1.2   Explain the reasons for the reclassification of living organisms into three domains.

©IBO 2007

Archaeabacteria are similar to other prokaryotes in most aspects of cell structure and metabolism. However, their transcription and replication do not show many typical bacterial features, and are in many aspects similar to those of eukaryotes.

Woese's three domain system was initially based upon comparing the sequences of nucleotides in ribosomal RNA (16S rRNA). Ribosomal RNA was chosen by Woese since it is the most conserved (least variable) gene in all cells. Later studies involved analysing the DNA sequences of the genes coding for RNA polymerase which is an enzyme involved in transcription *(see Topic 3.4).*

The base sequence in part of the gene for 16S RNA, the smaller of the two main RNA components of the ribosome was compared. Corresponding segments of nucleotides from a eukaryote (human), an archaebacterium (*Methanococcus jannaschii*) and a eubacterium (*E. coli*) were aligned as shown in Figure 1701.

The sequences from these three organisms all differ from one another to a similar degree. He concluded that the archaebacteria should be defined as a new domain or kingdom of life, in other words not all prokaryotes should be classified as bacteria. The data in Figure 1701 suggests that eubacteria branched off from the eukaryotes and

OPTION

Human	GTT CCG GGG GGA GTA TGG TTG CAA GCT GAA CTT AAA GGA ATT GAC GG..
Methanococcus	GCC GCC TGG GGA GTA CGG TCG CAA GAC TGA AAC TTA AAG GAA TTG GC..
E. coli	ACC GCC TGG GGA GTA CGG CCG CAA GGT TAA AAC TCA AAT GAA TTG AC..

Figure 1701   Matching Gene Sequences

archeabacteria relatively early, that is, eubacteria is the older kingdom.

Many strains of archaebacteria are **extremophiles** and live at high temperatures, but others live in very cold habitats or in highly saline (salty water) or acidic water. However, other archaebacteria are **mesophiles** and have been found in marshland, seage, soil and sea water. They are also found in the intestines of cows, termites and humans. Archaebacteria are not known to cause any diseases.

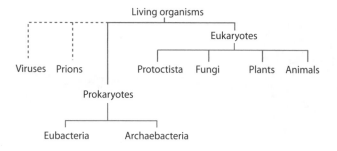

Figure 1702   A summary classification of living organisms

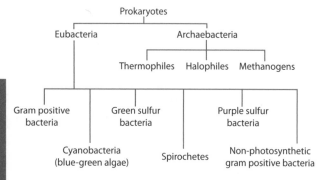

Figure 1703   Classification of bacteria

F.1.3   Distinguish between the characteristics of the three domains.

©IBO 2007

Archaebacteria differ from eubacteria with regard to their membrane structure, transfer RNA molecule structure and sensitivity to antibiotics *(see Topics 6.3.2 and F.6.5)*. The major differences between eubacteria, archaebacteria and eukaryotes are summarised in Figure 1704 *(see***&****)*.

*It binds to ribosomal protein and is found in all eubacteria;
**It is a sequence of bases on transfer RNA found in all eukaryotes and eubacteria.

F.1.4   Outline the wide diversity of habitat in the Archaebacteria as exemplified by methanogens, thermophiles and halophiles.

©IBO 2007

Archaeoglobus fulgidus is the first sulfate-reducing microorganism to have its genome sequence determined.

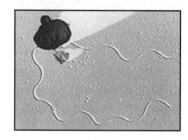

Figure 1705   Archaeoglobus fulgidus

Feature	Archaebacteria	Eubacteria	Eukaroytes
Cell wall	Varies in composition	Contains peptidoglycan	Varies in composition, contains carbohydrates
Membrane lipids	Composed of branched carbon chains attached to glycerol by an ether linkage (-C-O-)	Composed of straight carbon chains attached to glycerol by an ester linkage (-CO-O-)	Composed of straight chain carbon chains attached to glycerol by an ester linkage (-CO-O-)
Start signal for protein synthesis	Methionine	Formylmethionine	Methionine
Antibiotic sensitivity	No	Yes	No
Ribosomal RNA loop*	Lacking	Present	Lacking
Common arm of transfer RNA**	Lacking	Present	Present
Introns	Present	Absent	Present
Histones	Usually present	Absent	Present
Ribosome size	70S	70S	80S

Figure 1704   Comparing cell types

Archaebacteria often live in extreme environments and carry out unusual metabolic processes.

The archaebacteria are classified into three groups:
- methanogens
- halophiles
- thermophile

METHANOGENS

Methanogens are anaerobic and are rapidly killed by the presence of oxygen. Some strains termed **hydrotropic**, use carbon dioxide as a source of carbon and, hydrogen as a reducing agent). Some of the carbon dioxide is reacted with the hydrogen to produce methane, which produces a proton motive force across a membrane to generate ATP. They are common in wetland, where they are responsible for marsh gas, and in the intestines of cows where they are responsible for wind. They are also common in soils in which the oxygen has been depleted. Others are extremophiles and live in hot springs and submarine hydrothermal vents.

HALOPHILES

Extreme **halophiles** or haloarchaea are found in salt lakes, inland seas, and evaporating lakes of seawater, such as the Dead Sea. They require sodium chloride for growth. They are heterotrophs and respire aerobically.

THERMOPHILES

Thermophiles have been found in hot and deep sea hydrothermal vents. Thermophiles contain enzymes that can function at high temperature. Some of these enzymes are used in molecular biology (for example, heat-stable DNA polymerases for polymerase chain reaction (PCR)), and in washing agents.

Figure 1706   A hydrothermal vent

F.1.5	Outline the diversity of Eubacteria, including shape and cell wall structure.

©IBO 2007

An early attempt at bacterial classification was based upon their shape when viewed with a light microscope:
- bacilli (singular *bacillus)* – rod shaped
- cocci (singular *coccus*) – spherical
- spirilli (singular *spirillum*)
- vibrio – comma-shaped

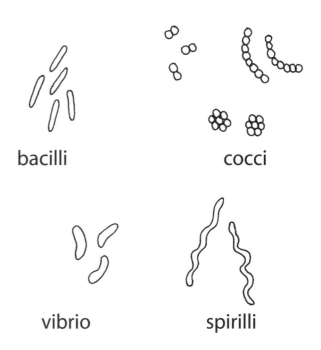

Figure 1707   Bacterial shapes

It should be noted that bacteria can alter their shape as a result of ageing, or due to an environmental shock, such as a rapid change in temperature – a phenomenon known as **pleomorphy**. This can cause confusion if the identification of bacteria strains if based only on morphological features.

Further classification considered whether the cells were single or formed chains and clusters and whether or not flagella were present. Many bacteria possess **flagella** (singular: flagellum) and these may occur all over the cell, limited to a group at one end, or singly.

Different positions in which flagella occur in bacterial:
a) polar attachment
   flagella attached at one or both ends
b) peritrichous attachment
   flagella dispersed randomly over the surface of the bacterium

OPTION

number of fimbriae may help to prevent phagocytosis by host cells.

Endospore formation occurs in some Gram positive bacteria. **Endospores** are dormant structures that develop when environmental conditions are unfavourable, for example, when it is dry and nutrients are depleted. The bacterium becomes covered by a thick protective coat, which protects the bacterium from desiccation (drying out). It also resistant to ultraviolet radiation and toxic chemicals.

The **capsule** is a barrier between the bacterium and its environment. It is composed of gum-like polysaccharide molecules which are secreted through the cell wall by the cell membrane. The capsule is critical to disease-causing or pathogen bacteria as it increases their **virulence**, that is, their ability to infect cells. This is because the capsule prevents binding of antibodies to the bacterium's surface.

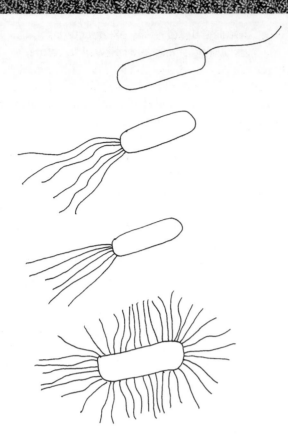

Figure 1708   Attachment of flagella

Bacteria can be divided into two different groups based upon a simple staining technique *(see Topic F.1.6)* known as **Gram staining**. **Gram positive** bacteria include *Bacillus* and the majority of cocci, such as *Staphylococcus*. **Gram negative** bacteria include *Escherichia coli* (E. coli), *Salmonella* and some cocci.

Fimbriae are short and rigid bristle-like projections from the bacterial plasma membrane through the cell wall. They act as antigens and interact with molecules of the host cell membrane. In pathogenic bacteria, the presence of a large

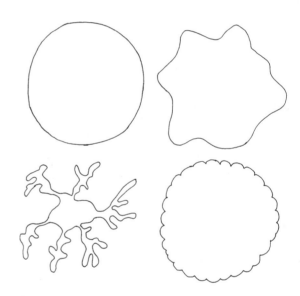

Figure 1710   Different shapes of bacterial colonies

Method	Description and comments
Microscopic morphology	Cell shape, cell size, presence of flagella, pilli, fimbriae, capsules and endopsores
Macroscopic morphology	Appearance of colony in broth or on solid media (see Figure 1710)
Biochemical characteristics	Ability to ferment sugars; breakdown specific proteins or polysaccharides
Chemical characteristics	Presence of certain compounds in the cell wall and membrane
Presence of specific antigens	Antibodies are produced in response to specific antigens; used in the identification of pathogens in specimens and cultures
Use of gene probes	Small single-stranded fragments of DNA (gene probes), labeled with a dye or radioactive isotope, are mixed with unknown DNA; if there is a match, hybridisation occurs between the probe and target DNA

Figure 1709   Summary of identification and classification of bacteria

F.1.6   State, with one example, that some
         bacteria form aggregates that show
         characteristics not seen in individual
         bacteria.

©IBO 2007

Vibrio fischeri is a rod-shaped bacterium found in warm sea water. It is heterotrophic and has flagella. Free living *Vibrio fischeri* is usually a saprotroph and survives on decaying organic matter.

The bacterium has **bioluminescent** properties, and is often found in symbiosis with the bobtail squid (*Euprymna scolopes*). Free-living *Vibrio fischeri* enters and 'inoculates' the light organs of juvenile squid. Ciliated cells within the squid light organs draw in the symbiotic bacteria. These cells promote the growth of the symbionts and actively reject any competitors.

Figure 1711   Sketch of Vibrio fischeri

There is a twenty four hour cycle during which the bacteria grow to high density in the light organ and **bioluminesce** occurs and then the majority of the bacteria are ejected from the light organ by the squid leaving only a few bacteria which act as the starting innoculum for the next cycle of bacterial growth

Inside the squid the population can reach high cell densities and under these conditions the bacteria bio-luminesce. The light organs are an ideal environment since the squid provides a nutrient rich solution which promotes rapid bacterial growth to densities which are sufficient to trigger bioluminescence. In return the squid uses the bacterial bioluminescence to hide its silhouette when viewed from below by matching the amount of light striking the top of the squid's body.

Quorum sensing is the regulation of a bacterial process that depends on the density of the bacterial population. In the case of *Vibrio fischeri* bioluminescence is under the control of quorum sensing. The process relies upon the bacteria producing and releasing signal molecules which diffuse outwards from the bacterium. This allows the bacteria population to communicate with each other and coordinate their behaviour when a certain population size is reached.

Quorum sensing signaling molecules are known as **autoinducers** and are detected by specific receptors in the bacterial cell membrane which detect the autoinducer signal. When the autoinducer binds to the receptor, it activates or represses transcription of target genes which include those for inducer synthesis.

When the bacterial population is low diffusion reduces the concentration of the autoinducer in the surroundings to almost zero. As the population increases the concentration of the autoinducer reaches a threshold, gene expression occurs and more autoinducer is synthesised. This forms a positive feedback loop for autoinducer production and also induces the production of enzymes in *Vibrio fischeri* for **luciferase**, an enzyme involved in bioluminescence.

Pseudomonas aeruginosa is a motile Gram-negative, aerobic, rod-shaped bacterium. It is an opportunistic pathogen in AIDS patients. It infects the pulmonary tract, urinary tract, burns and wounds. Cystic fibrosis patients are also predisposed to *Pseudomonas aeruginosa* infection of the lungs.

Cystic fibrosis is a relatively common genetic disease that affects the entire body, causing progressive disability and early death. Difficulty in breathing and excessive mucus production are the most common symptoms and results from frequent lung infections, often involving large colonies of *pseudomonas aeruginosa*, which are resistant to antibiotics. For information about the structure and function of the lungs refer to *Topic 6.4*.

Pseudomonas aeruginosa controls the production of enzymes and the formation of biofilms. Both of these processes are under the control of quorum sensing. The production of the biofilm provides the organism with protection against antibiotics and the enzymes damage the lung epithelium.

Biologists hope that treatments will be developed that will degrade autoinducers or compete with the autoinducer and inhibit quorum sensing and prevent secretion of enzymes and formation of biofilms. Disrupting the signalling process in this way is called '**quorum quenching**' or 'quorum sensing blocking'.

A **biofilm** is a complex aggregation of microorganisms marked by the excretion of a protective and adhesive extracellular matrix. Biofilms can contain many different types of microorganism, for example:

* bacteria
* archaebacteria
* protozoa
* algae.

OPTION

299

Each group cooperates and performs specialised metabolic functions. Biofilms have been found to be involved in a wide variety of microbial infections in the body, for example, urinary tract infections, catheter infections, middle-ear infections, formation of dental plaque and coating contact lenses.

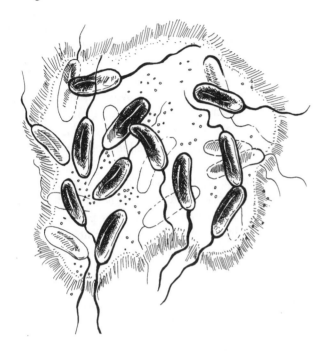

Figure 1712   Quorum sensing in Vibrio fischeri

F.1.7   Compare the structure of the cell walls of Gram-positive and Gram-negative Eubacteria.

©IBO 2007

The bacterial cell wall is mainly composed of a complex mixed polymer of hexose (C_6) sugars and amino acids called **peptidoglycan** or murein. It provides a strong but flexible framework, supporting the bacterial cell contents and protecting the bacterial cells from lysis in concentrated solutions.

Eubacteria can be divided into two groups based upon a simple staining test. A dye known as crystal violet is applied to a bacterial smear on a slide. Iodine solution is then applied and the preparations are then rinsed in ethanol (alcohol) and counterstained with the red dye, safranin.

Eubacteria with thick cell walls retain the crystal violet and it is not washed out by ethanol. In such bacteria, counterstaining with safranin has no effect and they are termed Gram positive bacteria. However, in eubacteria with thinner cell walls, the ethanol dissolves the lipids on the surface and subsequently removes the dye from the peptidoglycan layer. Counterstaining with safranin leaves the cells stained pink. This group of eubacteria are termed Gram negative.

Electron microscopy has revealed the nature of the differences in cell wall structure and these are summarised in the Figure 1713 and illustrated in Figure 1714.

Feature	Gram positive bacteria	Gram negative bacteria
Overall thickness	20 to 80 nm	8 to 11 nm
Thickness of peptidoglycan layer	20 to 80 nm	1 to 2 nm
Outer membrane with lipoprotein and protein lipopolysaccharides	No	Yes
Protein channels spanning outer membrane (porins)	No	Yes
Space between cell membrane and cell wall (periplasmic space)	Sometimes present	Always present

Figure 1713   Cell wall structure

Porins are integral proteins which and act as a pore through which molecules can diffuse. Unlike other membrane transport proteins, porins are large enough to allow passive diffusion.

The lipid rich outer layer of Gram negative bacteria protects them from **lysozyme**, an antibacterial enzyme found in saliva and tears. The lipid layer also provides protection against the antibiotic penicillin.

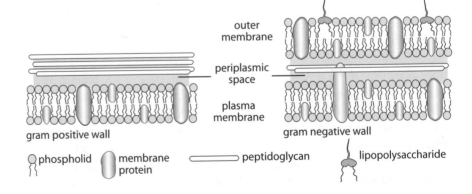

Figure 1714   The difference in cell wall structure

> **F.1.8** Outline the diversity of structure in viruses including: naked capsid versus enveloped capsid; DNA *versus* RNA; and single stranded versus double stranded DNA or RNA.
>
> ©IBO 2007

Viruses are the smallest living organisms and range in size from about 20 nm to 300 nm. They can only be observed with an electron microscope. They are obligate parasites and can only reproduce inside living cells. Inside the host cell their genome instructs the cell to make new copies of the virus. Viruses are transferred between cells as inert particles (**virions**).

Viruses contain a core of nucleic acid (RNA or DNA), often associated with protein, surrounded by an outer covering of protein termed a **capsid**. The capsid is composed of sub-units called **capsomeres**, each consisting of protein molecules. The capsomeres spontaneously associate to form a regular structure. The combination of the nucleic acid and protein coat is termed the **nucleocapsid**.

The shape and arrangement of the capsomeres determines whether the virus is classified as helical, polyhedral, for example, the tobacco mosaic virus (a plant virus) for example, the HIV virus and the adenovirus or complex,

for example, **bacteriophage**. A bacteriophage is a virus which uses a bacterium as its host.

Helical capsids are composed of rod-shaped capsomeres which assemble to form a continuous helix, inside which the nucleic acid strand is coiled. In polyhedral viruses, the capsid is usually an icosahedron (a regular polygon with 20 sides and 12 corners).

The nucleic acid may be single stranded or double stranded RNA or DNA. In **retroviruses** the enzyme **reverse transcriptase** (*see Topic F.3.1*) synthesis a single strand of DNA from single stranded RNA. It then directs the formation of a complementary double strand of DNA which is then inserted, under enzyme control, into a chromosome in the host cell, where it codes for retroviral proteins.

There may also be an external **envelope**, consisting of the plasma membrane derived from the host cell. Within this envelope some or all of the host cell membrane proteins may be replaced by viral proteins, often glycoproteins.

The functions of the capsid and envelope include:
- protecting the nuclei acid of the virus from enzymes and chemicals when the virus is outside the host cell
- binding to the surface of the host cell
- assisting in the penetration of the host cell and the introduction of the viral nucleic acid

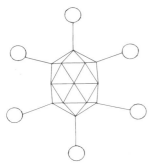

Figure 1715
Structure of an Adenovirus

Figure 1716   Structure of a Bacteriophage

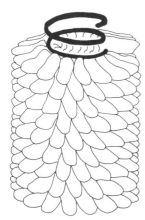

Figure 1717
Structure of Tobacco Mosaic Virus (TMV)

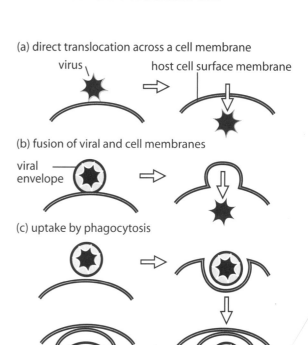

(a) direct translocation across a cell membrane

virus   host cell surface membrane

(b) fusion of viral and cell membranes

viral envelope

(c) uptake by phagocytosis

phagosome (phagocytic vesicle)

Figure 1718   Methods of entry into host c

F.1.9   Outline the diversity of microscopic eukaryotes as illustrated by *Saccharomyces, Amoeba, Plasmodium, Paramecium, Euglena* and *Chlorella*.

©IBO 2007

SACCHAROMYCES

Saccharomyces is a genus of single-celled fungus. They are known as yeasts and are employed in the fermentation processes associated with the baking and brewing industries. Yeast cells take the form of ellipses or spheres. They are surrounded by a cell wall containing the polymers of glucose and mannose. In the cytoplasm, the nucleus is situated to one side of large central vacuole. The cytoplasm usually contains glycogen granules and the vacuole may contain lipid droplets. See Figure 1719.

Saccharomyces reproduces asexually by **budding**, during which a daughter cell develops as an outgrowth from the end of a mature yeast cell. See Figure 1720.

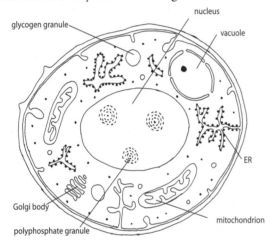

Figure 1719 Structure of a yeast cell in cross section

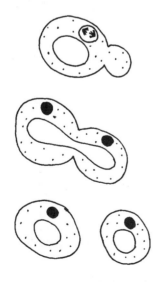

Figure 1720   Budding in yeast

AMOBEA

Amobea inhabits the bottom sediments of freshwater ponds. The cytoplasm is in the form of two layers: an outer transparent **ectoplasm** and an inner jelly-like **endoplasm**. Amoeba has a relatively large surface area to volume ratio and performs gas exchange and excretion by simple diffusion across its plasma membrane.

Movement and food capture occur by **pseudopodia** (singular: pseudopodium). Pseudopodia are pushed out to surround the prey or food particle and engulf it completely, forming a food vacuole. See Figure 1721.

PLASMODIUM

Plasmodium is a genus of parasitic protozoa. Infection with this genus is known as malaria *(see Topic F.6.9)*. The parasite always has two hosts in its complex life cycle: a mosquito vector and a vertebrate host. At least ten species infect humans.

Cell motility is accomplished through the action of a single flagellum that emerges from the basal body apparatus near the posterior end of the cell. The flagellum is surrounded by its own membrane that is distinct from, the plasma membrane. See Figure 1722.

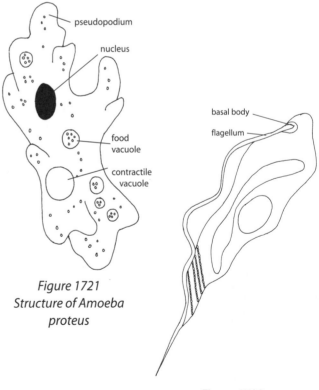

Figure 1721 Structure of Amoeba proteus

Figure 1722 Structure of Plasmodium

PARAMECIUM

Paramecium is a ciliated protozoan. The cilia beat with a coordinated rhythm and mover the organism rapidly through its freshwater environment. The structure of a large ciliate, *Paramecium caudatum* is shown below. The bases of the cilia are embedded in stiff outer covering called the **pellicle** which gives the organism a fixed slipper-like shape. Osmoregulation is performed by two **contractile vacuoles**. *Paramecium* feeds on bacteria which are collected from the water by the beating of the cilia lining the **oral groove**. Captured bacteria are then transferred via the gullet to the **cytosome** where food vacuoles are formed. See Figure 1723.

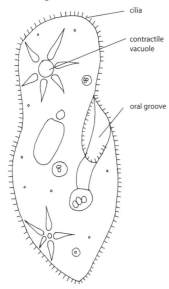

Figure 1723
Structure of Paramecium caudatum

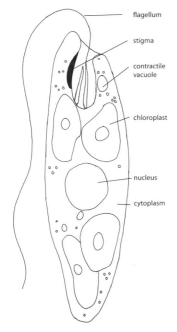

Figure 1724 Structure of Euglena

EUGLENA

Euglena is flagellated protozoan and commonly present in pond water. Near the base of the flagellum is a light absorbing red granule known as the **stigma**. Its function is to orientate the organism towards light to optimize its photosynthetic rate. Euglena contains chloroplasts, but lack a cellulose cell wall and does not store starch. See Figure 1724.

CHLORELLA

Chlorella is genus of unicellular green algae in the phylum Chlorophyta. It possesses a single, cup shaped chloroplast with chlorophylls very similar to those in green plants. The cytoplasm contains starch grains and oil droplets and a crystalline structure, termed a **pyrenoid**, is embedded in the chloroplast. It is concerned with the formation of starch.

Chlorella is and can be easily cultured in the laboratory and has been used in experiments investigating photosynthetic pathways. It has a high protein content and could be a possible food source. See Figure 1725.

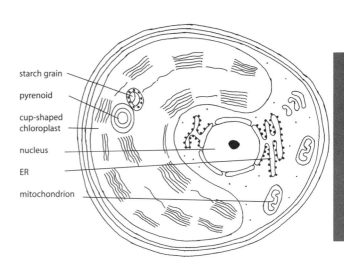

Figure 1725   The structure of Chlorella

OPTION

F2   MICROBES AND THE ENVIRONMENT

OPTION

> **F.2.1   List the roles of microbes in ecosystems, including producers, nitrogen fixers and decomposers.**
>
> ©IBO 2007

Bacteria play a major role in recycling many chemical elements and compounds in ecosystems, both on land and in water. The chemical elements involved include phosphorus, sulfur, carbon and nitrogen.

A number of bacteria are **decomposers** and breakdown the remains of dead organisms to release nutrients which re-enter the environment. Decomposers play very important roles in the carbon cycle and the nitrogen cycle (*see Topic F.2.2*).

Strains of specialised bacteria known as nitrogen fixers convert gaseous nitrogen into nitrates or nitrites as part of their metabolism, and the resulting products are released into the environment. They form an important part in the **nitrogen cycle** (*see Topic F.2.2*).

Producers convert raw energy to organic molecules and nutrients useful to themselves and other organisms. This is a varied group of bacteria and includes photosynthetic bacteria, for example, the cyanobacteria and chemosynthetic bacteria (*see Topic F.5*).

> **F.2.2   Draw and label a diagram of the nitrogen cycle.**
>
> ©IBO 2007

Refer to Figure 1726.

> **F.2.3   State the roles of *Rhizobium*, *Azotobacter*, *Nitrosomonas*, *Nitrobacter* and *Pseudomonas denitrificans* in the nitrogen cycle.**
>
> ©IBO 2007

Nitrogen gas forms about 80% by volume of the atmosphere. It is an important constituent of all living organisms (*see Topic 3, The chemistry of life*). Nitrogen gas exists in the form of diatomic molecules held together by a strong triple covalent bond.

Very few organisms possess the enzymes needed to split nitrogen molecules and use the gas directly. The majority of living organisms must obtain nitrogen in a fixed form, that is, in the form of nitrogen-containing compounds.

In the case of plants, the most accessible form are nitrate ions, NO_3^- (aq), although they can also absorb ammonium ions, NH_4^+ (aq) or urea, $CO(NH_2)_2$. Animals require nitrogen in an organic form, usually in the form of amino acids.

NITROGEN FIXATION

In this process nitrogen gas from the atmosphere is incorporated into nitrogen compounds, such as nitrates (NO_3^-), nitrites (NO_2^-) or ammonia (NH_3). Lightning is one source of **nitrogen fixation**: the high temperatures cause nitrogen and oxygen to form nitrogen monoxide. This is then oxidized by oxygen to form nitrogen dioxide which reacts with water to form nitrate ions:

$$N_2 \text{ (g)} + O_2 \text{ (g)} \rightarrow 2NO \text{ (g)}$$
$$2NO \text{ (g)} + O_2 \text{ (g)} \rightarrow 2NO_2 \text{ (g)}$$
$$3NO_2 \text{ (g)} + H_2O \text{ (l)} \rightarrow 2H^+ \text{ (aq)} + 2NO_3^- \text{ (aq)} + NO \text{ (g)}$$

Nitrogen fixation is also performed by a number of organisms. Examples include *Rhizobium* bacteria living in root nodules (see below) and the free living

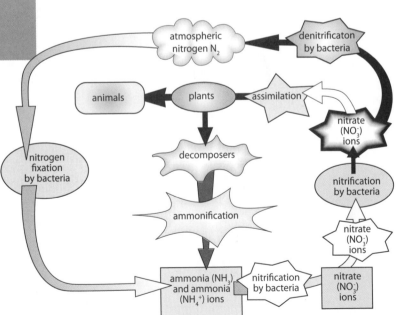

Figure 1726   *Simplified diagram of the nitrogen cycle*

bacteria *Azotobacter*. Some species of cyanobacteria *(see Topic F.5.5)* are able to fix nitrogen. Both of these **nitrogen fixing bacteria** utilise an enzyme known as nitrogenase. The process of nitrogen fixation also requires large amounts of ATP. Ammonia is produced which is then incorporated into proteins, nucleic acids and other nitrogenous biological chemicals.

$$N_2 + 6NADH + H^+ + 16ATP \rightarrow 16ADP + 16P_i + 2NH_3$$

Nitrogen fixation occurs in the Haber Process in which hydrogen and nitrogen gases are reacted together at high temperature and pressure in the presence of an iron catalyst to form ammonia.

$$N_2 (g) + 3H_2 (g) \rightarrow 2NH_3 (g)$$

This method is used to manufacture artificial fertilisers, for example, ammonium nitrate and ammonium sulfate.

ROOT NODULES

Some plants, including peas, beans and clover, and other plants known as **legumes**, have roots which are capable of forming a mutualistic association with nitrogen-fixing bacteria such as *Rhizobium*. They multiply inside small swellings called **root nodules**. The bacteria are chemically attracted to the legume root and they enter into the cells of the cortex by means of tiny channels called **infection threads**. Once inside the host the bacteria multiply and become non-motile. Nitrogenase only functions in the absence of oxygen, so the nodule contain **leghemoglobin** which has a high affinity for oxygen and storing as it enters the root cells.

> F.2.4   Outline the conditions that favour denitrification and nitrification.
> ©IBO 2007

NITRIFICATION

This process involves the oxidation of nitrogen compounds to produce nitrate ions in the soil. Nitrate ions are often absorbed via active transport by the root hairs from the soil. They are then incorporated by metabolic pathways into proteins and nucleic acids. They are then passed through the various trophic levels in a food pyramid in organic form. The compounds return to the soil in faeces or contained in dead material. These are then broken down by decomposers in a process called **deamination** which results in the release of ammonia. A more direct process of recycling occurs through the excretion by animals of urea or uric acid.

Ammonia in the soil can be used as an energy source by nitrifying bacteria, for example, *Nitrosomonas*, which oxidises ammonia molecules to nitrite ions.

$$2NH_3 + 3O_2 \rightarrow 2NO_2^- + 2H_2O + 2H^+ + energy$$

Nitrobacter is another group of nitrifying bacteria. It oxidizes nitrite ions to nitrate ions.

$$2NO_2^- + O_2 \rightarrow 2NO_3^- + energy$$

Both groups of bacteria require carbon dioxide. Nitrification occurs in well aerated soil and water.

Most of the ammonium and nitrate compounds produced by nitrifying bacteria are reused by living organisms. Ammonium ions tend to be retained by soil, but nitrate ions can be washed into lakes and rivers *(see Topic F.2.5)* and cause pollution.

DENITRIFICATION

Some of the nitrogen contained in nitrates is returned to the atmosphere through the action of denitrifying bacteria. They live in soil or water where oxygen is in short supply and use nitrate ions as a source of oxygen for aerobic respiration. Nitrogen gas is released a waste product form this process. *Pseudomonas denitrificans* is an example of a denitrifying bacterium.

$$2NO_3^- + 10 e^- + 12H^+ \rightarrow N_2 + 6H_2O$$

> F.2.5   Explain the consequences of releasing raw sewage and nitrate fertilizer into rivers.
> ©IBO 2007

Sewage from houses consists mainly of human faeces and kitchen waste which will include food residues and detergents. Sewage is also likely to include industrial waste which contain strongly acidic or alkaline chemicals. Toxic metals ions, such as chromium, copper and zinc may also be present. Water pollution may also result from the leakage of animal slurries from farm waste. Run off water from farm fields may also contain artificial fertilizers, especially nitrates.

If raw sewage and nitrate polluted run off water from farms is discharged into a river there will be rapid changes in the physical factors of the environment. Figure 1728 outlines the major components of sewage and summarises some of their effects in a fast flowing river. Figure 1727 shows in detail the various stages downstream.

OPTION

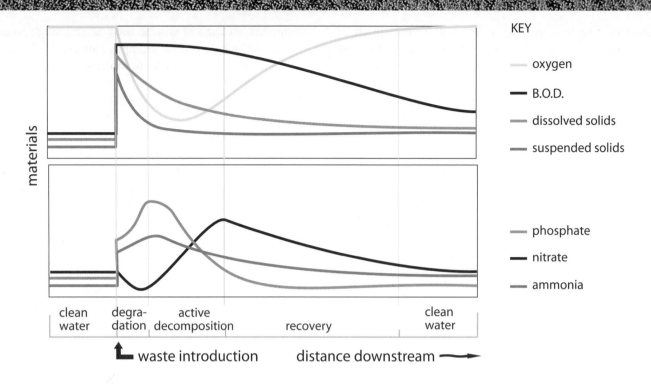

Figure 1727   *Typical changes in water quality after the introduction of raw sewage*

Component of sewage	Impact on environment
Suspended solids	Reduction in penetration of sunlight
	Increases demand for oxygen during breakdown of organic material by microorganisms
Phosphate	Eutrophication
Heavy metals	Toxic to aquatic organisms and to humans if untreated water is drunk
Microorganisms (viruses, bacteria, viruses, fungi and protozoa)	Possibility of disease if the untreated water is drunk
Detergents	• Foams on the surface of the water affect the aeration of the water • Eutrophication
Nitrogenous compounds	• Ammonium ions are toxic to fish • Eutrophication • Eutrophication may encourage algal blooms • Respiration of algae at night leads to an increase in the BOD (biochemical oxygen demand), resulting in depletion of dissolved oxygen in the water • Death of algae results in an increase in the BOD (while the algae are being broken down) • Toxins are produced during the growth of algal blooms by certain strains of blue-green bacteria • High nitrate concentrations are toxic if the water is drunk

Figure 1728   *The main components of sewage and their effects in a river*

The **biochemical oxygen demand** (BOD) of a sample of water is measured under standard conditions at 20 °C over a period of five days. The presence of polluting organic material leads to increased activity from bacteria involved in the decomposition of this material, resulting in a high demand for dissolved oxygen. The BOD measurement thus gives an indication of the level of organic pollution.

In the initial stage, just below the point at which the raw sewage enters the river, there is immediate decomposition of organic material by aerobic bacteria. The demand for dissolved oxygen in the water is high, resulting in a rapid decrease in the concentration of oxygen. This 'oxygen sag' occurs when the rate of consumption during respiration is greater than the rate at which oxygen is produced. As the organic material is decomposed, the numbers of aerobic bacteria decrease, but the numbers of protozoa *(see Topic F.1.9)*, which feed on other organisms, increases.

The numbers of algae increase when the suspended solids begin to settle and the water becomes clearer allowing light to penetrate and photosynthesis to occur. Consequently, levels of dissolved oxygen rise. The nitrate and phosphate ions will be absorbed by the increasing population of algae. **Eutrophication** refers to the artificial enrichment of nutrients in a river or lake. The excess nutrients in the water encourages rapid growth of algae and blue-green bacteria *(see Topic F.5.5)* resulting in an **algal bloom**.

When the algae die, they are broken down by the aerobic bacteria and if the oxygen level falls very low, there may be a sudden death of masses of fish, a fish kill. If the water is anaerobic then hydrogen sulfide and methane may be produced. Certain strains of blue green bacteria produce toxins which may also cause the death of fish and other animals, including humans. The recovery of the river occurs when the oxygenation of the water improves as well as dilution of the sewage and nutrients.

F.2.6   Outline the role of saprotrophic bacteria in the treatment of sewage using trickling filter beds and reed bed systems.

©IBO 2007

A sewage treatment plant uses natural decay processes and provides the best possible conditions for the growth of microorganisms and hence the breakdown or decomposition of organic material. The final breakdown products from aerobic processes are carbon dioxide, which is released to the atmosphere and nitrate, sulfate and phosphate ions, which remain dissolved in the water. A large amount of sediment and sludge accumulates which is decomposed anaerobically to produce methane.

The first step of sewage treatment involves screening the water and allowing it to enter a grit settlement tank. Grit (sand and small stones) settle out and some

OPTION

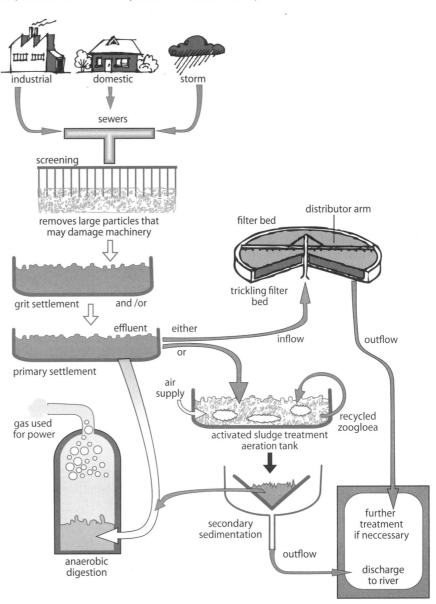

Figure 1729   The main stages in sewage purification

organic materials flocculate (clump together). After grit settlement the water is then passed to a trickling filter.

The trickling filter bed is made from carefully graded stones, grit and clinker. Clinker is a general name given to waste from industrial processes - particularly those that involve smelting metals or burning fossil fuels. Clinker often forms a loose, black deposit that can consist of coke, coal, slag, charcoal, grit and other waste materials. Bacteria, fungi and protozoa degrade organic matter as the waste water (**effluent**) trickles through the bed and these are consumed by predatory protozoa and insect larvae.

An alternative and organic alternative to traditional methods of sewage treatment is the use of a **reed bed**. A reed bed is an artificially created wetland planted with specially selected species of reed that have the ability to absorb oxygen from the air and release it through their roots. This creates ideal conditions for the development of huge numbers of micro-organisms which are able to break down any soluble material present. The need for chemical treatment is avoided.

F.2.7	State that biomass can be used as raw material for the production of fuels such as methane and ethanol.

©IBO 2007

Biomass is defined as the total mass of living material in an area. Plants use solar energy in the process of photosynthesis. Solar energy is hence incorporated into biomass, a potential human fuel. The biomass value is the dry mass in kilograms per square metre. Biomass includes plants, animals and microorganisms, but is usually restricted to the plant mass above the ground.

Fermentation *(see Topic F.4.1)* of sugar by yeasts (*Saccharomyces*) can convert the energy in biomass into ethanol, which can be used a fuel. An example is the fuel **gasohol** which consists of unleaded petrol mixed with ethanol (10 – 20%) and used in modified motor vehicles. The sugar is obtained from sugar cane, grown in tropical countries, and sugar beet, grown in temperate countries.

Fermentation by bacteria can convert the energy in biomass into **biogas**, a gaseous fuel which consists mainly of methane, CH_4, the major component of natural gas. However, carbon dioxide will be present together with traces of hydrogen sulfide and ammonia. Biogas generation exploits the metabolism of several different groups of bacteria which digest organic matter, for example, animal faeces, under aerobic conditions.

F.2.8	Explain the principles involved in the generation of methane from biomass, including the conditions needed, organisms involved and the basic chemical reactions that occur.

©IBO 2007

During the fermentation of faeces aerobic bacteria initially hydrolyse any carbohydrate, lipids and protein to sugars, fatty acids, glycerol and amino acids. As the available oxygen is used up, **acetogenic bacteria** convert the sugars to short chain fatty acids, especially ethanoate ions (acetate), together with some carbon dioxide and hydrogen. This stage is termed **acetogenesis**.

The final stage is **methanogenesis** which is carried out in anaerobic conditions by methanogenic bacteria. It involves the conversion of ethanoate and other acids to methane. Methanogenic bacteria are obligate anaerobes and are only active in the absence of oxygen. They are members of the archaebacteria *(see Topic F.1.1)*.

$$CH_3COOH \rightarrow CH_4 + CO_2$$

Successful biogas production depends on a temperature of between 30 to 40 degrees Celsius being maintained. Biogas production is often performed in an enclosed tank called a digester. These can be found in countries like China, Nepal and India. In developed countries they are used to dispose of large quantities of animal waste from intensive farming.

OPTION

F3 MICROBES AND BIOTECHNOLOGY

F.3.1   State that reverse transcriptase catalyses the production of DNA from RNA.

©IBO 2007

Reverse transcriptase is an enzyme that transcribes single-stranded RNA into double-stranded DNA. Normal transcription involves the synthesis of RNA from DNA, hence reverse transcription is the reverse of this, as it synthesises DNA from RNA. The gene encoding reverse transcriptase is present in HIV and other **retroviruses**.

F.3.2   Explain how reverse transcriptase is used in molecular biology.

©IBO 2007

Reverse transcriptase is commonly used in molecular biology to apply the polymerase chain reaction (PCR) *(see Topic 4.4.1)* technique to RNA in a technique called **reverse transcription polymerase chain reaction** (RT-PCR). PCR can only be applied to DNA strands, but with reverse transcriptase, RNA can be transcribed into DNA, thus making PCR analysis of RNA molecules possible. Reverse transcription polymerase chain reaction is widely used in the diagnosis of genetic diseases and studying gene expression in cells or tissues.

Reverse transcriptase is also used to create **complementary DNA** (cDNA) libraries from messenger RNA (mRNA). A cDNA library refers to a complete set of all the molecules contained within a cell or organism. Because working with messenger RNA is difficult (since messenger RNA is unstable and is easily degraded by RNAases), researchers use reverse transcriptase to produce a DNA copy of each mRNA strand. Referred to as cDNA these reverse transcribed mRNAs are collectively known as a cDNA library.

Such a **DNA library** has several uses. A cDNA of an organism can be cloned into a bacterium, and expressed (translated into the appropriate protein). The complete cDNA library of an organism gives the total of the proteins it can possibly express. Comparison between the cDNA libraries from different species offers an opportunity to examine the evolutionary relationship between those species in terms of their encoded proteins *(see Topic D.5.3)*.

F.3.3   Distinguish between *somatic* and *germ line* therapy.

©IBO 2007

Gene therapy involves the replacement or modification of a gene to restore or enhance cellular function.

Somatic cell therapy involves human cells other than germ cells (gametes or cells that divide to form gametes) which are genetically altered and **germ line therapy**, in which a replacement gene is integrated into the genome of human gametes, resulting in transmission of the change to the next generation, and expression of the new gene in the patient's children and their offspring.

The fundamental difference between germ line therapy and somatic cell therapy is that germ line therapy affects subsequent generations and may be associated with increased risk and the potential for unpredictable and irreversible consequences.

F.3.4   Outline the use of viral vectors in gene therapy.

©IBO 2007

Gene therapy is the introduction of genes into an individual's cells and tissues to treat a genetic disorder or disease. Gene therapy aims to replace a defective mutant allele with a functional one.

In most gene therapy studies, a normal gene is inserted into the genome to replace a mutated disease-causing gene. A **vector** must be used to deliver the gene to the patient's target cells.

Currently, the most common vector is a virus that has been genetically altered to carry normal human DNA. Viruses have evolved a way of delivering their genes to human cells *(see Topic F.1.8)*. Most viruses have specific cell-type targets. Molecular Biologists have taken advantage of this capability and manipulated the virus genome via use of restriction enzymes to remove disease-causing versions genes with modified or repaired genes.

Target cells are exposed to the vector. The virus then unloads into the target cells its genetic material containing the modified human gene into the target cell. The generation of a functional protein product from the modified gene restores the target cell to a normal state.

OPTION

Adenoviruses *(see Topic F.1.8)* are commonly used viral vectors and their genomes are composed of double-stranded DNA. They cause respiratory infections in humans. When these viruses infect a host cell, they introduce their DNA molecule into the host. The genome of the adenovirus is not incorporated into the host cell's genetic material. The DNA molecule is left free in the nucleus of the host cell, and this extra DNA molecule can be transcribed.

Severe Combined Immunodeficiency, or SCID, is a genetic disorder involving the lymphocytes of the immune system *(see Topic 6.3.6)*. SCID patients cannot mount an effective immune response to pathogens and have to live in a sterile environment free of bacteria. SCID displays an autosomal recessive pattern of inheritance.

Many SCID patients lack an active version of the enzyme adenosine deaminase (ADA), which is concerned with recycling the breakdown products of nucleic acids. The absence of ADA activity leads to the accumulation of metabolites that are toxic to lymphocyte development.

ADA deficiency is a suitable candidate for gene therapy because bone marrow cells (which play an important roles in the development of lymphocytes) or lymphocytes are suitable targets for the transfer of functional ADA gene sequences.

Functioning genes have been introduced to the patients via use of retroviruses *(see Topic F.1.8)* to restore the missing ADA enzyme activity and hence immune function. Clinical trials have met with some success, but have been associated with high rates of leukemia in treated SCID patients *(see Topic F.3.5)*.

F.3.5	Discuss the risks of gene therapy.
	©IBO 2007

SHORT-LIVED NATURE OF GENE THERAPY

The DNA introduced into target cells must remain functional and the cells containing the DNA must be long-lived and stable. Problems achieving the integration of modified DNA into the genome and the rapidly dividing nature of many cells may prevent gene therapy from achieving any long-term benefits. Patients may have to undergo multiple rounds of gene therapy.

IMMUNE RESPONSE

The risk of stimulating the immune system (due to the appearance of new (foreign) proteins)) in a way that reduces gene therapy effectiveness is a potential risk. In addition the immune system's enhanced response to antigens it has encountered before makes it difficult for gene therapy to be repeated in patients.

PROBLEMS WITH VIRAL VECTORS

Viruses present a variety of potential problems to the patient - toxicity, immune and inflammatory responses, and gene control and targeting issues. In addition, there is always the possibility that a slightly modified viral vector, once inside the patient, may recover its ability to cause disease. Hence the need for removing all crucial viral genes related to pathogencity.

MULTIGENE DISORDERS

Conditions or disorders that arise from mutations in a single gene are the best targets for gene therapy. However, some of the most commonly occurring disorders, such as heart disease, high blood pressure, Alzheimer's disease, arthritis, and diabetes, are caused by the combined effects of variations in many genes. **Multigene disorders** such as these would be particularly difficult to treat effectively using gene therapy.

CHANCE OF INDUCING A TUMOR

If the DNA is integrated in a place in the genome, and disrupts genomic function, for example, if the insertion disrupts a **tumor suppressor gene**, it could induce a tumor.

TOK   What are the risks in gene therapy?

All medical procedures carry some risk. However, participation in research carries a greater risk, as it is, by its very nature, exploratory. There are many ethical considerations involved in such research. In most cases, those participating in gene therapy research are very ill and they or their guardians must make informed choices as to whether or not to participate in research or continue with it as new information comes to light. There has been at least one death as a consequence of a gene therapy trial. In another trial a number of children being treated for SCID (severe combined immunodeficiency disease) using gene therapy developed leukaemia, most likely as a result of the gene therapy itself. Other participants in the trial were informed and made decisions about continuation based on this outcome. Researchers learnt more about the mechanism of gene therapy but some question whether the knowledge gained and future speculated benefits are worth the cost.

OPTION

F4 MICROBES AND FOOD PRODUCTION

F.4.1   Explain the use of *Saccharomyces* in the production of beer, wine and bread.

©IBO 2007

BEER

Beer is made from barley grains which are moistened and allowed to sprout. During germination a proportion of the starch reserves are converted by enzymes to maltose. However, in addition the process allows the development of enzymes which are important in the later stages of brewing. The process is known as **malting** and requires oxygen. The sprouting barley is termed **malt**.

Crushing and roasting the sprouted grains gives a darker colour and richer flavours. This process is known as **kilning** and allows brewers to store it for up to a year. Gentle heating produces a light malt, used in light ales, bitters and lagers. Further roasting gives a darker malt used for brown ales and stout.

The resulting grist is then mashed with hot water. This gelatinises the starch and further enzyme action in the mash produces glucose and simple nitrogen-containing compounds. This nutrient rich liquid is termed **wort**. It is filtered and the spent grain removed.

The higher the sugar content of the mash the higher the percentage of ethanol made. Brewers may also add additional enzymes, for example, amylase, to the mash to maximize the amount of sugar. This results in a low carbohydrate or 'lite' beer.

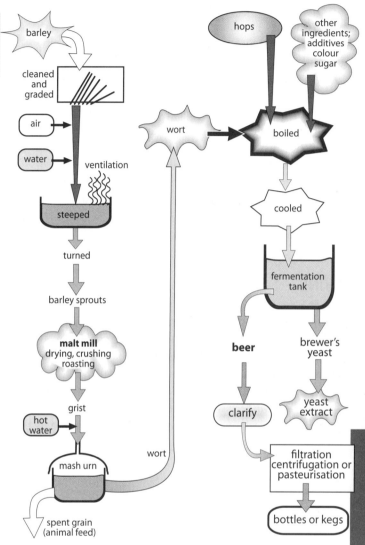

Figure 1731   A summary of the brewing process

OPTION

Figure 1730   Fermenting vessels in a brewery

Hops or hop extract are added to the wort with colourings and the mash is boiled. The hops give beer it characteristic bitter flavour and also have anti-microbial activity (by allowing movement across bacterial membranes). The bitterness is enhanced by the production of resins from an isomerisation process during the boiling of the hops.

After cooling, the mixture is run into a fermentation tank and inoculated with strains of *Saccharomyces cerevisiae*, brewer's yeast. The wort contains dissolved air and hence initially the yeast respires aerobically and multiplies rapidly. Later when the oxygen is consumed the yeast respires anaerobically and cell division stops. The dense layer of carbon dioxide generated by the activity of the yeast ensure that the tank is anaerobic thereby ensuring fermentation occurs. *Refer to Figure 1730.*

Top fermenting yeasts are those strains which float to the top of the beer after fermentation. In contrast, bottom fermenting yeasts sink to the bottom. Traditionally, ales were made with the former; lagers with the latter. Other beers, such as sorghum beer which is made in Africa mainly from sorghum, millet and maize, are brewed using similar principles

Hard water is used in brewing beer and traditionally breweries have been located where the water contains dissolved calcium sulfate. Calcium ions play an important role in amylase activity and yeast flocculation. Ethanol is produced as a result of the anaerobic fermentation of sugars. Fermentation usually stops when the fermentable sugars have been used up. The beer is then separated from the yeast, clarified, treated to prevent spoilage, carbonated and packaged.

WINE

Wines were traditionally made with mild yeast found on the skins of the grapes. Different yeast strains are often confined to small areas and each gives a particular flavour and aroma (smell) to the wine which is characteristic of that region. Each grape type has a slightly different chemical composition in its fruit which affects the wine it is made into. Modern wineries use specific strains of yeast which give consistency to the wine and reduce souring by bacteria.

The grapes are picked and gently crushed which loosens the soft skins and stems resulting in the formation of a **must**. The must is then screened to remove stems and treated with sulfur dioxide gas to kill microorganisms that cause spoilage.

Wine yeasts are then added to convert the sugars to ethanol. White wine is made when the skins are removed early. The fermentation is performed at 25 °C; anthocyanin and tannin pigments are leached out of the grape skins. The wine is run off and 'racked': the pulp is allowed to settle and then removed and pressed. It is then reintroduced to the wine and the fermentation allowed to finish. The dregs or 'lees' are allowed to settle. It is then stored and allowed to mature. It is then filtered, fined and bottled.

BREAD

When flour is made into a dough, amylases from the original wheat grain act on starch to produce a mixture of glucose and maltose. Specialised varieties of the yeast strain *Saccharomyces cerevisiae* ferment these sugars generating carbon dioxide gas. This makes the dough rise as bubbles of gas are caught in the mixture. Water

and ethanol are also generated, but are driven off as gases during the baking of the dough. The high temperatures kill the yeast, preventing further action.

F.4.2	Outline the production of soy sauce using *Aspergillus oryzae*.
	©IBO 2007

Soya beans are a rich source of protein and are an important component of the diets of many people around the world. Soya beans can be cooked or fermented in a variety of ways to make many foods. Soy sauce is made from soya beans and wheat. It is food flavour and has a high salt and peptide content. It is a very important ingredient in Asian cooking and is used to enhance the flavour of fish, rice, bean curd (tofu) and boiled vegetables.

Soy sauce is prepared on the industrial scale by using enzymes to hydrolyse beans and cereal proteins. The fungi *Aspergillus oryzae* and *Rhizopus* together with *lactobacilli* and yeasts provide the enzymes to break down proteins and starch. The soya beans are soaked and boiled and the wheat is rusted and crushed. They are then mixed together and inoculated with a culture of *Aspergillus oryzae*. The fungus grows for several days on the mixture, which is aerated and spread out. Salt water is added and the mash left in deep, cool fermentation tanks for several months. The *lactobacilli* and the yeasts grow and lactic acid and alcohol fermentations occur and the mixture is aged to make raw soy sauce. It is then filtered, pasteurised and the sediments and oils removed.

F.4.3	Explain the use of acids and high salt or sugar concentrations in food preservation.
	©IBO 2007

Many foods are preserved using salt or sugar. The majority of microorganisms will not be able to grow under such conditions, due to water loss via osmosis. Jams contain a very high concentration of sugar, typically fifty to seventy per cent. They are boiled before pouring into hot glass jars. This sterilises the jam which is then sealed to prevent further contamination from air borne fungi and bacteria. Once the jar is opened, bacteria cannot grow, but some strains of yeast and fungi can tolerate the high dissolved sugar content. Both salt and sugar absorb moisture from the atmosphere and this accelerates the spoilage process as the concentration of sugar or salt falls with time. Salting and brining uses salt (sodium chloride) concentrations of twenty to thirty percent and is used for meat, fish and vegetables which are not cooked before brining.

F.4.4	Outline the symptoms, method of transmission and treatment of one named example of food poisoning.

©IBO 2007

Food poisoning is best described as food infection since it is caused by pathogenic bacteria, viruses or fungi. Such contamination usually arises from improper handling, preparation, or food storage. Good hygiene practices before, during, and after food preparation can reduce the chances of contracting an illness. Bacteria are a common cause of food poisoning. *Salmonella* is a Gram negative genus of bacteria commonly responsible for food poisoning.

Salmonella produce enterotoxins, which are active in the human gut. An **enterotoxin** is a toxin released by a micro-organism in the lower intestine. The enterotoxin alters the permeability of the intestinal wall. This causes water and electrolytes to leak into the intestinal tract, causing diarrhea. In more serious cases the bacteria may enter the lymphatic system.

Salmonella also produces **endotoxins** *(see Topic F.6.3)*, which when present in large amounts cause fever, diarrhea and inflammation in the human host. However, with *Salmonella* infection the diarrhea does not occur until one to two days after eating infected eggs or uncooked fish or chicken. The delay occurs because the bacteria from the infected food stick to the surface of epithelial cells lining the intestine. The *Salmonella* bacteria then enter the cells via phagocytosis. The cells are damaged when the *Salmonella* bacteria multiply and produce endotoxins.

Most mild types of salmonella infection clear up in four to seven days without requiring any treatment other than rest and plenty of liquid. A more severe infection may cause excessive diarrhea, stomach cramps, severe dehydration and jaundice. In such cases, treatment with antibiotics *(see Topic F.6.5)* may be necessary and a doctor should be consulted.

TOK   When does correlation mean causation?

Epidemiology is a field of science where factors effecting heath are studied. Epidemiologists acknowledge that correlation between a factor and a disease does not mean that that factor is the cause of the disease. Carefully controlled experiments can determine cause, but this is extremely difficult in the area of human health, hence our reliance on epidemiological studies to determine risk of illness. An early case in which epidemiology was used was the linking of cholera to contaminated water by John Snow in London's Soho district in 1854. Snow collected data on the distribution of cholera cases in this part of London and linked them to a single public water pump in Broad Street, Soho. He insisted that the handle of the pump be removed to prevent further cases of Cholera. Snow could not prove that the water was the cause of the disease as the germ theory had not yet been proposed, but the correlation was accurate and the cause of the disease was eventually found to be the water borne bacterium, *Vibrio cholerae*.

Today cholera still kills thousands each year due to poor sanitation and treatment. More than ninety-five percent of the cholera deaths are in Africa. Sanitation (the provision of clean drinking water and proper disposal of sewage) can prevent the bacterium being consumed. For those at risk of contracting cholera education is needed that they should boil questionable water and to explain the effectiveness and ease of preparation of oral rehydration therapy. The treatment with one teaspoon of salt and eight teaspoons of sugar per one litre of clean water will save a Cholera sufferer from a horrible and easily avoided death.

OPTION

F5 METABOLISM OF MICROBES

F.5.1   Define the terms *photoautotroph, photoheterotroph, chemoautotroph* and *chemoheterotroph*.

F.5.2   State one example of a photoautotroph, photoheterotroph, chemoautotroph and chemoheterotroph.

©IBO 2007

PHOTOAUTOTROPHS

Photoautotrophs are bacteria that carry out a form of phosynthesis according to the following equation:

$CO_2 + 2H_2X \rightarrow (CH_2O) + H_2O + 2X$, where H_2X represents a hydrogen donor and (CH_2O) represents carbohydrate

In three groups of bacteria the hydrogen donor is never water; in the green **sulfur bacteria** (for example, *Chlorobium*) and the purple sulfur bacteria (for example, *Chromatium*) it is hydrogen sulfide and in the purple non-sulfur bacteria (for example, *Rhodospirillium*) it is lactic acid, pyruvic acid or ethanol.

Photosynthetic bacteria contain **bacteriochlorophyll** which absorbs light in the extreme ultra violet and infra-red parts of the electromagnetic spectrum which is outside the range used by chlorophyll.

The green sulfur bacteria are confined to oxygen-free environments and are found in shallow ponds with other bacteria which also thrive in the low oxygen concentration.

Cyanobacteria *(see Topic F.5.5)* live in fresh water, seas, soil and lichen, and use a plant-like photosynthesis which uses water as a hydrogen donor and releases oxygen as a by-product. They contain chlorophyll and depend on photosynthesis for both energy and carbon compounds.

PHOTOHETEROTROPHS

Certain bacteria are capable of obtaining energy from light, but are not capable of reducing carbon dioxide. Such bacteria must decompose the remains of other organisms to obtain their reduced-carbon compounds, but can generate energy from light. Such organisms are described as **photoheterotrophs** and include a few strains of purple non-sulfur bacteria. For example, *Chloroflexus* species are photoheterotrophic green non-sulfur bacteria

CHEMOAUTOTROPHS

Chemoautotrophs or chemosynthetic organisms are bacteria that use carbon dioxide as a carbon source but obtain their energy from chemical reactions rather than light. The bacteria obtain energy from inorganic substances such as hydrogen, hydrogen sulfide, iron(II) ions, ammonia and nitrite ions. They are widespread in soils and water.

Iron bacteria, for example, *Leptothrix*

Half equation
$Fe^{2+} \rightarrow Fe^{3+}$ + energy

Full equation
$4FeCO_3 + O_2 + 6 H_2O \rightarrow 4Fe(OH)_3 + 4CO_2$ + energy

It is thought many of the naturally occurring pure iron ore and sulfur deposits are due to bacterial activity.

Colourless sulfur bacteria, for example, *Thiobacillus*

Unbalanced half equation
$S \rightarrow SO_4^{2-}$ + energy

Full equation
$2S + 3O_2 + 2H_2O \rightarrow H_2SO_4$ + energy

Under anaerobic condition some species use nitrate ions as a hydrogen acceptor, thereby carrying out **denitrification** *(see Topic F.2.2)*. Nitrifying bacteria, for example, *Nitrobacter* and *Nitrosomonas* *(see Topic F.2.2)* are also examples of chemautotrophic bacteria.

CHEMOHETEROTROPHS

Organisms that use preformed organic compounds as their source of carbon and energy are called **chemoheterotrophs**. Chemoheterotrophs exhibit two basic methods of energy production: respiration and fermentation. Many chemoheterotrophic bacteria are saprotrophic, feeding on dead organic material by releasing enzymes and absorbing the soluble products of enzyme action. They play an important as decomposers in the nitrogen cycle *(see Topic F.2.2)*.

Chemoheterotroph can respire or ferment a wide range of chemical compounds, see the table below. All of the chemicals are metabolised to a form that can enter the respiratory pathway and generate ATP.

OPTION

	Photoautotrophic	Chemoautotrophic	Photoheterotrophic	Chemoheterotrophic
Energy source	Light	Chemical – from the oxidation of inorganic substances during respiration	Light	Chemical – from the oxidation of inorganic substances during respiration
Types	Green bacteria, cyanobacteria (blue-green bacteria), sulfur bacteria and some purple non-sulfur bacteria	Nitrifying and sulfur bacteria	Purple non-sulfur bacteria (very few)	Most bacteria – saprotrophs, parasites and mutualists.

Figure 1732   Nutritional characteristics of bacteria (table)

Some carbon-containing compounds metabolised by bacteria include:

- Alcohols
- Chitin
- Methane
- Monocarboxylic acids
- Polyurethanes
- Pyramides
- Cellulose
- Hydrocarbons
- Methanol
- Polyethene
- Purines
- Steroids.

Some bacteria are aerobic, using molecular oxygen in respiration and releasing carbon dioxide. Anaerobic bacteria use nitrate or sulfate ions, instead of oxygen. Fermenters are examples of anaerobic bacteria. They break down glucose to pyruvate which is then converted into lactic acid, ethanol or other compounds. Fermenters grow in mud, animal intestines and dead tissues.

An example of a chemoheterotroph is *Clostridium acetobutylicum*, an obligate anaerobe: it can only use anaerobic respiration.

F.5.3	Compare photoautotrophs with photoheterotrophs in terms of energy sources and carbon sources.
F.5.4	Compare chemoautotrophs with chemoheterotrophs in terms of energy sources and carbon sources.

©IBO 2007

A table summarising the four nutritional characteristics of bacteria and some of their characteristics is shown in Figure 1732.

The photoautotrophic and photoheterotrophic bacteria comprise the photosynthetic bacteria. In autotrophs the carbon source is carbon dioxide (inorganic); in heterotrophs the carbon source is organic compounds synthesised by other organisms.

F.5.5	Draw and label a diagram of a filamentous cyanobacterium.

©IBO 2007

The distinguishing features of **cyanobacteria**, formerly known as blue-green algae, are the presence of chlorophyll a (found in higher plants) and the production of oxygen during photosynthesis *(see Topic F.4.4)*. They contain protective blue and red pigments known as **phycobilins**. Certain strains of cyanobacteria, for example, the freshwater species *Nostoc*, are also unique in their ability to perform nitrogen fixation and photosynthesis.

Cyanobacteria are found in fresh and marine water around the globe with the exception of very acidic waters. They can also tolerate high levels of pollution and a wide range of temperatures. They are also found in jungle soils and live symbiotically with amoebae, diatoms, some fungi and in the roots of **cycads**.

The cells of cyanobacteria, which are occasionally branched, often occur in chains or in filaments. A number of species occur in colonies with individual cells held together by gelatinous sheaths, which are frequently pigmented.

Nitrogen fixation *(see Topic F2)* occurs only inside specialised thick-walled cells called **heterocysts**. The thick walls are necessary to exclude oxygen which disrupts the structure of nitrogenase.

Certain cyanobacteria produce toxins. Sometimes a mass-reproduction of cyanobacteria results in algal blooms *(see Topic F.2.5)*. Some freshwater cyanobacteria are marketed as having nutritional and health value, such as *spirulina*.

OPTION

Figure 1733 shows the structure of *Anabaena*, a nitogen fixing, filamentous cyanobacterium.

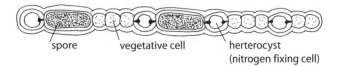

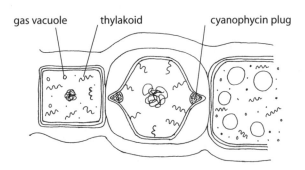

Figure 1733   Anabaena

F.5.6	Explain the use of bacteria in the bioremediation of soil and water.

©IBO 2007

Bioremediation can be defined as any process that uses bacteria, fungi, plants or their enzymes to return the environment altered by contaminants to its original condition. Bioremediation may be employed to degrade and remove specific soil contaminants, such as chlorinated hydrocarbons (solvents and pesticides) by bacteria. An example of a more general approach is the cleanup of oil spills by the addition of nitrate and/or sulfate fertilisers to facilitate the decomposition of crude oil by indigenous (native) or exogenous (introduced) bacteria.

Selenium is a toxic element found in drainage water from farm land. In water the element exists as SeO_4^{2-} and SeO_3^{2-}. It is also produced by oil refineries. At high concentrations it can kill animals and at lower concentrations cause deformities. It has been found that *Enterobacter cloacea* can convert the selenate ions into the less harmful and insoluble selenium.

Bacteria involved in bioremediation require sufficient oxygen to support aerobic respiration. The soil should be moist and the optimum pH range for microbial activity is between 6.5 and 7.5. Commercial companies now mass produce and supply standardised bacteria in concentrated liquid formats and dry endospores. They are the then introduced into suitable soil.

F6 MICROBES AND DISEASE

F.6.1	List six methods by which pathogens are transmitted and gain entry to the body.

©IBO 2007

A disease which can be passed from one sufferer to another is described as an **infectious disease** or communicable disease. A micro-organism which causes a disease when it infects is termed a pathogenic species or **pathogen**. The ability of a pathogen to cause disease is termed **virulence**.

Disease can be transmitted by direct contact from one infected individual to another via the mucous membranes, which are thinner, softer and moister than the epidermis of the skin.

A few diseases are spread directly into the blood. Transfer occurs when blood or body secretions from one individual enter the bloodstream of another person. This can happen when semen or saliva comes into physical contact with a damaged mucous membrane allowing entry directly into the capillaries.

Pregnant women may pass bacterial infections across the placenta to the developing embryo. Unprotected sexual activity and the use of infected hypodermic needles are other common ways of transferring pathogens.

Micro-organisms which enter the body through broken skin are often opportunistic. They are normally confined to the skin, but a wound in the protective surface caused by an accident provides an entry point for pathogens.

Micro-organisms can be transmitted in air currents: many fungi rely upon air currents or rain drops to disperse their spores. Organisms that infect animal respiratory tracts, for example, the influenza and SARS viruses, are spread by exhaled air or by droplets of mucus spread by coughs or sneezes. The smaller droplets take a long time to settle and are easily inhaled by another person.

Pathogens can enter the food with the raw ingredients, by the activity of insects, for example, house flies and poor hygiene, for example, failing to wash hands with soap after visiting the toilet. Typhoid and cholera bacteria may be present in sewage-contaminated drinking water. Raw meat may be infected with salmonella bacteria which cause 'food poisoning'.

Disease	Pathogen	Transmission
Athelete's foot	*Trichophyton rubrum*	Soil and water borne spores
Measles	*Measles virus (RNA virus)*	Inhalation of virus
Polio	*Poliomyelitis virus (RNA virus)*	Drinking water
Sleeping sickness	*Trypanosome*	Bite by tsetse fly
Syphilis	*Treponema pallidium*	Direct sexual contact
Influenza	*Myxovirus (DNA virus)*	Droplet infection
Common cold	*Rhinovirus (RNA virus)*	Droplet infection
German measles (rubella)	*Rubella virus*	Droplet infection
AIDS	*HIV (retrovirus)*	Unprotected sexual intercourse
Mumps	*Paramyxovirus (RNA virus)*	Droplet infection
Chlorea	*Vibrio cholerae*	Faecal contamination
Tuberculosis (TB)	*Mycobacterium tuberculosis*	Droplet infection; drinking contaminated milk
Whooping cough	*Bordetella pertussis*	Droplet infection
Tetanus	*Clostridium tetani*	Wound infection
Food poisoning	*Salmonella*	Eating meat from infected animals
Syphilis	*Treponema pallidum*	Sexual contact
Rabies	*Lyssavirus virus (RNA virus)*	By bite
Smallpox*	*Variola virus (DNA virus)*	Droplet infection

* The disease is believed to be extinct, but the virus is stored in several laboratories.

Figure 1734   Selected human pathogenic diseases and their means of transmission

Many viruses and protozoans are transmitted by vectors. Insects are a common vector. Mosquitoes have mouthparts adapted to penetrate through skin and between cells.

F.6.2	Distinguish between *intracellular* and *extracellular* bacterial infection using *Chlamydia* and *Streptococcus* as examples.
	©IBO 2007

EXTRACELLULAR BACTERIA

Extracellular bacteria, for example, *Streptococcus,* damage tissues from outside cells. Their presence usually results in the production of a class of antibodies known as **opsonins**. They produce acute diseases which are disease that last a short time, come on rapidly, and is accompanied by distinct symptoms.

Streptococcus are a genus of gram positive bacteria. Some species cause infections, for example, strep throat, tonsillitis, rheumatic fever and scarlet fever. Streptococcus produces **virulence factors.** Virulence factors are proteins produced by the bacterial chromosome or plasmids - they account for the pathogenicity. The capsule of *streptococcus pneumonia* produces proteins that inhibits pahgocytosis of the bacterium by the human's immune system.

INTRACELLULAR BACTERIA

Intracellular bacteria, for example, *Chlamydia,* multiply within cells, typically phagocytes or epithelial cells. They cause **chronic diseases** which are diseases that persists for a long time.

Chlamydia is a sexually transmitted infection caused by a bacterium *Chlamydia trachomatis*. It is curable with antibiotics, but if left untreated can lead to unfertility. The chlamydial infectious particle, called the elementary body. It enters a host cell and changes to a metabolically active and larger **reticulate body** that divides by binary fission. The entire growth cycle occurs within a vacuole that segregates the chlamydia from the cytoplasm of the host cell. The reticulate bodies change back to elementary bodies, and then the cell lyses and the infectious bacteria are released.

OPTION

317

F.6.3   Distinguish between *endotoxins* and *exotoxins*.

©IBO 2007

TOXINS

Toxins are chemicals released by pathogens, in particular bacteria, that have harmful effects on the body. The effects are felt throughout the body as the toxin is transported through the body tissues from bacteria present in other tissues.

EXOTOXINS

Exotoxins are soluble compounds secreted by the bacteria into their environments; they interact with cells in the immune system resulting in fevers and headaches.

Both gram negative and gram positive bacteria produce exotoxins. Exotoxins may be secreted, or may be released during lysis of the cell. The majority of exotoxins can be destroyed by heating. Exotoxins can be destroyed by antibodies produced by the immune system, but many exotoxins are so toxic that they may be fatal before the immune system can respond.

There are three main types of exotoxins:
- toxins that act upon connective tissue - this allows the further spread of bacteria and therefore the infection into underlying tissues
- toxins that act as enzymes, enter cells and effect their metabolism
- membrane damaging toxins - these toxins are designed primarily to puncture the cell membrane killing cells

Tetanus is a medical condition characterised by a sustained contraction of skeletal muscle, the symptoms are caused by tetanospasmin, an exotoxin and **neutrotoxin** produced by the Gram positive bacterium *Clostridium tetani*.

Infection generally occurs through wound contamination, and often involves a cut or deep puncture wound. As the infection progresses, muscle spasms in the jaw develop, hence the common name, **lockjaw**. This is followed by difficulty in swallowing and muscle stiffness and spasms.

ENDOTOXINS

Endotoxins are produced by Gram negative bacteria, for example, *Salmonella*. They are not released from the bacteria until the cell wall is damaged or lysis occurs. Endotoxins need to be present in relatively large amounts to have any effect, such as causing a fever, inflammation or diarrhoea. Endotoxins are lipopolysaccharides that form part of the outer membrane of the Gram negative cell wall. The only gram positive bacteria that produces endotoxins is *Listeria monocytogenes*.

F.6.4   Evaluate methods of controlling microbial growth by irradiation, pasteurization, antiseptics and disinfectants.

©IBO 2007

ANTISEPTICS

Antiseptics are chemicals used to prevent **sepsis** or infection of wounds. The first antiseptic used in hospitals was carbolic acid (phenol). Antiseptics commonly used today include **chlorhexidine** and alcohols such as ethanol and *iso*propanol (propan-2-ol). Chlorhexidine is often used as an active ingredient in mouthwash designed to kill dental plaque.

DISINFECTION

Disinfection is the destruction of infective organisms. Hypochlorite (chlorate(I)) disinfectants are used to purify water and in the water in public swimming pools. They are also used at home to disinfect babies' feeding bottles and toilets (in the form of bleach).

Disinfectants are most effective in warm solution since the increase in temperature raises the average kinetic energy

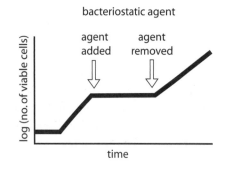

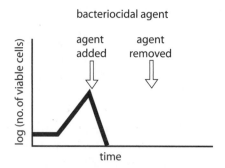

Figure 1735   The action of bacteriocidal and bacteriostatic agents

of the disinfectant molecules causing them to move more quickly. This increases the probability of the molecules colliding with a bacterium or virus in a given period of time. At low concentrations there may be insufficient disinfectant molecules in contact with the target organisms to kill them (**bacteriocidal**), but the there may be sufficient to prevent them form multiplying (**bacteriostatic**).

Bleaches are most effective at pH 5 since at this pH they form the highest concentration of hypochlorous acid (chloric(I) acid), HOCl, the active ingredient. The acid kills bacteria by releasing its oxygen and act as an oxidising agent. If spores are present then a high concentration of bleach is needed.

PASTUERISATION

Pastuerisation is used to sterilise foods, especially milk. It involves rapid heating followed by rapid cooling, for example, milk is pasteurised at 72°C for 15 seconds. This kills many bacteria that cause spoilage or potential pathogens.

RADIATION

Radiation, especially gamma radiation, is used to sterilise culture media for growing bacteria, medical supplies and drugs. The dose required varies: bacterial and fungal cells need low doses, but spores and viruses need higher doses.

CULTURE MEDIA

Bacteria are generally grown in a **medium** which contains all the nutrients need for bacterial growth. Some media are specific for a particular bacterial strain. Culture media can be prepared by mixing together known amounts of specific chemicals (a defined or synthetic medium) or they can be made from a natural source, such as boiled meat, which contains the nutrients required by most bacterial strains (an undefined or complex medium).

(See 'The Student Guide to Internal Assessment – Biology' from IBID Press on guidance on the precautions that must be observed when working with microorganisms).

Agar

Agar is often mixed with a liquid medium to prepare a solid medium, which is useful to observe, separate and store bacteria cultures. A solid medium in a Petri dish is known as an agar plate. Agar is a complex polysaccharide extracted from seaweed and can be warmed to 37 °C. It is a transparent jelly and is not broken down by bacteria.

Once bacteria have been introduced to the agar medium (a process known as **inoculation**) they are allowed to grow under defined conditions in an incubator, a thermostatically controlled oven. Liquid media or **broths** are often incubated in a water bath.

Culture

A **culture** is a growth of bacteria in a medium. The culture may be pure, that is, one bacterial strain may be present, or mixed, that is, many strains growing together. A colony is a visible growth of bacteria on an agar plate containing many millions of bacterial cells. Each colony has grown from a single original bacterial cell.

Streak plate

A **streak plate** is a method of inoculating an agar plate with bacteria so that they are gradually diluted. The aim is to separate individual bacterial cells which can grow into visible colonies. This method is used to separate pure cultures of bacteria from a mixed starting culture, such as soil or food.

Lawn

A **lawn** is a layer of bacteria growing on the surface of an agar plate. This is useful to test the effectiveness of antibiotics or antiseptics. In the pure plate method a bottle of warm, sterile, molten agar is inoculated with bacteria, stirred, and then the agar poured into the plate. In the spread plate method an agar plate is inoculated with a small volume of broth culture, which is then spread evenly over the surface.

Viruses

Because viruses are obligate parasites, they cannot be cultured in the laboratory like bacteria. They must be grown inside their specific living host cells. Traditionally, this involved infecting whole animals or plants, but with tissue culture techniques specific host cells can be grown and infected with a virus.

The growth of bacterial cells is generally measured by simply counting the number of cells. Some methods give total cell counts, which include both living and dead bacterial cells, while others give viable cell counts, which only include living cells.

CELL COUNTER (HEMEOCYTOMETER)

This approach counts the total cells by observing the individual cells under a light microscope. This is relatively easy for large cells such as yeast, but more difficult for the smaller bacterial cells.

OPTION

TURBIDOMETRY

This technique also counts cells, it is more rapid than using a hemeocytometer, but less accurate. A sample of the liquid culture is placed in a cuvette in a colorimeter or spectrophotometer and the absorbance of light is measured. The greater the concentration of the bacterial cells, the more cloudy or turbid the liquid is, so the more light it scatters, so the less light is transmitted to the detector. If the same sample is counted in a hemeocytometer and its absorbance measured, then a calibration curve can be plotted.

In general the bacterial growth rate increases with temperature until the enzymes undergo denaturation. Bacteria can grow within a wide range of temperatures, with archaebacteria (see Topic F.1.4) in particular growing at the extremes of the range. Most bacteria grow in neutral pH and die in extremely acidic or alkaline conditions, due to enzyme denaturation. The pH of a growth medium can change over time due to production of acids or alkalis, hence it is important to use a buffer when growing bacteria. Many bacteria are obligate aerobes and require molecular oxygen for respiration. In a solid agar medium these bacteria will only grow on the surface and hence a liquid medium must be well aerated.

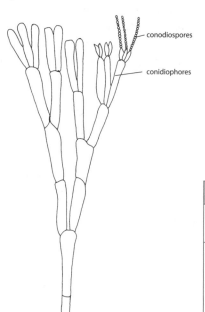

conodiospores

conidiophores

Figure 1736
The structure of
Penicillium notatum

F.6.5	Outline the mechanism of the action of antibiotics, including inhibition of synthesis of cell walls, proteins and nucleic acids.

©IBO 2007

Antibiotics were originally defined as substances produced by microorganisms that kill or inhibit growth of bacteria or other microorganisms. However the term has been broadened to include synthetic and semi-synthetic antimicrobial compounds. Penicillin was the first antibiotic discovered by Sir Alexander Fleming in 1928 and later produced for medical use. It is obtained from the fungus *Penicillium notatum* as shown in Figure 1736.

Antibiotics are used to treat infectious bacterial diseases. If the antibiotic kills the bacteria it is described as microbicidal; if the antibiotic inhibits or slows down the growth of bacteria it is described as microbistatic. The effect may vary with the concentration of the antibiotic. Generally Gram positive bacteria are more sensitive to antibiotics than Gram negative bacteria.

A broad spectrum antibiotic acts on a wide range of Gram positive and Gram negative bacteria, for example, tetracyclines and chloramphenicol. A narrow spectrum antibiotic is much more specific and will target a limited range of bacteria, sometimes only one strain.

Antibiotic mechanism of action depend on both the antibiotic and the bacterium affected, but include interference with bacterial cell wall synthesis, cell membrane function or cellular synthesis. Figure 1737 shows a summary of the action and mechanisms for antibiotics on selected bacteria (and fungi).

Site of action	Example of antibiotic	Mechanism of action
Cell wall synthesis	Penicillin, cephalosporin, vancomycin, bacitracin	Inhibits the formation peptide bonds that strengthen the bacterial cell wall
Protein synthesis	Chloramphenicol, tetracyclines, erythromycin, streptomycin, neomycin, streptomycin, gentamicin	Bind to bacterial 70S ribosomes, interfering and inhibiting protein synthesis Causes misreading of the genetic code thereby leading to synthesis of abnormal proteins
Nuclei acid synthesis	Rifampicin, anthracylines	Rifampicin selectively binds to bacterial RNA polymerase to prevent initiation of transcription Anthracylines inhibit DNA synthesis
Cell membrane function	Polymixin B	Damages cell membranes
Microtubules	Griseofulvin	Binds to fungal microtubules

Figure 1737   Action of antibiotics

However, the effectiveness of antibiotics has decreased significantly because of increasing resistance to antibiotics (*see Topic 5.4.8*). Some bacteria are naturally resistant, others have acquired the resistance through mutation but many have acquired resistance by conjugation (*see Topic 2.2.2*).

F.6.6	Outline the lytic life cycle of the influenza virus.

©IBO 2007

The **lytic cycle** is on method of viral reproduction. It is usually the main method of viral replication and involves the destruction of the infected cell.

The lytic cycle is a four-stage process:
- penetration
- biosynthesis
- maturation
- lysis

PENETRATION

To infect a cell, a virus must first enter the cell through the plasma membrane by either attaching to a receptor on the cell's surface. The virus then releases its genome (either single- or double-stranded DNA or RNA) into the cell. Once inside the host cell, the virus loses its ability to infect other cells and is in the eclipse stage.

BIOSYNTHESIS

The virus' nucleic acid uses the host cell's metabolism to make large amounts of viral components. In the case of DNA viruses, the DNA transcribes itself into messenger RNA (mRNA) molecules that are then used to direct the cell's ribosomes. In retroviruses (which inject an RNA strand), a reverse transcriptase transcribes the viral RNA into DNA, which is then transcribed again into messenger RNA. See Figure 1738.

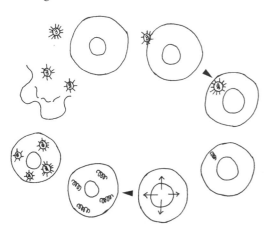

Figure 1738   Lytic cycle of the influenza virus

MATURATION AND LYSIS

After many copies of viral components are made, they are assembled into complete viruses. The cell eventually becomes filled with viruses and bursts, or lyses; thus giving the lytic cycle its name. The new viruses are then free to infect other cells.

F.6.7	Define *epidemiology*.

©IBO 2007

Epidemiology is the study of the spread of disease and the factors that influence its spread. If enough scientific information is known about the spread of an infectious disease then measures can be introduced to control, or even eradicate, a disease from an area. The first task of an epidemiologist will try to find the source of an infection and establish the mechanism of transmission.

Pathogens come from infected individuals or from other reservoirs of infection. There are three main reservoirs of human infection which have to be dealt with by an epidemiologist:
- Individuals who have had an infection but are symptomless carriers. They do not show any signs of infection, but excrete the pathogen.
- Some animals contain pathogens; a disease caused by a pathogen which infects both humans and animals is called a **zoonosis**.
- Many pathogens are found in soil and water and infection can be contracted by contact with them.

Disease	Organism	Reservoir
Plague (see Topic F.6.8)	*Yersinia pestsis*	Rats and other rodents
Rabies	Rhabdovirus	Dogs and related mammals
Ebola (see Topic F.6.8)	Ebolavirus	Possibly a fruit bat
Avian bird flu (see Topic F.6.8)	Influenza A virus subtype H5N1	Birds
Severe acute respiratory syndrome or SARS	SARS coronavirus	Bats and civet cats

Figure 1739   Some pathogens

An early example of simple epidemiology in action is provided by Edward Jenner. He was an English country doctor who in 1799 was the first to use a **vaccine** to successfully prevent a human disease. He had noticed that dairy maids who had milked cows suffering from cowpox were far less susceptible to the more virulent small pox *(see Topic F.6.8).* However, the dairy maids did display mild symptoms of the disease, for example, hand sores.

Jenner removed some of the **pus** from the sore of a diary maid suffering from small pox and scratched it into the skin of a young boy. He found the boy to be immune to small pox. Jenner has used an antigen to produce immunity against a pathogen. The reaction of the body to the cowpox vaccine is an example of **active immunisation** in which the body makes its own antibodies against the antigen.

These early public health experiments did not benefit from statistical and methodological principles characterising clinical trials today, nor would they now pass ethical review boards.

However, the 'Father' of epidemiology is considered to be John Snow, a London Physician who traced the source of a cholera outbreak London in 1854. He believed that cholera was transmitted by water contaminated by the faeces of cholera patients. However, the dominant theory at the time was that disease were caused by 'bad air'. By plotting the clusters of cholera on a map he identified a public water pump to be the source of the outbreak. He took a water sample and viewed it under a microscope and observed bacteria. The well pump was disabled and the outbreak was ended. He also used statistics to show the connection between the quality of the source of water and cholera cases.

Modern epidemiological studies are concerned with establishing a statistical correlation, for example, the HIV virus and AIDS, smoking and lung cancer. However, just because the two phenomena are associated it does not mean that one causes one another. In other words a correlation does not imply causality.

For example, the incidence of cirrhosis of the liver is associated with cigarette smoking, but it is believed that excessive consumption of alcohol is a more probable cause. However, as heavy drinkers tend to be heavy smokers, there is a statistical association, but in this case it is a confounding variable.

To establish a causal link you would need to set up a controlled experiment treating one group of animals with a variable (for example, a pathogen or chemical) and having a second control group without the variable but otherwise treated the same (thus avoiding confounding variables).

OPTION

TOK   The distinction between correlation and cause

Epidemiology is a field of science where factors effecting heath are studied. Epidemiologists acknowledge that correlation between a factor and a disease does not mean that that factor is the cause of the disease. Carefully controlled experiments can determine cause, but this is extremely difficult in the area of human health, hence our reliance on epidemiological studies to determine risk of illness. An early case in which epidemiology was used was the linking of cholera to contaminated water by John Snow in London's Soho district in 1854. Snow collected data on the distribution of cholera cases in this part of London and linked them to a single public water pump in Broad Street, Soho. He insisted that the handle of the pump be removed to prevent further cases of Cholera. Snow could not prove that the water was the cause of the disease as the germ theory had not yet been proposed, but the correlation was accurate and the cause of the disease was eventually found to be the water borne bacterium, *Vibrio cholerae*.

Today cholera still kills thousands each year due to poor sanitation and treatment. More than ninety-five percent of the cholera deaths are in Africa. Sanitation (the provision of clean drinking water and proper disposal of sewage) can prevent the bacterium being consumed. For those at risk of contracting cholera education is needed that they should boil questionable water and to explain the effectiveness and ease of preparation of oral rehydration therapy. The treatment with one teaspoon of salt and eight teaspoons of sugar per one litre of clean water will save a Cholera sufferer from a horrible and easily avoided death.

F.6.8   Discuss the origin and epidemiology of one example of a pandemic.

©IBO 2007

In any population of organisms there will always be a small number of people suffering from an infection caused by a micro-organism. An outbreak refers to a small number of people in a small area suffering from a disease. An **epidemic** occurs when a large number of people in several communities suffer from the same infection. A **pandemic** occurs when very large numbers of people in different countries all suffer from the same infection.

According to the World Heath Organisation (WHO), a pandemic may start when the emergence of a disease or disease strain new to the human population, the pathogen infects humans, causing serious illness and the agent spreads among humans.

Four strains of the influenza or flu virus are known: A, B, C and D. Strains C and D are stable, but new strains of A commonly emerge. Epidemics of influenza occur on a regular seasonal basis and pandemics also occur, for example, in 1918 when the Spanish flu (A_2 strain), killed more than twenty million people worldwide.

The influenza virus enters the respiratory system in infected droplets and then attacks the epithelial lining of the bronchioles. The symptoms include fever, shivering, headaches, sore throats and a blocked nose. Adults often have aches in the back and limbs. A cough often develops due to damage to the trachea and bronchioles. Pathogenic bacteria often invade the damaged air passages leading to bronchitis and pneumonia.

In 2004 an avian influenza virus was detected in birds in South East Asia. It has the ability to infect humans with a virulent form of the flu who come into close physical contact with infected birds. Biologists are concerned that the avian virus (known as H5N1) could combine with a human flu virus to create a subtype that could be highly contagious and lethal in humans. Human-human to transmission of avian flu has not been demonstrated.

The most famous pandemic of recorded history is the Black Death which was introduced to Europe in the 1300's from Asia. A quarter of Europe's population were killed. It has been traditionally assumed that the Black Death was an example of the bubonic plague, caused by the bacterium *Yersina pestis* and spread by fleas on the black rat. However some recent research suggests that the Black Death may have been caused by an Ebola type virus.

Many Biologists consider HIV infection to be a global pandemic. The WHO estimates that 25 million people have died since 1981 (when the HIV virus was first identified). 40 million people are estimated to be HIV positive. Retroviral drugs prolong life spans of HIV positive individuals, but there is currently no cure or vaccine.

The World Health Organisation (WHO) is an agency of the United Nations (UN) concerned with international public health. Its major task is to combat infectious diseases, for example, Asian bird flu, malaria and AIDS, and to promote the health of the world's population. It also has programs to develop and distribute vaccines and low cost HIV test kits. The WHO's vaccination program resulted in the eradication of small pox in 1979. It currently aims to eradicate polio within the next few years.

F.6.9   Describe the cause, transmission and effects of malaria, as an example of disease caused by a protozoan.

©IBO 2007

Globally at least 200 million people suffer from malaria, with an estimated two million deaths annually. Four species of *plasmodium* can infect man, but the two most important are *Plasmodium vivax* (found in temperate and subtropical areas) and *Plasmodium falciparum* (found only in tropical regions). Malaria is transmitted by the females of several species of the genus *Anopheles*. The females require several meals of blood before laying a batch of eggs, but males feed harmlessly on fruit juices or nectar. (The factors in blood required for egg production are unknown).

The life cycle of *Plasmodium vivax* is shown in Figure 1740. The cycle in the human host begins with the bite of an infected female inject salvia containing an anticoagulant together with **sporozoites**, the infective form of the *plasmodium* parasite.

They are transported via the blood to the liver where they asexually reproduce inside liver cells by a process of multiple cell fission called **schizogony**. The resulting **merozites** leave the damaged liver cells and pass out of the organ through blood vessels. However, in *Plasmodium vivax*, a small proportion remains to infect other liver cells.

A similar phase of asexual reproduction occurs in red blood cells (erythrocytes). After about forty eight hours, the red blood cells rupture to release new merozites. Repeated cycles produce the periodic bouts of fever characteristic of the disease in its early stages. See Figure 1740.

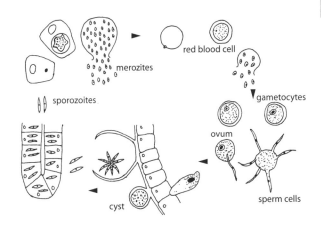

Figure 1740   Life cycle of the malarial parasite Plasmodium vivax

OPTION

After a period of time, some parasites develop into male and female **gametocytes** which circulate in the blood. New vectors (female *Anopheles* mosquitoes) are infected when these sexual forms form part of a blood meal. Inside the mosquito's stomach, ova and sperms develop and fertilization takes place. The zygote burrows through the wall of the stomach and forms a small cyst on the exterior. **Sporozites** from the cyst migrate to the salivary glands to infect a new human host.

F.6.10   Discuss the prion hypothesis for the cause of spongiform encephalopathy.

©IBO 2007

Spongiform encephalopathy is a group of progressive conditions that affects the brain and nervous system of humans and animals. It is transmitted by **prions**. Tiny holes appear in the cortex of the brain making it look like a sponge. Brain function is impaired resulting in memory and personality changes and problems with movement. **Creutzfeldt-Jacob disease** (CJD) is the most common form of Spongiform encephalopathy. It is very rare and commonly appears in people between the ages of 60 and 65.

Prions are misfolded proteins which carry the disease between individuals and cause the deterioration of the brain leading to death. They can be inherited, occur spontaneously or spread via infection. Transmission occurs when healthy animals eat infected tissues. This occurred in Britain during the 1980's when cows were infected by eating the processed remains of sheep nervous systems. This bovine form of spongiform encephalopathy (BSE or 'mad cow disease') spread through the cattle in an epidemic.

Prions cannot be transmitted through the air, via touching but they may be transmitted via contact with infected tissue or contaminated medical instruments. A new variant Creutzfeldt-Jacob (nvCJD) disease occurs in people very early in their life, typically in their twenties. It is believed that nvCJD is transmitted by eating nervous tissue of cows infected with bovine spongiform encephalopathy (BSE).

Prions, short for 'proteinaceous particles' - lack nucleic acid and are made of a single type of protein. They are believed to infect and propagate by refolding into an abnormal shape. They are very resistant to denaturation, radiation and heat.

The prion hypothesis was first proposed in the 1960's when the infectious agent of spongiform encephalopathy was found to resist the effects of ultra violet radiation (which breaks down nucleic acids) and yet responded to chemicals and treatments that disrupt proteins.

TOK   What is the cause and transmission of BSE?

Spongiform encephalopathies illustrate how natural sciences deal with information that does not fit into current models. Epidemiology has been used to investigate the diseases, but the small numbers of cases in humans has made its study difficult and led to argument about its origin and transmission. A perceived link between human cases and infected beef led to the culling of cattle in the UK in the 1990's. However the number of human cases reported were much lower than the number expected given the large number of cattle infected with the disease. It has been hypothesised that this is because humans in the UK generally only eat beef from parts of the animal that do not contain the causative prion. The publicity that this disease received and some initial, incorrect advice, led to confusion and some hysteria. Some suggest that the disease was taken advantage of by some governments to restrict imports of beef and assist their own farmers. One of the outcomes of this story was decreased trust in the scientific process of knowledge generation.

In 1982 *Stanley Prusiner* purified the infectious material confirming the presence of a specific protein. The prion hypothesis was controversial since it contradicts the central dogma of molecular biology which states that information flows from nucleic acid to proteins.

Further research showed that the protein that prions are made of is found in the bodies of healthy people and animals. However, the prion protein found in infectious material has a different structure and is resistant to proteases.

F1 DIVERSITY OF MICROBES

1. Which group of prokaryotes is often found living in harsh environments?
   A Fungi
   B Protists
   C Prions
   D Archaebacteria

2. Which two classification groups contain prokaryotic cells?
   A Archaebacteria and protists
   B Eubacteria and prions
   C Eubacteria and archaebacteria
   D Archaebacteria

3. Originally, organisms were classified as bacteria or eukaryotes. A three-domain system of classification has been proposed in which bacteria are divided into archaeabacteria and eubacteria. Why was this proposal made?
   A The number of prokaryotes is enormous,
   B There is a large genetic difference between the archaeabacteria and the eubacteria
   C The nucleus of the archaebacteria and eukaryotes are structurally similar
   D The archaeabacteria live in a range of inhospitable environments

4. Which of the following groups of organisms does not belong in the Archaebacteria?
   A Thermophiles
   B Halophiles
   C Methanogens
   D Glucophiles

5. Which of the following terms is used to describe bacteria with round cells?
   A Coccus
   B Pilus
   C Bacillus
   D Spirillus

6. What term is used to describe the ability of the bacterium *Vibrio fischeri* to produce bioluminescence only when a certain population density has been reached?
   A Quorum sensing
   B Aggregation
   C Induction
   D Morphogenesis

7. Which of the following is not a description of a virus?
   A A extremely small infectious particle that can pass through a filter that retains all bacteria
   B A non-metabolising protein and nucleic acid mixture
   C An infectious agent that requires entry into living cells in order to replicate.
   D An infectious protein

8. Which of the following processes is performed by both cells and viruses?
   A Synthesising carbohydrates b
   B Synthesising new RNA or DNA
   C Transporting signaling molecules through the endoplasmic reticulum
   D Aerobic respiration within mitochondria

9. How do viruses reproduce?
   A Directly attacking a host cell's membrane and then waiting for cell to lyse and die
   B Dividing by binary fission once they enter a host cell
   C Dividing by the process of mitosis followed by meiosis
   D Using the host cell's ribosomes to create proteins which self assemble into virus particles

10. What is the name given to a virus that attacks a bacterium?
    A Prion
    B Provirus
    C Bacillus
    D Bacteriophage

11. What does the term streptococcus imply about the arrangement of bacteria?
    A Cocci in clusters
    B Bacilli in clusters
    C Cocci in pairs
    D Cocci in chains

12. Bacteria which do not possess flagella cannot?
    A Move
    B Undergo binary division
    C Perform respiration
    D Grow in nutrient agar

13. What colour will a Gram-positive bacterium appear at the end of the Gram stain technique?
    A Yellow-green
    B Orange-red
    C Blue-purple
    D Black

14 From which structure is the envelope of an enveloped virus derived from?
A   The mitochondria of the cell
B   The cell membrane
C   The nuclear membrane
D   The endoplasmic reticulum of the cell

15 How does the protozoan amoeba move?
A   Cilia
B   Cilia and flagella
C   Pseudopodia
D   Flagella

16 What term is used to describe a dense bacterial population living in a complex secreted layer sticking to a surface?
A   coagulation
B   a biodisc
C   a biofilm
D   a bioinformatic

17 What is the highest temperature at which bacteria are likely to be found?
A   20 °C
B   40 °C
C   110 °C
D   400 °C

18 What does the term quorum sensing refer to?
A   The combined action of secondary messengers to form a single signal
B   Regulation that responds to population density
C   Feedback inhbition
D   Production of several proteins from a single operon

19 Which is a true statement about the cell membrane of bacteria?
A   It is impermeable to all molecules
B   It is permeable to water
C   It provides structural integrity and support
D   It is chemically unique compared to eukaryotic cells

20 Which of the following statements is false?
A   Gram positive bacteria do not possess a cell membrane
B   Gram negative bacteria have an outer membrane
C   Gram positive bacteria have a thick peptidoglycan or murein cell wall
D   Lipopolysaccharide is present in the Gram negative outer membrane

21 What is being compared during DNA hybridisation studies of two bacteria?
A   The rate of DNA replication in plasmids
B   The mechanism of RNA synthesis from DNA
C   The similarity of messenger RNA sequences
D   The nature of the 16S RNA component

22. Even though the two domains are procaryotic, the archaeabacteria differ from the eubacteria in that the archaeabacteria
I   lack muramic acid or peptidoglycan in their cell walls.
II   possess membrane lipids with ether-linked branched aliphatic chains.
A   I only is true
B   II only is true
C   Both I and II are true
D   Neither I or II are true

23 Which one of the following are not archaebacteria?
A   Thermoacidophiles
B   Methanogens
C   Halophiles
D   Spirochetes

24 How does amoeba reproduce?
A   fusion
B   binary fission
C   conjugation
D   exocytosis

25 Which structure is the light sensing organ in Euglena?
A   flagellum
B   contractile vacuole
C   cell membrane
D   stigma

26 The difference between Gram positive and Gram negative bacteria occurs in their?
A   organelles
B   outer membrane
C   structure of the 70S ribosomes
D   DNA sequence

27 (a) sketch and label a diagram of a typical eubacterium cell
    (b) Explain why Gram negative and Gram positive bacteria exhibit different appearances after staining.
    (c) Give a genus of gram negative bacteria.
    (d) Both gram negative and gram positive bacteria both exhibit quorum sensing. Briefly outline what happens during this process.
    (e) State two unique features of eubacteria not found in archaebacteria.

OPTION

F2 MICROBES AND THE ENVIRONMENT

1   What does the term Biological Oxygen Demand (BOD) refer to?
   A   amount of oxygen used by microbes present in the water
   B   concentration of decomposed waste in water
   C   percentage of oxygen left in water after organic matter is removed
   D   number of living organisms that a body of water can support

2   What is the underlying cause of the death of a river initiated by environmental pollutants?
   A   The overpopulation of green algae
   B   An excess of toxic soluble proteins
   C   The depletion of dissolved oxygen
   D   The buildup of sediment on the river bottom

3   What substance do most methanogens use to reduce carbon dioxide to hydrogen?
   A   Primary and secondary alcohols
   B   Glucose
   C   Hydrogen
   D   Iron(II) ions

4   Which one of the following sequences correctly describes the action of nitrifying bacteria?
   A   ammonium ions → nitrite ions → nitrate ions
   B   ammonium ions → nitrate ions → nitrite ions
   C   nitrate ions → ammonium ions → nitrite ions
   D   nitrite ions → ammonium ions → nitrite ions

5   Which one of the following pairs of bacteria are able to perform a process of nitrification?
   A   *Nitrosomonas* and *Rhizobium*
   B   *Azotobacter* and *Rhizobium*
   C   *Nitrosomonas* and *Nitrobacter*
   D   *Nitrosomonas* and *Azotobacter*

6   Anaerobic strains of bacteria are abundant in water-logged soils. What effect, if any, does this have on soil fertility and why?

	Soil fertility	Reason
A	None	None
B	Decreased	Bacteria convert nitrate ions to ammonia molecules
C	Decreased	Bacteria convert nitrate ions to nitrogen molecules
D	Increased	Bacteria carry out nitrogen fixation

7   Excess nitrate ions (NO_3^- (aq)) are a common pollutant in rivers and lakes causing rapid growth of algae and the death of submerged plants rooted in the mud.

   Lack of which factor causes the death of the submerged plants?
   A   dissolved carbon dioxide
   B   light energy
   C   oxygen
   D   suspended organic debris

8   Drawn and label a flow diagram representing the nitrogen cycle.

F3 MICROBES AND BIOTECHNOLOGY

1   How does yeast reproduce?
   A   Budding
   B   Binary division
   C   Parthenogenesis
   D   Allopolyploidy

2   Which bacterial enzymes are required for removing genes from DNA sequences?
   A   Splicases
   B   Restriction endonucleases
   C   Degradases
   D   Chaperonases

3   What is a DNA library?
   A   A database containing DNA sequences of all genes that have been sequenced
   B   All DNA fragment identified with a radioactive probe
   C   A DNA fragment inserted into a plasmid
   D   A collection of DNA fragments that make up the genome of a specific organism

4   Which is the correct description for germ-line therapy?
   A   Heritable
   B   Occasionally heritable
   C   Never heritable
   D   Totally unrelated to heritability

5   Which type of cell would not be a target for gene therapy?
   A   Alpha cells of the pancreas
   B   Red blood cell
   C   Hepatocytes in the liver
   D   Endothelial cells lining blood vessels

OPTION

6   Which one of the following primers, used with PCR, would allow copying of the single stranded DNA sequence 5'-ATGCCTAGGTC-3'?
A   5'-ATGCT-3'
B   5'-TACAG-3'
C   5'-CTGGA-3'
D   5'-GACCT-3'

7   What is the study of DNA sequence information to help explain cell functions?
A   Proteomics
B   Polymerase chain reaction
C   Transformation
D   Genomics

8   What is the first step in the polymersase chain reaction (PCR)?
A   Denaturation
B   Primer extension
C   Cooling
D   Annealing

9   Which technique is used to produce a library of DNA fragments?
A   Restriction enzymes
B   Plasmids
C   DNA ligases
D   Polymerase chain reaction

10   Both bacteriophages and plasmids can be used as cloning vectors. Which of the following is true and distinguishes a virus from a plasmid?
A   Plasmids use the translation machinery of the cell.
B   Viruses have a protein capsid.
C   Viruses can replicate in the absence of a cellular host.
D   Plasmids carry genes.

F4   MICROBES AND FOOD PRODUCTION

1   Which micro-organism is responsible for the production of bread, beer and wine?
A   *Acetobacter aceti*
B   *Saccharomyces cerevisiae*
C   *Penicillium roqueforti*
D   *Aspergillus oryzae*

2   In the production of beer, what is the term for the liquid to which the yeast is added?
A   Malt
B   Hops
C   Lager
D   Wort

3   Food may be preserved in brine, which is a 30% salt solution. How does this method of preservation prevent contamination by bacteria?
A   High salt concentration lowers the pH, thus inhibiting bacterial metabolism.
B   High salt concentration raises the pH, thus inhibiting bacterial metabolism.
C   A 30% salt solution is hypotonic to the bacteria, so they gain water and burst.
D   A 30% salt solution is hypertonic to the bacteria, so they lose water

4   Which of the following organisms are common pathogens which cause foodborne illness?
A   *E. coli, Aspergillus oryzae* and *Saccharomyces cerevisiae*
B   *Campylobacter, Salmonella* and *E .coli*
C   *E. coli, Thiomargarita namibiensis* and *Epulopiscium fishelsoni*
D   *E. coli, V. fischeri* and *nitrobacter*

5   Sake is a Japanese alcoholic drink produced from steamed rice (starch) by the combined activities of *Saccharomyces cerevisiae* and one other microorganism. From this it can be deduced that?
A   The other organism is one that excretes amylases, such as *Aspergillus oryzae*
B   Sake is a wine rather than a beer
C   The other organism is a species of *Acetobacter*
D   The other organism must act on the rice after *Saccharomyces cerevisiae*

OPTION

F5 METABOLISM OF MICROBES

1 What is the term given to the concept of using micro-organisms to clean up a polluted environment?
   A   Pasteurisation
   B   Bioremediation
   C   Fermentation
   D   Reverse phasing

2 Identify the structures which cyanobacteria lack but which most other prokaryotes possess?
   A   flagella
   B   photosynthetic membranes
   C   70S ribosomes
   D   nucleic acids

3 Which of the following is autotophic?
   A   paramecium
   B   amoeba
   C   euglena
   D   plasmodium

4. Which of the following organisms is unicellular and heterotrophic?
   A   amoeba
   B   paramecium
   C   chlorella
   D   both amoeba and paramecium

5 What is the function of heterocysts in the cyanobacteria?
   A   nitrogen fixation
   B   asexual reproduction by endopsore formation
   C   sexual reproduction by conjugation
   D   respiration

F6 MICROBES AND DISEASE

1 Which type of viral infection literally takes over and quickly destroys the host cell?
   A   Lytic cycle.
   B   Lysogenic cycle.
   C   Parthenogenetic cycle.
   D   Conjugation cycle.

2 Viruses can cause diseases in which of the following organisms?
   A   Bacteria
   B   Plants
   C   All organisms
   D   Animals

3 What term describes a disease that breaks out in explosive proportions within a population?
   A   Endemic
   B   Systemic
   C   Epidemic
   D   Pandemic

4. What term describes the situation when a virus enters a cell but does not undergo immediate replication?
   A   Lysogeny
   B   Transposition
   C   Endosymbiosis
   D   Synergism

5 Which group of organisms is the researcher Stanley Prusiner is associated with work on?
   A   Archaebacteria
   B   Prions
   C   Viroids
   D   Bacteriophages

6 Which infectious disease has been eradicated from the world by a WHO vaccination programme?
   A   Polio
   B   Smallpox
   C   Rabies
   D   Ebola

7 What do scrapie and Creutzfeldt Jakob disease (CJD) both have in common?
   A   They are diseases transmitted by bacterial vectors.
   B   The same vaccine protects against all of them.
   C   They are caused by prions.
   D   They are caused by retroviruses

OPTION

329

8   The parasitic protist that causes malaria, Plasmodium, must spend part of its life cycle in a non-human host. What organism serves as the vector for this life cycle?
   A   amoeba proteus
   B   house fly (musca domestica)
   C   mosquitoes (anopheles)
   D   tse-tse fly

9   What is the end result of a viral lytic cycle?
   A   The integration of the viral genome in the host cell genome
   B   The conversion of the virus into a prophage
   C   The release of mature and infectious viruses
   D   The release of reverse transcriptase via the cell membrane

10 Which of the following groups of infectious agents does not contain nucleic acids?
   A   Viruses
   B   Bacteria
   C   Prions
   D   Protists

11 Why is penicillin ineffective against viruses?
   A   Viruses do not perform meiosis
   B   Viruses lack a metabolism
   C   Viruses lack cell walls
   D   Viruses contain pencillinase

12 What is a complex bacterial medium?
   A   A medium whose pH changes during the growth of organisms
   B   A medium that includes many constituents
   C   A medium that includes organic compounds and growth factors;
   D   A medium that includes undefined substances such as fetal serum

13 What is a defined culture medium for the growth of bacteria?
   A   A medium made from constituents of all whose chemical formulas are known
   B   A medium made by adding constituents in a prescribed order and then aerating
   C   A medium that cannot be sterilised by filtration
   D   A medium that must be prepared in the absence of air

14 Most of the methods for estimating cells below gives an estimate that is relatable to cells per cubic centimetre. Which method below must be calibrated with one of the other methods?
   A   turbidity
   B   direct counts using a hemocytometer
   C   spread plates
   D   viable count

15 A patient has died of Creutzfeldt-Jacob disease (CJD). What would you expect to observe in a section of his brain?
   A   Viral bodies in the nucleus of neurons
   B   Viral bodies in the cytoplasm of neurons
   C   Aggregates largely composed of a single protein
   D   Aggregates of RNA containing virus particles

16 A patient is diagnosed with Creutzfeldt-Jacob disease (CJD). Which statement about this condition is correct?
   A   Protein deposits form in the central nervous system
   B   In cases transmitted by infection, the time lag between infection and disease is very short
   C   Only peripheral nerves are damaged
   D   Brain tissue is non-infectious

17. When bacteria such as Escherichia coli grow at their maximum rate, they population size doubles about every?
   A   20 days
   B   2 days
   C   20 minutes
   D   20 hours

ECOLOGY AND CONSERVATION

18

G1   Community ecology

G2   Ecosystems and biomes

G3   Impacts of humans on ecosystems

G4   Conservation of biodiversity

G5   Population ecology

G1 COMMUNITY ECOLOGY

> **G.1.1**   Outline the factors that affect the distribution of plant species, including temperature, water, light, soil pH, salinity and mineral nutrients.
>
> ©IBO 2007

The presence or absence of a certain plant species in a certain environment depends on several factors, including the characteristics of the abiotic environment.

The main factors affecting plant distribution are:
- temperature
- water
- light
- soil pH
- salinity
- levels of mineral nutrients

TEMPERATURE

Pine trees from the Austrian Alps photosynthesize best at 15°C but the Hammada bush (found in the Israeli desert) has an optimum temperature of 44°C for photosynthesis.

WATER

Xerophytes (plants that live in dry areas, e.g. cacti, pine trees) have several adaptations to conserve water. Hydrophytes (waterplants, e.g. duckweed, water lily) do not have these adaptations.

LIGHT

As plants need to photosynthesise, insufficient light will hamper their growth and may even cause death. Some plants are adapted to receiving a lot of light. These are known as sun plants and include lavender. Shade plants do not benefit from a lot of light and can survive in low light areas where other plants would not survive. An example of a shade plant is 'forget-me-not'.

The right side of the hills shown in Figure 1801 has different plants than the left side. This may be caused by a difference in the amount of light (note the position of the shadows).

Figure 1801   A north-south slope in southern England

SOIL pH

The **pH** of soil affects its capacity to retain minerals. In acid soil, H^+ ions replace the positive ions clinging to the clay particles and the positive ions leach out of the soil. Calcium becomes more soluble (and hence more available to plant roots) as pH increases, whereas iron becomes less soluble as pH increases. Alfalfa, clover and other leguminosae require high calcium, i.e. alkaline soil. Rhododendron and azalea require high iron, i.e. acidic soil.

SALINITY

The **salinity** of the soil refers to its salt content. The salt in the soil will dissolve in water. This water then has a relatively high osmotic value. Since roots take up water by osmosis, salt water is more difficult to take up and many plants cannot survive this. The plants which are adapted to high salinity often have some of the characteristics of xerophytes.

MINERAL NUTRIENTS

The **mineral** content of soil depends on several factors. One factor is the rock from which the soil was formed. Another factor is the size of the particles which make up the soil. Minerals (and water) drain rapidly through sand (large particles) and are held by clay (small particles). Since clay particles carry a negative charge, they bind positively charged particles such as Ca^{2+}, K^+ and Mg^{2+}.

The most important factors affecting mineral content of the soil are biological factors. An undisturbed environment will recycle nutrients via soil, plants, animals and microorganisms. Harvesting can quickly deplete the soil when the nutrients removed are not replaced (fertiliser). In some countries too much manure is put on the land resulting in a very high mineral content. The minerals will leach into the streams and lakes and cause eutrophication which is rapid growth of algae which depletes the oxygen in the water when they die and are broken down by bacteria.

G.1.2	Explain the factors that affect the distribution of animal species, including temperature, water, breeding sites, food supply and territory.
	©IBO 2007

The presence or absence of a certain animal species in a certain environment depends on several factors. They can be biotic and abiotic. Factors affecting animal distribution are:
- temperature
- water
- breeding sites
- food supply
- territory

TEMPERATURE

When cells freeze, they are damaged by the formation of ice crystals. When the temperature becomes too high, enzymes are denatured. ('Too high' is different for different enzymes. Some algae live in hot springs at 80°C.) Some animals have thermoregulation, others do not.

Thermoregulation refers to the ability to maintain a body temperature either at a constant level or within an acceptable range. An advantage is that optimum temperature makes enzymes more effective and allows species to live in more different environments. A disadvantage is that it costs a lot of energy so more food is required.

Homeotherms are able to regulate body temperature whereas **poikilotherms** do not. **Heterotherms** are oraganisms that can regulate body temperature part of the time.

Ways to warm up the body
Endothermic

Heat is generated through internal metabolic processes. The hypothalamus in the brain is the control centre.

Ectothermic

Use of external heat sources by behavioural means. For example, reptiles lie in the sun in the morning to warm up and look for a shady place when it becomes too hot.

Example 1   Owlet moth

The Owlet moth is a heterotherm: its body temperature is equal to its surroundings when at rest. Preparing for flight, they become endothermic so that the flight muscles can function properly. A counter-current blood flow retains heat in the body. *See Figure 1802.*

Figure 1802
The owlet moth

Figure 1803
The blue fin tuna

OPTION

Figure 1804   A shrew

Figure 1805   A gerbil

Figure 1806   Frog spawn
(frog eggs)

Example 2   Bluefin tuna

The Bluefin Tuna is endothermic (unusual for fish). The swimming muscles produce heat. Heat is then retained in the core of the body by an efficient counter-current system in the blood. *See Figure 1803.*

Example 3   Birds and mammals

A decrease in body size means an increase in metabolic rate. The small shrew consumes 100 times as much oxygen per gram of body mass than the elephant. *See Figure 1804.*

WATER

The amount of water that animals need in order to be able to survive in an area, differs a lot from one species to the next. Fish need a lot of water since they live in it, beavers use water for keeping their lodge safe as well as a providing food nearby. On the other hand, gerbils have evolved special kidneys and some other adaptations to survive with very little, if any, water. *See Figure 1805.*

BREEDING SITES

Many animals need special circumstances in order to reproduce. Many birds need a nesting site that has certain characteristics; amphibians need water in which to lay their eggs. *See Figure 1806.*

Figure 1808
A Japanese fighting fish

Figure 1807
A koala eating eucalyptus

FOOD SUPPLY

Some animals can adapt to a range of different foods. It is one of the reasons that rats are such a successful species. Koalas *(Figure 1807)* will not survive without eucalyptus and pandas need bamboo. The species will cease to exist in an area where its food is no longer available.

TERRITORY

A territory is an area that an animal defends against others of its species. The area may provide food and shelter/nesting space(s). Some birds "mark" their territory by singing whilst some mammals will do so by planting scent flags, e.g. with urine or droppings. Japanese fighting fish are territorial. *See Figure 1808.*

> G.1.3   Describe one method of random sampling, based on quadrat methods, that is used to compare the population size of two plant or two animal species.
>
> ©IBO 2007

A very simple tool which is often used in estimating plant populations is the **quadrat**. A quadrat is a wire, shaped into a square of a known size, for example 0.25 m² (50 cm x 50 cm).

When you want to know the population size of one (or more) plant species in a uniform area, you can take random samples of this area by throwing the quadrat and investigating the area inside the quadrat. A better method is to set out two axes at right angles along two sides of the area. Generate random numbers, e.g. using a calculator, and use each pair of numbers as the coordinates for placing the quadrat. Count the number of individuals of the species inside the quadrat and repeat in a new location. After a number of samples, the average number of individuals per quadrat can be calculated. Divide this by the area of the quadrat which yields the number of individuals per m².

OPTION

G.1.4   Outline the use of a transect to correlate the distribution of plant or animal species with an abiotic variable.

©IBO 2007

When the area shows variation (slope or seashore), then the quadrat can be used together with a line transect. You take some string to make a line across the area (across the variation) e.g. from the water edge up into the dunes. You can either investigate all plants touching the line or you can place your quadrat at regular intervals and investigate the area within the quadrat. It is also necessary to keep a measurement of the distance from the water edge or the increase in elevation. *See Figure 1809.*

Figure 1809   IB students at work

G.1.5   Explain what is meant by the niche concept, including an organism's spatial habitat, its feeding activities and its interactions with other species.

©IBO 2007

An species' **niche** is its role in an ecosystem. It includes the **spacial habitat** (where the species lives) but also what it feeds on and also how it interacts with other species in the ecosystem. The niche includes information on both biotic (e.g. food, predators) and abiotic factors (e.g. nesting space, temperature) in the environment as they affect the species.

To describe the niche of a species, usually at least a paragraph will be required. An example is given below. *See Figure 1810.*

The hedgehog
The niche of the hedgehog includes its habitat. This can be in a garden with a lot of shelter, such as dead leaves. It also includes its feeding habits which are that it eats insects and snails. The hedgehog's interactions with other animals are that its spines protect it well from predators but also make it a good home for parasites (fleas).

Figure 1810   A hedgehog

G.1.6   Outline the following interactions between species, giving two examples of each: competition, herbivory, predation, parasitism and mutualism.

©IBO 2007

Individuals of one species obviously interact with each other. This interaction can be intense (ants in a colony) or rare (spiders for reproduction). Individuals of different species also interact in various ways.

COMPETITION

Competition occurs when two or more organisms attempt to exploit the same limited resource such as food or space. This can occur between members of the same species (intraspecific competition) or between individuals of different species (interspecific competition).

An example of the latter kind is competition for food between 5 different species of warbler (a small bird) in a spruce tree in North America. This has been solved by niche differentiation (or resource partitioning). Each species has a preferred area of the tree for feeding so that these species are not really sharing the same niche. *See Figure 1811.*

Another example of interspecific competition can be found between different species of duckweed. *Lemna gibba* (*see Figure 1812*) and *Lemna polyrrhiza* (*see Figure 1813*) can be found in similar ponds and lakes and will compete mainly for light. *L. gibba* grows more slowly than *L. polyrrhiza* but since it has tiny air filled sacs, it will float on the surface, shading other species and winning the competition for light.

HERBIVORY

Herbivory is the eating of plants. This has been compared to parasitism since neither herbivores nor parasites intend to kill their source of food. Examples of herbivory are any herbivorous animal (e.g. deer, cattle, goats, zooplankton). Figure 1814 shows deer feeding on plants.

PREDATION

Predation is the eating of live organisms. In some definitions this includes plants as well as animals. Venus flytrap is a carnivorous plant which will capture insects and digest them to supplement its minerals. Of course, the lion is a well known example of a predator and its prey consists of zebra, gazelles, wildebeest, etc. (Often, the lion will steal the prey from, for example, hyenas). Another example could be the praying mantis. *See Figure 1815.*

PARASITISM

Parasitism is a long-lasting relationship between individuals of different species where one individual benefits (the parasite) and the other is harmed (the host). The other difference from predation is that the parasite is considerably smaller than its host. Examples are fleas on a dog and the fungus which causes athlete's foot. See *Figure 1816.*

MUTUALISM

Mutualism is the long-lasting relationship between individuals of different species where both benefit. Examples are lichens which are a symbiosis between an algae (photosynthesis) and a fungus (water and minerals). The algae will photosynthesise and share the products of photosynthesis with the fungus. The fungus grows the roots and is responsible for the uptake of water. *See Figure 1817.*

Another example is the relationship between the clownfish and sea anemones. The clownfish will chase away other fish trying to eat the sea anemone. In return, the tentacles of the sea anemone will not sting the clown fish and it can safely swim in between them, hiding from its predators. *See Figure 1818.*

Figure 1811   A new world warbler

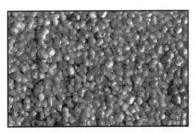

Figure 1812   Lemna gibba

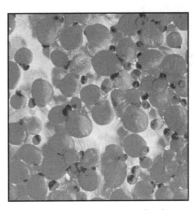

Figure 1813   Lemna polyrrhiza

Figure 1814   Deer are herbivores

Figure 1815   A lion with prey

Figure 1816   A flea

Figure 1817   Lichen

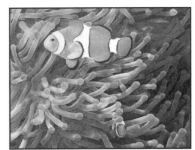

Figure 1818   A clown fish and sea anemones

OPTION

OPTION

G.1.7 Explain the principle of competitive exclusion.

©IBO 2007

The **competitive exclusion principle** states that two different species do not share the same niche. If they are found to do so, either the niche has been subdivided (*see Figure 1819*) or the species are competing with each other for everything and only the best adapted to that particular niche will remain. Sometimes birds "divide" the tree into separate niches so that different species are not sharing the same niche.

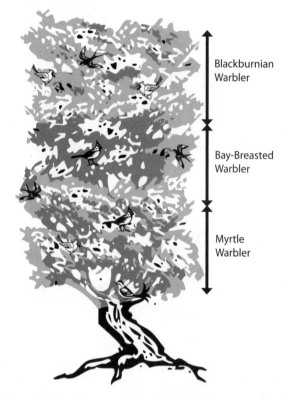

Figure 1819   Three species of warbler share a tree habitat

G.1.8 Distinguish between *fundamental* and *realized* niches.

©IBO 2007

FUNDAMENTAL NICHE

The **fundamental niche** of a species is the potential mode of existence, given the adaptations of the species.

REALIZED NICHE

The **realized niche** of a species is the actual mode of existence, which results from its adaptations and competition with other species.

G.1.9 Define *biomass*.

©IBO 2007

Biomass is the organic mass in an ecosystem. This does not include the water that is part of all living things, because water is not organic matter. Biomass is measured in g, kg or tonnes and often expressed in mass / area, e.g. kg Ha^{-1}.

G.1.10 Describe one method for the measurement of biomass of different trophic levels in an ecosystem.

©IBO 2007

In order to measure biomass, it is necessary to remove the water from the organisms. This cannot be done without destroying the organism.

To obtain the biomass of an organism, it needs to be cut into small pieces and placed in an oven (70°C) for 24 h (or longer if necessary) until all water has evaporated.

To obtain the biomass of an area, it is necessary to take several samples of a known size, e.g. using a quadrat. Remove all living organisms from inside the quadrat, cut them into small pieces and dry them in the oven as described above. Calculate the average biomass per m^2 and multiply by the surface area of the ecosystem.

If it is necessary to relate the information to the trophic levels, then the organisms collected need to be sorted and placed in the correct trophic level. This can then be followed by measuring the biomass in each trophic level.

This technique is very destructive and should only be used when the information is vital and cannot be obtained in other ways.

G2 ECOSYSTEMS AND BIOMES

G.2.1 Define *gross production, net production* and *biomass.*

©IBO 2007

GROSS PRODUCTION

Gross production is the amount of organic matter produced by photosynthesis in plants. (Approx 2% of the light striking a forest will be used for photosynthesis.)

NET PRODUCTION

Net production is the part of gross production not used in plant respiration.

BIOMASS

Biomass is the organic mass in an ecosystem as stated in G1.9. This does not include the water that is part of all living things, because water is not organic matter. Biomass is measured in g, kg or tonnes.

The total biomas of krill is around 0.6% of the total biomass of all species on Earth. This is the highest contribution to the total biomass of any single species. Figure 1820 shows an Antarctic krill.

Figure 1820   Antarctic krill

G.2.2 Calculate values for gross production and net production using the equation: gross production – respiration = net production.

©IBO 2007

Gross Production(GP)-Respiration(R)=Net Production (NP)

If a plant's gross production is 2 kg over a month and 0.95 kg is lost through respiration, then the net production is: 2 – 0.95 = 1.05 kg.

In plants, on average, net production is about half of gross production (i.e. 50% of the captured energy is used in cellular respiration).

G.2.3 Discuss the difficulties of classifying organisms into trophic levels.

©IBO 2007

In *Topic 5.1.6 and 5.1.7*, the flow of energy through a food chain and a food web was discussed. The first organisms in a food chain (or food web) must always be the producer or autotroph. It is relatively simple to decide if an organism is a producer or not. It becomes more difficult when we try to place predators as secondary or tertiary consumers. Since few predators prey on only one species, any one predator can be a secondary consumer (eating a herbivore) today and a tertiary consumer (eating another carnivore) tomorrow. Omnivores are always primary as well as secondary consumers. This shows again the discrepancy between a nicely ordered food chain and the reality of an ever changing food web.

G.2.4 Explain the small biomass and low numbers of organisms in higher trophic levels.

©IBO 2007

Food chains on land are rarely longer than four links. Those in the oceans may have up to seven steps. (In both cases, parasites and detritivores are not included.) This is caused by the fact that most energy contained in one trophic level is not used to create biomass in the next level, because usually not all organisms in the trophic level are eaten by those in the next level. Also, the metabolism of the consumer requires most of the energy contained in its

OPTION

337

food and very little is converted into biomass, which then is potentially available for the following level.

On average, the biomass found at a trophic level is 10% of that found at the previous trophic level. Consider the following example.

10 000 kg of waterplants can produce 1000 kg of insects, which produce 100 kg of small carnivorous fish, which produces 10 kg of bass which produces 1 kg of human. *See Figure 1821.*

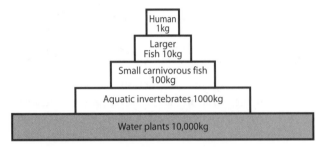

Figure 1821   The masses of various trophic levels

However, should the human decide to dine on aquatic invertebrates, 1 kg human would be sustained by 10 kg of invertebrates, which would require 100 kg water plants.

To sustain a reasonable biomass at the end of a long food chain, you need very large amounts of biomass at the level of the producer. Since the organisms at the end of the food chain are usually large, this means that you can only afford to sustain a small number of individuals at the highest trophic level.

G.2.5	Construct a pyramid of energy, given appropriate information.
	©IBO 2007

The units used for a pyramid of energy are kJ m^{-2} yr^{-1}.

A **pyramid of energy** will never be 'inverted' in shape since this employs figures of the amount of energy per unit area (or volume) that flows through the trophic level in a given time period.

This can help to explain an ecosystem that might otherwise seem rather strange. An example of such an ecosystem is found in the English Channel, where the biomass of the phytoplankton is about one-fifth of the biomass of the zooplankton. Initially, this seems to be a fast route to disaster, until the energy flow through the trophic levels is considered.

Let us assume that one individual of zooplankton needs to eat two individuals of phytoplankton every day. Yet every phytoplankton individual can produce eleven offspring a day. So if ten offspring are eaten, one individual of phytoplankton can sustain five individuals of zooplankton. So in a pyramid of energy high production of the algae in the English Channel is taken into account.

A pyramid of energy requires the following information:
- which species belong to each trophic level (*see Topic G.2.3*)
- how many individuals of the species are found per m^2
- what is the biomass of each individual (see G.1.10)
- how much energy does this biomass represent (in kJ)
- what is the productivity of each organism (per year)

The lowest bar of the pyramid of energy represents gross primary production. Figure 1822 shows and example of a pyramid of energy.

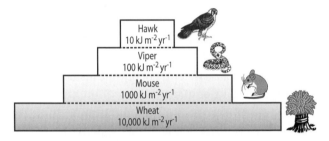

Figure 1822   A pyramid of energy

G.2.6	Distinguish between *primary* and *secondary* succession, using an example of each.
	©IBO 2007

SUCCESSION

Succession is the process of gradual changes over time in the occurrence of species in an ecosystem. Succession will eventually lead to the establishment of a **climax community**. A climax community is a group of populations of the species that are best adapted to that environment.

Primary succession

When the site has never sustained life before, it is called **primary succession.** When all life in a site has been destroyed (e.g. by fire), **secondary succession** will take place.

Primary succession takes place in a habitat that has never been colonised before.

An example of primary succession is the colonisation of an exposed rock.. Weathering (heat, water, freezing) will break large rocks into smaller ones. The first organisms (pioneer species) in primary succession on an exposed rock are often <u>lichens</u>. They cling to irregularities in the rocks with root-like rhizoids and secrete acid to dissolve the rocks. When lichens die, their remains are added to the soil. When a little soil has accumulated, <u>mosses</u> often follow lichens and will shade them, causing the lichens to die. This way, more organic material is added to the soil. Figure 1823 shows primary succession on a rock wall in Montreux, Switzerland. The light patches on the stone are lichens. In small hollows, the mosses, which are the next step in succession, are visible.

Figure 1823   Primary succession on a rock wall

Eventually, the mosses will be replaced by <u>ferns</u>, <u>grasses</u> and <u>shrubs</u> and eventually <u>trees</u> (coniferous, possibly followed by deciduous). The roots of all these plants will break rocks apart adding to the formation of the soil. Figure 1824 shows a later stage of primary succession on the south side of the same rock wall in Montreux.

Figure 1824   A later stage of succession on the same rock wall

Secondary succession

Secondary succession takes place after an area has been disturbed, e.g. by fire.

A drawing of four stages of this process is shown in Figure 1825.

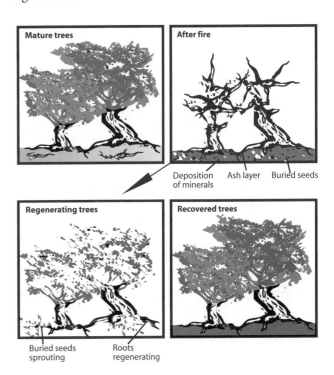

Figure 1825   Stages of secondary succession after a fire

Contrary to primary succession, in secondary succession the soil is already present. In the soil, seeds can be found from the species that were present before the fire. It is possible that even some parts of roots survived. The soil was already fertile but burning the previously existing vegetation adds minerals to the soil. This further improves the quality of the soil.

G.2.7	Outline the changes in species diversity and production during primary succession.

©IBO 2007

Only a few species are capable of living in an environment that has never sustained life before. As these pioneer species affect their environment, it gradually becomes more suitable for a larger diversity of species. So during primary succession, diversity increases until it reaches a maximum.

The same applies for **productivity**. Productivity increases as primary succession proceeds until a maximum is reached.

OPTION

A Scientist, *John Lichter* found in his research of primary succession in the dunes at the shores of Lake Michigan that maximum diversity and maximum productivity was found during the process of succession when plants involved in early succession were still present. After some time, the disappearance of these early successional species may have decreased diversity and productivity to the level of the climax community.

> **G.2.8** Explain the effects of living organisms on the abiotic environment with reference to the changes occurring during primary succession.
>
> ©IBO 2007

As lichens and mosses use acids to break up the rocks, small amounts of **soil** are produced. Subsequent species will continue this process and more soil will be produced. As the leaves, plants and possibly animals die and drop on the ground, decomposers (bacteria and fungi) will use the organic materials for respiration and release **minerals** into the soil. Depending on the kind of soil, the temperature and the amount of water, the process of breaking down the dead organic materials can take several months to many years. Some soil holds minerals better than other kinds where minerals are easily dissolved in water which drains into a stream or river. In many cases, the minerals will accumulate, promoting further plant growth. As more plants are growing in the site, **erosion** will decrease. The roots of the plants hold the soil and prevent it from being blown away. Plants also acts as a wind break, reducing the speed of the air over the ground, which also reduces erosion. Plants provide shade which leads to the soil holding more water and reduces erosion since dry soil erodes faster than damp soil.

> **G.2.9** Distinguish between *biome* and *biosphere*.
>
> ©IBO 2007

BIOME

Biome is a large geographical area that has a certain kind of climate and sustains specific communities of plants and animals.

BIOSPHERE

Biosphere is the total of all areas where living things are found, including the deep ocean and the lower part of the atmosphere. The biosphere contains a number of biomes.

> **G.2.10** Explain how rainfall and temperature affect the distribution of biomes.
>
> ©IBO 2007

Biomes are defined by temperature and the amount of rainfall.

- Tundra is dry and cold.
- Shrubland is colder than deciduous forest and often dryer.
- Desert is dry and hot.
- Grassland is quite dry and warm.
- Deciduous forest has a moderate amount of rain and a moderate temperature
- Tropical rainforest is wet and hot.

A **climograph** provides information on the amount of precipitation and the temperature. This information can be provided as an overall picture for several biomes, as shown in Figure 1826.

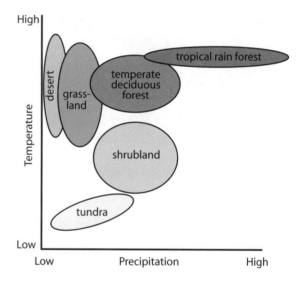

Figure 1826   An example of a climograph

A climograph can also contain more detailed information about the average amount of precipitation and temperature per month for each biome. Figure 1827 shows climographs for several of the major biomes.

> **G.2.11** Outline the characteristics of six major biomes.
>
> ©IBO 2007

Figure 1828 summarises the characteristics of the six major biomes. Of course, there are intermediate biomes as well.

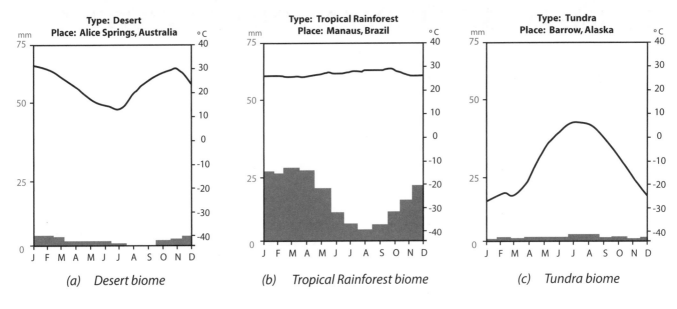

Figure 1827   Climographs for several of the major biomes

BIOME	Desert	Grassland	Shrub land	Temperate deciduous forest	Tropical rainforest	Tundra
Temperature	Summer: during the day 50°C Winter: at night -18°C	-30°C to 30°C	Summer: hot and dry Winter: cool and moist	-30°C to 30°C	20 - 35 °C	Winter: -70°C to - 10°C Summer: 3 - 15 °C
Precipitation	less than 300 mm/year	500 - 900 mm/year	200 - 1000 mm/year	500 - 1500 mm/year	above 1500 mm/year	150 - 250 mm/year
Comments on vegetation	• xerophytes are plants whose structure is adapted to conserving water • reduced leaves to reduce surface where transpiration could take place • photosynthesis takes place in the swollen stem • can store water	• grass and small herbs • trees do not grow well due to infrequent rain • frequent fires • grass tends to be taller if there is more rain • parts of plant above the ground dies during winter, roots grow new plant in spring • species diversity in grassland is very high	• frequent bushfire in the dry season • plants need to conserve water • small needle-like leaves to reduce surface area • thick waxy cuticle reduces transpiration • often adaptations to survive frequent fires	• trees drop leaves in autumn to reduce water loss in winter • leaves that stay on could be damaged by frost • in winter not much photosynthesis is possible due to lower light intensity	• high diversity of plants • high competition, e.g. for light so many trees grow straight up to reach light before being shaded by other plants • leaves high up will be exposed to a lot of heat and light so leaves are smaller to reduce transpiration and dark green to make most use of the light • only a small percentage of the light reaches the floor of the rainforest so not many plants can grow there and the ones that do have large leaves to catch most light • plants have adaptations to help water run off them quickly e.g. grooved leaves • plants called epiphytes may grow (high) on other plants to catch more light. • bougainvillea plants have thin smooth bark (not much protection against dehydration is needed). • plants often have a limited root system since water is easy to obtain.	• subsoil is permanently frozen, so no trees can grow here • in summer, waterlogged soil since it cannot drain because of the permafrost • very windy • plants are small and stunted: little water, short growing season
Example	cactus	milkweed	rosemary	oak tree	orchid (an epiphyte), bougainvillea	mosses and tussock grass

Figure 1828   A summary of the characteristics of the six major biomes.

OPTION

G3 IMPACTS OF HUMANS ON ECOSYSTEMS

G.3.1 Calculate the Simpson diversity index for two local communities.

©IBO 2007

We calculate diversity by using the **Simpson formula**. It takes into account the number of species present, as well as the abundance of each species.

$$D = \frac{N(N-1)}{\sum n(n-1)}$$

where N is the total number of individuals in the area, n is the number of individuals per species and D is the diversity index.

Example

Two islands each have populations of four plant species:

Island 1

Species	n	$n-1$	$n(n-1)$
daisy	345	344	118 680
buttercup	260	259	67 340
dandelion	342	341	116 622
clover	598	597	357 006
Totals	$N = 1545$		$\Sigma n(n-1) = 659\ 648$

Figure 1829   Plant species on island 1

Island 2

Species	n	$n-1$	$n(n-1)$
daisy	50	49	2 450
buttercup	20	19	380
dandelion	40	39	1 560
clover	1250	1249	1 561 250
Totals	$N = 1360$		$\Sigma n(n-1) = 1\ 565\ 640$

Figure 1830   Plant species on island 1

The diversity index for island 1 is:

$$D_1 = \frac{N(N-1)}{\sum n(n-1)}$$

$$= \frac{1545(1545-1)}{(345(345-1) + 260(260-1) + 342(342-1) + 598(598-1))}$$

$$= 3.62$$

and for island 2:

$$D_1 = \frac{N(N-1)}{\sum n(n-1)}$$

$$= \frac{1360(1360-1)}{(50(50-1) + 20(20-1) + 40(40-1) + 1250(1250-1))}$$

$$= 1.18$$

G.3.2 Analyse the biodiversity of the two local communities using the Simpson index.

©IBO 2007

So, even though both islands have the same number of species and a similar total number of individuals, island 1 has a greater diversity than island 2. If one or two species are present in much higher numbers than the other species, the site is considered to be less diverse than when all species are present in similar numbers.

A high diversity, i.e. a high value for D, suggests a stable and ancient site. A low D value could suggest pollution, recent colonisation or agricultural management. The index of diversity is usually used in studies of vegetation but can also be applied to animals or diversity of all species.

One of the consequences of the pollution caused by the marine oil spills during the Gulf War, was that the diversity of marine species around Bahrain dropped dramatically. The current war in Iraq seems to be having a similar impact, although it mainly affects terrestrial species.

G.3.3 Discuss reasons for the conservation of biodiversity using rainforests as an example.

©IBO 2007

ETHICAL REASONS

Local, indigenous, cultures usually do not survive when the biodiversity in the rainforest is destroyed. "Extinction is forever". If species become extinct, future generations will not be able to experience them.

ECOLOGICAL REASONS

Reducing biodiversity will interfere with the balance of the ecosystem. Changes to one biome may affect factors such as the weather patterns elsewhere and therefore indirectly affect other biomes.

A reduced biodiversity is likely to affect the recycling of nutrients.

Rainforests hold the soil in place. Reducing biodiversity may lead to erosion and, as this soil needs to go somewhere, it may block waterways and cause floods.

ECONOMICAL REASONS

Traditional medicine has already been useful in developing cures for diseases. These medicines are often based on plants from the rainforest that could disappear completely if biodiversity is reduced.

Rainforests produce valuable materials such as timber and dyes.

AESTHETIC REASONS

A tropical rainforest can be a very beautiful place, from which people can relax, gain pleasure and/or be inspired to produce works of art.

> G.3.4 List three examples of the introduction of alien species that have had significant impacts on ecosystems.
>
> ©IBO 2007

It is quite common to find a species absent from an areas that belongs to its fundamental niche *(see Topic G.1.8)*. Sometimes the species simply never colonised this area and will be able to survive very well, once it is introduced. If this is the case, this **alien invasive species** may even be better adapted to survive and may not have many parasites, predators or diseaeses in this "new environment". It may cause a decrease in the numbers of one or more established species. Under the competitive exclusion principle *(see Topic G.1.7)*, it could lead to these established species disappearing from this area.

BIOLOGICAL CONTROL

Release of ladybird beetles *(Coccinellidae)*. These beetles eat aphids which are a pest and can damage crops. Both the adults and the larvae will consume hundreds of aphids per day and they are a very useful biological control species. Unfortunately, both the Ladybird adults and the larvae are very mobile so these biocontrol species are not likely to limit themselves to a certain area. They are used very successfully in greenhouses. *See Figure 1831.*

Figure 1831   A ladybird eating an aphid

ACCIDENTAL RELEASE

Sometimes the alien invasive species escapes from where it is kept and is accidentally introduced into the environment. An example is the Golden apple snail. This species of the genus *Pomacea* was introduced in Taiwan so that they could serve as a source of food. Unfortunately, not many people wanted to eat the snail and it escaped and became an alien invasive species. As the snails are herbivores, they will eat the rice plants. As a result of the snails eating the rice, the nutrients are returned to the ecosystem and are available to algae which will grow at a much increased rate (algae bloom).

DELIBERATE RELEASE

Golden apple snails have been deliberately introduced in Africa and Asia in order to compete with local snails of the genus *Planorbidae* and reduce their numbers. *Planorbidae* are intermediate hosts for parasitic flukes which, at another stage of their life cycle, causes bilharzia (a disease) in humans. The parasitic flukes cannot complete their life cycle in Golden apple snails, so the incidence of bilharzia would be reduced if the Golden apple snail successfully competes with the *Planorbidae* snail.

> G.3.5 Discuss the impacts of alien species on ecosystems.
>
> ©IBO 2007

INTERSPECIFIC COMPETITION

Alien species of trees (on Hawaii) that grow very large leaves (e.g. *Miconia calvescens*, from South and Central America) cause shaded conditions where seeds of native species will germinate but do not receive sufficient light to grow. Alien invasive plants that are adapted to growing in low light will be able to grow and will replace the native species. *Miconia* has a shallow root system which does not hold the soil as well as the native plants so with more *miconia*, erosion increased. *See Figure 1832.*

Figure 1832   Miconia calvescens

Figure 1833   The cane toad (Bufo marinus)

Figure 1834   A rabbit with myxomatosis.

OPTION

PREDATION

Cane toads (*Bufo marinus*), from Central and South America (*see Figure 1833*) were brought to Australia to serve as **biological control** for cane beetles that were damaging crops. Cane toads are large (2.5 kg) predators with poisonous glands on their backs. They have a variety of natural predators in Central and South America but not many in Australia.

The cane toads preferred small vertebrates and other invertebrates for their prey over Cane beetles. They reduce biodiversity by preying on many species, competing with others and poisoning those who attacked them.

SPECIES EXTINCTION

The brown treesnake (*Boiga irregularis*) was accidently introduced on the island of Guam around 1950. Guam had no other snakes, nor did it have any species that is a predator to the snake. There were no organisms on Guam that cause disease to the brown Treesnake. As there was an abundant food supply, the number of snakes increased exponentially and they became a pest. Since their introduction the snakes have caused the extinction of 9 species of native bird and 2 species of native lizards. The birds include the Mariana Fruit Dove, the Guam Flycatcher, the Rufous Fantail and the Cardinal Honeyeater.

BIOLOGICAL CONTROL OF PEST SPECIES

In Australia, rabbits brought by Europeans escaped or were set free, survived very well in the environment. Without significant predators, their numbers increased exponentially, eventually doing significant damage to the environment. Rabbits eat grass and other vegetation including stripping the bark from trees (which kills them) and digging up roots. Their burrowing and grazing reduces plant cover and increases erosion. In 1950, the Australian government introduced the disease myxomatosis (*see Figure 1834*), a disease caused by the **myxoma virus** which affects only rabbits. Myxomatosis initially killed 90% of the rabbits but some rabbits appeared to be resistant and the population increased again. However, the virus myxomatosis continues to affect the rabbit population and keeps their numbers down.

G.3.6	Outline one example of biological control of invasive species.
	©IBO 2007

Rabbits are an invasive species in Australia. Currently biological control works reasonably well through myxomatosis. See section above for more details.

G.3.7	Define *biomagnification*.
	©IBO 2007

Biomagnification is a process in which chemical substances become more concentrated at each trophic level of the food chain.

Bioaccumulation can take place in an organism. It refers to the process where an organism takes in many small amounts of a chemical without egesting or excreting it. Hence the chemical accummulates in the organism.

G.3.8 Explain the cause and consequences of biomagnification, using a named example.

©IBO 2007

Biomagnification is caused by many organisms in a lower trophic level containing a low amount of a certain chemical, e.g. **DDT**. These organisms are then eaten by those of a higher trophic level. So all the DDT that was found in a large number of organisms at a lower trophic level is now concentrated into a few organisms at a higher trophic level. If all of these then get eaten by a top carnivore, the amount of the chemical that originally spread over hundreds of organisms is now all found in one top carnivore. *See Figure 1835.*

DDT is probably the best known organic insecticide. It does not dissolve well in water which means it tends to stay where it is sprayed. It takes 2-15 years to break down DDT which means that it is effective against insects for a long time.

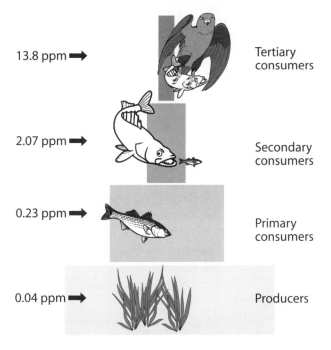

13.8 ppm ➡ Tertiary consumers

2.07 ppm ➡ Secondary consumers

0.23 ppm ➡ Primary consumers

0.04 ppm ➡ Producers

Figure 1835   The accumulation of DDT in a food chain

DDT sprayed on water to eliminate mosquito larvae will be taken up by algae. As each level of the food chain is eaten, DDT levels increase because it cannot be excreted with urine due to its poor solubility. Hence it accumulates within the organism and then is magnified as many organisms from one trophic level are eaten by a few from the next trophic level.

G.3.9 Outline the effects of ultraviolet (UV) radiation on living tissues and biological productivity.

©IBO 2007

The main effect of **UV radiation** on living tissues is found in the harm it does to DNA. *Refer to Figure 1836.* High levels of UV radiation alter the structure of DNA which eventually may cause (skin) cancer.

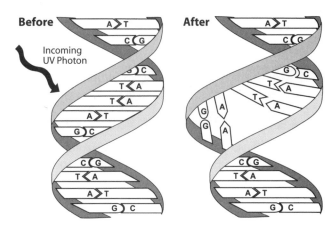

Before   Incoming UV Photon   **After**

Figure 1836   How ultraviolet rays cause mutations

UV light is harmful to the eyes and can cause cataracts (lens becoming less transparant) or pterygium (growths on the conjunctiva).

UV light can be absorbed by organic molecules causing them to dissociate forming atoms or groups with unpaired electrons. These substances are very reactive and can cause unusual reactions to take place.

A number of schools, particularly in Australia, now have a uniform with long sleeves and a hat so that students are less exposed to UV light. *Refer to Figure 1837.*

OPTION

Figure 1837   Wearing hats is 'sunsmart'

Phytoplankton are very sensitive to UV light. These organisms at the base of aquatic food chains function less well in even only moderate levels of UV light. Higher levels cause them to die. Since phytoplankton also contribute significantly to the total oxygen production on Earth, damage to these organisms will have far reaching consequences.

Terrestrial plants have been shown to have a lower yield when UV levels are increased. Nitrogen-fixing bacteria have been shown to be killed by high levels of UV light.

G.3.10   Outline the effect of chlorofluorocarbons (CFCs) on the ozone layer.

©IBO 2007

The major cause of the depletion of the ozone layer are **CFCs**. This abbreviation stands for chlorofluorocarbons. These molecules are very useful in refrigerators, air conditioners, fire extinguishers and as propellants in aerosol sprays. They were used in large amounts and were thought to diffuse harmlessly into the stratosphere where they were broken down by sunlight. *See Figure 1838.*

This is true except that in the process of breaking them down, a chlorine atom (Cl) is produced. The effect of chlorine on the ozone layer is very serious. The very reactive chlorine will react with an ozone molecule and break it apart into oxygen (O_2), which will not reform into ozone. One chlorine atom can destroy 100 000 ozone molecules.

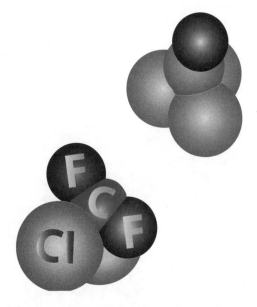

Figure 1838   Model of a molecule of CFC.

G.3.11   State that ozone in the stratosphere absorbs UV radiation.

©IBO 2007

The **ozone layer** in the stratosphere (10-45 km above the surface of the Earth) stops 99% of the UV radiation from the Sun. Ozone (O_3) *(see Figure 1839)* is formed spontaneously when UV light strikes the atmosphere. When UV light strikes an oxygen molecule, the energy of the UV radiation is absorbed. It is used to separate the oxygen molecule (O_2) into two oxygen atoms which are very reactive. Each of these will combine with an oxygen molecule, forming ozone, releasing the absorbed energy as heat. This reduces the level of UV radiation that gets through the ozone layer to reach the surface of the Earth.

Figure 1839   A molecule of ozone (O_3)

Ozone is necessary at high altitudes but a pollutant near the Earth's surface (the troposphere, 0-10 km above the surface of the Earth). Here it is a component of smog and a greenhouse gas. Ozone in the lower atmosphere is converted back to oxygen in a few days and does not replenish the ozone layer in the stratosphere. In plants, the presence of ozone inhibits photosynthesis, probably by altering the permeability of cell membranes. *See Figure 1840.*

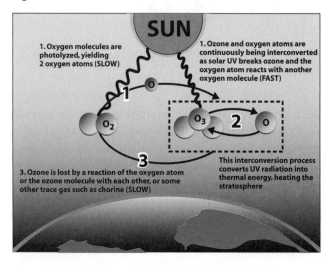

Figure 1840   The ozone cycle

G4 CONSERVATION OF BIODIVERSITY (HL ONLY)

> **G.4.1** Explain the use of biotic indices and indicator species in monitoring environmental change.
>
> ©IBO 2007

> **G.4.2** Outline the factors that contributed to the extinction of one named animal species.
>
> ©IBO 2007

It is important to know when and how much the environment changes. This is especially true if human actions might have caused the change. Careful environmental monitoring can warn us in advance of undesired changes and we may be able to take some action which prevents the damage from becoming worse.

Here we will consider monitoring **eutrophication**. Eutrophication means nutrient enrichment (of an aquatic environment) which results in an explosive growth of water plants, particularly algae. The large number of algae growing at the surface of the water will block the light which causes lower plants or algae to die. Bacteria will decompose the dead material, using up oxygen in the process. The overall result is a significant decrease in oxygen levels in the water which may cause heterotrophs like fish or crustaceans to die. These, of course, are then also decomposed, further reducing oxygen levels.

Eutrophication can be measured chemically, for example, by measuring oxygen levels. The rate of oxygen depletion by organisms is the biochemical oxygen demand (BOD). It reflects the activity of micro-organisms in decomposing organic material.

However, it is often easier to measure eutrophication biologically by using indicator species. The Trent Biotic Index (TBI) and the Chandler Biotic Score (CBS) are often used for measuring the organic pollution in water.

TBI monitors presence/absence of key macroinvertebrate species together with diversity. Eutrophic waters show a high abundance of some species but low overall species diversity. In addition, certain species can tolerate higher levels of pollution than others. All this has given rise to the TBI tables which link the presence of certain species etc. to certain levels of pollution.

Examples of indicator species of reasonably <u>high oxygen levels</u> are:
- mayfly larvae
- stoneflies

Indicator species for <u>low levels of oxygen</u> are:
- higher number of aquatic worms
- higher number of midge larvae

In 1991, 1.7 million species of plants and animals had been identified, but many scientists believe that as many as 40 million different species may inhabit our planet. Many of the known animal species belong to the phylum of the Arthropods (approx 750 000). Scientists now suspect that species are becoming extinct before they have even be classified.

The approximate number of known species are:

Viruses	1 000
Prokaryota	30 000
Protoctista	30 000
Fungi	70 000
Plantae	250 000
Animalia	1 030 000

According to the theory of evolution, many species that once lived on Earth are no longer around. They have become extinct. There are many ways in which a species can become extinct. Currently about 4 500 animal and 20 000 plant species are endangered and may become extinct.

The **dodo** (*Raphus cucullatus*) *(see Figure 1841)* is one of the species to recently become extinct. Dodos used to live on the small island of Mauritius. Mauritius lies in the Indian Ocean, 2000 km east of Africa, 900 km east of Madagascar.

Mauritius was discovered in the early sixteenth century and quickly became a place for ships to stop and collect fresh food and water. Sailors found a species of bird on Mauritius that had not been seen elsewhere. These birds were called dodos. Dodos lived on fruit and nested on the ground. They were unable to fly and had no natural predators.

Since dodos were not afraid of people, they could be approached easily. It is reported that many dodos were

Figure 1841   The dodo is now extinct

OPTION

killed by sailors. Some may have been killed because this provided a source of entertainment it is unclear how many were eaten by humans.

Eventually people settled on Mauritius and brought with them cats, dogs, pigs and, unintentionally, rats. These animals found dodos an easy prey; they attacked and ate the flightless birds or its eggs or chicks found in nests on the ground and the dodo became extinct by 1680.

> **G.4.3**   Outline the biogeographical features of nature reserves that promote the conservation of diversity.
>
> ©IBO 2007

SIZE

According to the IB syllabus promoting large nature reserves usually promotes conservation of biodiversity more effectively than small ones. However, this is disputed in a study by *F. Götmark* and *M. Thorell* in 2003 (*Biodiversity and Conservation, June 2003*). They found that the density of large trees and dead wood decreased when the size of the reserve was larger. They found that biodiversity in small patches of forest was generally very high.

EDGE EFFECT

The ecology of the edge of a nature reserve, for example where a forest borders on meadows, is different from that found in the core. On the edge of the forest, there is more light and more wind so more loss of water but also more photosynthesis at lower levels. Therefore, biodiversity is usually greater at the edges than in the core.

An example of an **edge effect** is seen in the egg-laying habits of the cowbird of the western United States. It feeds in open areas, but it lays its eggs in the nests of other birds, near the edges of forests. Fragmentation of forests has led to a considerable increase in cowbird populations because of the increase in forest edge.

The same surface area to volume concept can be applied to this situation: the larger the reserve is, the smaller the relative size of the edge and vice versa. So, there is a relatively large edge effect in smaller reserves and a more limited edge effect in larger reserves.

WILDLIFE CORRIDORS

Wildlife corridors allow organisms to move between different parts of a fragmented habitat, for example, tunnels under busy roads or passages built above them.

Wildlife corridors allow individuals of populations previously separated to mix which expands the gene pool. Figure 1842 shows a wildlife corridor at Terlet in the Netherlands which connects two nature reserves.

> **G.4.4**   Discuss the role of active management techniques in conservation.
>
> ©IBO 2007

The management of nature reserves involves:
- control of alien species
- restoration of degraded areas
- promotion of recovery of threatened species
- control of exploitation by humans

Almost every nature programme on television about nature reserves (e.g. Serengeti) will have information, directly or indirectly, on management of nature reserves. Alien species are those that originally did not belong in the ecosystem but are capable of surviving and competing with the original species. To protect the original species, individuals of the alien species are removed and their reproduction is discouraged for example by making breeding sites unsuitable.

Areas that have been damaged by human activity or by natural causes need to be restored so that they can again be used by various species as (part of) their habitat. Populations where there is a very low number of individuals may need additional support to increase their number. This could be done by providing food, nesting space or planting seeds, sometimes in combination with clearing an area of other plants.

None of the above measures will be effective unless the exploitation of the species by humans is carefully controlled. Removing trees for wood or killing elephants for their ivory tusks reduces the number of individuals of a population. This may be possible without a negative impact on the overall population size but the effects must be carefully monitered and human actions adjusted during times of hardship (e.g. drought or disease).

> **G.4.5**   Discuss the advantages of *in situ* conservation of endangered species (terrestrial and aquatic nature reserves).
>
> ©IBO 2007

In situ **conservation** means that one (or more) endangered species are protected in an area where they would normally be found. Usually this means in a nature reserve.

Figure 1842   A wildlife corridor

Figure 1843   Royal Botanical Gardens, UK

they could be seen easily. This was then called a zoo. Was this an improvement on shooting the animal and using its skin for a rug or did it only prolong the animal's misery?

Advantages of *in situ* conservation are:

- some species are very hard to breed in captivity
- the population remains adapted to its original habitat
- individuals maintain their natural behaviour
- the species interacts with others and fulfils its role in the ecosystem
- the habitat remains available for the endangered species (and others)
- it requires a larger gene pool but then conserves this variation between individuals

As the Chinese found out, pandas are very hard to breed in captivity. Therefore they set up 'panda farms' which are essentially nature reserves in areas where pandas normally live. Breeding has been more successful here. Most commonly *in situ* preserved plants are those related to our agricultural crops. Examples are the conservation of teosinte, relatives of *Zea mays* (corn) in Latin America and coffee landraces in Ethiopia.

The conservation of species is not an easy task at any time, even *ex situ*. Plants are easier to conserve since they can be kept as seeds. Conserving an animal species means keeping alive a certain population of animals and having them breed successfully. Many animals do not thrive in captivity and even if they do reproduce, there are often signs of reduced welfare. All this reflects on the animals' health. The more conditions differ from the animals' normal habitat, the more difficult it becomes to keep them.

> G.4.6   Outline the use of *ex situ* conservation measures, including captive breeding of animals, botanic gardens and seed banks.
>
> ©IBO 2007

To see a species in its natural environment, it might be necessary to travel a long way and even then it may be hard to find. Plants might live in less accessible places and animals might prefer to hide from visitors. So people have captured the animals and put them in small cages so that

Capturing animals is hard work. They tend not to cooperate and often many are killed in the process. It might be easier to shoot the mother and then take the young. The young must then be transported and many do not survive, especially if they need to be smuggled. Finally, many species die younger in captivity (sea mammals) or fail to reproduce. Some species are more successful in captive breeding than others.

Some of this is also true for plants kept in botanic gardens. To maintain a climate in which the plant will grow, often a lot of energy might have to be spent. Any plant that would not normally grow in the area of the botanic garden, is not part of the climax community for that area and hence will be replaced by others unless action is taken to prevent this. A famous example is the Royal Botanical Gardens, Kew, in the UK. *See Figure 1843.*

Of course plants are easily kept as seeds for a long time and seed banks are set up to do exactly this and preserve as many species as possible with a minimum investment of energy. These seedbanks are a valuable back up and play an important role in preservation of certain genes.

However, zoos and botanical gardens do raise awareness of regions other than the one in which people live and might make them more concerned about global issues. Although we have seen elephants roam in the Serengeti on television, seeing a real living elephant still inspires a sense of awe. Zoos have also changed very much over the last few decades and are now concerned about the living conditions of the animals and play an important role in breeding programmes. The lion in the small cage is a thing of the past.

The importance of surveys of biodiversity, environmental monitoring and environmental impact assessment is to note changes on time, as they happen. No one noticed that the numbers of salmon in the Rhine were decreasing until they had entirely disappeared. By continuous monitoring, changes can be detected early and, hopefully, it will be possible to do something about them.

OPTION

G5 POPULATION ECOLOGY

G.5.1	Distinguish between *r-strategies* and *K-strategies*.

©IBO 2007

In *Topic 5.3*, processes affecting population size were discussed. Natality (birth rate) is one of the processes that can increase population size. There are two extreme **reproductive strategies** as follows.

r-STRATEGY

An **r-strategy** involves investing more resources into producing many offspring, having a short life span, early maturity, reproducing only once and having a small body size.

K-STRATEGY

A **K-strategy** involves investing more resources into development and long-term survival. This involves a longer life span, late maturity, is more likely to involve parental care, the production of few offspring, and reproducing more than once.

There are organisms that display extreme r- or K-strategies, but most organisms have life histories that are intermediate on the continuum, displaying some r-traits but also some K-traits. *See Figure 1844.*

	K-strategy	r-strategy
Trees	Live a long time	Very large number of seeds
	Good competitors	Spread over a large area
Turtles	Live a long time	Many eggs
		No care for young
		Many young die very early

Figure 1844   K - and r- strategies table

Some organisms such as the vinegar fly *Drosophila melanogaster* switch strategies depending on environmental conditions.

G.5.2	Discuss the environmental conditions that favour either r-strategies or K-strategies.

©IBO 2007

r-strategies tend to be found in unstable or unpredictable environments. As the environment may change quickly, survival of the species is more likely to be increased if there is a large population where some individuals may be able to cope with the change. So rapid production of large numbers of offspring tends to be an advantageous strategy in an unstable environment.

Examples of organisms that favour an r-strategy are:
- mice
- weeds
- insects

K-strategies are more common in a stable and/or predictable environment where each organism needs to compete for limited resources. Long term development caused by a longer life span and extensive care of young, tend to work to the advantage of the species in a stable environment.

Examples of organisms that favour a K-strategy are:
- elephants
- whales
- humans

When an environment has been disrupted, possibly but not necessarily by human influence, the species using r-strategies are favoured. Pathogens and pests are typical r-strategists.

G.5.3	Describe one technique used to estimate the population size of an animal species based on a capture–mark–release–recapture method.

©IBO 2007

If we want to know the size of a certain population, we can use the technique known as 'capture - mark - release - recapture' and a calculation known as **Lincoln Index**.

This sounds a lot more complicated that it really is. What needs to be done is to capture a number of organisms (random sample) and mark them (without harming them or changing their behaviour). They are then released them back into their original population. The assumption is that they will mix with the unmarked individuals in a random way.

After a suitable time a second random sample of the population must be captured. A certain proportion of this second sample will be marked from the first capture. This is the same proportion as the original first (marked) sample was to the entire population. This techniques assumes that natality, mortality, immigration and emigration are zero.

There are different ways of understanding this calculation. A method based on an equation and a visual approach are presented below.

Lincoln index

In every case

n_1 = number in the <u>first sample</u> captured and marked
n_2 = <u>total</u> number in the <u>second sample</u>
n_3 = number of <u>marked</u> individuals in the <u>second sample</u>
N = number of individuals in the <u>total population</u>

Equation

The proportion that n_3 is to n_2 is equal to that of n_1 to the entire population. In an equation this becomes:

$$\frac{n_3}{n_2} = \frac{n_1}{N}$$

From the above, the following equation can be obtained. It is possible to just memorise and use the equation to estimate the total size of the population.

$$\text{population size } N = \frac{n_1 \times n_2}{n_3}$$

A visual approach

It is possible to imagine the total population as a square. The first sample (n_1) is a number of individuals from the total population. The same applies for the second sample (n_2) but, of course, they are different individuals so cannot be drawn the same as the first sample. Some individuals of the second sample are marked (n_3). *See Figure 1845.*

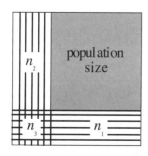

Figure 1845   The principle of capture-recapture

It can be seen that this is really no different from using an equation. The first sample (n_1) is a proportion of the entire population but at the time of sampling, it is not known what that proportion is. After the second sample (n_2), it becomes clear that the marked individuals of this sample (n_3) are a certain proportion of the second sample (n_2). The assumption is that this proportion is the same for n_1 to the entire population. Animals can be 'marked' in a variety of ways depending on the species. Marking with tags and collars are common examples.

The accuracy of using Lincoln index based on data from a mark-recapture investigation depends on several factors:

- the population needs to have very low natality, mortality, immigration and emigration.
- the method of capturing needs to have little effect on the animal.
  - If being captured is pleasant (e.g. awarded with food), then animals become "trap-happy". They will allow themselves to be caught again in larger numbers. This increases the size of n_3 which will decrease the estimate for N.
  - If being captured is negative, they become "trap-shy" which will decrease n_3 and inflate N.
- the method of being marked must have little effect on the animal. If the mark makes them more visible, they become prey in larger numbers, reducing n_3 and inflating N and vice versa. Marks must also remain in place for the appropriate period but should disappear after some time. Insects have been marked with a text marker which turned out to be toxic to them.

| G.5.4 | Describe the methods used to estimate the size of commercial fish stocks. |

©IBO 2007

The International Council for the Exploration of the Sea (ICES) is an organisation which provides estimates of fish stock in the North Atlantic. Scientists from 19 countries work together, collecting and interpreting data. In general, the scientists aim to take a sample of 200 fish from every 1000 tonnes of fish brought into port. They collect data on age, length, and breeding condition of the fish.

Most years, more than 8 million tonnes of fish are brought in, giving the scientists information about 1.6 million fish. Figure 1846 shows that fish sampling is an important part of the work of ICES.

Every year, fish grow a ring on the small bones, involved in balance, on either side of the brain. This is used to decide their age. The fish caught should be a broad range of ages. If only young fish are caught, it might mean that the total number of fish of that species (the stock) is reducing,

Figure 1846   ICES Fish sampling

possibly due to overfishing. Not all fish caught are brought into port. Scientists sometimes travel on fishing boats to see which fish are being thrown back. Sometimes they will mark a fish and put it back to obtain mark-recapture data. They also may check the diaries of the fishing boat to see how long it took to collect the catch. If it takes longer to catch a certain number of fish, the stock may be decreasing, possibly due to overfishing.

The scientists also catch fish in a standard manner. They go to a randomly assigned grid section, and fish for a standard amount of time, using standard equipment. The catch is then compared to that caught at other sites and/or at other times. This also provides information about fish stocks. Research vessels also use echo sound equipment to detect schools of fish. The equipment can tell them the size of the school but sometimes it is difficult to decide exactly which species. In those cases, they may trawl (fish) to confirm the species they were studying.

Yet another method employed is to use a very fine net to catch eggs and larvae as they float in between plankton. As only adult fish produce eggs, the number of eggs and larvae gives an indication of the number of adult fish of the species. Every May and October, mathematical models are used to estimate the size of the fish stock. One of the more commonly used models is the Virtual Population Analysis (VPA). It uses the number and age of fish caught to estimate the number of fish that were around before the start of the data collection. The estimates are given to the EU and to each of the 19 countries that are members of ICES.

| G.5.5 | Outline the concept of maximum sustainable yield in the conservation of fish stocks. |

©IBO 2007

ICES gives advice on limits to catching fish. They base their advice on the concept that there should be enough fish left to ensure production of a sufficiently large next generation. In order to safeguard this concept, ICES uses a biomass limit which is the lowest amount of fish a stock should be allowed to fall to. If it drops below the biomass limit, it is likely that reproduction will be reduced and the next year's stock will be lower in numbers.

The precautionary **biomass limit** is higher than the biomass limit. It allows for the difficulty of estimating the total biomass of a species.

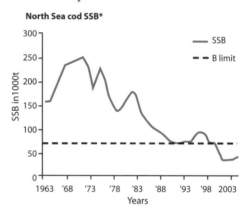

This figure shows the decline of the North Sea cod stock to a level below the biomass limit
* Spawning Stock Biomass (total weight of mature fish)

Figure 1847   Cod numbers in the North Sea

As can be seen in Figure 1847, the cod stock in the North Sea has been declining since 1973 and now numbers are below the biomass limit. In contrast, Figure 1848 show the recovery of the herring.

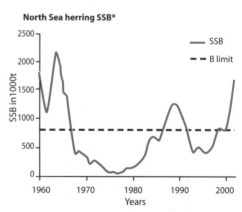

This figure shows the rollercoaster of the North Sea herring stock.
* Spawning Stock Biomass (total weight of mature fish)

Figure 1848   Herring numbers in the North Sea

OPTION

ICES limits itself to the biological aspect of fishing. It passes on its recommendations to the authorities who need to weigh the advice and consider social and economic issues. Reducing the amount of fish allowed to be caught can cause fishermen severe economic difficulties as they often have made investments into the latest technology on their vessels which need to be paid off.

Volendam, in the Netherlands, was a fishing village at the beginning of the 20th century. Many people are still involved in fishing and limiting the amount of fish caught reduces the income of many. As a result, the financial repercussions are felt throughout the village, although today the town depends heavily on tourism.

Figure 1849 (a)
Volendam about 100 years ago on the sea

Figure 1849 (b)
Volendam today on a lake

TOK   How should fish stocks be managed?

Some argue that we know more about the Moon than Earths oceans. More than seventy percent of the surface of the Earth is ocean and our knowledge of marine ecology is limited. As a result of limited data there are often widely opposed interpretations and conflicting points of view on the ecology and consequent human interaction with marine ecosystems. The whale hunting issue illustrates this clearly where some countries argue for commercial hunting while others call for the cessation of such hunting. To complicate this issue further other countries support the right of their indigenous people to hunt as a central part of their cultural identity.

Oceans have many political borders and representatives of these countries battle in international meetings and on the surface of the oceans themselves. What is needed is research to generate sufficient data to allow conclusions to be drawn that all can agree and act upon. There are also important economic issues involved in this area that make decisions based on data and ethics difficult as they may affect the livelihood of many.

G.5.6   Discuss international measures that would promote the conservation of fish.
©IBO 2007

QUOTA

An example of the advice of ICES for cod in the Kattegat is that " *There should therefore be no fishing on this stock in 2007.*"

INCLUDING FISH DISCARDED AT SEA

In Canada, there are observers on fishing vessels and fish discarded at sea will be counted against quota. This increases accuracy.

AQUACULTURE/FISH FARMING/HATCHERIES

There are many fish farms throughout the world, successfully breeding and growing many different species. Areas or artificial ponds are created where fish eggs can be hatched and reared to be returned to the seas to support dwindling stocks. An example of this is the Stock Enhancement Research Facility in Florida. Conversely, growing fish under controlled circumstances may reduce the amount caught from the seas.

MESH SIZE

Setting a minimum mesh size will allow small sized fish to escape the net.

IDENTIFYING NO FISHING ZONES

Certain areas could be declared no fishing zones and become marine nature reserves. Fish could use these for breeding. This would promote the amount of eggs and increase the size of the next generation. Examples include one third of the Great Barrier Reef in Australia but also an area east of the island Lundy in the UK. *See Figure 1850.*

Figure 1850   Lundy is a no-fishing zone

OPTION

OPTION

EXERCISES

1. Compare parasitism and mutualism.

2. (a) Define gross production.
    (b) Compare gross and net production.
    (c) Outline how diversity and production change during primary succession

3. Students sampled two fresh water habitats at different sites.
    They found the following results

	Site 1	Site 2
water beetle	19	
water snail	66	
mosquito fish	19	
leech	11	
diptera larvae	11	
bivalve	786	
Ostracada	5	16
tadpoles	8	32
true worms	74	39
water hoglouse		157
swimming mayfly nymph		102
dusky mayfly nymph		16
non biting midge larva		614
'Hawker' dragon fly		16

    (a) Calculate Simpson's diversity index for both sites.
    (b) Interpret the significance of the numbers found.
    (c) Discuss a possible cause for the difference found.

4. (a) Give an example of in situ and one of ex situ conservation.
    (b) Compare the benefits of in situ and ex situ conservation.

5. Prepare a table to compare r and K strategies of reproduction.

6. Students were investigating a woodlice population in an abandoned shed in the woods. They caught a number of woodlice and marked them with a non-toxic paint and returned them to the population. The next day, they returned and caught another sample, some of which were marked. There results are given below.

first sample	n1	78
second sample	n2	83
marked in second sample	n3	8

    Estimate the size of the population of woodlice in the shed. Assume there is no natality, mortality, emigration or immigration.

FURTHER HUMAN PHYSIOLOGY

H1   Hormonal control

H2   Digestion

H3   Absorption of digested foods

H4   Functions of the liver

H5   The transport system

H6   Gas exchange

H1 HORMONAL CONTROL

> **H.1.1**   State that hormones are chemical messengers secreted by endocrine glands into the blood and transported to specific target cells.
>
> ©IBO 2007

The endocrine system consists of **endocrine glands** which produce **hormones** which are released to the blood. Endocrine glands are ductless glands; they do not secrete their product into a duct, as exocrine glands, such as sweat glands do. Instead, endocrine glands secrete their product (hormones) into the blood which transports it around the body. As the hormone passes cells, only those with special receptors will react to the presence of the hormone. These cells are called **target cells.**

> **H.1.2**   State that hormones can be steroids, proteins and tyrosine derivatives, with one example of each.
>
> ©IBO 2007

The term 'hormones' refers to a group of substances, produced by endocrine cells and transported by the bloodstream to their target cells.

Hormones can be
* steroids (e.g. testosterone)
* proteins (e.g. insulin)
* tyrosine derivatives (e.g. thyroxine).

> **H.1.3**   Distinguish between the mode of action of *steroid* hormones and *protein* hormones.
>
> ©IBO 2007

Once hormones have reached their target cells, they need to effect a change inside the cell. There are essentially two different ways of achieving this, depending on the chemical nature of the hormone.

STEROID HORMONES

Steroid hormone receptors are intracellular (usually cytoplasmic), as shown in Figure 1901. Because steroid hormones are hydrophobic, they generally can pass quite easily through the cell membrane, so don't require a receptor on the cell surface membrane. There they will bind to receptors in the cytoplasm or nucleus. The **hormone-receptor complex** will then switch specific genes on or off (see **lac operon model**).

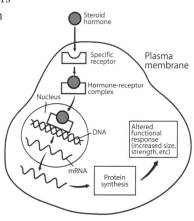

Figure 1901   How steroid hormones work

OPTION

355

OPTION

PROTEIN HORMONES

Polypeptide hormones will also bind to receptors on the cell surface membrane. The binding of the polypeptide hormone to the outside of the cell surface membrane will cause a change on the inside of the cell surface membrane. This will change the concentration of a substance known as the second(ary) messenger which will e.g. activate a specific enzyme. An example of a second messenger is cyclic AMP (cAMP). *See Figure 1902.*

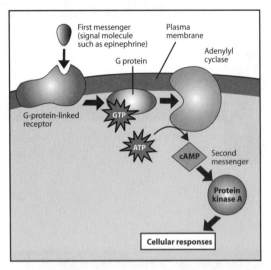

Figure 1902   How protein hormones work

H.1.4	Outline the relationship between the hypothalamus and the pituitary gland.

©IBO 2007

The **hypothalamus** is a very important section of the brain that connects the nervous system with the endocrine system. The **pituitary gland** is an endocrine gland which lies just below the hypothalamus in the brain, as shown in Figure 1903. The pituitary consists of two lobes:

- anterior lobe
- posterior lobe

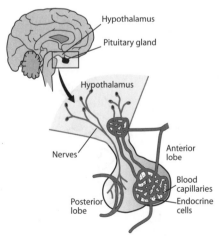

Figure 1903   The hypothalamus and the pituitary gland

There are two related systems to regulate the hormones released from the pituitary gland:

POSTERIOR LOBE

Neurosecretory cells that have their cell bodies in the hypothalamus produce protein hormones (ADH and oxytocin). The hormones are transported through the axons and are released into the blood from the nerve endings which are located in the posterior lobe of the pituitary gland.

ANTERIOR LOBE

Neurosecretory cells in the hypothalamus produce hormones (sometimes called releasing factors) which are released into capillaries in the hypothalamus. These capillaries are part of a portal system which has a second capillary bed in the anterior lobe of the pituitary gland. The releasing factors will travel through the blood, directly from the hypothalamus to the anterior lobe. There they will cause the release of one of six protein hormones (prolactin, GH, TSH, ACTH, FSH, LH) that are produced by, and released from, the anterior lobe of the pituitary gland.

H.1.5	Explain the control of ADH (vasopressin) secretion by negative feedback.

©IBO 2007

The kidneys are the organs responsible for maintaining the water potential in the mammal. Large volumes of water pass through the kidneys and are (mostly) reabsorbed into the blood. The exact amount reabsorbed is regulated by the hormone **antidiuretic hormone** (ADH), produced by the hypothalamus and secreted from the posterior pituitary gland. ADH is produced by the cell bodies of the neurosecretory cells in the hypothalamus. It is transported via the axons of these cells to be stored in the nerve endings which are located in the posterior lobe of the pituitary gland.

The hypothalamus contains **osmoreceptors** which will detect changes in the concentration of dissolved particles in the blood plasma. When an increase in concentration is detected, an impulse will be sent down the axon of the neurosecretory cell and ADH will be released from its nerve end into the blood capillaries in the posterior lobe of the pituitary gland. ADH will travel to the kidney and make the walls of the collecting duct more permeable so that more water is reabsorbed and less is excreted.

If the plasma is dilute, no ADH will be released so the walls of the collecting duct will be fairly impermeable to water. Less water is reabsorbed so more dilute urine is produced and the concentration of dissolved particles in the blood will increase. This is an example of **negative feedback.**

H2 DIGESTION

H.2.1 State that digestive juices are secreted into the alimentary canal by glands, including salivary glands, gastric glands in the stomach wall, the pancreas and the wall of the small intestine.

©IBO 2007

The process of **digestion** requires a number of different enzymes. They are secreted at different places, under different conditions. Some of the main digestive juices are:

- saliva - from salivary glands in the mouth
- gastric juice - from gastric glands in the stomach wall
- pancreatic juice - from the pancreas, released into the duodenum
- intestinal juice - from the wall of the small intestine.

H.2.2 Explain the structural features of exocrine gland cells.

©IBO 2007

Exocrine glands have a duct into which they secrete their products. They are grouped around hollow spaces (acini) which join to form ducts. Examples of exocrine glands are sweat glands and glands producing digestive enzymes (e.g. chief cells). *See Figure 1904.*

The secretory cells of an exocrine gland produce the product and secrete it into the acinus. The acini collect the product and pass it into the duct which leads into a lumen or out of the body.

Endocrine glands have 'internal secretion' which means that they do not possess a duct and secrete their product into the blood. Hormone-producing cells form endocrine glands.

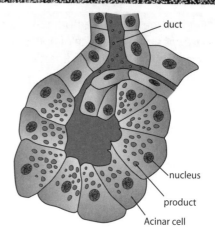

Figure 1904   The structure of exocrine gland cells

H.2.3 Compare the composition of saliva, gastric juice and pancreatic juice.

©IBO 2007

Refer to Figure 1905.

H.2.4 Outline the control of digestive juice secretion by nerves and hormones, using the example of secretion of gastric juice.

©IBO 2007

When the brain perceives food (sight or smell), it will send nerve impulses to the stomach to start releasing gastric juice. During and after a meal, gastrin will be released by the stomach as a response to the presence of particular polypeptides and amino acids as well as physical stretching of the wall of the stomach.

Gastrin is a hormone which travels from the stomach via the blood to the gastric glands and stimulates the release of gastric juice.

OPTION

Place released	pH	Gland	Secretion	Enzyme	Substrate	Product
mouth	7	salivary glands	saliva	salivary amylase	starch	maltose
stomach (chief cells and parietal cells)	2	gastric glands	gastric juice hydrochloric acid	pepsin(ogen)	protein	polypeptides
small intestine	8	pancreas	pancreatic juice	pancreatic amylase trypsin(ogen) lipase phospholipase	starch protein lipid phospholipids	maltose polypeptides glycerol + fatty acids phosphate, glycerol + fatty acids
			bicarbonate ions	not an enzyme	neutralises stomach acid	

Figure 1905   Comparison of digestive juices

357

H.2.5 Outline the role of membrane-bound enzymes on the surface of epithelial cells in the small intestine in digestion.

©IBO 2007

Some digestive enzymes, e.g. maltase, are immobilised in the plasma membrane of epithelial cells on the surface of intestinal villi. They are situated in the membrane in such a way that the active site is towards the lumen of the small intestine. When a substrate (maltose) binds to the active site, it is broken down into product (glucose) which is then immediately absorbed into the epithelial cell and passed on to the capillary.

H.2.6 Outline the reasons for cellulose not being digested in the alimentary canal.

©IBO 2007

Like starch, cellulose is a polysaccharide. Cellulose does not dissolve in water which causes the first problem in its digestion.

Starch is made up of both amylose, which only has alpha 1,4 linkages, as well as amylopectin which has alpha 1,4 linkages as well as alpha 1,6 linkages (to make branch points in the molecule). **Cellulose**, on the other hand, contains beta 1,4 linkages which make the chain undigestable by amylase. Consequenlty cellulose cannot be digested by mamals. Mammals do not possess the enzyme cellulase to digest cellulose. Some bacteria do and they can live in a mutualistic relationship with herbivores.

H.2.7 Explain why pepsin and trypsin are initially synthesized as inactive precursors and how they are subsequently activated.

©IBO 2007

Pepsin and trypsin are proteases. If they were produced in their active form, they would digest the cell which made them. So they are produced as inactive precursors (pepsinogen and trypsinogen) and are activated by the presence of hydrochloric acid (HCl) and enterokinase (an enzyme in the small intestine) respectively. Since hydrochloric acid and enterokinase are produced seperately from the enzyme precursors, the precursor and the activator do not meet until they are in the lumen of the digestive tract. This is there the enzyme becomes active.

H.2.8 Discuss the roles of gastric acid and *Helicobacter pylori* in the development of stomach ulcers and stomach cancers.

©IBO 2007

The human stomach is not a very hospitable place for bacteria to live. Secretions of hydrochloric acid and protein-digesting enzymes create an environment in which bacteria cannot readily survive. Yet *H. pylori* has been found in the stomach. The bacteria *H. pylori* can survive in the stomach because it does not live in the lumen with the acid and pepsin, but in the mucous layer, close to the cells of the stomach wall. The pH there is much higher (i.e. less acidic) and enzymes do not penetrate the mucus.

The immune system detects the presence of *H. pylori* and will respond by sending white blood cells to the area. However, they cannot act because they cannot penetrate the mucous layer. They will remain in the area and this accumulation of white blood cells may damage the tissue and cause an ulcer.

Figure 1906   Helicobacter pylori (x40000)

H. pylori may reduce the amount of gastric acid, which increases the chances of developing gastric ulcers and, eventually gastric cancer. It may also increase the amount of gastric acid which will lead to duodenal ulcers. About 30% of the people with stomach ulcers are not infected with *H. pylori* . These ulcers are often due to the use of aspirin or other medicines that affect the mucous lining of the stomach.

Many people who are infected with *H. pylori* do not develop stomach ulcers.

A chronic infection with *H. pylori* makes it much more likely that the person will eventually develop cancer of the stomach. Of the people with stomach cancer, 70-90% are, or have been, infected with *H. pylori* . The World Health Organisation now considers the risk of *H. pylori* in stomach cancer similar to the risk of smoking for lung cancer.

358

H.2.9   Explain the problem of lipid digestion in a hydrophilic medium and the role of bile in overcoming this.

©IBO 2007

Lipids are difficult to digest since they do not dissolve in water. The lipid molecules will group together (coalesce) forming droplets of fat. The enzyme (lipase) is water soluble because it needs to work in a watery environment. Lipase has an active site for the hydrophobic lipid molecules to bind. It can only work at the lipid-water interface, on the surface of the lipid sphere. This makes digestion very slow.

Bile salts emulsify fats, meaning that they divide big drops of fats into smaller droplets. Bile salts have a hydrophilic end and a lipophilic (hydrophobic) end. The hydrophobic end will bind to the lipid, leaving the hydrophilic end to stick out and interact with water, thereby preventing other lipid molecules attaching there. This emulsifies fats, i.e. divides it into smaller droplets, increasing the surface area and therefore increasing the rate with which the lipase can digest the lipid. *See Figure 1907.*

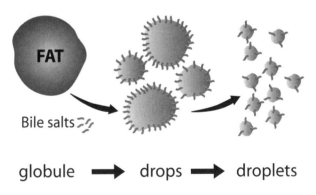

globule ➡ drops ➡ droplets

Figure 1907   Bile salts cause emulsification

TOK   An example of a paradigm shift

The stomach's acidic gastric juice not only begins protein digestion, it also digests pathogens, making it an extremely effective defence against infection. This fact made the suggestion that a bacterium was the cause of stomach disorders such as ulcers sound far-fetched.

There is some historical evidence of bacteria being found in gastric juice, but these findings were rare and could easily be dismissed as due to poor isolation technique rather than accurate data collection.

In the late 1970's Australian scientists Robin Warren and Barry Marshall isolated *Helicobacter pylori* from the stomach, successfully cultured it and argued that it, rather than stress or spicy food, was the cause of gastric ulcers and gastritis as had been considered at the time.

The medical community was slow to respond to such evidence, but took notice when Marshall famously drank a sample of *H. pylori* to infect himself, then treated himself with antibiotics to rid himself of the infection.

In 2005 Warren and Marshall were awarded the Nobel Prize for medicine. Their story illustrates a paradigm shift and the value of questioning 'fact' and trusting the scientific method.

OPTION

H3   ABSORPTION OF DIGESTED FOODS

H.3.1	Draw and label a transverse section of the ileum as seen under a light microscope.
	©IBO 2007

Figure 1908 illustrates the structure of the ileum in cross section.

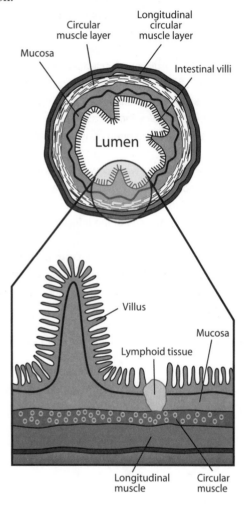

Figure 1908   The TS and LS of the small intestine

H.3.2	Explain the structural features of an epithelial cell of a villus as seen in electron micrographs, including microvilli, mitochondria, pinocytotic vesicles and tight junctions.
	©IBO 2007

Figure 1908 illustrates the structure of a villus (*see also Topic 6.1.7*). The structure of the villus greatly increases the surface area of the small intestine which improves its function of absorbing digested food.

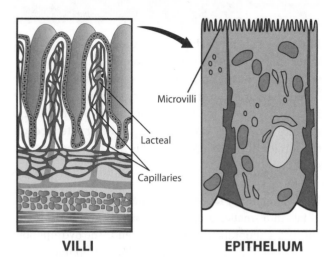

Figure 1909   The structure of villi

The **microvilli** are folds in the plasma membrane at the side of the lumen of the small intestine. They further increase the surface area (as villi do) of the membrane exposed to the lumen. Therefore, more food nutrients can be absorbed by diffusion at the same time. *See Figure 1909.*

Tight junctions are connections between epithelial cells that serve to maintain the integrity of the tissue. Tight junctions are fusions of adjacent cell surface membranes which form a continuous seal around each cell in the tissue.

Pinocytotic vesicles are present are present in the epithelial cells since some food is taken up by **endocytosis**.

Mitochondria are present in the epithelial cells to provide the energy required for active transport by which some nutrients are absorbed. *See Figure 1910.*

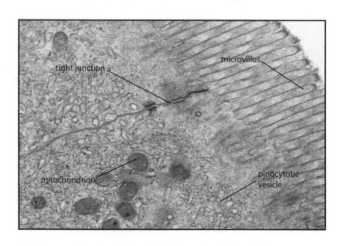

Figure 1910   EM of an epithelial cell

OPTION

H.3.3	Explain the mechanisms used by the ileum to absorb and transport food, including facilitated diffusion, active transport and endocytosis.
	©IBO 2007

Digested food materials needs to be moved into cells in order to be used. Transport across membranes may occur passively (no energy needed) or actively (energy needed).

PASSIVE TRANSPORT

Diffusion and facilitated diffusion are driven by the concentration differences on either side of the membrane. Neither process requires energy. The molecules go down the concentration gradient, either simply moving through the membrane (diffusion), or, if their structure will not permit this, through pores or carrier proteins that change shape allowing the molecule (e.g. amino acid) to pass through the membrane (facilitated diffusion). *See Figure 1911.*

Transport that does not require energy:
- simple diffusion, e.g. lipids
- facilitated diffusion, e.g. amino acids and glucose*

*Glucose can also be transported actively, e.g. from the filtrate to the blood in the nephron of the kidney.

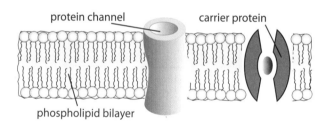

protein channel   carrier protein

phospholipid bilayer

Figure 1911   Passive transport

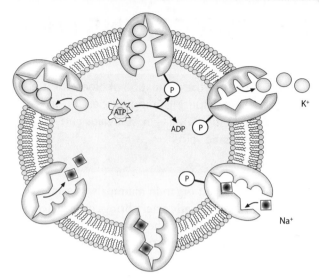

Figure 1912   Active transport

ACTIVE TRANSPORT

Active transport requires energy in the form of ATP. Often active transport moves molecules against their concentration gradient. *See Figure 1912.*

Transport that requires energy:
- active transport, e.g. sodium ions
- endocytosis, e.g. DNA is too large to be taken up any other way

ENDOCYTOSIS

Endocytosis is another way of using energy to absorb materials into the cell, as shown in Figure 1913.

H.3.4	List the materials that are not absorbed and are egested.
	©IBO 2007

Cellulose, lignin, bile pigments, bacteria and intestinal cells are not absorbed but egested from the body in the feces.

OPTION

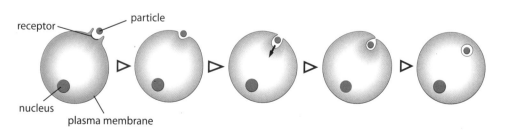

receptor   particle

nucleus

plasma membrane

Figure 1913   Endocytosis

H4   FUNCTIONS OF THE LIVER

> **H.4.1**   Outline the circulation of blood through liver tissue, including the hepatic artery, hepatic portal vein, sinusoids and hepatic vein.
>
> ©IBO 2007

The **liver**, the largest organ in mammals, has an excellent blood supply. The **hepatic artery** brings oxygenated blood from the heart to the liver. The **hepatic portal vein** delivers the blood from the digestive tract to the liver. This blood is deoxygenated but, at time, contains high levels of absorbed nutrients. The hepatic vein takes de-oxygenated blood away from the liver back to the heart. *See Figure 1914.*

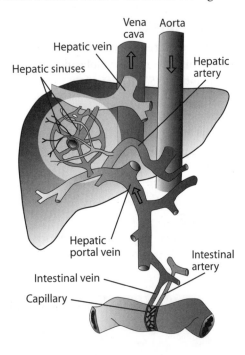

Figure 1914   Blood flow to and from the liver

The liver is divided into many liver lobules. Between the lobules, branches of the hepatic artery and the hepatic portal vein are found, as well as bile tubules. A branch of the hepatic vein, called the central vein, is found in the centre of each lobule.

The functional unit of the liver is called the **acinus**. An acinus contains branches of the three blood vessels, the bile ductule and many hepatocytes, arranged in rows.

The blood flows from the hepatic arteriole and the hepatic portal venule through the sinusoids to the hepatic venule. During this process, there is close contact between the blood and the hepatocytes.

Sinusoids differ from capillaries in three ways:
1. they have a dilated, large, irregular lumen.
2. there are spaces between the endothelial cells which line the sinusoid; they facilitate exchange between the sinusoids and adjacent tissues.
3. the basement membrane-like material is not continuous but forms barrel hoop-like rings around the endothelial walls.

As a result of these differences, the blood flows very slowly through the sinusoids. The slow moving blood together with the spaces between the endothelial cells and non-continuous basement membrane facilitate the exchange of materials between the blood in the sinusoid and the hepatocytes of the tissue of the liver.

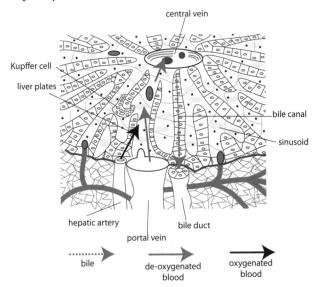

Figure 1915   The internal strucure of the liver

The Kupffer cells line the sinusoids. They ingest foreign particles and are involved in the breakdown of old erythrocytes. Bile is produced by the hepatocytes and moves in the opposite direction of the blood, towards the edge of the lobule, into the bile ductules. *See Figure 1915.*

> **H.4.2**   Explain the role of the liver in regulating levels of nutrients in the blood.
>
> ©IBO 2007

The liver regulates the levels of nutrients in the blood. This is important because the rate at which nutrients are used is not always constant and certainly the supply of nutrients depends on how recently a meal was ingested. Some time after eating, a lot of nutrients will enter the blood causing a sharp increase in, for example, the blood glucose level.

Too high levels of glucose can do damage, for example, to the retina so a regulating mechanism which keeps levels of nutrients in the blood constant is required.

The liver, receiving all the blood from the small intestine, will temporarily store excess glucose (see Topic H.1) and release it into the blood as blood glucose levels drop due to glucose being used (for cellular respiration).

Glucose is stored as glycogen under the influence of the hormone insulin (produced by the β cells of the Islets of Langerhans in the pancreas). When blood glucose levels are low, glucagon (produced by the α cells of the Islets of Langerhans in the pancreas) stimulates the breakdown of glycogen and release of glucose to the blood.

Proteins are broken down by proteases and the individual amino acids can be used to build proteins. Some amino acids can be made from other amino acids in the process of trans amination and amino acids can also be used for energy after de-amination and trans-amination. Some amino acids cannot be stored.

H.4.3	Outline the role of the liver in the storage of nutrients, including carbohydrate, iron, vitamin A and vitamin D.
	©IBO 2007

CARBOHYDRATE STORAGE

The liver plays a vital role in **carbohydrate** metabolism. The role of insulin and glucagon is described in Topic 6.5.

The following processes are involved in glucose metabolism:

$$\text{glucose} \; \underset{\text{glucagon}}{\overset{\text{insulin}}{\rightleftharpoons}} \; \text{glycogen}$$

It is important to remember that insulin and glucagon are hormones, NOT enzymes.

Although the intake of carbohydrates during meals creates fluctuating blood glucoses levels in the hepatic portal vein (the blood vessel which takes the blood from the small intestine to the liver), the level of glucose in the blood at other places is remarkably constant (around 90 mg glucose/100 cm^3 blood). The liver converts all monosaccharides into glucose and stores any surplus as glycogen, an insoluble polysaccharide. The liver can store up to 100 g of glycogen. Muscles can also store glycogen.

When the blood glucose level falls below 60 mg/100 cm^3, the liver converts glycogen back into glucose.

The hormones glucagon (from the pancreas), adrenaline (from the adrenal medulla) and nor-adrenaline (from the nerve endings of sympathetic neurons) stimulate the breakdown of glycogen into glucose.

Muscles lack some of the required enzymes and convert glycogen into pyruvate which can be used for (an)aerobic respiration.

STORAGE OF IRON

Iron is a component of hemoglobin. Hemoglobin is found in erythrocytes. Erythrocytes last about 120 days before they are broken down. After the hemoglobin from the erythrocytes has been broken down, the iron is carefully stored.

Although several kinds of food contain iron, this element is difficult to absorb. The iron from the broken down hemoglobin will be used again to produce new hemoglobin. In the meantime, it will be stored in the liver in the form of ferritin, a complex of iron and globulin. The human liver contains approximately 1 mg iron per gm dry mass.

STORAGE OF VITAMIN A AND VITAMIN D

The liver is capable of storing water soluble vitamins, but the main vitamins stored in the liver are fat soluble, such as vitamin A (retinol) and vitamin D (calciferol).

Vitamin A is found in dairy products and carrots. It is part of a visual pigment (rhodopsin) and a deficiency of retinol can lead to night blindness.

Vitamin D is found in cod liver oil and dairy products. It is also made by the skin under the influence of UV light. Vitamin D helps in the uptake of calcium and a calciferol deficiency can lead to rickets in a child.

H.4.4	State that the liver synthesizes plasma proteins and cholesterol.
	©IBO 2007

The liver produces cholesterol and uses most of it to produce bile salts. Cholesterol is a component of cell membranes and also a precursor for steroid hormones and vitamin D. Since the liver plays an important role in the amino acid metabolism, it stands to reason that it is involved in the production of plasma proteins, e.g. albumin and fibrinogen.

Plasma proteins are an extremely important constituent of blood plasma. The most common plasma protein is albumin, which transports a variety of molecules including calcium, some amino acids and/or some hormones. Other examples are fibrinogen and globulins such as gamma globulins which are antibodies. The concentration of plasma proteins determines the distribution of water between blood and interstitial (intercellular) fluid. Since this process takes place by hydrostatic pressure and osmosis, a small change in the number of dissolved particles can change the rate of movement of the water molecules.

H.4.5	State that the liver has a role in detoxification.
	©IBO 2007

The liver is the main organ for detoxification. Not only pesticides are broken down in the liver but also medicines and alcohol.

H.4.6	Describe the process of erythrocyte and hemoglobin breakdown in the liver, including phagocytosis, digestion of globin and bile pigment formation.
	©IBO 2007

Humans have approximately 5×10^9 erythrocytes per cm³ blood. If we assume that you have 5 litres of blood, this means a total of $(5 \times 10^3) \times (5 \times 10^9) = 250 \times 10^{11}$ in your body.

Since erythrocytes, on average, last 120 days, every day

$$\frac{250 \times 10^{11}}{120} \approx 2 \times 10^{11}$$

new erythrocytes are formed every day and the old ones are broken down. This requires an efficient process without too many components being lost.

The breakdown of erythrocytes is one of the functions of the liver. Old erythrocytes are broken down by **phagocytosis** (macrophages) in the liver (Kupffer cells), spleen and bone marrow. The hemoglobin which was packed in the erythrocytes is released and broken down into heme and globin.

Heme is an iron-containing prosthetic group. The iron is stored in the liver before being transported to the bone marrow where it is used to make hemoglobin for new erythrocytes. The remainder of the heme group becomes **biliverdin** (a green bile pigment) which in turn becomes bilirubin (a reddish-yellow pigment) and is secreted into the small intestine via the bile duct. Bacteria in the gut further change bilirubin into a pigment which gives the characteristic colour to feces.

Globin is a protein and is broken down to its constituent amino acids. These are then treated as any other amino acid and may be used to make a protein, trans-aminated or de- aminated for energy. This may take place in the liver; alternatively, the amino acids are released into the blood.

H.4.7	Explain the liver damage caused by excessive alcohol consumption.
	©IBO 2007

Alcohol is absorbed from the digestive system. The liver breaks down alcohol in the following pathway:

alcohol → acetaldehyde → acetic acid → carbon dioxide

The first step of the reaction is:

alcohol + NAD^+ → acetaldehyde + NADH + H^+

Acetaldehyde may bind to proteins, lipids or DNA, forming adducts which interfere with the normal functions of these molecules and/or can cause an inflammation response. (*Note: The systematic name for alcohol is ethanol, acetaldehyde is ethanal and acetic acid is ethanoic acid.*)

Excess NADH can cause the following:
- excessive production of lactic acid
  pyruvate + NADH + H^+ → lactic acid + NAD^+
- accumulation of fat in the liver by:
  -synthesis of glycerol and fatty acids
  -reduction of breakdown of fatty acids

Breakdown of alcohol produces free radicals and other reactive molecules that damage proteins, lipids and DNA. The hepatocytes in the liver will be replaced by fatty tissue and eventually by scar tissue which does not carry out any of the normal liver functions.

Having to break down excessive amounts of alcohol regularly for a long time, seems to interfere with the normal liver metabolism of protein, fat and carbohydrates. Whereas not every person who consumes large amounts of alcohol frequently will develop Alcoholic Liver Disease, others show symptoms with only a few glasses a day. Alcoholic Liver Disease may lead to cirrhosis of the liver. Some of the damage to the liver in Alcoholic Liver Disease may be reversible. **Cirrhosis** is irreversible and advanced cirrhosis can only be treated by a liver transplant.

Symptoms of cirrhosis include:
- bruising due to disturbed process of blood clotting (clotting factors are made by the liver)
- impotence and infertility
- jaundice: yellowing of the skin due to increased bilirubin (bile salt) levels

H5 THE TRANSPORT SYSTEM

H.5.1	Explain the events of the cardiac cycle, including atrial and ventricular systole and diastole, and heart sounds.

©IBO 2007

H.5.2	Analyse data showing pressure and volume changes in the left atrium, left ventricle and the aorta, during the cardiac cycle.

©IBO 2007

Refer also to Topic 6.2.

One heart-beat is really one cardiac cycle. One cardiac cycle involves the following phases:

- blood enters the atria; the bicuspid and tricuspid valves open when atrial pressure exceeds ventricular pressure. This resting period is called **diastole**.
- the two atria contract simultaneously (atrial **systole**), causing the blood to be pushed into the ventricles.
- almost immediately the ventricles contract (ventricular systole); this increases the pressure in the ventricle which closes the tricuspid and the bicuspid valves and opens the semilunar valves, pushing the blood into the aorta and pulmonary artery. The atria relax.
- the ventricles then relax (ventricular diastole) and some of the blood in the aorta and pulmonary artery will try to flow back and will close the semilunar valves. *See Figure 1916.*

The sound that the heart makes is usually considered to be a 'lub-dub' sound. The 'lub' is caused by the closing of the bicuspid and tricuspid and the 'dub' is caused by the closing of the semilunar valves in the arteries. So ventricular systole = 'lub'; ventricular diastole = 'dub'.

Figure 1916 contains a lot of information about what happens in the heart during a cardiac cycle. Starting at the bottom, the phonocardiogram is a visual representation of the heart sounds as described in *Topic H.5.1*. The sound labelled "1st" is the lub and the sound labelled "2nd" is dub.

LEFT ATRIUM

We start by looking at the left atrium from the beginning of phase C. The atrium has some blood but continues to fill. The left Atrio-Ventricular valve (A-V valve = bicuspid) is open so the blood flows from the atrium into the ventricle. Then the atrium starts to contract in the last part of C. The volume of the atrium decreases and the pressure increases. The blood is pumped into the left ventricle and the atrium relaxes which causes a decrease in pressure in the atrium and an increase in atrial volume. The atrium will start to fill again with blood from the pulmonary vein. The changes in pressure and volume are very small compared to those taking place in the ventricle. The changes in pressure in the left ventricle are much greater than those in the right ventricle because blood is being pumped to the body.

OPTION

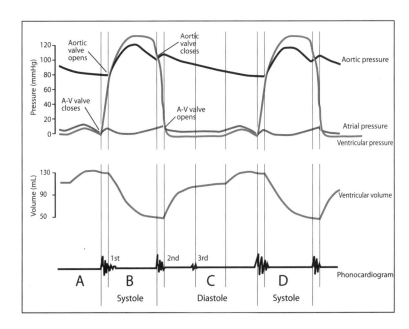

Figure 1916   *Volume and pressure changes in the heart*

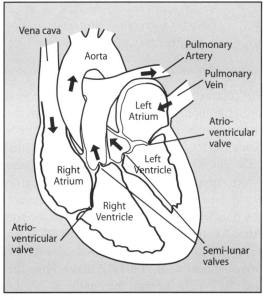

Figure 1917   *The structure of the heart*

VENTRICLE

The left ventricle fills with blood during phase C. The volume of the ventricle increases so the pressure does not immediately change a lot. When the atrium contracts (phase a), more blood flows into the ventricle, further increasing its volume and having a small effect on the pressure in the left ventricle. When the atrium relaxes and atrial volume increases, atrial pressure drops. As soon as atrial pressure drops below ventricular pressure, blood from the ventricle starts to flow back into the atrium. This closes the left AV valve, stopping the backflow, and causes the first heart sound.

The ventricles then start to contract, rapidly decreasing ventricular volume and hence increasing ventricular pressure (phase D and B). This is called ventricular systole. As soon as ventricular pressure is greater than aortic pressure, the aortic valves (= semilunar valves) to the aorta open and blood flows from the ventricle into the aorta.

The ventricle continues to contract, decreasing volume and increasing pressure until the end of phase D and B. Then, the ventricles are empty so the pressure drops rapidly. As soon as the pressure of the left ventricle is smaller than that of the aorta, blood from the aorta starts to flow back which closes the semi-lunar valves, stops the backflow of blood and causes the second heart sound.

The ventricle relaxes, increasing volume and decreasing pressure. The pressure in the left atrium is now greater than that in the left ventricle. This opens the AV valve and blood starts to fill the ventricle.

H.5.3	Outline the mechanisms that control the heartbeat, including the roles of the SA (sinoatrial) node, AV (atrioventricular) node and conducting fibres in the ventricular walls.
	©IBO 2007

The contractions of the cardiac muscles are brought about by nerve impulses which originate not from the brain but from a specific region of the right atrium: the **Sino-Atrial Node** (SAN). The SAN is made from specialised muscle cells. The SAN releases an impulse at regular intervals which spreads across the walls of the atria, causing simultaneous contractions. The impulse cannot spread to the muscles of the ventricles except in the region of the **Atrio-Ventricular Node** (AVN). The AVN is connected to the bundle of His (specialised cardiac fibres) which branches out into the **Purkinje tissue**. From the AVN, the impulse travels through the bundle of His down to the apex of the heart and from there spreads up through the

Purkinje tissue. This causes the ventricular contractions to start at the apex and push the blood up into the arteries. *See Figure 1918.*

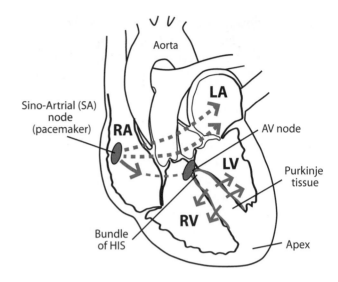

Figure 1918   The control of heartbeat

Although the heart is largely autonomous in its contractions, the brain and some hormones can influence the frequency of the heart-beats. Impulses from a nerve from the sympathetic nervous system will increase the heart rate, messages from the vagus nerve (part of the parasympathetic system) will decrease the cardiac frequency. Some hormones also have an effect on the heart rate: adrenaline (epinephrine) increases cardiac frequency.

If the SAN does not function properly, it is quite easy to implant an artificial pacemaker to carry out this function. With a well adjusted pacemaker, a person with a malfunctioning SAN can live a long and active life.

H.5.4	Outline atherosclerosis and the causes of coronary thrombosis.
	©IBO 2007

Atherosclerosis is the hardening and narrowing of arteries caused by chronic inflammation of the walls of arteries, which can be caused by the accumulation of lipids on the inner surface. This hinders normal blood flow and may cause the formation of blood clots. All this can lead to a blockage in the coronary artery (coronary thrombosis) which causes a heart attack (myocardial infarction).

OPTION

H.5.5 Discuss factors that affect the incidence of coronary heart disease.

©IBO 2007

There is an overlap with A.3.6

Risk factors for coronary heart disease include:

- genetic factors - if one or more family members have CHD, the risk is increased
- age - CHD is more common with increasing age
- gender - CHD is more common among males
- smoking - smoking increases the chance of CHD
- obesity - obesity increases the chance of CHD
- diet - a diet high in cholesterol and saturated fats increases the chances of CHD; there is evidence that trans fatty acids are particularly unhealthy
- lack of exercise - exercise seems to decrease levels of LDL cholesterol and reduces chances of CHD.

TOK   How important are risk factors?

Epidemiology is a field of science where factors effecting heath are studied. Epidemiologists acknowledge that correlation between a factor and a disease does not mean that that factor is the cause of the disease. A link between high saturated fat intake and heart disease is widely understood to exist.

However Maasai people have a very high intake of saturated fat and extremely low incidence of cardiovascular disease, contradicting this observation. This reinforces the nature of epidemiology, that correlation is not the same as cause. Carefully controlled experiments can determine cause, but this is extremely difficult in the area of human health, hence our reliance on epidemiological studies to determine risk of illness.

H6   GAS EXCHANGE

H.6.1 Define *partial pressure*.

©IBO 2007

Partial pressure refers to the pressure exerted by each component in a mixture. The pressure of a gas in a mixture is the same as the pressure it would exert if it occupied the same volume alone at the same temperature.

H.6.2 Explain the oxygen dissociation curves of adult hemoglobin, fetal hemoglobin and myoglobin.

©IBO 2007

The oxygen that enters the blood in the lungs, will bind with the hemoglobin in the erythrocytes. Each molecule of hemoglobin can bind a maximum of four molecules of oxygen. If the maximum number of oxygen molecules have attached to hemoglobin, it is said to be fully saturated. Hemoglobin with oxygen is known as oxyhemoglobin (HbO_2).

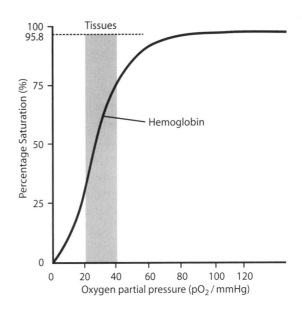

Figure 1919   How oxygen is carried in the blood

The amount of saturation of the hemoglobin depends on the concentration of oxygen in the air.

The amount of saturation of the hemoglobin is expressed as a figure percentage with 0% indicating no oxygen binding and 100% complete saturation with four oxygen molecules attached to every hemoglobin. *See Figure 1919.*

OPTION

The concentration of oxygen in the air is noted as pO_2, the partial pressure of oxygen in the air.

The pO_2 depends on the concentration of oxygen in the air and the air pressure. If the concentration of oxygen decreases, so does the pO_2. But if the air pressure decreases, as it does at high altitudes, there is also a drop in the pO_2. The saturation of hemoglobin is then lowered and hence so is the amount of oxygen transported by hemoglobin. The body will, in time, compensate by increasing the number of erythrocytes.

At sea level, air pressure is 760 mm Hg. As there is 21% oxygen by volume in air, the partial pressure of oxygen (pO_2) is $0.21 \times 760 = 159$ mm Hg. However, by the time the air reaches the alveoli, it has been warmed and water vapour has been added. The air in the alveoli is not completely refreshed because with each breath, some air stays behind in the lungs. As a result, when the air is in the alveoli, the pO_2 has dropped to about 100 mm Hg. The pO_2 in active muscles is around 20 mm Hg.

OXYGEN DISSOCIATION CURVE OF
HEMOGLOBIN

Erythrocytes going through the capillaries in the lung are exposed to a partial pressure of oxygen (pO_2) of around 100 mm Hg. This means that the hemoglobin will be almost 100% saturated with oxygen. As the erythrocytes travel through the body, the levels of oxygen will drop. Reaching the active muscle, with a pO_2 of 20 mm Hg, hemoglobin will only be about 30% saturated.

(Note: Check this by using a ruler to work out where 20 mm Hg is on the x-axis. Draw a line straight up to meet the graph and another line left to the y-axis and determine the value. You need to be able to do this accurately as it is a skill often needed in IB exams.)

If the hemoglobin is still 30% saturated in the muscles, then 70% of the oxygen taken up in the lungs has been given off to the cells in the muscles. This is the oxygen available for cellular respiration. *Refer to Figure 1919.*

The sigmoid shape (S-shape) of the curve is caused by cooperative binding. Cooperative binding is the phenomenon that binding the first oxygen to a molecule of hemoglobin will cause a small change in the structure of the hemoglobin making it easier to bind the next oxygen molecules.

FETAL HEMOGLOBIN

Since mother and child have separate circulatory systems, the hemoglobin of the fetus must be capable of taking oxygen from the mother's hemoglobin in the placenta. Due to a slight difference in structure between fetal and 'normal' hemoglobin, the affinity for oxygen is slightly greater in the case of the fetal hemoglobin. So any oxygen released by the maternal hemoglobin is bonded to the fetal hemoglobin and transported to the fetus.

Assuming again a pO_2 of 100 mm Hg and 20 mm Hg in the placenta, it can be seen that the saturation of the mother's hemoglobin is 100% in her lungs. When her blood arrives at the placenta, about 70% of the oxygen will be released as maternal hemoglobin will be only 30% saturated. According to the graph, fetal hemoglobin will be 55% saturated, so the fetal hemoglobin can take up the oxygen released by the maternal hemoglobin.

HEMOGLOBIN AND MYOGLOBIN

Hemoglobin carries oxygen around the body, but when it reaches the muscles, the oxygen is taken over and stored by myoglobin. To be able to do this, myoglobin must have a higher affinity for oxygen than hemoglobin (at equal pO_2), but still be able to release the oxygen when the muscles need it at very low pO_2. *Refer to Figure 1919.*

Hemoglobin is made of four polypeptide chains and each chain has a heme group which can bind a molecule of oxygen. **Myoglobin** is only made of one polypeptide chain, so only has one heme group and binds only one molecule of oxygen. As a result, there is no cooperative binding. Therefore, the oxygen dissociation curve of myoglobin is not sigmoidal. *See Figure 1920.*

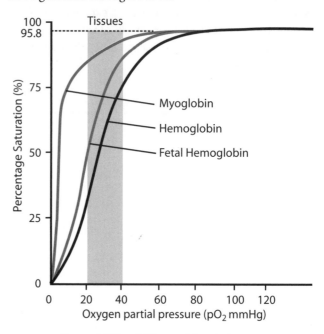

Figure 1920   Different blood pigments

H.6.3   Describe how carbon dioxide is carried
         by the blood, including the action of
         carbonic anhydrase, the chloride shift
         and buffering by plasma proteins.

©IBO 2007

TRANSPORT OF OXYGEN AND

CARBON DIOXIDE

Oxygen is transported from the lungs to the tissues by hemoglobin in the erythrocytes. It then becomes oxyhemoglobin (HbO_2).

Carbon dioxide is carried from the tissues to the lungs in different ways:

- some is bound to hemoglobin forming carbamino-hemoglobin (as $HbCO_2$).
- very little is directly dissolved in the plasma.
- most enters the erythrocyte, changes to HCO_3^- and goes into the plasma.

The CO_2 produced by the tissue cells diffuses into the plasma and directly into the erythrocyte. In the erythrocyte, the enzyme carbonic anhydrase turns it into H_2CO_3 which then splits into H^+ and HCO_3^-. The HCO_3^- leaves the erythrocyte (and is exchanged for Cl^-, the so-called chloride shift). The H^+ causes the HbO_2 to dissociate (releasing O_2 to the tissue cells) and binds with Hb to form HHb. *See Figure 1921.*

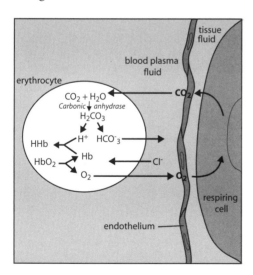

Figure 1921   The transport of carbon dioxide

The HbO_2 is weakly acidic and associated with K^+. It can be referred to as $KHbO_2$. When oxygen is released and carbon dioxide taken up, the following buffer reaction takes place:

$$KHbO_2 \rightarrow KHb + O_2$$

$$H^+ + HCO_3^- + KHb \rightarrow HHb + KHCO_3$$

By accepting hydrogen ions, hemoglobin acts as a buffer molecule and so enables large quantities of carbonic acid to be carried to the lungs without any major change in blood pH.

H.6.4   Explain the role of the Bohr shift in the
         supply of oxygen to respiring tissues.

©IBO 2007

THE BOHR EFFECT

The pH of the blood (the amount of free H^+), is directly related to the carbon dioxide (CO_2) concentration. As the amount of CO_2 increases (and the pH lowers), the oxygen dissociation curve for hemoglobin shifts to the right. The effect, as you can see in Figures 1921 and 1922, is that the saturation of hemoglobin is reduced. In other words, more oxygen is released from the hemoglobin. The CO_2 is produced in cellular respiration. The more energy the cells need, the more cellular respiration takes place and the more CO_2 is produced. The increased CO_2 concentration will reduce the saturation of hemoglobin and release more oxygen to the cells.

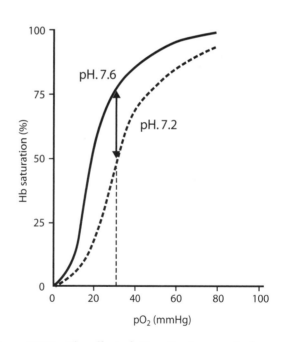

Figure 1922   The effect of pH on the transport of oxygen

H.6.5   Explain how and why ventilation rate
         varies with exercise.

©IBO 2007

During exercise, more oxygen is used but also more carbon dioxide is produced. Since carbon dioxide is transported by the blood plasma as HCO_3^-, the pH of the blood will be lowered by large amounts of carbon dioxide.

Chemosensors (found in the aorta and carotid arteries) will detect this change and send impulses to the breathing centre in the brain. This centre compares the incoming information with the desired value (the set point) and if the blood pH is too low, impulses will be sent to the intercostal muscles and the diaphragm to increase the rate and depth of lung ventilation. This entire system is under involuntary control, although some voluntary control is possible.

> **H.6.6**   Outline the possible causes of asthma and its effects on the gas exchange system.
>
> ©IBO 2007

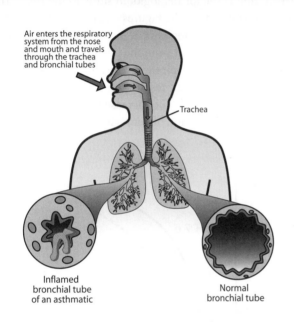

Air enters the respiratory system from the nose and mouth and travels through the trachea and bronchial tubes

Trachea

Inflamed bronchial tube of an asthmatic

Normal bronchial tube

Figure 1923   The symptoms of asthma

Asthma is a disease of the respiratory system. Asthma is chronic with recurring attacks. During an asthma attack, the airpassages constrict and it becomes very difficult to breathe and get enough air into the lungs.

CAUSE OF ASTHMA

An asthma attack is often triggered by allergens e.g. pollen, house dust mites, certain animals, certain foods etc. but can also be triggered factors such as vigorous exercise. These factors are the direct cause of the attack. The cause of the condition may be hereditary, although some evidence now suggests that children growing up in very clean environments are more likely to develop asthma. Figure 1923 illustrates how the bronchioles of an asthmatic person tighten and thicken and the air passages may become mucous-filled and inflamed making it difficult to breathe.

EFFECTS OF ASTHMA

Some effects of asthma include inflammation and constriction of bronchial tubes leading to wheezing, coughing and respiratory distress. Asthma can usually be controlled by medication and (trying to) avoid known "triggers", but a very severe attack is potentially life-threatening.

> **H.6.7**   Explain the problem of gas exchange at high altitudes and the way the body acclimatizes.
>
> ©IBO 2007

At high altitudes, the pressure is lower and therefore the partial pressure of oxygen is also lower. This makes it more difficult for the body to take up oxygen. As a result of lower levels of oxygen, the person might suffer from mountain sickness (fatigue, nausea, breathlessness and headaches). This may be caused by too rapid and very deep breathing, losing too much carbon dioxide with a subsequent change in blood pH (alkalaemia).

This will be solved in a few days, by the kidneys which will excrete alkaline urine. Pulmonary ventilation increases and the bone marrow produces greater numbers of red blood cells to assist in the process of oxygen transport. People who live at high altitudes have greater lung surface and larger vital capacity than those living at sea level. Athletes competing in the Olympics in Mexico City had to arrive several weeks early in order to acclimatise to the altitude.

OPTION

EXERCISES

1. (a) State the other name for vasopressin.
   (b) State where vasopressin is produced.
   (c) State where vasopressin is released.
   (d) State the target cells of ADH.
   (e) Explain the mechanism for control of ADH levels

2. (a) Explain why pepsin and trypsin are produced as inactive precursors
   (b) Name the compound that activate them.

3. (a) List which structures of the epithelium cell of a villus make it particularly suitable to its function.
   (b) Explain how each structure supports the function of the cell.

4. (a) List the nutrients in the blood that are controlled by the liver
   (b) Outline the role of the liver in controlling nutrients in the blood

5. List factors that can contribute to CHD and explain their risks

6. (a) Explain the shape to the oxygen dissociation curve for adult hemoglobin.
   (b) Explain how the Bohr shift helps to increase oxygen given off to the tissue.

OPTION

CHAPTER 1

1   The mean is determined by adding the data to obtain 27. The mean is now found by dividing by the number of items of data (10) to obtain a mean of 2.7.

Direct entry of the data into a graphic calculator (in this case a Texas TI-83) gives an immediate answer.

First use the STAT mode and enter the data as a list.

Mean ⎯

Standard deviation ⎯

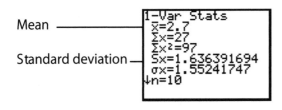

To calculate the standard deviation manually using the formula

$$\sqrt{\dfrac{\sum (x - \bar{x})^2}{n - 1}},$$

we could use a table.

Number of eggs	$x - \bar{x}$	$(x - \bar{x})^2$
5	2.3	5.29
3	0.3	0.09
5	2.3	5.29
3	0.3	0.09
4	1.3	1.69
2	-0.7	0.49
0	-2.7	7.29
2	-0.7	0.49
1	-1.7	2.89
2	-0.7	0.49

The sum of the third column gives

$$\sum (x - \bar{x})^2$$

$$= 24.1$$

The sample standard deviation

$$= \sqrt{\dfrac{\sum (x - \bar{x})^2}{n - 1}} = \sqrt{\dfrac{24.1}{10 - 1}} = 1.6363917$$

2   (i)   The population means for drugs A and B are the same.
    (ii) The population means for drugs A and B are different.
    (iii) 3.899
    (iv) 2.10
    (v)   Greater
    (vi) Yes

CHAPTER 2

1B, 2C, 3D, 4A, 5C, 6B, 7B, 8C, 9A, 10B, 11A, 12B, 13D, 14A, 15B, 16A, 17B, 18A

19 The correct order is: atom, DNA double helix (thickness, length is much more), thickness of membrane, organelle, prokaryotic cell, eukaryotic cell

20 (a)   The child has the larger surface area.
    (b)   dog: SA/V = 0.13/2 = 0.065
          child: SA/V = 0.9/24 = 0.0375
          the dog has a higher SA/V ratio than the child
    (c)   If the SA/V ratio is larger, the organism is likely to loose more heat so based on this, the dog would need more food per kg bodyweight than the child. However, as the child is likely to be growing and the dog is fully grown, the child is likely to eat more. The level of activity may also be different which would affect the amount of food needed.

21 (a)   Refer to Figure 215.
    (b)   Refer to Figure 222.
    (c)

organelle	structure	function
rER	small structures, consisting of 2 subunits, each made of RNA and protein	proteins for use outside the cell are produced here
lysosome	membrane surrounding (hydrolytic) enzymes	intracellular digestion and autolysis
Golgi apparatus	stack of flattened, membrane bound sacs, forming an extensive network in the cell	intracellular transport, processing and packaging
mitochondrion	double membrane, inner membrane folded into cristae, surrounding matrix.	involved in the release of energy from organic molecules
nucleus	contains DNA in linear chromosomes, surrounded by nuclear envelope	controls the activity of the cell by transcribing certain genes and not others (see 3.5)

22 (a) Refer to Figure 233

The membrane is made of a phopholipid bilayer. This consists of a number of phosholipid molecule. Each phospholipid molecule is made of a polar/hydrophilic phosphate, attached to a central glycerol molecule which also has 2 nonpolar/hydrophobic lipid tails. In the phospholipid bilayer, the phosphate molecules are found on either side of the layer and the lipid tails are facing each other in the centre.

In between the phospholipid molecules, there are cholesterol molecules and proteins. Integral proteins are proteins which are mostly found in between the phospholipid molecules of the membrane and peripheral proteins are mostly found outside the phospholipid bilayer but interacting with the phosphate heads.

(b) the middle of the phospholipid bilayer is hydrophobic/non-polar which means that the part of the protein that is found in this area also needs to be non-polar. If it were polar, it would move through the phospholipid bilayer to find other polar molecules to make hydrogen bonds. This would obviously disrupt the structure of the membrane.

23

creation of two genetically identical nuclei	mitosis	telophase
biochemical reactions	interphase	
separation of sister chromatids	mitosis	anaphase
DNA replication	interphase	S-stage
chromosomes moving to the equator	mitosis	metaphase
protein synthesis	interphase	

24 Asexual reproduction, cloning, growth, repair. Mitosis, with meiosis, is also part of the process of producing gametes.

25 Volume is length x width x height so as the cell gets bigger, volume increases to the power 3. Surface area is length x width so surface area incrases to the power 2.

Rate of use of resources (food, oxygen) and the rate of heat and waste production (urea, carbon dioxide) are linked to the volume of the cell. Rate of exchange (of e.g. oxygen) is linked to the surface area. So the need for e.g. oxygen will increase faster than the ability to take it up.

26 real size × magnification = measured size

real size = measured size / magnificatio

$8 \times 10^{-3} / 400$

the actual size of the nucleus is 20 micrometres.

CHAPTER 3

1D, 2C, 3B, 4A, 5D, 6A, 7D, 8A, 9D, 10A

11 Thermal properties: water needs a lot of energy to warm up and a lot of energy to go from solid to liquid or liquid to gas. This is because of the strong cohesion forces between molecules.

Water molecules have a negative and a positive side. This means that they are polar. There are hydrogen bonds (attraction forces) between the negative side of one molecule and the positive side of another which causes the cohesion forces between water molecules.

Water is a good solvent for polar molecules. Polar molecules can interact with water molecules in the same way that other water molecules do. Non-polar molecules do not interact with water molecules and therefore do not dissolve well.

12 (a) carbohydrates: carbon, hydrogen, oxygen
(b) lipids: carbon, hydrogen, oxygen
(c) proteins: carbon, hydrogen, oxygen, nitrogen

13 (a) carbohydrates: e.g. glucose - *see Figure 313*
(b) lipids: glycerol and fatty acids - *see Figure 317*
(c) proteins: amino acids - *see Figure 319*

14 The condensation reaction between monosaccharides is between two OH groups, forming water. This leaves one O in place which forms an oxygen bridge between the monosaccharides. The condensation reaction between two amino acids is between NH_2 of one amino acid and COOH of the other amino acid. The H of the NH_2 group combines with the OH of the COOH group, forming water and a peptide bond.

15 (a) Enzymes are proteins. Increasing the temperature changes the three dimensional shape of any protein, so also that of the active site of the enzyme. If the active site changes shape, then the substrate will no longer fit and the enzyme does not work anymore.

(b) Increasing substrate concentration will make it more likely that the active site of any enzyme has a substrate attached. Therefore the speed of the reaction will increase untill all active sites are filled with substrate at any time. Further increasing the substrate concentration will not increase the rate of reaction.

(c) Denaturation occurs when the shape of the active site of the enzyme changes. The substrate no longer fits and the rate of the reaction becomes very low.

16 (a) covalent bond caused by a condensation reaction

(b) covalent bond caused by a condensation reaction

(c) hydrogen bonding caused by positive-negative attraction forces between either oxygen or nitrogen in one base and hydrogen in the other.

(d) covalent bonds are stronger because they involve sharing electrons.

(e) because A and T both form two Hydrogen bonds and C and G both form 3 Hydrogen bonds. Also, A and G are purines (have two rings) while C and T are pyrimidines (have one ring) and there is room for exactly three rings between the sides of the DNA ladder.

17 *Similarities*:

Both are nucleic acids, made of nucleotides. Nucleotides contain a pentose sugar, a phophate and an organic base.

Differences:

DNA has de-oxyribose, RNA has ribose.
DNA has thymine, RNA has uracil
DNA has two strands, RNA has one strand
DNA is usually in the shape of a double helix, RNA is not.

18 (a) light intensity, colour of the light, amount of carbon dioxide available, temperature.

(b) oxygen, ATP (and NADPH)

19 (a) ATP, NADH and pyruvate

(b) ATP, CO_2, ethanol, lactic acid, heat

20 It is done by attaching the enzyme lactase to a large molecule and then bringing it into contact with milk. Any lactose present will be broken down into glucose and galactose by the lactase.

CHAPTER 4

1A, 2B, 3D, 4D, 5B, 6A, 7C, 8B, 9D, 10D,

11 Refer to Figure 413
The results of the self-fertilisation of the F1 will be:
genotypes: 25% TT, 50% Tt, 25% tt
phenotypes: 75% tall, 25% short

12 w+ = wild type
w = black
A x B gives only wild type colour so at least one parent must be w+w+
A x C gives some black (ww) so both A and C must have a w allele and be w+w
B x C gives only wild type colour so at least one parent must be w+w+

Therefore   A is w+w
                   B is w+w+
                   C is w+w

A × black will give 50% wild, 50% black (same for C)
B × Black will give 100% wild type.

13 (a)   Exp A: Yellow is dominant over white
           Exp B: Short is dominant over long

(b)

phenotypes possible	genotypes
yellow	YY or Yy
white	yy
short	SS or Ss
long	ss

(c) since the F1 contains some long plants with white flowers, their genotype is yyss. The genotype of the parent plant with white flowers and long stems is also yyss. So the yellow flowered short stemmed parent must be heterozygous YySs.

Punnett square		yyss	genotype parent
		ys	gametes
YySs	YS	YySs	genotype offspring
		yellow short	phenotype offspring
	Ys	Yyss	genotype offspring
		yellow long	phenotype offspring
	yS	yySs	genotype offspring
		white short	phenotype offspring
	ys	yyss	genotype offspring
		white long	phenotype offspring
genotype parent	gametes		

There is 25% chance of each of the types of offspring. The results found match this ratio

14 If a mouse has two c alleles, it will not be able to produce pigment, so it will be albino. It will still have the alleles for wild type colour or black colour but they will not be seen because the mouse will be albino. If a mouse is wild-type colour or black colour, it has at least one allele for making pigmnt (C).

phenotypes possible	genotypes
albino	ccAA or ccAa or ccaa
wild type	CCAA or CCAa or CcAA or CcAa
black	CCaa or Ccaa

(a)

Punnett square		ccAA (albino)	genotype parent
		cA	gametes
CCaa (black)	Ca	CcAa wild type	genotype offspring phenotype offspring
genotype parent	gametes		

(b)

Punnett square		CcAa				genotype parent
		CA	Ca	cA	ca	gametes
CcAa	CA	CCAA wild type	CCAa wild type	CcAA wild type	CcAa wild type	genotype offspring phenotype offspring
	Ca	CCAa wild type	CCaa black	CcAa wild type	Ccaa black	genotype offspring phenotype offspring
	cA	CcAA wild type	CcAa wild type	ccAA albino	ccAa albino	genotype offspring phenotype offspring
	ca	CcAa wild type	Ccaa black	ccAa albino	ccaa albino	genotype offspring phenotype offspring
genotype parent	gametes					

The ratio of the phenotypes of the offspring will be
wildtype: 9
black: 3
albino: 4

15 (a) *Refer to Figure 414.*
Baby has phenotype B so can have genotype $I^B I^B$ or $I^B i$.
Mother is type A so can be genotype $I^A I^A$ or $I^A i$.
Father's father is type A so can be genotype $I^A I^A$ or $I^A i$.
Father's mother is type B so can have genotype $I^B I^B$ or $I^B i$.
Baby does not have an allele I^A so he must have received allele I from his mother.
Baby is type B so he must be $I^B i$, as he has received I from his mother.

(b) In order to be $I^B i$, he must have received I^B from his father who must have been $I^B i$, having received I from his father (the paternal grandfather of the baby who was type A) and I^B from his mother (the paternal grandmother who was type B).
Paternal grandfather must have been $I^A i$.
Paternal grandmother was either $I^B I^B$ or $I^B i$.

16

possible phenotypes	genotypes
red polled	$C^R C^R PP$ or $C^R C^R Pp$
red horned	$C^R C^R pp$
roan polled	$C^R C^W PP$ or $C^R C^W Pp$
roan horned	$C^R C^W pp$
white polled	$C^W C^W PP$ or $C^W C^W Pp$
white horned	$C^W C^W pp$

(a) P: red polled   x   white horned
(phenotypes)

$C^R C^R P^P$ x $C^W C^W pp$
(genotypes)

$C^R P$ x $C^W p$
(gametes)

F1 $C^R C^W Pp$ *(genotype)*
roan polled *(phenotype)*

(b) A Punnett square can be used to help work out the F2 generation

Punnett square		CR CW Pp				genotype F1
		$C^R P$	$C^R p$	$C^W P$	$C^W p$	gametes
CR CW Pp	$C^R P$	CR CR PP red polled	CR CR Pp red polled	CR CW PP roan	CR CW Pp roan polled	genotype F2 phenotype F2
	$C^R p$	CR CR Pp red polled	CR CR pp red horned	CR CW Pp roan polled	CR CW pp roan horned	genotype F2 phenotype F2
	$C^W P$	CR CW PP Roan polled	CR CW Pp roan polled	CW CW PP white polled	CW CW Pp white polled	genotype F2 phenotype F2
	$C^W p$	CR CW Pp roan polled	CR CW pp roan horned	CW CW Pp white polled	CW CW pp white horned	genotype F2 phenotype F2
genotype F1	gametes					

F2: red polled (3) + red horned (1) + roan polled (6) + roan horned (2) + white polled (3) + white horned (1)

17

phenotypes possible	genotypes
male normal	X^HY
male haemophiliac	X^hY
female normal	X^HX^H
female carrier	X^HX^h
female haemophiliac	X^hX^h (usually fatal)

(a) Mother must be carrier XHXh. Father is normal XHY. Since Mohammed is male, he cannot be a carrier so he has no chance of passing on the haemophilia allele to his children. He could have children with haemophilia if his wife is a carrier.

(b) Latifa inherits a normal allele from her father XH. She has 50% chance of inheriting a normal allele from her mother XH but also 50% chance of inheriting the haemophila allele from her mother Xh. So she has a 50% chance of being a carrier. If she is a carrier, she will pass her haemophilia allele on to 50% of her children. That means that each of her sons will have a 50% of being a haemophiliac and each of her daughters will have a 50% chance of being a carrier.. So if Latifa is a carrier, 25% of her children are likely to be haemophiliacs.
The above is based on the assumption that Latifa's husband is not a haemophiliac.

18 *Similarities*:
- in both divisions, chromosomes move to the equator
- meiosis II is similar to mitosis
- both involve spindle formation
- in both chromosomes/homologous pairs move to the poles
- both increase the number of cells

Differences

	mitosis	meiosis
purpose	growth, repair	production of gametes
number of divisions	one	two
number of cells produced	two	four
possible in	haploid/diploid nuclei	diploid (or more) nuclei
nuclei produced	as parent	haploid (reduction division)
chromosome movement	chromosomes line up at the equator	meiosis I: homologous pairs line up at the equator
crossing over	no	possible
chiasmata	no	possible

19 Just match the shapes.

CHAPTER 5

1B, 2D, 3A, 4C, 5A, 6D, 7A, 8C, 9A, 10A, 11C, 12C, 13C, 14B, 15A, 16D,

17 There are many possibilities here but one example is given below:

1. a. *insect has wings* . . *go to 2*
   b. *insect does not have wings* . *go to 6*

2. a. *wings are shorter than body* . *go to 3*
   b. *wings are as long as body* .. *go to 4*

3. a. *body is gray* .. .. *E*
   b. *body is striped* . . *F*

4. a. *antennae are short* . .. *G*
   b. *antennae are long* . . *go to 5*

5. a. *antennae are feathered* . *H*
   b. *antennae are not feathered* . *I*

6. a. *insect has tails* . . *go to 7*
   b. *insect does not have tails* .. *go to 8*

7. a. *insect has two tails* . .. *A*
   b. *insect has three tails* . .. *B*

8. a. *insect has antennae* . .. *C*
   b. *insect does not have antennae* . *D*

18 (a) Species: a group of organisms that can interbreed and produce fertile offspring.

(b) A habitat describes just the environment in which a species normally lives while an ecosystem describes the community and its environment.

19 (a) Carbondioxide levels increase from 315 ppm in 1960 to 368 ppm in 2000. Each year, carbondioxide levels fluctuate around the mean value. The fluctuation is about 4 ppm above and below the mean value.

(b) Suggest reasons for these changes.
- The overall increase from 1960 to 2000 can be related to the increased use of fossil fuel which produces carbondioxide when burned.
- Deforestation has reduced the number of plants available to reduce carbondioxide levels by photosynthesis.
- The yearly fluctuations are caused by the seasons: in summer, plants photosynthesize more which reduced carbon dioxide levels while they increase in winter when plants have

dropped their leaves and reduced/stopped photosyntesis.

20 (a) Methane and nitrous oxided

(b) Energy from the sun reaches Earth as light rays with a short wavelength. 70% of this will warm up the Earth surface, be changed into Infra Red radiation (with a longer wavelength) and re-radiate into space. Green house gases absorb some of this IR radiation which causes an increase in the temperature of the atmosphere.

21 (a) The precautionary principle comes from the concept of do no harm. Normally, if there is a certain change planned, e.g. building a nuclear power station at a new site, those against the change (e.g. people living in the area) will have to prove that it will be harmful. This is sometimes difficult to do which would make the change go ahead.

If the precautionary principle is applied, then those who want the change (e.g. those building the nuclear power station) will have to prove that it will not do harm. This may also be difficult but failure to do so will stop the change from taking place.

(b) When it is not certain to what degree a species is endangered, the precautionary principle will dictate that they are placed on the level of the most endangered species, giving it the highest level of protection. If it turns out that the species is indeed endangered, then it is placed correctly. Should it be less endangered than originally thought, the higher level of protection has not caused harm to the species. However, if the species were to be placed incorrectly and too low, then it will be given less protection and the species may be seriously reduced in numbers. This would do a considerable amount of damage to the species.

22 It should look something like this:

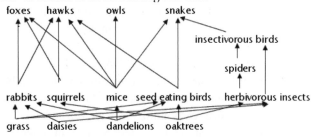

23 Sexual reproduction increases variation because the genetic material of each individual comes from a sperm and an egg cell.

Mendels first law (law of segregation) says that each trait has two alleles but they are seperated during the formation of gametes so that a gamete has only one allele for each gene.

Mendel's second law (law of independent assortment) says that the combination of alleles from different genes is random and that therefore the gametes of one organism are not all the same.

As a result, the combination of male and female gametes (which is sexual reproduction) will lead to a number of different individuals. This should be knows because it is clear that siblings from one set of parents are not identical to each other.

In addition, it is possible that during Prophase I of Meiosis, an exchange of genetic material between non-sister chromatids occus. This is called crossing over and will lead to more new combinations of genes, causing further variation.

24 The Peppered Moth rests on tree trunks covered in off-white lichens. The moth is the same colour and will spread its wings to blend in with their background. Occasionally a black one appears which is quickly seen and eaten by birds.

As a result of the industrial revolution, trees were covered in soot. Lichens died and the tree trunks became black. The white moth now were eaten more often and the few black ones had the advantage. In only a few years, the black moths were more common than the white ones.

25 (a) *Homo sapiens.* Notice that the name should be in intalics or underlined (when writing by hand). The first letter of the genus name is capitalised, everything else in small print.

(b) Kingdom, phylum, class, order, family, genus, species.

26 *Similarities*: both

- are autotrophs/producers
- have chlorophyll for photosyntesis
- have true roots, stems, leaves
- produce seeds

Differences

coniferophyta	angiosperma
have needles	have leaves
no flowers	flowers (although small in wind pollinated plants)
seeds in cones	seeds in ovaries which become fruits

27 (a) all except porifera

(b) all except porifera

(c) platyhelminthes, annelida, mollusca and arthropoda.

(d) porifera, cnidaria

CHAPTER 6

1C, 2B, 3C, 4A, 5B, 6B, 7C, 8A, 9D, 10A, 11B, 12D, 13B, 14B, 15A, 16A, 17B,

18 (a) Refer to Figure 603

(b)

structure	function
whole villus	increase surface area which increases absorption
epithelial cells	these cells are permeable to nutrients which need to be absorbed
microvilli	increase surface area which increases absorption
capillary bed near surface of villus	removes absorbed nutrients and maintains concentration gradient proximity to surface reduces distance and speeds up absorption
lacteal	part of the lymphatic system which absorbs and tranports lipids

19 (a) The blood pressure in arteries can be high and a thick wall is needed to prevent the artery from bursting.

(b) Because a lot of the plasma has left the capillary to become tissue fluid and the remaining fluid is more viscous. This is an advantage because there is more time to exchange materials with the tissue

(c) To prevent backflow of blood. Due to the higher pressure and speed of the blood in arteries, there is no risk of back flow there but the low pressure in veins makes it likely to flow in the wrong direction, e.g in the legs when we are standing up.

20 • nutrients
   • oxygen
   • hormones
   • antibodies
   • heat
   • waste: urea and carbon dioxide

21 (a) antigen enters the organism
   (b) lymphocyte that produces the correct antibody will recognise the antigen
   (c) lymphocyte will form a clone
   (d) all cloned cells produce the same antibody
   (e) antibody will make antigen harmless

22 HIV reduces the number of lymphocytes. Lymphocytes make antibodies so HIV reduces antibody production.

23 (a) Refer to Figures 620 and 621.
   (b)

structure	function
large surface area	a lot of gas exchange can take place at the same time
thin	short diffusion distance
moist	gases can only cross a membrane when dissolved
good blood supply	maintains concentration gradient

(c) An alvelous privides a large surface area for diffusion of gases into and out of the blood.

(d) To maintain the higher concentration of oxygen and the lower concentration of carbondioxide in the lungs so that oxygen will diffuse from the air in the lungs into the blood and carbondioxide from the blood into the air in the lungs.

24 Both refer to a difference in charge across the membrane of a neuron. A resting potential is fairly stable and usually around -70 mV. An action potential is a change in the potential across the membrane. The electric potential will change from -70 mV to +30 mV and back again. An action potential is what is measured as an impulse is conducted through the neuron.

25 (a) Heat centre in the hypothalamus which senses the temperature and compares it to the desired value. Skin arterioles, muscles that flatten or raise up hairs and sweat glands are all effectors.

(b) • vasodilation
   • sweating
   • Increased metabolism
   • 'fluffing' of hair or feathers
   • thick layer of brown fat or of blubber
   • special structure hair

26 Both estrogen and progesterone inhibit secretion of FSH which is necessary for the development of a follicle and hence an egg cell. In the absence of FSH, no follicle will ripen and no egg cell can mature so no fertilisation can take place.

27 • dry skin is difficult to penetrate because it is made of tough cells and there are only few gaps
   • normal bacteria growing on the skin will make it more difficult for pathenogenic bacteria to grow
   • pH of skin is slightly acidic and many pathogens cannot grow there

- mucus is found where there is not enough protection e.g. air passages
- sticky mucus traps bacteria and stops them from spreading

CHAPTER 7

1B, 2C, 3A, 4D, 5B, 6D, 7D, 8B, 9D, 10A,

11 Refer to Figure 703 and mention these points
- DNA is made of two strands
- strands are antiparallel
- strands are kept together by hydrogen bonds between the organic bases
- building blocks of DNA are nucleotides
- nucleotides are linked together by covalent bonds
- covalent bonds are created by condensation reactions
- nucleotide consist of a deoxyribose, a phosphate and an organic base
- base is atached to C1, phosphate to C 5
- organic base can be Adenine, Thymine, Cytosine, Guanine
- a base pair between the strands is always A-T or C-G
- ladder is twisted
- approx 10 nucleotides per full turn

12 (a) helicase unwinds the twisted ladder and breaks the hydrogen bonds between the strands which separates the strands
   (b) RNA primase will form covalent bonds between the RNA nucleotides to form the RNA primer
   (c) DNA polymerase III will form covalent bonds between the DNA nucleotides and the growing strand. It works in a 5' to 3' direction.
   (d) DNA polymerase I removes the RNA primers (mostly from Okazaki fragments) and replace RNA nucleotides with DNA nucleotides
   (e) DNA ligase will attach the DNA fragments that were the Okazaki fragments to form a complete strand

13 Both need energy and work in the same direction (5' to 3')

transcription	translation
DNA to RNA	RNA to protein
more limited number of mRNA is made each time.	many protein molecules are made almost at the sme time
enzymes needed	enzymes and ribosomes and tRNA needed
in nucleus	in cytoplasm

14 (a) mRNA is an RNA copy of the nonsense strand of the DNA. The sequence of the mRNA codons determines the sequence of the amino acids in the polypeptide.
   (b) ribosomes are needed for the tRNA anticodon to bind to the mRNA codon so that the amino acid of the tRNA can be attached to the growing polypeptide chain.
   (c) a codon is a sequence of 3 organic bases that codes for a specific amino acid; an anticodon is a sequence of three organic bases(found on tRNA) complementary to the codon.
   (d) each tRNA has a specific anticodon. Related to this anticodon, tRNA also carries a particular amino acid so that the same amino acid is always found with the same anticodon. tRNA takes the amino acid to the ribosome and allows it to attach to the growing polypeptide chain.

15 • primary structure: covalent bonds
   • secondary structure: hydrogen bonds
   • tertiary structure: hydrophobic interactions, disulfide bonds, hydrogen bonds
   • quaternary structure: hydrogen bonds, positive/negative attraction forces, hydrophobic forces, disulfide bridges

16 • enzymes e.g. maltase which breaks down maltose into glucose and fructose
   • hormones e.g. insulin
   • defense e.g. antibodies/immunoglobins
   • strucrure e.g. spindle fibre in cell division
   • transport e.g. hemoglobin for oxygen transport

17 • they are used to keep the protein in its place: polar amino acids interact with water on either side of the membrane, non-polar amino acids interact with the non-polar lipid bilayer in the centre of the membrane
   • a hollow tube can be created, using polar amino acids at the ends, interacting with the water on either side of the membrane. In the centre, the inside of the cylinder is made of non-polar acids, creating a hydrophilic channel through the membrane.
   • polar and non-polar amino acids can help create the shape of the active site of an enzyme and help provide the forces that keep the substrate in the active site and make sure that other substrate do not fit well and do not stay there.

18 (a) at the active site
   (b) anywhere on the enzyme as long as it is away from the active site
   (c) competitive inhibitor: prontosil non-competitive inhibitor: cyanide

19
- allostery is non-competitive inhibition
- end product is the inhibitor
- end product will attach to the enzyme
- of an reaction earlier in the metabolic reactions
- at a place which is NOT the active site
- will change the shape of the active site
- enzyme no longer works
- no more product produced
- when product runs out
- then no more product to act as allosteric inhibitor
- so reactiom proceeds
- new product formed.

20
- if reaction is A + B → C
- A and B may need to collide with a high amount of energy
- in order to have reaction take place
- only few particles have this energy
- increasing temperature will increase the number of partciples with sufficient energy
- but this could denature proteins in a living system
- when substrates meet at the active site
- the conditions are such that it is easier for the reaction to take place
- less activation energy is needed
- more particles can react at the same time
- rate of reaction increases.

CHAPTER 8

1D, 2A, 3B, 4A, 5D, 6D, 7B, 8D,

9 (a) in the cytoplasm
   (b) in the matrix of the mitochondria
   (c) on the cristae (inner membranes of the mitochondria)

10 Refer to Figure 804

11 (a) The site for the Krebs cycle is the matrix of the mitochondria. It is a watery fluid containing all the enzymes and compounds needed for the Krebs cycle to proceed.
    (b) The site for the electron transport chain is the cristae (folded inner membrane) of the mitochondrion. It has a large surface area so there is a lot of room for many ATP synthetase molecules. It is also impermeable to protons (except where there are ATPase molecules).

(c) Then it would not be possible to build up a higher concentration of protons and chemiosmosis would not work. As a result, no ATP would be produced.

12 Refer to Figure 809.

13 Refer to Figure 810.
The light dependent stage produces ATP and NADPH which are needed to drive the Calvin cycle in the light independent stage. The light independent stage fixes carbon dioxide to produce a triose. This process requires ATP and NADPH, made in the light dependent stage: ATP is needed to phosphorylate GP and to change TP into RuBP. NADPH is needed to reduce glycerate diphosphate into anther triose.

14 (a) they provide the energy and the reducing power to drive the Calvin cycle in the light independent stage.
    (b) it is a simple method of producing ATP
    (c) non-cyclic photophosphorylation produces NADPH which is needed to drive the light independent stage. The advantage of the light independent stage is that it makes carbohydrates which can be used for long term energy storage but also as building materials for new cells so that the plant can grow and reproduce.
    (d) in the Calvin cycle, 3 molecules of carbon dioxide are combined to form a triose molecule; 2 triose molecules will be combined to form glucose.

15 The grana thylakoid provide a large surface for absorbing light the membrane of the grana allows the electron carriers needed for photophosphorylation to be kept in the right order, helping the reaction to proceed. The volume inside the grana is small so that a relatively small number of protons will cause a large difference in concentration across the membrane the stroma is a watery fluid which contains all enzymes and intermediates needed for the Calvin cycle.

16 *Similarities*:
- both use chemiosmosis
- both involve transport of electrons and protons
- both use ATP synthetase to produce ATP from ADP and Pi
- both take place across a membrane which is impermeable to protons
- both buld up a proton gradient across the membrane
- both transport protons into a small space

Differences:

	chloroplasts	mitochondria
site	membrane of granum	membrane of crista
organelle	chloroplast	mitochondrion
source of electrons	water (photolysis)	NADH + H+
ultipmate electron acceptor	NADP	oxygen
protons are pumped into	lumen of the grana	intermembrane space
protons diffuse via ATPase into	stroma	matrix

CHAPTER 9

1C, 2A, 3C, 4D, 5A, 6D, 7A,

8 (a) Refer to Figure 903
   (b) *upper epidermis* reduces water loss
       prevent gas exchange
       allows light to pass
       secretes cuticle
       barrier against infection
   palisade layer photosynthesis
   spongy layer allows rapid diffusion of oxygen and carbon dioxide through air spaces
       photosynthesis
   lower epidermis stomata open/close to allow gas exchange but reduce water loss
       secrete cuticle
       barrier against infection
   vascular tissue **xylem** transports water and mineral from roots to leaves
       phloem transports carbohydrates from source to sink
   (c) *upper epidermis* cells close together - no space between for pathogens to enter or water to evaporate
       transparent (no chloroplasts) - light can pass easily
   palisade layer tighly packed, narrow end to top - maximum exposure to light
   spongy layer air spaces allow rapid diffusion of respiratory gases
       chloroplasts for photosynthesis
   lower epidermis cells close together - no space between for pathogens to enter or water to evaporate
       no chloroplasts
       stomata allows rapid gas exchange

vascular tissue **xylem** dead cells - no cross walls - facilitates transport of water and minerals
   phloem living cells - active transport of carbohydrates

9

	monocotyledenous plants	dicotyledenous plants
veins in leaf	parallel	reticulate (net-like)
distribution of vascular tissue	scattered	in a ring
number of cotyledons in seed	one	two
floral organs	multiples of three	four or five
roots	unbranched	branched
examples	grass, onion, lily and tulip	daisy, oak tree and rose

10 • auxin is group of plant hormones
   • auxin is produced by the apical bud of a plant
   • auxin is transported down the stem as needed
   • auxin stimulates growth
   • by promoting cell division and cell stretching
   • auxin accumulates on the shaded side of the stem
   • which makes the shaded side grow faster
   • so the plant grows towards the light
   • this increases the amount of light on the leaves
   • which increases photosynthesis

11 Water is taken up by osmosis because the concentration of dissolved particles in the root hair cell is greater than that outside. The plant roots take up minerals by active transport this increases the concentration of dissolved particles in the root hair cells. Root hairs increase surface area roots need a large surface area to allow a lot of water uptake at the same time water is taken from roots by xylem. Transpiration pull moves water up the xylem. Cohesion is the force needed for transpiration pull, adhesion enables the water creep up the sides of a capillary tube and supports the flow of water in the plant.

12 Phloem transports sugars and amino acids by pressure flow hypothesis from source (area of production/storage) e.g. leaves or roots to sink (area of use/storage) e.g.fruits/growing points or roots. So carbohydrates/amino acids may go up or down stem at different times. Phloem is made of living cells and transport involves active transport i.e. energy is needed, energy is supplied by companion cells.

13 Please refer to Figure 925.

14 Water is absorbed, gibberelins are made in the cotyledons, amylase is made, starch broken down to maltose which is used to release energy and enable growth.

15 (a) oxygen, water, suitable temperature
   (b) *oxygen*: respiration requires energy and oxygen is needed to release energy
   water: seeds swell up after taking up water which bursts the testa and the presence of water activates enzymes which hydrolyses large molecules
   suitable temperature: germination requires enzymes which need to have a temperature suitable for them to work

16 • there are long day plants, e.g.carnations and clover, and short day plants, e.g. coffee and strawberries
   • long day plants flower in summer, short day plants in autumn (and spring)
   • long day plants only flower when nights are short
   • short day plants only flower when nights are long
   • phytochrome regulates the flowering of plants
   • two states: Pr and Pfr
   • Pr becomes Pfr quickly when exposed to red light
   • Pfr becomes Pr slowly in darkness
   • long day plants need Pfr to flower
   • short day plants only flower when Pfr is absent

CHAPTER 10

1B, 2D, 3C, 4C, 5C, 6A, 7B, 8A

9 Refer to Figure 1001
   Interphase: DNA replication.
   Prophase I: Chromosomes condense.
   Nucleolus becomes invisible.
   Spindle formation.
   Synapsis: homologous chromosomes side by side.
   (the pair is now called a bivalent, the crossover points are called chiasmata).
   *Nuclear membrane disappears (sometimes considered as early metaphase).
   Metaphase I: Bivalents move to the equator.
   Anaphase I: Homologous pairs split up, one chromosome of each pair goes to each pole.

Telophase I: Chromosomes arrive at poles.
   *Spindle disappears.
Prophase II: New spindle is formed at right angles to the previous spindle.
Metaphase I: Chromosomes move to the equator.
Anaphase II: Chromosomes separate, chromatids move to opposite poles.
Telophase II: Chromosomes have arrived at poles.
   Spindle disappears.
   Nuclear membrane reappears.
   Nucleolus becomes visible.
   Chromosomes become chromatin.

10 (a) Mendel's second law: law of independent assortment.
   Any one of a pair of characteristics may combine with either one of another pair.
   (b) Mendel's second law does not apply to linked genes. They inherit together except for those cases where crossing over occurs.

11 (a) wild type colour, wild type wings
   (b) All possible phenotypes and genotypes are:
   r^+ is red eyes, r is white eyes
   w^+ is normal wings, w is vestigial wings

possible phenotypes	corresponding genotypes
red normal	$r^+r^+w^+w^+$, $r^+r\ w^+w^+$, $r^+r^+w^+w$, $r^+r\ w^+w$
red vestigial	r^+r^+ww, $r^+r\ ww$
white normal	$rr\ w^+w^+$, $rr\ w^+w$
white vestigial	$rr\ ww$

Possible genotypes of the parents:

parent	phenotype	possible genotypes
1	white eyes, vestigial wings	$rr\ ww$
2	red eyes, normal wings	$r^+r^+w^+w^+$, $r^+r\ w^+w^+$, $r^+r^+w^+w$, $r^+r\ w^+w$

(c)

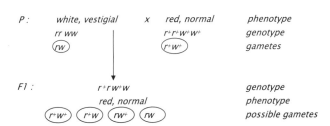

PUNNET SQUARE		Red, normal			
		r⁺w⁺	r⁺w	rw⁺	rw
Red, normal	r⁺w⁺	r⁺r⁺ w⁺w⁺ red, normal	r⁺r⁺ w⁺w red, normal	r⁺r w⁺w⁺ red, normal	r⁺r w⁺w red, normal
	r⁺w	r⁺r⁺ w⁺w red, normal	r⁺r⁺ ww red, vestigial	r⁺r w⁺w red, normal	r⁺r ww red, vestigial
	rw⁺	r⁺r w⁺w⁺ red, normal	r⁺r w⁺w red, normal	rr w⁺w⁺ white, normal	rr w⁺w white, normal
	rw	r⁺r w⁺w red, normal	r⁺r ww red, vestigial	rr w⁺w white, normal	rr ww white, vestigial

(d) *genotypes of the F2:*

r⁺r⁺ w⁺w⁺: 1	r⁺r w⁺w⁺: 2	rr w⁺w⁺: 1
r⁺r⁺ w⁺w: 2	r⁺r w⁺w: 4	rr w⁺w: 2
r⁺r⁺ ww: 1	r⁺r ww: 2	rr ww: 1

phenotypes of the F2:

red, normal:	9
red, vestigial:	3
white, normal:	3
white, vestigial:	1

12 Since haemophilia is a sex-linked trait, boys either display the disease or do not possess the allele. Girls may be carriers, i.e. appear healthy but be able to pass on the trait.

Edward VII was Queen Victoria's oldest son. He did not display hemophilia so did not possess the trait so could not pass it on to his children. Several of Victoria's daughters probably were carriers and passed the trait on to their offspring. Males would display the trait, e.g. Alexis, son of Nicolas II of Russia and Alexandra (granddaughter of Queen Victoria). Daughters could be carriers.

13 (a)

possible phenotypes	corresponding genotypes
grey, straight	g⁺g⁺s⁺s⁺, g⁺g s⁺s⁺, g⁺g⁺s⁺s, g⁺g s⁺s
grey, curly	g⁺g⁺ss, g⁺g ss
black, straight	gg s⁺s⁺, gg s⁺s
black, curly	gg ss

A heterozygous grey, straight winged fly has genotype g⁺g s⁺s.
A black, curly winged fly has genotype gg ss.

P :	grey, straight		black, curly	phenotype
	g⁺g s⁺s	x	gg ss	genotype
	g⁺s⁺, g⁺s, gs⁺, gs		gs	possible gametes

F1	g⁺g s⁺s	g⁺g ss	gg s⁺s	gg ss	genotypes
	grey straight	grey curly	black straight	black curly	phenotypes

(b) The expected ratios for the phenotypes would be grey straight: grey curly: black straight: black curly = 1 : 1 : 1 : 1

(c) As the ratios found show a much higher occurrence of the parental phenotypes, it suggests that the Law of independent assortment did not apply here, which suggests that the traits are linked.

14 (a) C = coloured, c = albino; G = grey, g = black

possible phenotypes	corresponding genotypes
coloured grey	CCGG, CCGg, CcGG, CcGg
coloured black	CCgg, Ccgg
albino	ccGG, ccGg, ccgg

Parent 1: homozygous recessive albino: ccgg
Parent 2: homozygous grey: CCGG

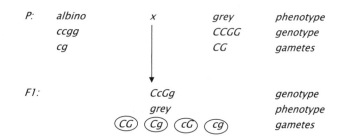

All F1 have the phenotype grey and the genotype CcGg.

(b & c) The predicted ratios of the genotypes of the F2 can be found using a Punnett square. The results will be

CCGG:	1	CcGG:	2	ccGG:	1
CCGg:	2	CcGG:	4	ccGg:	2
CCgg:	1	CcGG:	2	ccgg:	1

(d & e) The predicted ratios of the phenotype of the F2 can be found by using a Punnett square. They are grey : black : albino = 9 : 3 : 4

Normally, the phenotypic ratio of this kind of dihybrid cross is 9:3:3:1 but in this case the "albino grey" and "albino black" are both albino and therefore have the same phenotype. Hence the numbers are added, giving the above ratio.

CHAPTER 11

1D, 2B, 3C, 4A, 5B, 6C, 7C, 8A, 9B, 10D, 11B, 12B, 13A, 14C, !5C, 16D, 17C, 18D, 19B, 20A, 21D,

22 (a) Helper T cells will form a clone and select and activate the correct B cells.

(b) B cells divide to form clones which produce plasma cells and memory cells. Plasma cells produce antibodies against the antigen detected. Memory cells remain present after the infection has passed in order to speed up the production of antibodies in case the antigen is detected again.

23 (a) *Benefits:*
- total elimination of the disease (e.g. smallpox)
- prevention of pandemics and epidemics
- decrease health care costs
- prevent harmful side effects of diseases (e.g. paralysis after polio or problems with eyesight of the child after rubella infection of the mother.

(b) Dangers:
- some vaccines contained the preservative Thimerosal which contains mercury which, at high levels, causes damage to the brain, especially in babies and infants. The preservative was needed to make sure that no other pathogens would grow in the solution with the vaccine. No evidence was found of harmful effects of mercury in vaccinations but as a precaution, it is now used less and less.
- it is possible that an overload of the immune system, e.g. caused by vaccinations against many different diseases in a short time, may make the vaccination less effective and/or cause other problems. It has been speculated that Gulf War syndrome may have been caused by the many vaccinations to protect soldiers from agents of biological warfare.
- a possible link between MMR vaccination and an increased chance of autism; studies carried out since have failed to confirm this link.

24 When a nerve impulse arrives at the muscle, the depolarisation of the motor end plate is passed on to the sarcoplasmic reticulum which causes it to release calcium ions (Ca^{2+}) into the sacroplasm. The calcium ions attach to the troponin which is attached to the tropomyosin. This uncovers the binding sites on the actin for the myosin hooks. The muscle will now contract.

(a) Ca^{2+} is released from the sarcoplasmic reticulum into the sarcoplasm. The calcium ions attach to the troponin which is attached to the tropomyosin.

(b) When troponin binds to calcium ions, it changes its shape. As troponin is attached to tropomyosin, this then makes the tropomyosin move and uncovers the binding sites on actin for the myosin hooks.

(c.) Hooks on myosin will attach to the binding sites on actin. The hooks will then release and repeat the action further down the actin. This is called the ratchet mechanism.

(d) ATP is hydrolysed to ADP. In this process, energy is released which drives the ratchet mechanism.

25
- muscles only contract when they receive an impulse from a nerve
- nerve cells carry depolarisations to muscles
- impulse causes release of calcium in the muscle
- muscle contracts
- muscle is attached to at least 2 bones via tendons
- bones are attached to each other via joint and ligaments
- leverage of bone will make the distance of movement of the bone more than the distance the muscle contracted
- bones move relative to each other (using joints)
- different joints allow different kinds of movement
- antagonistic muscles cause opposite movement

26 *Similarities:*

All blood cells and proteins should remain in the blood.

Since glucose and proteins will not be excreted, the amounts should remain the same. However, it is possible that the concentration has increased if water has been removed.

Differences:

	renal artery	renal vein
urea	more	less
oxygen	more	less
carbon dioxide	less	more
salt	usually more	usually less
hormones	more	less
toxins (e.g. medicin)	more	less

27 (a) oogenesis is the process of forming ova (egg cells).

(b) mitosis occurs in the germination epithelium. One cell mitotically divides into two, one of them proceeds with oogenesis (the primary oocyte), the other remains as germination cell and can have another mitotic division.

(c) meiosis reduces the number of chromosomes in the gamete. Since a gamete needs to fuse with another gamete to start a new individual, each gamete must have half the number of chromosomes so that the new organism has the same number as either parent.

(d) spermatozoa are very small and the 4 spermatids that result from Meiosis I and II can all become spermatozoa. Ova are very large since they need to contain reserve food for the zygote. If each of the cells produced in Meiosis I and II would be an ovum, then each ovum would only contain one quarter of the reserve food of the original primary oocyte. As it is, two or three polar bodies are produced to reduce the amount of genetic material but almost all the cell material goes to one ovum, giving it the best chance to grow out to a new individual if it is fertilised.

28 (a) HCG is secreted by the trophoblastic cells of the developing embryo

(b) HCG maintains the corpus luteum which produces progesterone

(c) At a later stage, the placenta will start to produce progesterone so the corpus luteum no longer is needed.

(d) Obtain monoclonal antibodies against the HCG (human chorionic gonadotropin). Fix them in place on a testing stick/strip. Add urine to the testing stick/strip. If the HCG is present in the urine (as it will be if the woman is pregnant), it will attach to the antibodies. The test has been so designed that this will give a colour showing a positive test.

CHAPTER 12

1   • not enough proteins in the blood
    • tissue fluid is not returned to the blood
    • fluid retention
    • retardation of mental and physical growth.

2 (a) PKU is phenylketouria.

(b) PKU is a genetic disorder. PKU patients lack the gene to produce functioning phenylalanine hydroxylase.

(c) Phenylalanine hydroxylase changes phenylalanine into tyrosine. Without this enzyme, phenylalanine accumulates and is changed into phenylpyruvic acid which causes retardation.

(d) PKU causes severe problems unless it is diagnosed early and a special diet is followed. So in many countries all babies are screened within hours after birth.

(e) The diet focusses on avoiding most protein since levels of phenylalanine (an amino acid) must be kept low. With low levels of phenylalanine in the diet, the affected children lead normal lives.

3 (a) antioxidant activity
       collagen synthesis
       role in immune system
       reduce chance of forming arterial plaque

(b) Current FDA recommendation is 70 mg/day.

(c) megavitamin therapy of vitamin C may reduce chance of respiratory infection and/or cancer.

(d) rebound malnutrition is caused by taking larger doses of e.g. vitamin C for an extended time. The organism will excrete the surplus and if levels are then reduced back to normal, it may take time to stop the excretion so that the organism actually suffers from a lack of vitamin C.

4 (a) sex (male/female); level of activity; age (which also relates to activity, size and growth); special circumstances e.g. disease or pregnancy/nursing.

(b) sex: males need more energy than females because males tend to be larger and females tend to have more subcutaneous fat (less heat lost).
level of activity: the more active a person, the more energy is needed.
age: younger is smaller smaller people need less energy but (fast) growing people need more energy whereas older people are often less active so need less energy.
special circumstances:
recovering from illness make require extra energy
pregnancy/breastfeeding will require extra energy

5   • fibre is not digested
    • causes slight irritation of the wall of the intestine
    • increases peristalsis
    • moves food faster through intestine
    • softer stools (feces)
    • reduced constipation and hemaroids
    • may help weight loss as people feel full sooner on high fibre diet
    • may reduce cholesterol levels but not proven

6   (a)

	Human milk	Artificial milk
monosaccharide	rich in lactose	no or little lactose
protein	more whey, less casein	less whey, more casein
antibodies	present	absent
fats	rich in omega-3 fatty acids (DHA)	some brands add DHA but usually less than in human milk
enzyme	contains lipase	no lipase
minerals	most iron absorbed	most iron not absorbed

(b)   *advantages of breastfeeding*:
   - breast milk contains antibodies which help the baby fight infections
   - proteins in breast milk are easier digested than those in artificial milk
   - calcium and iron in breast milk are better absorbed
   - breast feeding helps the uterus contract so that the bleeding after delivery will be shorter
   - breast feeding reduces the risk of breast cancer
   - breast feeding improves the bond between mother and child
   - breast feeding is cheaper - very important in some parts of the world
   - mother usually does not ovulate while breast feeding (natural contraception)

   disadvantages of breast feeding
   - if the mother takes medication for an illness, it may also be found in breast milk
   - breast feeding requires more strength from the baby than bottle feeding so weak/ill babies may not be able to get enough milk
   - there may be an increased chance of post natal depression but this is not proven

CHAPTER 13

1   - muscles need energy to contract
   - glycogen can be broken down to glucose
   - glucose can be used to release energy/ATP
   - in aerobic and anaerobic respiration
   - aerobic respiration releases most energy/ATP
   - and takes place in mitochondria
   - if sufficient oxygen is available

2   - myoglobin is protein
   - made of one chain of polypeptide
   - able to bind oxygen
   - stored in muscles
   - myoglobin has greater affinity for oxygen than haemoglobin
   - makes myoglobin store oxygen
   - oxygen released from myoglobin when all available oxygen used up.

3   (a)   *Benefits*
   - increased amount of oxygen can be taken to muscles
   - so more aerobic respiration/less anaerobic respiration
   - more energy yielded per molecule of glucose
   - more energy available/energy available for longer time
   - less lactate produced - lactate can lead to fatigue and muscle cramp
   - more chance to win
     personal achievement/honour
     team achievement/honour
     prize money / scholarship / commercial opportunities

   Risks
   - to be disqualilfied and/or prosecuted
   - knowledge that you gained an unfair advantage
   - anabolic steroids: liver damage, fertility problems, females become more masculin
   - blood doping:
   - more viscous blood - heart failure, stroke
   - improperly stored - infection
   - using donor blood - transmission of e.g. HIV or hepatitis
   - EPO: more viscous blood - heart failure, stroke

4

Sprains	overstretching of a ligament in a joint
Torn ligaments	overstretching of a ligament causing rupture
Torn muscle	most severe case of muscle strain; muscle fibres may tear
Dislocation of joints	the bones in the joint are moved, relative to each other, and do not return to their original position
Intervertebral disc damage	one of the discs may may buldge out and put pressure on the nerves in the spinal cord.

CHAPTER 14

1D, 2A, 3D, 4A, 5B, 6A, 7D, 8D, 9B, 10D,

11 • primary structure: covalent bonds
  • secondary structure: hydrogen bonds
  • tertiary structure: hydrophobic interactions, disulfide bonds, hydrogen bonds
  • quaternary structure: hydrogen bonds, positive/negative attraction forces, hydrophobic forces, disulfide bridges

12 • enzymes e.g. maltase which breaks down maltose into glucose and fructose
  • hormones e.g. insulin
  • defense e.g. antibodies/immunoglobins
  • strucrure e.g. spindle fibre in cell division
  • transport e.g. hemoglobin for oxygen transport

13 • they are used to keep the protein in its place: polar amino acids interact with water on either side of the membrane, non-polar amino acids interact with the non-polar lipid bilayer in the centre of the membrane
  • a hollow tube can be created, using polar amino acids at the ends, interacting with the water on either side of the membrane. In the centre, the inside of the cylinder is made of non-polar acids, creating a hydrophilic channel through the membrane.
  • polar and non-polar amino acids can help create the shape of the active site of an enzyme and help provide the forces that keep the substrate in the active site and make sure that other substrate do not fit well and do not stay there.

14 (a) at the active site
  (b) anywhere on the enzyme as long as it is away from the active site
  (c) competitive inhibitor: prontosil
      non-competitive inhibitor: cyanide

15 • allostery is non-competitive inhibition
  • end product is the inhibitor
  • end product will attach to the enzyme
  • of an reaction earlier in the metabolic reactions
  • at a place which is NOT the active site
  • will change the shape of the active site
  • enzyme no longer works
  • no more product produced
  • when product runs out
  • then no more product to act as allosteric inhibitor
  • so reactiom proceeds
  • new product formed.

16 • if reaction is A + B → C
  • A and B may need to collide with a high amount of energy
  • in order to have reaction take place
  • only few particles have this energy
  • increasing temperature will increase the number of partciples with sufficient energy
  • but this could denature proteins in a living system
  • when substrates meet at the active site
  • the conditions are such that it is easier for the reaction to take place
  • less activation energy is needed
  • more particles can react at the same time
  • rate of reaction increases.

17 (a) in the cytoplasm
  (b) in the matrix of the mitochondria
  (c) on the cristae (inner membranes of the mitochondria)

18 Refer to Figure 804

19 (a) The site for the Krebs cycle is the matrix of the mitochondria. It is a watery fluid contaning all the enzymes and compounds needed for the Krebs cycle to proceed.
  (b) The site for the electron transport chain is the cristae (folded inner membrane) of the mitochondrion. It has a large surface area so there is a lot of room for many ATP synthetase molecules. It is also impermeable to protons (except where there are ATPase molecules).
  (c) Then it would not be possible to build up a higher concentration of protons and chemiosmosis would not work. As a result, no ATP would be produced.

20 Refer to Figure 809.

21 Refer to Figure 810.
  The light dependent stage produces ATP and NADPH which are needed to drive the Calvin cycle in the light independent stage. The light independent stage fixes carbon dioxide to produce a triose. This process requires ATP and NADPH, made in the light dependent stage: ATP is needed to phosphorylate GP and to change TP into RuBP. NADPH is needed to reduce glycerate diphosphate into anther triose.

22 (a) they provide the energy and the reducing power to drive the Calvin cycle in the light independent stage.
  (b) it is a simple method of producing ATP

(c) non-cyclic photophosphorylation produces NADPH which is needed to drive the light independent stage. The advantage of the light independent stage is that it makes carbohydrates which can be used for long term energy storage but also as building materials for new cells so that the plant can grow and reproduce.

(d) in the Calvin cycle, 3 molecules of carbon dioxide are combined to form a triose molecule; 2 triose molecules will be combined to form glucose.

23 The grana thylakoid provide a large surface for absorbing light the membrane of the grana allows the electron carriers needed for photophosphorylation to be kept in the right order, helping the reaction to proceed. The volume inside the grana is small so that a relatively small number of protons will cause a large difference in concentration across the membrane the stroma is a watery fluid which contains all enzymes and intermediates needed for the Calvin cycle.

24 *Similarities*:
- both use chemiosmosis
- both involve transport of electrons and protons
- both use ATP synthetase to produce ATP from ADP and Pi
- both take place across a membrane which is impermeable to protons
- both buld up a proton gradient across the membrane
- both transport protons into a small space

Differences:

	chloroplasts	mitochondria
site	membrane of granum	membrane of crista
organelle	chloroplast	mitochondrion
source of electrons	water (photolysis)	NADH + H+
ultimpate electron acceptor	NADP	oxygen
protons are pumped into	lumen of the grana	intermembrane space
protons diffuse via ATPase into	stroma	matrix

CHAPTER 15

D1 ORIGIN OF LIFE ON EARTH

1. A Miller and Urey placed methane, ammonia, water and hydrogen into their apparatus to stimulate the hydrogen-rich reducing atmosphere believed to have been present on the pre-biotic Earth.

2. D An endosymbiont is an organism that has a mutally beneficial symbiotic relationship with a host organism while living in the host. Eukaryotes probably evolved when larger prokaryotes absorbed smaller prokaryotes and formed a symbiotic relationship.

3. B Current living organisms on the Earth's surface are protected from the harmful and damaging effects of ultraviolet radiation by the ozone layer in the upper atmosphere. The ozone molecules absorb solar ultraviolet radiation.

4. A The early atmosphere of the pre-biotic Earth is thought to have been reducing in nature due to the absence of oxygen. It is believed that oxygen only entered the atmosphere following the appearance of photosynthetic prokaryotes.

5. A The first organic molecule able to replicate on the pre-biotic Earth is currently believed by many Molecular Biologists to have been RNA. This hypothesis has been strengthened by the discovery of ribozymes which consist of short lengths of catalytic RNA. The ribosome may also employ catalytic RNA during protein synthesis.

6. C The pre-biotic atmosphere is thought to been reducing in nature and characterised by hydrogen and carbon rich molecules. The presence of oxygen would have made the atmosphere oxidising in nature and prevented the pre-biotic synthesis reactions.

7. C The endosymbiotic theory suggests that the ancestors of some eukaryotic organelles, notably the chloroplast and mitochondria, were originally free-living prokaryotes that entered into a symbiotic relationship with another prokaryote to form an ancestral eukaryote cell.

8. D There is no atmosphere or liquid water on the Moon and the daily range in surface temperatures is too high to support life.

9. D A common feature of all living organisms, including viruses, is that they contain nucleic acids (DNA and /or RNA).

10. A Oxygen was probably not present in the Earth's early atmosphere. The majority of the oxygen present in the current atmosphere was generated by photosynthesis. The Earth's early pre-biotic atmosphere probably originated from volcanic gases - free oxygen gas was not present.

11. B   The current estimate of the Earth's age, based upon dating of the oldest rocks, is about 4.5 billion years ago.

12. B   Clays may have catalysed the formation of organic polymers, such as proteins and nucleic acids, on the surface of their lattices.

13. D   The observation that DNA in the eukaryotic nucleus codes for many of the enzymes in mitochondria is not strong and direct evidence for the role of endosymbiosis in the origin of eukaryotes. (However, it could be argued that over time many mitochondrial genes were transferred to the nucleus).

14. B   Proteinoid microspheres are only formed when amino acids are heated at relatively high temperatures for a prolonged period of time.

15. D   This is a description of the endosymbiotic theory.

16. A   Prokaroytes do not possess lysosomes or Golgi apparatus. Their digestive enzymes are present in the cytoplasm.

17. C   The theory that life on Earth was initiated by the arrival of organic molecules and, perhaps even bacteria on asteroids and meteorites, is termed panspermia.

18   Both mitochondria and chloroplasts can arise only from pre-existing mitochondria and chloroplasts by a process of binary fission. (They cannot be formed in a cell that lacks them because nuclear genes encode only some of the proteins of which they are composed).
Both mitochondria and chloroplasts have their own genome and it resembles that of prokaryotes not that of the nuclear genome: both genomes consist of a single circular molecule of DNA and there are no histones associated with the DNA.
Both mitochondria and chloroplasts have their own ribosomes (70S), which closely resemble that of prokaryotes not the 80S ribosomes found in the cytoplasm of eukaryotes.
A number of antibiotics that act by blocking protein synthesis in bacteria also block protein synthesis within mitochondria and chloroplasts. They do not interfere with protein synthesis in the cytoplasm of the eukaryotes.
Conversely, inhibitors of protein synthesis by eukaryotic ribosomes do not have any effect on bacterial protein synthesis nor on protein synthesis within mitochondria and chloroplasts.

19   Miller and Urey used a reflux apparatus to re-circulate water vapour and a mixture of methane, ammonia and hydrogen (believed to reflect the composition of the early atmosphere) through a chamber where they were exposed to a continuous high voltage electrical discharge (spark) that stimulated lightning. After several days Miller and Urey analysed the mixture and detected a number of amino acids. Later experiments involving hydrogen cyanide and ammonia resulted in the formation of the base adenine.

20   Panspermia is a theory or hypothesis, that suggests that the 'seeds' of life are prevalent throughout the Universe and life on Earth began by such 'seeds' landing on Earth and replicating. One line of evidence comes from research that shows there are many more potential habitats for life than Earth-like planets. There is some evidence to suggest that bacteria may be able to survive for very long periods of time even in deep space (and may therefore be the underlying mechanism behind Panspermia). Bacteria and more complex organisms have been found in more extreme environments, such as black smokers or oceanic volcanic vents. Some strains of bacteria have been found living at temperatures above 100 °C, others in strongly alkaline environments, and others in extreme acidic conditions. Semi-dormant bacteria have been found in ice cores over a mile beneath the Antarctic - this lends credibility to the concept of sustaining the components of life on the surface of icy comets. The presence of past liquid water on the planet Mars, suggested by river-like formations, was confirmed by the Mars Exploration Rover missions. Possible water oceans on Europa, one of Saturn's moons, and perhaps other moons in the Solar system.

21   Ribose sugars (found in RNA) are much easier to synthesis under simulated pre-biotic conditions than are deoxyribose sugars (found in DNA). Single stranded RNA, unlike single stranded DNA, can form, via hydrogen bonding a variety of complex three-dimensional configurations. It is suspected that ribosomal RNA plays an active role in the synthesis of proteins in ribosomes. Several RNA sequences have been demonstrated to be catalytic, for example, self-splicing introns – so-called ribozymes.

D2 SPECIES AND SPECIATION

1.   C   The finches, although originating from the same ancestral species, evolved separately due to the different habitats colonised. A process of adaptive radiation occurred resulting in the formation of

the thirteen new species each adapted to a unique habitat on the island.

2. D The relatively sudden appearance of a number of new species, without intermediates, is termed punctuated equilibrium.

3. A Natural selection is slowest when migration is absent (no new variation is introduced into the population); when the selection pressure is low the rate of evolution will be low and when variation due to gene mutation is low, consequently there will be little genetic variation for natural selection to act on.

4. B All the alleles present in the gametes of a sexually reproducing population are known as the population's gene pool.

5. B Birds A and B successfully interbreed and produce viable offspring. This is the Biological definition of a species (that reproduces sexually)

6. C The term 'Gradualism' in Darwin's theory of evolution refers to the emergence of complex Biological adaptations, for example, the eye, evolved in many small incremental steps.

7. D Members of the same species do vary in phenotype, frequently, two or more varieties or morphs can be identified.

8. B Reproductive barriers prevent different species from successfully interbreeding. The various reproductive barriers which isolate species can be classified as either prezygotic or postzygotic. Prezygotic barriers are mechanisms which prevent the fusion of the ovum and the sperm so that no zygote can form. Postzygotic barriers are mechanisms that prevent a zygote from developing into a fertile adult offspring.

9. A The periodic events in which extinction rates increase dramatically are termed mass extinction events. They may be caused by volcanic eruptions, meteor impacts and/or long term changes in the global climate.

10. A Adaptive radiation is the production of ecologically diverse species from a common ancestral stock or population, for example, Darwin's finches.

11. B The term microevolution refers to an increase or decrease of allele frequencies within a gene pool.

12. C One form of reproductive isolation is spatial isolation. If members of two populations never encounter each other, they will never mate and no gene flow will occur.

13. A Punctuated equilibrium does not invoke large evolutionary steps via macromutations with large effects on the phenotype.

14. D Behavioural isolation involves genetic modifications to behaviour that lead to lack of mating between two groups of a species. Its continued presence may eventually result in speciation.

15. A A pre-zygotic isolating mechanism prevents fertilisation (the fusion of the sperm and ovum nuclei).

16. D Transient polymorphism is being exhibited: there is clearly no balancing selection occurring since there is random mating and both morphs are exhibiting equal reproductive success.

17. D The maintenance of the frequency of both dominant and recessive genes over a number of generations by selecting for the heterozygotes. Balanced polymorphism explains the discrepancy in number of individuals with sickle-cell disease compared to sickle-cell trait in Africa compared to North American blacks.

18. C The increase in the frequency of the dark melanic form of Biston betularia is thought to be the result of natural selection. The dark forms were better camouflaged on the soot covered trunks and thus prone to less predation by birds. The mutation rate would have been approximately constant during this period of time.

19 (a) $2.6\% = 2.6/100 = 0.026$ (b) $p^2 + 2pq + q^2 = 1$
Let q represent the frequency of the HbS allele
$q^2 = 0.026$; $q = \sqrt{0.026} = 0.161$

(b) Let p represent the frequency of the HbA allele $p + q = 1$; $p = 1 - 0.161 = 0.839$ Hence, frequency of heterozygotes $= 2pq = 2 \times 0.839 \times 0.161 = 0.270$ Number of heterozygotes in population $= 600 \times 0.270 = 162$.

(c) Balanced polymorphism is being exhibited.

(d) The force responsible for maintaining this polymorphism is termed heterozygote advantage – the heterozygote is fitter than either homozygote, since it is immune to malaria.

20 (a) Let p represent the frequency of M; p = 0.5 and let q represent the frequency of m; q = 0.5.

At equilibrium the genotype frequencies will be 0.25 MM, 0.5 Mm and 0.25 mm, according to the Hardy-Weinberg equation. Therefore the phenotypic ratio is 0.75 melanic: 0.25 pale.

(b) 500 mm moths will be eaten leaving 500 MM and 1000 mm.

Number of alleles remaining = (2 x 1500) = 3000

Number of M alleles = (2 x 500) + 1000 = 2000

Number of m alleles = 1000

Frequency of M = 2000/3000 = 0.667

Frequency of m = 1000/3000 = 0.333

(c) Out of 2000 moths, 500 mm will survive. There are no melanic forms, so the frequency of m = 1.0.

(d) m and M.

(e) Transient polymorphism is being exhibited.

D3 HUMAN EVOLUTION

1. B A. erectus is not a species of Australopithecus. Homo erectus is in a different genus and species.

2. C Anatomical and biochemical evidence, especially maternal mitochondrial DNA sequence analysis, strongly suggest that modern man evolved in Africa. The so-called 'Out of Africa' hypothesis.

3. A The species of Homo in order of evolutionary appearance are: H. habils, H. erectus, H. neanderthalensis and H. sapiens.

4. A In modern humans the head is not kept in position by powerful neck muscles.

5. A Cultural evolution is learned behaviour which is passed from generation to generation via non-genetic processes, for example, transmission of knowledge via books and the passing on of religious beliefs and cultural practices or language.

6. B The first Australopithecine fossils date back to approximately 5 million years ago. They have only been found in Africa.

7. C Binocular vision is a characteristic of the order primates.

8. D The genus Homo lived with the genus Australopithecus in East Africa for about 1 million years.

9. C Homo sapiens made the most sophisticated tools.

10. D All of the hominid skeletons show evidence of bipedalism to some degree.

11. B Tool use is probably restricted to the genus Homo – Homo habilis was the first member of this genus.

12. D Humans and apes are presently classified in the same category at all of the following levels except genus. Humans belong in their own genus (Homo). Apes are divided among four genera. Humans and apes belong in the same Order: Primates, Class: Mammalia, Phylum: Chordata, Kingdom: Animalia.

13. D Of the living genera of apes, the one most closely related to humans are the chimpanzees (that is, the common chimpanzee and the pygmy chimpanzee or bonobo).

14. C Opposable thumbs is a feature that sets primates apart from all other mammals. The ability to produce milk is a characteristic of all mammals that distinguishes them from the other vertebrate Classes; placental embryonic development is a characteristic of the placental mammals that distinguishes them from the marsupials and monotremes.

15. B Two important characteristics of the first hominids were bipedal locomotion and relatively small brains.

16. C The oldest hominid fossils have all been discovered in Africa.

17. B Early hominids dating to between 6 and 3 million years ago are considered primitive because they possessed many ancestral characteristics common to all hominids.

18. B The fossil specimen nicknamed "Lucy" is an example of Australopithecus afarensis.

19. D The fossil footprints at Laetoli show clear bipedal characteristics which include: non-divergent big toe, heel strike and a well developed arch on the foot.

20. A The fossil record strongly suggests that bipedalism evolved 3.5 million years before tool use.

21. C Neoteny refers to a delay in the maturation process, especially that of the cerebral cortex. It is therefore possible that intelligence and learning are enhanced before the organism reaches sexual maturity.

22. D Fossils of Homo erectus have only been found in tropical Africa and Asia, for example, Indonesia.

23. B Cultural evolution is a rapid and powerful force, for example, the transmission of knowledge and skills via learning.

24. C When fossils are unearthed, it is generally found that the bones or shells of the dead organism have been replaced by hard minerals, for example, calcium carbonate.

25. B Water with dissolved oxygen is a poor preservative medium for the remains of animals and plants. These conditions would encourage the growth of bacteria which would digest the remains.

26. C The half life of carbon-14 is relatively short it can only be used to date organic remains that are less than 70,000 years old

27 (a) (i) The genus is Homo; the species is floresiensis.
      (ii) To demonstrate that LB1 is not an aberrant individual, but was a typical member of the population.
   (b) (i) Dwarfing may be common on islands due to the relatively limited amount of resources, for example, food supply and breeding space and lack of predators. Smaller animals may also be able to achieve thermoregulation on smaller amounts of food.
       (ii) A general increase.
   (c) It suggests that how the brain is 'wired up', namely, its complexity (the number of neuronal synapses), is perhaps more important than its absolute size or brain to body size ratio.
   (d) The use of tools.

28 (a) There are fewer complementary base pairs and hence fewer hydrogen bonds to hold the two strands together.
   (b) The DNA of distantly genetically related species has less complementary base pairs and hence there will a greater number of mismatched base pairs. Fewer hydrogen bonds are formed and hence less heat is required to separate or 'melt' the strands. Closely related species will have more complementary based pairs and hence a greater

number of matched base pairs. A larger number of hydrogen bonds are formed and hence more heat is required to separate or 'melt' the strands.
   (c) 30/7.3= 4.1 million years
   (d) 4.1 million years x 1.9 = 7.8 million years
   (e) A = gibbons; B = orang-utan
       Palaeontology – the study of fossils; study of amino acid sequences in proteins, for example, hemoglobin and cytochrome c oxidase.

D4 THE HARDY-WEINBERG PRINCIPLE

1. A For a Hardy-Weinberg equilibrium to be maintained and for evolution not occur, there has to be a large population, isolation from other populations (that is, no immigration or migration), no mutations, random mating and no selection pressure.

2. A $p^2 + 2pq + q^2 =1$ represents the Hardy-Weinberg equation.

3. D In the Hardy-Weinberg equation, p represents the frequency of a dominant allele.

4. B In the Hardy-Weinberg equation, q represents the frequency of a recessive allele.

5. C The Hardy-Weinberg principle assumes that the population is not experiencing mutation.

6. B $p^2 + 2pq + q^2 =1$; p = 0.7; q = 0.3; 2pq = (2 x 0.7 x 0.3) = 0.42

7. D Significant deviations from the frequencies predicted by the Hardy-Weinberg principle may indicate that natural selection is occurring and hence altering allele and genotype frequencies over time.

8. D $p^2 + 2pq + q^2 =1$; $q^2=0.09$; q = 0.09 =0.3

9. B $p^2 + 2pq + q^2 =1$; q = 0.3, hence p = 0.7; 2pq = (2 x 07 x 0.3) = 0.42

10. C The Hardy-Weinberg principle can be applied to three or more alleles. For example, the expression when applied to three alleles takes the form of $(p + q + r)^2$, which when expanded gives $p^2 + q^2 + r^2 + 2pq + 2rq + 2rp = 1$.

11. A Random mating will maintain the proportion of dominant to recessive characteristics in a population from generation to generation. This

is because the population is in Hardy-Weinberg equilibrium and allele frequencies remain constant over time.

12 Frequency of genotype BB = p^2 = 0.8^2 = 0.64
Frequency of genotype Bb = 2pq = 2 x 0.8 x 0.2 = 0.32
Frequency of genotype bb = q^2 = 0.2^2 = 0.04

13 p^2 = frequency of AA 2pq = frequency of Aa
q^2 = frequency of aa, whose frequency is 1 in 20000 q^2
= 1/20000 = 0.00005
Therefore, q = $\sqrt{0.00005}$ = 0.007 p = 1 – q = 0.933
Hence, the frequency of heterozygotes
= 2 x 0.993 x 0.007 = 0.014

14 (a) Let q^2 represent the frequency of the homozygous recessive genotype.
q^2 = = 0.23
In males q = 0.48.
q^2 = = 0.16.
In females q = 0.40.

(b) The samples of males and females are small and the differences in calculated allele frequencies is due to sampling error.

15 (a) q^2=1/1000 = 0.0001, therefore, q = $\sqrt{0.0001}$ = 0.01
p + q = 1; p = 1 – 0.99
Let 2pq represent the frequency of the heterozygotes.
2pq = 2 x 0.01 x 0.99 = 0.0198
2000 x 0.0198 = 39.6
Hence about 40 people in 2000 would be expected to be heterozygous.

(b) If the couple have already had one phenylketonuric child, they must both be heterozygous. The probability of two heterozygotes having a heterozygous child is or 50%.

16 (a) The 53% resistant rats have the genotypes RR or Rr. The 47% non-resistant rats have the genotype rr.
q^2 = 0.53, therefore q = 0.73; p + q = 1,
therefore p = 1 – q; p = 0.27
Therefore frequency of R allele = 0.27.

(b) p = 0.27 and q = 0.73; p2 = 0.073 (RR); 2pq = 0.39 (Rr); q^2= 0.53
Out of 100 rats, 7 are RR, 40 are Rr and 53 are rr. Non-resistant rats have the genotype rr. If all these rats were killed, there would be 7 RR and 40 Rr rats remaining.

(c) 7 + 40 = 47 animals remaining. 2 x 47 = 94 alleles.
Number of r alleles = 47; frequency of r allele = = 0.5.

Substituting q = 0.5 into the Hardy-Weinberg equation, the frequency of non-resistant rats (rr) = q^2 = 0.25.

D5 PHYLOGENY AND SYSTEMATICS

1. C The universality of the genetic code is strong evidence for a single or unitary origin of life on Earth. It is very conserved and arose early in evolution.

2. C Homology refers to the appearance of a trait that was present in a common ancestor of two or more related groups of organisms.

3. D This phenomenon is known as an evolutionary or molecular clock. It is a consequence of the neutral theory of evolution which holds that in any given DNA sequence, mutations accumulate at an approximately constant rate as long as the DNA sequence retains its original function.

4. D Homologous features imply structural and developmental similarities, where the structures concerned may not perform the same function. The human hand and whale fin both share the same basic pentadactyl limb structure.

5. A This suggests that reptiles, birds, and mammals have a common evolutionary ancestor.

6. B The toad, the amphibian, is the most distantly related, in evolutionary terms, of the organisms. The common ancestor of all toads and all the organisms evolved before the common ancestor of the other organisms.

7. B The term phylogeny describes the branching sequence of the evolution by natural selection of organisms.

CHAPTER 16

1 (a) retina
(b) rods and cones
(c) rods
Several rods are linked to one bipolar neuron. This means that their impulses are 'added up' and this explains their higher light sensitivity. However it also reduces accuracy.

(d) Rods and cones contain photopigments that are broken down when exposed to light. This causes the cells to send an action potential to the brain.

2 (a) behaviour which normally occurs in all members of a species, including in young and inexperienced animals.
   (b) innate behaviour is controlled by genes
   (c) taxes and kineses
   Euglena going towards the light is a phototaxis. Woodlice moving faster and turning more often is a kinesis.

3 • learning may benefit individual and/or group
   • animals can learn how to catch food efficiently or avoid food
   • e.g. bear catching salmon and bird avoiding to eat wasps
   • which makes it more efficient
   • warning calls increase safety of all individuals in the group
   • e.g. monkeys
   • other cooperative behaviour
   • e.g. hunting of dolphins

4 • **psychoactive** drugs influence the brain by affecting it at the level of the neurotransmitters.
   • They can increase or decrease postsynaptic transmission.
   • psychoactive drugs can cause dependence
   • *excitatory* drugs work by releasing the neurotransmittor, mimicing its effect or reducing or delaying the re-uptake of the neurotransmittor, prolonging its effect
     nicotine stimulates receptors that respond to acetyl choline causes increase in adrenaline making people feel more alert
     cocaine blocks the re-uptake of dopamine causing people to feel happy
     amphetamines release dopamine causing improved concentration and performance
   • *inhibitory* drugs block neurotransmittor receptors
     benzodiazepines increases the inhibitory effect of GABA slow down the brain and calm people down
     alcohol increases the inhibitory effect of GABA and reduces inhibitions
     tetrahydrocannabinol THC blocks cannaboid receptors and cause relaxation and pain relief

5 (a) The sympathetic nervous system is part of the autonomous nervous system and not under voluntary control. The sympathetic nervous system is involved in action e.g. fright, fight, flight response
   (b) It increases heart rate, contracts the radial muscles of the iris and reduce the blood flow to the gut.
   (c) Increasing heart rate will pump more blood round the body, also to the muscles. Blood carries food and oxygen, needed to release energy by cellular respiration. Contracting radial muscles in iris will increase size of pupil which will allow more light into the eye and better vision. Blood will be redirected from the gut to e.g. muscles, increasing speed or strength.

6 (a) Altruism is behaviour which benefits another individual but at cost to the performer
   (b) (i) A worker bee being killed while defending the hive
       (ii) A male blue throated side blotched lizards form partnerships; occasionally one of them spends so much time defending the territory that he does not mate - the other one can mate because the territory is defended
       (iii) Vampire bats regurgitating blood for another bat that did not feed for some days
   (c) Genetically related individuals benefit if another individual carrying some of their genes increases its chances of survival.
   Reciprocal altruism in bats: individuals benefit from blood regurgitated by others only if they themselves also feed others when needed

CHAPTER 17

F1 DIVERSITY OF MICROBES

1.D, 2C, 3B, 4D, 5A, 6A, 7D, 8B, 9D, 10D, 11D, 12A, 13C, 14B, 15C, 16C, 17C, 18B, 19B, 20A, 21D, 22A, 23D, 24B, 25D, 26B,

27 (a) Refer to Figures 215 and 1707 in text book
   (b) Gram negative bacteria have a much thinner cell wall than Gram positive bacteria. Hence, the cell wall does not retain the stain (crystal iodine complex).
   (c) Escherichia and Salmonella.
   (d) Both gram negative and gram positive bacteria both exhibit quorum sensing. Briefly outline what happens during this process.
   (e) The membrane lipids are composed of straight carbon chains attached to glycerol by an ester linkage (-CO-O-); histones and introns are absent.

F2 MICROBES AND THE ENVIRONMENT

1A, 2C, 3C, 4A, 5C, 6C, 7B

8   Refer to Figure 1726 in the text book

F3   MICROBES AND BIOTECHNOLOGY

1A, 2B, 3D, 4A, 5B, 6D, 7D, 8A, 9A, 10B

F4   MICROBES AND FOOD RODUCTION

1B, 2D, 3D, 4B, 5A

F5   METABOLISM OF MICROBES

1B, 2A, 3C, 4D, 5A

F6   MICROBES AND DISEASE

1A, 2C, 3C, 4A, 5B, 6B, 7C, 8C, 9C, 10C, 11C, 12D, 13A, 14A, 15C, 16A, 17C.

CHAPTER 18

1   *Similarities*

Both

- are long term relationships
- between organisms of different species
- where at least one of them benefits

Differences:

parasitism	mutualism
one organims benefits, the other is harmed	both organisms benefit
e.g. athlete's foot: fungus growing on damp skin; fungus obtains nutrients from host which loses nutrients	e.g. algae and fungus in lichen algae photosynthesis, fungus takes up water and minerals
e.g. fleas on a dog fleas drink blood from dog which loses blood	sea anemone and clown fish clown fish chases away fish that eat anemones; tentacles of anemone protect clownfish

2   (a)   gross production is the amount of organic matter produced by photosynthesis in plants.

(b)   net production is gross production minus respiration.

(c)   diversity increases as succession proceeds until a maximum, then it reduces some until a climax community is reached. Production increases until a maximum is reached and stabilizes.

3   (a)

	SITE 1		
	n	n-1	n(n-1)
water beetle	19	18	342
water snail	66	65	4290
mosquito fish	19	18	342
leech	11	10	110
diptera larvae	11	10	110
bivalve	786	785	617010
Ostracada	5	4	20
tadpoles	8	7	56
true worms	74	73	5402
sum	999		627682

	SITE 2		
	n	n-1	n(n-1)
Ostracada	16	15	240
tadpoles	32	31	992
true worms	39	38	1482
water hoglouse	157	156	24492
swimming mayfly nymph	102	101	10302
dusky mayfly nymph	16	15	240
non biting midge larva	614	613	376382
'Hawker' dragon fly	16	15	240
sum	992		414370

	site 1	site 2
total number of individuals at each site N	999	992
N-1	998	991
N(N-1)	997002	983072
sum of n(n-1) for all species at one site	627682	414370
simpson's index	1.588	2.372

(b)   Simpson's index for site 2 is bigger than for site 1. This means that the diversity at site 2 is greater than at site 1 despite the fact that site 2 has fewer species. The smaller divesity index at site 1 is caused by the fact that only one species is present in large numbers while in site 2 more species have a larger number of individuals.

(c) Site 1 could be more polluted than site 2. Only some species are capable of competing successfully in a polluted environment so the diversity of a polluted area is generally less than that of an unpolluted area. If both sites are from the same stream, it is likely that site 2 was higher upstream than site 1.

Another possiblity is that succession has proceeded further at site 2 than at site 1, unless site 1 was the climax community.

4 (a) *in situ*: nature reserves e.g. Great Barrier Reef Marine Park in Australia and Yellowstone National Park in the USA.

ex situ: zoos, e.g London Zoo
botanic gardens e.g. New Botanic Garden of the University of Helsinki at Kumpula Manor
seed banks e.g. Millenium Seed Bank Project in Kew (UK)

(b) *benefit of in-situ*
- some species are very hard to breed in captivity
- the population remains adapted to its original habitat, e.g. continue it natural diet
- individuals maintain their natural behaviour
- species interacts with others and fulfills its role in the ecosystem
- the habitat remains available for the endangered species (and others)
- it requires a larger gene pool but then conserves this variation between individuals
- species continues to evolve
- individuals can have more space, e.g. for a territory
- individuals may not need to be transported

uses of ex situ
- protect individuals of a nearly extinct species
- captive breeding programmes can increase number of individuals and maintain some biodiversity
- increasing awareness about exotic or endangered species

5

	r-strategy	**K-strategy**
body size	small	large
life span	short	long
maturity	early	late
offspring	many	few
care for offspring	little	extensive
population size	fluctuates	stable
environment	unstable	stable
description	opportunistic	stable
example	pathogens and pests e.g. mice	whales and elephants

6 Population size N = n1 x n2 / n3 = 809.25

So the estimate of the total population size would be just over 800 woodlice. Be aware that if the numbers were the same but 9 of the woodlice had been marked, the estimated population size would have been just over 700.

CHAPTER 19

1 (a) Anti-Diuretic Hormone (ADH)

(b) ADH is produced by cell bodies of neurosecretory cells in the hypothalamus

(c) ADH is stored in the posterior lobe of the pituitary gland and released from the nerve endings of neurosecretory cells there

(d) cells of the wall of the collecting duct

(e) The mechanism is an example of negative feedback: Osmoreceptors in the hypothalamus detect an increase in the concentration of dissolved particles in the blood plasma and cause the release of ADH. ADH travels to the kidneys via the blood, makes the walls of the collecting duct more permeable so more was is reabsorbed and less urine is produced which decreases the concentration of dissolved particles in the blood so stops the release of ADH.

2 (a) Pepsin and trypsin are proteases, if produced in active form would digest the cell that produces them so they are made as pepsinogen and trypsinogen

(b) Pepsinogen is activated by HCl in the stomach. Trypsinogen is activated by enterokinase in the small intestine.

HCl and enterokinase are made by different cells than those who make pepsinogen and trypsinogen.

3 (a) microvilli, mitochondria, pinocytotic vesicles, mitochondria.

(b) *microvilli* increase the surface area, allowing more food to be absorbed at the same time

mitochondria provide energy since some of the processes of absorption are active transport which requires energy

pinocytotic vesicles as a result of endocytosis

tight junctions to prevent particles from entering in between cells

4 (a) glucose, amino acids, hormones, vitamins, cholesterol,

(b) *glucose* is taken up, converted to glycogen and stored

amino acids are used to make (blood) proteins, surplus amino acids are broken down for energy and urea produced as a waste product

vitamins A and D are stored in the liver

cholesterol levels are controlled

5 • genetic factors - if one or more family members have CHD, the risk is increased
   • age - CHD is more common with increasing age
   • gender - CHD is more common among males
   • smoking - smoking increases the chance of CHD
   • obesity - obesity increases the chance of CHD
   • diet - a diet high in cholesterol and saturated fats increases the chances of CHD; there is evidence that trans fatty acids are particulary unhealthy
   • lack of exercise - exercise seems to decrease levels of LDL cholesterol and reduces chances of CHD.

6 (a) As the partial pressure of oxygen increases, the percentage saturation of hemoglobin with oxygen increases as shown by the sigmoid curve. First oxygen is more difficult to attach but it facilitates binding of subsequent oxygen molecules. In lungs, pO_2 is high so hemoglobin is (almost) saturated with oxygen. In tissue, pO_2 is low so hemoglobin releases oxygen (to respiring cells).

(b) Bohr shift = Bohr effect takes place when CO_2 levels are high

e.g. in actively respiring tissues like muscle

High CO_2 levels causes drop in pH, drop in pH makes oxygen dissociation curve go to the right. So at a specific pO_2, hemoglobin will have less oxygen with the Bohr effect, that means more oxygen is released to the tissue which is available for cellular respiration

A

abiogenesis
The origin of life. It refers to the various hypotheses about the chemical origin of life.

absolute dating
A date for a fossil or artefact, for example, tool, derived by measuring the age of the sediments in which it is found, usually by radiometric methods.

absorption
taking in substances through cell membranes or layers of cells.

acetogenesis
The conversion by bacteria of soluble acids to acetate, carbon dioxide and methane, and of carbohydrates, hydrogen and carbon dioxide to acetic acid

acetogenic bacteria
Bacteria capable of reducing carbon dioxide to acetic (ethanoic) acid or converting sugars quantitatively into acetate (ethanoic acid).

acetylcholine
a common neurotransmitter

acinus
hollow space in exocrine gland where product is collected

acrosome reaction
the reaction where the sperm touches the cells of the corona radiata, the membrane around the acrosome fuses with the membrane of the cells, releasing the proteolytic enzyme and digesting the cell.

acrosome
part of the sperm cell, contains proteolytic enzymes

actin
a protein and thinner myofilament

action potential
the localised reversal and then restoration of the electrical potential (measured in millivolts) across the membrane of a neuron as the impulse passes along it.

activation energy
the energy that must be added in order for a chemical reaction to occur

active immunity
immunity due to the production of antibodies by the organism itself after the body's defence mechanisms have been stimulated by antigens

active site
place where the substrate binds (to the enzyme) and where the reaction occurs

acute disease
A disease that develops rapidly, shows substantial symptoms, and then comes to a climax.

adaptation
In the evolutionary sense, some heritable feature of an individual's phenotype that improves its fitness, that is, chances of survival and reproduction in the existing environment.

adaptive radiation
The relatively rapid diversification of a species into several forms as a result of a single species invading different habitats and evolving under different selective pressures in those habits so that they are each adaptively specialised to a specific environmental niche.

addiction
the repeated and compulsive use of psychoactive drugs.

adenovirus
An icosahedral DNA virus involved in respiratory infections, viral meningitis, and viral conjunctivitis.

ADH
see anti diuretic hormone

adhesion
attraction between different kinds of molecules

aerobic respiration
release of energy in the presence of oxygen

afferent vessel
blood vessel leading away from the glomerulus

agar
A derivative of marine seaweed used as a solidifying agent in many microbiological media.

algal bloom
Algal blooms can occur when certain types of microscopic algae grow quickly in water, forming visible patches that may harm the health of the environment, plants, or animals. Algal blooms can deplete the oxygen and block the sunlight that other organisms need to live, and some algae release toxins.

alien invasive species
species not native to a particular area, often causing environmental damage

allele frequency
For a specific gene, the relative proportion of each allele of that gene found in a population.

allopatric speciation

Speciation that occurs when two populations are separated by a physical barrier that prevents gene flow between them.

allosteric effector

compound which bind to the enzyme at a specific site, well away from the active site. They cause a reversible change in the structure of the active site.

allostery

a special kind of non-competitive inhibition

altruism

a behaviour which benefits another individual but at cost or direct benefit to the performer.

alveolus

airsac in the lungs, major site for gas exchange

amino acid

molecule that contains an amine and a carboxyl group, subunits of proteins

amniote

the group of reptiles, birds and amphibians. They all develop through an embryo that is enclosed within a membrane called an amnion.

analogous structures

Structures found in various species that may have the same appearance function, but have different evolutionary origins. The similarities are due to similar selective pressure, rather than common ancestery.

anorexia nervosa

the condition where the person is obsessive about his (but usually her) weight

anti diuretic hormone (ADH)

protein hormone released by posterior lobe of the pituitary gland in the brain; it increases reabsorption of water (reduced the volume of urine but makes it more concentrated)

antibiotic resistance

bacteria can survive in the presence of an antibiotic, it is inherited not acquired

antibody

a soluble protein produced by a plasma cell. It is produced by the immune system as a response to the presence of an antigen

anticodon

sequence of three nucleotides on the tRNA that correspond to a codon on the mRNA

antigen

a molecule that is recognised by the organism as foreign. It will usually cause an immune response.

antisense strand

the DNA strand which is transcribed

antiseptic

A substance that prevents the growth of microorganisms.

apes

the groups of primates that includes chimpanzees, gorillas, and the orangutan (the great apes); and the gibbons and siamangs (the lesser apes).

appetite control centre

part of the hypothalamus of the brain that controls the feeling of hunger

arboreal

an animal that is tree-living.

archaebacteria

A group of prokaryotic microorganisms that are only distantly related to eukaryotes and the other prokaryotes and are members of the domain Archaea.

Ardipithecus ramidus

The oldest known hominid; it shares many features with both apes and humans but is thought to be bipedal. It is dated to around 4.4 million years ago, and is found only in Africa.

assimilation

the conversion of nutrients into fluid or solid parts of the organism.

assortative mating

The tendency of like to mate with like.

asthma

chronic disease of the respiratory system

atherosclerosis

caused by an inflammation of the walls of arteries, which can be caused by the accumulation of lipids on the inner surface.

Atrio Ventricular Node (AVN)

section between atria and ventricles which conducts impulses

Australopithecines

The first hominids that lived on the Africa savannas between about 4.4 and 1.5 million years ago.

Australopithecus afarensis
an australopithecine species that was bipedal but had many primitive features of the skeleton. It is dated to between 3.9 and 3.0 million years ago, and is found only in Africa.

autoclave
A laboratory instrument that sterilises microbiological materials by means of steam under pressure.

autoinducer
Autoinducers are signaling molecules in bacterial quorum sensing that regulate mRNA production for specific genes in response to population density.

autolysis
when the lysosome(s) burst and the cell digests itself

autonomic nervous system
part of the nervous system not under voluntary control

autopolyploidy
Pololyploidy in which all the chromosomes come from the same species; the polyploid is formed by the doubling of a single genome

autosome
any chromosome which is not a sex chromosome

autotroph
an organism that synthesises its organic molecules from simple inorganic substances.

auxins
a group of plant hormones

B

bacitracin
An antibiotic derived from a Bacillus species and effective against Gram-positive bacteria when used topically.

bacteriochlorophyll
A pigment located in bacterial membrane systems that upon excitement by light loses electrons and initiates photosynthetic reactions.

bacteriocidal
a substance capable of killing bacteria.

bacteriophage
A virus that infects and lyses certain bacteria.

bacteriostatic
a substance capable of inhibiting or slowing the reproduction of bacteria.

balanced polymorphism
The prolonged maintenance of two or more alleles in a population, usually because the phenotypes they determine are favoured by different selective forces; it may also arise from the increased fitness of the heterozygote over the homozygote at a particular locus. e.g. light and dark coloured peppered moths.

balanced selection
occurs when all parents have equal contributions to the next generation

basal body
Tiny cylindrical structure in the cytoplasm located at the base of flagella and cilia, in eukaryotic cells.

basement membrane
a protein membrane between the cells that form the walls of the glomerulus and those that form the walls of Bowman's capsule

bicuspid
valve between left atrium and ventricle

bilirubin
yellow bile pigment

biliverdin
green bile pigment

binomial system (of nomenclature)
every species has a Latin name, made up of two parts. The first part is the name of the genus, the second part specifies the species.

bioaccumulation
the accumulation of substances in the bodies of organisms as matter passes up the food chain

Biochemical Oxygen Demand (BOD)
A number referring to the amount of oxygen utilised by the microorganisms in a sample of water during a five day period of incubation.

biofilm
A layer of microoganisms on an aqueous surface protected within a matrix of polysaccharides and glycoproteins secreted by the organisms. These microorganisms have distinct physiological properties separate from free-floating microorganisms.

biogas
A product of the anaerobic digester that is a combination of methane, carbon dioxide and trace levels of other gases produced by the decomposition of organic matter.

biological control
using one species to attempt to control the population of another

bioluminescence
The ability of organisms to produce light.

biomagnification
the increase in levels of substance(s) in the bodies of organisms as matter passes up the food chain

biomass limit
the lowest amount of (e.g. fish) a stock (e.g. fish) should be allowed to fall to or it is likely that reproduction will be reduced and next year's stock is lower in numbers

biomass
The total mass (in grams or kilograms) of living matter within a given unit of environmental area.

biome
A general type of ecosystem occupying extensive geographical areas, characterised by similar plant communities, for example, deserts.

bioremediation
The use of microorganisms to treat environmental problems.

biosphere
total of all areas where living things are found; including the deep ocean and the lower part of the atmosphere. The biosphere contains a number of biomes.

bipedalism
Upright walking on two legs.

bivalent
the pair of homologous chromosomes as they are aligned side by side

blood doping
injecting additional erythrocytes to the organism to enhance performance in a competition

Bohr effect (also Bohr shift)
reduction in affinity for oxygen of hemoglobin which releases more oxygen

Bovine Spongiform Encephalopathy (BSE)
infected brain tissue become soft and spongy; accompanied by neurogical defects; also called 'mad cow disease.

Bowman's capsule
first part of the nephron, site of filtration

brachiation
Movement through trees by hanging from branches and swinging alternate arms from branch to branch.

brain imaging
creating a visual image of brain activity

breathing
ventilation of the lungs

broad spectrum antibiotic
An antibiotic useful for treating many groups of microorganisms including Gram-positive and Gram negative bacteria, fungi, and protozoa.

bronchiole
branch of a bronchus, leading air to the alveoli

bronchus
branch of the trachea, leading air into the lungs

broth
Any of a variety of liquid media, especially nutrient broth or any liquid medium based on nutrient broth and/or hydrolysed protein.

brow ridge
Ridge of bone above the eye sockets.

budding
Asexual reproduction of some unicellular organisms by growth and specialisation followed by the separation by constriction of a part of the parent.

bulb
stem that grows underground and has modified leaves for storing food

bundle of His
specialised muscle cells which conduct impulse from the AVN to Purkinje tissue

C

Calvin cycle
cyclic process in the stroma of the chloroplast where three carbondioxide molecules are combined in the process of forming glucose

capsid
The protein coat of a virus.

capsomere
One of the individual subunits that makes up a capsid.

capsule
Compact layer of polysaccharide exterior to the cell wall in some bacteria.

carbon dating
A chemical analysis used to determine the age of organic materials based on their content of the radioisotope carbon-14.

cardiac cycle
contactions of atria followed by contractions of ventricles

cardiac output
volume of blood pumped out by the heart per minute.

carrier
One who has recovered from a disease but retains live organisms in the body and continues to shed them.

carrying capacity
the maximum number of individuals of a species that can be sustainably supported by the environment.

cell respiration
process of releasing energy from food (large organic molecules), often using oxygen as the ultimate electron acceptor

Central Nervous System (CNS)
consists of the brain and spinal cord

centromere
point where spindle fibres attach and where two sister chromatids are kept together

cephalosporins
A group of antibiotics derived from the mould Cephalosporium and used against Gram-positive bacteria and certain Gram-negative bacteria and certain Gram-negative bacteria.

CFC
(Chlorinated fluorocarbons) are gases which reduce the amount of ozone in the atmosphere which results in higher levels of ultraviolet light reaching earth

chemical evolution
The pre-biological changes that transformed simple atoms and molecules into the more complex chemicals needed for the origin of life.

chemiosmosis
the process where protons, driven by a difference in their concentration, move through ATP synthetase and cause the production of ATP

chemoautotrophs
Organisms that need only carbon dioxide as a carbon source, but that obtain their energy by oxidising inorganic substances

chemoheterotrophs
An organism that derived energy from chemical reactions and utilises the energy to synthesize nutrients from carbon compounds other than carbon dioxide.

chemoreceptor
cells that detect the presence of chemical and sent an electrical impulse

chiasma (singular chiasmata)
cross over point of chromatids of homologous chromosomes during synapsis

chlorhexidine
A bisphenol compound widely used as an antiseptic and disinfectant.

cholera
A food borne and waterborne bacterial disease of the intestine caused by Vibro cholerae and accompanied massive diarrhea, fluid and electrolyte imbalance, and severe dehydration.

cholesterol
lipid, found in cell membranes, precursor to vitamin D and steroid hormones

cholinesterase
enzyme which breaks down acetylcholine

chronic disease
A disease that develops slowly tends to linger for a long time, and requires long convalescence.

cirrhosis
liver tissue is replaced by scar tissue, sometimes as a result of alcoholism; liver cirrhosis reduced the working of the liver

citric acid cycle (TCA)
cyclic process in the matrix of the mitochondria where a two carbon compound is changed into two molecules of carbon dioxide, producing energy

clade
A group of species that contains the common ancestor of a group and its descendants.

cladistic species concept
A concept of a species, according to which a species is a lineage of populations between two phylogenetic branch points (or speciation events).

cladistics
The school of evolutionary biology that seeks relationships among species based on the polarity (primitive or derived) of characters.

cladogram
A branching diagram representing the most parsimonious distribution of derived characters within a set of taxa.

cleavage division
first mitotic division of zygote, not followed by growth

climax community

A mature stage in ecological development in which a community of organisms, especially plants, is stable and capable of perpetuating itself.

climograph

a graph that provides information on the amount of precipitation and temperature

clonal expansion

the process of T-cells and B-cells forming clones by mitosis to produce the large numbers of cells required to deal with the infection

clonal selection

the process of the macrophage selecting which T-cells and B-cells have the required surface receptor

Clostridium tetani

A Gram-positive anaerobic spore-forming bacterium that causes tetanus.

coacervates

A spherical aggregation of lipid molecules is held together by hydrophobic forces. Coacervates measure 1 to 100 micrometers across, possess osmotic properties, and form spontaneously from certain weak organic solutions. Coacervates may have played a significant role in the evolution of cells.

coalesce

group together (lipid molecules will coalesce)

codon

a sequence of three nucleotides that codes for a specific amino acid

cohesion

the attraction between molecules of the same kind resulting from intermolecular forces

collecting duct

tubule leading to the renal pelvis where final amount of water are reabsorbed

colourless sulfur bacteria

A diverse group of non-photosynthetic proteobacteria that can oxidise reduced sulfur compounds such as hydrogen sulfide. Many are lithotrophs and derive energy from sulfur oxidation. Some are unicellular, whereas others are filamentous gliding bacteria.

communicable disease

A disease that a transmissible among various hosts.

community

a group of populations living and interacting with each other in an area.

competition

The simultaneous demand by two or more organisms for limited environmental resources, such as nutrients, living space, or light.

competitive exclusion principle

states that two different species do not share the same niche

competitive inhibitor

an inhibitor whose structure is so similar to the structure of the substrate molecule that it binds to the active site of the enzyme and prevents the substrate from binding.

complemental air

inspiratory reserve volume

complementary DNA

A DNA that is complementary to a given RNA which serves as a template for synthesis of the DNA in the presence of reverse transcriptase.

condensation

reaction in which a new covalent bond is formed between two molecules and water is produced

cone

photoreceptor in the retina responsible for seeing colours

conjugated protein

a protein with a prosthetic group

conjugation

A type of bacterial recombination in which genetic material passes from a live donor cell into a live donor cell into a live recipient cell during a period of contact.

conservation

The preservation of the function of a given gene through evolutionary time. This normally occurs in genes that play a fundamental role in basic biological processes, such as growth and physiology.

consumer

an organism that ingests other organic matter that is living or recently killed.

contagious disease

A communicable disease whose agent passes with particular ease among hosts.

contractile vacuole

A small vesicle located in the cytoplasm of many freshwater protozoans that expels excess water.

contralateral processing

some of the nerve fibres in the optic nerve will cross before reaching the brain

convergent evolution
The independent evolution of similar structures among unrelated organisms, due to similar selective pressures.

corona radiata
layer of follicle cells surrounding the zona pellucida.

correlation
statistical relationship between two variables.

correlation coefficient
is a measure of the linear association between two variables.

cortical granules
special structures containing enzymes to thicken the zona pellucida

cortical reaction
the fusion between the head of the sperm cell with the membrane of the secondary oocyte and special structures, the cortical granules, will release enzyme to thicken the zona pellucida so that it becomes a fertilisation membrane

Cory cycle
glucose-lactate interconversion in liver and muscles

Creutzfeldt-Jakob Disease (CJD)
A rare but fatal brain disease with unusually long incubation periods (measured in years) and which usually strikes people over 65.

cristae
folds in the inner membrane of a mitochondrion

crossing over
process during prophase I where non-sister chromatids exchange information leading to the formation of recombinants

cultural evolution
Changes in the behaviour of a population of organisms, usually humans, by learning behaviours acquired by members of previous generations.

culture
Population of microorganisms cultivated in an artificial growth medium. A pure culture is grown from a single cell; a mixed culture consists of two or more microbial species or strains growing together.

cyanobacteria
Photosynthetic bacterium generally blue-green in colour and in some species capable of nitrogen fixation. Sometimes called blue green algae.

cycads
Cycads are tropical plants that resemble palms but reproduce by means of spermatozoids.

cystic fibrosis
A genetic disease characterised by an excessive secretion of mucus and consequent vulnerability to lung infection.

cytokinesis
cell division (not nuclear division)

cytosome
Cell opening through which protozoa ingest food (mouth) or secrete wastes.

D

DDT
(dichlorodipheyltrichloroethane) an insecticide which was once widely used but has caused damage to the environment

dead air
the amount of air that is NOT refreshed during a ventilation

deamination
Production of ammonia from nitrogen-containing compounds.

decarboxylation
reaction in which a molecule of carbon dioxide is removed from an existing molecule

decomposers
organisms that obtain their energy from dead organisms. Two main groups are detritivores (e.g. earthworms and dung beetles) and saprotrophs (fungi and bacteria).

defined medium
A medium in which the nature and quantity of each component are identified; also called a ,synthetic medium,

denitrification
To reduce nitrates or nitrites to nitrogen-containing gases, as by bacterial action on soil.

denitrifying bacteria
Anaerobic strains of bacteria in soil which decompose nitrate ions into nitrogen and oxygen.

deoxyribonucleosides triphosphates
DNA nucleotides (deoxyribose, organic base and a phosphate) with two extra phosphates which provide the energy necessary to bind to other nucleotides in forming a new DNA strand

depolarisation
when the potential difference across the membrane become less (valuegoes from -70 mV to 0 mV)

derived character

A character acquired by some members of an evolutionary group, and therefore serves to unite them in a taxonomic sense and distinguish them form other species in the group.

detritivore

an organism that ingests dead organic matter.

diabetes

disease where glucose can not be used fully by the bidy and too much urine is produced, often containing glucose

diastole

relaxation of the heart muscle

diet

the food consumed by an individual

digester

A solid waste management facility that uses bacteria to break down manure from a dairy into biogas and sludge.

dihybrid cross

cross involving two different genes

directional selection

Directional selection favours those individuals who have extreme variations in traits within a population.

disinfectant

A chemical agent used to destroy virtually all recognized pathogenic microorganisms, but not necessarily all microbial forms (for example, bacterial endospores).

disinfection

A process which destroys or irreversibly inactivates micro-organisms and reduces their number to a non-hazardous level.

dislocation

the bones in the joint are moved, relative to each other, and do not return to their original position.

disruptive selection

A type of natural selection in which both extreme phenotypes are favoured over the average phenotype.

distal convoluted tubule

tubule, part of the nephron where active transport take place

distance

In taxonomy it refers to the quantitatively measured difference between the phenetic appearance of two groups of individuals, such as populations or species (phentic distance), or the difference in their gene frequencies (genetic distance).

disulfide bridge

covalent bond between two sulfur atoms of two amino acids

divergent evolution

Divergent evolution is a process where one species begins to separate into two distinct species through the process of natural selection.

DNA library

An unordered collection of clones (i.e., cloned DNA from a particular organism) whose relationship to each other can be established by physical mapping.

DNA ligase

enzyme that forms bonds attaching the DNA fragments of the lagging strand to become one strand

DNA polymerase I

enzyme that removes the RNA primer of the Okazaki fragment and replaces the RNA nucleotides with DNA nucleotides

DNA polymerase III

enzyme that works only in a 5' to 3' direction and forms covalent bonds between the individual nucleotides

Dodo

an extinct flightless bird

domain

A domain is a taxon (group) in the highest rank of organisms, higher than a kingdom.

DRI

dietary reference intake

drugs

chemicals that affect physiological processes

E

eardrum

membrane in the ear that changes sound into movement

ebola virus

An RNA virus existing in Africa and causing a form of a type of hemorrhagic fever called 'Ebola fever'.

ecological isolation

A form of reproductive isolation in which two species are separated by what is often a slight difference in the niches they occupy.

ecology

the study of relationships between living organisms and between organisms and their environment.

ecosystem
a community and its abiotic environment.

ectoplasm
Outer layer of the cytoplasm of a cell.

edge effect
On the edge of the forest, there is more light and more wind so more loss of water but also more photosynthesis at lower levels. Therefore, biodiversity is usually greater at the edges than in the core.

edge enhancement
makes the edge of something dark even darker and creates a "halo" of light around it, enhancing the contrast

effector
the muscle or gland that produces the response to a stimulus.

efferent vessel
blood vessel leading to the glomerulus

effluent
Wastewater or other liquid - raw (untreated), partially or completely treated - flowing from a reservoir, basin, treatment process, or treatment plant.

elongation
adding amino acids to the growing polypeptide chain

emigration
an organism leaving an area permanently

emulsify
divide into smaller droplets (bile emulsifies lipids)

end product inhibition
process that takes place when the end product of a metabolic pathway is an allosteric effector for an earlier reaction

endocrine gland
ductless gland that produces hormones and secretes them into the blood

endocytosis
process of taking up substances by surrounding them with a membrane

endomitosis
Duplication of chromosomes without division of the nucleus, resulting in increased chromosome number within a cell. Chromosome strands separate, but the cell does not divide.

endoplasm
The granular portion of the cytoplasm surrounding the nucleus.

endopsores
A thick-walled spore formed in a bacterial cell. It is very resistant to being killed by heat and various other chemical and physical agents.

endosymbiotic theory
The widely accepted theory that mitochondria and chloroplasts evolved from mutually beneficial associations between the ancestors of eukaryotic cells and captured bacteria living within the cytoplasm of the pre-eukaroytic cell.

endothermic reaction
chemical reaction which needs to take in energy in order to take place

endotoxin
A metabolic poison produced chiefly by Gram- negative bacteria, endotoxins are part of the bacterial cell wall and consequently, are release on cell disintegration; they are composed of lipid-polysaccharide- peptide complexes,

enterokinase
an enzyme in the small intestine that activates trypsinogen

enterotoxin
A toxin that is active in the gastrointestinal tract of the host.

enterovirus
A virus that infects intestinal cells.

envelope
A lipid membrane enveloping a virus particle.

epidemic
A widespread outbreak of an infectious disease where many people are infected at the same time.

epidemiology
The branch of medical science dealing with the incidence, distribution and control of disease in a population.

EPO (see erythropoietin)

equilibrium population
A population in which allele frequencies and the distribution of genotypes do not change from generation to generation.

error bars
an error bar indicates the range of values when several measurements are used to generate a single point on a graph, or the maximum possible error in measuring or calculating the position of the point.

erythromycin
An antibiotic derived from a streptomycin species; used against Gram-positive bacteria.

erythropoietin
naturally occuring hormone that stimulates the bone marrow to produce more erythrocytes. Sometimes used illegally by athletes to enhance performace.

eubacteria
One of the three major evolutionary lines of cellular life forms, primarily prokaryotic micro-organisms which possess a peptidoglycan cell wall.

eutrophication
Water rich in minerals and organic nutrients that promotes a proliferation of plant life, especially algae, which reduces the dissolved oxygen content and often causes the extinction of other organisms.

evolution
Changes in the proportions of different genotypes in a population or species over time.

evolutionary clock
The molecular clock is a concept which is based on the idea that spontaneous mutations accumulate at a constant speed within a particular gene during evolutionary time. Hence accumulated mutations can be used as a measure of the passage of time.

excitatory post-synaptic potential (EPSP)
this depolarizes the post-synaptic membrane, making it easier to reach the threshold potential

excretion
the removal from the body of the waste products of metabolic pathways.

exocrine glands
gland that secretes its products in ducts which take it to its destination

exons
coding sections of DNA which are expressed (used to make proteins)

exothermic reaction
chemical reaction which will give off energy (heat) as it takes place

exotoxin
A metabolic poison produced chiefly by Gram-positive bacteria. Exotoxins are released to the environment on production; they are composed of protein and affect various organs and systems of the body.

expiration
breathing out

expiratory reserve volume
amount of air that can be breathed out after a normal expiration (around 1.1 dm3)

exponential growth phase
unlimited growth of the population due to the absence of limiting factors.

extinction
The state in which all members of a group of organisms, such as a species, population, family or class, have disappeared from a given habitat, geographic area, or the entire world.

extracellular bacteria
Bacteria that do not enter cells and damage the cells from the outside.

extremophiles
Bacteria that live comfortably in environments formerly considered lethal, such as those that are very hot or lack oxygen.

F

fatty acid
carboxylic acid, often with long unbranched chain, can be part of lipid

fenestrated
have small "holes" (windows); the wall of the glomerulus is fenestrated

fermentation
A form of anaerobic respiration found in yeast and plants that converts pyruvic acid produced by glycolysis into lactic acid or alcohol (ethanol) and carbon dioxide.

fertilization
the fusion of male and female gametes to form a new organism

fimbria (singular: fimbriae)
Thin, short filaments protruding from some bacteria; involved in attachment.

fish kill
A die off of fishes within a relatively short period due to the onset of man-caused or, more rarely, natural factors.

fitness
the physical condition of the body which suits it to the particular exercise which it performs

flocculation
The water-treatment process after coagulation that uses gentle stirring to cause suspended particles to form larger, aggregated masses (flocs). The aggregates are removed from the water by a separation process (for example, sedimentation, flotation, or filtration).

food chain
the feeding relationships between species in a community.

food miles
the distance the food has travelled from where it is produced to where it is consumed

food vacuole
A membrane-bound space within a unicellular organism in which food particles are enclosed. Digestive enzymes are released into the vacuole, where intracellular digestion occurs.

food web
shows a more accurate representation of the very complex feeding interactions between species.

foraging behaviour
finding food

foramen magnum
The opening at the base of the skull through which the spinal cord passes.

formyl methionine
An amino acid derivative used, together with a special tRNAf, to initiate translation. tRNAf bears the same anticodon as the tRNA for methionine.

fossil record
all fossils, discovered and undiscovered that exist.

fossil
A remnant or trace of an organism of a past geologic age, such as a skeleton or leaf imprint, embedded and preserved in the Earth's crust.

fossilisation
The process of converting, or of being converted, into a fossil.

founder effect
The result of starting a new population with a low number of individuals (founders), so that, as result of sampling error, their gene pool may not contain the same proportions of alleles for a particular locus as in the original population.

fundamental niche
is the potential mode of existence, given the adaptations of the species.

gametocyte
The sexual stage of malaria parasites. Male gametocytes (microgametocytes) and female gametocytes (macrogametocytes) are inside red blood cells in the circulation. If they are ingested by a female Anopheles mosquito, they undergo sexual reproduction which starts the extrinsic (sporogonic) cycle of the parasite in the mosquito.

gametogenesis
production of gametes

gas exchange
the intake of oxygen and excretion of carbon dioxide which takes place at the (specialised respiratory) surface of an organism

gasohol
Gasohol refers to petrol or gasoline that contains 10% ethanol by volume.

gastrin
hormone produced by cells in the duodenum and stomach which causes release of hydrochloric acid gastric juice

Gaussian curve
bell-shaped curve resulting from a normal distribution.

gene family
A set of related genes occupying various loci in the DNA, almost certainly formed by duplication of an ancestral gene.

gene pool
The collective genetic information contained within a population of sexually reproducing organisms.

gene probe
An artificially prepared DNA sequence made radioactive with carbon-14, coding for a particular amino acid residue sequence.

gene therapy
The treatment of certain disorders, especially those caused by genetic anomalies or deficiencies, by introducing specific engineered genes into a patient's cells.

genetic drift
Random fluctuations in the frequency of the appearance of a gene in a small isolated population, presumably owing to chance rather than natural selection

genetic isolation
The failure of two forms to produce fertile offspring even when in breeding contact.

genetic polymorphism

The presence in a population of two or more forms, produced when different alleles of a gene occur in the same population and the rarest allele is not maintained by merely by repeated mutation.

geographical isolation

Geographic isolation is the physical separation between members of a population.

geophytes

storage organs for water or food or the plants that possess these storage organs

germ line therapy

Transmission of a gene into egg or sperm cells and thus the passing on of this gene to future generations.

germination epithelium

layer of cells which divides and gives rise to gametes

glomerular filtrate

found in Bowman's capsule, is similar to blood plasma without large proteins

glomerulus

capillary bed in the kidney

glycogen

polysaccharide, chain of glucose molecules, used for short time energy storage in animals

glycolysis

breakdown of glucose into two pyruvate

goitre

swelling in the neck due to an enlarged thryroid gland

gracile

an organinsl that is small and lightly built

gradualism

The view that evolution proceeds by small, cumulative steps over long periods of time rather than by abrupt, major changes.

gram negative

To describe a prokaryotic cell whose cell wall stains pink (negative) in Gram stain. The cell wall of a gram-negative bacterium contains relatively little peptidoglycan but contains an outer membrane composed of lipopolysaccharide, lipoprotein, and other complex macromolecules.

gram positive

To describe a prokaryotic cell whose cell wall stains purple (positive) in Gram stain. The cell wall of a gram-positive bacterium consists chiefly of peptidoglycan and lacks the outer membrane of gram-negative cells.

gram stain

A differential stain that divides bacteria into two groups, gram-positive and gram-negative based on the ability to retain crystal violet when decolourised with an organic solvent such as ethanol.

granum (thylakoid)

stacks of membrane where the light dependent stage of photosynthesis takes place

great apes

Chimpanzees and gorillas (in Africa) and orangutans (in Asia).

green sulfur bacteria

Anoxygenic phototrophs containing chlorosomes and bacteriochlorophyll and light harvesting chlorophyll.

greenhouse effect

the observation that the temperature inside a greenhouse (made of glass) is higher than outside. This also happens on Earth but the mechanism that keeps the heat inside a greenhouse is different from the mechanism of absorption of infrared radiation by the Earth's atmosphere.

gross production

The rate at which photosynthetic products are formed in a green plant from the solar energy received. (The units are J/kJ or g/kg per unit time).

H

habitat

the environment in which a species normally lives or the location of a living organism.

half life

The time required for half the atoms in a radioactive substance to undergo radioactive decay.

halophile

Microorganisms that live in environments that have concentrations of salt.

Hardy-Weinberg principle

The stable frequency distribution of genotypes, AA, Aa, and aa, are in the proportions p^2, 2pq, and q^2 respectively (where p and q are the frequencies of the alleles, A and a) due to random mating. This occurs in a large population in the absence of mutation, immigration, migration or natural selection.

heart rate

number of contractions of the heart per minute.

heavy metal

A metal with a relatively high density, especially one that is poisonous.

helicase
enzyme that unwinds DNA and breaks hydrogen bonds between anti-parallel DNA strands which separates the strands

hemorrhagic fever
Any of a series of viral diseases characterised by high fever and hemorrhagic lesions of the throat and internal organs.

hepatic artery
bloodvessel from heart to liver

hepatic portal vein
bloodvessel from small intestine to liver

herbivory
the eating of plants by organisms

heterocyst
Specialised cell in filamentous cyanobacteria frequently associated with nitrogen fixation.

heterotroph
an organism that obtains organic molecules from other organisms.

heterozygosity
The presence of different alleles on homologous chromosomes.

heterozygote advantage
The greater reproductive success of heterozygous individuals compared to homozygotes.

heterozygous
having two different alleles for the same gene

hexose
monosaccharide containing 6 Carbon atoms

homeostasis
the maintenance of the internal environment within acceptable limits, despite possible fluctuations in the external environment

homeotherm
An organism, such as a mammal or a bird, having a body temperature that is constant and largely independent of the temperature of its surroundings.

hominid
A general term applied to all humans and their ancestors (known collectively as the Hominidae). beginning with the Australopithecines. Homo sapiens is the only living species.

hominisation
The evolutionary process by which Homo sapiens evolved from primates.

hominoid
group including humans and apes.

Homo erectus
The first species in the genus Homo to leave Africa. There is an increase in brain size from earlier to later Homo erectus. It is dated to between 1.8 million and 300,000 years ago, and is found in Africa, Europe, and Asia.

Homo habilis
the first species in the genus Homo. It had some primitive features of the skeleton but shows an increase in brain size from earlier australopithecines. It is dated to between 1.9 and 1.8 million years ago, and is found only in Africa.

homologous proteins
Proteins having sequences and functions in different species, for example, the haemoglobins.

homologous structures
Biological structures derived from the same evolutionary origins and hence having similar anatomy.

homozygosity
The presence of identical alleles for a particular gene on both (or all, in the case of a polyploidy) matching chromosomes; no genetic variation for the gene in that individual.

homozygous
having two identical alleles for the same gene

hops
The cones or flowers of the female Humulus lupulus plant. They may be dried whole hops or may be used after being dried into pellets.

hormone
chemical messenger produced by endocrine cells and tranported by blood

hybrid sterility
Pertaining to the sterility of animals produced from matings between members of two different species

hybrid vigour
Increased vigour or other superior qualities arising from the crossbreeding of genetically different plants or animals.

hybridisation
The process of mixing differing gene pools by crossing to produce offspring of combined parental characteristics.

hydrolysis
reaction in which water is added to split a molecule into smaller molecules

hydrothermal vent
An opening in the sea floor through which super-heated water and other material are discharged into the surrounding seawater.

hydrotropic
Archaebacteria that use carbon dioxide as a source of carbon and hydrogen as a source of energy (hydrogen functions as a reducing agent).

hypothalamus
part of the brain, linking the endocrine system with the nervous system

I

ice age
When glaciers and ice caps were much more extensive than they are today. The world's climate was much colder and drier, and sea levels were much lower.

immigration
moving into an area from somewhere else

immunoglobulin
a soluble protein produced by a plasma cell. It is produced by the immune system as a response to the presence of an antigen

in vitro fertilisation (IVF)
the procedure where the egg and sperm cells are fertilised outside the female's body

inbreeding depression
A reduction in viability or fertility resulting from increased homozygosity through inbreeding.

independent assortment
the orientation of different homologous chromosomes to each other in metaphase I.

industrial melanism
A situation in which the frequency of alleles for dark colour increases in relation to alleles for light colour in response to changes in the environment due to pollution caused by increasing industrialisation.

infection thread
The specialized hypha of a pathogenic fungus that invades tissue of the susceptible plant
Infection
a successful invasion of the body by pathogens

influenza
A disease of the lungs caused by helical RNA virus.

inhibitor
a molecule which can reduce the rate of an enzyme cntrolled reaction

inhibitory post-synaptic potential (IPSP)
this hyperpolarizes the post-synaptic membrane, making it more difficult to reach the threshold potential

initiation
binding of the ribosome to the mRNA to begin translation

innate behaviour
behaviour which normally occurs in all members of a species, including in young and inexperienced animals

inoculation
Initiation of microbial growth by adding an inoculum.

inoculum
A culture medium in which microorganisms are implanted.

inspiration
breathing in

inspiratory reserve volume
extra amount of air that can be taken in after a normal breath (around 3 dm^3)

interglacial
Between two glacial periods (ice ages). The world is an interglacial period at the moment.

intracellular bacteria
Bacteria that reproduce within cells.

intracellular digestion
digestion inside the cell with the help of enzymes in the lysososme

introns
non-coding sections of DNA which are not expressed

invasiveness
The ability of a parasite to invade the tissues of the host and cause structural damage to the tissues.

isolating mechanism
Any mechanism that results in reproductive isolation between the species.

isotope
One of two or more atoms having the same atomic number but different mass numbers.

IVF
see in vitro fertilisation

J

jaundice
yellowing of the skin due to increased bilirubin (bile salt) levels

K

kilning
An important step in the malting process, whereby germinated barley is dried in a kiln. By applying differing amounts of heat during the kilning process, various types of malt can be produced, which in turn influence the flavour and colour of the beer produced.

kingdom
the largest group in the system of classification

knuckle-walking
Quadrupedal mode of locomotion, on the knuckles of the hands and the soles of the feet, by chimpanzees and gorillas.

Kreb's cycle
cyclic process in the matrix of the mitochondria where a two carbon compound is changed into two molecules of carbondioxide, producing energy

K-strategy
a reproductive strategy in stable communities, usually larger organisms and lower reproduction rates

L

lactate
alkanoic acid produced during anaerobic respiration in animals

lagging strand
new DNA strand forming in the 3' to 5' direction by formation of Okazaki fragments

lawn (bacterial)
An even growth of a specific bacterial culture across a Petri plate.

leading strand
new DNA strand forming in the 5' to 3' direction
learned behaviour develops as a result of experience

leghemoglobin
A protein containing heme which functions to bind oxygen in leguminous root nodules.

legumes
A family of plants characterised by root swellings which are occupied by nitrogen-fixing bacteria.

ligament
fibrous tissue that connects bones in a joint

limiting factor
the factor the furthest away from its optimum value which will limit the rate of a biological process

Lincoln Index
a technique for estimating the population of a species

line graph
graph in which points representing the value of a variable at selected values of the dependent variable are connected by straight lines or a smooth curve.

line transect
a line along which the distribution of organisms will be surveyed

linkage group
a group of genes whose loci are on the same chromosome

'lock-jaw'
A colloquial expression for tetanus based on the spasms on the jaw muscles.

locus
position of a gene on the chromosome

loop of Henle
tubule, part of the nephron where water and salt reabsorption are regulated via counter current mechanism

luciferase
This gene encodes an enzyme that catalyzes a reaction that produces light.

lymphocytes
white blood cells that help defend the body against infection

lysis
reaction in which a molecule is split into smaller molecules

lysogenic bacterium
A bacterium that carries a prophage.

lysogeny
The phenomenon in which the virus remains in the cell cytoplasm as a fragment of DNA or attaches to the chromosome, but fails to replicate in or destroy the cell.

lysozyme
An enzyme occurring naturally in egg white, human tears, saliva, and other body fluids, capable of destroying the cell walls of certain bacteria and thereby acting as a mild antiseptic.

lytic cycle
The process in which the virus replicates within the host cell and destroys the host cell the process of replicating.

M

macroevolution
Large-scale evolution occurring over geological time that results in the formation of new taxonomic groups (usually above the level of species).

mad cow disease (BSE)
A common term for bovine spongiform encephalopathy.

malaria
A serious protozoal disease of the red blood cells caused by Plasmodium species transmitted by mosquitoes and accompanied by high fever, anemia, and blood clotting.

malnutrition
the lack of a proper diet : not enough food, food lacking some minerals, vitamins, etc, but also too much food.

malt
Barley or other grain which has been soaked with water, allowed to sprout, and then dried. Sprouting allows development of the enzymes that bring about starch conversion in the mash.

malting
The process through which barley is transformed into malt, by artificially starting up its germination process, which will eventually be stopped at the kilning stage

mass-extinction event
A time when vast numbers of species abruptly vanish.

matrix
watery fluid inside mitochondria

mean
the mean is the arithmetic average of a set of numbers.

measles
A communicable respiratory disease caused by the RNA helical virus and accompanied by respiratory symptoms and a skin rash.

medium
Any liquid or solid materials which is prepared for the growth, maintenance, or storage of microorganisms.

megavitamin therapy
taken doses larger then the RDI in order to achieve a beneficial effect.

meristem
undifferentiated tissue and generates new cells for growth of the plant

merozoite
A stage in the life cycle of the plasmodium species parasites invades the red blood cells in this form.

mesophiles
Organisms that grow at the temperature range of 20-40 degrees Celsius.

mesophyte
a plant adapted to conditions of average water supply, i.e. not a xerophyte or a hydrophyte.

messenger RNA
strand of RNA transcribed from DNA in the nucleus containing information about the sequence of the amino acids in the protein that it codes for

methanogenesis
The biological production of methane.

methanogens
A methane-producing prokaryote; member of the Archaeabacteria.

MHC (major histocompatability complex) proteins
membrane proteins found on macrophages

microevolution
Evolution, below the species level, resulting from a succession of relatively small genetic variations.

microspheres
Microscopic, firm spherules which form on the cooling of hot saturated solutions of proteins, that are sensitive to heat. Microspheres might represent a significant early stage in pre-cellular evolution.

Miller-Urey Experiment
An experiment that simulated the conditions on primitive Earth that led to the origin of life.

mineral (nutrients)
elements in ionic form such as calcium (Ca^{2+})

missing link
An absent member needed to complete an evolutionary lineage.

mitochondrion
large cell organelle where aerobic respiration takes place

monophyletic group
A set of species containing a common ancestor and all of its descendants.

morph
One of various distinct forms of an organism or species.

mortality
death rate

motor neuron
nerve cell which transmits impulses from the brain to an effector (muscle or gland)

mRNA
see messenger RNA

multi gene disorder
A disorder involving more than one gene.

mumps
A communicable disease caused by an icosahedral DNA virus and accompanied by a swelling of the salivary glands.

must
The must is the mixture of fermenting grape juice, pips, skins and stalks.

mutualism
A symbiotic association between organisms of two different species in which each member benefits.

Mycobacterium tuberculosis
An acid-fast bacterium that causes tuberculosis.

myofibrils
thin fibres inside muscle cell, capable of contraction

myogenic
originate from within the heart

myoglobin
a protein made of one polypeptide chain which has the ability to bind oxygen, similar to haemoglobin

myosin
thicker myofilament

myxoma virus
a virus that is used to control the population of rabbits, especially in Australia

N

narrow-spectrum antibiotic
An antibiotic that is useful for a restricted group of microorganisms.

natality
birth rate

natural selection
The process by which those individuals of a species with characters or traits that help them to become better adapted and hence increase in frequency as compared to those less well adapted.

neanderthals
A population of archaic humans that lived in Europe and the Middle East. It is dated to between 150,000 and 30,000 years ago. Many believe that this group is a geographic variant of Homo sapiens, and not a separate species.

negative feedback
the control of a process by the result or effect of the process in such a way that an increase or decrease in the results or effects is always reversed.

neomycin
An amino glycoside antibiotic derived from a Streptomyces species, used topically for infections caused by Gram-negative bacteria, especially in the eye.

neoteny
The retention of juvenile characteristics in the adults of a species.

nephron
functional unit in the kidney

net(t) production
is the amount of energy trapped in organic matter at a given trophic level less that lost by the respiration of the organisms at that level.

neuron
nerve cell

neurosecretory cells
neurons which produce hormones which are released from nerve endings as a result of a stimulus

neurotoxin
A neurotoxin is a chemical whose primary action is on the CNS (Central Nervous System)

neurotransmitter
chemical which carries information across the synapse

niche
The role played by the organism in its community. It includes its abiotic requirements and tolerances, as well as its interactions with the other organisms.

nitrification

To oxidise an ammonium compound into nitric acid, nitrous acid, or any nitrate or nitrite, especially by the action of nitrobacteria.

nitrogen cycle

The transformation of nitrogen from an atmospheric gas to organic compounds in the soil, then to compounds in plants and eventually the release of nitrogen gas back into the atmosphere.

nitrogen fixation

The process of chemically combining atmospheric nitrogen with hydrogen to form ammonia or ammonium ions.

nitrogenase

An enzyme system that catalyzes the reaction of molecular nitrogen to ammonia.

node

A branch-point on a cladogram.

normal distribution

the normal distribution is a type of bell-shaped frequency polygon centred around the mean.

nucleocapsid

The combination of genome and capsid in the virus.

nucleolus

one or more darker sections in the nucleus which contain DNA coding for rRNA

nucleoside tri phosphate

RNA nucleotides (ribose, organic base and a phosphate) with two extra phosphates which provide the energy necessary to bind to other nucleotides in forming a new RNA strand

nutrient

a chemical substance found in foods that is used in the human body.

O

obesity

condition where more than the usual amount of fat is present in the organism

Okazaki fragments

segments of 100-200 nucleotides formed in the 5' to 3' direction on the lagging strand

oogenesis

production of egg cells

opposable thumb

a thumb that can rotate along its axis so that the fleshy tip can touch and push against other fingertips.

opsonins

Antibodies that function by preparing microorganisms for engulfment by white blood cells.

oral groove

In ciliates, the membrane structure that functions in food uptake.

osmoreceptors

cells that sense a change in concentration of dissolved particles

osmoregulation

the control of the water balance of the blood, tissue or cytoplasm of a living organism

Out of Africa (model)

The hypothesis that modern humans originated first in Africa and then migrated into the rest of the Old World; based principally on fossil evidence.

oval window

membrane that seperates middle ear from inner ear

oxidation

oxidation is loss of electrons

oxygen sag

The depletion of oxygen caused by the introduction of oxygen-demanding chemicals or microorganisms into a stream.

ozone layer

the layer of ozone (O_3) in the upper atmosphere

P

pacemaker

sino atrial node determines the frequency of the contractions

palaeontology

The science that studies fossil organisms and related remains.

pandemic

A worldwide epidemic.

panspermia

The theory that micro-organisms or biochemical compounds from outer space are responsible for originating life on Earth and possibly in other parts of the universe where suitable atmospheric conditions exist.

parallel evolution
The evolution of similar characters in related lineages whose common ancestor was phenotypically different.

parapatric speciation
Speciation in which the evolution of reproductive isolating mechanisms occurs when a population enters a new niche or habitat within the range of the parent species.

paraphyletic group
Set of species containing an ancestral species together with some, but not all, of its descendants. The species included in the group are those that have continued to resemble the ancestor; the excluded species have evolved rapidly and no longer resemble their ancestor.

parasitism
when one organism lives on or in another organism and causes some harm

parsimony (technique)
A method for seeking the most likely set of relationships among species/populations as a way of establishing their history.

parsimony (principle)
The concept that evolution has followed the most economical route, involving the assumption that closely related species will have consistently fewer differences.

partial pressure
pressure exerted by each component in a mixture

passive immunity
immunity due to the acquisition of antibodies from another organism in which active immunity has been stimulated, including via the placenta, colostrum, or by injection of antibodies

pasteurisation
A heating process that destroys pathogenic bacteria in a fluid such as milk and lowers the overall number of bacteria in the fluid.

pathogen
An agent that causes disease, especially a living micro-organism such as a bacterium or fungus.

pellicle
A rigid covering layer of certain protozoa composed in part of chitin-like material.

pentadactyl limb
A limb with five digits which is characteristic of virtually all vertebrates.

pentose
monosaccharide containing 5 Carbon atoms

pepsin
protein digesting enzyme

pepsinogen
inactive precursor to pepsin

peptidoglycan
The rigid layer of cell walls of Bacteria, a thin sheet composed of N-acetylglucosamine,

peripatric speciation
A form of allopatric speciation in which the new species is formed from a small population isolated at the edge of the ancestral population's geographic range.

Peripheral Nervous System (PNS)
all nerves not in the brain or spinal cord

periplasmic space
The space between the cytoplasmic membrane and the outer membrane of Gram-negative bacteria.

peritrichous bacteria
Bacteria that possess flagella over the entire of the cell.

pH
the scale of acidity from 0 to 14

phagocytosis
one form of endocytosis in which particels are engulfed by a cell

phenetic classification
Method of classification in which species are grouped together with other species that they most closely resemble phenotypically.

phenetic species concept
Concept of a species, according to which a set of species is a set of organisms that are phenetically similar to one another.

phosphorylation
reacttion which adds a phosphate group to an existing molecule; e.g. ADP + P → ATP

photoactivation
electrons are excited and move away from the atom because they have absorbed light energy.

photoautotroph
Photoautotroph are organisms that are capable of synthesizing organic substances by the process of photosynthesis using solar energy.

photoheterotroph
A microorganism that utilises light energy while assimilating organic compounds as a carbon source.

photoperiodicity
the plant's responses to the length of the night

photophosphorylation
reaction which uses light energy to add phosphate to an existing molecule

photoreceptor
a protein that can absorb light

phototropism
a growth response or growth movement of a plant in response to light coming from a specific direction

phycobilins
Reddish and bluish photosynthetic pigments found in cyanobacteria.

phyletic change
The evolution of a new species through the gradual change of an existing species, resulting in no increase in species diversity.

phylogeny
The line of genetic relationship (or descent) involved in the evolutionary development of a species or taxonomic group of organisms.

phytochrome
a photoreceptor

pili (singular: pilus)
Pili are tiny, hollow projections made of protein used to attach bacteria to surfaces - but are not involved in movement.

pinocytosis
one form of endocytosis

pituitary gland
an endocrine gland which lies just below the hypothalamus

plaque
A clear area on a lawn of bacteria where viruses have destroyed the bacteria; also, the gummy layer of gelatinous material consisting of bacteria and organic matter on the teeth.

plateau phase
the number of individuals of the population no longer increases due to limiting factors.

pleomorphy
An organism that appears in a variety of shapes.

poikilotherm
An organism, such as a fish or a reptile, having a body temperature that varies with the temperature of its surroundings.

pollination
the tranfer of pollen grains from the anther to the carpel

polygenic inheritance
the inheritance of a characteristic which is controlled by more than one gene

polyphyletic group
A set of species descended from more than one common ancestor.

polyploidy
An organism having one or more extra sets of chromosomes.

polysome
cluster of ribosomes on a strand of mRNA

population genetics
The study of processes influencing gene frequencies.

population
a group of organisms of teh same species who live in the same area at the same time.

porin
A protein channel in the lipopolysaccharide layer of gram-negative bacteria.

portal system
sequence of two sets of capillaries, e.g. hepatic portal system (small intestine and live) and pituitary portal system (hypothalamus and anterior lobe of pituitary)

post zygotic isolation
Reproductive isolation in which a zygote is successfully formed but then either fails to develop or develops into a sterile adult.

potassium-argon dating
A radiometric technique for dating volcanic rock, based on the decay of potassium-40 to argon-40.

pox
Pitted scars remaining in recovers from small pox.

prebiotic evolution
Evolution before life existed; chemical evolution and the abiotic synthesis of organic molecules.

precautionary principle
the concept that someone wishing to take a certain kind of action should prove that the action does not cause serious or irreversible harm to the public if there is no scientific consensus about the outcome of the action.

predation
when one organism eats another live organism

prehensile tail
A tail adapted for grasping.

pressure flow hypothesis
explanation for the movement of fluid in the phloem

pre-zygotic isolation
A form of reproductive isolation in which the two species never reach the stage of successful mating, and thus no zygote is formed.

primaeval soup
Mixture of water and chemicals that constituted the oceans on Earth about three billion years ago. Among the chemicals were simple organic molecules. The primeval soup is thought to have been the place where life originated.

primary succession
Succession that occurs in an environment, such as bare rock, in which no trace of a previous community is present.

primate
A member of the mammalian order Primates which have nails, usually a thumb and a big toes which are opposable to the other digits. All possess a relatively large brain and have well developed eye sight, often with binocular vision.

prions
Infectious particles of protein possibly involved in human diseases of the brain.

productivity
The amount of biomass fixed by primary producers (photosynthetically).

promoter region
the site for binding RNA polymerase to the 3' end of the structural gene in prokaryotic cells

protease
enzyme that digests protein, e.g. pepsin
protease enzyme that digests protein, e.g. pepsin

proteobacteria
A large diverse group of gram negative bacteria.

protobionts
Aggregates of abiotically produced molecules.

proximal convoluted tubule
tubule, part of the nephron where most substances are reabsorbed

Pseudomonas aeruginosa
A Gram-negative bacterium transmitted by contaminated materials and involve in disease of burnt tissue and the urinary tract.

pseudopodium (plural: pseudopodia)
A temporary extension of an amoeboid cell, by which movement or feeding may occur.

punctuated equilibrium
An evolutionary process involving long periods without change (stasis) punctuated by short periods of rapid speciation.

Punnett square
notation for helping to work out possible genotypes in a cross

pupil reflex
cranial reflex of reducing pupil size in bright light

pure culture
A culture or colony of microorganisms of one type.

Purkinje tissue
special muscle fibres which conduct impulse to ventricles

purple non-sulfur bacteria
A group of photosynthetic bacteria classified in the Proteobacteria that do not deposit

purple sulfur bacteria
Photosynthetic bacteria classified as Proteobacteria that can deposit sulfur granules in their cells.

pus
A mixture of serum, dead tissue cells, leucocytes and bacteria that accumulates at the site of infection.

pyramid of energy
a graphical representation of the amount of energy of each trophic level in a food chain in kJ/m2/yr.

pyrenoid
a region of the chloroplast in algae involved in the polymerisation of polysaccharides.

pyruvate
three carbon compound produced in glycolysis

Q

quadrat
A small, usually rectangular plot of land arranged for close study of the distribution of plants or animals in an area.

quorum quenching
Quorum-quenching stops bacterial cells from producing disease-causing pathogenic factors.

quorum sensing

A process by which bacteria regulate gene expression on the basis of their population density; once a critical population density has been reached, gene expression is altered.

R

rabies

A serious nervous system disease due to a helical RNA virus, transmitted by an animal bite and characterised by destruction of the brain tissue leading to paralysis and death.

radioactive decay

Spontaneous disintegration of an atom accompanied by the emission of ionising or nuclear radiation.

radiocarbon dating

An age estimate based on the amount of a natural radioactive carbon isotope (carbon-14) that remains in any organic matter.

radiometric dating

Absolute dating methods based on the measurement of radioactive decay.

RDA

recommended daily allowance

RDI

reference daily intake

realized niche

is the actual mode of existence of a species, which results from its adaptations and competition with other species.

receptor

specialised cells that detect a stimulus and change it into an electrical impulse

recombinants

chromosomes or gametes which contain new combinations of alleles as a result of crossing over

redox reaction

reduction-oxidation reaction where one compound loses some electrons and the other compound gains them.

reducing atmosphere

An atmosphere of a planet or moon which has a high hydrogen content, either in the form of hydrogen or hydrogen-containing compounds, such as methane or ammonia.

reducing power

the ability to reduce another compound.

reduction

reduction is gain of electrons

reed bed

A reed bed consist of a shallow soil filter planted with reed. Wastewater flows through and undergoes treatment by means of settling, biological decomposition, filtration and adsorption to humus and clay

reflex

a rapid sub-conscious response

refractory period

the time during which no new action potential will be generated

regression

aims to find a linear relationship between two variables by the method of least squares.

relative dating

A method of dating rock layers by their relationships or proximity to each other.

relay neuron

nerve cell which transmits impulses from one neuron to another inside the CNS

repolarisation

when the potential difference across the membrane becomes larger (value goes from 0 mV to -70 mV)

reproductive isolation

Reproductive isolation is the inability of formerly interbreeding organisms to produce offspring.

reproductive strategies

strategies of reproduction used by various species (see r- and K-)

reservoir

A human or other animal that retains disease organisms in the body, but has not experienced disease and shows no evidence of illness.

response

an action resulting from the perception of a stimulus. It is a reaction to a change perceived by the nervous system. The total of responses to stimuli is often called behaviour.

resting potential

the electrical potential (measured in millivolts) across a cell membrane when not propagating an impulse.

reticulate bodies

The metabolically more active form of elementary bodies of Chlamydia.

reverse transcriptase
An enzyme, requiring a DNA primer, that catalyses the synthesis of a DNA strand from an RNA template.

reverse transcription polymerase chain reaction
A variation of the PCR technique allowing to amplify a RNA sequence after synthesis of a complementary DNA. cDNA is made from RNA by the enzyme reverse transcriptase. The resultant cDNA is then amplified using PCR technique.

rhinovirus
An icosahedra DNA that causes diseases of the upper respiratory tract that commonly called 'head colds.'

ribosomal RNA
A type of RNA that combines with ribosomal proteins to form ribosomes.

ribozyme
An RNA molecule that can catalyse certain chemical reactions, especially those involved in the synthesis and processing of RNA itself.

rickets
condition where children have soft and weak bones, due to a lack of Calcium and/or vitamin D

ring species
A ring species is a situation in which two populations which do not interbreed are living in the same region and connected by a geographic ring of populations that can interbreed.

RNA primase
enzyme that forms the RNA primer

RNA primer
section of RNA nucleotides at the beginning of the forming new DNA strand

RNA World
The RNA World referred to a hypothetical stage in the origin of life on Earth where RNA stored genetic information and acted as a catalyst in a very primitive self-replicating system.

robust
an organism that is large and heavily built

rod
photoreceptor in the retina responsible for seeing black and white

root nodule
A structure developed on the roots of most legumes and some other plants in response to the stimulus of root nodule bacteria.

round window
allows the vibrations of the fluid inside the cochlea to occur without an increase in pressure

rRNA
ribosomal RNA

r-strategy
a reproductive strategy favoured by organisms in succession communities, usually by small organisms that reproduce quickly

rubella
A communicable skin disease caused by an icosahedral RNA virus and accompanied by mild respiratory symptoms and measles like rash; can cause damage in fetus if contracted by a pregnant woman.

S

salinity
the amount of salt peresent in the soil or water

saprotroph
A plant or micro-organism that obtains its nutrients from dead or decaying organisms in the form of organic substances in solution.

sarcolemma
the membrane surrounding the muscle cell.

sarcomere
functional unit of the muscle

sarcoplasm
cytoplasm inside a muscle cell

sarcoplasmic reticulum.
internal membrane within the sarcoplasm

savanna
Subtropical grassland with scattered shrubs and trees and pronounced dry season, typical of Eastern Africa.

scattergram
the scattergram visualises a relation (correlation) between two variables. Individual data points are represented in two-dimensional space where axes represent the two variables.

schizogony
Asexual reproductive stage of malaria parasites. In red blood cells, schizogony entails development of a single trophozoite into numerous merozoites. A similar process happens in infected liver cells.

secondary disease
A disease that develops in a weakened individual.

secondary messenger
substance produced inside the cell causing a reaction as a response to binding of a signal molecule outside the cell

secondary succession
succession or species on soil already formed, in which the community has been disturbed.

seed dispersal
moving the seeds away from the parent plant to reduce competition.

self-replication
Self-replication is the process by which a molecule may act, and thereby make a copy of itself.

seminiferous tubule
tubule in testis where spermatogenesis takes place

sense strand
the DNA strand that is not transcribed; the sequence of the organic bases is the same as that of the mRNA (except that DNA has T where RNA has U)

sensory neurons
receive action potentials from receptors and conduct them towards the CNS where they connect to relay neurons

sepsis
Sepsis is a serious medical condition characterized by a whole-body inflammatory state caused by infection.

Sertoli cell
cell in seminiferouw tubule which nourish developing sperm cells

severe Combined Immunodeficiency (SCID)
An immune disease in which the lymph nodes lack both B-lymphocytes and T-

sex chromosome
a chromosome which helps in determining the sex of an individual

sickle-cell anemia
A chronic, usually fatal anemia marked by sickle-shaped red blood cells. The disease occurs in individuals who are homozygous for a mutant haemoglobin gene.

sickle-cell trait
the inheritance of one gene for hemoglobin and one gene for sickle hemoglobin.

sigmoid
s-shaped

Simpson formula.
A method used to calculate diversity takings into account the number of species present, as well as the abundance of each species.

Sino-Atrial Node (SAN)
specialised muscle cells in the wall of the left atrium, responsible for generating impulses that causes cardiac contractions

sinusoid
space filled with blood or other fluid

smallpox
A now-extinct viral disease of the skin and body organs caused by a complex DNA virus and accompanied by bleeding skin pustules, disfigurements, and multiple organ involvements.

somatic gene therapy
The introduction of genes into tissue or cells to treat a genetic related disease in an individual.

spacial habitat
the space where an organism lives

speciation
The evolutionary formation of new species, usually by the division of a single species into two or more genetically distinct ones, thus increasing species diversity.

species
A category of taxonomic classification, ranking below a genus and consisting of related organisms, that closely resemble each other, and are capable of interbreeding and producing fertile offspring

spermatogenesis
production of sperm cells

spike
A functional projection of the viral envelope.

spirochete
A twisted bacterial rod with a flexible cell wall containing axial filaments for motility.

splicing
the process of enzymes cutting the bond between exon and intron nucleotides and attaching the remaining exon nucleotides to each other

sporozoite
A stage in the life cycle of the malaria parasite. Sporozoites are produced in the mosquito and migrate to the mosquito's salivary glands.

sprain
the overstretching of a ligament in a joint

stabilising selection
A type of natural selection in which those organisms displaying extreme phenotypes are selected against.

standard deviation
standard deviation is a measure of the spread or dispersion of a set of data. The more widely the values are spread out, the larger the standard deviation.

stasis
A period of equilibrium during which change appears to be absent.

stem tuber
stem modified for food storage which can form roots.

stigma
The dense region of pigments found in many photosynthetic protists which is sensitive to light.

stimulus
a change in the environment that is detected by a receptor and elicits a response.

storage roots
modified to store water or food

streak plate
The streak plate method is a rapid and simple technique of mechanically diluting a relatively large concentration of microorganisms to a small, scattered population of cells. The aim is to obtain isolated colonies on a large part of the agar surface, so that desired species can then be brought into pure culture.

streptomycin
An antibiotic derived from *Streptomyces griseus* that is effective against Gram-negative bacteria and the tubercule bacillus; streptomycin interferes with protein synthesis.

stroke volume
volume of blood pumped out with each contraction of the heart.

stroma
watery fluid inside chloroplast

succession
The gradual and orderly process of ecosystem development brought about by changes in community composition and the production of a climax characteristic of a particular geographic region.

supplemental air
expiratory reserve volume

sympatric speciation
Speciation of populations that are not physically divided; usually due to ecological isolation or polyploidy.

synapse
the connection between two neurons

synapsis
homologous chromosomes align side by side

syndrome
A collection of symptoms.

systole
contraction of the heart muscle

T

t test
statistical test used to evaluate the differences in means between two groups.

target cell
cells with special receptors that react to the hormone

TCA cycle
cyclic process in the matrix of the mitochondria where a two carbon compound is changed into two molecules of carbon dioxide, producing energy

tendril
specialised stem or leaf which will attach the plant to something

termination
release of the polypeptide chain when a stop codon is reached

terminator
the site for stopping transcription, found at the 5' end of the structural gene in prokaryotic cells

tetanus
A soil borne bacterial disease of the muscles and nerves caused by toxins produced by Clostridium tetani and accompanied by uncontrolled muscles spasms.

thermophiles
Organisms that grow at high temperature ranges of 40 to 90 degrees Celsisus.

thermoregulation
the regulation of its body temperature by an organism

theshold potential
value (around -50 mV) which must be reached before an action potential is generated

thylakoid membrane
membrane inside the chloroplast

tidal volume

amount of air breathed in and out during a normal breath (around 500 cm3)

tight junctions

connections between cells to maintain the integrity of the tissue; fusions of adjacent cell surface membranes which form a continuous seal around each cell in the tissue
total lung capacity
volume of air in the lungs after a maximum inhalation.

toxin

A poisonous substance produced by a species of microorganisms; bacterial toxins are classified as exotoxins or endotoxins.

trachea

windpipe that transports air to and from the lungs

transcription

the process of synthesizing RNA from a DNA template

transfer RNA (tRNA)

strand of RNA which carries a specific amino acid to the growing polypeptide chain; the amino acid carried on the 3' end is decided by the anticodon of the tRNA

transient polymorphism

A temporary form of genetic polymorphism existing at a time when an allele is being replaced by a superior one.

transitional phase

limiting factors start influencing the rate of increase of the population.

translation

the process of converting the information from a sequence of mRNA codons (mRNA) into a sequence of amino acids (polypeptide)

translocation

the movement of sugars and amino acids from source to sink

transpiration pull

the force which makes all the water molecules in the xylem move up when one molecule from evaporates from a leaf; it also pulls new water molecules into the roots

transpiration stream

the movement of water and minerals from the roots to the leaves

transpiration

the loss of water vapour from the leaves and stems of plants.

tricuspid

valve between right atrium and ventricle

triose

monosaccharide containing 3 Carbon atoms

tRNA

see transfer RNA

trophic level

the position of the organism in a food chain. Producers are on the first trophic level, primary consumers on the second.

trypsin

protein digesting enzyme

trypsinogen

inactive precursor to trypsin

tuberculosis

An airborne bacterial disease of the lungs caused by Mycobacterium tuberculosis and accompanied by degeneration of the lung tissue and spread to other organs.

tumor suppressor gene

A tumor suppressor gene is a gene that reduces the probability that a cell in a multicellular organism will turn into a tumor cell. A mutation or deletion of such a gene will increase the probability of the formation of a tumor.

type II diabetes

body no longer produces enough insulin and/or the receptors in the target cells (liver and muscle) are less sensitive to the presence of insulin

typhoid fever

A food borne and waterborne bacterial disease of the intestine caused by Salmonella typhi and accompanied by intestinal ulcers, severe fever, and blood involvement.

U

ultra-filtration

process in kidney where some of the liquid and dissolved particles are pushed out of the glomerulus into Bowman's capsule by the pressure of the blood in the glomerulus

UV radiation

a part of the radiation from the sun, known to cause mutations in the DNA of living organisms

V

Vancomycin
An antibiotic used in therapy of diseases caused by Gram-positive bacteria, especially staphylococci.

variation
the concept that individuals of one species are different from each other

vasa recta
blood vessels around the nephrons

vasoconstriction
the blood vessels in the skin contract which decreases the flow of blood to the skin; as a result the skin becomes colder reducing the heat loss to the environment

vasodilation
the blood vessels in the skin become wider which increases the flow of blood to the skin.

vector
A bacteriophage, plasmid or other agent that transfers genetic material from one cell to another. It also refers to a disease causing organism, for example, a bacterium or virus.

venous return
volume of blood returning to the heart via the veins per minute.

ventilation rate
number of inhalations or exhalations per minute.

ventilation
the process of moving air into and out of lungs

vibrio cholerae
A Gram-negative curved bacterium transmitted by food/ and or water and the cause of cholera.

vibrio
A form of bacterium occurring as a curved rod; resembles a comma.

virion
A complete viral particle, consisting of RNA or DNA surrounded by a protein capsid and constituting the infective form of a virus.

virulence factor
A virulence factor is a feature of a pathogenic organism that enhances its ability to cause disease. This might be a structure, an enzyme, a transport system, or any other cellular function that makes the bacteria more successful in infecting some other organism

virulence
The degree of ability of an organism to cause disease.

virulent phage
A bacteriophage that replicates within a bacterium and destroys the bacterium.

vital capacity
maximum amount of air that can be breathed out after a maximum inspiration (around 4.5 dm3)

vitamin
organic compound that the organism cannot synthesize

VO_2 max
the highest possible volume of oxygen taken up per minute by a specific individual.

VO_2
volume of oxygen taken up per minute

W

wort
A sugar solution derived from grain by mashing.

xerophyte
a plants that can tolerate dry conditions

Yersinia pestis
A Gram-negative bacterium that displays bipolar staining and causes plague.

zona pellucida
a mucoprotein (a complex of protein and polysaccharide) membrane surrounding the secondary oocyte of mammals

zoonosis
Any disease in humans acquired from an animal of any type.

zygomatic arch
The cheek bone.

F

G

H